A Companion to the Philosophy
of Literature

Blackwell Companions to Philosophy

This outstanding student reference series offers a comprehensive and authoritative survey of philosophy as a whole. Written by today's leading philosophers, each volume provides lucid and engaging coverage of the key figures, terms, topics, and problems of the field. Taken together, the volumes provide the ideal basis for course use, representing an unparalleled work of reference for students and specialists alike.

Already published in the series:

1. The Blackwell Companion to Philosophy, Second Edition
   Edited by Nicholas Bunnin and Eric Tsui-James
2. A Companion to Ethics
   Edited by Peter Singer
3. A Companion to Aesthetics, Second Edition
   Edited by Stephen Davies, Kathleen Marie Higgins, Robert Hopkins, Robert Stecker, and David E. Cooper
4. A Companion to Epistemology, Second Edition
   Edited by Jonathan Dancy, Ernest Sosa and Matthias Steup
5. A Companion to Contemporary Political Philosophy (two-volume set), Second Edition
   Edited by Robert E. Goodin and Philip Pettit
6. A Companion to Philosophy of Mind
   Edited by Samuel Guttenplan
7. A Companion to Metaphysics, Second Edition
   Edited by Jaegwon Kim, Ernest Sosa and Gary S. Rosenkrantz
8. A Companion to Philosophy of Law and Legal Theory, Second Edition
   Edited by Dennis Patterson
9. A Companion to Philosophy of Religion, Second Edition
   Edited by Charles Taliaferro, Paul Draper, and Philip L. Quinn
10. A Companion to the Philosophy of Language
    Edited by Bob Hale and Crispin Wright
11. A Companion to World Philosophies
    Edited by Eliot Deutsch and Ron Bontekoe
12. A Companion to Continental Philosophy
    Edited by Simon Critchley and William Schroeder
13. A Companion to Feminist Philosophy
    Edited by Alison M. Jaggar and Iris Marion Young
14. A Companion to Cognitive Science
    Edited by William Bechtel and George Graham
15. A Companion to Bioethics, Second Edition
    Edited by Helga Kuhse and Peter Singer
16. A Companion to the Philosophers
    Edited by Robert L. Arrington
17. A Companion to Business Ethics
    Edited by Robert E. Frederick
18. A Companion to the Philosophy of Science
    Edited by W. H. Newton-Smith
19. A Companion to Environmental Philosophy
    Edited by Dale Jamieson
20. A Companion to Analytic Philosophy
    Edited by A. P. Martinich and David Sosa
21. A Companion to Genethics
    Edited by Justine Burley and John Harris
22. A Companion to Philosophical Logic
    Edited by Dale Jacquette
23. A Companion to Early Modern Philosophy
    Edited by Steven Nadler
24. A Companion to Philosophy in the Middle Ages
    Edited by Jorge J. E. Gracia and Timothy B. Noone
25. A Companion to African-American Philosophy
    Edited by Tommy L. Lott and John P. Pittman
26. A Companion to Applied Ethics
    Edited by R. G. Frey and Christopher Heath Wellman
27. A Companion to the Philosophy of Education
    Edited by Randall Curren
28. A Companion to African Philosophy
    Edited by Kwasi Wiredu
29. A Companion to Heidegger
    Edited by Hubert L. Dreyfus and Mark A. Wrathall
30. A Companion to Rationalism
    Edited by Alan Nelson
31. A Companion to Pragmatism
    Edited by John R. Shook and Joseph Margolis
32. A Companion to Ancient Philosophy
    Edited by Mary Louise Gill and Pierre Pellegrin
33. A Companion to Nietzsche
    Edited by Keith Ansell Pearson
34. A Companion to Socrates
    Edited by Sara Ahbel-Rappe and Rachana Kamtekar
35. A Companion to Phenomenology and Existentialism
    Edited by Hubert L. Dreyfus and Mark A. Wrathall
36. A Companion to Kant
    Edited by Graham Bird
37. A Companion to Plato
    Edited by Hugh H. Benson
38. A Companion to Descartes
    Edited by Janet Broughton and John Carriero
39. A Companion to the Philosophy of Biology
    Edited by Sahotra Sarkar and Anya Plutynski
40. A Companion to Hume
    Edited by Elizabeth S. Radcliffe
41. A Companion to the Philosophy of History and Historiography
    Edited by Aviezer Tucker
42. A Companion to Aristotle
    Edited by Georgios Anagnostopoulos
43. A Companion to the Philosophy of Technology
    Edited by Jan-Kyrre Berg Olsen, Stig Andur Pedersen, and Vincent F. Hendricks
44. A Companion to Latin American Philosophy
    Edited by Susana Nuccetelli, Ofelia Schutte, and Otávio Bueno
45. A Companion to the Philosophy of Literature
    Edited by Garry L. Hagberg and Walter Jost
46. A Companion to the Philosophy of Action
    Edited by Timothy O'Connor and Constantine Sandis
47. A Companion to Relativism
    Edited by Steven D. Hales
48. A Companion to Hegel
    Edited by Stephen Houlgate and Michael Baur
49. A Companion to Schopenhauer
    Edited by Bart Vandenabeele
50. A Companion to Buddhist Philosophy
    Edited by Steven M. Emmanuel
51. A Companion to Foucault
    Edited by Christopher Falzon, Timothy O'Leary, and Jana Sawicki
52. A Companion to the Philosophy of Time
    Edited by Heather Dyke and Adrian Bardon
53. A Companion to Donald Davidson
    Edited by Ernest Lepore and Kirk Ludwig
54. A Companion to Rawls
    Edited by Jon Mandle and David Reidy
55. A Companion to W.V.O Quine
    Edited by Gilbert Harman and Ernest Lepore
56. A Companion to Derrida
    Edited by Leonard Lawlor and Zeynep Direk
57. A Companion to David Lewis
    Edited by Barry Loewer and Jonathan Schaffer

A Companion to the Philosophy of Literature

Edited by
Garry L. Hagberg
and
Walter Jost

WILEY Blackwell

This paperback edition first published 2015
© 2010 John Wiley & Sons, Ltd

Edition history: Blackwell Publishing Ltd (hardback, 2010)

Registered Office
John Wiley & Sons Ltd, The Atrium, Southern Gate, Chichester, West Sussex, PO19 8SQ, UK

Editorial Offices
350 Main Street, Malden, MA 02148-5020, USA
9600 Garsington Road, Oxford, OX4 2DQ, UK
The Atrium, Southern Gate, Chichester, West Sussex, PO19 8SQ, UK

For details of our global editorial offices, for customer services, and for information about how to apply for permission to reuse the copyright material in this book please see our website at www.wiley.com/wiley-blackwell.

The right of Garry L. Hagberg and Walter Jost to be identified as the authors of the editorial material in this work has been asserted in accordance with the UK Copyright, Designs and Patents Act 1988.

All rights reserved. No part of this publication may be reproduced, stored in a retrieval system, or transmitted, in any form or by any means, electronic, mechanical, photocopying, recording or otherwise, except as permitted by the UK Copyright, Designs and Patents Act 1988, without the prior permission of the publisher.

Wiley also publishes its books in a variety of electronic formats. Some content that appears in print may not be available in electronic books.

Designations used by companies to distinguish their products are often claimed as trademarks. All brand names and product names used in this book are trade names, service marks, trademarks or registered trademarks of their respective owners. The publisher is not associated with any product or vendor mentioned in this book.

Limit of Liability/Disclaimer of Warranty: While the publisher and authors have used their best efforts in preparing this book, they make no representations or warranties with respect to the accuracy or completeness of the contents of this book and specifically disclaim any implied warranties of merchantability or fitness for a particular purpose. It is sold on the understanding that the publisher is not engaged in rendering professional services and neither the publisher nor the author shall be liable for damages arising herefrom. If professional advice or other expert assistance is required, the services of a competent professional should be sought.

Library of Congress Cataloging-in-Publication Data

A companion to the philosophy of literature / edited by Garry L. Hagberg and Walter Jost.
  p. cm. – (Blackwell companions to philosophy)
  Includes bibliographical references and index.
  ISBN 978-1-4051-4170-3 (hardcover : alk. paper)–ISBN 978-1-118-96387-6 (paperback)
 1. Literature–History and criticism.   2. Literature–Philosophy.   I. Hagberg, Garry, 1952–
II. Jost, Walter, 1951–
  PN501.C626 2010
  801–dc22
                                        2009018607

A catalogue record for this book is available from the British Library.

Cover image: Peter Paul Rubens, The Four Philosophers. Florence, Galleria Palatina. © Photo Scala Florence, 2014, courtesy of the Ministero Beni e Att. Culturali

Set in 10/13pt Photina by SPi Publisher Services, Pondicherry, India

Contents

Notes on Contributors   viii

Acknowledgments   xiii

Introduction   1
Garry L. Hagberg and Walter Jost

Part I   Relations between Philosophy and Literature   5

1   Philosophy as Literature and More than Literature   7
    Richard Shusterman

2   Philosophy and Literature: Friends of the Earth?   22
    Roger A. Shiner

3   Philosophy and Literature – and Rhetoric: Adventures in Polytopia   38
    Walter Jost

4   Philosophy and/as/of Literature   52
    Arthur C. Danto

Part II   Emotional Engagement and the Experience of Reading   69

5   Emotion and the Understanding of Narrative   71
    Jenefer Robinson

6   Feeling Fictions   93
    Roger Scruton

7   The Experience of Reading   106
    Peter Kivy

8   Self-Defining Reading: Literature and the Constitution of Personhood   120
    Garry L. Hagberg

Part III Philosophy, Tragedy, and Literary Form — 159

9 Tragedy and Philosophy — 161
   Anthony J. Cascardi

10 Iago's Elenchus: Shakespeare, *Othello*, and the Platonic Inheritance — 174
   M. W. Rowe

11 Catharsis — 193
   Jonathan Lear

12 Passion, Counter-Passion, Catharsis: Flaubert (and Beckett) on Feeling Nothing — 218
   Joshua Landy

Part IV Literature and the Moral Life — 239

13 Perceptive Equilibrium: Literary Theory and Ethical Theory — 241
   Martha C. Nussbaum

14 Henry James, Moral Philosophers, Moralism — 268
   Cora Diamond

15 Literature and the Idea of Morality — 285
   Eileen John

16 Styles of Self-Absorption — 300
   Daniel Brudney

Part V Narrative and the Question of Literary Truth — 329

17 Narration, Imitation, and Point of View — 331
   Gregory Currie

18 How and What We Can Learn from Fiction — 350
   Mitchell Green

19 Literature and Truth — 367
   Peter Lamarque

20 Truth in Poetry: Particulars and Universals — 385
   Richard Eldridge

Part VI Intention and Biography in Criticism — 399

21 Authorial Intention and the Varieties of Intentionalism — 401
   Paisley Livingston

22	Art as Techne, or, The Intentional Fallacy and the Unfinished Project of Formalism *Henry Staten*	420
23	Biography in Literary Criticism *Stein Haugom Olsen*	436
24	Getting Inside Heisenberg's Head *Ray Monk*	453

Part VII On Literary Language 465

25	Wittgenstein and Literary Language *Jon Cook and Rupert Read*	467
26	Exemplification and Expression *Charles Altieri*	491
27	At Play in the Fields of Metaphor *Ted Cohen*	507
28	Macbeth Appalled *Stanley Cavell*	521

Index 541

Notes on Contributors

Charles Altieri teaches modern poetry and literary theory at the University of California, Berkeley. His two most recent books are *The Particulars of Rapture* and *The Art of Modernist American Poetry*. He is working on a book on Wallace Stevens.

Daniel Brudney is Associate Professor of Philosophy at the University of Chicago. He is the author of *Marx's Attempt to Leave Philosophy*. His work in philosophy and literature includes "Lord Jim and Moral Judgment: Literature and Moral Philosophy," in *Journal of Aesthetics and Art Criticism*, and "Marlow's Morality," in *Philosophy and Literature*.

Anthony J. Cascardi is Director of the Townsend Center for the Humanities and Margaret and Sidney Ancker Professor of Comparative Literature, Rhetoric, and Spanish at the University of California, Berkeley. His publications on literature, philosophy, and aesthetics include *The Subject of Modernity, Consequences of Enlightenment*, and *Literature and the Question of Philosophy*. Since 1995 he has been General Editor of the Penn State Press series of books on literature and philosophy.

Stanley Cavell is the Walter M. Cabot Professor Emeritus of Aesthetics and the General Theory of Value, Harvard University. He is the author of many influential and groundbreaking books, including *The Claim of Reason, Cities of Words*, and *Philosophy the Day After Tomorrow*. His work has been the subject of numerous books, edited volumes, and journal issues.

Ted Cohen is Professor of Philosophy at the University of Chicago. In addition to a series of widely influential articles in philosophical aesthetics, he published *Jokes: Philosophical Thoughts on Joking Matters* a few years ago, and *Thinking of Others: On the Talent for Metaphor* recently. He is a past president of the American Society for Aesthetics and of the Central Division of the American Philosophical Association.

Jon Cook is Professor of Literature and Dean of the Faculty of Arts and Humanities at the University of East Anglia. His recent publications include *Hazlitt in Love* and *Poetry in Theory*. He has taught at universities in the United States, Europe, and India, most recently as a Hurst Visiting Professor at Washington University in St Louis.

NOTES ON CONTRIBUTORS

Gregory Currie teaches philosophy at the University of Nottingham. Before that he taught in New Zealand and Australia. He was a Fulbright Fellow, and more recently a British Academy/Leverhulme Research Fellow. He has held visiting positions at Cambridge, the Australian National University, Maryland, and Oxford. His latest book, *Narratives and Narrators: A Philosophy of Stories*, is due to appear with Oxford University Press in 2010. His current project, on aesthetics and the sciences of mind, is supported by a grant from the Arts and Humanities Research Council.

Arthur C. Danto is Johnsonian Professor Emeritus in Philosophy at Columbia University. He is the author of numerous books, including *Nietzsche as Philosopher*, *Mysticism and Morality*, *The Transfiguration of the Commonplace*, *Connections to the World: The Basic Concepts of Philosophy*, and *Encounters and Reflections: Art in the Historical Present*, a collection of art criticism which won the National Book Critics Circle Prize for Criticism, 1990. Among his most recent books are *Unnatural Wonders: Essays from the Gap Between Art and Life* and *Andy Warhol*.

Cora Diamond is the William R. Kenan Jr. Professor of Philosophy at the University of Virginia and Professor of Law at its law school. Diamond's scholarly interests are in Wittgenstein, Frege and the philosophy of language, moral and political philosophy, and philosophy and literature. She is the author of *The Realistic Spirit: Wittgenstein, Philosophy, and the Mind* and the editor of *Wittgenstein's Lectures on the Philosophy of Mathematics* and *Intention and Intentionality*.

Richard Eldridge is Charles and Harriett Cox McDowell Professor of Philosophy at Swarthmore College. He is the author, among other volumes, of *Literature, Life, and Modernity* and *The Persistence of Romanticism*, and he is the editor of *The Oxford Handbook of Philosophy and Literature* and *Stanley Cavell*.

Mitchell Green is the NEH/Horace W. Goldsmith Distinguished Teaching Professor at the University of Virginia. His research is in the philosophy of language, aesthetics, and the philosophy of mind. Major publications include *Self-Expression* and *Moore's Paradox* (co-editor). He has held grants from the National Endowment for the Humanities, the American Council of Learned Societies, and the National Science Foundation. He is currently working on empathy, the epistemic value of literature, and the evolution of language.

Garry L. Hagberg is the James H. Ottaway Professor of Philosophy and Aesthetics at Bard College, and has in recent years held a Chair in the School of Philosophy at the University of East Anglia. He writes at the intersection of aesthetics and the philosophy of language, and is the author of *Meaning and Interpretation: Wittgenstein, Henry James, and Literary Knowledge* and *Art as Language: Wittgenstein, Meaning, and Aesthetic Theory*. He has recently completed *Describing Ourselves: Wittgenstein and Autobiographical Consciousness* for Oxford University Press and an edited volume, *Art and Ethical Criticism*, for Wiley-Blackwell, and is presently writing on literature and self-formation. He is joint editor of the journal *Philosophy and Literature*.

NOTES ON CONTRIBUTORS

Eileen John is an Associate Professor of Philosophy at the University of Warwick. She has written on art and knowledge, and on moral and aesthetic value, and has a special interest in philosophical questions arising from literature. She is co-editor of an anthology, Wiley-Blackwell's *Philosophy of Literature: Contemporary and Classic Readings.*

Walter Jost is Professor of English at the University of Virginia. He is the author of *Rhetorical Thought in John Henry Newman* and *Rhetorical Investigations: Studies in Ordinary Language Criticism*, and editor or co-editor of six previous books, including *A Companion to Rhetoric and Rhetorical Criticism.*

Peter Kivy is Board of Governors Professor of Philosophy at Rutgers University, New Brunswick, and a past president of the American Society for Aesthetics. He has published numerous books and articles on the philosophy of art, in the sub-fields of eighteenth-century British aesthetics, aesthetic concepts, philosophy of music, and philosophy of literature. His most recent book, from Oxford University Press, is *Antithetical Arts: On the Ancient Quarrel Between Literature and Music.*

Peter Lamarque is Professor of Philosophy at the University of York. He was editor of the *British Journal of Aesthetics* from 1995 to 2008 and is author of *Truth, Fiction, and Literature* (with Stein Haugom Olsen), *Fictional Points of View*, and *The Philosophy of Literature*. He edited the *Concise Encyclopedia of Philosophy of Language* and *Aesthetics and the Philosophy of Art: The Analytic Tradition: An Anthology* (with Stein Haugom Olsen).

Joshua Landy is Associate Professor of French at Stanford University, where he co-directs Stanford's Initiative in Philosophy and Literature. He is author of *Philosophy as Fiction: Self, Deception, and Knowledge in Proust*; editor, with Claude Bremond and Thomas Pavel, of *Thematics: New Approaches*; and editor, with Michael Saler, of *The Re-Enchantment of the World: Secular Magic in a Rational Age*. He is currently completing a second book, *How to Do Things With Fictions.*

Jonathan Lear is the John U. Nef Distinguished Service Professor at the Committee on Social Thought and in the Department of Philosophy at the University of Chicago. He works primarily on philosophical conceptions of the human psyche from Socrates to the present. His books include *Aristotle and Logical Theory*, *Aristotle: The Desire to Understand*, *Love and its Place in Nature: A Philosophical Interpretation of Freudian Psychoanalysis*, *Open Minded: Working out the Logic of the Soul*, *Happiness, Death and the Remainder of Life*, *Therapeutic Action: An Earnest Plea for Irony*; *Freud*, and *Radical Hope: Ethics in the Face of Cultural Devastation.*

Paisley Livingston is Chair Professor of Philosophy and Academic Dean of Humanities at Lingnan University, Hong Kong. Author of a number of volumes in philosophical aesthetics, his most recent book is *Cinema, Philosophy, Bergman: On Film as Philosophy.*

Ray Monk is Professor of Philosophy at the University of Southampton. He is author of the award-winning biographies *Wittgenstein: The Duty of Genius*, *Bertrand Russell: The Spirit of Solitude 1872–1921*, and *Bertrand Russell: The Ghost of Madness 1921–1970*, and he is presently working on a biography of Robert Oppenheimer. He has also written on Wittgenstein's philosophy of mathematics, an introduction to Wittgenstein's philosophy, *How to Read Wittgenstein*, and on philosophical issues in biography.

Martha C. Nussbaum is the Ernst Freund Distinguished Service Professor of Law and Ethics, appointed in the Philosophy Department, Law School, and Divinity School at the University of Chicago. Her many publications include *The Fragility of Goodness: Luck and Ethics in Greek Tragedy and Philosophy*, *Love's Knowledge*, *The Therapy of Desire*, *Cultivating Humanity: A Classical Defense of Reform in Liberal Education*, *Sex and Social Justice*, *Women and Human Development*, and *Upheavals of Thought: The Intelligence of Emotions*.

Stein Haugom Olsen, having held chairs at the University of Oslo, Norway, and Lingnan University, Hong Kong, is head of the Department of Linguistic, Literary, and Aesthetic Studies at the University of Bergen, Norway. He has written books and articles on problems in literary theory, literary criticism, and aesthetics. He is currently working on a book on the origin of academic literary criticism.

Rupert Read is Reader in Philosophy at the University of East Anglia, where he specializes in Wittgenstein, in literature and philosophy, and in environmental and political philosophy. His *Applying Wittgenstein* has recently appeared with Continuum Press, and his *There is No Such Thing as Social Science* with Ashgate. Perhaps his most famous book remains *The New Wittgenstein*, a Routledge edited collection of essays.

Jenefer Robinson is Professor of Philosophy at the University of Cincinnati. She is author of *Deeper than Reason: Emotion and its Role in Literature, Music, and Art*, editor of *Music and Meaning*, and Area Editor for Aesthetics, *Encyclopedia of Philosophy*. Her articles have appeared in numerous books and journals including *Journal of Philosophy*, *Philosophical Review*, *Australasian Journal of Philosophy*, *Erkenntnis*, *Philosophy*, *Philosophical Quarterly*, *Behavioral and Brain Sciences*, *Emotion Review*, and *Journal of Aesthetics and Art Criticism*.

M. W. Rowe is Senior Lecturer in Philosophy at the University of East Anglia. He is particularly interested in aesthetics, the intersections between philosophy and literature, Shakespeare, Larkin, and nineteenth-century music, and his recent publications include *Philosophy and Literature: A Book of Essays* and *Heinrich Wilhelm Ernst: Virtuoso Violinist*. He is currently finishing a book entitled, *Philip Larkin: Art and Self*.

Roger Scruton is currently a resident scholar at the American Enterprise Institute in Washington. He taught philosophy at Birkbeck College, University of London, until 1990 and then, after a brief spell at Boston University, pursued a career as a writer and in business. His books include *The Aesthetics of Architecture*, *The Aesthetics of Music*, and *Beauty*. He has tried to explain himself in *On Hunting*, *News from Somewhere*, and *Gentle Regrets*.

Roger A. Shiner taught aesthetics and philosophy of law at the University of Alberta for 35 years, and is now Adjunct and Visiting Professor at the University of British Columbia Okanagan. He has published numerous articles in aesthetics and philosophy of law. He is the author of *Legal Institutions and the Sources of Law*, *Freedom of Commercial Expression*, and *Norm and Nature: The Movements of Legal Thought*. He is a former Secretary-Treasurer of the American Society for Aesthetics.

Richard Shusterman is the Dorothy F. Schmidt Eminent Scholar in the Humanities at Florida Atlantic University and directs its Center for Body, Mind, and Culture. His authored books include *Surface and Depth*, *Performing Live*, *Practicing Philosophy*, *T. S. Eliot and the Philosophy of Criticism*, *The Object of Literary Criticism*, *Pragmatist Aesthetics* (translated into 12 languages), and most recently *Body Consciousness*. He also edited *Analytic Aesthetics* and *The Range of Pragmatism and the Limits of Philosophy*.

Henry Staten is Lockwood Professor in the Humanities and Adjunct Professor of Philosophy at the University of Washington. He is the author of *Wittgenstein and Derrida*, the first book-length study in English of the philosophical pertinence of deconstruction, *Nietzsche's Voice*, and *Eros in Mourning*. His current work focuses on the theory of "art as techne."

Acknowledgments

First and foremost we editors are extremely grateful to each of the contributors to this volume, for his or her willingness to support and participate in the original idea, for the willingness to revise in the light of suggestions, and not least for the cheerful and supportive patience they showed during the extended process of getting all the pieces finished and fitted together. Jeff Dean at Wiley-Blackwell has been a model of wise counsel and indefatigable support from the beginning, giving the project his unique blend of steadfast confidence, discernment, and expert advice; we all have benefited much from having him at the editorial helm throughout the process. We benefited much from a good number of hardworking anonymous readers of the plans for this volume at the early stages. We are also very grateful to Tiffany Mok, to Claire Creffield, and to Barbara Duke, all at Wiley-Blackwell, for playing their parts so effectively, and we thank Jeanette McDonald at Bard College and Elizabeth Leis at the University of Virginia for their precise work in assembling the final manuscript. We also thank the University of East Anglia for much-valued research support and both its School of Philosophy and its School of Literature for providing such an engaging environment for a project of this kind; and the University of Virginia for a Sesquicentennial research award during which the project was initially launched. And special thanks to Liz Granger for preparing a thoroughly useable comprehensive index. We hope that these sustained efforts on the part of everyone involved combine to make this Companion – well, a good companion.

Text Credits

The editors and publisher gratefully acknowledge the permission granted to reproduce the copyright material in this book:

Chapter 4: Arthur C. Danto, "Philosophy and/as/of Literature," originally appeared in the *Proceedings and Addresses of The American Philosophical Association* 58:1 (September 1984).

Chapter 8: Lines from Virgil, *The Aeneid*, trans. Robert Fitzgerald (New York: Random House, 1983).

ACKNOWLEDGMENTS

Chapter 11: Jonathan Lear, "Catharsis," is reprinted from "Katharsis," *Phronesis* 33:3 (1988). With permission of Koninklijke Brill NV.

Chapter 13: Martha Nussbaum, "Perceptive Equilibrium: Literary Theory and Ethical Theory," is reprinted from Ralph Cohen (ed.), *The Future of Literary Theory* (New York: Routledge, 1989). © Taylor & Francis Group LLC.

Chapter 28: Stanley Cavell, "Macbeth Appalled," originally appeared as "Macbeth," in *Raritan* 12:2 (Fall 1992) and 12:3 (Winter 1993).

Every effort has been made to trace copyright holders and to obtain their permission for the use of copyright material. The publisher apologizes for any errors or omissions in the above list and would be grateful if notified of any corrections that should be incorporated in future reprints or editions of this book.

Introduction

GARRY L. HAGBERG AND WALTER JOST

The time seems right for a Companion like the present one – but then, perhaps, the time has never not been right, for, as is well known, the "philosophy of literature" (the thing, not the phrase) traces its unbroken cultural lineage back to Aristotle and Plato. Relations between these two matters, however people have named them – philosophy and literature, moral philosophy and belles-lettres, theoretical knowledge and aesthetic production bridged by ethical and political commitments – have always fascinated thoughtful people, and the discussion naturally continues unabated into our own time. Indeed it has been accelerated by the increasing blurring of disciplinary genres over the last few decades and the increasing cross-fertilizations among "fields," "subjects," "area studies" (everyone's metaphorical nomenclature is clearly wobbling here). All the more reason, then, for this present Companion, the first to bring together such a number of eminent scholars and leaders in their respective areas to take the measure of both long-standing preoccupations and dynamic new developments.

Even as these essays may be read as a series of reports from the field, they were intended from the start also to function individually and in ensemble in a variety of interlocking ways. The editors first set out to get some of the best thinkers to write essays that would provide a solid grounding in the central questions, groundings (or perhaps a better metaphor, soundings?) useful for both students and advanced scholars alike; in this we believe we have, thanks to our hardworking contributors, quite happily succeeded. Equally important, from the start both editors and authors committed to two parallel goals: we agreed that we would seek the clearest possible conceptual language and presentation (diction, tone, structure, style, argument) for our respective inquiries, and we tried whenever possible to illustrate and exemplify our conceptual issues by turning concretely to literary texts, refreshing the memories of those familiar with those works, and including enough relevant details so that their content and point were comprehensible to those unfamiliar with them. Many who work in the philosophy of literature already know – and those of us who are teachers might particularly appreciate this – that sometimes essays in philosophy ascend brilliantly but too far out of range to remain connected to the richness of literature – just as any literary work is potentially too overwhelming in speaking for itself, and literary

---

A Companion to the Philosophy of Literature, First Edition. Edited by Garry L. Hagberg and Walter Jost.
© 2010 John Wiley & Sons Ltd. Published 2015 by John Wiley & Sons, Ltd.

criticism often over-self-involved in doing so. Yet matters needn't be like this (although literature will always outrun us, of course, as will philosophy), so we have tried to keep the two terminal points of the work contained here, philosophy and literature, always in contact with each other, and in such a way that that they engage each other clearly, concretely, precisely, and humanely.

Additionally, this Companion was designed to be reasonably comprehensive in various ways, at least regarding fairly canonical literature in English and regarding contemporary philosophy in the UK, Europe, and the United States as it pertains to the complex relations between philosophy and literature. At the same time it has tried to show how much remains to be done along these and other, as yet uncharted, directions. Comprehensiveness is temporal as well as geographical, and several of the essays show the contemporary relevance of issues or works one might have mistakenly relegated to historical or specialized interest. Other essays call for, or display their own particular blend of, methodological pluralism. Still others, in debating recent authors (and in a number of cases debating each other) show precisely what led to the current state of a philosophico-literary question and point out directions for future work. And some, synthesizing historical and contemporary positions and advancing them to a new stage of development, show how a composite or "mosaic" perspective can illuminate things we might otherwise have missed.

Finally, viewing the book more synoptically, these 28 chapters, presented within sectionally-divided groups of four, offer for the first time a large-scale perspective that makes it possible for contemporary readers to discern links and survey the lay of the land in new ways. Taken as a whole the volume easily lends itself either to sequential study or to selecting sections or chapters individually, as interests and needs dictate. In only a few cases – this will be plainly evident within the chapters – will it be strongly preferable to have read a preceding chapter.

The first of the seven parts of the volume concerns ways of characterizing, and ways of showing, the relation or the complex set of relations that connects philosophy and literature. Here questions arise concerning whether philosophy can be reduced to a kind or special genre of literature, what it is about philosophical content that might resist any such attempted reduction, what literature might show that philosophy (construed one way) can only say, and the distinctive self-transformative philosophical role that literature might play.

Part II concerns, first, our emotional engagement with, and responses to, narrative fiction, and, second, some ways of describing the experience of reading as one kind of performing art and the special self-defining power that, given a distinctive kind of doubly-focused identification with a protagonist, the act of absorbed literary reading can exert.

Part III investigates the relations between the genre of tragedy and the issue of philosophical content in literature, some Platonic themes discernible in Shakespeare, and both ancient and modern conceptions of catharsis as they inform our understanding of literary experience.

In part IV we have detailed inquiries into the intricate interconnections between literary and ethical theory, literature as it may be read under the influence of competing conceptions of morality, and ways in which literature can mimetically reflect, and bring about change to, our ways of seeing the world and others in it.

Questions concerning narrative, point of view, how and what we learn from literature, and the possibility of truth in literature generally and poetry in particular are discussed in part V, while competing conceptions of literary intention, the critical relevance of such intentions, the role of biographical information, and the very possibility of (as we say under the telling influence of a spatial metaphor) getting inside the head of another are treated in part VI.

The seventh and final part concerns the nature of literary language, the relations between exemplification and expression in literary writing, the role and strength of metaphorical description and re-description, and the role of language in understanding and recognizing the autonomy, and yet human interrelatedness, of others.

It will be clear even from these prefatory notes on the content to follow that, as mentioned above, the 28 chapters speak to each other in many ways; in this respect, the more closely one looks, the more one sees. We hope that, rather like the readers of Borges' Book of Sand (see chapter 8), this volume's readers will thus find ever-new things – or at least seemingly ever-new connections – in it.

Part I

Relations between Philosophy and Literature

1

Philosophy as Literature and More than Literature

RICHARD SHUSTERMAN

Philosophy without Literature

If philosophy is conceived primarily in terms of definitional "what is?" questions, then "philosophy of literature" should take as its initial task the definition of literature, and that seems to mean that it should examine the nature of literature with objective, critical distance, as it were from the outside. But if philosophy is itself a form of literature, is this external perspective really possible? And how can we convincingly deny that philosophy is literature, given the enormous breadth of the concept of literature? We cannot exclude philosophy from literature by reducing literature to fictional discourse, since so much literature is non-fictional and aims at truth. Philosophy, moreover, displays a variety of recognized literary genres: essays, dialogues, poems, meditations, treatises, speeches, confessions, memoirs, letters, discourses, journals, commentaries, investigations, sermons, notes, lectures, fragments, aphorisms, inquiries, outlines, sketches – and the list could be doubled and will grow with the arrival of new literary genres, such as the blog, which has already been enlisted into philosophical use.

Nor can we deny that philosophy is literature by arguing that some philosophers (including the great Socrates) never wrote philosophical texts but only communicated their views in oral dialogue. Even if the term "literature" derives from the Latin root for "letter," and thus suggests writing, the concept of literature clearly includes also oral literature, and we know that ancient Greek poetry was essentially intended for oral transmission and was largely preserved through oral traditions before being committed to textual form.

To award philosophy the privilege of defining literature, but at the same time to acknowledge that literature is itself the broader genus needed for defining philosophy as one of its species, suggests a disconcerting circularity. Even if circularity can be avoided, moreover, philosophy seems compelled to cede to literature the status of generic primacy, in which philosophy is a subsumed species. Such concession is something that philosophers are rarely happy to give, since philosophy first emerged as a major force in ancient Greece through its struggle to assert its superiority to poetry and rhetoric

---

A Companion to the Philosophy of Literature, First Edition. Edited by Garry L. Hagberg and Walter Jost.
© 2010 John Wiley & Sons Ltd. Published 2015 by John Wiley & Sons, Ltd.

not only in providing truth for the conduct of life but also (as argued in Plato's *Symposium*) for the realization of the highest kind of beauty and happiness.

To distinguish philosophy as more than "mere" literature (whether poetic or rhetorical, written or oral), ancient philosophers often insisted that their enterprise was essentially a way of life rather than a form of language, that it had to be expressed in action beyond mere utterances or textual inscriptions. In this tradition, philosophers like Cicero, Epictetus, Seneca, and later Renaissance philosophers like Montaigne, disparage as mere "grammarians" or "mathematicians" those philosophers who devote more "care and attention to their speech . . . than to their lives," and thus "teach us how to argue instead of how to live." Philosophy in this tradition derives her value and "authority over other arts" by being the "most valuable of all arts, the art of living well." "Philosophy," says Seneca, "takes as her aim the state of happiness," not book learning or textual production whose zealous pursuit can be harmful. Diogenes Laertius reports that Socrates was not alone among the eminent ancient philosophers who "wrote nothing at all" but instead conveyed their teaching primarily through the conduct of their exemplary lives. As Montaigne writes, "To compose our character is our duty, not to compose books . . . Our great and glorious masterpiece is to live appropriately."

Though this tradition of philosophy as a way of life has waned in modern times with the institutionalization of philosophy as an academic profession of theoretical writing, we still hear echoes in Thoreau's famous complaint: "There are nowadays professors of philosophy, but not philosophers. Yet it is admirable to profess because it was once admirable to live."[1] And the insistence on philosophy as a way of life that goes beyond textual practice has been reasserted in contemporary times by philosophers as different as Foucault, Wittgenstein, and John Dewey.[2]

There is, of course, no contradiction between living and writing philosophy. Indeed the most successful ancient philosophies combined discourse and deeds, theory and practice. The Stoic life of simple consistency with nature and tranquil acceptance of its providence was, for example, both justified and facilitated by philosophical discourse that viewed the whole world as a perfect, living, organic unity, whose parts, as necessary to the whole, must be accepted. The same symbiosis exists between the Epicurean life of unmixed tranquil pleasures and its discourse on the nature and limits of human sensations and sentience. If philosophy is supposed to assert truths about the world, it must do so in some literary form, through some discursive linguistic expression. The point of asserting philosophy as a way of life, rather than merely as a form of literature, could still be important as underlining that philosophy needs to go beyond mere discourse and engage a world beyond that of words. Yet how could it really do this effectively and lastingly without relying on words and, eventually, writing? Even if it is the philosopher's actual embodied life rather than her discourse that is most important, the exemplary meaning of that life could not long survive her death without an enduring literary expression of discursive testimony. The tradition of the embodied philosophical life thus requires the literary genre of biography (including autobiography), and philosophy seems to have first firmly established itself through Plato's brilliantly literary account of Socrates' life and death for the sake of philosophy.

If both philosophical theories and philosophical life-stories require some literary formulation, then what kind of philosophy might exist without literary form? Perhaps the most likely candidate would be what Socrates identifies as the most basic and essential philosophical task, the one that prompted his philosophical quest – the Delphic injunction to "know thyself," which he also closely connected with the idea of caring for oneself.[3] Unlike narrating philosophical lives or expressing theories about knowledge, being, justice, and beauty, the task of self-knowledge and self-care would seem, prima facie, to be a matter of silent introspection and discipline. Philosophy, as such, would apparently require no special literary formulation.

In the *Phaedrus*, for example, Socrates tells us that he cannot concern himself with all sorts of speculative knowledge because he is wholly engaged and "still unable" to do

> as the Delphic inscription orders, to know myself; and it really seems to me ridiculous to look into other things before I have understood that. This is why I do not concern myself with them. I accept what is generally believed, and, as I was just saying, I look not into them but into my own self.[4]

Having identified self-examination as the philosophical project par excellence, the very same dialogue strikingly offers Plato's most vigorous critique of writing as a mode of philosophy. Socrates does not condemn writing in general; he even affirms its value for literary arts, since it provides a man "gardens of letters for amusing himself." But unlike literature, philosophy is too serious a matter to be identified with even "noble amusement," since it concerns the essential health of the mind. Written formulations of knowledge make the mind weak by undermining the cultivation of memory. Writing fills men with an empty conceit of their own wisdom, which, without memory, is shallow and unabiding. Written philosophy is further censured as epistemologically inadequate, because, orphaned from the voice of its author who could explain or define it, it cannot speak to answer interrogators and is helplessly exposed to misinterpretation. Finally, the written word is metaphysically inferior, a lifeless image of oral communication and thus, as it were, two removes from "the living, breathing discourse of the man who knows," "a discourse that is written with knowledge in the soul" (*Phaedrus* 276a). The Greek term, translated here as "discourse," also often translated (in this dialogue and elsewhere) as "word" (among several other possibilities) is the seminal notion of *logos*. This term denotes not only the discursive expression (or words) of a thought but the unexpressed "inward thought itself."[5]

If the possibility of wordless thinking is granted (and even Wittgenstein seems to allow this possibility), then *logos*, despite its intimate connection with words, might also signify such silent, wordless thinking.[6] Moreover, even if silent thinking requires some link to concepts or words, it can hardly be considered literature; and this would suggest that philosophical self-knowledge could then apparently be pursued through introspection without the need of literary form whether written texts or oral soliloquies. Moreover, in the Platonic dialogues *Alcibiades* (131b) and *Charmides* (164d), the philosophical project of knowing oneself is identified with being "self-controlled" or being "temperate" rather than with a specifically discursive knowledge about one's person or mind. The work of philosophy as perfecting greater self-control would likewise seem not to require any real literary performance.

Having identified this option of philosophy without literature, I want to consider it more critically. Even if philosophical self-examination and self-mastery are matters of introspective discipline, such introspection, I shall argue, requires careful literary formulation for its most successful pursuit. Further, philosophical self-examination and self-mastery require more than introspection. Finally, I maintain that these philosophical activities also require more than literary means, so that philosophy is both literature and "more" than literature.

The Literary Formulation of Introspection

We should begin by underlining the psychological dangers of such silent introspection, first by recalling that the dominant ancient meaning of the Delphic injunction to know thyself was in fact a critical warning for mortals to know their place and limitations by acknowledging their inferiority to the gods. The project of self-knowledge was thus, from the outset, bound up with self-criticism, just as self-care highlighted recognizing the flaws in oneself that required amelioration. We see that quite clearly in *Alcibiades*, where Socrates convinces the talented, proud, and ambitious young Athenian that he is in fact hopelessly unready to pursue his political ambitions because he is miserably deficient in self-knowledge and self-cultivation, hence requiring a friend like Socrates to put him on the right path through a combination of dialogical criticism and friendly encouragement.

The project of solitary absorption in one's self and its inadequacies seems a recipe for depression and frustration. Even Montaigne, surely among the greatest advocates of solitary self-study, warned of its psychological dangers, since honest self-examination reveals

> an object that fills us with discontent; we see nothing in us but misery and vanity. In order not to dishearten us, Nature has very appropriately thrown the action of our vision outward.[7]

Likewise, Kant, while insisting that "the First Command of all Duties to Oneself . . . is "*know* (scrutinize, fathom) *yourself*," warns that this involves a "descent into the hell of self-cognition," even though such descent is necessary to "pave the way to godliness."[8] Nietzsche similarly cautions that introspective "digging into oneself, this straight, violent descent into the pit of one's being, is a painful and dangerous undertaking." Nietzsche thus gives preference to the creative, dynamic project of self-transformation, "to become what one is" by changing one's current self – a project for which the merely introspective "*nosce te ipsum* [know yourself] would be the recipe for destruction."[9] Goethe goes even further by protesting this emphasis on solitary self-examination that brings "psychological torments" and unhealthily directs us "away from the activities of the outer world to an inner false contemplation." Instead, he argues, one can know oneself better by knowing one's world, which includes knowing one's place in it among other things and other persons. By comparing our views of life with others, we can gain a more objective and nuanced self-knowledge than we could through isolated introspection.[10]

We thus move beyond the charge that silent and solitary introspection is psychologically morbid to the critique of its own epistemological inadequacy. Several arguments can be brought to support the claim that effective self-knowledge requires some form of mindful literary practice and even, preferably, a form of writing. First, there is a need to objectify the self in some way in order to examine it. The examining subjectivity (or "I") must be directed at some representation of the self (or "me"). Verbal descriptions and expressions of that self provide such representations. Without gainsaying the important presence of nameless feelings and non-verbal images that stream through consciousness, it is clear that our most precise, articulate, and examinable representations of the self are expressed in language, and thus formulated in terms of words and meanings that are public and shared.

Secondly, uttered or written formulation gives thought an exterior expression that enables the subject herself to experience it in a different way, allowing for more critical distance. What seems right in one's interior thinking may ring false and inadequate once it is actually said or written down. If critical thinking rather than mere thinking is essential to philosophical self-examination, then literary expression is also essential. Moreover, as Horace proverbially put it in his *littera scripta manet* (the written word remains), literary inscriptions have a durability and accessibility that neither silent thought nor oral expression could provide (though recording technology has now supplied oral literature with powers of permanence and reproducibility similar to written texts). Such durability enables continued consultation and re-examination of self-analysis essential for measuring one's progress in self-knowledge and self-cultivation. Though it may weaken the powers of spontaneous memory, the use of writing and other technologies of recording in fact extends our abilities to remember by providing enduring reminders.

Writing, with its graphic spatial features, can be particularly effective in sustained efforts at self-knowledge and self-improvement. Consider, for example, Benjamin Franklin's autobiographical account of the little book of virtues he devised "for Self Examination" and for progress toward "moral perfection." It was composed of an inventory of 13 virtues, vertically listed on each page, with the days of the week running horizontally and perpendicular to the top of the list, creating a grid of empty squares where he would "mark by a little black spot every Fault [he] found upon Examination to have been committed respecting that Virtue upon that Day."[11] Such a method prevented him from deceiving himself about his progress, even if his desire to think well of himself would incline his memory to forget his faults. Those faults would be marked there in baleful black to remind him, displaying with graphic clarity, in the immediacy of a quick glance, precisely those virtues in which he had been the weakest and which required the greatest efforts to improve.

Franklin's book, it might be objected, is more a matter of accounting charts than the conventional stuff of literature, even though his book also includes for each virtue an aphoristic precept and a few hortatory literary fragments from famous authors. But books that are instead composed with a concern for fine literary style can also, by that very character, serve as enduring means for self-examination and its work of memory. When oral or written texts are well-wrought with engaging literary qualities, they are more likely to be cherished, consulted, preserved, remembered, and hence can provide better service to philosophical investigations. It is therefore not surprising that philosophers take considerable pains to express their self-examining thoughts in attractive literary form, even if they are inscribed initially in the form of notes made for one's private contemplation and use. Consider the wonderfully evocative aphorisms and literary fragments that Wittgenstein secretly recorded in his so called "coded notebooks," a collection of which have been posthumously decoded and published in *Culture and Value*.[12]

The effort to pursue one's self-examining inquiries in literary form has a fourth advantage. Vague feelings can be rendered more precise and discriminating through literary expression. The care that one takes in giving one's thoughts and feelings an adequate and attractive literary formulation can, moreover, prompt and guide one's mind to new insights. Language does not so much mirror thought as shape it. William James notes how the different names of wines help us discriminate their subtly different flavors far more clearly than we could without the use of such names, while T. S. Eliot argues that the poet's role of forging new language enables us to feel things that could not otherwise be felt, thus "making possible a greater range of emotion and perception for other men, because he gives them the speech in which more can be expressed."[13]

So far, we have concentrated on how the process, discipline, and techniques of careful literary expression can improve the individual's efficacy in exercising solitary philosophical self-examination and self-care. But we must not forget that an undeniably major merit of expressing one's efforts of self-examination in well-crafted literary formulation concerns the ways that such literary expression reaches out to other people who can then encourage, advise, comfort, and otherwise support the individual in her quest for self-knowledge and self-improvement.

As already noted, an honest critical examination of the self is likely to be a painful process that brings up disturbing personal flaws, ills, feelings of guilt, and fears – problems that one's consciousness may not have merely overlooked but even suppressed for the individual's own mental health and stability. In such circumstances it is extremely valuable to have a caring friend or interlocutor with whom one can share one's self-revelations and whose continuing friendship affirms that one's self, despite all the faults uncovered, is still worthy of friendship and respect, not least in part because of one's disciplined efforts at self-examination and self-improvement. This need for a dialogical friend in the pursuit of self-knowledge and self-improvement is already clear in Plato's *Alcibiades*, where Socrates not only uses his external perspective to show his interlocutor's lack of self-knowledge and need for self-cultivation, but also repeatedly frames his exhortation to undertake this pursuit by underlining his enduring love for Alcibiades and assuring him of his faithful, affectionate support in this self-ameliorative struggle: "[S]omeone who loves your soul, will not leave you as long as you're making progress" (*Alcibiades* 131d). And the dialogue closes with the hope that Socrates' own pursuit of self-cultivation "will be cared for in return" by his beloved young friend

(*Alcibiades* 135e). It should be obvious, moreover, that when such self-revealing dialogical exchange between friends is expressed in an attractive literary form, the rewarding pleasures of literary style add zest to the communication and can even deepen the bonds of friendly affection and mutual appreciation.

Moreover, because one is revealing oneself to someone whose love and loyalty is trusted and respected, there is a powerful incentive, both emotional and moral, to do one's best to be as honest, clear, insightful, and articulate as possible in expressing oneself. Among the many interdependent complementarities of self and other, one's sense of responsibility to an intimate other can drive the self to be more responsibly frank and diligently rigorous in self-examination than when one is left to one's own devices. And when there is no fear that one might have to face an embarrassed, bored, or disappointed look from one's interlocutor at the very moment of one's self-expression (say, because that interlocutor is not physically present but is being addressed in a letter), then self-exposure can be freer still. In today's very different world, intimately detailed self-revelations are exchanged over email that might never have been expressed if the interlocutors were confined to real-time and face-to-face communication (despite the ever-present risk of interception).

It is, therefore, not surprising that the Socratic idea of self-examination and self-transformation through open yet mindfully focused and stylistically attractive communication with friends soon evolved in antiquity from the form of oral dialogue to the genre of letters. Written expression has distinct advantages. It allows one to take more time to compose one's thought in a more careful, critical, and attractive form without making one's interlocutor wait in silence during the time needed for formulating one's views. This extra time enables one to probe deeper in introspective analysis, providing more detail and nuance of one's mood and following a line of inquiry at greater length than one could do in oral communication with a friend. The written technology of "introspection" can thus be seen as changing the very practice and experience of philosophical self-examination. As Foucault argues, citing, for example, the loving correspondence between the young emperor-to-be Marcus Aurelius and his rhetoric teacher Fronto (a relationship rather parallel to that of Alcibiades and Socrates), "A relation developed between writing and vigilance. Attention was paid to nuances of life, mood, and reading, and the experience of oneself was intensified and widened by virtue of this act of writing."[14]

Besides, because writing is recorded and hence preserved beyond its immediate context of production, one's soul-searching message can be composed at one's leisure and in tranquil privacy, yet nonetheless be faithfully communicated without the need for one's interlocutor to be physically present. Indeed, through copying and forwarding, the message can reach more than one friend. Moreover, the written form allows the receiver of the message to examine it at his convenience and pace and even re-examine it repeatedly so as to insure a better understanding and thus provide better critical feedback to the philosophical friend who composed it. One prominent example of this genre of philosophical writing is Seneca's famous *Epistulae morales ad Lucilium* (a collection of 124 letters dealing with ethical issues and written to his friend Lucilius).[15] Because words do not simply clothe thoughts but rather shape them, it follows that greater literary skill in formulating the letters should also enhance the revelatory insights of the self-analysis. And such improvement in the style and insights of the letters encourages repeated perusal by their readers and thus inspires more attentive and perceptive feedback from them. The powers of the epistolary form, with its sense of direct, personal communication, are such that it has even been deployed as a fictional device for philosophical composition, in which we find the putative philosophical correspondence between two friends who are but the creations of a different philosophical author (for example, the Julius and Raphael of Schiller's *Philosophical Letters*).

Given the proven powers of friendship-grounded epistolary self-examination and self-cultivation in philosophy's ancient pursuit of the art of living, it is not surprising that Saint Augustine's *Confessions*, though not formally composed as letters, is rhetorically directed not to the general public of readers but directly to God as a dialogical partner. God is here addressed as an intimate, loving, caring, attentive (though infinitely superior) friend with whom one could share one's deepest secrets, struggles, and hopes for self-knowledge, self-improvement, and salvation, and who provides the sturdiest support for this pursuit of the good while also being the ultimate judge of its success. In this path-breaking philosophical and literary work of art, which innovatively combines the verbal music of the Latin rhetorical tradition with the sweet sacred language of Christian prayer, "The pronoun *tu* – "Thou," "You" – occurs in 381 out of the [book's] 453 paragraphs."[16]

If the psychological advantages of externalizing one's self-analysis in literary form are now evident, the epistemological advantages should be no less so. Solitary introspection for self-analysis and self-care faces the unavoidable problem that one's view of oneself is always partial, in both senses of "biased" and "incomplete." One cannot even view the surface of one's body without the help of a mirror or other reflecting device. The depths of one's soul, the complex layers, quirks, and weaknesses of one's personality, are hardly transparent to one's own consciousness, either because they are implicitly repressed or because, as part of one's second nature, they are so close that they escape attention. Even if one subjects oneself to the strictest scrutiny that one's own critical perception and reason can muster, one's purely self-directed self-analysis always remains within the limits of one's own subjective capacities. Subject-centered reason must therefore yield to the greater power of communicative rationality, even within the quest for self-knowledge.

Goethe, we may recall, in sharply criticizing the traditional ideal of introspective self-examination, insisted that a healthier and more reliable self-knowledge can be gleaned not only by looking outward to the world to teach us about ourselves and our place in it, but also, and especially, by learning about ourselves through the testimony of others.

> Most effective are our neighbors, who have the advantage, from their standpoint, of comparing us to the world, and therefore of achieving a better knowledge of us than we ourselves could acquire. In my riper years, I have given great attention to how others have been inclined to know me, by which, as if through so many mirrors, myself and my inner being could become clearer.[17]

While adversaries' views of him could not be taken to heart because of their essential negative bias, Goethe claims that he "readily and without limit depends for guidance" on those views of himself held "by his friends and always regards them with pure trust as truly edifying."[18] Contemporary experimental studies in psychology confirm that one's well-intentioned teachers and sympathetic colleagues provide a surer sense of one's abilities than can be discerned by one's own self-reflection. Students, asked to evaluate themselves honestly, consistently overvalue their abilities and even actual performance, while their teachers and peers give more accurate judgments of them. Moreover, feedback from peers (as from teachers) tends to improve both the self-knowledge and the performance of students.[19]

What an individual can learn from others about one's self is not, however, confined to others' expressed opinions about that self or their reactions to one's own formulations of self-analysis. It just as importantly includes the others' articulated views on a whole range of topics that concern the wider world. Because a great many of the self's beliefs are so implicit that it takes contrast to bring them to full consciousness, by discovering what others think about things, and especially how their views and interests differ from one's own, an individual can come to distinguish more clearly and know more deeply her own opinions and values. This encounter with different views has always been one of the highly touted benefits that literature offers for philosophical and personal insight. Thinkers as different as T. S. Eliot and T. W. Adorno have insisted that when we read a literary work of art we must, in order simply to grasp its meanings and achieve the aesthetic experience it offers, immerse ourselves empathetically into its world and the beliefs that structure it, though one should thereafter proceed to a second stage where those views are subjected to critical questioning from other viewpoints, including one's own perspective.[20] Yet one's own perspective can be transformed by a powerful author: "[Y]ou have to give yourself up, and then recover yourself," Eliot claimed, but "the self recovered is never the same as the self before it was given."[21] Wide reading is especially valuable, Eliot argues, because it prevents an overwhelming of the self, "an invasion of the underdeveloped personality . . . by the stronger personality of the poet." In caring for the self, the need to read widely in literature is not so much for accumulation of informational knowledge; rather, it is

> because in the process of being affected by one powerful personality after another, we cease to be dominated by any one, or by any small number. The very different views of life, cohabiting in our minds, affect each other, and our own personality asserts itself and gives each a place in some arrangement peculiar to ourself.[22]

Public Self-Transformation

Eliot's remarks on reading display the general tendency to blend the projects of self-knowledge and self-cultivation, whose connection is highlighted in Plato's *Alcibiades* and elsewhere in antiquity. The Greek term for this second project, *epimelia*, implies the notions of caring for or carefully attending to something, of showing concern for something, of taking charge, managing, or governing something. Because the originally dominant meaning of the Delphic command to "know thyself" was to humbly note one's human and personal limitations so as not, through *hubris*, to risk punishment from the gods and the powerful, the relationship of self-knowledge to self-care was initially clear and unproblematic. However, when self-knowledge is construed more in terms of rigorously analyzing one's self and inner character, then there is the possibility of a serious tension between self-examination and self-care, because too much ruminative self-analysis can be detrimental to psychological health.

This worry is what drives Nietzsche and Goethe to prefer creative self-transformation through one's activities in the world to an introverted preoccupation with one's private consciousness. If William James and John Dewey also express this worry in different ways, Michel Foucault (explicitly building on Nietzsche) is more forthright in urging that self-care is more important than self-knowledge, and that philosophical literature (even with respect to the self) should be more focused on transforming the self, on escaping (rather than dwelling on) the limits of its present state. If "the main interest in life and work is to become someone else that you were not in the beginning," then literary writing provides an excellent way both to transform oneself and to hide one's self behind a faceless labyrinth of words. "I am no doubt not the only one who writes in order to have no face," claims Foucault. "Do not ask who I am and do not ask me to remain the same."[23] By creating a textual persona to conceal and thus protect the self-examining self from physical exposure to the public, an exposure that could be much too inhibiting and risky, one can provide greater freedom for imaginative experiments to question one's self and the social conventions that define it, to challenge one's own limits (and society's) in a more adventurous quest for self-transformation.

But for all its values of concealing the individual behind the veils of textual constructions and even fictional pseudonyms, literary form is also a crucial device for bringing oneself into the public and thus transforming oneself productively precisely through the public exposure that literary composition brings to the subject herself and that rescues her from the privacy of her thoughts, feelings, and imaginative efforts of self-knowledge and self-care. I use the feminine pronoun here pointedly, because two of the twentieth century's most important female philosophers (Hannah Arendt and Simone de Beauvoir) have insisted on the value of literature for the project of woman's emancipatory self-realization by liberating that project of self-recognition from the oppressively stifling confinement of self-examining introspection, of private, ephemeral interiority.

Arendt, for example, in her book on Rahel Varnhagen (*née* Levin, a turn-of-the-nineteenth-century Jewish salon intellectual), stresses the importance of Rahel's chosen literary practice of letter writing as necessary for her quest of self-realization by insuring that her rich inner life found external expression in a literary form that made it no longer ephemeral and private. In the same way, Rahel's reading of literature (especially Goethe) gave her the tools not only to experience life more subtly but also to capture and convey that experience in precise and preserving language: "The function of language is preservation," writes Arendt, and what literature embodies can "remain longer than is possible for ephemeral human beings." Through her absorption in literature's "absolute precision in the use of words," "Rahel acquired to the point of mastery the art of representing her own life" to others and thus emerging more confidently beyond her inner world into the real "intricacies of social life." "She had learned that the pure subjectivity which makes a point of 'bearing a world within itself' is doomed because this inner world" rests too narrowly on the mere contingency of the individual's experience without sufficient support by broader social existence and recognition.[24] Through literary writing, even in the form of letters which she circulated among her friends, social recognition of one's distinctive personhood could be achieved, and through such recognitional processes the self could be transformed.

In *The Second Sex*, Simone de Beauvoir continuously cautions against the special dangers that introspective self-examination poses for women. Distanced from the life of public action and essentially confined to the private domains of caring for home, husband, and children, women are already overly inclined to "being occupied with [themselves]" in the realm of contemplative interiority. Relegated to the essential role of ornament, whose value depends on its always presenting a charming appearance, the female sex is already too absorbed in critical self-analysis of what she is and how she looks to achieve a radical transformation of her condition in the world. "She still regards her life as an immanent enterprise," measured by "subjective success." Rather than self-analysis, "what woman essentially lacks today for doing great things is forgetfulness of herself," an escape from critical subjective immanence that enables the transcendence of projecting oneself boldly and forcefully into the world of action.[25]

Given the societal conventions that have constrained the possibilities of women to make a public mark in the world, writing presents an extremely important mode of transcendence and public recognition. Beauvoir always proudly defined herself as a writer rather than a philosopher, and it is clear from her extensive autobiographical writings that she regarded writing as an indispensable tool for converting self-analysis into active transcendence in the public sphere. "This was the meaning behind my vocation," she writes in examining her early years, "I would take my childhood in hand again and make of it a faultless work of art. I saw myself as the basis of my own apotheosis."[26] To transcribe one's life, feelings, and thoughts in a literary form can thus transform the self not only by taking it beyond its interior experience so that it can play a more public role, but by reshaping the self into a more coherent and effective narrative that supports further activity of transformational transcendence.

Another way that writing the self can help care for and transform the self is by enlisting others to encourage and assist us in that pursuit. Instead of struggling alone with its efforts at self-reform, the self can acquire, by expressing that struggle in a literary form attractive to others, an extensive support group to cheer it on but also to admonish it when it strays or lapses. An interesting contemporary example of this can be found in the increasingly popular genre of blogs devoted to debt. In these blogs (with such names as "bloggingawaydebt.com," "wereindebt.com," and "makelovenotdebt.com"), the individual bloggers (who typically remain anonymous) try to get a handle on their struggle with debt and irresponsible credit card spending by reaching out to a wide, anonymous internet audience with whom to share their struggle, revealing to an extensive public intimate financial details and personal feelings that they dare not share with their family and close friends. In order to connect to these unknown people through the internet, the bloggers claim to rely on their "good communication skills." And without sufficient literary skills to recount, with poignancy and humor, their struggles with debt and spending, how could they succeed in engaging this initially unknown audience? The bloggers also claim that feedback from their internet public has helped their self-discipline, not only through the "supportive" comments but through "the fear of censure" for their failures.[27]

Philosophy as More than Literature

Having thus far urged the need for literature in pursuit of the philosophical tasks of self-examination and self-care, I wish to conclude by briefly arguing that philosophy in this sense must also be "more" than literature. Discourse, no matter how powerful and exquisite, is not enough. To know oneself requires knowing one's deeds as well as one's words, just as judgments of others are more reliable if based also on their actions beyond the speech acts they perform in utterance or writing. Formulations of one's philosophical ethos must be tested in trials of experience, especially since philosophical views can often be a contrasting compensation for one's own life rather than a faithful expression of one's experience or character.[28] To explore the value of philosophical views by examining the quality of life of the person expounding them can be seen as a form of *argumentum ad hominem*, which is today considered a glaring logical fallacy and is surely irrelevant to philosophy's more formal, abstract issues. But in earlier times, it was common to test a philosopher's views by his manner of life, often with special emphasis on his way of facing death. As Montaigne praises Socrates, Cleanthes, and Seneca for how they managed, and ended, their lives, so he condemns Cicero for the wretched, cowardly way he met his death. In fact, Socrates, who produced no writings and whose words we only know through their interpretation by others, gave philosophy its inspirational power largely by his heroic model of living and dying in the courageous pursuit of wisdom rather than by any specific doctrine or literary masterpiece that he left us. Similarly, when Plato uses his persona in the *Phaedo* to argue for the immortality of the soul, the Socratic example of actually meeting death with cheerful welcome rather than cowering fear gives a more powerful aura of credibility to the discursive arguments Plato offers. Other ancient philosophers (either inspired by Socrates' example or preceding it) also insisted on embodying their philosophies not merely in discourse but in forms of concrete embodied practice, including distinctive somatic disciplines that were alleged to contribute to philosophical insight, virtue, and happiness. Though philosophy in modern times has largely neglected such forms of embodied practice to confine itself to literary or conceptual expression, there are some very important philosophers who do insist on the somatic dimension of their enterprise.[29]

Thus far, I have dealt only with philosophy and literature in the Western context. Let me conclude by reminding readers that philosophy and literature are also intimately intertwined in the Asian philosophical traditions, which have not suffered from Plato's foundationally formative attack on mimetic literature as essentially deceptive and morally destructive. Yet Asian traditions also emphasize with particular force that the philosophical quest for self-knowledge and self-improvement cannot be a mere matter of words alone. The *Bhagavad Gita* (or "Song of God"), a poem that forms part of the *The Mahabharata* (one of the two major Sanskrit epics of ancient India), is a key text for yogic and vedantic doctrines, and thus is often described as a basic guide to Hindu philosophy. But, when it comes to the yogic practice of philosophy – whether we are dealing with yoga of action, yoga of devotion, or yoga of meditation (all delineated in the *Gita*), we obviously cannot limit philosophical practice to the realm of mere words.

The same twofold message of philosophy as literature and more than literature is evident in the Confucian tradition. On the one hand, Confucius insists on the importance of poetry, repeatedly affirming the value of the *Shih Ching* or *Book of Songs* for guiding one's thought and efforts at self-cultivation. "My young friends, why don't you study the *Songs*? Reciting the *Songs* can arouse your sensibilities, strengthen your powers of observation, enhance your ability to get on with others, and sharpen your critical skills."[30] On the other hand, Confucius repeatedly insists that fine words are not enough, that they require fine action to make them convincing, and that without such action words in themselves are suspicious. "What can possibly be done with people who find pleasure in polite language but do not draw out its meaning, or who comply with model sayings but do not reform their ways." "Exemplary persons would feel shame if their words were better than their deeds" (9:24; 14:27). Moreover, right action for Confucianism is not merely performing the proper act but also requires performing it with the "proper countenance" or "demeanor" that expresses the proper attitude (2:8; 8:4). Similarly, the Confucian tradition emphasizes that some of the most persuasive lessons in the philosophical art of self-cultivation can be conveyed without words, through the wordless, radiating power of the bodily bearing and gracious action of the teacher, who instructs by the exemplarity of his being and behavior, in ways that both interpret and complement the words of his teaching. As Mencius says of Confucius, "His every limb bears wordless testimony."[31]

The view that philosophy is both literature and more than literature poses a double challenge for students and teachers of philosophy. It is not enough to compose our texts and refine them with logical and literary skill – we must also take real pains, in practicing philosophy, to give careful composition to our character, behavior, and bearing, and to refine them through harmonizing grace and attractive style that is artfully appealing though not artificial or insincere.

Notes

1   See Epictetus, *The Handbook*, trans. Nicolas White (Indianapolis, IN: Hackett, 1983), 28; Seneca, *Letters from a Stoic*, trans. Robin Campbell (London: Penguin, 1969), 160, 171, 207; Montaigne, *The Complete Essays of Montaigne*, trans. Donald Frame (Stanford, CA: Stanford University Press, 1992), 124 (quoting Cicero), 850–51; Diogenes Laertius, *Lives of Eminent Philosophers*, trans. R. D. Hicks (Cambridge, MA: Harvard University Press, 1991), vol.1, 17; Henry David Thoreau, *Walden*, in *The Portable Thoreau* (New York: Viking, 1969), 270.

2   See Richard Shusterman, *Practicing Philosophy: Pragmatism and the Philosophical Life* (London: Routledge, 1997).
3   Self-knowledge, of course, also forms an essential part of larger philosophical projects, as, for example, when Descartes makes the self-knowledge of the knowing subject a crucial first step in his general theory of knowledge.
4   Plato, *Phaedrus*, in *Plato: Complete Works*, ed. John Cooper (Indianapolis, IN: Hackett, 1997), 510. The Stephanus page reference is 230a. I will henceforth quote from this Hackett edition but give the standard Stephanus page references.
5   See *An Intermediate Greek-English Lexicon, Founded upon the Seventh Edition of Liddell and Scott's Greek-English Lexicon* (Oxford: Oxford University Press, 1997), 476–7.
6   Cf. Ludwig Wittgenstein, *Zettel*, trans. G. E. M. Anscombe (Oxford: Blackwell, 1967), paragraph 122.
7   *The Complete Essays of Montaigne*, 766.
8   Immanuel Kant, *The Metaphysics of Morals*, trans. Mary Gregor (Cambridge: Cambridge University Press, 1991), 191.
9   Friedrich Nietzsche, I translate from the authoritative 15-volume critical scholarly collection of Nietzsche's work, edited by G. Colli and M. Montinari (Berlin: de Gruyter, 1999). See "Schopenhauer als Erzieher" (§1), vol. 1, 340; "Über Wahrheit und Luege im aussermoralischen Sinne," vol. 1, 877; *Ecce Homo*, vol 6, 293.
10 I translate from J. W. von Goethe, *Maximen und Reflexionen*, in Erich Trunz, ed., *Goethes Werke* (Christian Wegner Verlag: Hamburg, 1966), vol. 12, 413; and *Zur Naturwissenschaft im Allgemeinen*, in Trunz, *Goethes Werke*, vol. 13, 38.
11 Benjamin Franklin, *The Autobiography and Other Writings* (London: Penguin, 1986), 90–100.
12 Ludwig Wittgenstein, *Culture and Value*, trans. Peter Winch (Oxford: Blackwell, 1980).
13 William James, *The Principles of Psychology* [1890] (Cambridge: Harvard University Press, 1983), 483. T. S. Eliot, *To Criticize the Critic* (London: Faber, 1978), 134.
14 Michel Foucault, *Technologies of the Self*, ed. L. H. Hutton, H. Gutman, and P. H. Hutton (Amherst, MA: University of Massachusetts Press, 1988), 28.
15 Seneca, *Letters from a Stoic*, trans. Robin Campbell (London: Penguin, 1969).
16 See Peter Brown, "Introduction," in Augustine, *Confessions*, trans. F. J. Sheed (Indianapolis, IN: Hackett, 1992), xiii, who notes that *Confessions* would have struck its first readers as "a literary work" that was "almost without parallel," "creating a new sacred rhetoric" (xi, xii).
17 J. W. von Goethe, *Zur Naturwissenschaft im Allgemeinen*, 38.
18 Ibid.
19 David Dunning, *Self-Insight: Roadblocks and Detours on the Path to Knowing Thyself* (London: Psychology Press, 2005).
20 On the one hand, claims Adorno, "one must enter into the work" and "give oneself over to the work"; but on the other hand, "Those who have only an inside view of art do not understand it." See T. W. Adorno, *Aesthetic Theory* (London: Routledge, 1984), 346, 387, 479. Eliot similarly describes "two attitudes both of which are necessary and right to adopt in considering the work of any poet." First is to "try to understand the rules of his own game, adopt his own point of view" but secondly we must go beyond the poet's world, rules, and viewpoint so as to "measure him by outside standards." See T. S. Eliot, *On Poetry and Poets* (London: Faber, 1957), 145. For more on the two-stage theory of reading shared by Eliot and Adorno, see Richard Shusterman, *Surface and Depth* (Ithaca: Cornell University Press, 2000), chapter 8.

21 Quoted from a letter to Stephen Spender that Spender cites in his "Remembering Eliot," in Alan Tate, ed., *T. S. Eliot: The Man and his Work* (New York: Delacorte Press, 1966), 55–6.
22 T. S. Eliot, *Essays Ancient and Modern* (London: Faber, 1936), 103–4.
23 Foucault, *Technologies of the Self*, 9; *The Archeology of Knowledge* (New York: Pantheon, 1972), 17.
24 Hannah Arendt, *Rahel Varnhagen: The Life of a Jewess* (Baltimore, MD: Johns Hopkins University Press, 1997), 170–73.
25 Simone de Beauvoir, *The Second Sex* (New York: Vintage, 1989), 623, 626, 702.
26 Simone de Beauvoir, *Memoirs of a Dutiful Daughter* (New York: Harper, 1959), 57.
27 See John Leland, "Debtors Search For Discipline Through Blogs," *New York Times*, February 18, 2007, 1, 23.
28 For more on this point, see the "Introduction" in Shusterman, *Practicing Philosophy*.
29 Michel Foucault, John Dewey, and William James are three examples. See my discussions of them in *Practicing Philosophy* and in *Body Consciousness: A Philosophy of Mindfulness and Somaesthetics* (Cambridge: Cambridge University Press, 2008).
30 See *The Analects of Confucius: A Philosophical Translation*, trans. Roger Ames and Henry Rosemont, Jr. (New York: Ballantine, 2002), book 16, §13. Future references to the *Analects* similarly use the standard form of book and section number, and employ the Ames and Rosemont translation. The *Songs* are an anthology of 305 poems compiled about 600 BCE from a selection of already existing poems some of which date back several hundred years earlier. According to one tradition, Confucius personally selected these works from an earlier collection of over 3000 poems, choosing and arranging them to exemplify his ideas about government and harmonious personal relations.
31 *Mencius: A New Translation*, trans. W. A. C. H. Dobson (Toronto: University of Toronto Press, 1963), 181.

2

Philosophy and Literature: Friends of the Earth?

ROGER A. SHINER

The final words of Stanley Cavell's *The Claim of Reason*[1] pose this arch question: Can philosophy become literature and still know itself? This question provokes various further questions. For example: Does philosophy already have a sufficiently stable state of mind that could credibly be called "self-knowledge"? Suppose it did, is there anything about the influence of literature on philosophy which could block, eliminate, or deconstruct that self-knowledge? Suppose it did, there was, and it could, would that be so bad a thing anyway? Philosophers may traditionally fall down wells through staring at stars. But at least if staring at stars they are staring at something real; it is not clear this is so when they embark on omphalic contemplation.

One cannot consider whether philosophy can become literature and still know itself without having first some idea of what philosophy is, what literature is, and what the possibilities are for a relationship between them. It will come as no surprise that the history of philosophy reflects a variety of responses to these issues. The historian, passing rapidly by Heraclitean arcanities over the fundamental ubiquity of Logos, would come first to a narrative that has the vices as well as the virtues of simplicity, Plato's war with the poets. Plato distinguished sharply between reason and emotion, argument and rhetoric, and he associated philosophy exclusively with the first of each pair and literature with the second.[2] Plato's answer to Cavell's question is clear. Philosophy that became literature would lose the ability to execute those routines which constitute its very nature. Philosophy become literature could not know itself because it could not know anything. Knowledge implies reason, and philosophy become literature could not reason. The alienation of philosophy and literature is utter. We shall not follow Plato here.

Another view, scarcely less divisive, would acknowledge that philosophy may need literature, its figures and its feats, as a politician or preacher may need a good joke or epigram – a need backed by psychology for the sake of persuasion rather than a need backed by logic for the sake of argument. This view displays the Platonic antipathies, and makes but a pragmatic concession to the constraints of the Cave. It is a hard professional truth to face that the odd joke goes as well in a lecture to the British Academy or the Canadian Philosophical Association as in a freshman class. But perhaps we are never nearer to the Forms than when we begin philosophy.

A Companion to the Philosophy of Literature, First Edition. Edited by Garry L. Hagberg and Walter Jost.
© 2010 John Wiley & Sons Ltd. Published 2015 by John Wiley & Sons, Ltd.

A more articulate and irenic conception of how philosophy relates to literature which nonetheless still stays close to the Platonic conceptualization has received a clear formulation by McTaggart:

> Philosophy is the systematic study of the ultimate nature of reality. The scientist studies systematically the nature of reality, but not its ultimate nature. The poet does not study the nature of reality systematically, but he does study its ultimate nature.[3]

The thought here is of philosophy and literature working side by side in advancing our understanding of how things are, in different but complementary ways. On this McTaggartian conception, if philosophy becomes literature, it would not so much have gone over to the enemy, but acquired a different set of skills – transubstantiated, not transmogrified. Philosophy could still know itself in a sense of a common goal with literature, but the new method for philosophy would be radically unrecognizable. McTaggart's view implies that philosophy is defined by method, not by aim: change the method and you change philosophy.

In contrast to those strategies for opposing philosophy and literature, consider now one for assimilating them. This strategy begins with the recognition of a point McTaggart also recognized. Suppose that, give or take the odd photon, quark, or gene, we say that the objects of science are part of the everyday furniture of the world. It is a commonplace that the statements of the philosopher do not refer in any straightforward way to the furniture of the world as do the statements of the scientist or of the ordinary person. This thought is often expressed by saying that the philosopher is concerned with the *concept* of Mind, or of Courage, or of Justice, or of Law, rather than with an individual mind or individual act of courage or of justice or individual law. But the ontological status of these "concepts" is problematic, and this problem leads to remarks like the following by Ellen Esrock:

> If the subjects of philosophical inquiry do not have referents of the extensional sort in the worlds of objects, then, like the creations of literature, they must be understood as intensional semantic constructions.[4]

Esrock goes on to quote approvingly a remark by Richard Rorty that "philosophy is best seen as a kind of writing, . . . delimited not by form or matter but by tradition."[5] She ends her paper with these claims:

> Both texts [literary and philosophical] are constructions. When understood in this way, neither text can be compared with an external reality, a physical fact or metaphysical essence. These inventions can be judged interesting, profound or innovative, not by extensional standards but only against the traditions from which they arise. Only the tradition, the great texts that precede a work, provides the grounds for assessment.[6]

As a set of constructions, as a series of contributing voices to an ongoing conversation of mankind, of course philosophy can then become literature and still know itself, for philosophy would be nothing other than literature – a genteel and elegant pastime, the cultural garnish on the plate of serious pursuits like politics, commerce, or professional sport. Call such an approach the Rortification of philosophy.

Philosophers who reject the Rortification of philosophy need not have a monopoly on the rejection of Rortification. Although perhaps these days it would lead to difficulties in getting published in the journals, there are those in literature who reject the Rortification of literature also, the reduction of literature itself to mere conversation within a tradition. And so we come to the problematic that this paper addresses. Is Rortification the price that philosophy has to pay for becoming literature and still knowing itself – being allowed still to call itself philosophy, for remaining a distinct kind of enterprise? Is the only hope for the individuation of philosophy as an enterprise the historically distinct conversation of philosophers? As myself a philosopher, my main interest is in the problematic so phrased. But one could reverse Cavell's question and ask: Can literature become philosophy and still know itself? Rortification can then seem attractive to literature as the only way to preserve its identity from the encroachments of philosophy. So my chapter may also be taken to address a secondary problematic: is Rortification the price that literature has to pay to keep philosophy from becoming literature and still knowing itself?

Esrock in the passage quoted above refers to tradition: assessment by the tradition is equated with Rortification. Indeed I do not believe that either literature or philosophy either has or should have the ability to escape its tradition. I do not beyond a certain point take seriously Wittgenstein's idea that he thought and wrote simply as the heir of what used to be called philosophy.[7] In literature, analogously, the work of F. R. Leavis reminds us that membership in a tradition does not require that literary texts be understood simply as "intensional semantic constructions." Nor do I wish to dishonor the legitimate claims of modernism in any form of art. As long as art is creative, and as long as philosophy is creative, then any generation sets problems for those that come after it. We are all post-modernists now, let alone modernists. By way of showing how philosophy might become literature and still know itself, I shall offer some considerations in favor of saying, as a fundamental truth about both philosophy and literature, that, when it comes to the deepest things of metaphysics, philosophy and literature are not merely both engaged in the same task, but so engaged in an importantly similar kind of way. The brilliance of technical achievements in exploiting the outer limits of bequeathed art forms must not be allowed to conceal what has been lost, and I do not join with those who would celebrate that loss. What has been lost is consciousness of what I shall call the *ontological function* of literature and of philosophy. The fault here lies with philosophy itself and with the nature of its attempts to understand the possibilities for this function. Philosophy has tended to want to understand the function in terms of a simple model of extensional referentiality, and this will not do – to that extent my sympathies are with those who reject the dominance of the metaphysics of presence. But we must be wary of too cramped an idea of how an ontological function may be performed by literature and by philosophy. The strategies reviewed above suffer from such a cramped idea. I will not here explain further what I mean. The remainder of the paper will serve as explanation of the point.

Reference and Literary Language

I want to begin by considering whether the very idea of an ontological function for literature and for philosophy makes any antecedent sense. Even the briefest acquaintance with either philosophy or literature reveals what makes philosophers uneasy with the talk of "ontological function." The philosopher who asks whether this is a dagger is not asking Macbeth's question, for she would not accept any proof Macbeth would accept for the reality of the dagger. When asking whether Aunt Agatha is really in pain, the philosopher is not concerned with proofs of sincerity or sedation. The language of the philosopher is not ordinary language, for the philosopher's questions are not the ordinary questions which her words in ordinary language would be used to put.[8] Likewise, whether one is faced with the created world of a novel or drama, or the subjective world explored by the poets, ordinary language in its relationship to the ordinary world is left behind. Neither Soames Forsyte nor the chair she sat in like a burnished throne exists as does the good ship *Queen Elizabeth II*. So, if there is a radical problem of reference for philosophical and literary language, how can we talk about an ontological function for philosophy and for literature?

Let me leave philosophy for a while to fend for itself, and concentrate on literature. We must, first, refine the ancient notion of literature as presenting the universal through the particular. One can in fact distinguish here three different kinds of presentation, and the distinction between these three kinds is essential to the notion of "ontological function."

First, though this will not be true of all literary works, there are some which concern an actual particular, rather than simply an imagined one. Hochhuth's play about Winston Churchill is a play about a historical figure. Perhaps also *Macbeth* or *Hamlet*: *Julius Caesar* and *Anthony and Cleopatra* certainly are. Pinter's *Homecoming* or *The Tempest* are not such plays. Likewise, J. Alfred Prufrock is not a historical figure, but there are such birds as falcons about which Hopkins wrote such a stunning poem. In the case of literature with a historical reference, literature may reveal truths about that historical figure which historical biographies and treatises may not have been able to reveal, or may have revealed only to the extent that they ceased being treatises and became literature. Here, the idea of the universal in the particular plays no special role; the particular itself is the object of attention.

A *second* kind of presentation is the universalization from that particular – any ambitious man or woman, anyone who is torn between passion and duty, anyone who has heard the eternal footman snicker, any soaring and hovering bird. Distinct again from this is a third kind of presentation, and I understand the idea of "ontological function" in terms of this third kind. Here what is presented is not just the characteristics of a certain type of person, but of *any* person; not just the characteristics of a certain type of human predicament, but of the human predicament itself. This third kind of presentation is "ontological" because it is about how things ultimately are, about the nature of human being in general, about that realm where being reaches its ground. We may see each of these three different kinds of presentation quite clearly in Hopkins's short, but typically dense and crafted, poem – the first kind:

> I caught this morning morning's minion, kingdom
> of daylight's dauphin, dapple-dawn Falcon, in his
> riding of the rolling underneath him steady air . . .

The second kind:

> . . . how he rung upon the rein of wimpling wing
> In his ecstasy . . .
> . . . My heart in hiding
> Stirred for a bird – the achieve of, the mastery of
>   the thing.

The third kind:

> Brute beauty and valour and act, oh, air, pride, plume, here
> Buckle! AND the fire that breaks from thee then, a billion
> Times told lovelier, more dangerous, O my chevalier!

How might we characterize the workings of this third kind of presentation of the universal, the achievement of which counts as performing an ontological function? One answer to this question is that given by Heidegger in his essay, "The Origin of the Work of Art."[9] Heidegger confronts the problem of reference head-on by accepting that the relation of artworks to being indeed is not "reference"; he construes it instead as "unconcealing":

> The world is the self-disclosing openness of the broad paths of the simple and essential decisions in the destiny of a historical people. The earth is the spontaneous forthcoming of that which is continually self-secluding and to that extent sheltering and concealing.[10]

> Projective saying is poetry . . . Poetry is the saying of the Unconcealedness of what is . . . Projective saying which, in preparing the sayable, simultaneously brings the unsayable as such into a world.[11]

> The poet, if he is a poet, does not describe the mere appearance of sky and earth. The poet calls, in the sights of the sky, that which in its very self-disclosure causes the appearance of that which conceals itself, and indeed as that which conceals itself. In the familiar appearances; the poet calls the alien as that to which the invisible imparts itself in order to remain what it is – unknown.[12]

In these three passages we note the key concepts that Heidegger uses to flesh out his position: those of *world* and *earth*. Heidegger both does and does not mean by these terms what they would ordinarily be taken to mean – thus *showing*, and I cannot resist pointing this out in passing, that philosophy, supposing Heidegger here to be doing philosophy, is similarly located between ordinary language and an ideal of purity. Let us examine these concepts in more detail.

World, Heidegger says, is "das immer Ungegenständliche." That is to say, we do not stand over against the world as objective: rather, we inhabit a non-objective world which is our own historical creation. Individuals, peoples, races all have their own non-objective worlds. The proper task of art is to establish a world, and "in setting up a world, the work sets forth the earth."[13] The essence of the earth is to be ontologically basic, but as such also to be invisible, concealed, and to be momentarily unconcealed only via the medium of art.

I shall try to state what is happening here in plainer language – at least, if I understand Heidegger. Two things must be noted. Not only is the referential function of ordinary language here being distinguished from the ontological function of art, especially poetry. In addition, a very particular interpretation is being given to each of these notions, an interpretation which is an expression of Heidegger's existentialism. All that is objective is Being Itself, the earth; but that lies beyond the reference of ordinary language, which can only be to beings. Beings, however, are inhabitants of non-objective, historicist worlds. The references of their language can only be to the constituents of a non-objective world. As a corollary, the language of a literary text, as Paul Ricoeur, following Heidegger, has explicitly argued, has reference only to the world that is established by that literary work.[14] As the author creates the world of his or her text, and the language of the text refers only to that created world and its contents, or to the created worlds of other texts, so also humans create worlds and human language refers only to those humanly constructed worlds and their contents.

At first sight, such conventionalism is counterintuitive. Karsten Harries has argued however that as far as concerns literature, Ricoeur's conclusion, that reference in literature is only to the world of a text, is not required by the general Heideggerian position.[15] The ontological function of literature, a genuine thrust towards something beyond the text compatible with a historicist account of that text, is achieved, according to Harries, if we are able to recognize in the world established by the literary work the world that assigns us our place, into which we have been thrown. Reference in the literary text in the strict sense is certainly to the non-objective (our world), but it is still reference, and reference not merely to the world of the text itself. Harries is trying to show that rejecting the claim that ordinary language refers to an objective world, to something beyond itself, does not necessitate maintaining the claim that the language of a literary text refers only to that text and not to a world beyond the text. If you like, intertextuality as the essence of ordinary language does not imply intertextuality as the essence of literary language.

It is important for my purposes to realize that Harries' argument is unsound, and that ordinary and literary language cannot thus be prized apart. In the argument, the claim to reference to something beyond the world of the text is supposedly secured by the world that assigns us our place. The existence of *that* world separate from the world of the text is supposedly secured by the Heideggerian earth. So, in literature, we move from the world of the text to our non-objective world, not via the reference of the text's language, but via the earth it unconceals. Thus the whole weight of the idea that literature construed as Harries and Heidegger construe it has an ontological function must be carried by the idea that literature unconceals the earth, the groundedness of Being.

There are two difficulties with this idea. First, if the idea of an ontological function for literature so construed is to stand up at all, then the use of language to unconceal must be deemed primary. Heidegger does in fact acknowledge and maintain this view:

> Language itself is poetry in the essential sense. But since language is the happening in which for man beings first disclose themselves to him each time as beings, poesy – or poetry in the narrower sense – is the most original form of poetry in the essential sense. Language is not poetry because it is the primal poesy; rather, poesy takes place in language because language preserves the original nature of poetry.[16]

I take this difficult passage to deny, on the one hand, that poetry in the narrow sense is fundamental to language, but, on the other hand, to assert that something that is the heart of such poetry in the narrow sense *is* fundamental to language, namely, the essentially poetical activity of revealing the earth. That thought, however, only leaves as born only of existential finitude rather than of necessity the fact that the poet *uses language* – a consequence acknowledged by Harries in his thought that in the very process of using language "the poet is forced to use a medium that is not his own."[17] Heidegger repeats this thought in a later essay in *Poetry, Language, Truth* on "Language": "Poetry proper is never merely a higher mode (*melos*) of everyday language. It is rather the reverse; everyday language is a forgotten and therefore used-up poem, from which there hardly resounds a call any longer."[18] I do not understand, and therefore cannot accept, what is meant by this supposed ideally pure *Ursprache* of poetry in the essential sense. To a degree I understand what is meant by talk of "transcending" everyday language for certain purposes, primarily aesthetic, religious, and metaphysical purposes. But such transcending leaves everyday language in place as the point at which the climb starts. To take that away and leave behind a pure language makes no sense to me.

In the second place, if we do take the idea that the writer "creates a world" seriously, then the systematic denial that this characterization is compatible with an ontological function for literature simply conflates patent distinctions between the ways that literary works do create worlds. Consider the difference between the way that Margaret Drabble's *The Ice Age* is quite simply about Britain in the late 1970s or *The Radiant Way* about Britain in the 1980s; the way that Camus's *The Outsider* is set in, but is not quite simply about, pre-World War II Algeria; and the way that science fiction like Lawrence Sanders's *The Tomorrow File* or Ursula Le Guin's *The Left Hand of Darkness* creates future worlds fundamentally unlike ours in that gender differences there are genuinely of no social relevance. In the sense in which science fiction creates a world, Margaret Drabble does not "create a world": she describes a world in which people actually live, in order to help them better understand that world. Granted, it is a very particular world; her novels are not entirely accessible to people from the Southern USA, any more than Flannery O'Connor or William Faulkner will be entirely accessible to the British middle class of the time about which Drabble wrote. *The Outsider* of course does better than either in terms of universal accessibility. Moreover, even science fiction is still "about" our world in an intelligible way. It sheds light on how things are in our world by describing a world in which things are very different, thus shedding a refracted light into the dark corners of our world. In short, it is a *philosophical* description, and therefore a contestable description, to say of every literary work that it creates a world – a description not merely contestable, in fact, but also false.

I conclude, then, that *pace* Harries, we may still regard ordinary language and literary language as having essentially similar claims to refer to the world. The issue still remains, of course, of whether Heidegger is correct to deny both claims, and to limit the ontological function of language to "unconcealing the earth." Let us continue with that issue.

The Second Inheritance: Revealing the World through Metaphor and Paradox

Let us first of all assume that McTaggart and Heidegger are right in their joint assumption that literature reveals (in some sense) "ultimate reality," and does so (in some sense) unsystematically. Despite this agreement, McTaggart and Heidegger, as one would expect of a neo-Hegelian and an existentialist, differ profoundly on whether "ultimate reality" or "Being itself" is capable in principle of having its nature revealed systematically by philosophy. McTaggart urges as a difference between philosophy and literature that the nature of ultimate reality can in principle be revealed systematically by philosophy. Heidegger urges as a similarity between philosophy and literature that the nature of ultimate reality can be revealed systematically by neither one. Let me now try to urge a third view – that both philosophy and literature refer to a reality that can be distinguished from the empirical reality described systematically by science, and that both philosophy and literature perform this referential function in a manner that, while not being systematic like science or philosophy on a Hegelian model, is not either utterly unsystematic like a Heideggerian unconcealing of the earth.

I want to begin the presentation of this third view by an examination of Heidegger's language. Consider the metaphors that run through Heidegger's exposition, and in which it is so deeply rooted that one may not even notice them as metaphors. Beginning even with the basic "trans-" in "transcendence," these metaphors are three-dimensional, spatial, synchronic, static. They treat reality as something that exists at a point in time as a three-dimensional entity. Opening up, sheltering, grounding, calling, secluding, opposing – all these metaphors imply a distancing spatiality, a distinction in fact as well as in logic between world and earth. If we are to progress towards a more satisfactory understanding of the ontological function of literature, and ultimately of philosophy, we need to break the hold that these spatial metaphors have on our thinking about ontological reference. That can only be done by sensing the power of a different set of metaphors, metaphors that are different precisely in being four-dimensional, temporal, diachronic, and dynamic.

Such a set of metaphors is found in Cavell's work, and the key metaphor is in the following passage:

> Language is not only an acquirement but a bequest; . . . we are stingy in what we attempt to inherit. One might think of poetry as the second inheritance of language. Or, if

learning a first language is thought of as the child's acquiring of it, then poetry can be thought of as the adult's acquiring of it, as coming into possession of his or her own language, full citizenship ... Poetry thereby celebrates its language by making it a return on its birth, by reciprocating.[19]

The metaphor of language as a bequest is dynamic. A bequest takes place from one generation to another; it is a passing on; it takes place in time and signals the passing of time, evolution and change, the old yielding place to the new.

There are three aspects to the inheritance metaphor as Cavell uses it that need emphasis. First, notice the order of priority in the metaphor. The child's learning of language is prior and the adult's learning, though leading to a fuller appreciation of things, is still secondary. The reason: "it becomes important to say that meaning words literally is not just one way among others of meaning them. If it were, a child would learn to speak if we *always* spoke to it ironically, metaphorically, parabolically,"[20] clearly an absurdly counterfactual suggestion. The underlying point here is epistemological.[21] The child learns as it enters into its first inheritance, not the appearance of things, but realities, how things literally and actually are. The child inherits a form of life, the human form of life with its fundamental grammar, its constitutive ways of knowing, responding, reasoning, feeling, understanding about, of, and in the world. It is true that the child inherits a particular culture, a particular historical tradition. This is not merely a matter of the child inheriting "a world" in Heidegger's sense. The child is in part "thrown into" a world insofar as the child learns its own country's literature and history. But mostly not – fire burns, mothers love, peers scorn, food nourishes, eyes see, and calculations add up in any culture. These things are part of *the world*, this world that is ineluctably real and ineluctably ours. The reality of this world, its mental and material furniture, shows the falsity of conventionalism and of the textualizing of ordinary discourse.

For Cavell, however, and this is the second aspect of the inheritance metaphor that needs to be mentioned, there is also a truth to conventionalism, or, rather, a philosophical authenticity to the threat of conventionalism. There is no foundation of human knowledge beyond that which Cavell has called "our mutual attunement or agreement in our criteria,"[22] what Wittgenstein has called "agreement in judgments" and "agreement in form of life."[23] Human knowledge, human ethics, human politics, human art, are each a matter of community, and each one of us bears responsibility for the maintenance of this community. The human form of life is that there is in Heidegger's sense no earth. We are not statically related to some genuine and "unconcealable," even if unsayable, ground of our existence. Our existence is its own earth through its continuing dynamic. Heidegger, in thinking that an ungrounded world is a world of simply human construction and historical tradition, is being as "foundationalist" as any rationalist metaphysician or empiricist scientist. Heidegger's earth is not Wittgenstein's *das Mystische*, for of *that* we must be silent, and not even write poetry. True, for Wittgenstein, the limiting structure of human thought cannot be said, but can only be shown. Wittgenstein's "showing," however, is not Heidegger's "unconcealing." Human language and knowledge function successfully to describe the world because of the mutual attunement, the agreement in our criteria, the agreement in judgments. These agreements do not depend on the human form of life in the sense that the latter comes first and the former subsequently, as if we had discovered the hard way that a life with attunement was a saner way of living than one without such an attunement. On the other hand, as implied by Wittgenstein's thought that philosophy supplies remarks on the natural history of human beings,[24] the agreement in judgments, the mutual attunement, is inseparable from the existence of language and knowledge viewed as ongoing human enterprises. The natural necessity here that is, if anything is, the earth of human knowledge is human life itself. We live as persons who are present in the world and to whom the world is present: we just do.

The third aspect of the inheritance metaphor to which I shall draw attention is integral to its meaning for Cavell, though he does not make this explicit. In a bequest, title passes absolutely to the legatee, even if the testator hedges around the bequest with conditions. If a father bequeaths title in his house to his son, then the house becomes the son's, to dwell in, to sell, to rent for exorbitant sums. There is no redress except from competing legatees. We need this part of the metaphor of language as a bequest. Just before the passage quoted,[25] with Wittgenstein's notions of meaning as related to use and of what it is to follow a rule both in the background, Cavell argues that language itself, and *a fortiori* the use of language by a given generation, cannot determine what future generations will mean by any given term. Title to the terms of a language passes absolutely: that is why language is a bequest. *But*, and it is an important "but," though title does pass, the new generation cannot, any more than Lewis Carroll's Humpty Dumpty, make words mean whatever they like. "Words come to us from a distance; they were there before we were; we are born into them. Meaning is accepting that fact of their condition."[26] If I inherit a house, then, though I may do with it what I may, given that it is a suburban semi-detached, I cannot use it as a safari park. And so it is with language. Striking new idioms, metaphors, conceits enter into language, and many that are not so striking, or striking only in their barbarity. But these new uses must be seen as acceptable evolutions from, or as having ancestry traceable to, old uses: otherwise they will make no sense and will not survive.

In his metaphor of inheritance, Cavell also distinguishes the first and the second inheritance. Let us examine this distinction. As noted already, it is easy to see what is meant by "first inheritance" – the newborn child is thrown into a culture and a world, and grows up with it. The child takes on board all those crucial parts of what will give that child his or her identity as the person they will become. "Second inheritance" is a trickier notion. I take it to refer to a process of autonomous or authentic assimilation or acknowledgment of that inherited background – perhaps after conscious repudiation of that background, perhaps not. Elsewhere, Cavell deploys the genre of 1930s and 1940s "comedies of remarriage" as an extended image for this notion of "second inheritance."[27]

This philosophical metaphor of "inheritance" in the context of the present chapter requires an account of its method. Here I draw on the work of John Wisdom. The second inheritance, for which philosophy and literature are the facilitating counsel, is not the discovery of new information in the manner of Nobel-prizewinning scientific research. Rather, it consists in enlightenment engendered by putting in a new light the familiar, the first inheritance. Wisdom continually emphasizes the vital role in philosophy of philosophical paradoxes – that we do not know the sun will rise tomorrow, that we do not know the material world or the mind of another. He insists that these paradoxes are symptoms of linguistic penetration as much as of linguistic confusion.[28] This emphasis is not only stated but also shown in his own practice: the great paradoxes of metaphysics are time and again shown to be powerful lights shining into ontological darkness. Wisdom wants to make us realize two things. First, philosophical insight is often engendered by techniques at first sight radically different from conventional uses of reason (the uses, that is, that are the official techniques of the philosopher) and which are the stock-in-trade of the poet. Second, the exotic techniques of the poet and prophet have as much claim as familiar linear reasoning to be regarded as argument once all these techniques – the conventional and the unconventional – are seen as examples of the procedure of setting one case beside another, of reflective argument by the presentation of parallel cases.

The issue here is not the adequacy of words as such. It is not a matter of poetry and philosophy resorting to paradox and metaphor to overcome the inadequacies of words. Eliot in *The Four Quartets* muses in philosophic mode about the inadequacies of words. But elsewhere when he speaks of the still point of the turning world and of the fire and the rose being one, we who love know that fused into anything that might be called a magnificent inadequacy is an equally magnificent adequacy. The issue is not whether, but *how* words are adequate – how it is that both the accountant's use of deduction and the poet's use of extravagant comparison do what is also done by counsel in the courtroom and philosophers in the classroom and study – namely, reveal what is hidden in the obvious, and so perform their ontological function.

The dramatic way in which paradox and metaphor are successful in revealing what is hidden in the familiar itself dramatically illuminates the affinities between philosophy and poetry that the traditional McTaggartian definition obscures. Wisdom comes nearer to the truth than does McTaggart when Wisdom says: "In a sense, like poetry, metaphysics is synthetic because it reveals something which is hidden in a way which logical definitions never do."[29] Tom Stoppard's Guildenstern observes: "All your life you live so close to truth, it becomes a permanent blur in the corner of your eye, and when something nudges it into outlines it is like being ambushed by a grotesque."[30] For the deepest metaphysical truths concealed in the familiar, only an ambush by a grotesque will do. We know that paradox and metaphor, poetry and extravagance, parable and proverb *do* work, *do* bring enlightenment. In the attempt to gain a philosophical view of how they work, and in particular of how they work in philosophy, and so of philosophy itself, the twofold insistence that reflective reasoning by the presentation of parallels is a form of reasoning and argument, and that it is the technique employed by poetry is a paradox. But it is an important and revealing paradox, for it is needed as a balancing antidote to the correlative paradox that what cannot be defined by necessary and sufficient conditions and by analysis is not worth knowing.

Initiation into the World: Appreciating the Adequacy of Words

There is also another deep affinity between philosophy and literature. The second inheritance is in an important sense the separate inheritance of a new set of gifts – figurative or metaphysical (in a *very* broad sense) language. But in another equally important sense the second inheritance is not a separate inheritance at all, as is marked by the terminology of "full citizenship." The child is already at birth and by birth a citizen. He or she becomes no more of a citizen by becoming an adult, but rather takes on different civic responsibilities. Both the philosopher and the poet or novelist or dramatist are citizens of the/our world, implicated in it: they cannot escape that. Title has passed to them; they have new responsibilities. They can avoid acknowledging these responsibilities, but such is what the philosophic and the poetic predicament come to – conventionalism, nihilism, and despair are not modes forced upon the philosopher and poet, but stances that each only chooses to take out of avoidance of responsibility.

Both poetry and philosophy have the capacity to perform an ontological function, to reveal the profoundest things. To be a philosopher, then, as to be a poet, is to be called to live a certain kind of life in the world, a life of assisting one's fellow human beings to full citizenship. This must be done in the right spirit:

> If philosophy is the criticism a culture produces of itself, and proceeds essentially by criticising past efforts at this criticism, then Wittgenstein's originality lies in having developed modes of criticism that are not moralistic, that is, that do not leave the critic imagining himself free of the faults he sees around him, and which proceed not by trying to argue a given statement false or wrong, but by showing that the person making an assertion does not really know what he means, has not really said what he wished.[31]

It is perhaps humanly too much to demand of philosophers that they take as inspiration only their own questioning wonder, and never what other philosophers have said – that they never take part, or never see themselves as taking part, in a conversation whose rules are set by tradition. But philosophers will only assist themselves, and therefore only have the capacity to assist others, into full citizenship if they acknowledge their implication in the puzzlements at hand. How often does Wittgenstein begin, "We have the idea that . . ."! This assistance of others and of oneself, even though it must deploy metaphor, is mediated by the ontological function of philosophic and poetic writing. In the end it is the philosophic and the poetic life – that is, actualized philosophy and poetry – that because of the naturalness of that life guarantee fulfillment of the ontological function of each.

Cavell characterizes the history of philosophy as the Rejection of the Human. The human form of life is ultimately nothing more (and nothing less) than a mutual attunement of judgments. What is transmitted from one generation to the next is in part, but for certain not merely, a way of talking: it is also a way of knowing and understanding and living in the world. Children at first by adults, and adults at second by philosophy and literature, are initiated into the world, and only the world, taken in its proper, not its Heideggerian, sense. There is no Heideggerian "earth," no foundation for the world, but this lack does not make the world a mere stream of history, convention, and conversation. The "voices of the earth" – the voices that ambush us when they nudge the truth into outline – are but some of the voices of the world: the philosophical and literary voices. The notion of inheriting a language, both the first and second inheritance, has an ontological dimension, of initiation into the world. Harries rightly says that the origin of words is forgotten, their adequacy taken for granted, and that thereby we are bound to the community and to reality.[32] But he puts these facts in the wrong light. It is not that ordinary people in their dogmatic slumber forget the origin of words, or mistakenly take the adequacy of words for granted, or are bound where they should be free with philosophers and poets standing by to liberate them. To bemoan forgetfulness of the origin of words is to join in the rejection of the human. The adequacy of words can be taken for granted, for it is presupposed by there being human life at all. Indeed language binds us to the community and to reality – any other view of language, or of reality, is mistaken.

The adequacy of words itself has no "earth": it simply is. The adequacy of words both is an integral part of human life and that life's "earth." We need philosophy and we need literature to inherit anew full membership of humanity, and full appreciation of the full adequacy of words. The poet and the writer who seek the earth, and in seeking fall inevitably into figurative language, are indispensable, for only by seeking the philosopher's idealized earth will the real truth about the earth be found and understood. Equally, only by realizing that the philosopher's idealizations obscure the familiar will the real world be found and understood. Without the philosopher's and the writer's and the poet's struggles with the ontological function of figurative language, we would never see that philosophy and literature reveal, that the depths each plumbs are the depths of the human and not of what transcends the human. We need philosophy and literature and figure, not to make our own what is not our own, but to make again our own what is already our own.

The Continuum between Philosophy and Literature

It is certainly possible to overstate the case for the parallels between philosophy and literature that I am urging here, as arguably I once did in over-assimilating the former to the latter.[33] Francis Sparshott has not only been one of the foremost philosophers writing in aesthetics in the twentieth century, but is also a frequently published poet of some repute. He himself sees these two activities as altogether different, and my attempt to use his work as a pretext for assimilating them was soundly and correctly rebuked.[34] All the same, there are two complementary errors that might be made here. Suppose there is a meaningful continuum between philosophy and literature. One mistake is to infer from the existence of the continuum that the distance between the extremes is illusory. One might say that Sparshott criticizes my earlier remarks for making that mistake. The other mistake is to take the distance between the extremes as grounds for denying the continuum. I would like to say that Sparshott's rebuke makes this mistake. Consider the work of a different contemporary Canadian philosopher who is also a widely published and indeed honored poet, Jan Zwicky.[35] Zwicky does not accept any supposed discontinuity in technique between philosophy and poetry. She has spent her career exploring, and even, one might be tempted to say, creating the middle ground between the two. Her poetry ("mainstream poetry," if you like) ranges from the compactly imagistic to the discursively metaphysical. *Wittgenstein Elegies*[36] takes as its starting point a comment by Wittgenstein in his original (1930) preface to *Philosophical Remarks* about the kind of system-building that "tries to grasp the world by way of its periphery" and the kind of striving after clarity that reaches the world at its centre, its essence.[37] The book is a series of philosophical meditations in poetic form on texts of Wittgenstein and Georg Trakl that seeks just such clarity. The theme of clarity and perspicuity in opposition to discursive system-building is further pursued in *Lyric Philosophy*.[38] Two parallel texts on facing pages run through the book, one by Zwicky herself that ranges from aphorisms to lengthy expository paragraphs and the other a series of quotations, many from philosophers, but also from writers and fragments of musical composition also. The thought behind the book is that what the book has to teach is not found in the texts themselves, but in the spaces between the texts, in the synergy between the ideas presented simultaneously as one takes in what is printed in the book. *Wisdom and Metaphor*[39] continues the project, except that now the texts by Zwicky are typically brief and aphoristic, while the texts by poets and writers are more discursive.

It is not necessary for my argument here that her writings achieve their goal of clarity, though I believe a reader with an open mind will see that they do. All I need is that the project makes meta-philosophical sense. Things can be as Zwicky says they are. Say, if you like, that the poet lights flares or drops bombs, while the novelist and the philosopher draw maps. But the poet's wrestling with the limits of language, and with the spaces beyond and within ordinary words that the poet seeks to describe, is in the end no different from the philosopher's wrestling with the limits of language, and with the spaces between the attunement of our judgments that the philosopher seeks to describe. The ontological function, whose own proper mode is acknowledgment, not description or reference, must in its own turn be the object of acknowledgment in order to be understood. The poet and the philosopher are each trying to respond to and to express ontological wonder, puzzlement, despair, with no resources to employ save that language whose embedded pictures caused the original problems.[40]

Conclusion

I do not claim in the preceding pages to have proved to supporters of a view about philosophy and literature like McTaggart's or Plato's by an argument from premises they would accept via rules of inference they would accept that such a view is false. Nor should I be trying to prove such a view is false – for it is the classic picture of philosophy, and if it were not we would not have philosophy as we know it. Rather, I have tried as a philosopher to show how far controversial methodological and metaphysical assumptions within philosophy itself and about philosophy itself play a role in shaping the problem of defining the relation between philosophy and literature. If those assumptions are abandoned, then an interesting affirmative answer is at least possible to the question whether philosophy can become literature and still know itself. An affirmative answer to the question may even be warranted, if it is a form of metaphysical avoidance to concentrate on the separatenesses between philosophy and literature, and not to acknowledge their fundamental kinship.

Notes

Earlier versions of this paper were presented to the University of Waterloo, the University of Alberta, the University of Gdansk, and the International Association for Philosophy and Literature. I am grateful to Annette Barnes, Robert Burch, Bohdan Dziemidok, and Rick Eldridge for comments and encouragement at different times, and most recently to Garry Hagberg. My greatest debt is to Jan Zwicky, not only for detailed and invaluable criticism, and not only for pathbreaking work, but also for the faith that somewhere in all the confusion with which I surrounded myself there was a paper that someone ought to write. I hope this is it, or something enough like it.

1. Stanley Cavell, *The Claim of Reason: Wittgenstein, Skepticism, Morality, and Tragedy* (New York: Oxford University Press, 1979), 496.
2. This is of course something of an oversimplification: see among other possibilities Jan Zwicky, "Plato's *Phaedrus*: Philosophy as Dialogue with the Dead," *APEIRON: A Journal for Ancient Philosophy and Science* 30 (1997): 19–48.
3. The quotation does not appear in McTaggart's published writings. It is reported by John Wisdom in his *Paradox and Discovery* (Oxford: Blackwell, 1965), 59.
4. Ellen Esrock, "Literature and Philosophy as Narrative Writing," *Comparative Literature Studies* 17 (1980): 459.
5. Richard Rorty, "Philosophy as a Kind of Writing: An Essay on Derrida," *New Literary History* 10 (1978–9): 143.
6. Esrock, 467, *Literature and Philosophy*.
7. Cf. Ludwig Wittgenstein, *The Blue and Brown Books*, 2nd edn. (Oxford: Blackwell, 1960), 28.
8. See especially "Metaphysics and Verification," in John Wisdom, *Philosophy and Psychoanalysis* (Oxford: Blackwell, 1957), 51–101.
9. Martin Heidegger, "The Origin of the Work of Art," in *Poetry, Language, Truth*, trans. Alfred Hofstadter (New York: Harper and Row, 1875), 15–88.
10. Ibid., 48.
11. Ibid., 74.
12. Martin Heidegger, essay on Hölderlin, in *Poetry, Language, Truth*, trans. Alfred Hofstadter (New York: Harper and Row, 1875), 225.
13. Heidegger, "The Origin of the Work of Art," 46.
14. Paul Ricoeur, "Metaphor and the Main Problem of Hermeneutics," *New Literary History* 6 (1974–5): 107.
15. Karsten Harries, "Metaphors and Transcendence," in Sheldon Sacks, ed., *On Metaphor* (Chicago, IL: University of Chicago Press, 1979), 71–88.
16. Heidegger, *Poetry, Language, Truth*, 74.
17. Harries, "Metaphors and Transcendence," 78.
18. Heidegger, *Poetry, Language, Truth*, 208.

19 Cavell, *Claim of Reason*, 189.
20 Ibid., 333.
21 See here Roger A. Shiner, "Wittgenstein and the Foundations of Knowledge," *Proceedings of the Aristotelian Society* 78 (1977–8): 103–24; Roger A. Shiner, "Canfield, Cavell, and Criteria," *Dialogue* 22 (1983): 253–72.
22 Cavell, *Claim of Reason*, 168.
23 Ludwig Wittgenstein, *Philosophical Investigations*, trans. G. E. M. Anscombe (Oxford: Blackwell, 1958), §§241–2.
24 Wittgenstein, *Philosophical Investigations*, §415.
25 That is, Cavell, *Claim of Reason*, 189.
26 Stanley Cavell, *The Senses of Walden* (New York: Viking, 1972), 63.
27 Stanley Cavell, *Pursuits of Happiness* (Cambridge, MA: Harvard University Press, 1982). See also Roger A. Shiner, "Getting to Know You," *Philosophy and Literature* 10 (1985): 80–94.
28 Wisdom, *Philosophy and Psychoanalysis*, 41. See also Roger A. Shiner, "From Epistemology to Romance Via Wisdom," in Ilham Dilman, ed., *Philosophy and Life: Essays on John Wisdom* (Boston, MA: Martinus Nijhoff, 1984), 291–316.
29 Wisdom, *Philosophy and Psychoanalysis*, 56.
30 Tom Stoppard, *Rosencrantz and Guildenstern Are Dead* (London: Faber and Faber, 1967), 28.
31 Cavell, *Claim of Reason*, 175.
32 Harries, "Metaphors and Transcendence," 81, 87.
33 Roger A. Shiner, "Sparshott and the Philosophy of Philosophy," *Journal of Aesthetic Education* 31 (1997): 3–8.
34 Francis Sparshott, "Reply to Commentators," *Journal of Aesthetic Education* 31 (1997): 63–4.
35 Her book *Songs for Relinquishing the Earth* won the Governor General's Award for Poetry, Canada's most prestigious poetry award, in 1999: Jan Zwicky, *Songs for Relinquishing the Earth* (London, ON: Brick Books, 1998).
36 Jan Zwicky, *Wittgenstein Elegies* (Edmonton, AB/Ilderton, ON: Academic Printing and Publishing/Brick Books, 1986).
37 Ludwig Wittgenstein, *Philosophical Remarks*, ed. Rush Rhees, trans. Raymond Hargreaves and Roger White (Oxford: Blackwell, 1975), vii. Think also of the remarks of McTaggart discussed above: he implies philosophy is essentially systematic.
38 Jan Zwicky, *Lyric Philosophy* (Toronto: University of Toronto Press, 1992).
39 Jan Zwicky, *Wisdom and Metaphor* (Kentville, NS: Gaspereau Press, 2003).
40 Cf. "A *picture* held us captive. And we could not get outside it, for it lay in our language and language seemed to repeat it to us inexorably" (Wittgenstein, *Philosophical Investigations*, §115, his emphasis).

3

Philosophy and Literature – and Rhetoric: Adventures in Polytopia

WALTER JOST

The word "dwelling" derives from the Middle English *dwellen*, meaning "to reside" or "to inhabit" (no surprise there). Dwelling also appears to have been influenced by the Old Norse *dvelja*, meaning "to sojourn," that is, to travel by taking up temporary residence as one goes. "Dwelling," then, in the way that I wish to use the word here, signifies the paradoxical status of being permanently "home away from home" – not displaced or in exile, but as though one lived in a tent. It was Hegel's idea, later elaborated by modernist authors and theorists, that we human beings are "divided selves." (A Zulu saying puts this well: "A person is a person through other people").[1] The late Lithuanian-cum-Californian, Czeslaw Milosz, also thought of individuals as internally divided but reversed the relationship of self-as-sojourner by describing the "I" as its *own* place *through* which other "I's" come and go:

> The purpose of poetry is to remind us
> How difficult it is to remain just one person,
> For our house is open, there are no keys in the door,
> And invisible guests come in and out at will.[2]

For my purposes, these reverse-images amount to the same thing: the nomadic-sojourning self (or the self as host to travelers) comes to be "through" other people, is a divided self comprised "of" other people (places, things, events, and so on). Each of us, therefore, lives in what might be called Polytopia, or a "place of many places" – meaning not merely that there are many places in our discursive worlds, but rather that *each* place in our world is itself (and always already) "many places." One can begin to appreciate the need for different images to evoke such a strange place as Polytopia.

"Place," accordingly, a concept involved in the concepts of "dwelling" and "sojourn," is a term of art I need to describe Polytopia and us Polytopians – at least those among us interested, as I am here, in reading American poetry. My concern is not primarily with what certain poets explicitly intend in their poems or in their poetics, important and useful as this is to me and to others. For example, Charles Bernstein has noted that Charles Reznikoff's poems "move from site to site without destination, each site

---

A Companion to the Philosophy of Literature, First Edition. Edited by Garry L. Hagberg and Walter Jost.
© 2010 John Wiley & Sons Ltd. Published 2015 by John Wiley & Sons, Ltd.

inscribing an inhabitation, every dwelling temporary. . . ."[3] That kind of empirical observation aligns with Reznikoff's inferable purposes. In a similar way the literary theorist and critic Gerald L. Bruns has recently developed a similar insight about contemporary language poets (in particular Charles Bernstein), in "The Accomplishment Of Inhabitation," trying to clarify these poets' self-conscious, "nomadic" worldviews and poetic practices.[4]

My particular interest, however, is less an empirical than a philosophical and critical invitation to *look* briefly at poetry (American "modernist" poetry in particular) *in a certain way*. What I am after is related to the interests of those just mentioned, but differs by shifting from a predominantly descriptive to a prescriptive register – that is, not only a seeing but a "seeing-as." To paraphrase Hegel, who maintained that if you look at the world rationally the world will look back at you rationally, I propose that if we look at the world *rhetorically*, the world will look back at us rhetorically. The world will look at us, we will see it "as," a rhetorical Polytopia. What I am asking, then, is: What happens when modern American poetry is understood as a kind of discourse which the many resources of rhetoric might illuminate?

I take pluralism seriously and recognize that there are many ways to organize our world(s) discursively.[5] Let "poetry," if we wish, keep its generic distinctions from rhetoric.[6] Let a Plato banish it, or a Coleridge subordinate it to his own post-Kantian dialectic. Let High Modernist poets inveigh against "rhetoric" (however inadequately they conceived it).[7] Above all, let us keep and cherish other perspectives on, and languages for, poetry, for there are always many, and sometimes new ones, as Angus Fletcher has recently demonstrated to such good effect in *A New Theory for American Poetry*.[8] What remains (and what explains why my essay is an "invitation") is the philosophical-critical option of looking at the world, and the poems and people in it, in an explicitly rhetorical way.

Rhetorical literary critics have traditionally taken "style" as their turf. Jane Hirshfield argues that rhetoric locates "words and readers in time and place, in situation and point of view."[9] By adding "situation" and "point of view," Hirshfield suggests that not style alone but also content are the purview of rhetorical study. This claim is acceptable, so long as we emphasize that rhetorical analysis should treat all points of view, all poetic "claims" or "positions" or "content," "*as*" mediations – that is, as interpretations in and of a time and place. Reading rhetorically does not exhaust a poem, but it can help us mine a poem's inexhaustible riches.

In "Voice as Summons for Belief: Literature, Faith, and the Divided Self," Walter Ong invokes the ancient use of the dramatic mask as an image and trope to show how communication, including literature, mediates between author and reader by enabling *another* to reside *in* oneself. Masks and roles, like language itself, are public properties. Words as signs are not vessels containing mental contents, but public events in which those speaking and hearing "take on" the roles and masks performed by others: "It is as though this ability to take on the role of another shows [one's] own humanity, shows that the other is already within him."[10] Roles and masks, and the words and sign-systems from which they are constructed, move in the realm of "beliefs," meaning a continuum of facts ("belief-that") and values ("belief-in") that pervades every aspect of the event-world.

When we communicate, words (especially literary works) stage a "between-ness," a potential bridge (or barrier) which requires us to select from various possibilities for belief and action already in us. We can communicate just because we *already* share at least some "commonplaces."

At Home in the Commonplace

While I refer to literature-as-communication-of-the-commonplace, literature can also communicate *new* "places" – new values, experiences, emotions, imaginations, "masks," and the rest. From the Romantics on, this communication of the new has been regarded as literature's *chief* function, evident today in the highly contested nature of the concepts "art" and "literature." Stanley Cavell argues that what is "modern" about modern art is precisely its shattering of traditions and conventions.[11] Still, the new is never simply and wholly new, for if it were it would be wholly alien and unintelligible. Cavell argues, in a Kantian manner, that modernist artists face the challenge of claiming and earning for their art the objective status of "art" precisely *because*, by defying conventions, they nevertheless display possible new conventions that can be acknowledged by others as shareable, as real, even as "objective" and "universal." Another way to put this is to say that everything we know depends upon tacit knowledge of contexts, upon widening circles of commonplaces – interests, values, commitments – of which we are largely unaware, and whose unseen possibilities art displays.[12]

As a rhetorical theorist and critic, I am interested in precisely such commonplaces established in or emerging from the "everyday and ordinary." All rhetoric presupposes a more or less stable, communal background of habit, routine, ritual, and beliefs, even when (or especially when) the object is to disturb these and reshape them into new commonplaces. The physical scenes of such habit and routine are houses and homes, work places and play places, indeed *any* "place" subject to, subject of, or subjecting old ways to new ways of habit and routine, repetition and ritual. A word or two, then, about the "commonplace," and we will have successfully passed customs at the frontier of Polytopia and outfitted ourselves to visit some of these "places."

As an adjective "commonplace" denotes all those familiar everyday objects, people, situations, routines – the "given," the "everyday and ordinary," "what goes without saying" – among which we habitually dwell. We sense the commonplace around us, and in us, in our felt sense of repetitive place and time. Shared or oft-repeated things and situations are commonplace. If one were to challenge them – with, say, something we might call the "monumental" or "sublime" – new phenomena can be judged only *by means of what is already* valued, what "goes without saying," the commonplace.

Of course my commonplace is not simply equivalent to everyone else's "everyday." Although everyone *has* an everyday, not everyone has the *same* everyday, the same commonplaces. Nevertheless, from day to day the commonplace may be said to comprise a given people's "equipment for living." It is no accident that terrorists target the commonplace – the restaurant, the bus, the school building, even the monumental World Trade Center – for those are the very hub of our society, where life quickens and circulates. We too, however, are destroyers in our own fashion, inclined to dismiss or destroy our own common, everyday surroundings. Aristotle, in the *Rhetoric*, notes that "Men value what is rare." The corollary of this is " 'People-in-the-know' look down on the everyday and ordinary." Indeed this perceived poverty of the commonplace may be a defining trait of post-Romantic, modern(ist) art. Yet nothing like the prospect of annihilation by, for example, global warming or terrorism more powerfully brings home to us the value of ordinary everyday life.

A second meaning of the word "commonplace" comes from the tradition of rhetoric. This usage refers to those common objects, experiences, actions, values, and so on of people mentioned above. But now such matters are understood as discursive symbols that we routinely exchange with others, the coin of the realm of Polytopia – our basic rhetorical "resources." They are also *re*-sources, since we can use them again and again in new ways. Rhetorical commonplaces, known as "topics,"[13] we use automatically and tacitly to make sense of our lives.

In order to understand commonplaces as topics, several brief distinctions may be helpful. First, commonplaces easily degrade into clichés or (worse) the next person's zealously-held ideology, so everything depends on what we do with it or them. To be merely useful, commonplaces need not be (*pace* Wordsworth) socially or spiritually redemptive, but neither should they numb the mind. The question is: how does a writer interpret the world?

Second, rhetorical topics take a variety of forms, including: (1) single or doubled guiding terms ("commonplace" is a single-term commonplace for thinking about commonplaces; "theory-practice" and "words-things," mentioned above, are double-termed topics); (2) propositions or claims widely accepted by a group (e.g., "Men value what is rare"; "Poetically, man dwells"; "Sophisticates condescend to the everyday"); and (3) structures of reasoning (e.g., argument "from cause to effect" ["If A then B"]; argument "from division" ["Either A or B or C"]; argument "from circumstance" ["It's my party and I'll cry if I want to"]; and other forms like these).[14]

Finally, rhetorical commonplaces help us to discover relevant materials for talk, for discussion, ultimately for persuasion or meaning or identification of an important problem. We may think or argue badly or well, but "argument," in a broad sense of the word – making the case for something, getting others to see it "as" this rather than that – is the name of the game, at least as pursued here.

Think of Polytopia, then, as the "Commonplace of Commonplaces," "the place in which the certainties of the familiar are brought into contact with the transformations of innovation."[15] Polytopians innovate, well or poorly: it's what we do. Like bathtubs, or fuel and fertilizer, or trains, planes, and automobiles, rhetorical commonplaces are widely and readily available, and more combustible by far than any other resource.

Re-Thinking Proto-Modernism: Dickinson

One example of a high-explosive package of rhetorical commonplaces is this poem by Emily Dickinson.[16]

403

> I reason, earth is short –
> And Anguish – absolute –
> And many hurt,
> But, what of that?
>
> I reason, we could die –
> The best Vitality
> Cannot excel Decay,
> But, what of that?
>
> I reason, that in Heaven –
> Somehow, it will be even –
> Some new Equation, given –
> But, what of that?

This poem is rhetorically loaded in a hundred different ways. I am interested in two different but compatible readings of the poem: the first moderates the implicit threat in the poem; the second allows it to ramify.

The first reading is produced by taking the refrain of each stanza as a "rhetorical question," that is, as a question whose answer is already known. Dickinson's "what of that?" then reads as the "So what?" of summary dismissal. Taken this way, the poem implies a skeptical and even nihilistic reaction of the speaker to the usual problematics of theodicy, defending the ways of God to man. To be clear about these problematics, however, the reader would have to track down the possibilities arising from the implied arguments of each ambiguous stanza. This reading, which emphasizes its question–answer format (Dickinson's "So what?"), veers towards the arch-skeptic's dismissal of everything.

A second plausible reading, however, building on the first, takes the poet's "But, what of that?" as a virtuoso stylization of the "mystery" of persuasion itself. Taken as a genuine *inquiry*, not dismissal, Dickinson's "What of that?" rephrases the rhetorician's most fundamental attitude: how shall I "take" something, what shall I "see it 'as'?" In Cicero's *On the Orator*, Antonius says that

> the orator should master everything that is relevant to the practices of citizens and the ways humans behave: all that is connected with normal life, the functioning of the State, our social order, as well as the way people usually think, human nature and character.[17]

He means that all such materials can be used as commonplaces, as topics, to interpret and "pose"[18] situations. All literature, all history, all art, all politics, are potential resources for rhetorical thinkers and doers and can be used and re-used to make persuasive affirmations, decisions, choices, judgments. In Cicero's work, the term "orator" can extend methodologically to anyone who uses intellectual and verbal resources innovatively.[19] Cicero's portrait of the rhetorician offers us learning topically rather than through specialized principles and knowledge. The imperious scope of this ideal is nevertheless moderated (though it is still daunting), because thinking, writing, speaking, and acting effectively require being open to challenge by the full range of human experience.

In reading of Dickinson's poem as a dismissive rhetorical question, we notice that each stanza sets up its own persuasive argument(s). The poet leaves her elliptical arguments unfinished because, like any good rhetorician, she trusts her readers to fill in what is needed. Rhetorical theorists call such an argument an enthymeme ("a kind of syllogism"[20]), meaning not only that it may be left to the audience to complete, but that it is comprised, in part, of commonplace facts, values, and beliefs not tethered to specialized knowledge (*en-thymos* translates as in the "heart" or "gut"):

> [T]he enthymematic gap . . . exemplifies the ellipses that rhetoric exploits, on the plausible psychological assumption that the auditor will span the gap himself and, by an almost inevitable movement of mind, persuade himself more effectively than he could be by others, the rhetorician himself simply exploiting the auditor's own momentum.[21]

"People suffer," "Life is short," "Suffering consumes everything," "People die," "In Heaven is our reward": Who hasn't created enthymematic gaps (that is, gaps that one expects others to complete) by calling on such commonplaces?

Having heard or said them, however, the reader must still complete them: "Therefore . . . what?" The problem in this poem is not that we can't know how to complete the arguments. It's rather that we can draw on so many further commonplaces (combined with the poet's factual claims) to solve her puzzles. To wit: "Many hurt." [We add: But God in His Mercy knows this and looks out for all. Therefore, all will be well.] Or: "Many hurt." [But we are our brothers' keeper. Therefore, we must help them.] Or, a little more complex: "Many hurt." [And therefore we must help. But, after all, "You have to look out for Number One" first. Therefore, they're not *my* problem.] Or, more complicated still: "Many hurt." [And anguish is absolute, and life is nasty, brutish, and short. In Heaven, however, God will give us a new "Equation" to calculate our sufferings. But then: what good is *that*, if my own human life has ended (for death excels all)? An infinity of Equations butters no bread *now*. Therefore, to Hell with Heaven.]

This last version works well with Dickinson's "Earth is short," since the latter suggests not only that "*Life* is short" (and therefore, perhaps, "Grab all the gusto you can" because "Life wants to go on living"), but that "It's impossible to take the long view, to see beyond" and therefore, "to Hell . . ." etc. Whatever version we choose – and many more versions are possible – we come to particular conclusions, holding or rejecting them with whatever degree of probability or faithful certitude seems right.

But what if, on my second reading, we do *not* read the refrain as a series of merely skeptical rhetorical questions? What if (skeptical) "conclusions" are not exclusively, or not at all, Dickinson's intent? What happens when we take these questions as genuine confrontations with, among other things, what it is to listen to and weigh arguments built out of such materials? In this case the poem may be inquiring not only into philosophical-theological matters of morals and faith, but also into what it means to *argue* about such things. Her "what of that?" then becomes an inquiry into the conclusions one might draw (skeptically or not), as well as into whether the method of persuasion itself avails in such matters at all. In this reading, her commonplaces – meaning now both her propositions and their implicit binaries of "human–divine," "belief–doubt," and "reason–feeling" – can go on almost indefinitely, suggesting further lines of inquiry and discussion into moral and methodological questions. In other words, her rhetorical topics do not eventuate but remain as open-ended topics for ongoing discovery.

Dickinson herself does not make us choose between these two readings – for they are not incompatible. On the contrary: only by trying out the arguments can we get into a position to test their possible value and to reflect on the persuasive power of belief, on the very mystery of how such rhetorical argument works, or possibly deludes. Whether we cast these commonplaces in straightforward enthymematic arguments, as I have done, or mix and match others in more complex rhetorical arrangements; and whether we take them as obvious facts ("Earth is short") or "probabilities" ("I *could* die today, but it's unlikely") or theological beliefs or absurdities ("In Heaven it will be different"), they, and the further ideas with which the poet expects us to combine them, are the very stuff of rhetorical appeals, at once intellectual and emotional and imaginative. We expect the poet to know this, as she expects *us* to know this, not because we were trained in rhetoric (although she was), but because we are beings for whom rhetoric is a constitutive part of the human condition.

I will not pursue that argument here, but Dickinson, like other American writers, frequently uses topics in various senses to think about or display rhetoric and its possibilities:

76

The rainbow never tells me
That gust and storm are by –
Yet she is more convincing
Than Philosophy.

My flowers turn from Forums –
Yet eloquent declare
What Cato couldn't prove me
Except the *birds* were here!

It may be that the commonplaces in this poem are not as familiar as those in poem 403 above. Nevertheless the poem offers what many expect from nineteenth-century lyrics – namely a heartfelt celebration of the natural world. At the same time, Dickinson's praise is a rhetorical *argument*, running something like this: "It is only 'real life' that makes a thought or language convincing or compelling – take my rainbow, flowers, and birds, as proof!" Is this a *non sequitur*? Irrational? Absurd? In any case our experiences with flowers and birds are commonplace enough, while the poem's topical structuring again hinges on implied binaries or contrasts – especially "words–things," "philosophy–eloquence," and "convincing–persuading" – entirely familiar to those who consider such matters (not least theorists and philosophers of literature and rhetoric). Discussion of those larger topics we must defer, confining ourselves to Dickinson's attitudes towards speech and persuasion in this particular poem.

Consider the Roman statesman Marcus Cato (234–149 BCE), mentioned in line 7. In his own time Cato was widely celebrated, and is often cited by Cicero, as a man of notable eloquence. However, according to Antonius (again) in *De oratore*, Cato was one of those speakers who

> had no idea by what means speech is given distinction – such things [i.e., rhetorical matters], after all, have only recently been introduced here –, and who suppose that, provided what they say is understood, the sole virtue of speaking is brevity.[22]

Cato was, in other words, an accomplished orator but not adept, as Dickinson appears to be, in rhetorical theory.

As to "what gives speech distinction," several points can be made about Dickinson. For most in the nineteenth century, as for Cicero in republican Rome, "speech" referred to both oral and written words, and normally to words *as heard*. Emily Dickinson had a woman's, and a poet's, and an orator's, if not the then-scholar's sense of language:

> [T]he word *scholar* signified power. The word suggested closed clubs. Scholar was "other." Scholar was male. In the Victorian middle and upper class world of expansive intellectual gesturing, men gesticulated and lectured, while women sat in parlors or lecture halls *listening*.[23]

Dickinson listened to innumerable lectures and sermons, some of which, as she states in her letters, impressed her as being of great power and eloquence. (She also lived next door to the great orator Emerson, though she never visited him.) She very likely read Cato at Amherst Academy in the 1840s, recently opened to young girls, while studying Latin from 1841 to 1845, including Virgil's *Aeneid*. That Latin was important to her sense of written English is evident, as has been noted by others, "in her extreme dislocations of standard English word order."[24] Those dislocations themselves "eloquent declare" some of her own rhetorical (and scholarly) distinction of speech.

In "The rainbow never tells me," Dickinson's admiration of High Latin eloquence seems to be undercut by her advertence to everyday things, as if, in lawyer-speak, *res ipsa loquitur*. On the other hand, the lyric presents a series of argumentative *instances* (rainbow, flowers, birds), commonplace events or things placed within sets of indeterminate controlling terms, either explicit or implied ("words–world," "philosophy–eloquence," and so on), for further inquiry. The rainbow or flowers may assert more convincingly "than Philosophy" and declare more eloquently than Cato's oratory, but it takes the orator-poet in us to innovate on an old *topos*, turning the trope of "reading the book of Nature" (yet another commonplace) into *listening* to it (even as the birds "here/hear"). Furthermore, having her "flowers *turn* from Forums" eloquently declares the poet's own rhetorical wit, for she is aware not only that words are needed to speak for things, but that "flowers" is a common metaphor for rhetorical tropes themselves (trope in Greek means "turning," which tropes/turnings are but the nether side of rhetorical topics). Topics need not but can be tropes, but tropes seem to presuppose topics: "'tropes' have been connected closely with 'topos' in the history of devices of placing and turning" since time immemorial.[25]

In short: in poem 76 Dickinson's attitude towards speech is as suspicious as in poem 403, and yet she is at once beguiling and beguiled by speech. On the face of it, she speaks as though "things" might replace thoughts or words, whether those of philosophy or rhetoric (with nothing much to distinguish those two). But then the poet herself argues the matter in enthymemes of her own, speaking philosophically for the verbally inarticulate rainbow, flowers, and birds. Perhaps she here invokes, as in poem 403, Tertullian's *credibile est, quia ineptum est* ("believable because it is absurd").[26] Perhaps she is suggesting that genuine persuasion and conviction occur only when words remain unprized from her own close experience with the common, and commonplace, world. In any case, enlarging on John Hollander's view that what poets do is trope poetic forms (rhymes, meters, genres, etc.),[27] I suggest that poets trope "forms" *as such*, not least rhetorical topics of all kinds.

Re-Thinking High Modernism: Stevens

Wallace Stevens, though anti-rhetorical in many ways, shares Dickinson's preoccupation with rhetoric. To read Steven's "Theory" as a moment of specifically rhetorical theory and rhetorical methods of interpretation may seem counterintuitive, but to do so presents a neglected possibility for literary modernism and provides an opportunity for rhetorical study and practice. Stevens's "Theory" presents the averted gaze of high modernist literature, but it is also part of the unrecognized troping of rhetoric after Romanticism:[28]

Theory
I am what is around me.

Women understand this.
One is not duchess
A hundred yards from a carriage.

These, then are portraits:
A black vestibule;
A high bed sheltered by curtains.

These are merely instances.

I mean by the term "high modernist" that the poem is self-consciously ironic in suggesting both that something so grand as what we call a "Theory" might fit neatly inside a poem, and that so otherwise-unassuming a lyric as this can handle such a Big Bad Wolf as "Theory." I also mean that the poem is, like much high modernist art and literature, at least on its face "*anti*-rhetorical" – in its formal abstraction, in its speaker's various refusals to make explicit connections among diverse thoughts, in its refusal to identify an exigent indeterminate situation or even a relevant problem or audience, much less a specific purpose for theorizing, or to apologize for (not to mention avoiding in the first place) the minimalist bathos in concluding that "These are merely instances." Stevens *features* these instances; why call them "mere?" If they are "instances," instances of what, and for what? Moreover, just *how* are a carriage, a vestibule, a bed, "*portraits*"? These are peculiarly blank portraits, in any case, "a sheltered bed," "a black vestibule," not unlike Gertrude Stein's "A CARAFE, THAT IS A BLIND GLASS" that begins *Tender Buttons* (1914), which also purports to offer "portraits of objects, food, rooms" – none of which are the generalizations that normally belong to Theory. Is the vestibule an anteroom to someone's bedroom? To the duchess's? What duchess?

Such "anti-rhetoric" may even be said to approach *ressentiment*, an "imaginary revenge" on the audience, saying "No to what is 'outside,' what is 'different,' what is 'not itself.'"[29] Such a claim against abstract modernism, to the effect that individual consciousness gets strictly confined (especially in Stevens) within its own insular borders, would, as my undergraduate student Margaret Rennix pointed out in a class paper, "present an obvious problem for rhetoric" – "*unless*," she adds, "one considers the possibility that the second party in modernist discourse is not another character or the reader but an opposing facet of the central character." Not all high modernist literature operates this way; but it's a fair appraisal of *one* way to read it "rhetorically": the "divided self," the "self as a field of selves"[30] rather than the self-as-colonialist narcissistically incorporating all others, or narcissistically standing alone.

Such questions in any case are likely to be less difficult for us than for Stevens's contemporaries. We are after all their heirs, steeped in high modernist irony, parataxis (one thing after another without explicit connections), impersonality and abstraction (Is the *speaker* a duchess? *This* duchess? A woman?), paradox (a poem = a theory = a poem), and obscurity ("black vestibule," "sheltered by curtains"), so that we are, at least generally, prepared to understand such dislocations. When my students first come to read this poem they often feel initial hesitation, but they are not offended by the poem's abruptions as such (they have all seen *Traffic*, and *Magnolia*, and *Memento*, and a dozen other films dislocated by extreme parataxis). The more experienced students are likely to invoke some version of the widely disseminated, modernist notion of the "divided self," or the modern-postmodern "contextualist" theory of meaning (reality, self, etc.),[31] to explain what they take to be the poet's point, which goes something like this: I am who I am by virtue of the innumerable identifications I make with things around me – my family, neighborhood, school, job, political party, race, class, gender, country, hemisphere. These (asymptotically) constitute me."[32] As William Carlos Williams says in his epic poem *Paterson*, "an identity – it can't be otherwise – an interpenetration, both ways." From this angle Stevens suddenly seems less solipsistic. While many of my literature students have encountered some version or other of the divided self or even of rhetoric (the latter usually as destabilizing tropes), it does not occur to most of them that Stevens's poem is both self-consciously a rhetorical argument and, more obscurely still, a rhetorical instrument for inquiry (a "theory," to use the word) into the rhetorical, the divided, self.

Consider how the initial claim, "I am what is around me," is backed by several condensed arguments. First, "Women understand this" may be taken in various ways. Among them, to signify what half the population of the world "understands" may be taken as *prima facie* evidence for the speaker's initial claim. Second, the citation of "duchess" also supports and deepens, while it illustrates, that claim, while the other "portraits" mirror (as further supporting illustrative elaborations) whatever they are around. The poet-speaker himself, in having such examples around *him*, "is" self-reflexively what *they* betoken, even while his ironic tone qualifies whatever we might make of it or them.

But what *do* we make of it? What is this supposed to be a theory *of* – and what, in our own present context, is it *for*? I have hinted that, whatever they're about, the portraits Stevens presents are far too thin, obscure, even empty, for the purpose of an abstract theory of ironic consciousness or the divided self or alienation or perspectivism or contextualism. Nearly everything we would ask of a scientific or philosophical theory is missing.

Looked at *rhetorically*, however, almost nothing is missing that should be there, at least for the first beginnings of a rhetorology. The reason for this is that only *as* relatively empty ideas (gaps) can Stevens's images begin to perform like rhetorical commonplaces, as guides requiring the reader to invest them with meanings not simply provided by the rhetor-speaker himself (the enthymematic gap now as "topical" gap). In fact, *only* as relatively empty can his images provoke the reader to imagine a world for the duchess; only a relatively unencumbered everyday world can prompt the reader to determinations of his or her *own* everyday world; and only as "mere" instances of just what it is that women in particular understand – namely, *what is around us* – can the images function as "instances" at all: more than illustrations, but less than strict rules about what the reader might care to imagine about any possible world.

But what is around us, making us what we are? The first possibility is the commonplace – even when the commonplace is a carriage and a high bed. In fact, that carriage and high bed are wonderful innovations in context, for, although commonplace to a duchess, they are strange to us, made stranger by what we are inclined to take as reticent withholdings of the speaker. But "reticent" can't be quite right, since one cannot be said to withhold what is *already* given as the commonplace. As readers we already possess our own everyday and ordinary, inside and outside ourselves, although we may not know how or where (if only we would look!), much less how to project it onto the duchess for transformation. It is precisely by declining (not "refusing") to say "what goes without saying" that the good rhetorician Stevens invites the audience to fill in, as Dickinson did, from out of its own provisions, what will make the argument relevant and sound *to them*, bridging the gap.

We are likely to overlook not the high modernist tactics of the past (absence, irony, defamiliarization, abstraction, absent authorial commentary, and so on) but what I call its "low modernist" strategy, one that invites the reader to theorize *rhetorically* about what post-Romantic rhetoric can provide in an everyday that does not speak for itself; and to *innovate*, as Stevens does (so that he himself becomes "merely an instance" in the reader's repertory for invention of the everyday). Reading rhetorically, we gather and deploy relatively indeterminate intellectual resources, including images, characters, scenes, and the like, as provocations for discovery-invention, in this case not only of what Stevens is "about" but of what *we* are about.

In this way we can use the poem as a topical instrument to sound out what is around us, not least the conventional narratives about high modernism, narratives that have in the past routinely been taken to express contempt for the role of rhetoric ("the rhetoric of anti-rhetoric"), the routine, the commonplace, the everyday and ordinary. Stevens's use of paratactic absences may once have been relatively experimental and even "subversive" and may still be so to some. But for all that, his experimentation is no less an employment of a rhetorical mode of teaching and learning by *experience* with words. It is a pragmatic mode of rhetorical practice and theory which was familiar to that earlier modern minimalist, Emily Dickinson.

Notes

1. See G. F. W. Hegel, *The Phenomenology of Spirit*, trans. A. V. Miller (Oxford: Oxford University Press, 1977), especially on the "unhappy consciousness"; and, for example, Michael Bell, "The Metaphysics of Modernism," in Michael Levenson, ed., *The Cambridge Companion to Modernism* (Cambridge: Cambridge University Press, 1999), 9–32.
2. Czselaw Milosz, "Ars Poetica?" in *New and Collected Poems: 1931–2001* (New York: HarperCollins, 2003), 240–41.
3. Charles Bernstein, "Reznikoff's Nearness," in *My Way* (Chicago, IL: University of Chicago Press, 1999), 205.
4. Gerald L. Bruns, "The Accomplishment of Inhabitation: Danto, Cavell, and the Argument of American Poetry," in *Tragic Thoughts at the End of Philosophy: Language, Literature, and Ethical Theory* (Evanston, IL: Northwestern University Press, 1999), 133–63.
5. For two different but parallel efforts, see Stephen C. Pepper, *World Hypotheses: Prolegomena to a Systematic Philosophy and a Complete Survey of Metaphysics* (Berkeley, CA: University of California Press, 1942); and Walter Watson, *The Architectonics of Meaning: Foundations of the New Pluralism* (Chicago, IL: University of Chicago Press, 1985). For more philosophically advanced work, see Zahava K. McKeon and William G. Swenson, eds., *The Selected Writings of Richard McKeon*, 2 vols. (Chicago, IL: University of Chicago Press, 1998, 2005).
6. For a good example of the desire to keep this distinction, and the difficulties in doing so, see Charles Altieri, "Rhetoric and Poetics: How to Use the Inevitable Return of the Repressed," in Walter Jost and Wendy Olmsted, eds., *A Companion to Rhetoric and Rhetorical Criticism* (Oxford: Blackwell, 2004), 473–93.
7. On the modernists' turn against rhetoric, see (for a beginning) Kenneth Burke, *Counter-Statement* (Berkeley, CA: University of California Press, 1931), especially 210–11.
8. For an interesting approach different from mine, see Angus Fletcher, *A New Theory for American Poetry: Democracy, the Environment, and the Future of the Imagination* (Cambridge, MA: Harvard University Press, 2004). Milosz reminds us: "serious combat, where life is at stake, / Is fought in prose. It was not always so" (*New and Collected Poems*, "Preface" to "A Treatise on Poetry," 109).
9. Jane Hirshfield, *Nine Gates: Entering the Mind of Poetry* (New York: HarperCollins, 1997), 11. For a fuller sense of rhetoric in poetry, see Shira Wolosky, *The Art of Poetry* (Oxford: Oxford University Press, 2001), especially chapter 6; and my *Rhetorical Investigations* (Charlottesville, VA: University of Virginia Press, 2004).

10. Walter J. Ong, "Voice as Summons for Belief: Literature, Faith, and the Divided Self," in *The Barbarian Within and Other Fugitive Essays and Studies* (New York: Macmillan, 1968), 49–67.
11. See especially "Aesthetic Problems of Modern Philosophy," in Stanley Cavell, *Must We Mean What We Say?* (Cambridge: Cambridge University Press, 1969), 73–96.
12. I am alluding to the work of Michael Polanyi, particularly *The Tacit Dimension* and *Personal Knowledge*. See also the article by Robert L. Scott on tacit knowledge in *The Encyclopedia of Rhetoric*. For a good essay on Cavell and modernism, see J. M. Bernstein, "Aesthetics, Modernism, Literature: Cavell's Transformations of Philosophy," in Richard Eldridge, ed., *Stanley Cavell* (Cambridge: Cambridge University Press, 2003), 107–42.
13. In Greek, *topoi*, in Latin *loci* = "places." But we should include also the Latin *situs* and *sedes* = sites (hence, rhetorical "situations;" also "websites") and "seats" (e.g., of agency, as in an office, or "the County seat").
14. And note that a commonplace fact is not a rhetorical commonplace until it is used as a discursive resource. The fact that Napoleon was victorious at Austerlitz only becomes a rhetorical resource when its treatment allows room for persuasive interpretation (for example, as an analogy for another military escapade, or of foresight or discipline, or even, as in Tolstoy, unfathomable collocations of unknown causes). For recent excellent work on topics, see Christof Rapp, "The *topoi* of [Aristotle's *Rhetoric*]," at http://plato.Stanford.edu/entries/Aristotle-rhetoric/supplement2.html.
15. Richard McKeon, *Rhetoric: Essays in Invention and Discovery*, ed. Mark Backman (Woodbridge, CT: Ox Bow Press, 1987).
16. All citations of Dickinson's work are from R. W. Franklin, ed., *The Poems of Emily Dickinson* (Cambridge, MA: Harvard University Press, 1998).
17. Cicero, *De Oratore*, 2.68.
18. Ibid.
19. See Michael J. Buckley, "Operational Method," in *Motion and Motion's God: Thematic Variations in Aristotle, Cicero, Newton, and Hegel* (Princeton, NJ: Princeton University Press, 1971), 89–103.
20. *Rhetoric* 1.1 1355a; see also Jeffrey Walker, "Lyric Enthymemes," in *Rhetoric and Poetics in Antiquity* (New York: Oxford University Press, 2000), 154–83; and Thomas Conley, "What Jokes Can Tell us About Arguments," in Jost and Olmsted, *Companion to Rhetoric and Rhetorical Criticism*, 266–77. For related but differing views, see E. F. Dyck, "Topos and Enthymeme," http://www.wtc.ab.ca/tedyck/top.enth.00.htm.
21. Arthur C. Danto, *The Transfiguration of the Commonplace* (Cambridge, MA: Harvard University Press, 1981), 170.
22. Cicero, *De oratore* 2.53.
23. Susan Howe, *My Emily Dickinson* (Berkeley, CA: North Atlantic Books, 1985), 15.
24. Alfred Habegger, *My Wars Are Laid Away in Books: The Life of Emily Dickinson* (New York: Random House, 2001), 141, 310–12ff. See also Lois A. Cuddy, "The Latin Imprint on Emily Dickinson's Poetry: Theory and Practice," *American Literature* 50 (March 1978): 74–84. Latin syntax is quite malleable because word inflection displays the part of speech.
25. McKeon, *Rhetoric*, 32. See also E. F. Dyck, "Topos in Rhetorical Argumentation: From Enthymeme to Figure," www.wtc.ab.ca/tedyck/2.Topos.Rhet.Argt.htm.
26. Tertullian, *De carne Christi* 5.4.
27. Quoted in Fletcher, *A New Theory for American Poetry*, 148.

28 For support for this claim and for the importance of the "surround," see Fletcher, *A New Theory for American Poetry*. On p. 25 Fletcher uses the term "Low Romanticism" consonant with my use of low modernism.
29 Friedrich Nietzsche, *On the Genealogy of Morals and Ecce Homo*, trans Walter Kaufmann and R. J. Hollingdale (New York: Vintage Books, 1989), vol. 1, 10, 36.
30 Wayne C. Booth, *Modern Dogma and the Rhetoric of Assent* (Chicago, IL: University of Chicago Press, 1974).
31 For one account see Michael Bell in Levenson, *Cambridge Companion to Modernism*.
32 On the divided self, see for examples Richard Ellman and Charles Feidelson, Jr., *The Modern Tradition: Backgrounds of Modern Literature* (New York: Oxford University Press, 1965).

4

Philosophy and/as/of Literature

ARTHUR C. DANTO

> By displaying what is subjective, the work, in its whole presentation, reveals its purpose as existing for the subject, for the spectator and not on its own account. The spectator is, as it were, in it from the beginning, is counted in with it, and the work exists only for this point, i.e., for the individual apprehending it.
>
> Hegel, *Aesthetik*, trans. T. M. Knox

Philosophy seems so singular a crossbreed of art and science that it is somewhat surprising that only lately has it seemed imperative to some that philosophy be viewed as literature: surprising and somewhat alarming. Of course, so much has been enfranchised as literature in recent times that it would have been inevitable that literary theorists should have turned from the comic strip, the movie magazine, the disposable romance – from science fiction, pornography, and graffiti – to the texts of philosophy. This is in virtue of a vastly widened conception of the text which enables us to apply the strategies of hermeneutical interpretation to bus tickets and baggage checks, want ads and weather reports, laundry lists and postage cancellations, savings certificates and address books, medical prescriptions, pastry recipes, olive oil cans, and cognac labels – so why not meditations, examinations, and critiques? Admittedly this is not the exalted sense of literature we have in mind in speaking of philosophy as an art, but even if we retain the normative connotations of the term, there is something disturbing in the fact that this particular face of philosophy should have now become visible enough that we should have been enjoined to treat its texts as a particular literary genre. For, after all, the imperatives that have governed the transformation of philosophy into a profession have stressed our community with the sciences. Were a kind of semiotic egalitarianism to direct us to regard as so many texts the papers that regularly appear in the *Physical Review*, their literary dimension must seem deeply secondary, as ours has always seemed to us to be; so to treat it suddenly as primary has to be unsettling.

Philosophy-as-literature carries implications in excess of the claim that philosophical texts have at times a degree of literary merit. We take a remote satisfaction that some of us – Strawson, Ryle, and Quine, let alone Santayana, Russell, and James – write

---

A Companion to the Philosophy of Literature, First Edition. Edited by Garry L. Hagberg and Walter Jost.
© 2010 John Wiley & Sons Ltd. Published 2015 by John Wiley & Sons, Ltd.

distinguished prose, and we would all regard as astute a teacher of English who took pages from any of these as compositional paradigms. Still, our tendency is to regard style, save to the degree that it enhances perspicuity, as adventitious and superfluous to that for the sake of which we finally address these texts: as mere _Farbung_, to use Frege's dismissive term. So to rotate these texts in such a way that the secondary facets catch the light of intellectual concern puts what we regard as the primary facets in shadow; and to acquiesce in the concept of philosophy-as-literature just now seems tacitly to acquiesce in the view that the austere imperatives of philosophy-as-science have lost their energy. Considering what has been happening to texts when treated in recent times, our canon seems suddenly fragile, and it pains the heart to think of them enduring the frivolous sadism of the deconstructionist. But the perspective of philosophy-as-literature is an uncomfortable one for us to occupy, quite apart from these unedifying violations.

Consider the comparable perspective of the Bible-as-literature. Certainly it can be read as such, its poetry and narrative responded to as poetry and narrative, its images appreciated for their power, and its moral representations as a kind of drama. But to treat it so is to put at an important distance the Bible considered as a body of revelations, of saving truths and ethical certitudes: a text of which a thinker like Philo could believe that everything in it and nothing outside of it is true. So some fundamental relationship to the book will have changed when it sustains transfer to the curriculum as "living literature." Of course some aspect of its style has from the beginning of its historical importance played a role in biblical epistemology. The language of the Koran is said so to transcend in its beauty the powers of human expressiveness as virtually to guarantee its own claim to have been dictated by an angel and to be, not even metaphorically, the word of God: so its style is taken to be the best evidence for its truth. Biblical writing, by contrast, was taken to be the record of human witnesses; and much of it was so offensive to literary taste that it had to be true. A second-century apologist writes, "When I was giving my most earnest attention to discover the truth I happened to meet with certain barbaric writings . . . and I was led to put faith in these by the unpretending cast of the language." Origen, admitting the stylistic inferiority of Scripture by specific comparison with Plato, finds in this evidence that it is exactly the word of God, since if written by men it would be classier: its rudeness is a further weapon for confounding the wise. "However roughly, as regards mere authorship, my hook should be got up," Poe has his fictional hero write in the arch foreword to _The Narrative of Arthur Gordon Pym_, "its very uncouthness, if there were any, would give it all the better chance of being received as truth." That plain prose has a better chance of being received as true is a stylistic maxim not unknown in adopting a philosophical diction – think of Moore – but my point is only that there is a profound contrast between taking the Bible as literature and viewing it as the Word, and I would suspect disjoint classes of passages to become prominent depending on which view we take. The remaining music of the Bible must count as small compensation when the truth-claims made on its behalf are no longer felt to be compelling, and something like this contrast arises with philosophy-as-literature set against philosophy-as-truth. On the other hand, it provides an occasion to reflect on how philosophical truth has been regarded if we approach philosophy for the moment as though it were a genre of literature: it enables us to see how we constructed truth when we hadn't thought of ourselves as producing literature. And so we may reflect on the ways in which the dimensions of our professional being are connected.

For a period roughly coeval with that in which philosophy attained professionalization, the canonical literary format has been the professional philosophy paper. Our practice as philosophers consists in reading and writing such papers; in training our students to read and write them; in inviting others to come read us a paper, to which we respond by posing questions which in effect are editorial recommendations, typically incorporated and acknowledged in the first or last footnote of the paper, in which we are exempted from such errors and infelicities as may remain and thanked for our helpful suggestions. The journals in which these papers finally are printed, whatever incidental features useful to the profession at large they may carry, are not otherwise terribly distinct from one another, any more than the papers themselves characteristically are. If, under the constraints of blind review, we black out name and institutional affiliation, there will be no internal evidence of authorial presence, but only a unit of pure philosophy, to the presentation of which the author will have sacrificed all identity. This implies a noble vision of ourselves as vehicles for the transmission of an utterly impersonal philosophical truth, and it implies a vision of philosophical reality as constituted of isolable, difficult, but not finally intractable problems, which, if not altogether soluble in 15 pages more or less, can be brought closer to resolution in that many pages. The paper is then an impersonal report of limited results for a severely restricted readership, consisting of those who have some use for that result, since they are engaged with the writers of the papers in a collaborative enterprise, building the edifice of philosophical knowledge.

It is perfectly plain that the implied vision of philosophical reality, as well as of the form of life evolved to discover it and the form of literature in which it is suitable to represent it, is closely modeled on the view of reality, life, and literature which composes what Thomas Kuhn has instructed us to think of as normal science. Mastery of the literary form is the key to success in the form of life, bringing tenure and the kind of recognition which consists in being invited to read papers widely and perhaps in attaining the presidency of one or another division of the American Philosophical Association. These practical benefits aside, no one could conceivably be interested in participating in the form of life defined by the literary form in issue, were it not believed that this is the avenue to philosophical truth. It is less obviously a matter of agreement that philosophical truth is defined by this being believed to be the way to find it.

It is not my purpose here to criticize a form of life in which I after all participate, nor to criticize the format of speech and writing that, after all, reinforces the virtues of clarity, brevity, and competence in those compelled to use it. I only mean to emphasize that the concept of philosophical truth and the form of philosophical expression are internally enough related that we may want to recognize that when we turn to other forms we may also be turning to other conceptions of philosophical truth. Consider the way in which we address our predecessors, for example. Much of what

I have read on Plato reads much as though he, to whom the whole of subsequent philosophy is said to be so many footnotes, were in effect a footnote to himself and were being coached to get a paper accepted by the *Philosophical Review*. And a good bit of the writing on Descartes is by way of chivying his argumentation into notations we are certain he would have adopted had he lived to appreciate their advantages, since it is now so clear where he went wrong. But in both cases it might at least have been asked whether what either writer was up to can that easily be separated from forms of presentation that may have seemed inevitable, so that the dialogue or meditation flattened into conventional periodical prose might not in the process have lost something central to those ways of writing. The form in which the truth as they understood it must be grasped just might require a form of reading, hence a kind of relationship to those texts, altogether different from that appropriate to a paper, or to what we sometimes refer as a "contribution." And this is because something is intended to happen to the reader other than or in addition to being informed. It is after all not simply that the texts may lose something when flattened into papers: life may have lost something when philosophy was flattened out to the production and transmission of papers, noble as the correlative vision is. So addressing philosophy as literature is not meant to stultify the aspiration to philosophical truth so much as to propose a caveat against a reduced concept of reading, just because we realize that more is involved even in contemporary analytical philosophy than merely stating the truth: to get at that kind of truth involves some kind of transformation of the audience, and the acquiescence in a certain form of initiation and life.

I cannot think of a field of writing as fertile as philosophy has been in generating forms of literary expression. Ours has been – to use a partial list I once attempted – a history of dialogues, lecture notes, fragments, poems, examinations, essays, aphorisms, meditations, discourses, hymns, critiques, letters, *summae*, encyclopedias, testaments, commentaries, investigations, tractatuses, *Vorlesungen*, *Aufbauen*, *prolegomena*, *parerga*, *pensées*, sermons, supplements, confessions, *sententiae*, inquiries, diaries, outlines, sketches, commonplace books, addresses, and innumerable forms that have no generic identity or that themselves constitute distinct genres: *Holzwege*, Grammatologies, Unscientific Postscripts, Genealogies, Natural Histories, Phenomenologies, and whatever the *World as Will and Idea* may be or the posthumous corpus of Husserl, or the later writings of Derrida, and forgetting the standard sorts of literary forms – novels, plays, and the like – which philosophers have turned to when gifted those ways. One has to ask what cognitive significance is conveyed by the fact that the classic texts of China are typically composed of conversational bits, a question vividly brought home to me when a scholar I respect complained that it is terribly hard to get any propositions out of Chuang Tzu: for this may be the beginning of an understanding of how that elusive sage is to be addressed, and what it means to read him. Responding to a review of *The Realm of Truth* by his amanuensis, Santayana wrote:

> It is well that now you can take a holiday: which doesn't exclude the possibility of returning to them with freshness of judgement and apperception. Perhaps then you might not deprecate my purple passages, and might see, which is the historical fact, that they

are not applied ornaments but natural growths and *realizations* of the thought moving previously in a limbo of verbal abstractions.

It is arguable that the professional philosophical paper is an evolutionary product, emerging by natural selection from a wild profusion of forms Darwinized into oblivion through maladaptation, stages in the advance of philosophy toward consciousness of its true identity, a rockier road than most. But it is equally arguable that philosophers with really new thoughts have simply had to invent new forms with which to convey them, and that it may be possible that from the perspective of the standard format no way into these other forms, hence no way into these systems or structures of thought, can be found. This claim may be supported, perhaps, by the consideration that pretty much the only way in which literature of the non-philosophical kind has impinged upon philosophical awareness has been from the perspective of truth-or-falsity. The philosopher would cheerfully consign the entirety of fiction to the domain of falsehood but for the nagging concern that there is a difference between sentences that miss the mark and those that have no mark to miss and are threatened in consequence of prevailing theories of meaning with meaninglessness. Some way must therefore be found for them to have meaning before they can be dismissed as false, and pretty much the entirety of the analytical – and I may as well add the phenomenological – corpus has been massively addressed to the question of fictive reference. Literature sets up obstacles to the passage of semantical theories, which would go through a great deal more easily if literature did not exist. By assessing it against the concept of reference, literature derives what intellectual dignity philosophy can bestow, with the incidental benefit that if literature is merely a matter of skillfully relating words to the world, and if philosophy is literature, literature is meaningful, providing it can show how. And philosophy's way of relating literature to reality may make philosophy-as-literature one with philosophy-as-truth.

This is scarcely the place to tell the chilling tale of fictional reference, in part because it seems not to have reached an end, there being no accepted theory of how it works. But if there ever was an argument for philosophy as a kind of literature, it might be found in the extravagant ontological imagination of semantical theorists in proposing things for fictive terms to designate. Since Don Quixote is meaningful, "Don Quixote" must refer, not to some specific addled Spaniard in La Mancha, but to Don Quixote himself, a subsistent entity, which *Don Quixote* can now be about in just the way it would if he were indeed an addled Spaniard in La Mancha. How such subsistent entities confer meaning, or at least how they explain the fact that we grasp it, was never particularly explained, causal transactions between the domain of subsistent entities and existent entities such as we being surely ruled out of question. This problem is aggravated when we purge the universe of fictive beings by waving a Quinean wand which changes names into predicates, Don Quixote becoming the x that quixotizes all over the y that lamanchas. The prodigality complained of in manufacturing entities to order is evidently unnoticed when it comes to manufacturing predicates to order, and the change from *Gegenstände* to *Gedanke* leaves the question of meaning and its being grasped about as dark as ever. Nor is the matter especially mitigated when we allow *Don Quixote* to pick a possible world to be about, for the relationship of it to ours and finally to us remains as obscure as that between Don Quixote and us when he was a homeless wraith, an ontological ghost wandering in worlds undreamt of by poets.

From this point of view Nelson Goodman's elegant theory of secondary extensions is particularly welcome, first from the perspective of ontology, since secondary extensions are composed of things we can put our hands on, like inscriptions, and second from the point of view of epistemology, since pictures play a prominent part in the secondary extension of a term and we in fact begin our adventures into literature with picture books. It does on the other hand throw an immense semantical burden on illustrated editions and the like and tangles us in puzzles of its own, since the set of pictures ostensibly of the same thing may look so little alike that we may have severe doubts as to what their subject would look like if it existed, while pictures of altogether different subjects may look so alike that we could not tell them apart were they to be real. Whether we must ascend to tertiary extensions and beyond, and how these would solve our further problems, are matters not to be taken up here, for the question I want to raise is why, whichever of these theories is true, we, as readers, should have the slightest interest in *Don Quixote* if what it is about is an unactualized thin man in a region of being I would have no reason to know about save for the interventions of semantical theory: or if it were about the x that quixotizes (there being none) or a set of possible worlds other than my own, or primarily about nothing but secondarily about such things as a set of engravings by Gustave Doré.

I raise the question because literature, certainly in its greatest exemplars, seems to have something important to do with our lives, important enough that the study of it should form an essential part of our educational program, and this is utterly unexplained if its meaning is a matter of its reference, and if its candidate referenda are as bizarre a menagerie of imaginabilia as the fancy of man has framed. And it may be that when we show the kind of connection there is, there will not be a problem of the sort to which semantical theory has been so elaborate a response. Well, it may be said, this might simply remove literature from the sphere of philosophical concern, a welcome enough removal but for the fact that it might remove philosophy itself from the domain of philosophical concern if philosophy itself is literature. And my insinuation has been that the sorts of things philosophy has laid down to connect literature in order to give it meaning – *Gegenstände*, intensions, fictive worlds – are themselves as much in need of ontological redemption as the beings to whose rescue they were enlisted: Don Quixote, Mr Pickwick, Gandalf the Grey. To believe we can save fiction by means of fiction is one of the endearing innocences of a discipline that takes pride in what it likes to think is its skeptical circumspection.

Semantical theory does the best it can in striving to connect literature to the world through what after all are the only kinds of connections it understands: reference, truth, instantiation, exemplification, satisfaction, and the like. If this means distorting the universe in order that it can receive literary representations, this has never been reckoned a high price for philosophy to pay but a creative opportunity, and it remains to the credit of this enterprise that it at least believes *some* connection between literature and the world is required. In this it contrasts with literary theory as currently practiced, which impugns philosophical preoccupations with semantical ligatures as but a further instance of what one leading theoretician dismisses as the Referential Fallacy. Literature does not refer at all to reality, according to this view, but at best to other literature, and a concept of *intertextualiy* is advanced according to which a literary work is to be understood, so far as referentiality facilitates understanding, only in terms of other works a given work refers to, so that no one equipped with less than the literary culture of the writer of a work up for interpretation can be certain of having understood the work at all. There is certainly something to this view if Northrop Frye is correct in claiming of Blake's line "O Earth, O Earth return" that "though it contains only five words and only three different words" – five tokens and three types, as we might more briskly say – "it contains also about seven direct allusions to the Bible." The author of the Referential Fallacy, whom I prefer for somewhat complex reasons to refer to simply as R (he after all speaks for his profession) assures us that "the poetic text is self-sufficient." But "if there is external reference, it is not to reality – far from it! Any such reference is to other texts." This extreme view merits some examination, if only for its vivid opposition to the standard philosophical view.

Consider one of his examples, the last line of Wordsworth's poem "Written in March," which goes, "Small clouds are sailing,/Blue skies prevailing,/The rain is over and done." This line, together with the title, might lead the reader to suppose that the poem refers to the end of winter and expresses the poet's gratitude that spring has come at last – but this easy reading is, according to R, quite seriously and fallaciously wrong: it refers in fact to the Song of Songs, from which Wordsworth's line is taken verbatim, and is in fact a fragment of the biblical line that begins "For lo! The winter is past . . ." Now it can hardly be doubted that Wordsworth knew the Song of Songs, and it is certain that literary scholarship, in explaining the sources of the poem, will refer to it as an ultimate source for the last line. Perhaps every line or phrase in a poem may be explained with reference to something in the literary culture of the writer. But not every literary effect necessarily refers to its causes, and there is a considerable difference between understanding a poem, which may require understanding its references when it makes them, and understanding the provenances of a poem, which is quite another matter: it is specialist knowledge, and likely incidental to understanding a poem.

Let me offer an illustration from another art, in part to make my argument more general, in part to confirm a claim about pictorial semantics. Raphael's beautiful *Madonna della sedia* is composed within a circular frame – a *tondo* – not, as Gombrich points out, because Raphael one day seized a handy barrelhead in order to paint an innkeeper's daughter who charmed him, together with her pretty child, as Madonna and Infant, which is the tour guide's lovely explanation; but rather because, like many of his contemporaries, Raphael was excited by some recently exhibited drawings of Leonardo, among them some circular compositions. Every painter in the region would have known about those drawings, and hence the provenance of Raphael's painting, but for all that Raphael was not referring to the drawings that inspired him. By contrast, the American painter Benjamin West did a portrait of his wife and son in *tondo* form, her garment the garment of Raphael's Madonna, not as a copy of but in *reference to* Raphael's painting. It was an exceedingly pretentious reference, depicting his wife as Madonna, his child as the Baby Jesus, *his* painting as the *Madonna della sedia*, and himself as Raphael. But to understand the painting is to understand those allusions, for he is representing his family *as* the Holy Pair *as* depicted by Raphael, and a very self-exalting metaphor is being transacted. (What a humiliation to have had this hopeful vision de-accessioned by the Reynolds's collection in exchange for a merely typical Thomas Cole!)

It was a triumph of art historical scholarship to demonstrate the unmistakable use made by Manet of an arrangement of figures in an engraving by Marcantonio Raimondi in setting the figures in his *Déjeuner sur l'herbe*. This by no means excludes the possibility, or rather the fact, that Manet was representing friends of his, wits and demimondaines, enjoying an elegant outing. Of course it is a different painting depending upon whether he was referring to or merely using Raimondi's work. If he was referring to it, then his subject is *that* outing *as* a feast of the gods, which is the subject of the original engraving. Raimondi was the most famous engraver of his age (as well as a notorious forger), but in Manet's world he was doubtless too obscure for such an allusion to be made, by contrast perhaps with biblical references in Wordsworth's world; and probably obviousness is a condition of allusion as banality is a condition of validity in the enthymeme. But even so Manet's use of that engraving must be distinguished from a use made by the American painter John Trumbull, in his famous portrait of General Washington with his horse, of a certain pre-existing form of horse-representation. Far from being the finely observed depiction of Washington's elegant steed, Washington's horse, as shown, is but one in a long historical sequence of similar horses which Leo Steinberg has traced back to a Roman cameo, and which probably could be traced even farther. Still, it is Washington with his horse that is being referred to, and not any member of this series, each of which but conforms to a pattern. The pattern, which may be an example of what Gombrich speaks of as a *schema*, is a very satisfactory way of representing horses, which are, as we know, very difficult to observe – until Muybridge nobody knew whether all four legs were altogether off the ground in the gallop – and yields up a kind of representational *a priori* of a sort whose narrative and lyrical counterparts may be found in literature; and, though this is not my topic, there may be profound similarities to scientific representations as well.

In all these cases and countless others, reference to the world works together with references to other art, when there are such references, to make a complex representation; so why should or must it be different in the case of Wordsworth? R writes thus:

> The key word – *winter* – absent from Wordsworth, is the matrix penetrating every Spring detail in the poem . . . now perceived as the converse of an image that has been effaced, so that the poem is not a direct depiction of reality, but a negative version of a latent text on the opposite of Spring.

This is the kind of hermeneutic contortion that earns interpreters of literature distinguished chairs in universities – the kind that argues, for example, that *Hamlet* is a negative version of a latent text about Fortinbras, the true hero of the play, which is perceived now as comedy rather than tragedy, since the hero is alive at the end, thus making Shakespeare a clever forerunner of Tom Stoppard. But my concern is not to argue with the interpretation but with the "so" to which R is not entitled: a proper interpretation would have to show why Wordsworth referred to the season through the medium of a biblical allusion if in fact it was an allusion and not a cliché of the sort that has simply entered language the way so much of *Hamlet* has that a student is said to have criticized it for being too full of clichés, though a pretty exciting story. And what of the Song of Songs itself, if poetry: is it about winter, or, to use the other option offered us, altogether self-contained?

In a famous letter to his mistress, Louise Colet, Flaubert lays out his own ideal as an artist:

> What I should like to write is a book about nothing, a book dependent upon nothing external, which would be held together by the internal strength of its style, just as the earth, suspended in the void, depends upon nothing external for its support: a book which would have almost no subject, or at least in which the subject would be invisible, if such a thing is possible.

Flaubert's astronomy is appalling, and if R is right he could not have failed of his purpose, all literature, just so far as it is literature, being about nothing. Or at best it is about other literature, work holding work in referential orbit, to give Flaubert a happier physical metaphor, but basically untethered to reality. The question is, what considerations recommend the guaranteed irrelevancy of literature to life?

"In everyday language," the author of the Referential Fallacy writes,

> words seem to refer vertically, each to the reality it seems to render, like the labels on a barrelhead, each a semantic unit, while in literature the unit of meaning is the text itself. The reciprocal effect of its words on one another, as members of a finite network, replaces the vertical semantical relationship with a lateral one, forged along the written line, tending to cancel the dictionary meanings of the words.

Now I want to applaud the concept of a text as a network of reciprocal effects. Not original with R, of course, it has entered our world from European sources, making an immense impact upon literary theorists while leaving philosophy so far untouched. I feel that were the concept of the text to become as central in analytical philosophy as the sentence has been since Frege gave it primacy, or as the term has been since Aristotle, a vast world for philosophical research will have opened up. For the concept of the text is considerably wider than literary texts alone. It applies to musical compositions and to architectural structures, art forms whose referentiality has been in occasional question, and to personalities, whole lives in the biographical sense of the term, families, villages, cultures, things for which the question of referentiality has hardly been raised at all. And the expression "a network of reciprocal effects" will come to be exchanged for a class of relationships as various as and perhaps as important as those that bind sentences into arguments and that have been so massively explored in contemporary philosophical thought. Even so, it is altogether compatible with being united through a network of reciprocal effects that a literary work should refer, as it were extratextually, though the reference may be complicated as much by intra- as by intertextual references. The Prelude and Finale of *Middlemarch* refer reciprocally, as well as to the novel they frame, and both refer or allude to Saint Theresa, herself not a text save in so wide a sense as to make R's theory timid and disappointing. They refer to her to provide a metaphor for Dorothea Brooke – Miss Brooke as erotic ascetic perhaps – proving that her character has remained constant through two marriages, and saying finally something deep about the narrow space there after all is for being different from what we are.

But this goes well beyond what philosophers have wanted to say in supposing *Middlemarch* refers, say, to a world of its own or to some fleshless subsistent woman, Dorothea Brooke. And it goes well beyond what R will allow, who leaves us with the same question philosophical discussions of fictional reference did, namely why should we be interested in *Middlemarch*? Why, since not ourselves literary scholars, should we concern ourselves with these intricate networks of reciprocal effects? "Because they are there" was not even a good reason for climbing mountains, but I am struck by the fact that philosophers seem only to understand vertical references and literary theorists, if R is right, only horizontal ones. On this coordinate scheme it is difficult to locate literature in the plane of human concern at all. Clearly we need a z-coordinate; we must open a dimension of reference neither vertical nor horizontal reference quite reveals, if we are to get an answer.

"The distinction between historian and poet is not in the one writing prose and the other verse," Aristotle writes, helpfully as always. "You might put the work of Herodotus into verse and it would still be a species of history." Though he neglects the reverse possibility, I take Aristotle to mean that one ought to be unable to tell by mere examination of a text whether it is poetry or something else, which gives my own question an immediate philosophical structure. The form of a philosophical question is given – I would venture to say always but lack an immediate proof – when indiscriminable pairs with nevertheless distinct ontological locations may be found or imagined found, and we then must make plain in what the difference consists or could consist. The classical case is matching dream experience with waking experience in such a way that, as Descartes required, nothing internal to either mode of experience will serve as differentiating criterion. So whatever internal criterion we in fact, and, as it happens, pre-analytically, employ will be irrelevant to the solution of the problem, for example, that dreams are vague and incoherent. For dreams may be imagined, and possibly had, which are as like waking experience as we require to void the criterion. So the difference must come in at right angles to the plane of what we experience, and philosophy here consists in saying what it can be. Kant discovers the same thing in moral theory, since he imagines it possible that a set of actions should perfectly conform to principle and yet have no moral worth, because that requires a different relationship to those principles than mere conformity, and outward observation cannot settle the matter. And Adeimanthus furnishes the stunning example that generates the *Republic*, that of a perfectly just man whose behavior is indiscriminable from that of a man perfectly unjust: the example requires that justice be orthogonal to conduct, and entails as uniquely possible the kind of theory Plato gives us. Other examples lie ready to hand. The present state of the world is compatible with the world being any age at all, including five minutes old, and nothing on the surface of the world will arbitrate without begging the question. A mere bodily movement and a basic action might appear exactly alike, just as what we take to be an expression of a feeling may be but a kind of rictus. Nothing open to observation discriminates a pair of connected events, to use Hume's distinction, from a pair merely conjoined. And in my own investigations into the philosophy of art, I have benefited immensely from Duchamp's discovery that nothing the eye can reveal will arbitrate the difference between a work of art and a mere real thing that resembles it in every outward particular. So any proposed distinction based upon perceptual differences, even in the visual arts, will have proved, as with the Linnaean system in botany, to be artificial, however useful in practice. Duchamp consigned all past theories to oblivion by proving that the problem was philosophical. And here is Aristotle, telling us that the difference between poetry and history does not lie on the surfaces of texts, and that distinguishing them is not an ordinary matter of classification but a philosophical matter of explanation.

It is indeed not at all difficult to imagine two quite sustained pieces of writing which belong to relevantly distinct genres, without there being so much difference as a semicolon. I once imagined a pair of indiscriminable texts, one a novel, one a piece of history. My colleague Stern, suppose, comes across an archive containing the papers of a Polish noblewoman of the last century, who died, characteristically, in a convent. Incredibly, she was the mistress of Talleyrand, Metternich, the younger Garibaldi, Jeremy Bentham, Eugene Delacroix, Frederic Chopin, and Czar Nicholas of Russia, though the great loves of her life were George Sand and the nubile Sarah Bernhardt. Published by Viking, it wins the Pulitzer Prize in history in the same year as a novel with exactly the same name wins it in literature – *Maria Mazurka, Mistress to Genius*. The novel was written by Erica Jong, who was inspired to invent a heroine who dies appropriately in a convent, but who in her time had been the mistress of Talleyrand, Metternich, the younger Garibaldi, Jeremy Bentham, Eugene Delacroix, Frederic Chopin, and Czar Nicholas of Russia, though the great loves of her life were George Sand and the nubile Sarah Bernhardt. Jong's novel, unfortunately, is too improbable, has too many characters, sprawls all over the place, as Jong is wont to do these days, and bears critical comparison with Stern's marvelous book, which manages to keep track of all its characters, is tightly regimented given the diversity of materials, and contains not a fact in excess. So Jong's book, to the despair of the author and Random House, is soon remaindered, and for $2.98 you can get a lot of pages which cannot be told apart from Stern's book, on special at $19.99 through the History Book Club – though none of Stern's readers would be caught dead reading a mere novel. Stern's book, of course, refers vertically, while Jong's, being a novel, is a network of reciprocal effects, and self-sustained or nearly so, characterized only by horizontal reference. I realize I am slipping out of philosophy into literature, but the point is that whatever is to mark the difference must survive examples such as these.

Aristotle's famous suggestion, of course, is that "poetry is something more philosophical and of graver import than history, since its statements are of the nature of universals, whereas those of history are singular." It is plain that this difference is not registered grammatically or syntactically, if the example just constructed is possible, and in the Aristotelian spirit. So there must be a way in which Jong's book, for all its failings, is universal, and in which Stern's book, splendid as it is as historiography, remains for just that reason singular – about that specific woman in just those steamy liaisons. On the other hand, there must be some way in which Jong's book, if universal and hence more philosophical than Stern's, is not quite so philosophical as philosophy itself is. Otherwise the problem of construing philosophy as a form of literature would be solved at the cost of so widening philosophy, since nothing could be more philosophical than it, as to compass whatever Aristotle would consider poetry. In whatever way philosophy is to be literature, if it is to be literature at all, it must respect whatever differences there may be with literature, which is not philosophy, however necessarily philosophical it has to be in order to be distinguished from mere history.

My own view is that philosophy wants to be more than universal; it wants necessity as well: truth for all the worlds that are possible. In this respect it contrasts with history, or for that matter with science, concerned with the truths of just this particular, uniquely actual world, and happy if it can achieve that much. My contention here has been that philosophical semantics renders literature true of possible worlds, to lapse into the vernacular, in such a way that it would be history for any of them if actual instead of ours. *Gulliver's Travels* would just be anthropology for a world in which there were Lilliputians instead of Melanesians. This, I am afraid, is very close to Aristotle's own view, history dealing, according to him, with the thing that has been, while poetry is concerned with "a kind of thing that might be." And that sounds too much like being true of a possible world for me to be comfortable with it as an analysis. I nevertheless believe that literature has a kind of universality worth considering, different from this, and I shall now try to say what it is in my own way, recognizing that if philosophy is also literature, it might have to be universal and possibly even necessary in two kinds of ways.

The thought I want to advance is that literature is not universal in the sense of being about every possible world insofar as possible, as philosophy in its non-literary dimension aspires to be, nor about what may happen to be the case in just this particular world, as history, taken in this respect as exemplificatory science, aspires to be, but rather about each reader who experiences it. It is not, of course, about its readers as a book about reading is, which happens incidentally to be about its readers just as a subclass of its subject, but rather in the way in which, though you will look for him in vain, Benjamin West's pretentious family portrait is about him. He does not show himself in the manner of Velasquez in *Las Meninas*, but still, the painting is about Benjamin West *as* Raphael *as* painter of the Holy Family, through an allusive and metaphoric identification: he informs the work as a kind of *dieu caché*. A literary work is about its readers in this metaphoric and allusive way, in an exact mirror image of the way West's painting is about him. In Hegel's wonderful thought, the work exists for the spectator and not on its own account: it exists, as he says, only for the individual apprehending it, so that the apprehension completes the work and gives it final substance. The difficult claim I am making can be put somewhat formally as follows: the usual analysis of universality is that (x)Fx is via the mechanisms of natural deduction equivalent to a conjunction of all the values on x, true in the event each is F. The universality of literary reference is only that it is about each individual that reads the text at the moment that individual reads it, and it contains an implied indexical. Each work is about the "I" that reads the text, identifying himself not with the implied reader for whom the implied narrator writes but with the actual subject of the text in such a way that each work becomes a metaphor for each reader: perhaps the same metaphor for each.

It is a metaphor, of course, in part because it is literally false that I am Achilles, or Leopold Bloom, or Anna or Oedipus or King Lear or Hyacinth Robinson or Strether or Lady Glencora; or a man hounded by an abstract bureaucracy because of an unspecified or suspected accusation; or the sexual slave O; or the raft rider responsible to a moral being whom an unspeakable nation refuses to countenance as a man; or the obsessive narrator of the violence of my ancestors, which is my own violence, since their story is in the end my story; or one who stands to Jay Gatsby as Jay Gatz stood to the same dream as mine of "love, accomplishment, beauty, elegance, wealth" (which is a list I just found in a marvelous story by Gail Godwin). It is literature when, for each reader I, I is the subject of the story. The work finds its subject only when read.

Because of this immediacy of identification, it is natural to think, as theorists from Hamlet onward have done, of literature as a kind of mirror, not simply in the sense of rendering an external reality, but as giving me to myself for each self peering into it, showing each of us something inaccessible without mirrors, namely that each has an external aspect and what that external aspect is. Each work of literature shows in this sense an aspect we would not know was ours without benefit of that mirror: each discovers – in the eighteenth-century meaning of the term – an unguessed dimension of the self. It is a mirror less in passively returning an image than in transforming the self-consciousness of the reader who in virtue of identifying with the image recognizes what he is. Literature is in this sense transfigurative, and in a way that cuts across the distinction between fiction and truth. There are metaphors for every life in Herodotus and Gibbon.

The great paradigm for such transfiguration must be Don Quixote, Cervantes having to be credited not only with the invention of the novel but with discovering the perversion of its philosophy. Quixote is transformed, through reading romances, into an errant knight while his world is transformed into one of knightly opportunities, wenches turning into virgins and innkeepers into kings, nags into steeds and windmills into monsters. Yet it is a perversion of the relationship between reader and romance because Quixote's own sense of his identity was so antecedently weak that he failed to retain it through the transformation, and his own sense of reality was so weak that he lost his grip on the difference between literature and life. Or he read poetry as though it were history, so not philosophical but particular. He would be like those who, through reading Descartes, seriously come to believe that "they are kings while they are paupers, that they are clothed in gold and purple while they are naked; or imagine that their head is made of clay or that they are gourds, or that their bodies are glass." Or that there is an Evil Genius, or that there is no world or that the belief in material objects is misguided. These are failures to distinguish philosophy from life, whose counterpart in Cervantes induces an illusion so powerful that the distinction is lost: which may be a formula for happiness – living in an illusion – making *Don Quixote* genuinely comic.

I have encountered the tragic obverse of this, where one's sense of self is strong but one's sense of reality has become desperate through literature having thrown a bitter discrepancy into the relationship between the two. I knew a lady who discovered the truth from Proust's novel that she really was the Duchess of Guermantes, as unavailing, in her case, unfortunately, as the Prince's knowledge of who he really is, when a spell has nevertheless required that he live in the investitures of a frog. Her land was Combray and the Faubourg St Germain, an air of wit and exquisite behavior and perfect taste – not the Upper West Side, falling plaster, children with colds, a distracted husband, never enough money, and nobody who understood. Her moments of happiness came when reality on occasion agreed to cooperate with metaphor, when she could coincide with an alien grace, too ephemeral alas, leaving her with the dishes to clear and the bills to pay and a terrible exhaustion. Unlike Quixote, her illusions were never strong enough to swamp reality, only in a sense to poison it; and while she maintained that her greatest happiness consisted in reading Proust, in truth he only caused her anguish.

I should like to place the theorist R alongside these two readers of fiction, one of whom happens to be in fiction as well, since R himself could be a fictional being and the Referential Fallacy a fiction within a fiction, both of them created by me. In fact both the theorist and article are real. R is a man of great pride and passion, who has lived through times of extremity and has known, as much as anyone I know has known, the defining tribulations of the full human life. Surely he cannot have been drawn to literature simply to be a reader of literature through literature to literature, unless, like the professor in Mann's *Disorder and Early Sorrow*, he meant to draw a circle in order to exclude life. If it were a piece of literature, the Referential Fallacy would offer a metaphor of extreme dislocation, putting life as a whole beyond the range of reference, displaying an existence lived out in an infinite windowless library, where book sends us to book in a network of reciprocal relationships the reader can inhabit like a spider. Imagine that it had been written by Borges, whose life was almost like that, and included in *Ficciones!* But it in fact is by R and it gives us a misanalysis rather than a metaphor; it refers vertically to readers whose relationship to texts it gets wrong, rather than to the reader of the text whose life it metaphorically depicts. If this chapter were art, it would be a mirror only for R, who seeing his own image reflected back, might find his consciousness entrapped and mend his thought.

R's text, which I have sought to view once as literature and once as science, illustrates, since it is about reading, the two ways in which a text might refer to readers, and with these two modes of reference in mind, we may return to philosophy as literature, not by way of treating philosophical texts as literature, which would be merely a conceit if they were not that, as R's text is not that, but by way rather of displaying one of the ways in which philosophy really does relate to life. *One* of the ways. There is a celebrated deconstructionist text that holds that philosophy must be treated as a genre of literature because it is ineluctably metaphoric, when in fact it only becomes interestingly metaphoric when it is first decided to treat it as literature, and that text begs just the question it has been taken by its enthusiasts to have settled. Metaphors have in common with texts as such that they do not necessarily wear their metaphoricity on their surfaces, and what looks like an image may really be a structural hypothesis of how a reality we heretofore lacked words for is to be understood. One mark of metaphors is their ineliminability, a feature that makes them paraintensional if not fully intensional. But in philosophical as in scientific writing, what looks like a metaphor in the beginning ends as a fact, and it may be eliminated in favor of a technical term, as Locke begins with the natural light – with "the candle within us" – and ends with the technical term *intuition*. So what appear to be metaphors, what have been taken by deconstructionists to be metaphors, belong to philosophy as science, rather than to philosophy as literature.

There is a view abroad, credited to Nietzsche, that in metaphor we have the growing edge of language, assimilating by its means the unknown to the known, where the latter must originally have been metaphor now grown cold and desiccated and taken for fact. It is difficult to understand how, on its own view, this process got started, but I think it must be appreciated as a transvaluational and necessarily paradoxical view, like saying that the first shall be last or that the meek shall inherit the earth, giving poetry the place science has presumed was its own. But it is a view lent credibility by the fact that structural hypotheses look enough like metaphors to be taken for metaphors by theorists resolved to view an activity like philosophy as largely if not altogether metaphorical. It is my own thought that philosophical texts are kept alive as metaphors when they have long-since stopped seeming plausible as structural hypotheses, a tribute to their vivacity and power, their status as literature being a consolation prize for failing to be true. But this is to overlook the way in which philosophy functions as literature does, not in the sense of extravagant verbal artifacts, but as engaging with readers in search of that sort of universality I have supposed to characterize literary reference: as being about the reader at the moment of reading through the process of reading. We read them as literature in this sense because, as Hegel said, they exist for the reader who is "in them from the beginning." The texts require the act of reading in order to be complete, and it is as readers of a certain type that philosophical texts address us all. The wild variety of philosophical texts implies a correspondingly wild variety of possible kinds of readers, and hence of theories of what we are in the dimension of the reading. And each such text finds a kind of ontological proof of its claims through the fact that it can be read in the way it requires.

The most conspicuous example of such a text is obliged to be the *Meditations*, where the reader is forced to co-meditate with the writer and to discover in the act of co-meditation his philosophical identity: he must be the kind of individual the text requires if he can read it, and the text must be true if it can be read. He finds himself there, since he was in it from the beginning. How astonishing I find it that precisely those who insist that philosophy is merely a genre of literature offer readings of Descartes so external that the possibility of their being universal in the way literature demands is excluded from the outset. To treat philosophical texts after the manner of Derrida, simply as networks of reciprocal relationships, is precisely to put them at a distance from their readers so intraversable as to make it impossible that they be about us in the way literature requires, if my conjecture is correct. They become simply artifacts made of words, with no references save internal ones or incidental external ones. And reading them becomes external, as though they had nothing to do with us, were merely there, intricately wrought composites of logical lacework, puzzling and pretty and pointless. The history of philosophy is then like a museum of costumes we forget were meant to be worn.

The variety of philosophical texts, then, subtend a variety of philosophical anthropologies, and though each text is about the reader of it and so is a piece of literature by that criterion, it does not offer a metaphor but a truth internally related to the reading of it. Even now when textual innovativeness has abated in philosophy and all texts are pretty much alike, so much so that the address to the reader has thinned almost to nothingness, the reader in the act of reading exercises some control over what the text says, since what the text says must be compatible with its being read. A text, thus, that set out to prove the impossibility of reading would have a paradox of sorts on its hands. Less flagrantly, there are texts in philosophy, current reading among us, which if true would entail their own logical illegibility. It is inconceivable that philosophers would have fallen into such incoherences if they had not, as it were, forgotten that their texts, in addition to being representations of a kind of reality, were things to be *read*. We pay a price for forgetting this in the current style of writing, since it enables us to depict worlds in which readers cannot fit.

The propensity to overlook the reader goes hand in hand with the propensity to leave beings of the sort readers exemplify outside the world the text describes. Contemporary philosophies of mind, language, humanity, may be striking examples of an oversight encouraged by a view of philosophical writing which makes the reader ontologically weightless, a sort of disembodied professional conscience. Science, often and perhaps typically, can get away with this, largely because, even when about its readers, is not about them as readers and so lacks the internal connection philosophical texts demand because they are about their readers *as* readers. So philosophy is literature in that among its truth conditions are those connected with being read, and reading those texts is supposed then to reveal us for what we are in virtue of our reading. This revelation is not metaphorical, however, which is why I cannot finally acquiesce in the thought that philosophy is literature. It continues to aim at truth, but when false, seriously false, it is often also so fascinatingly false as to retain a kind of perpetual vitality as a metaphor. It is this that makes our history so impossible to relinquish, since the power is always there, and the texts engage us when we read them vitally as readers whose philosophical portraits materialize about us as we enter that place that awaited us from the beginning.

Part II

Emotional Engagement and the Experience of Reading

5

Emotion and the Understanding of Narrative

JENEFER ROBINSON

How to Read a Story

A good story makes us curious and suspenseful about what is going to happen. It may make us laugh and cry, tremble and sweat. It may make us feel horror, disgust, anger, fear, love, compassion, and many other emotions from the repertoire available in our culture. In this essay, I'll first explain how the emotions function when we respond emotionally to characters and events in novels, plays, and movies, arguing that an emotional process works in basically the same way when we respond to characters and events in novels, plays, and movies as when we respond to people and events in real life.[1] Secondly, I'll argue that our emotional responses to novels, plays, and movies can help us to understand them, to understand characters and grasp the significance of events in the plot. Our emotional responses, guided or managed by the author (or implied author[2]) of the work, can serve as important data on which to base an interpretation of the work as a whole. This may not be true of all novels, plays, and movies; some post-modern stories that foreground form or structure may not work in quite this way. But it is certainly true for the great realistic novels by the likes of Leo Tolstoy, Henry James, and George Eliot, on which I'll be focusing.

It might seem puzzling how having one's emotions aroused can help us to understand anything at all. After all, if I am in a state of intense fear or grief, I am not in a very good position to understand anything. Moreover, rather than furthering understanding, some of the emotions that a novel evokes may distract my attention from it. If I read in a novel a description of a handsome young fighter-pilot who dies in the Second World War, and fall into a tender reverie about my fiancé who flies a plane for Fed-Ex, my feelings of tenderness may have nothing to do with the way the fighter-pilot is depicted in the novel. What's more, in such a case my attention seems to be directed not at the novel but at my fiancé.

Many of the emotions aroused by reading a novel, however, are important – even essential – to a proper understanding of the novel. This idea is not new.[3] What's new in my treatment is (1) the application of recent results in emotion theory, and (2) the

---

A Companion to the Philosophy of Literature, First Edition. Edited by Garry L. Hagberg and Walter Jost.
© 2010 John Wiley & Sons Ltd. Published 2015 by John Wiley & Sons, Ltd.

explicit defense of the idea that appropriate emotional responses by the reader are essential to understanding some novels.

What is Emotional Involvement?

What does it mean to get emotionally involved in the characters, situations, and events recounted in a novel such as George Eliot's *Middlemarch*, Tolstoy's *Anna Karenina*, or Henry James's *The Ambassadors*? In my view, an emotion is a process of interaction between an organism and its environment. When human beings have an emotional response to something in the (internal or external) environment, they make an automatic affective appraisal that picks that thing out as significant to them (given their wants, goals, and interests) and requiring attention. This affective appraisal causes physiological changes, tendencies to act, and expressive gestures, including characteristic facial and vocal expressions, which may be subjectively experienced as feelings, and the whole process is then modified by cognitive monitoring. The various aspects of the emotion process are interconnected in various ways. For example, physiological responses reinforce attention. Expressive gestures, action tendencies, and behavior may change the environment so that the emotional situation changes or dissipates. Cognitive monitoring may confirm or disconfirm affective appraisals. In short, the process is constantly modulating in response to feedback from the various elements in the process.[4]

This account of emotion emphasizes several features of emotion about which there is relatively widespread agreement:

First, there's general agreement that emotional responses occur in situations where what is deemed to be at stake are goals, interests, and wants of mine that are important to me or mine, in terms of my survival and that of my "group," and, more generally, the well-being of me and my group.[5]

Second, there's wide agreement that emotional responses are bodily responses. There is good evidence that different facial and vocal expressions differentiate among certain so-called basic emotions, and there is also some evidence that different emotion types exhibit different patterns of autonomic nervous system activity as well as distinct motor responses and action tendencies.[6]

Third, it is also widely agreed that emotions involve some kind of evaluation or appraisal of the environment (whether internal or external). Emotions are special devices for processing information. Some writers on emotion think of emotions as cognitive states, such as beliefs or judgments, or as caused by such states. I have been arguing for many years, however, that what triggers an emotional (physiological) response is not a cognitive state such as a belief or judgment, but an automatic, instinctive, non-cognitive appraisal (an affective appraisal) of the (internal or external) environment. As I once expressed the point, the body itself registers what's important to the person (or other animal).[7]

I think of this appraisal as a "meta-appraisal" that registers in the body what's important to the person (or other animal) in a crude, coarse-grained way: That's BAD or that's

GOOD, that's a THREAT or an OFFENSE, and so on. In general, however, I think we should be agnostic about exactly how to conceptualize these affective appraisals, which by definition, occur pre-linguistically.[8]

Fourth, emotions focus attention on those things in which we have a personal stake or interest.[9] Moreover, they seem to focus attention in a bodily way, by putting the body into a state of action readiness. Thus the (angry) affective appraisal OFFENSE! is registered in bodily changes such as increased heart rate, sweating, fist-clenching, and so on, and these very bodily changes themselves help to keep attention fixed on the (perceived) offense.

Fifth, there is also evidence from Joseph LeDoux and others that there are special emotional memory systems, activated, for example, in phobias, that are independent of declarative memory (so that I may have forgotten the details of an accident I was in when a child, but the sound of screeching brakes can turn me white-faced and trembling, perhaps without my even knowing why.)[10] Some believe that emotional responses are stored in motor memory. And if Antonio Damasio is right, the brain classifies scenarios as harmful or beneficial, based on past experience with similar such scenarios, and it does this by marking these categories of scenario in a bodily (somatic) way, which we may access by means of the corresponding feelings of bodily change.[11]

Sixth, emotion is not just a physiological response caused by an affective appraisal, however. Even in the most primitive cases, like the startle mechanism, the automatic, instinctive (affective) appraisal gives way immediately to a cognitive appraisal, which monitors the affective appraisal and modifies subsequent behavior and physiological responses. For example, after an affective appraisal of THREAT! a cognitive appraisal may confirm the affective appraisal (yes, danger is nigh; that's a mugger over there in the dark); or it can deny the affective appraisal and abort the physiological changes (there's no danger: that's not a mugger lurking in the darkness; it's the shadow of a tree); or it can lead to a new affective appraisal: FRIEND! (that's not a mugger; it's my beloved come home unexpectedly from the war) and a new sequence of physiological and motor changes.

In summary, on the model I defend, emotion is a process at the core of which is a set of bodily responses activated by an affective appraisal that is "instinctive" and automatic. This automatic appraisal gives way to cognitive monitoring of the situation, which reflects back on the instinctive appraisal and modifies expressive, motor, and autonomic activity accordingly, as well as actions and action tendencies. Emotions are special kinds of information devices that also prepare us to act on or deal with the information processed.

What, then, does it mean to say we are getting emotionally involved in a novel? My claim is that we respond emotionally to people and events in novels in just the same way as we respond to people and events in real life. If this is true, then my analysis of emotion has a number of implications for our emotional experience of a novel. (1) Emotional appraisals occur in situations in which our wants, interests, or goals are deemed to be at stake, so somehow our wants, interests, and goals have to be at stake in our encounter with the novel. (2) Emotional responses are bodily responses, so we have to respond in a bodily way to what's going on in the novel. (3) Emotional appraisals are instinctive, automatic, and non-cognitive, or pre-cognitive. So our responses to characters and events in the novel are (in part) non-cognitive. Obviously we have to understand what we read before we can respond emotionally in this way. We don't respond emotionally to the inscriptions on the page, but to what they mean and the images they induce in our minds. The affective appraisal is a meta-appraisal of these images and ideas.[12] (4) Emotions focus attention in a bodily way. This means that bodily changes help to focus attention on events that are important in the novel. (5) Emotional situations are stored in emotional memory, possibly in motor memory, in which case the characters and events in a novel may elicit bodily responses based on our own emotional memories of similar people and events. More importantly, if my emotional reactions to the novel are strong enough, then they in turn may become encoded in emotional memory, making new connections between affective appraisals and bodily responses (somatic markers) and influencing my thoughts and behavior long after I have finished the novel. Finally, (6) in the emotion process, cognitive monitoring modifies the results of the affective appraisal. Our emotional responses to what's going on in a novel give way to reflections that modify and moderate those responses.

In what follows I want to emphasize in particular that, in becoming emotionally engaged with a novel, a reader finds her own wants and interests to be at stake; that she makes affective appraisals of what she reads that fix her attention on salient events, characters, and character traits; that these affective appraisals affect her physiologically; and that she cognitively monitors these affective appraisals and the bodily changes they set off. Thus I won't experience any emotional response to a story unless I sense that my own interests, goals, and wants are somehow at stake. The story has to be told in such a way that the reader cares about the events it recounts. If I am going to respond emotionally to the character Dorothea Brooke, what happens to her has to be important to me in some way. I appraise her situation affectively, as one who cares about her: I don't want her to give up all her youthful idealism in the service of her husband's crabbed idea of scholarship. I don't like it that her uncle fails to exert himself to try to stop her marriage. I wish Casaubon were more understanding, less resentful and cold in his attitude towards her.

If I am in an emotional state, that means that I get emotionally or physiologically worked up – perhaps my heart rate increases, perhaps my muscles tense, perhaps I frown. I may also want to help Dorothea by giving her some good advice, and find myself in the relevant state of action readiness. My physiological responses help to focus my attention on what's most important in the unfolding events. Thus, knowing that Celia is the voice of practical reason, and knowing too her deep affection (mixed with some feelings of superiority) for Dorothea, I react in a bodily way when Celia learns that Dorothea is engaged to Casaubon:

> Perhaps Celia had never turned so pale before. The paper man she was making would have had his leg injured, but for her habitual care of whatever she held in her hands. She laid the fragile figure down at once, and sat perfectly still for a few moments. When she spoke there was a tear gathering. "O Dodo, I hope you will be happy." Her sisterly tenderness could not but surmount other feelings at this moment, and her fears were the fears of affection.[13]

My emotional response to this little scene is complex. It is not until I "see" Celia's reaction that I fully realize what a horrible mistake Dorothea may be making. I am made to share Celia's fears, and I become anxious about Dorothea. I also feel compassion for both sisters, the one because she is afraid for Dorothea yet powerless to stop her taking the fateful step, and the other because she is trying so hard to lead a virtuous life, yet is so ignorant of what she is about.

After reacting emotionally to this incident, I may cognitively monitor the initial affective appraisal, judging it to have been appropriate or not. In this particular case I may well decide that my fears and anxiety were justified, that they did indeed alert me to important aspects of Dorothea's character (as well as Celia's), and that they prepared me to some extent for the disappointments and regrets that lie ahead for Dorothea. Something very similar can happen in real life: an anxious reaction to a friend's decision may alert me to the dangers it might imply. It might also teach me something about my friend's character, something perhaps that I have never noticed before. In short, I respond emotionally to my friend and her decision and then I reflect upon the appropriateness or otherwise of my emotional response. And I react in a very similar way to Dorothea.

Even though I react to Dorothea as if she were a real person, however, this does not mean that I am unaware that Dorothea is a character, not a real English lady, and that the events Eliot recounts are fictional. Cognitive monitoring of my initial affective appraisal will affect my physiological responses, my focus of attention, and also my actions and action tendencies. If I feel compassion for my friend, there is probably something I can do to help that friend, whereas if I feel compassion for the victims of massacre in the Sudan, I may want to help but be unable to. Similarly, there is nothing I can do to help Dorothea. Most readers of the novel make a cognitive appraisal that this is a story we are engaged with and that there is no appropriate action to take. Even if I want to help her, and have a tendency to lecture her in my head ("Don't marry him! You'll regret it!"), I know perfectly well that I can't help her, can't lecture her, and can't nudge her from her chosen path. Indeed, part of my anxiety derives from the cognitive appraisal: "I am not in control of this series of events."

Cognitive monitoring has other important roles, in readjusting attention and in reflecting on initial affective appraisals. In reading a complex novel like Middlemarch, we don't just emote about Dorothea. We use our emotional responses towards her as data in arriving at an interpretation of her character. And although, of course, there are many other aspects of the novel, I think we'll all agree that an interpretation of Dorothea's character is crucial to any interpretation of the novel as a whole, including its plot and its theme. Cognitive monitoring of our emotional responses to Dorothea provides crucial data for an interpretation of the book as a whole.

Processing a Narrative

The reader-response theorist and critic Wolfgang Iser has emphasized that an author cannot tell us everything in a story.[14] A text is always and necessarily full of gaps, and understanding a text is necessarily a matter of filling in the gaps. The fairy story begins: "Once upon a time there was a boy called Jack." It doesn't say: "Jack had two arms, two legs, a head, a liver, a pancreas, two kidneys, and a heart," but the reader assumes that if he is a boy, then he has all these things: we fill in the gaps appropriately. It would be willfully to misunderstand the text to think of Jack as having one leg or a heart condition. (With only one leg and a heart condition he wouldn't be able to climb the beanstalk.) In short, an author relies upon our making inferences all the time as we read, in order to fill in what the text does not explicitly say. One of the main kinds of inference we draw is causal. We read: "Jack's mother threw the beans out of the window. The next day there was a giant beanstalk growing outside the window." We make the causal inference that the beanstalk grew from the magic beans.

According to McKoon's and Ratcliff's "minimalist hypothesis," for which there is considerable empirical support, as we read a narrative "only two classes of inferences, those based on easily available information and those required for local coherence, are encoded during reading, unless a reader adopts special goals or strategies."[15] For example, if we are told that Jack's mother sends Jack to bed without any supper, we do not automatically imagine Jack going to his bedroom. The idea is that we imagine only so much as we need to make sense of the ongoing narrative. Unless the fact that Jack goes to his bedroom turns out to be vital to the plot, we won't ever think about it as we read.

Tom Trabasso and his colleagues have shown that understanding a narrative consists in understanding "a causal network that represents the relationships between the causes and the consequences of events in a story." As readers read moment to moment in a text, they "derive a main causal chain for the story, which preserves the sequence of causally important events that serves as the backbone for the story." Trabasso has "demonstrated that the importance and memorability of the clauses in [certain short] texts can be predicted by the causal connectedness of each clause as well as by whether it lies along the main causal chain."[16]

Similarly, other researchers have suggested that "readers build causal networks by strategically deploying the resources of working memory" and that "the causal structure of a narrative controls the allocation of attention as it is read."[17] Fletcher and associates advocate a model they call the "current state selection strategy," designed to use working memory to best advantage. Readers identify the most current clause with causal antecedents – but no consequences – in the preceding text. All propositions that contribute to the causal role of this clause remain in short-term [working] memory as the following sentence is read.[18]

The idea is that the reader assumes that "any clause that has not yet yielded causal consequences is likely to do so as the text continues,"[19] and so readers should keep it in working memory. Some clever experiments suggest that this is indeed what happens as readers process a text. For example, if we read a series of sentences, each one describing an event in a causal series, we tend to push out of working memory the steps in the causal chain as their consequences become known. If it turns out that some future event relies causally on some step that came earlier in the causal sequence, it takes longer for the reader to understand it and make the causal connection. (For example,

"Sally was baking a cake in the kitchen. Her sister said that the oven was broken. Sally decided to borrow the neighbor's oven. From the living room her mother heard voices in the kitchen.")

All these inferences are cognitive, not emotional. Gerrig does not specifically focus on emotional responses, although he does discuss what he calls "participatory responses," which he describes as heterogeneous "noninferential responses" that include the readers' emotional responses to a suspenseful situation in a thriller or the kinds of hopes and fears that readers entertain for a character as the plot develops. But such "participatory responses," he says, "do not fill gaps in the text" and so "do not fit the classic definition for inferences."[20]

But I would urge, on the contrary, that many of our emotional responses to texts do indeed fill in gaps in the text, for they alert the reader to important information about character and plot that is not explicitly asserted in the text. In *The Ambassadors* Henry James does not say "Strether is a mildly comic character." He induces us to laugh (rather quietly!) at Strether. Similarly, George Eliot does not say that Dorothea is in a difficult situation in the early parts of *Middlemarch*: she describes Dorothea's situation and lets us experience it emotionally for ourselves. It is through our emotional responses that we gather important information about characters and plot.

Interpretation as Reflection on Emotional Responses to a Text

On this way of thinking, our emotional experience of a novel is itself a form of understanding, even if it is an inarticulate or relatively inarticulate understanding: if I laugh and cry, shiver, tense, and relax in all the "right" places, then I have in some sense understood the story.[21] But if I want not just to have a rich emotional experience while reading the novel but also to give a critical account – a "reading" or an "interpretation" – of it, this requires reflecting on my emotional experience. I need to reflect upon my affective appraisals, figure out what they were, what it was in the story that provoked them, and whether they were justified. In this way I may arrive at an overall interpretation of the novel, which is the result of affective responses and subsequent cognitive monitoring of those responses, including judgments about whether my initial responses were appropriate. This means that in order to come up with a convincing interpretation of a great realistic novel such as *Middlemarch*, a critic typically needs to rely on a prior emotional experience of it. The initial affective appraisals of the work are a crucial part of the data that the critic draws upon when giving a reflective interpretation of the work as a whole.

If I experience anxiety on Dorothea's account before her marriage and compassion for her afterwards, and if I respond to Casaubon with, say, a mixture of anger, contempt, and pity, then I am in a much better position than a disinterested observer to reflect upon these characters and the role they play in the novel as a whole. I am in a better position to give a critical interpretive account of it. For what I am reflecting upon is not just a set of words and their literal descriptive meanings but my experience of what is described, my feelings about the characters, my emotional responses to them. These experiences, feelings, and responses can then form the basis for a critical reading of the work. "The work" is not just a set of words and their literal meanings, but descriptions, dialogue, etc., as experienced by the reader. A critical interpretation of a work becomes a reflection upon one's emotional experience of the work.

Obviously emotion isn't everything: you have to understand the meanings of the words in a literary work before you can get off the ground at all. And if you are reading a novel, you probably need some background information about its place in the history of literature and how it fits or fails to fit the general conventions of the genre of novels. You also need to be able to make appropriate inferences. But what I'm emphasizing here is that appropriate emotional reactions to a novel are evidence that we understand the novel, and an important source of data for an interpretation of the novel.

Why Be Emotionally Involved?

Even if it's granted, however, that responding emotionally to a literary work can be a mode of understanding the work and that it can give us data on which to rely in arriving at an interpretation of the work, someone might still object that the information we get via emotional involvement with a work could equally well be gathered by purely cognitive means. Why do I have to be amused by Strether or feel compassion for Dorothea in order to understand them? Can't I have a dispassionate understanding of Strether's predicament and see it as comic without actually being amused by it? Can't I grasp dispassionately that Dorothea's situation is difficult and that she is pitiable in some respects, without myself feeling compassion for Dorothea? Why do I need to become personally, emotionally involved in order to understand what is going on? More generally, why does a critic have to rely on a prior emotional experience of a work in order to come up with a convincing interpretation of it?

In replying to these questions, I wish to focus on the role of character in a novel, which, as I've already pointed out, is crucial to an understanding of a novel as a whole. The argument in a nutshell is this: (1) Understanding character is essential to understanding the great realist novels I have in mind; (2) understanding character is relevantly like understanding real people; and (3) understanding real people is impossible without emotional engagement with them and their predicaments. Now, these are large claims, and I don't purport to have a definitive proof of them. But I will try to demonstrate their plausibility.

Consider first the way in which emotions focus attention.[22] I might not even notice that Strether has a comic aspect unless he makes me smile. I might not notice Dorothea's vulnerability at the beginning of Middlemarch unless I respond to her with anxiety and compassion. In responding with amusement to Strether and with anxiety to Dorothea, I am focusing on important aspects of their characters. Indeed, if I do not notice that Strether is a comic character or Dorothea (at first) a vulnerable one, then I have missed an important aspect of the novels in question.

In general, our emotions let us know what is important to us by focusing attention through affective appraisals and consequent physiological responses. Dorothea is described as a person who is well-intentioned and idealistic, but also stubborn and inexperienced, and my emotional responses to her register these facts in a way that holds my attention willy-nilly. When she accepts Casaubon against the advice of all the "practical" characters around her, I make an affective appraisal that one of "my own" is faced with a threat. Physiological changes also reinforce the focus of my emotion; action tendencies and expressive gestures keep my body alert to how I am thinking of her. I feel my anxiety on her behalf in a bodily and instinctive way that is hard to eradicate. The emotions are ways of focusing attention on those things that are important to our wants, goals, and interests. So although it might seem that an unemotional "point of view" can serve the same purpose as a bona fide emotional response, in fact those who fail to respond emotionally to Dorothea won't be focused on her vulnerability with the same urgency and sense of its importance. Similarly, if I don't laugh affectionately with Strether, I may not notice his mildly comic innocence and lack of worldliness. It is not easy to detect James's subtle comedy, so unless I am amused by Strether, it is quite possible that this important aspect of his character will be completely lost on me. I suppose someone could just tell me that he is a comic character. But unless I am actually amused by Strether so that I laugh or smile at or with him, do I really understand that he is comic?[23] And if I don't understand why he is comic, why should I believe it when someone tells me I ought to find him funny? Perhaps I admit that this other person for some reason finds him funny, but I could attribute that to some quirk of this person's personality rather than to anything about Strether. On the other hand, if this other person is a friend on whose testimony I often rely, then perhaps I might bow to her superior understanding and grant that Strether is indeed a comic character, but still without understanding why. If my friend then explains why she finds him amusing, I may still remain mystified: perhaps I do now understand why my friend finds Strether comic, but that is not the same thing as my understanding why Strether is comic. The same thing is true in real life. You can tell me that some comedian is hilarious, and try to explain why, but unless I laugh myself, I do not really understand why he is funny; at best I begin to understand why you think he is funny.

This is related to a second point, namely that "understanding" a novel or the characters in a novel is not the same thing as understanding a proposition. There is a difference between smiling at Strether and understanding that we ought to smile, between feeling anxiety for Dorothea and figuring out cognitively that she's making a mistake. In general, there's a difference between cognitive understanding of propositions – that Strether is comic, that Dorothea is making a risky move – and understanding how people feel, and the emotional significance of a situation, event, or setting. Emotional understanding is in the first instance a kind of bodily understanding: my "affective appraisals" of characters, events, and situations are automatic and instinctive, and they immediately produce physiological and behavioral responses that reinforce these emotional appraisals. Consequently I feel my anxiety for Dorothea in a bodily and instinctive way. And although the bodily responses in question may be more subtle, I feel Strether's amusing qualities when I smile, however weakly, at his remarks.

Thirdly, emotional understanding "re-gestalts" the world in a global way: in responding emotionally to Dorothea, I see the whole world of the novel through the prism of those emotions. My feelings for her affect my feelings towards Celia, who has only a limited understanding of Dorothea, together with much affection and a touch of contempt. It affects my feelings for Casaubon, who, although a much less attractive figure than Dorothea, nevertheless has his own pitiable vulnerabilities. Feeling compassion for Dorothea is not just a response to her but a response with wide implications for my understanding of the novel as a whole. In particular, my different emotional responses to the different characters helps to set them in a moral matrix, whereby Dorothea, although more foolish than Celia in some ways, nevertheless has depths of character of which Celia is incapable, and Casaubon although deferred to by "the world" is more narrow-minded than either sister. My emotional responses to each character helps to establish their moral significance in the novel. Similarly, being amused by Strether colors my understanding of the whole structure of the novel, and of the moral balance among the characters: it contributes to my sense that Strether is a good and intelligent man who is also in some ways an "innocent abroad," out of his depth in the situation in which he finds himself.

When emotions re-gestalt the world in line with our wants, goals, and interests, they do this by affective appraisals of the world, reinforced by bodily changes, which register the world under a particular aspect, so that, for example, I register the world of *Middlemarch* as difficult for its heroine. I don't just dispassionately notice the emotional implications for Dorothea of Casaubon's desire for an uncritical and affectionate amanuensis: if I'm responding emotionally, then I feel its implications for Dorothea in a bodily way, which reinforces my sense of its importance to Dorothea (and thus to me). Recognizing cognitively that Dorothea's world is not the way she thought it was and hoped it to be is not the same as feeling for her as she reacts.[24]

But someone might still object that I can figure out that Strether is comic and Dorothea vulnerable without actually experiencing any emotion for these characters, and that I can figure out the ramifications of Dorothea's vulnerability for the wider context of the novel without any emotional prism to look through. Why insist that the proper understanding of a novel requires emotional understanding? The answer is that people who lack this kind of emotional understanding in real life are unable to understand other people very well, and this is true of people in novels as well as real life. Such people have a serious deficit that shows up in various social inadequacies. It seems that in real life we need emotional understanding and "fellow feeling" if we are to understand other people properly, and that cognition without emotion simply does not do as good a job. If this is true for our understanding of people in real life, it is likely to be true of fictional characters as well, at least when they are richly and realistically portrayed.

In ordinary life, we all agree that it is important to be capable of "fellow feeling" for other people; those who lack this ability have an emotional deficit, a lack of emotional intelligence, and they behave insensitively as a result. Fellow feeling is fellow *feeling*, not just an intellectual recognition that someone is in trouble, say, but a "gut reaction" of compassion, an emotional or bodily response, a response consisting in autonomic and motor changes. So-called "intuition" about people is probably just this kind of emotional sensitivity to others, and it is a valuable capacity. To see what happens when people lack this capacity, I'd like to look briefly at a range of examples. In general, I think that people who lack emotional understanding are unable to understand other people very well, and that this is true not just of understanding our neighbors and friends but also for understanding the characters we encounter in novels, plays, and movies. First, imagine a reader who doesn't notice that Strether is comic because the subtle Jamesian emotions are outside her emotional experience. For example, a precocious child reading *The Ambassadors* might "understand" what she reads in a sense if she understands the literal meaning of the words, but in another, deeper sense she won't understand because she won't understand the characters or their motivation. The book is "too old" for her in that it describes experiences outside her emotional range. Here cognition is clearly not enough. The little girl needs emotional sophistication as well.

But perhaps such an example will be deemed irrelevant to my case, since a little girl probably would not be able to grasp what is going on in a Henry James novel either emotionally or cognitively. So consider next a person with sophisticated cognitive powers but a low "EQ" or emotional intelligence. One of the marks of such people is that they fail to register other people's emotional gestures and expressions and consequently fail to understand other people's feelings and motivations. Peter Salovey reports that there are "individual differences in people's ability to perceive accurately, understand, and empathize with others' emotions" and suggests that "individuals who are best able to do so may be better able to respond to their social environment and build a supportive social network."[25] People who are relatively lacking in the ability to have or to access or interpret "gut reactions" of the sort I have described are much more likely to fail to perceive what emotions other people are experiencing and what motivations they have for their behavior.[26] This same ability to understand emotionally what other people are experiencing would seem to be an asset in our attempts to understand fictional characters as well as actual people. In movies, this point is even more obvious. As Paul Ekman has shown, facial expressions are an excellent guide to people's emotional states. Postures and gestures and tones of voice are also key to understanding other people.[27] But even though we don't perceive these things directly when reading a novel, authors describe not only the gestures, postures, and facial and vocal expressions of their characters, but also their trains of thought and imaginings, things that are more difficult to represent directly in a movie.

Finally, Damasio's patients. I mentioned earlier how Damasio has suggested that our brains are able to classify kinds of stimuli and link them with a particular kind of bodily feeling or "somatic marker." His idea is that when faced with a stimulus of the right sort, our body responds automatically with what I would call an affective appraisal of GOOD! or BAD! These pairings of groups of stimuli and somatic markers are stored in what LeDoux calls emotional memory. If this is right, then when my emotions for Dorothea or Strether are evoked, I may be drawing on associations from emotional memory, and, since these associations are stored in emotional memory, they are particularly insistent and hard to eradicate. It seems not unlikely that these "gut reactions" stored in emotional memory are necessary for my grasp of what people are like and how they are likely to act, and that they respond to fictional people as they would to any other people.

Damasio's patients with damage to the frontal lobe (probably to the ventromedial pre-frontal cortices) lacked "somatic markers" linking specific emotional responses and feelings to specific kinds of scenario, and so failed to make sensible decisions in his gambling experiments.[28] It may be that some deficit of this sort is also responsible for pathological failures to respond with appropriate emotions to the way other people behave and express themselves.[29] That such pathologies exist is itself suggestive that mere cognition is not enough for understanding other people and that emotional understanding is crucial. If this is right, then it seems reasonable to think that it is also crucial to understanding the "people" who populate well-crafted realistic novels.

Some of what I have been saying here is admittedly speculative. In particular, Damasio is discussing people's ability to make plans and decisions, not their ability to understand other people.[30] Nevertheless, I hope I have said enough to show that understanding other people in real life most likely requires a special kind of emotional or bodily understanding. We know this is so, because people who lack the ability to respond in a bodily, emotional way to other people – their expressions, behavior, and gestures as well as their thoughts and attitudes – simply don't understand other people very well. I suggest that it is reasonable to think that understanding characters in great realist novels requires the same kind of bodily understanding. And of course understanding characters is a *sine qua non* of understanding the works in which they figure. Here ends my positive defense of the thesis. In the remainder of the essay I'll consider some objections.

Objections

First objection: lots of novels don't require emotional involvement

I happily endorse the view that many novels do not require intense emotional involvement with the characters. I can read a "stock" detective novel or Harlequin romance without getting emotionally worked up about the characters, simply because I understand it as just a characteristic member of a particular genre. There is no need for me to enter into the feelings of the detective or the country squire or the butler: they are just stock characters behaving in a stock way. More interesting are those novels that deliberately attempt to prevent the reader from getting emotionally involved even in the development of the plot. Italo Calvino is a master of this sort of thing, haranguing the reader as if she were a misbehaving character and then turning the reader into just such a character. The reader is never allowed to "forget herself" and enter emotionally into the trials and tribulations of (other!) characters. Another trickster author, Robert Coover, fragments his narrative as Calvino does, and also invents characters that are quintessentially "characters," comic constructions, seen "from the outside." Ian McEwan's *Atonement* is a particularly interesting example, in that it purports to be a realistic "Victorian" novel, but turns out to have a post-modern bite in its tail.

Post-modern novels, however, are written in reaction against the kind of work that I have been discussing: they tend to foreground the formal aspects of the novel and downplay the content of the story. I am not denying the existence of novels that appeal more to the intellect than the heart. What I am suggesting is that an emotionless reading of George Eliot or Henry James or other traditional realistic novels, while no doubt revealing some of the important aspects of a novel, is seriously inadequate, and that a personal emotional involvement with the characters and the story is essential to a proper understanding of novels of this sort.

Second objection: we don't respond to novels in a bodily way

I have insisted that an emotional response is a physiological response. It could be objected that we do not in fact sweat and blush and weep and groan as we sit in the theater watching a play or in the living room curled up with a novel.

However, there is now empirical research that shows people do in fact experience the physiological changes characteristic of emotion when reading a text. For example, Vrana and colleagues showed that "recall of sentences that describe fearful situations resulted in greater heart-rate increase than recall of less affectively arousing text."[31] Paul Harris reviews a number of studies by Peter Lang and his group also showing that when reading a text that describes a frightening encounter, "some of the visceral accompaniments to fear (i.e., heart-rate acceleration and skin conductance) are triggered." Interestingly, fearful reactions to a passage about snakes produce a more powerful reaction in people who have a phobic fear of snakes.[32]

Perhaps it makes sense for people to respond fearfully to thoughts about critters that they fear in real life. But why get all excited about Dorothea Brooke? After all, none of us is really acquainted with her. Why should we respond physiologically to her troubles? There is some empirical evidence to shed light on this question. In an experiment by Jose and Brewer, children read stories and were then asked to rate "how similar they were to the main character, how much they liked that character and how much they worried about the character when he or she was in danger."[33] The experiment showed that the children were most anxious about the good characters in a story, that they liked those characters the most, and also that they judged themselves to be most similar to those characters. Jose and Brewer suggested that it was identification with the characters that made the children worried about them, but even if we do not make this assumption, the experiment suggests a connection between emotional involvement with characters and thinking of them as in some respect "like me," or, as I have put it in previously, as like "me or mine." So it makes sense that we would respond emotionally to Dorothea if we are responding to her as in certain respects someone like me (or like a friend of mine).

A qualification is in order here, however. It is possible in ordinary language or folk psychological terms to be anxious about something without getting emotional about it. ("I am anxious that you should meet my new husband.") Similarly, perhaps a novel or movie may succeed in getting us to form appropriate thoughts about the events and characters depicted but without our actually "getting emotional" about them. There are many reasons why this could happen, from inadequacy on the part of the author to distraction and fatigue on the part of the audience. In these cases, for whatever reasons, I presumably do not care enough about the characters, or – which is much the same thing – I do not feel my own interests and wishes to be sufficiently at stake to evoke an emotional (physiological) response. I have anxious thoughts about Dorothea but without the physiological concomitants of anxiety, or I feel compassion for Anna Karenina without changes in heart rate or skin conductance. Having said that, however, I would like to stress that having an anxious or compassionate point of view on someone or something typically does produce a physiological response, just because of the way we have been designed. And it remains to be seen whether it is empirically possible to have anxious or compassionate thoughts without any physiological disturbance.

Interestingly, as Paul Ekman has shown, emotional expressions are often suppressed, in accordance with the display rules for one's culture.[34] It may be that in the case of responses to fiction, the non-cognitive appraisal "I DON'T LIKE THIS" produces an emotional response but that this is quickly suppressed because of a succeeding cognitive appraisal: "It's only a story." Although some of us will admit to reading a novel with tears streaming down our faces, or cracking up with laughter over a story while all alone in our living rooms, many people no doubt just feel silly sitting all by themselves in tears for "no good reason." By the same token I suspect that, at least in our culture, women will have fewer inhibitions in this respect than men. Interestingly, in an experiment on music listening, Carol Krumhansl has noted that emotional responses to music are closer to the suppressed emotion condition in a study by Gross and Levenson.[35]

Third objection: the paradox of fiction

How can we feel anxiety for Dorothea or amusement at Strether when we know perfectly well that neither of these people really exists? Almost nobody who has written on this topic has had much of a theory of emotion,[36] yet how you respond to this issue will depend very largely on what you think an emotional experience is. The problem got going because most theorists were in thrall to the so-called "judgment" theory of emotion, according to which an emotion is partially constituted by a judgment to the effect (roughly) that someone is suffering (compassion) or that someone has offended me (anger) or that something threatening is in the offing (anxiety) and so on. But although Dorothea is described as having made a risky decision in marrying Casaubon and as suffering in its aftermath, it's not true that there is really something threatening in the offing or that anyone is really suffering, because neither Dorothea nor Casaubon nor the situation between them actually exists. How can I feel anxiety for a woman because she is suffering in an unhappy marriage when I am perfectly aware that there is no such woman and no such unhappy marriage?

In general, the answer to this question is that even when we know we are emotionally engaged with imaginary or fictional characters and events, this does not affect our non-cognitive affective appraisals. An emotional response to something or other does not require a judgment or belief that the something or other exists. If this is right then the "paradox of fiction" is not really a paradox at all. Let me explain.

We have emotional responses to all sorts of things, both real and imaginary, both perceived and merely thought about, both possible and impossible. I can smile to myself with love and tenderness as I think of my husband working away in his lab (which he is), but I can also make myself weep by imagining him dying in a plane crash (which he hasn't). I can feel compassion for my troubled next-door neighbor, who exists, as well as for Dorothea Brooke, who doesn't, but whose story could conceivably turn out to be non-fiction. (After all, the relationship between Tom and Maggie in *The Mill on the Floss* is based partly on Eliot's own troubled relationship with her brother, and one suspects there is also much of Eliot in the character of Dorothea.)

But I can also feel compassion for somebody whom I know cannot possibly exist, as when I feel compassion for Little Grey Rabbit who is captured by the wicked weasels and forced to keep house for them. I feel compassion for her, even though I have no inclination to acknowledge the possibility of the existence of a rabbit who wears a blue apron and keeps a neat little house with a squirrel and a hare.[37] I suspect that we can view anything emotionally, present or absent, existent or non-existent, concrete or abstract. After all, it seems that certain individuals can even view numbers emotionally:

> The mathematician Wim Klein has put this well: "Numbers are friends for me, more-or-less. It doesn't mean the same for you, does it – 3,844? For you it's just a three and an eight and a four and a four. But I say, 'Hi! 62 squared!'"[38]

We respond emotionally not just to what is happening in front of us but to whatever we are paying attention to, whether in the external environment or in the internal environment of our minds. All that's minimally required for an emotional response to occur is a non-cognitive, affective appraisal followed by physiological changes of a certain sort, followed in turn by a cognitive appraisal of the situation (each aspect of the process feeding back upon the others). I can respond emotionally to a conception of Dorothea as articulated in Eliot's novel even while firmly convinced of Dorothea's non-existence.

Some philosophers think it is absurd to say that I am responding emotionally to Dorothea because I know she does not exist, so maybe I am responding to some real-life counterpart of Dorothea: I am responding to a person who is just like Dorothea in all details except for the fact that this person, unlike Dorothea, exists. But then other philosophers counter with the argument that it's not some counterpart of Dorothea that we pity, but Dorothea herself. Again, some people say that our pity is directed at a thought of Dorothea, not a flesh-and-blood woman, but the reply to this argument is that we aren't compassionate towards a thought (whatever that would mean), but towards a woman. And so on and so forth for the past 30 years.[39]

What all this discussion ignores is the fact that although philosophers make their living by making these kinds of distinctions, our psychology does not. Pre-cognitive affective appraisals do not discriminate between real and imagined scenarios: I respond emotionally to whatever seems to have a bearing on my interests and the interests of those to whom I am close (my family, my group, my fellow humans). It does not matter to my emotion systems (fear, sadness, etc.) whether I am responding to the real, the merely imagined, the possible or the impossible. A sculpture of Christ's grieving mother can evoke compassion for her and a novel about a naïve and straitlaced American visitor to Europe can evoke amused affection for him, just as easily as a description or a perception or a thought about comparable real-life people and situations. Indeed, sometimes a vivid thought can evoke emotion more powerfully than a seriously held belief. After the initial response, however, there will be cognitive monitoring, which tells us right away whether we are weeping over a block of marble or a flesh-and-blood woman, whether we are feeling amused affection for a real or an imagined person. This cognitive monitoring will feed back on the original response and modify the physiological symptoms and action tendencies set off. We may weep, but we won't recommend grief counseling to the Holy Mother. We may smile but we won't write a letter of advice to Strether. Again there is empirical evidence to back up this claim. Paul Harris, for example, has studied how children respond emotionally to make-believe situations even when they know that the situations are only imaginary.[40] This might be irrational in some sense, but it happens all the time.[41]

Fourth objection: I'm ignoring authorial manipulation

Another objection to my picture of emotional involvement with characters in novels is that my responses may not in fact reflect my own interests, goals, wants and wishes, likes and dislikes. The author has manipulated me into abandoning my usual interests, goals, and wishes and adopting some new set just for the purposes of the novel.[42] A disturbing example occurs in the movie *Pulp Fiction*, when in one incident we are encouraged to find the sight of the John Travolta character shooting someone in the face amusing. If we laugh, we may be appalled later when we reflect on our emotional response and perhaps angry with the film's director, Quentin Tarantino, for manipulating us in this way. We resent being encouraged to act in ways that we deem on reflection to be immoral. (Alternatively, we may just be responding with amusement to the ironic juxtapositions Tarantino has arranged.) On the other side of the coin, Susan Feagin has pointed out that there are "selfish sentimentalists" who weep over fictional characters while ignoring their own families, the poor, the homeless etc.[43] Such folk are manipulated by the author to be (albeit briefly) better people than they really are, whereas in the *Pulp Fiction* example we are encouraged to be worse!

This phenomenon is a genuine concern, and one that raises the whole question of the role of the author in guiding our emotional responses.[44] Here, however, perhaps it is enough to note that while reading a novel or watching a movie or play, my interests, wants, and goals may indeed differ from those I have when I am not reading or watching. But this does not affect my basic point. We respond emotionally to what we perceive and think about, especially if it is presented in vivid images. We affectively appraise the situation presented as terrible or as wonderful or whatever, because it is presented to us as either thwarting or facilitating what at the time are our goals, wants, and interests. It is important to remember that emotional reactions are automatic and "instinctive": we do not pause to wonder whether all things considered we regard the heroine as suffering or the Travolta action as amusing (although later on, when "interpreting the movie," we may do just that).

Fifth objection: what about inappropriate emotional responses?

The theory I'm implicitly defending here is a version of reader-response theory. One corollary of this view is that different readers will come up with different interpretations based on their different emotional experiences of the work in question. This is a welcome result, I think. Most people agree that great works of art admit of a wide range of "valid" interpretations. My view explains how this can be. Because interpretations are the result of cognitive monitoring of our non-cognitive affective appraisals, and because those non-cognitive appraisals are likely to be somewhat different for different people with different goals, wants, and interests, there is likely to be disagreement about the resulting "cognitive" overview of plot, character, and theme.

But what about responses that seem to be plain inappropriate: implacable hatred for Strether or loathing and disgust for Dorothea Brooke? One can imagine situations in which a person might have such responses. For example, loathing and disgust for Dorothea might be experienced by a woman who thinks that a wife's attitude to her husband should be one of completely uncritical devotion. However, in order to allow these feelings to color her entire interpretation of the novel, such a reader would have to refuse to focus on Dorothea's actual situation; she would have to ignore large parts of what George Eliot wrote. Can I argue someone out of such an interpretation? It depends. The person may be uninterested or unwilling to experience the novel in any other way; she may refuse to "open" herself to the aspects of the novel that she is missing. But what I can do is show that this reader is ignoring large parts of the novel.

"An interpretation" claims to be an overview, making sense of as much of the work as possible in a consistent way.[45] This remains true even when the basis for our interpretations is a series of emotional experiences. Again, if I hate Dorothea from the word go, just because she rebels (in her heart!) against her husband, then I will be unable to respond sympathetically to her, and once again much of the significance of her story will pass me by. If I have no idea what it is like to live in another era or another culture, I may be simply bewildered by Dorothea's story or bored by my incomprehension: I do not have enough in common with the work for my emotions to get involved at all. If such readings sound so bizarre as to not be worth talking about, we should remember that most people respond to novels in personal ways. It is not necessarily a bad thing for people to respond in a personal way, connecting up what they read with their own experiences and able to respond emotionally because their own wants and interests have been successfully appealed to. It would be a bad thing, however, if our own lack of awareness or our own idiosyncratic personal interests forbade or prevented us from enlarging our emotional horizons by sympathetically engaging with people who are different from us in significant ways. If the reader is unable to treat these people as part of "our own," then they may miss the significance of the novel altogether.

It is not hard to root out all the interpretations which ignore huge chunks of the novel, or which do not show a basic understanding of the words on the page. But of necessity every interpretation can be shown to ignore some aspect of a work. Different interpretations necessarily emphasize some aspects and underemphasize others. That is why there will always be different interpretations that are all "valid" in that they account for "the work as a whole" (give or take a little). In the academy, readings of novels often suffer not from a naïve or dogmatic emotionalism, but from a different kind of problem: not enough emotional involvement. "Cognitive" ingenuity is often more prized than emotional insight. But a meaningful encounter with a great work of art is often a highly emotional set of experiences. In the view I have outlined here multiple interpretations of the same work of art are not just possible but to be encouraged and celebrated, for they represent reflections about a genuine emotional involvement with the work in question.

Notes

This essay is an adapted and abbreviated version of chapters 4 and 5 of my *Deeper Than Reason: Emotion and its Role in Literature, Music, and Art* (Oxford: Oxford University Press, 2005). Reprinted by permission of Oxford University Press.

1   The main difference is that when we read a novel or watch a movie or play, our responses are manipulated by the *formal* devices that the author employs to tell the story. See *Deeper Than Reason*, chapter 7.
2   The idea of the "implied author" was introduced by Wayne C. Booth in *The Rhetoric of Fiction* (Chicago, IL: University of Chicago Press, 1961). It refers to the author as (s)he seems to be from the evidence of the work. Since this "evidence" is interpreted *by a reader*, the implied author is also partly determined by the reader of the work, as I explain in *Deeper Than Reason*, chapter 6.
3   Its best-known exponent in recent times is probably Martha Nussbaum. See Nussbaum, *Love's Knowledge: Essays on Philosophy and Literature* (New York: Oxford University Press, 1990).
4   My view is laid out in more detail in *Deeper Than Reason*, chapters 1–3. For a condensed version of the view, see Robinson, "Emotion: Biological Fact or Social Construction?" in Robert C. Solomon, ed., *Thinking about Feeling: Contemporary Philosophers on Emotion* (New York: Oxford University Press, 2004), 28–43. I develop the view further in "Emotion," in Jesse Prinz, ed., *The Oxford Handbook of Philosophy of Psychology*, forthcoming.
5   This point was emphasized by Robert C. Solomon, *The Passions* (Garden City, NY: Anchor Press/Doubleday, 1976) and has been endorsed by most emotion theorists ever since.
6   The evidence on facial expression is outlined in Paul Ekman, *Emotions Revealed* (New York: Henry Holt, 2003). The evidence of differential autonomic activity is summarized in Robert Levenson, "The Search for Autonomic Specifity," in Paul Ekman and Richard J. Davidson, eds., The Nature of Emotion: Fundamental Questions (New York: Oxford University Press, 1994), 252–7. The notion of action tendencies is crucial to the account in Nico Frijda, *The Emotions* (Cambridge: Cambridge University Press, 1986).
7   See Jenefer Robinson, "Startle," *Journal of Philosophy* 92 (1995): 53–74. A similar view has been developed with great sophistication by Jesse Prinz (*Gut Reactions: A Perceptual Theory of Emotion*, Oxford: Oxford University Press, 2004). In "Emotion" (forthcoming) I suggest

that Prinz's view is in fact a plausible account of what *triggers* emotional responses, but that it cannot explain emotion *tout court*.

8   Different appraisal theorists take different approaches. Some think of emotion triggers as assessments of preference or aversion; others take a broader "componential" approach, including not only preference and aversion but also novelty, uncertainty, and other *components* of particular emotional evaluations, such as anger and fear; others again think they should be thought of in terms of the person's (or animal's) goals. The approach I leaned towards in *Deeper than Reason* was the "basic emotion" approach, according to which there is a limited set of non-cognitive appraisals corresponding to certain basic emotions: THREAT! OFFENSE! LOSS! GOOD THING! FRIEND! FOE! which roughly correspond to fear, anger, sadness, happiness, love and hate. In "Emotion" (forthcoming) I express some doubts about this approach.

9   This point is emphasized by Ronald de Sousa, *The Rationality of Emotion* (Cambridge, MA: MIT Press, 1987).

10 See Joseph LeDoux, *The Emotional Brain: The Mysterious Underpinnings of Emotional Life* (New York: Simon and Schuster, 1996).

11 See Antonio R. Damasio, *Descartes' Error: Emotion, Reason, and the Human Brain* (New York: G. P. Putnam, 1994). Patients with damage to the ventromedial region of the prefrontal cortices responded with pleasure or displeasure to good and bad draws from the packs in Damasio's gambling experiments, but showed no anticipatory responses. There was apparently no emotional/bodily memory of the bad/good packs.

12 In her review of Robinson, *Deeper Than Reason*, Kathleen Higgins (2007) says:

> To describe what we are doing while reading [a novel] as involving non-cognitive appraisals is strange. The only way we apprehend that something in a novel might appeal to our wants, interests, and values is by means of the conceptual mediation of interpreting the words on the page. Even to make sense of the incidents described, we must do a lot of mental processing, and neocortical processing at that.

But of course I do not deny this. The non-cognitive appraisals operate on what has already been cortically processed.

13 George Eliot, *Middlemarch*, ed. W. J. Harvey (Harmondsworth: Penguin, 1987), chapter 5, 72.

14 See Wolfgang Iser, *The Implied Reader: Patterns of Communication in Prose Fiction from Bunyan to Beckett* (Baltimore, MD: Johns Hopkins University Press, 1974); *The Act of Reading: A Theory of Aesthetic Response* (London: Routledge and Kegan Paul, 1978); and "The Reading Process: A Phenomenological Approach," in Jane P. Tompkins, ed., *Reader-Response Criticism: From Formalism to Post-Structuralism* (Baltimore, MD: Johns Hopkins University Press, 1980).

15 Richard J. Gerrig, *Experiencing Narrative Worlds: On the Psychological Activities of Reading* (New Haven, CT: Yale University Press, 1993), 31, quoting G. McKoon and R. Ratcliff, "Inference During Reading," *Psychological Review* 99 (1992): 440–66, 441.

16 Described in Gerrig, *Experiencing Narrative Worlds*, 46–7.

17 Ibid., 47, quoting C. R. Fletcher, J. E. Hummel, and C. J. Marsolek, "Causality and the Allocation of Attention During Comprehension," *Journal of Experimental Psychology: Learning, Memory, and Cognition* 16 (1990): 233–40, 239.

18 Gerrig, *Experiencing Narrative Worlds*, 47, quoting Fletcher, Hummel, and Marsolek, "Causality and the Allocation of Attention," 233.

19 Gerrig, *Experiencing Narrative Worlds*, 48.

20 Ibid., 66–7.
21 Leonard Meyer, *Emotion and Meaning in Music* (Chicago, IL: University of Chicago Press, 1956), defends a similar view about music.
22 Cf. Noel Carroll, "Art, Narrative, and Emotion," in Mette Hjort and Sue Laver, eds., *Emotion and the Arts* (New York: Oxford University Press, 1997), 192: "The emotions in life and in art have the function of focusing attention." Carroll cites my "Startle," in support of this contention. The view that emotions are primarily devices for focusing attention has been most forcefully defended in De Sousa, *The Rationality of Emotion*.
23 Miss Gostrey has just learned that Strether's full name is "Mr Lewis Lambert Strether," and she comments that she likes it.

> "particularly the Lewis Lambert. It's the name of a novel of Balzac's."
> "Oh, I know that!" said Strether.
> "But the novel's an awfully bad one."
> "I know that too." Strether smiled. To which he added with an irrelevance that was only superficial:
> "I come from Woollett, Massachusetts."

The remark amuses us not just by its apparent inconsequence but also because Strether is so anxious to avow his origins, as though, as Maria Gostrey points out, he wants to prepare her for "the worst." There is also the comic incongruity between the reference to Balzac and the reference to Woollett. As Maria Gostrey reflects: "Balzac had described many cities, but he had not described Woollett, Massachusetts."

24 We might also feel her reactions empathically as well as feeling *for* her. There is a huge literature on empathy and simulation, which I am not going to discuss as it is not directly relevant to my concerns. I claim that emotional involvement with characters in realistic novels is necessary to understanding them, but I do not believe that that our emotional involvement with characters *has* to take the form of empathizing with them or simulating their emotions.
25 Peter Salovey, et al., "Current Directions in Emotional Intelligence Research," in Michael Lewis and Jeanette M. Haviland-Jones, eds., *Handbook of Emotions*, 2nd edn. (New York: Guilford, 2000), 504–20, 506.
26 A lot of people have argued that we need to explain "mind-reading" in terms of the concept of "simulation." By contrast, I am stressing here the role of emotional responses to what we *perceive* in other people's expressions and gestures, and what we are *told* about other people's thoughts and ways of seeing the world (as well what we are told about their expressions and gestures). See also note 24.
27 See Amy Coplan, "The Low Road to Affect: How Film Elicits Non-Cognitive Affective Responses," Invited Symposium, *The Nature of Film*, American Philosophical Association Pacific Division conference, San Francisco, April 2007.
28 The details are explained in Damasio, *Descartes' Error*.
29 Much has been written recently about people with *autism*, who typically have severe problems with social interaction. One of the deficits associated with autism lies in the ability to "mind-read," i.e., to understand what other people are feeling and thinking. In certain kinds of autism most cognitive abilities remain intact, yet even high-functioning autistic people fail to respond with appropriate emotions to others. It is possible, therefore, that such people have difficulty understanding others because, although they can grasp cognitively what is going on around them, they cannot understand emotionally what other people are

feeling and thinking. On the other hand, Shaun Nichols (personal communication) has pointed out to me that the research over the last decade or so has shown that children with autism and Asperger's are actually competent at identifying simple emotions and seem to experience at least some distress at others' suffering. Where they show clear emotional deficiencies is in the attribution of complex emotions such as pride. It is therefore possible that it is *cognitive* demands that interfere with success and that autism should be treated as a cognitive psychopathology rather than an emotional one. But all of this is contested territory.

30 Gregory Currie and Ian Ravenscroft (in *Recreative Minds: Imagination in Philosophy and Psychology*, Oxford: Clarendon Press, 2002, 198) link these two abilities by suggesting that both involve "modelling" in imagination.

31 S. R. Vrana, B. N. Cuthbert, and P. J. Lang, "Processing Fearful and Neutral Sentences: Memory and Heart Rate Change," *Cognition and Emotion* 3 (1989): 179–95.

32 Paul L. Harris, *The Work of the Imagination* (Oxford: Blackwell, 2000), 70–1.

33 Gerrig, *Experiencing Narrative Worlds*, 81, citing P. E. Jose and W. F. Brewer, "The Development of Story-Liking: Character Identification, Suspense, and Outcome Resolution," *Developmental Psychology* 20 (1984), 911–24.

34 Ekman, *Emotions Revealed*, 4.

35 Carol L. Krumhansl, "An Exploratory Study of Musical Emotions and Psychophysiology," *Canadian Journal of Experimental Psychology* 51 (1997): 336–52, 350.

36 Noel Carroll is an exception. In "Art, Narrative, and Emotion" he follows William E. Lyons, *Emotion*, Cambridge Studies in Philosophy (Cambridge: Cambridge University Press, 1980).

37 I refer to a series of children's books by Alison Uttley.

38 Oliver Sacks, *The Man Who Mistook his Wife for a Hat* (New York: Harper and Row, 1987), 208–9.

39 For a nice summary of the paradox and the various sorts of solutions that have been offered to it, see Jerrold Levinson, "Emotion in Response to Art: A Survey of the Terrain," in Mette Hjort and Sue Laver, eds., *Emotion and the Arts* (New York: Oxford University Press, 1997), 20–34. One of the leading alternative theories that I reject is found in Kendall Walton, "Fearing Fictions," *Journal of Philosophy* 75 (1978): 5–27; and *Mimesis as Make-Believe: On the Foundations of the Representational Arts* (Cambridge, MA: Harvard University Press, 1990).

40 Harris, *The Work of the Imagination*.

41 There are studies that show that people (as I would put it) respond affectively even when they know the response is rationally unjustified. Some good examples come from the literature on disgust: people refuse to eat fudge in the shape of a dog turd or to drink from a glass of juice into which a sterilized cockroach has been dunked. And if you pour sugar into two brand-new empty bottles, one of which is labeled as sugar and the other as poison, and then make sugar water in two beakers, one of which has sugar from the bottle marked "sugar" and the other from the bottle marked "poison," people much prefer to sample the sugar water made from the sugar in the bottle marked as sugar. See Paul Rozin and A. E. Fallon, "A Perspective on Disgust," *Psychological Review* 94 (1987): 23–41.

42 Thanks to Susan Feagin for pressing me on this point.

43 Susan Feagin, *Reading with Feeling: The Aesthetics of Appreciation* (Ithaca, NY: Cornell University Press, 1996). See also Roger Scruton, *Art and Imagination* (London: Methuen, 1974), 131.

44 The issue is addressed more fully in Robinson, *Deeper Than Reason*, chapters 6–7.

45 Monroe Beardsley once proposed two criteria of correctness for interpretations, the principle of congruence (make your interpretation of the parts of the text consistent), and the principle of plenitude (make your interpretation fit as much of the text as possible). His advice remains sound. Adjusting his view to my emotional reader-response perspective, I would propose that a "dispassionate" interpretation should take into account as many of our emotional responses as possible, provided that they are consistent with an overall reading of the text. See Monroe Beardsley, *Aesthetics: Problems in the Philosophy of Criticism* (New York: Harcourt Brace, 1958).

6

Feeling Fictions

ROGER SCRUTON

In plays, novels, and poems, imaginary beings rejoice and suffer and we respond in sympathy. Is that a puzzling fact? If so, where does the puzzle lie? The consensus among philosophers seems to be that there really is a puzzle, and that it has to do with the fictional nature of the situations presented. How can we feel real emotions towards unreal events? And if our feelings too are unreal, why should we value them? Is there not a "paradox of fiction," asking us simultaneously to believe that we readers feel great emotions, and also that we feel nothing at all?

Addressing this problem Kendall Walton has argued that we understand fictions by using them as props in a game of make-believe. Games of make-believe involve the elaboration of fictional worlds, in which we ourselves participate as spectators. It is not literally true that I feel pity for Desdemona; but – to use Walton's idiom, "it is fictional that" I pity her, and the unfolding of the story makes it "fictional that" (or fictionally true that) my emotions evolve in tandem with the events of the story.[1]

As Walton recognizes, this does not in itself answer the puzzle about fictions. It does not tell us whether our feelings towards the play are real or unreal. He goes on to argue, in effect, that I do not feel real pity towards Desdemona, but something that he calls quasi-pity. And what is that? Walton admits that there is a problem here. "But," he goes on, "it is not so much a problem for my account of the appreciation of works of fiction as one for theories of emotion."[2] Insofar as he is prepared to define quasi-pity, quasi-fear, etc., it is in the following roundabout way:

> Whatever it is that combines with the appropriate belief to constitute the emotion (in those instances in which such a belief is involved), I suggest that some such state or condition, or one that is naturally taken to make it fictional that the appreciator is in such a state or condition, helps to make it fictional that one admires or pities someone.[3]

There is much more to Walton's account, but I want to pause here, since Walton's way of putting the problem brings home just what is puzzling in the case of fictive emotions. What makes it true that John pities Mary is certainly a belief (that Mary is unfortunate), together with something else. Walton toys with the suggestion that the

---

A Companion to the Philosophy of Literature, First Edition. Edited by Garry L. Hagberg and Walter Jost.
© 2010 John Wiley & Sons Ltd. Published 2015 by John Wiley & Sons, Ltd.

"something else" is a "phenomenological experience." But, aside from all the difficulties presented by the recourse to phenomenology (difficulties associated with the attempt to give a purely "first-person" description of our mental states[4]), it is evident – and Walton admits as much – that for many of our most important emotions there is nothing inner to identify, or at least, nothing of importance. What significantly remains to an emotion when the element of belief has been substracted is not usually a passive inner "feel," but an outward-going motive to action. You act *out of* fear, pity, love, anger, and it is precisely because they are motives to action that emotions are so interesting. That is why we try to control them and to educate them, and also why we judge people in terms of them. (Just think why it is so severe a criticism of someone to say that he is heartless.) Take the belief that you have been wronged, and the resulting desire to harm the person responsible: what more is required for resentment? If someone says "there is also a phenomenological aspect, a "what it is like" that must be present if the emotion is to be correctly identified as resentment," then what do you say to the person who admits that he has both the belief and the desire, but denies the presence of anything "phenomenological"? Do you say that he is lying? That he is self-deceived? Or that it is not *resentment* that he feels? None of those responses, it seems to me, is justified by the given facts.

Pity involves a desire to help, to relieve, to console. It is not true that I desire to help, relieve, or console Desdemona, since I know that there is no such person. So this "extra" bit of the emotion which, added to the belief, constitutes pity, cannot in this case be added. Here we see the work assumed by the parenthesis in the last sentence quoted from Walton. His response will be – sure, you don't have a real desire to help Desdemona, but you are in a condition which makes it fictional that you desire to help her. But what condition is that? Well, it is a quasi-desire to help. And what are quasi-desires? Well, they are states of mind which stand to quasi-emotions as real desires stand to real emotions. In short, we are back where we started.

Throughout his book – which, let me say, I regard as a major and ingenious contribution to the subject – Walton makes use of the "it is fictional that" idiom, in order to slip sideways out of the puzzle posed by the unreality of fictions. If this idiom were being proposed as the first step in a semantic theory of fictions – in other words as a quantifier over possible worlds – then we would expect it to make an independent contribution to solving that puzzle. However, that is not how Walton treats the idiom, nor could it be so treated, since, as Aristotle pointed out long ago, fictional worlds are not necessarily possible worlds, nor is it possibility (as opposed to "probability") that is the mark of fictional success. It is impossible that a man should be transformed into a stag, but probable, in the context of the story of Actaeon and Diana, that Actaeon should suffer just such a change.[5]

Walton's use of the "it is fictional that" idiom should perhaps be seen as genealogical rather than semantic. The idiom summarizes what is carried over into our understanding of fiction from our childhood games of make-believe. These games involve role-playing, pretending, making one thing stand in for another, so that we too can stand in for other things. And this construction of a fictional world is both a necessary exercise of the childish mind – an extension into the world of rational communication of that instinct for play on which the free development of our capacities depends and which we share with other species – and also a first step towards the understanding of art. In exploring this suggestion Walton takes an interesting journey along a path first opened up by Schiller in his *Letters on the Aesthetic Education of Man* – the path towards art through the gateway of play. And there is surely something highly persuasive in the suggestion that those games of "let's pretend" are the ancestors of our sophisticated passions in the theatre. The problem is, however, that the puzzle about fictions is just as much a puzzle about make-believe. Walton's genealogy is plausible largely because he has identified in its childish form the very same puzzling fact that we encounter in our adult response to fiction: the fact that we direct our emotions towards purely imaginary things. How is that possible, and what do we gain from doing so? It would be an advance to say that this imagining of, and feeling towards, fictions is an exercise of "make-believe," only if "to make-believe that p" could be explained without assuming a theory of fiction. But the puzzles remain: how can you make-believe that p while believing not-p? How can you feel towards some object of make-believe an emotion that you might also feel towards an object of real belief? And how can you take what you learn from fiction into life, when what you learn from fiction is to be explained in terms of quasi-emotions, whose relation to real emotions remains as opaque as the relation of make-believe to real belief? When it comes to the philosophical puzzles, it seems to me, the concept of "make-believe" is doing no real work. Instead it is identifying a special case of imaginative narrative, every case of which presents the problem of our response to fiction.

Something similar should be said, it seems to me, of the idea of pretence, suggested by Walton, and explicitly built into his theory of fiction by Gregory Currie.[6] In reading fiction, according to Currie, we "go along with" the pretence, by adopting the point of view of a "fictional author." This exercise of the imagination engenders emotional affects which are to be understood as "quasi-emotions" in the manner of Walton. Once again, it seems to me, we have a theory that states the problem without offering a solution to it. In subsequent writings both Currie and Walton have tried to advance towards a solution by adopting "simulation theory" from cognitive science. This "theory" is not yet a theory, but rather the speculative suggestion that we understand another's psychology by simulating the beliefs and desires that we might have in his situation, and thereby experiencing some premonition of their emotional affect.[7] When we simulate a state of mind our motivational system runs "off-line," since the cognitive content is disconnected from our actual beliefs and desires, and by running that content "off-line" we gain insight into a hypothetical situation, experiencing some reverberation of the emotional affect which that situation would generate. This suggestion has been criticized, in that it limits emotional responses to fiction to those in which we can identify a model whose responses the reader can simulate.[8] It therefore involves a perpetuation of the implausible "fictional author" thesis of Currie's earlier work. More importantly, it seems to me, this kind of would-be cognitive science gets nowhere with the fundamental philosophical problem, which concerns the nature and intentionality of emotion, when emotion is not founded on belief. What do such emotions amount to, how do they connect with our real-life motives, and what, if anything, do we learn from them?

Here it seems appropriate to summarize a position that I have argued for in more detail elsewhere, and which I believe gets us over the first hurdle towards a theory of fiction.[9] Imagination, I suggest, is the capacity, which all rational beings exhibit to some degree, to entertain thoughts without affirming or asserting them, and to create an order among those thoughts which makes each in some way answerable or appropriate to the others. It is a cognitive capacity which, unlike belief or desire, is directly subject to the will. ("Imagine that p!" is a sensible order; "Believe that p!" is not.) It may or may not involve imagery, though not all imagery is an exercise of the imagination: dreams and hallucinations, for example, are "impressions" that severely limit one's freedom to alter or dissent from them. ("See a dagger before your eyes!", "Dream of Kitty!" are neither of them sensible orders.) Imagination, as I envisage it, is a response to the question "What if . . . ?" And it involves the construction of an imaginary world by unfolding a narrative, whether in literary form, as in a play or a novel, or in visual form, as in a painting. The relation of imagination to belief, I suggest, can best be understood in terms of two contrasts: that between unasserted and asserted sentences, and that between active and passive mental states – states which are, and states which are not, subject to the will. And Frege's proof that assertion is no part of the meaning of a sentence implies that when someone imagines that p, and when he believes that p, he is in one case imagining exactly what in the other case he is believing. Hence, what we learn from the imagination we might also apply in life.

It would seem to follow from that account that emotions arising in the course of imagining something cannot be of the same kind as those arising in real-life situations. Works of fiction, which are explicitly directed to the imagination, are asking us to conjure up thoughts without asserting them as true. Our ordinary emotional life, however, is a response to what we believe. That is not an arbitrary stipulation – as though I were to say that I am calling "emotion" only those states that are founded on belief. It is to point to a deep fact about human beings, which is that they are cognitive creatures, whose responses result not from mechanical instincts like the responses of insects, but from what they *take to be true*. Their motives are built upon assessments of reality, and in classifying these motives we are attempting to give a preliminary theory of human nature. For example, when we associate the belief in danger with the desire to flee, and construct a concept of "fear" whereby to embrace their conjunction, we are not producing an arbitrary definition: we are postulating the existence of a *natural kind*, namely a motive founded in cognition. The same is true of most of our ordinary emotional categories: joy, sadness, pride, anger, remorse, shame, affection are all explanatory concepts, part of the commonsense theory whereby we explain people's actions by describing their beliefs. This is why there is a real *problem* in asserting that we respond to fictions in something like the way that we respond to realities. For our responses to realities are deeply implanted motives, that could not possibly exist without the beliefs that cause them. Our classifications of these responses belong to an attempt – fundamental to human society and personal relations – to explain the way people behave, and also to influence their behavior by changing their beliefs.

Here I want to protest against a proposed solution to the paradox of fiction which has gathered ground in recent publications and which is defended by Jenefer Robinson.

According to Robinson there is a core element of "affective appraisal" in every emotion, which precedes cognitive evaluation, and which is the real source of "what we feel."[10] On this view, the model for emotional reaction is the fear that we feel in response to a sudden threat – the flinching, the flow of cortisone and adrenaline, and with them the hot flush of readiness, all of which precede that deliberative assessment which tells us that we are indeed in danger. On such a view there is a part to every emotion that precedes cognition and which is also the origin of our intensest response. Since this part is independent of cognition it can be reproduced even in those circumstances, such as the reading of fiction, where belief is "on hold."

Now I don't doubt that there are these "gut reactions," as I shall call them, residues of our animal instincts, which precede rational assessment. But that they are the main or even the normal response to reading literature is surely highly implausible. We do not feel some equivalent of the antelope's startled response to the smell of a cheetah when we read, in *Moby Dick*, of the first sighting of the White Whale. Or if we do feel some such thing, it is irrelevant to the expressive content of the passage. It is not *this* that the author intends to convey but something far more subtle – an emotional response entirely and minutely dependent upon the cognitive content which he carefully unfolds before our rational faculties. And the paradox of fiction arises because he is expressly asserting that content as something to be imagined but, for Heaven's sake, not believed.

The suggestion that emotions can be broken up into cognitive and non-cognitive components leads me to rephrase the paradox in a way that directly confronts Walton's account of fiction. If we are to define fear, say, as "belief in a threatened harm + X," we should *not* suppose that we can isolate the X and attach it to some other cognitive state – so as to define quasi-fear, for example, as "the imaginative thought of a threatened harm + X." X, being a motive to action, is bound up with the belief that engenders it, and cannot survive its excision. Or so it seems, at least. If that claim is false, then there is no paradox. But if it is true, as I think it is, then the paradox remains.

Three thoughts help us, I believe, to get round the problem. The first is due to Aristotle, who argued in the *Nicomachean Ethics* that virtue is acquired by imitation. We admire courage, but courageous actions are not produced by admiration: they are produced by the desire to do what is honorable and right, regardless of the danger. That desire is a very special kind of motive, which only a rational being can have. Nevertheless, you can acquire the motive in time, by imitating its outward expression. By repeatedly copying the actions of the virtuous person you translate your admiration for courage into the genuine article. For example, you begin by steeling yourself to stand firm, as courageous people do, even though it goes against the grain; you end by acting courageously – that is, from the very motive that distinguishes courage, the motive to pursue honor in the face of danger. This thought of Aristotle's is of wider application than the teaching of virtue, as he acknowledges in the *Rhetoric*, when discussing mimesis in literature and music. Motives are bound up with the actions that express them; and by imitating those actions we rehearse the motives. We equip ourselves with the ability to act from anger, remorse, pity, or whatever, by imitating the outward expression of those passions in dancing, marching, or play-acting.

An important case of this is the funeral rite – a ceremony in which ritual gestures and formalized words offer both support to the mourners and an example to the rest. You may not, yourself, feel any grief over the person who is being mourned. But the rituals offer you the outward forms of grief, and by copying them you rehearse the emotion. *This* is how grief is expressed, and this is how you too, will express it, when one day the grief is yours. There is evidence from modern culture that the decline in ritual expressions of these existentially challenging emotions has led to a crucial vagueness in acting from them. Grief, love, triumph, and the sense of collective threat, deprived of their ritual forms and their repertoire of religious gestures, have a tendency to dissipate, dwindling into sentimental simulacra which retreat from the real costs of feeling.[11]

That last observation connects with my second thought, which is that there is such a thing as knowing what to feel, and that this "knowing what" is, or ought to be, on a par with the "knowing that" and "knowing how" that are routinely distinguished in the literature. Psychotherapists speak, in this context, of "emotional knowledge" and "affective competence." It seems to me that we have the right to speak of knowledge, since the person who knows what to feel is someone who is "rightly guided," led by his own inner motives to do and feel what is right and appropriate in the circumstances. He is the person on whom you can rely, in this intricate matter of emotional competence. This kind of knowledge is, as Aristotle recognized, a part of virtue, since it conditions the motive from which virtuous action issues. The virtuous person is disposed to feel the right emotion, towards the right object, in the right circumstances, and to the right degree.[12] And just as there is emotional knowledge, which consists in a disposition to be rightly motivated, so is there emotional ignorance. Many of those vices that are condemned in art and literature – sentimentality, stereotyping, insincerity, false naivety, narcissism, and so on – correspond to familiar emotional disorders in people, of a kind that might reasonably be described as "feeling in ignorance." The sentimentalist is a dangerous example to follow, since he falsifies the world to suit his feelings, and to be guided by his love, his anger, his compassion, or whatever, is to risk falling into a trap, as reality is eclipsed by fantasy and the emotions trumpeted no longer match the thing observed.

In discussing emotional knowledge of this kind we are evidently steering close to the realm of literary criticism – or at least, of a certain kind of literary criticism. If we combine the two thoughts that I have sketched, we find ourselves in territory made familiar by T. S. Eliot in *The Sacred Wood* and F. R. Leavis in *Revaluation*. A work of literature, on the view implicit in those critics, is a vehicle through which we rehearse various emotions, and by rehearsing acquire them – not as occurrent motives, to be sure, but as dispositions which will eventually show themselves in actions. If this is so, then of course it matters very much what we read, and whether we read it critically.

If we are to establish such a conclusion, we shall need to say much more about the kind of "imitation" that goes on, when we read a work of literature and adopt its words and gestures as our own. So far I have relied on an intuitive idea of "rehearsal" which is, in itself, no more clearly defined than Walton's notion of make-believe or the notion of "simulation" subsequently adopted by both Walton and Currie. Before returning to this point, however, there is a third thought that I wish to put before the reader. While children's games of pretence usually involve the acting out of roles in an imagined drama, this is not true of our appreciation of literature – not even of a child's appreciation of literature. Here the roles are not acted out, nor are the emotions of the characters directly rehearsed. Whatever is felt by the reader is felt *in sympathy with* the emotions expressed by the work or displayed by the characters described in it.

"Sympathy" means "feeling with"; but this should not deceive us into thinking that, when I sympathize with Rachel, either in real life or in a work of fiction, I feel exactly what she feels, or that I am in any way "simulating" her emotion. There is, it is true, a kind of contagious "sympathy," exhibited by herds and crowds, in which a single emotion is spread from one creature to another, as flight is spread through the herd. But the normal case of human sympathy is not like that, not least because it involves a judgment. Sympathy for Rachel's suffering vanishes when I discover that she is pretending, exaggerating, suffering from an affliction that she has negligently brought upon herself, or suffering deservedly for some wrong of her own. The whole burden of the plot in children's stories is to distinguish those characters with whom it is right to sympathize from those whose triumphs are moral losses and whose sufferings are moral gains.

Suppose you sympathize with Rachel's grief. This does not mean that you too feel grief: the loss was hers, not yours. Nor does it mean that you suffer, or that you find yourself in an emotional condition from which you would wish to escape. On the contrary, your sadness, such as it is, is informed by a sense of its own rightness and fitness, and not to feel it would lower you in your own esteem. You owe it to Rachel to feel as you do, and there would be no comfort for her if you did not feel it. Quite clearly then, your sympathetic response is an entirely different kind of emotion from Rachel's grief. It is not pleasant, but not unpleasant either; it does not involve the deep frustration that comes from losing what you are attached to; it does not involve helpless longing or despair; it does not look backward to what has been lost. On the contrary, your sympathy is a form of closeness, of cherishing, a "being with" Rachel in her grief that comforts her only because it also comforts you.

Sympathetic emotion of this kind belongs with a class of responses that involve the *orientation* of the subject towards the object, rather than any direct readiness to act. Like amusement or admiration, sympathetic responses can be directed equally to past and present events, to real and imagined situations, to things that we can act upon and things forever removed from the possibility of change.

In his *Theory of the Moral Sentiments* Adam Smith gives many carefully described instances of sympathy, which he regards as a core component in social life, and the true foundation of moral sentiment. He points out that sympathetic emotions always involve a judgment of their appropriateness and that, in reaching this judgment, we adopt, or tend to adopt, the standpoint of the impartial spectator. He also points out that, while sympathetic emotions are not always enjoyable, they are not in themselves painful, even when experienced in the face of someone's pain. There is, for Smith, no paradox in the fact that we enjoy theatrical tragedies. For although we witness the image of pain and suffering, our response need be neither painful nor a form of suffering.

It would be painful, of course, if we believed that the dreadful events portrayed on the stage were actually occurring. But we believe no such thing: we have no motive to intervene, or to do anything save relish the sympathetic emotions with which we are filled by the action. This experience is usually not painful at all, since all sympathy, divorced from the emergencies that call on us to act and to suffer, conveys an intimation of our social togetherness. Comfort, and the reassurance of our common nature and mutual help, is intrinsic to the sympathetic response. And that is why we are drawn to tragic literature. It does not follow that we will *not* feel pain, just *because* we are confronting a fiction. Dr Johnson famously felt such pain at the death of Cordelia that he found himself unable to read the scene until he had, as he says, undertaken "to revise it as an editor." But when fictions are painful in this way it is not simply because they portray a distressing and distressful situation: it is because they undermine that residue of optimism upon which all our sympathies are, in the last analysis, founded.

I have drastically curtailed and adapted Smith's argument, for purposes of my own. And it should be obvious what those purposes are. In responding to literature we are responding *sympathetically* to an *imagined* situation, and we do this by "imitating" or, more properly, *rehearsing* the motives that would lead us to sympathize towards the real-life version of the characters and feelings described. In rehearsing these motives we are "learning what to feel," and the true work of art is the one that *teaches* us what to feel, so that we *know* what to feel towards situations of the kind that it portrays. Now sympathy is always concrete: its object is particular people, in the particular situation that is theirs. This "learning through sympathy" is not a matter of learning general maxims or acquiring a theoretical familiarity with the kinds of human fate. Whether or not we can generalize from the situation of Emma Bovary, Isabel Archer, or Huckleberry Finn, our sympathies are engaged by them on account of the concrete situation that is theirs, their character, their emotions, their life. Sympathy "individualizes," and at the same time distances: it is a reflective posture, alert to the rightness and wrongness of the feelings that it prompts.

This brings me to the crucial point. If emotions are motives, then we need to say something about the relation between sympathetic responses and human motivation, if we are to confront the problem of fiction. Of course, sympathetic responses are as various as the situations that cause them. But they have an important feature in common, which is that they involving *wanting something for someone else.* I want Rachel to be comforted. I want the lovers to be reunited. I want the villain to be killed. This "wanting something for someone else" is distinctive of our species, a natural outgrowth of self-consciousness, and of the knowledge that the Other is another like me.[13] This motive is, as Smith rightly observes, the root of moral feeling. And it is also the root of our response to fiction. For it is a motive that is, in an important sense, indifferent to the existence of its object. Whether Rachel is a real woman or a figment, it is equally true that I want her to be comforted. Of course, in the case of the figment there is nothing *I* can do to comfort her, so that this wanting does not provide me with a motive to action. But it is there in my heart for all that, and provides the core of my emotional response. And by following the story I rehearse that response, become familiar with it, come to know "what it is like," through the very process of "imagining what it is like" that is sparked off by the fiction. And fiction has the advantage over reality, in that it enables me to replay my sympathy and to correct it. At the start of *Vanity Fair*, we encounter Becky Sharp, dismissively treated by the snobbish Miss Pinkerton, as she takes her leave of the latter's academy for young ladies. Jemima, Miss Pinkerton's tender-hearted sister, endeavors to make up to Becky by presenting her with the official parting gift (Johnson's "Dixonary") that Miss Pinkerton had withheld. Thackeray so presents the situation that your sympathy is entirely with Becky who, for reasons that you have yet to learn, is an outsider in a society of heartless conventions. And then, as the carriage drives away, taking Becky and her friend Amelia, Becky throws the gift into the garden and shows her own original and far deeper heartlessness. Your sympathies are jolted out of their complacent espousal of the underdog, and for the rest of the novel you will be wary of taking sides. You don't know whether you want this girl to be happy; and after a while you cease very much to care whether she is.

That, of course, is art of the highest order. But it illustrates a point that is exemplified by the simplest fairy tale, which is that what we want for other people depends entirely on how they behave. And this is as true of fiction as it is of life: the very same principles govern our sympathies, whether we are reading of a conflict in a newspaper, witnessing a conflict at first hand, or seeing a conflict in the theatre. We want the good to triumph and the bad to be destroyed. We want grief to be comforted and love to be rewarded. And because nothing in real life is simple, nothing in fiction is simple either: the good and the bad come inextricably mixed, and our sympathies may veer now towards, now away from, the character who occupies the centre of the stage. Moreover, because things don't always turn out for the best, we need to come to terms with the fact that our sympathies will be frustrated; and we must find the route to consolation nonetheless. That, surely, is the point of tragedy – to make sympathy its own consolation, even when what is intensely wanted for the other is not to be. By "learning what to feel" towards fictional tragedies, we rehearse the emotions that we shall need in life, as one by one our hopes are dashed by misfortune, malice, and mortality.

Sympathetic responses are not the only responses aroused in us by art. There are also the "gut reactions" to which I earlier referred – residues of our real-life motivation that we cannot easily eradicate, even when faced with a situation that we know to be fictional. Walton discusses the example of a malevolent slime, that advances towards the spectator from the cinema screen, causing him to curl up in horror. For Walton this is a paradigm of our emotional response to fiction.[14] I would say rather that it is a residue of our instinctual response to something else. Consider a similar case: the training administered to a fighter-pilot, who is asked to stand in front of a machine which shoots out a heavy metallic cylinder at high speed, constructed, however, so as to stop dead a foot in front of him. This situation, which simulates many in which the would-be pilot will have to stay calm and unflinching, precipitates that gut reaction of recoil which no amount of *knowledge* can eradicate, but which may nevertheless be *trained* away. The trainee pilot knows that there is no danger, and he does not actually want to run away. Indeed, he does not fear for himself at all. But his instinctive recoil causes enormous stress, and there are trainees who cannot vanquish their reflex reactions, and thereby show their unfitness for such an aeronautical career.

Now the cinema, because it engages our eyes, engages all the reflexes that are set off by sudden movement or by the sight of violence and destruction. We cannot help ourselves, and these gut reactions are those on which second-rate film directors depend for their "effects." You won't find a Renoir or a Bergman having recourse to these startle effects, and for a very good reason. Startle effects do not belong to the flow of sympathetic emotion. On the contrary they interrupt it, precipitating gut reactions that have nothing to do with the drama. The Greek tragedians were aware of this, and therefore adopted the convention that death should not occur on stage, but should always be announced, so as to be experienced at second hand, through the veil of sympathy. Blood and entrails, screams and death throes, prompt in us quite different reactions from those of straightforward sympathy for the victim – reactions of horror, revulsion, and anxiety that eclipse the calm judicial approach which is the precondition of dramatic understanding. The all-but-unbearable scene of the tearing out of Gloucester's eyes is to some extent mitigated by the two servants who intervene on Gloucester's behalf, and who seem to be animated by our own anxious sympathy. But it is undeniable that Shakespeare went as far as a playwright can reasonably go, in displaying the horrors that the Greeks believed the tragedian should conceal behind a veil of narrative.

It seems to me that, by combining the theory of imagination as directed but unasserted thought with a Smithian account of the sympathetic emotions, we can dissolve the original puzzle about our response to fiction. However, there is one aspect of the theory that needs more detailed exposition: the idea that we can "rehearse" our sympathies through our encounter with fictions, and so come to "know what to feel" in situations that we have not previously encountered. In conclusion I want to illustrate this suggestion through criticism, beginning with the celebrated essay "Reality and Sincerity" which F. R. Leavis published in *Scrutiny* in 1952. Adversely comparing Emily Brontë's "Cold in the Earth" to Thomas Hardy's "After a Journey," Leavis writes:

> Emily Brontë conceives a situation in order to have the satisfaction of a disciplined imaginative exercise; the satisfaction of dramatizing herself in a tragic role – an attitude, nobly impressive, of sternly controlled passionate desolation.

And he contrasts Brontë's "talking *about*" emotion with Hardy's "quiet presentment of specific fact and concrete circumstance." Leavis fails to mention that Emily Brontë's poem was not written in her own voice, but in the imagined voice of Rosina Alcona in the Gondal Saga, which Brontë wrote in conjunction with her sister Anne. Leaving that (highly relevant) point to one side, however, I think it is true, as Leavis argues, that each poem leads us into a world and at the same time "invites a response" to that world. The response is not that of the poet, but that of the reader – though the goal of each author is to place reader and poet in sympathy. Writing of the first line of Hardy's poem ("Hither I come to view a voiceless ghost") Leavis writes that

> "view," we recognize, is no insensitive perversity; it is the word compelled by the intensely realized situation, and we feel it imposing itself on Hardy (and so on us) as right and irreplaceable.

The sincerity of the feeling expressed is one with the concrete nature of the situation represented – the refusal to retreat into heroic abstractions – and this sincerity compels our sympathy, as the words "imposed" on the poet impose themselves also on us.

Two points emerge from Leavis's analysis. The first is that the reader's sympathy is being invited towards the emotional state conveyed by the poem, and that this sympathy may be either offered or withheld. The second is that sympathy will certainly be withheld at the first hint of insincerity, and the sign of insincerity is a vagueness, a lack of concretion, in the situation presented. Words may flow mellifluously, inviting us to endorse the poem's willed sense of tragedy, as Leavis claims to be the case in the example from Brontë. Or they may, as in the example from Hardy, stumble over hard and recalcitrant facts, recognizing the complexity of grief and the imperfection of those remembered feelings. In the latter case the very concretion of the imagery elicits our sympathy. We move *with* the poet, compelled to imagine the situation exactly as it affects him. This concretion prompts that first act of judgment which sets sympathy in motion.

Literary devices have their own way of compelling an argument. Rhyme, rhythm, word sound, and word order coax us forward, towards a goal which they may make it difficult to resist. In such a case – and Leavis implies that this may be true of Brontë's poem – we may find ourselves rehearsing an emotion of sympathy towards a state of mind that deserves less than wholehearted endorsement. By contrast, a poem may, through its literary devices, coax us away from a state of mind that it seems to be expressing, so permitting sympathy despite toying with desolate or dreary states of mind. Consider this poem by Housman:

> I to my perils
>   Of cheat and charmer
>   Came clad in armour
>   By stars benign.
> Hope lies to mortals
>   And most believe her,
>   But man's deceiver
>   Was never mine.
>
> The thoughts of others
>   Were light and fleeting,
>   Of lovers' meeting
>   Or luck or fame.
> Mine were of trouble,
>   And mine were steady,
>   So I was ready
>   When trouble came.

Christopher Ricks writes that "the poem says a dour cramping thing, but how does it say it? With gaiety and wit. . . ."[15] The form of the poem, its dancing rhythms, and its wry reference to the unbearable sufferings of Job (quoted in the last line) all bespeak a conscious withdrawal from the posture of adolescent despair for which Housman is so often reproached, and – Ricks implies – this permits our sympathy, enabling us to "go along with" the feeling of the poem. The feeling is conditioned by the lightness of the poem's music, and in submitting to this music we also distance ourselves from the too-easy pathways of a callow misanthropy.

In the examples we see two critics showing how poems can teach us "what to feel" through the exercise of sympathy. The poem "points the way to" an emotion, and invites us to sympathize with it. But in that very act it opens the way to judgment. Is the situation precisely defined? Does the language, the rhythm, the literary technique seek to draw us on uncritically, or do they, on the contrary, invite us to see things as they are, and to offer our sympathy only on proof that it is rightly offered? These, and similar questions, all arise from an underlying thought, which is that sympathetic responses to fictional situations are also rehearsals of sympathies that could be applied in life. And that thought in turn suggests something important about the connection between life and literature. According to the Aristotelian idea of moral education, virtue is taught by imitation, imitation instills habits, and habits transform themselves into motives. If good literature has a moral value then it is surely because it feeds into that process, by teaching us "what to feel" towards the actions, characters, and fates of our fellow humans. And if bad literature is to be avoided, it is likewise because it misleads us into feeling sympathy where sympathy is mistaken.

Those observations are relevant, it seems to me, not only in describing the reading of fiction, but also in describing the writing of it. For Currie the object of the fictional response is either the "fictional author" (whose emotions the reader "simulates") or the characters whom that author presents. The fictional author is not, or not necessarily, the real author: he is the person imagined as the one who is telling the story – like the subject who is supposed to be speaking Hardy's lines. (We know that this subject is in fact Hardy and that he is writing of his dead wife and troubled marriage; but had we known no such thing the impact of the poem would have been the same.) It seems to me that this apparatus – which seems to be multiplying fictional entities beyond necessity – misrepresents the true nature of our sympathetic feelings. The response of the reader of a work of fiction is *of the same kind* as that of the writer. In the story "A Dove Descending," I invented a character, Zoë Costas, in whom I took a profound interest, and towards whom I felt real sympathy.[16] I did not share her emotions of indignation, shame, attraction, affection, or bewildered desire as I described or invoked them – but always I responded to them with concern, knowing her for a good person in a bad situation, and wanting what was best for her even while describing her downfall. That is how I hoped the reader would respond too: not to me feeling sympathy, still less to some "fictional author" created by my words, but to *Zoë*, the subject of the story. She does not exist, of course; but for both reader and author it is *as if* she exists – and this "as if," which describes the workings of the imagination, permeates every aspect of the story, including the name of the girl herself. Frege said of Zoë's archetype, Nausicaa, that it is "as if the name 'Nausicaa' referred to a girl." And what reader of Homer has not felt sympathy for that girl, and learned (I hope) to love the aspect of womanly virtue that she exemplifies?[17]

Notes

1. Kendall L. Walton, *Mimesis as Make-Believe* (Cambridge, MA: Harvard University Press, 1990), chapter 7.
2. Ibid., 251.
3. Ibid., 252.
4. Of the kind spelled out by Wittgenstein, in his celebrated "private language" argument, *Philosophical Investigations* (Oxford: Blackwell, 1958), §§243–330.
5. Any attempt at a formal theory of fictions will therefore need to look beyond semantics in general, and model theory in particular, if it is to give an account of what we understand when we understand a story. This is one reason for thinking, with Gregory Currie, that pragmatics has a large role to play in the interpretation of literary texts. See "Interpretation and Pragmatics," in Gregory Currie, *Arts and Minds* (Oxford: Clarendon Press, 2004), 107–33. Elsewhere in his writings Currie argues that, because "fictional worlds" are often vague, inconsistent, and gappy, they cannot be what we have in mind in interpreting fictions, and he compares them unfavorably with the possible worlds of the model theorist. Instead he offers, as the semantic background to a fiction, the world of the "fictional author's" literary community – the fictional author being himself a character in the fiction (*The Nature of Fiction*. Cambridge: Cambridge University Press, 1990, 54 ff). Though why that world should be consistent, determinate, and devoid of ontological gaps he does not say.
6. Currie, *The Nature of Fiction*, and also "Pretence and Pretending," in Currie, *Arts and Minds*.
7. Gregory Currie, "The Moral Psychology of Fiction," *Australasian Journal of Philosophy* 73 (1995): 250–59; Kendall L. Walton, "Spelunking, Simulation and Slime: On Being Moved by Fiction," in Mette Hjort and Sue Laver, eds., *Emotion and the Arts* (New York: Oxford University Press, 1997), 37–49.
8. See Aaron Meskin and Jonathan M. Weinberg, "Emotions, Fictions and Cognitive Architecture," *British Journal of Aesthetics* 43 (2003): 18–34.
9. See my *Art and Imagination* (London: Methuen, 1974; South Bend, IN: St Augustine's Press, 1998), chapters 7 and 8.
10. Jenefer Robinson, *Deeper than Reason: Emotion and its Role in Literature, Music, and Art* (Oxford: Clarendon Press, 2005). See also Robinson, "Emotion and the Understanding of Narrative," chapter 5 in this volume.
11. On this point see my "Emotion and Culture," in *The Aesthetic Understanding* (London: Methuen, 1983; South Bend, IN: St Augustine's Press, 1998), 163–79.
12. See the remarks about anger in *Nicomachean Ethics*.
13. Currie writes in this connection of our capacity for "de-centring" (*Arts and Minds*, 219–20); others (Frankfurt, Dennett, etc.) of "second-order" states of mind or "higher order intentionality," others still (Alan Leslie) of "metarepresentation," while some would wish to return to the original insights of Kant and Hegel, in recognizing "the transcendental unity of apperception" as the defining feature of the human condition. All are ways of joining the emerging consensus, that the transition from conscious animal to self-conscious person involves the crossing of a momentous ontological barrier.
14. Walton, *Mimesis as Make-Believe*, 196–204.
15. Christopher Ricks, *The Force of Poetry*, 165.
16. See *A Dove Descending and Other Stories* (London: Sinclair Stevenson, 1991).
17. Frege: "Der Name Nausikaa tut als ob er ein Mädchen bedeutet," in Further Notes on Sense and Reference.

7

The Experience of Reading

PETER KIVY

Introduction

The major fine arts, the *traditional* ones, in the Western canon, are the visual arts of painting and sculpture, music, dance, the literary arts of poetry, drama, and the novel, and the photographic arts of still photography and the moving picture. *All* of these but one, the *novel*, appeal directly to the external senses of vision and hearing for a very substantial part of their artistic and aesthetic effect. (Poetry is a problematic case which I will get to later on.) This is not to say that the experience of these arts is wholly visual or aural. For they are, clearly, of the mind as well as of the senses, not merely in the trivial sense of mental processes being essential to the kind of sense perception involved in their appreciation, but in the more important sense that when we have experience of these arts we are meant to *think* about them, and indeed cannot perceive them properly without thinking about them: we are meant to think about their representational, narrative, and perhaps their philosophical or other propositional content. Nevertheless, the aesthetic and artistic payoff of these fine arts lies, in very large part, in a direct visual or aural acquaintance: acquaintance with a singular physical object, or a complex physical event, be it a performance, in the case of music, dance, and the drama, or a "showing," in the case of cinema.

The novel, however, is in stark contrast to these other fine arts. Neither its entire aesthetic and artistic payoff, nor any part thereof, lies in direct aural or visual acquaintance with an object or event present to the external senses. It lies, rather, in the reader's direct acquaintance with his or her conscious states. Or, in other words, "it's all in the mind."

Of course the process of reading does require to begin with direct perceptual acquaintance with the novel's text, either by sight, or by touch (if it is in Braille), or aurally, if it is read aloud (and more of that anon). But no one thinks that either the aesthetic or artistic experience of the novel lies in sight or touch or sound. These are the instrumentalities, merely, that bring the novelistic artwork to the mind in which direct acquaintance with it takes place.

A Companion to the Philosophy of Literature, First Edition. Edited by Garry L. Hagberg and Walter Jost.
© 2010 John Wiley & Sons Ltd. Published 2015 by John Wiley & Sons, Ltd.

A second respect in which the novel at least *seems* to differ from the other traditional fine arts is, loosely speaking, in its "ontology." In *Languages of Art*, the late Nelson Goodman introduced to the philosophical community the terms "autographic" and "allographic," to refer, respectively, to those arts, such as easel painting or sculpture, in which there is but one singular object of direct acquaintance, *the* statue, or *the* picture, and those arts, such as drama or music, where there are numerous objects of direct acquaintance, namely, the performances of the dramatic or musical artworks.[1] Most philosophers of art have adopted Goodman's terminology, including the present writer, although most, including the present writer, have not adopted Goodman's well-known nominalism, and have construed allographic arts as arts in which works are types or universals, of *some* kind or other, with numerous tokens or instances.

Given this rough ontology, it can be seen that all of the major, traditional fine arts fit, more or less satisfactorily, into one or the other of Goodman's two categories, again, with the notable exception of the novel, and, again, with poetry as a special case, put aside for the time being. On the one hand, novels, unlike dramas and musical works, do not have performances. On the other, they are clearly not autographic arts, as they do, all would agree, have multiple instances, at least in the form of your copy of *Pride and Prejudice*, my copy of *Pride and Prejudice*, and all the other copies of *Pride and Prejudice* abroad in the land.

But in respect of copies, novels are certainly not unique. There is your script of *Hamlet*, my script of *Hamlet*, and all the other scripts of *Hamlet* abroad in the land. As well, there is your score of Beethoven's Ninth Symphony, my score of Beethoven's Ninth Symphony, and all the other scores of Beethoven's Ninth Symphony abroad in the land. Of course *Hamlet* and the Ninth Symphony *also* have performances realized from their scripts and scores; and there, apparently, the analogy breaks down. For the novel is not, at least in any obvious way, a performing art. Might it, perhaps, be a performing art in a *non-obvious* way? That is the question to be pursued in the present essay.[2] And it must be answered in light of the distinction made at the outset, between our experience of the other fine arts through the external senses of sight and hearing, and our experience of the novel, which is a "mental experience" solely, with the external senses (usually, of course, the sense of sight) in the process of reading as mere instruments for its facilitation.

Reading to Yourself

When I contrasted the novel with the other major, traditional fine arts, in the previous section, and maintained its singularity in two respects, I put aside the literary genre of poetry as a problematic case to be considered later on. It now must be worked into the equation.

It would seem, on first reflection, that everything said above, about the novel, in contrast with the other fine arts, can also be said of poems. After all, poems as well as novels are read, not seen or heard in the manner of the other fine arts. Thus poems, like novels, are things of the mind, in that they are experienced as artistic and aesthetic objects, in the mind, not in the flesh. I may decide, of an evening, to go to a performance of *Hamlet*, or of Beethoven's Ninth. But I might also decide to curl up with a good book. And the book could be the *Iliad* as well as *Pride and Prejudice*. So it would seem that in the contrast with the other fine arts, poetry and the novel are on all fours with one another. But this is too facile and ill-considered a conclusion, as a little historical reflection will make clear.

As we know from Plato's *Republic* and *Ion*, as well as from numerous other ancient texts, the Homeric epics were performed works, given to audiences in public recitations, and were no more intended primarily to be read to oneself in private, apparently, than was *Hamlet* or *Death of a Salesman*. This is not to say, of course, that one could not read the *Iliad* to oneself if one wanted to; but that was not its intended payoff. Poetry, in the ancient world, was a performing art. As well, a performing art, more or less, it must have remained, until well into the middle ages, and perhaps even later than that.

Furthermore, until the late middle ages, *silent* reading was, even if possible, surely rare. There is, indeed, some opposing opinion here. But the preponderance of evidence suggests that silent reading, although not unknown, could not have been the ordinary way of reading to oneself until that time for the simple reason that until the late middle ages *there was no space between words* in written manuscripts; rather, they were written in what is known to paleographers as *scriptura continua*. As Paul Saenger puts the point, in his copiously documented book, *Space Between Words: The Origins of Silent Reading*:

> In the West, the ability to read silently and rapidly is a result of the historical evolution of word separation that, beginning in the seventh century, changed the format of the written page, which had to be read orally and slowly in order to be comprehended.[3]

He continues: "We know that the reading habits of the ancient world . . . were profoundly oral and rhetorical by physiological necessity as well as by taste."[4]

The upshot was that even when one read to oneself, one read aloud, or, perhaps, was read to, since

> that the greater portion of the population should be autonomous and self-motivated readers was entirely foreign to the elitist literate world. For the literate, the reaction to the difficulties of lexical access arising from *scriptura continua* did not spark the desire to make script easier to decipher, but resulted instead in the delegation of much of the labor of reading and writing to skilled slaves who acted as professional readers and scribes.[5]

But if the experience of poems, until the late middle ages, was, like the experience of all other written texts, an aural experience, in which someone spoke aloud to you, or you spoke aloud to yourself, then poetry was, for most of its long history in the West, a performing art. Before the advent of written texts, poems like the *Iliad* and *Odyssey* existed, of course, in a completely oral tradition. Afterwards they were, as we know, recited by professional rhapsodes in public performances. And even when read in private, by servant to master, or read aloud to oneself, they were experienced aurally, as, perhaps, the limiting case of a performance, but a performance nevertheless.

I believe that most people, if asked to classify the fine arts along the lines I suggested at the outset, would place drama (obviously) in the class of performing arts, poetry of all kinds, and the novel in (unquestionably) the class of silently read fiction, palpably a non-performing art. Thus the picture is that of two historical streams, running parallel, since the beginning of written-down literature in the West, the stream of performed literature, starting with Greek tragedy, and the stream of silently read, non-performed fiction, starting with the Greek epics, and continuing into the modern era, in the novel, short story, and various poetic genres.

This picture is *clearly* inaccurate in one respect, and, I am suggesting, seriously inaccurate in another respect as well. It is inaccurate, to begin with, of course, because the Greek epics, as well as other non-dramatic poetry, were certainly performing arts in the ancient world, in that they were normally experienced in public recitations by professional rhapsodes. And there is good reason to believe, given the paucity of "books" before the invention and perfecting of printing and the proliferation of printed matter, that the public recitation of poetry remained for a long time – how long I do not know – the normal way of experiencing it.

Second, if Saenger is right, and I think he is, that reading aloud, even to yourself, was the norm at least until the advent of the space between words in the late middle ages and probably well after that, then even reading in private was an oral and aural affair, in the limiting case a performance, which is to say an oral and aural performance, to oneself.

What I want to propose, then, is a different way of looking at the literary arts, based on the above historical considerations. It is that there were not two parallel literary tracks from antiquity to the present, one the track of the performing dramatic arts, the other the track of the privately consumed, silently read, non-performing arts of poetry and (later) prose fiction. Rather, I propose we view our literary tradition as a single track of *performed* literary fiction that bifurcated at a point in time after word separation and the consequent development of silent reading into the two tracks of performed and silently read literary fiction we know today.

I propose, further, that because of this changed historical perspective we might seriously consider the following possibility. Given that silently read literary fiction – and I am thinking here, as I will be throughout this essay, principally of the novel – evolved, so to speak, out of a performance tradition, the possibility is that it retains vestiges of the performance tradition from which it evolved. In short, I propose to develop the view that the novel, the paradigm instance of silently read literary fiction, is, *au fond*, a performing art, its silent readings being its performances. The argument is not that its origins imply its present nature, which would, clearly, be an instance of the genetic fallacy. But what I *am* urging is that the historical origins of silently read fiction in a performing tradition suggest, though they do not imply, the plausibility of regarding silent readings of novels as self-directed performances.

I am not, I must add, the first to entertain the thesis that silent reading of literary fiction might be understood as a kind of performance. However, all of those who have entertained it before me – at least all of those I am acquainted with – have rejected it pretty much out of hand, without a hearing, or, in the rare instance, have accepted it, though with little attempt to elaborate on the possibility.[6] With that in mind, I turn now to how, in my view, that possibility might be cashed out.

Self-Performance and Silent Performance

Ion, the rhapsode in Plato's dialogue of the same name, recited the poetry of Homer and talked about Homer, which is to say eulogized him, and explicated his meaning to an audience: "on Homer I am the finest speaker of mankind, and full of things to say," he immodestly informs Socrates.[7] Thus Ion the rhapsode, and his *confrérie*, had, apparently, two functions to execute: they recited narrative poems and other forms of poetry to an audience, in the form of a dramatic performance, if Plato's description in book 3 of the *Republic* is to be credited, and, perhaps, in the same performance, offered critical exegesis of the works recited.[8]

In what follows I will try to work both of these functions into an integrated account of silent novel reading as performance. For now I am primarily interested in the former, on which I shall direct my attention for some considerable time.

It seems clear from various accounts that the normal and the common way in which the ancient world experienced narrative poetry in general, the Homeric epics in particular, was through fairly elaborate dramatic recitations by professional rhapsodes, of which Plato's Ion is, I am assuming, a *more or less* accurate depiction. Furthermore, if Saenger is right, when someone of the times experienced these poems in private, either they would be read *to* him by a second party, or he would read them aloud *to himself*.

And the first point to be made is that even in the case in which the reader read aloud *to himself*, it was a *performance* to himself, if a limiting case. For even when you read *to yourself* aloud, you read "with expression." (You have to *try* to read without it.)

But there is no need to be skeptical, anyway, of the concept of performing for oneself. We have a perfectly clear example of it in the case of the musician playing to herself. If, for instance, an amateur pianist, for her own pleasure, plays a sonata, while alone, to herself, listening the while to the sounds of her own playing with the kind of attention she would give to another's playing at a piano recital, it seems plain enough that the most felicitous way of describing her action is that of a performance by herself for herself. She is her own audience. Whatever of paradox there may be in self-deception, or duty to oneself, does not, I suggest, attach to performing to oneself. In rehearsal a musician does it as a matter of course.

Let us, then, take this line of thought one step further. Imagine now the advent of silent reading and the rise of the modern novel as the literary art form ideally suited – designed one might say – for the silent reading experience. My suggestion is that we view the step from reading aloud to yourself to reading silently to yourself – with perhaps silently moving your lips while you read, the way children do, as a halfway house – as a step from performance aloud to yourself, not to another thing altogether, but, rather, to another form of performance: a performance silently to yourself. Ion recited the *Iliad* to an audience, in a public performance. An Athenian citizen, alone, was read to by his servant, in a private performance, as it were; or he read aloud to himself in a private performance by himself to himself. Finally, to end this story, we have the silent reader of *Pride and Prejudice*, whose "inner Ion" recites the story silently, to her "inner ear."

Furthermore, just as we have a musical analogue to the ancient reader aloud, which is to say, the performer aloud to himself, in the pianist who plays for herself, to help make my claim more plausible, we have another musical analogue to the silent reader's silent performance to herself, to help make my claim more plausible, in the person of the silent reader of a modern musical score. *The Harvard Dictionary of Music* defines "Score reading" as follows: "The internal realization of the sound of a work by means of simply reading the score...."[9] In other words, the score reader, if he has the considerable training and musical "circuits" prerequisite for the task, "hears" a performance of the work scored "in his head." (Brahms is reported to have said about an opera performance he was invited to attend that he could "hear" a better performance reading his score at home.)

So if silently reading a score can provide a "heard in your head" performance of a musical work, might not silently reading a novel provide a "heard in your head" performance of a storytelling? If so, what kind of "performance" would that be? And are there serious objections to such a proposal?

Hearing Voices

The experience of thought as a kind of inner colloquy seems to be a common human experience. As Plato famously described it in the *Sophist*: "Are not thought and speech the same, with this exception, that what is called thought is the unuttered conversation of the soul with herself?"[10] Or, as Daniel Dennett put it: "Not only do we talk to ourselves silently, but sometimes we do this in a particular tone of voice."[11] Many other witnesses to the phenomenon could be called into the box.

What is particularly pertinent to present concerns is Dennett's observation that we not only speak silently to ourselves but do so "in a particular tone of voice," which is to say, I take it, "with expression," a notion I will return to later on. But all I want to get across right now is the simple idea that, in a perfectly benign sense, absent of mystery or any kind of outré metaphysics, and, I think, consistent with any philosophy of mind liberal enough to countenance human consciousness as something to be explained, not denied, it has been the human experience, at least the experience of great numbers of human beings, from Plato to Dennett, that conscious thought, at least *some* conscious thought, consists in "hearing" voices "in the head."

Thus it seems to me consistent with what we know about thought and consciousness that reading a story *might* be experienced as "hearing" a story told in your head, in the way that reading a score, we know, is experienced, by those few who can, as "hearing" music played in your head. For at least there is nothing, so I have been arguing, implausible about the underlying premise, that one hears a voice in one's head, with what we know about consciousness: first-person reports seem to confirm the experience.

My claim, however, is a stronger one than the bare bones suggestion that we hear in our heads, while reading novels silently, a recitation of the story. It is that we hear the recitation as a "performance"; for the argument is that the *seemingly* anomalous art of the novel displays, on the contrary, the same basic ontology and "phenomenology" (if I may so put it) as the performing arts of music and the drama, arts with "texts" (broadly speaking) from which performances are realized.[12] And there would seem, anyway, and not surprisingly, to be very serious objections to the view that my *silently* reading, *to myself*, *Pride and Prejudice*, constitutes a *performance*, if the word is being used in anything like the way it is in its canonical settings: the performance of *Hamlet* in the West End last night; the performance of the *Hammerklavier* Sonata last summer at Tanglewood; or even my performance, *to myself*, of Benjamin Britten's *Six Metamorphoses after Ovid*. I cannot deal with all of the possible objections in this place. But what I propose to do, in what follows, is to deal at least with what I take to be *some* of the principal ones. And to that task I now turn my attention.

Reading as Interpretation

It is common parlance to call performers "interpreters": Olivier's interpretation of Hamlet, Serkin's interpretation of the *Hammerklavier*. Some philosophers are inclined to say that these are not literal uses of the term. But others, myself included, take them literally. Performers are, when they are at a high level of achievement, anyway, interpreters of what they perform, and their performances *are* interpretations.

The first thing to notice is that unlike, for example, critics' interpretations of novels or plays, performers' interpretations are not stated (in writing or speech) but *shown*: a musical performance is the *showing*, the displaying forth of the performer's interpretation.

Second, performances are what might be called interpretation-driven. That is to say, a performer of any distinction at all has an interpretation of the work performed, or character portrayed, that informs the performance; that must be in place before the performance to serve, as it were, as its plan. In the case of a dramatic work, the interpretation would of course have largely to do with semantic and representational properties. To perform the character of Hamlet I must, obviously, have an idea of what Hamlet's speeches mean, and what the nature of his person is. And even when a work has *no* semantic or representational properties, as is the case with pure instrumental music, there is still an interpretation, properly so called, in the sense of an idea of how the music goes: what makes it tick as a structure in sound.

But if an interpretation in hand, prior to performance, is a prerequisite for a performance, and if, as well, a performance *is* an interpretation, then, it might be objected, a silent reading of a novel cannot be a performance because, in the usual case, the novel is read for the first time, so the reader cannot have a prior interpretation of it before the reading, to inform it. And that being the case, the reading cannot be the showing of an interpretation, since there is no interpretation in place to show.

Let me begin to answer this objection by stating the obvious. We interpret a novel, of course, as we go along. We interpret as we read – in the process of reading. How could we understand the deeper, non-obvious aspects of what we read without interpreting it?

Furthermore, it is something of an exaggeration to say that we have *no* prior interpretation *at all* of a novel we read for the first time. And to explain this claim it might be well to again seek a parallel in music.

A much-prized skill among players of musical instruments is playing at sight, or "sight-reading," as it is usually referred to. This is the ability to play on your instrument, from musical notation, a piece you have never played or even heard before, and not only that, but play it with some degree of musicality and "expression." How can one *do* that?

Obviously, one does not sight-read *de novo*, with one's mind a blank slate. If I am (say) playing viola in a string quartet, and we are reading at sight a quartet by Haydn that I have never played or heard before, I nevertheless have played and heard other string quartets by Haydn and his contemporaries. I have internalized that style, and can anticipate what is coming on the basis of that experiential base. In other words, I have a proto-interpretation of the work, if I am an experienced player, even before I have played or heard it. I have a proto-idea of "what makes it tick."

Similarly, when I pick up a novel for a first read (which is customarily my only read) I normally have a good deal of experience and background knowledge behind me of the novel I am about to devour. If it is a particular genre of novel, I have experience and knowledge of that genre; if it is a novel by an author whose work I have read before, I have experience and knowledge of other of her novels, and so on. I have, as in the sight-reading case, a proto-interpretation before I begin, which develops as I read, until, in the end, I know what the novel is about – which is to say, I have a full, albeit not perfect interpretation.

Thus, what I want to conclude is that the first reading of a novel, which for most of us, most of the time, is the only reading, fulfills both criteria of a genuine performance. It is interpretation-driven, in that it is driven by a proto-interpretation, as explained above, and is an interpretation in progress, which reaches completion at the end of the reading. Furthermore, like a performance of a musical work, the interpretation, in the event, is *shown*, not stated, *in* the reading.

So far, then, the claim that novel readings are, at least, performance-like, if not absolutely full-blown performances, has held up to criticism. But there are more problems to come. So on to the next.

Reading as Art

As we saw above, performers are referred to, and rightly so, as *interpreters* of what they perform. But performers are also referred to as *artists*: "performing artist" is a common description of the performer, at least a distinguished one. And if performers *are* performing *artists*, then it obviously follows that they must, in that office, produce *artworks*, which artworks, it would seem, could be only one thing: their *performances*. Performances, then, are *artworks*.

Now in calling performances *artworks*, I may raise some eyebrows. But if silent readings of novels are performances, then it seems inevitably to follow that if I call performances artworks, I must call silent novel readings artworks. And that *surely* will raise eyebrows. Surely that in itself is a *reductio ad absurdum* of the claim that silent novel readings are performances. So to defend my view I must first give some plausible idea of how ordinary performances can be artworks, and then go on to explain in a convincing way how *silent readings* can be artworks.

What is the relation of a musical performance to a musical work, when the work is a work of absolute music in the Western canon? Well one relation, and the only one I am interested in here, is that of a *version* of the work to the work. Let me explain.

Two of the "arts" closely related to the composer's art, and, as well, closely related to one another, are the arts of orchestrating and arranging. In the modern Western musical tradition, a composer usually composes an orchestral work in what is known as a "short score," a score with relatively few staves, and when the composition is complete, in this skeletal form, he "orchestrates" it, which is to say, he, as it were, makes it into an orchestral version of the short score. Nor is the task of orchestrating merely a cut and dried, mechanical affair. It is a much admired art in its own right, that can be done badly or outstandingly well, with composers like Berlioz, for example, singled out for special praise in this, or Schumann for rebuke (whether deserved or not an open question).

Furthermore, the art of orchestrating segues into the art of "arranging," when a pre-existent work is "arranged" or "transcribed" for an instrument or instruments other than the one or ones for which it was originally composed, Ravel's orchestral version of Mussorgsky's *Pictures at an Exhibition* being perhaps the most notable example, and the best known to music lovers. And all woodwind players, whose chamber music literature is limited, are acutely aware, of necessity, of the "art" of arranging, as they must use arrangements of music, originally written for strings, to augment their limited repertoire. Such musicians well know the difference between a pedestrian, mechanical transcription, and a genuine *version* of a work that is so "artfully" done that it is a true work of the arrangers "art." And I put "artfully" and "art" in scare quotes not to indicate non-literal uses but to call attention to their literal meanings. *Some* arrangements are works of the arranger's art.

Arrangers, then, at their best, are akin to composers (and are sometimes one and the same). Their products are works of the arranger's art, and are frequently referred to as "versions" of the works they are arrangements of, as Ravel's orchestral "version" of Moussorgsky's *Pictures at an Exhibition*, or his orchestral "version" of his own *Le Tombeau de Couperin*.

But performances are also referred to as "versions" of the works they are performances of: rightly so, I think. And it seems to me to make a good deal of sense to say, also, that, like arrangers' "versions" of musical works, performances of musical works are artworks in their own right, at least the best of them, as well. Performers are akin, then, to composers, as are artful arrangers in that, like composers, arrangers and performers produce musical artworks, albeit ones that are parasitic on those produced by composers. Performances, then, are artworks: versions of the musical works of which they are the performances.

The final step in this argument is to the conclusion that silent readings, like performances of musical works, are performances, are versions, and are artworks (or at least the limiting case thereof).

I believe the most easily accepted conclusion, for the initially skeptical, is that individual silent readings are versions of works. For when *anyone*, regardless of his or her literary sophistication, reads a novel with understanding, the reader must make out, at whatever level, what the novel is about. The reader must, in the process of reading, interpret and understand the work to the best of his or her abilities. And it seems fair to say that that interpretation cum understanding is his or her "version" of the work in a perfectly *echt* sense of the word. It is what he or she has made of the work: his or her version of it, which might well differ from other folks' versions, and might well, of course, be mistaken in some respect or other. But does it make sense to take the next step, and to say that the version, so described, is a "performance" of the work?

Let us begin with an easy case. It is clear that one can "perform" a novel in the perfectly literal sense of the word. When a great actress, for example, reads a novel aloud to be recorded for the blind, she will read the novel with all the nuance and expression she would bring to a part in a play. Surely it is completely uncontroversial to say that her reading of the novel aloud displays her version of the novel, is a performance of the novel, and is, by virtue of her status as a performing artist, a performance artwork. It, point for point, corresponds exactly to a great pianist's performance of a sonata.

Consider now the actress's reading of the novel to herself, silently, in preparation for the recording session. She will, in her mind's ear, as it were, "hear" her silent reading; and it will be a silent reading done with the same nuance and expression as she intends to bring to her out-loud performance to come. It is, in fact, precisely analogous to the gifted musician's silent reading of a score, in which he "hears" in *his* "mind's ear," a performance of the musical work that the score inscribes.

But what about the rest of us silent readers? Most of us are not, of course, gifted actors or actresses. When we read novels silently to ourselves, does it make any sense at all to call us performers of the works we read, our performances, if that is what they are, performance artworks, and we artists? It is hard to credit; and yet I am asking you to believe that the answer to all of these questions is: Yes.

Well why not begin with the "ordinary" reader, as we did with the actress, reading aloud to someone else. I might, for example, be reading *Winnie the Pooh* to a child, or perhaps reading aloud to my wife a passage from a novel I am engrossed in that I find particularly striking, and want to share with her. Obviously I do not have to be Laurence Olivier to read aloud with nuance and expression. I do not have *his* nuance and expression – who does? – but I am not a zombie, after all. I do the best I can with the gifts that I have, and try to make my "performance" as aesthetically interesting and convincing as possible. And surely *performance* is exactly the right word for what I am doing. It comes naturally to my lips in describing my act. There is an exact analogue here to the amateur musician playing a piece for himself or for others. It is not a virtuoso's performance, but surely it is a *performance*, in the literal sense of that word.

But if the "amateur" reader's out-loud recitation is a performance, properly so called, why not his silent reading as well? Here the analogy to the silent reading of a musical score partially breaks down; but not in a crucial respect for the thesis being floated here. It breaks down in that the amateur reader is, of course, fully capable of realizing his or her performance as a storytelling "in the head," whereas there are very few musicians, and essentially *no* amateur musicians, with the skill or mental equipment to fully realize a musical performance "in the head," although there *are* varying degrees of success in this regard, from hearing a melody "in the head," which most of us can do, lay persons and amateur musicians alike, to hearing (say) a symphony "in the head," an accomplishment of only the very gifted few.

Thus, there *is* a disanalogy here between the silent reading of novels and the silent reading of musical scores. The former is possible for *any* literate person, which means, potentially, *every* normal person, whereas the latter is possible for only the musically gifted few. But it is an irrelevant disanalogy for present purposes. The point is that what happens in the head of the novel reader is the same thing that happens in the head of the score reader: *a silent performance of the notated work.*

Furthermore, just as the out-loud performance-reading of a novel can be nuanced and expressive, even if the reader is just you or I, and not a professional actor or actress, so too can the silent performance. As Dennett says: "Not only do we talk to ourselves silently, sometimes we do this in a particular tone of voice." And, indeed, what I am claiming is that the mature and practiced reader of novels not only talks, which is to say, recites the novel he is reading to himself in *a* tone of voice, but he does so in many tones of voice, as the story requires. If you don't believe me, try catching yourself in the act. I have done that frequently; and I am convinced it is true of me, as well as others (if I am not a completely abnormal case).

Well now for the hard sell. If the skeptical have been willing to go along with me this far, and granted that silent readings of novels, by just ordinary folks, are performances, will they be willing to go the extra mile and say, with me, that they are therefore versions in the form of performance *artworks?* Those who do not share my view that performers literally are artists and their performances literally artworks will have no problem. Since they don't believe that being a performance implies being an artwork, they can accept the conclusion that silent readings are performances without having to accept the further, and, *prima facie*, more implausible conclusion that silent readings are artworks. They can get off here.

Middle ground might be found in the compromise position that only *some* performances are artworks – those by professional performers at a certain level of attainment. Thus, the argument would go, just as an ordinary person's reading aloud of a novel would be a performance, but not attain the level of an artwork, whereas a great actress's reading aloud would be both a performance and an artwork, in virtue of her performance artistry, so, *pari passu*, with their respective silent readings.

I think there is a good deal to be said for the moderate view; and I am inclined to accept it with the added proviso that the class of silent readers' performances that are artworks be drawn with wide rather than narrow boundaries. For I think there is at least a little bit of the artist in a lot of us, and that it is in performance that it most readily and most often emerges. But I must, of necessity, leave the argument here, and move on to other matters, and a suitable conclusion.[13]

Reading and Thinking

Finally, I want to return to the beginning again, to the *Ion*, in fact, to add another important dimension to the reading experience I am representing here as a silent performance of a storytelling to the "minds ear."

Recall that Ion's performance of Homer to his ancient audiences seems to have consisted, according to Plato, of two interlarded activities: reciting Homer's poetry in dramatic fashion, *and*, strange as it may seem to us, making explanatory comments on the *content* of the poems: interpreting to his hearers, as we might say, what theses about "life" (or whatever) he thought Homer meant to convey. As Plato has Socrates put it: "So you rhapsodes in turn interpret the words of the poets?" To which Ion replies: "You're right in that too."[14]

Now there is some question as to whether Plato is saying that Ion's comments on Homer occur during his performances of the poet's works, or at some other time. (In classes, or lectures, for example.) For reasons that it would take too long to explore in detail here, I am convinced that, at least some of the time, it is actually *in his performances* that Ion's critical comments on Homer are made (even though they may be made elsewhere as well).[15] But if, as I am maintaining, the experience of silent novel reading is the experience of a kind of inner "Ion," reciting to the mind's ear, then if we take this inner Ion to be as represented by Plato, it appears we will have to accept that we "hear in the head" not only a storytelling, but a storytelling cum critical commentary on the story being told. And this sounds very weird indeed, as would an out-loud recitation of a novel or poem with interlarded critical commentary (although in some public poetry and novel readings in bookstores, authors do comment as well as recite).

Obviously, the easy way out of this difficulty is just to excise the critical part of Ion's performance from our picture of what the inner Ion does in silent reading. Why not simply say that the inner Ion is a storyteller only, leave it at that, and not try to weave into the account a strange custom of an ancient civilization?

Well, I am made of sterner (or is it more foolhardy?) stuff. I believe there *is* an analogue to the "other Ion" – the critical, interpretive Ion – in the silent reading experience.[16]

Many people would agree to the notion that *one* of the functions of *some* great novels is the expression of important propositions of a philosophical, social, psychological, political, or moral interest and significance. I myself subscribe to this notion.

Many people would, as well, agree that a novel is more valuable for its expression of *true* propositions of the above described kind. I also agree, but to a *modified* version of this thesis. It is not the truth of its propositional content that matters in a novel, but that the propositional content is, at least, a *possible* candidate for truth: a "live" hypothesis, as opposed to a "dead" one, to lift some terminology from William James.[17]

It is *part* of the purpose of *some* novels, then, to convey live hypotheses, on matters of deep concern, to their readers, so that they may think about them, and, perhaps, decide for themselves for or against, *as part of the literary experience*. This thinking takes place, when it remains part of the literary experience of a novel, in what I have called elsewhere the "gaps" and the "afterlife," in other words, the times, during the reading of a serious novel, when one puts the novel down (as serious novels cannot be nor were they meant to be read at one sitting) and the time after the reading of a novel, when it still actively stimulates thought about its propositional content.[18] It is this thinking, in the gaps and the afterlife of the silent reading experience, that is the counterpart to the "other" Ion: the Ion who comments on the Homeric epics while he represents them to his audience.

So, I contend, the silent reader of serious novels has an Ion within, who tells the reader the story, as Ion of old, and, again, like Plato's Ion, comments on the serious propositional content of the story, if such content it has. In the latter capacity he (or she) is Plato's "unuttered conversation of the soul with herself."

Why Should You Believe Me?

There are a great many other problems for the view I am presenting here, of silent reading as performance, than I have had time to deal with. And the defense I have given is bound to seem to many too weak to credit. In the end, then, why should you believe me? The answer, I suppose, that is likely to have the most immediate appeal to the philosophically inclined, is the appeal to ontological parsimony. The silently read novel appears to be, like the notated performing arts, an art with a text, *but*, unlike the arts (say) of drama and music, in the Western tradition, an art without a clear type–token ontology. The tokens of the type *Hamlet* are the performances in conformity with the script. The tokens of the type Beethoven's Ninth Symphony are the performances in conformity with the score. What are the tokens of the type *Pride and Prejudice?* The ontologically attractive answer is: its "readings." And if readings are understood as performances in conformity with the text, there is no need of postulating an ontology for novels other than that of *Hamlet* and the Ninth Symphony. The law of parsimony has been satisfied.

But considerations of ontological economy are *not* what I want to appeal to, simply because they are *not* what drove *me* to the conclusion that silent novel reading is a form of performance. I reached that conclusion, rather, by catching myself in the act – by spying on myself reading, and coming, that way, to the conclusion that "This is the way it is with me." Is it the way it is with *you? That* is the question. Ontology must await the answer.

Notes

1. Nelson Goodman, *Languages of Art: An Approach to a Theory of Symbols* (Indianapolis and New York: Bobbs-Merrill, 1968), 112–23, *et passim*.
2. This question is pursued in greater depth and detail in Peter Kivy, *The Performance of Reading: An Essay in the Philosophy of Literature* (Oxford: Blackwell, 2006).
3. Paul Saenger, *Space Between Words: The Origins of Silent Reading* (Stanford, CA: Stanford University Press, 1997), 6. For a dissenting view, see A. K. Gavrilov, "Techniques of Reading in Classical Antiquity," *The Classical Quarterly*, New Series 47 (1997): 56–73.

Gavrilov's article was, as can be seen, published the same year as Saenger's book; so neither author could have had the other's work in hand. As for the layman in such matters, it is hard not to be convinced by a scholarly book of imposing dimensions as opposed to an equally scholarly article, but of less than 20 pages, written without the benefit of Saenger's imposing scholarship.

4   Saenger, *Space Between Words*, 11.
5   Ibid.
6   For some previous discussions, see: Edward T. Cone, *The Composer's Voice* (Berkeley, Los Angeles, and London: University of California Press, 1974), 160; Nelson Goodman, *Languages of Art*, 114; Barbara Herrnstein Smith, "Literature as Performance, Fiction and Art," *Journal of Philosophy* 67 (1970): 553–63; J. O. Urmson, "Literature," in George Dickie and Richard Sclafani, eds., *Aesthetics: A Critical Anthology* (New York: St Martin's Press, 1977); Richard Wollheim, *Art and Its Objects: Second Edition with Six Supplementary Essays* (Cambridge: Cambridge University Press, 1996), 167.
7   Plato, *Early Socratic Dialogues*, ed. Trevor J. Saunders (London: Penguin, 1987), 54.
8   On the question of what the nature of Ion's critical commentary was, see Kivy, *The Performance of Reading*, pp. 93–100.
9   Don Michael Randel, ed., *The Harvard Dictionary of Music*, 4th edn. (Cambridge, MA, and London: Belknap Press, 2001), 766.
10 Plato, *The Dialogues of Plato*, trans. Benjamin Jowett (New York: Random House, 1937), vol. 1, 274.
11 Daniel Dennett, *Consciousness Explained* (Boston, Toronto, and London: Little, Brown, 1991), 195.
12 Since the development of dance notation, of course, notated dance would also have the same ontology as texted drama and scored music.
13 For further reflections on this matter see Kivy, *The Performance of Reading*, 74–80, et passim.
14 Plato, *Early Socratic Dialogues*, p. 56.
15 For more on this debate see Kivy, *The Performance of Reading*, 93–100.
16 See ibid., §§25–8; and Peter Kivy, "On the Banality of Literary Truths," *Philosophic Exchange* 28 (1997–98); also, Peter Kivy, *Philosophies of Arts: An Essay in Differences* (Cambridge: Cambridge University Press, 1997), chapter 5.
17 William James, "The Will to Believe," in Alburey Castell, ed., *Essays in Pragmatism* (New York: Hafner, 1951), 89.
18 See Kivy, *The Performance of Reading*, §§25–8.

8

Self-Defining Reading: Literature and the Constitution of Personhood

GARRY L. HAGBERG

When we enter an imaginary fictional world, the referents of the "we" are not the stable entities our intuitions concerning selfhood may lead us to believe. Those intuitions are in part supported by experiential considerations, but also – of central importance to this chapter – in part by linguistic ones. Experientially, we of course do not emerge from a fictional world changed beyond recognition: we know that it is *we* who underwent the literary experience. Linguistically, we believe that the reflexive referent of the first person pronoun has not, by virtue of that literary engagement, changed in any wholesale sense from one entity to another. It is then all too easy to adopt, pre- or semi-reflectively, the strong presumption of identity-fixity across time – including the time spent in that other, imaginary fictional world. Here I want to suggest that this overarching presumption blinds us to a more nuanced, remarkable, and once one sees it for all its power, in fact rather unexpected, truth about this variety of aesthetic experience. To support this suggestion concerning the decisive power displayed by the kind of literary experience I have in mind I will look, in the first section of this chapter, at the concepts of fixity and flux as they apply to human selfhood and at the way in which beliefs (and the language in which we express those beliefs, as we will see in connection with some views of Donald Davidson and Richard Rorty) serve to do no less than to make us who we are. Under the heading "The Textually Cultivated 'I': Making up One's Mind," I will describe the three-level literary experience (introduced in sketch form in the preceding section) that, as seen in examples from Goethe, Borges, Iris Murdoch, and Virgil, occasions the acts of self-reflection that allow us to articulate ourselves but in a way where the articulation itself becomes self-constitutive, i.e. determinative of who we are at that moment and then binding upon who we are in the future. And in the final part of the chapter, I will look, in connection with a view advanced by Arthur Danto, at the metaphorical structure of the relation between self and text that allows us, in a distinctive sense herein described, to interact with literary texts in a self-constitutive way, or, in short, to make the texts our own.

A Companion to the Philosophy of Literature, First Edition. Edited by Garry L. Hagberg and Walter Jost.
© 2010 John Wiley & Sons Ltd. Published 2015 by John Wiley & Sons, Ltd.

Possible Selves and Webs of Belief

In *Four Quartets*,[1] T. S. Eliot captures in finely chiseled form the opposition in play here between (1) the idea of fixity-of-self across time in a way impervious to the vicissitudes of experience, and (2) the idea of experience leaving its mark in such a way – indeed in a way both indelible and cumulative – that the experience *becomes* a part of the person who has it. On this latter view, experience becomes, however small, one constituent part, one distinguishing and defining element, of the referent of the first-person pronoun. Eliot writes:

> Fare forward, travellers! not escaping from the past
> Into different lives, or into any future;
> You are not the same people who left that station
> Or who will arrive at any terminus,
> While the narrowing rails slide together behind you.

To not escape from the past into a different life is to preserve the fixity of the referent of the first-person pronoun. To not escape into any future is to not leave the content of one's present, one's identity, behind. Those words convey a sense of the permanence of selfhood, and they rely for their plausibility on the unspoken intuitions that support it. But then Eliot as quickly paints the opposing picture of personhood: in not being the same people who left the station, they are persons reshaped by the experience delivered to the self within that journey. And Eliot's line is delivered as a proclamation, as a strong rebuttal to the entrenched – and as we shall see blinding – presumption of fixity: "You are not the same people . . ." constitutes a polemical assertion designed to challenge the implicit assumption that they *of course* are the same people, to challenge the very self-referential belief he just articulated in the previous lines. But as a still stronger rebuttal, Eliot's next line aggressively asserts (against his imaginary interlocutors who presume fixity-across-experience) the more subtle point that they, as presently referred to, will not arrive at any terminus precisely because they, as a matter of ontological impossibility, cannot arrive there. Those who do, and can, arrive will of necessity – that is, by virtue of this easily concealed feature of personhood as it can be understood with heightened sensitivity to the self-formative power of experience – be different. To encapsulate, this contrasting picture, focused upon and respectful of the power experience possesses to effect real change in the self that undergoes the experience, sees experience as constitutive. Its previous, opposing picture sees experience as a set of mere accretions, layered upon an underlying, but ultimately unchanged, person.

But then Eliot is never too quick to accept as given, or to give the last word to, a polemical duality. He has indeed captured these two opposing pictures of fixity and flexibility, but in his next line he intimates a way out of this dichotomy (a we shall see, a false dichotomy) of self-understanding. He writes:

> And on the deck of the drumming liner
> Watching the furrow that widens behind you,

GARRY L. HAGBERG

> You shall not think "the past is finished"
> Or "the future is before us."

Here, in opposition to tracks that converge ultimately to a point (and indeed to one that vanishes), the liner carves a furrow in the sea that widens as it disperses. These are now the competing images for the relation between the self and its past – the first with an ever-diminishing record of its presence, the second with ever-broadening ripples of the implications of its actions. But it is, as he instructs through his admonishment ("You shall not . . ."), possible to think neither that the past is closed[2] and now diminished to invisibility and thus no longer a part of us, nor that the future lies before us as we, unchanged, move into it. Those words intimate a kind of freedom from a philosophical dichotomy that one does not simply announce, assert, or declare; instead, one earns such freedom of thought (in this case, as we shall see below, rather important self-constitutive thought) by working through the intellectual impulses that lead us into, keep us within, and then, if momentarily free of them, all-too-easily pull us back into, the presumptions and intuitions buttressing either side. We will return to this below, but first we need to ask: How do the beliefs we hold operate in connection with self-fixity or self-fluidity? I mentioned just above that some of the intuitions supporting the notion of the fixity of selfhood are linguistic: most briefly stated, in order for "I" to mean the same thing across time and differing circumstances, its referent, to ensure constancy of meaning, must, we all too easily think, remain the same. But there are further, and more subtle, linguistic intuitions that would blind us to literature's self-constitutive power. It is all too easy to think, as Donald Davidson[3] has observed, that the relation of thought to talk is one of complete dependency, with some philosophers taking it as obvious that thought is primary and psychologically prior, with speech being wholly dependent for its content on the thought that is separate from and prior to it.[4] (This picture is only encouraged by phrases such as "the articulation of thought" or "the expression of thought," where these are construed on dualistic terms.) And a polemically opposed group of philosophers have come to regard such priority as a myth now shattered, arguing that thought is in fact only possible once speech is in place.[5] Be all that as it may, what is of special importance for the present discussion is to bring to brighter light the deeply embedded influence exerted by the thought-dependency thesis specifically on our thinking about the nature of the self *as it is described in language*: we think (here once again all too easily) that just as the content of language is dependent upon the pre-linguistic thought that precedes it, so the self precedes, and is ontologically autonomous from, both (1) any third-person language used to describe it and (2) any first-person language used to express it.

The truth about this relation between thought and speech – I should say these relations – is I believe irreducibly complex,[6] and instructively so. And that complexity is something that is shown throughout whole stretches of literature in the finest detail. Davidson himself argues for a language-dependency position, and although I believe it can be shown that this position cannot accommodate all cases (specifically cases in which we exactly describe instances of thinking before speaking and some sensation-based cases of visual thinking) and is thus reductive in precisely the sense

Davidson himself finds objectionable, there are a number of points Davidson makes along the course of his argument that cast valuable light on present considerations. Davidson, as one foundational starting point for his larger discussion, emphasizes the centrality of belief to many subcategories of thought (he mentions desire, knowledge, fear, and interest as only a few of these), giving the example of a person being glad that, or noticing that, or remembering that, or knowing that, a gun is loaded. In each case, he claims, this person "must believe that the gun is loaded" (157). He writes:

> Even to wonder whether the gun is loaded, or to speculate on the possibility that the gun is loaded, requires the belief, for example, that a gun is a weapon, that it is a more or less enduring physical object, and so on. There are good reasons for not insisting on any particular list of beliefs that are needed if a creature is to wonder whether a gun is loaded. Nevertheless, it is necessary that there be endless interlocked beliefs. The system of such beliefs identifies a thought by locating it in a logical and epistemic space. (157)

Although I think there are indeed some problems with this overarching way of stating the preconditions of belief that run along Austinian and Wittgensteinian lines (do we believe this gun is an enduring physical object because the last one turned out to be a hologram?), at present what I want to pursue is the significance for selfhood of the notion of a system of interlocking beliefs making a thought *possible*. And what is significant for the special kind of self-defining reading that it is the task of this chapter to identify and describe is the point concerning the open status of belief with regard to the thought made possible by the background nets of beliefs, nets that provide what Davidson called the logical and epistemic space within which the thought has its place, within which that thought is made possible and brought to life. Davidson puts it this way:

> Having a thought requires that there be a background of beliefs, but having a particular thought does not depend on the state of belief with respect to that very thought. (157)

Seen one way, literature gives us a web of beliefs (to use W. V. O. Quine's phrase[7]) within which the thoughts of the characters living in that imaginary world are made possible. So in a sense – the more simple one – the world depicted in a literary text is a world within which we, as readers, witness fictional characters thinking thoughts rendered possible by the webs of belief, explicitly (Smith is glad the gun is loaded) or implicitly (Smith acts upon the unspoken belief that the gun is an enduring physical object) present, in that world. And in another sense – the more complex one – we as readers witness characters entertaining thoughts to which their belief is not yet (described by the author as) extended, but where these entertained possible beliefs are themselves rendered possible by the belief-web that locates them, gives them a home and a life, in logico-epistemic space. The simpler sense has been in place, one might say, from Homer (indeed from the first imaginary narrative). The second sense is also (but not ineliminably) woven throughout the history of literature; in recent times, Milan Kundera's and Iris Murdoch's novels are densely populated with such thought-entertaining characters (and this may be one of the indeterminate cluster of reasons they are classified as philosophical novels).

Now, Davidson's fundamental point (in the article being discussed presently, but this is also foundational to his larger philosophical project) is that to be able to so much as have thoughts, we must already be, as he puts it, "an interpreter of the speech of another" (157). By "interpretation" he does not at this stage mean anything frightfully complex: his example is that of interpreting a person's raising his arm as a manifestation of (1) his desire to attract the attention of his friend, and (2) his belief that raising his arm will do so. (Here again, one might well say on Austinian-Wittgensteinian grounds that such a person is not raising his arm, i.e. he is not volunteering for something, but rather waving to his friend; but that critique of this line of thinking, however important, is not germane to what I am presently trying to use Davidson to bring out.) What is here called an interpretation is thus really what Davidson indentifies as a "redescrib[ing] of certain events in a revealing way" (151).

A redescribing of certain events in a revealing way. That, I will go on to suggest, is not the worst way of capturing the special kind of self-reflective activity in which a reader (again, of the certain kind under investigation here) engages. The literary novel is a complex and extensive web of indeterminate reach that provides the logico-epistemic space within which thoughts, on the part of a character, become possible. And it is the space within which that character can be depicted as entertaining thoughts, thoughts themselves made possible by other strands in that background web (roughly, what Wittgenstein, in a related context, called "the scaffolding" of thought) of beliefs. Literature, seen in the light of this set of Quinean-Davidsonian ideas, can then be seen as mimetic in a somewhat special way: the reader, at the simplest level, sees a narrative world depicted, where the complex web of explicit and implicit beliefs within that world makes thought (and in Davidson's sense, interpretation of speech and action) possible. And then at one higher or second mimetic level the reader of imaginative literature sees belief-neutral thought – often of a self-reflective kind, i.e. where the character, inside his or her imaginative logico-epistemic space, reflects on his or her actions, desires, motives, fears, aspirations, romantic ambitions, and so forth (we will see a case of this in Iris Murdoch's *The Sea, The Sea* below). Within the novel, the granting of assent to the entertained belief by the character transforms it from an entertained belief to what I want now to call, in terms of the make-up of that character, a self-constitutive belief. The reader looks, as a spectator-outsider, into the mimetic world within which that process occurs, learns about it, and in a sense rehearses it (to which I will return below), in the act of reading. The reader indeed gets to know the character by witnessing the character's acquisition of beliefs, by witnessing the character's thoughts, and this itself is a mimetic reflection of the way we get to know people in life: people are defined in considerable part by their thought, and more specifically by the quality, character, moral content, degree of refinement, humane sensitivity, precision, and care shown in that thought.

At this second level, the reader, looking closely into that imaginative world, also sees the complexity of what one might call the negotiations involved in converting an entertained thought into a belief, where that belief then becomes both character-constitutive and part of the web-background for other now-possible thoughts. The reader sees, in an extended narrative depiction, the process, with all its subtle variations, of taking on a thought as one we would defend, or one we hold to, or one we are convinced of, or one we feel sure about, or one we are sure about, and so forth. And these processes are, like their end results, i.e. the beliefs we take on, subject to moral evaluation by the first-person holder of the belief, and by second- and third-person others. Belief-holders can be proud, ashamed, or anything in between not only of their beliefs, but also of how they came to hold them, and others can and certainly do evaluate these processes of belief-acquisition as well: that a holocaust denier[8] holds the belief he does is morally indicative of who and what he is, and how he came to that belief (it was consistent with or followed from his other intertwined beliefs; it was the result of his having been brutally tortured and brainwashed; it was subsequent to severe head trauma after which his epistemic responsibility was diminished, etc.) is similarly morally relevant in determining his character and condition. Again, the reader sees, in the highly variegated ways literature shows, the hardening of a possible view into a settled one. And in seeing this, the reader sees the forming, the strengthening, and the solidification of the morally constitutive epistemic content of a character.

Davidson emphasizes the easily forgotten truth that "uttering words is an action," and that, understood as such, a (linguistic) action "must draw for its teleological explanation on beliefs and desires" (161). The term "teleological" might here be taken as a kind of shorthand for the open-ended process of situating what a person says, as action, into the larger frame of reference, the web, that makes that action intelligible. One benefit of seeing an utterance as an action is that we would not find it intuitively plausible for an action to have something called a meaning independent from the circumstances within which that action was performed. Many do, however, find a parallel notion of pre-contextual word-meaning or sentence-meaning intuitively plausible, and the explicit categorization of speech as action helps to diminish the force of this misleading intuition. And it is precisely such linguistic actions, as they occur in the expanded contexts that make them possible for the actor and intelligible for the hearer (what Davidson calls, in his restricted sense, the "interpreter"), that are mimetically depicted in literature. Where revealing redescriptions of those linguistic actions are put forward and considered by the characters who utter them and their fictional interlocutors, we see the kind of interpretation that Davidson is discussing, indeed the processes that allow us to so much as make sense of ourselves and others – in action, or within what Wittgenstein called the stream of life. We see the processes within which characters have their own Davidsonian interpretations of themselves ("to explain why someone said something we need to know, among other things, his own interpretation of what he said, that is, what he believes his words mean in the circumstances under which he speaks," 161), sometimes maintaining these self-interpretations, and sometimes, through the process of revealing redescription, coming to a changed self-understanding. This process of self-understanding (and as we shall see more fully below, of self-constitution) – of central importance to the task of this chapter – very often takes the form of arriving at a changed understanding of what was meant by our words.[9] And this is often negotiated in terms of a speaker's beliefs concerning, as Davidson says, "how others will interpret his words" (161).

It is at this juncture, this stage of the three-level aesthetic experience I am presently sketching, that we move to the third level. As we have seen, as readers we (1) see the extended and indeterminately bounded contexts within which beliefs, actions, and expressions are possible, and we (2) see characters performing actions (often of a linguistic kind) whose meaning we grasp as a function of having grasped the larger context and where their actions evince the beliefs they either hold or entertain. But beyond this, we (3) can *identify* with the character in his or her context of action and web of beliefs in such a way that we (a) learn what it is, what it *means*, to perform expressive actions that evince belief in this highly particular way, (b) learn what it is like to *be* the kind of person who holds these narrated beliefs and acts upon them – and, importantly, a person who interacts with others in certain ways and not others on the basis of those beliefs –, and (c) see the narrated fictional content as a rather grand metaphor for our own real or possible life-circumstances. We can thus imagine in a full way – i.e. at the imaginative depth necessary to truly fathom, truly comprehend, both the possibility and the meaning of significant human actions – the circumstances as they take shape in external physical situations, in patterns and habits of human interaction, and in dispositions of character that would together lead us to be, indeed together *make* us to be, one kind of person or another. In these layered ways – ways considerably more complex than any oversimplified picture of lesson-learning literary didacticism could accommodate – much of moral significance is taking place within the imaginative world of aesthetic experience. And with the foregoing sketch (at this stage still only a sketch because not yet shown in detailed examples) of these three levels of the reader's experience behind us, we can begin to see how such aesthetic engagement can be of a kind that expands our imaginative reach, our understanding of others' webs of belief and the perhaps idiosyncratic ways in which a person's beliefs are interconnected, and – most importantly, I want to suggest – our understanding of what it means to hold those beliefs and the circumstances that make those beliefs and the actions that express them possible. Moreover, such aesthetic experience can be of a kind that is stronger still in terms of its self-constitutive power: it can elicit in the reader's consciousness an act of entertaining a belief (where this involves all that has been described at the first and second levels) that is, through the identification of the literary context as a metaphor for our own lives,[10] then taken on (through the process of epistemic acquisition to be shown more fully in the following sections) as one that we hold true. Such beliefs can be about the world, about others, or about ourselves – in all cases they are, because beliefs serve to define in part the content of personhood, self-constitutive. If about the world, (e.g. the history of the holocaust), they can determine the attitude (e.g. skeptical or immediately dismissive, or accepting and immediately supportive) with which we will approach many other intertwined possible beliefs. If about others, they can influence no less than the patterns, the character, the tone, and the content of our human interactions. And if about ourselves, such aesthetically occasioned beliefs can determine the extent to which we have earned self-understanding, the extent to which we possess self-knowledge, or in the negative case the extent to which we have become, as a matter of belief-hardened character, resistant to self-examination or given over to patterned or chronic self-deception.[11]

Richard Rorty has cast in high-relief – perhaps, as I will suggest, in too high a relief – a feature of our identities that he calls "the contingency of selfhood."[12] (This constitutes one important articulation of the flux or malleability of selfhood that would facilitate the recognition of literature's formative power.) Rorty embarks on his examination of this defining feature of selfhood by reading a poem of Philip Larkin's where Larkin describes the content of self-knowledge (gained as the result of "walk[ing] the length of your mind") as inescapably idiosyncratic to the self-examiner. That body of gained self-knowledge – in Larkin's words "as clear as a lading list" – is what makes the difference between the I and what Rorty calls "all the other I's," and it is this exclusively self-known idiosyncratic content that we fear will be lost forever at death ("[s]ince it applied only to one man once,/And that man dying," as Larkin expressed it). Rorty interestingly sees the fear as the symptom of an achievement of self-knowledge – the strength of the fear of the loss of the impress on the self of the experiential content that makes each of us unique is just a measure of our knowledge of that content. But Rorty also sees in these lines a novel expression of a classic tension, a new flare-up of the ancient quarrel between the particularity of poetry and the desired universality of philosophy: Rorty describes this as "the tension between an effort to achieve self-creation by the recognition of contingency and an effort to achieve universality by the transcendence of contingency" (25).

As Rorty has discussed extensively in his *Philosophy and the Mirror of Nature*,[13] the deeply-entrenched epistemology of universality – the discipline-hardened attitude which would discard the idiosyncratic, the particular, the contingent, as irrelevant "noise" from the outset – would lead us to value only that which, as experiencing selves, we have in common with all the other experiencing selves. Thus he writes:

> They [the defenders of universality throughout philosophy's history] would thereby inform us what we really are, what we are compelled to be by powers not ourselves. They would exhibit the stamp which had been impressed on *all* of us. This impress would not be blind, because it would not be a matter of chance, a mere contingency. It would be necessary, essential, telic, constitutive of what it is to be human. It would give us a goal, the only possible goal, namely, the full recognition of that very necessity, the self-consciousness of our essence. (26)

Rorty sets against this grand picture what he identifies as the view of Nietzsche, whom he credits with being the first to reject "the whole idea of 'knowing the truth'" (27). If Nietzsche's "perspectivism amounted to the claim that the universe had no lading-list to be known" (27), then, having

> realized that Plato's "true world" was just a fable, we would seek consolation, at the moment of death, not in having transcended the animal condition but in being that peculiar sort of dying animal who, by describing himself in his own terms, had created himself. More exactly, he would have created the only part of himself that mattered by constructing his own mind. (27)

Thus, on this view (one polemically opposed to the presupposition of fixity), the content of self-knowledge will not be gained as the result of a process of discovery, but rather as the result of a process of creative self-narration. Here the self, as reflexively engaged author, "writes" itself – the story of its accumulated "impress" of experience, ordered into a self-definition with the strength of what Rorty, borrowing the term from Harold Bloom, calls a "strong poet," i.e. one who creates his own unique language of self-description out of that utterly contingent and experientially unique body of experience. And such a self (here following some of Nietzsche's thoughts on the matter) will not – because it metaphysically could not – be a mere token of a pre-established type, or "a copy or replica of something which has already been identified" (28). The self, in this sense, is for Rorty in truth both ineliminably and inimitably contingent, as is the language, the narrative we assemble, to linguistically identify that self. This, again, would indeed all seem to go a long way toward describing the malleable self whose content is in part determined by the "impress" of literary content and the absorbed reader's reflections upon that content as sketched above.

The problem with this view, however – as I intimated – is that in placing itself *polemically* against the classically entrenched view, it dramatically overstates its case, ironically ascending to a universal claim concerning our identity that is designed to challenge the very possibility of making a universal claim concerning our identity. Rorty selectively assembles a mosaic from Nietzsche's writings, and then provides a summary that leaves out a number of other defining particularities of Nietzsche's work. Nietzsche does, in *The Twilight of the Idols*,[14] blast (he calls this slim volume a piece of dynamite) away at what he there calls "The Problem of Socrates,"[15] giving a sharp-toned voice to some observations that Rorty elevates to a generalized position. But Nietzsche also emphasizes – of great importance to understanding precisely how Rorty goes wrong on the subject of selfhood, despite his having identified an important kernel of truth concerning what it is to be human – that along with the historically entrenched idea of the real world (that has for millennia been taken to be philosophy's grand task to describe) being removed as an epistemic ideal or endpoint, the idea of the apparent world *goes out as well*. This, for Nietzsche, is hardly throwing out the baby with the bath water – for him, there was no baby to begin with. But for Rorty, it would be to do so, precisely because of his having first taken on the polemicized, ancient-quarrel structure of the argument requiring position-formulation and counter-formulation. In fact, in a spirit perhaps closer to that of (at least) the later Wittgenstein, Nietzsche is undercutting the presuppositions of the debate, suggesting that to banish the idea of the real world – for us the objective universal facts of human selfhood – is *not at all* to thus lay the foundation for a universalizing anti-objectivist, all-is-contingency (or like Heraclitus, all-is-flux) position. It is, rather, reminiscent of the lines of Eliot's work with which we began, to first break free of one constraining picture or conceptual model, but then also to come to see that this gives us the sense of liberation, of autonomy, to know how to resist that first constraining picture's polemically situated antithesis as well. In positioning Nietzsche as the *defender* of a grand view that stands in opposition to the classically entrenched epistemological presumption that Rorty has done so much to bring to light and to subject to scrutiny,[16] Rorty himself has failed to acknowledge, and to put to philosophical use, the very fine-grained particularities and contextually seated idiosyncrasies that, taken together, constitute Nietzsche's body of work. That body of work in this sense mimetically reflects the body of experience, the collective impress of life, that constitutes the content of self-knowledge, and it does so in highly particularized observations that – like human experience – take their meaning, their force, and their significance *within*, and not in any grander sense that serves a larger polemical purpose, above, the context of each utterance, each observation. Wittgenstein showed the profound importance of working through what one might call the etiologies of philosophically universalizing or over-generalizing positions, tracking closely and with exquisite care the pressures on thought, the intellectual attractions and snares that would lead us to turn away from what was misapprehended (often under the influence of entrenched epistemological presuppositions of just the kind Rorty has excavated) as the "noise" of particularities. But Wittgenstein, knowing where to stop, did so without then adopting an anti-objectivist position that itself amounted to an objective claim. It is all too easy, at just this juncture, to overstate the distinctive kind of fluidity, or, in a positive sense of the term, impressionability, of selfhood that I am suggesting is the raw material upon which formative literary experience acts.

Rorty, in what might fairly be called his polemical zeal (or at least a position-shaping exaggerated boldness), is perhaps too quick to equate the unique, the idiosyncratic, the highly particular, with contingency, and perhaps too quick to generically place those things, and other things in broad terms like them, into the category of "the contingent," which, also generically, is taken to oppose, indeed to preclude, the kind of stability that classical epistemology would, if true to its highest aspirations, correctly describe. As Austin and those in his tradition showed, shooting a donkey by mistake, by accident, inadvertently, by mishap, by misadventure, through confusion, through misidentification, and so forth, are, at the level of detailed particularity (and that is after all the level at which these words function), *very* different things: to generically group them all together as "unintentional action" and then to attempt to provide a general theory of that is, indeed, to obscure (rather than to reveal an imagined hidden essence of) the very specific action that drew our attention to the case in the first place.[17] And the making of these fine distinctions, and the describing of the detailed highly particularized contexts of human engagement within which we importantly distinguish the accident from the mistake, the inadvertent from the mishap, is one of the services philosophically significant literature performs. What Rorty's grand view (constructed out of an over-generalized and selective reading of Nietzsche that is positioned in opposition to a preceding grand view) misses, through the too-quick identification of the unique, the idiosyncratic, the particular with the generically contingent, is that a kind of objectivity is possible, a kind of descriptive veracity is possible, not despite, but rather *because of*, a clear focus on the unique, the idiosyncratic, the particular. It will not – and this is what Rorty is absolutely right about (where this rightness is not merely a function of his powers as a "strong poet," i.e. it is not merely because he said it in particularly convincing or resonant rhetoric) – be an objectivity or veracity born of verified correspondence between a *post factum* statement and pre-linguistic state of affairs. But to claim that then the content of self-knowledge will be purely, inescapably, and wholly a matter of self-descriptive *creativity* is to go too far, to cast the valuable point beneath all of this in far too high relief, which in turn blinds us to other meaning-determining nuance. Indeed to see the extreme claim Rorty is making as plausible, one might already be woven into a web – in this case caught in it – of belief that intertwines with (and makes possible and gives a home to) this too-bold claim, and one of these inter-webbed beliefs may well be that language is, in its most fundamental nature, descriptive, rather than constitutive, of complex entities like human selves. That presumption would prevent us from seeing the "bootstrapping" character of self-definition where that definition advances incrementally by the accrued items of self-constitutive language. The stability of selfhood that Rorty's strong neo-Heraclitean thesis declares mythical may well be real enough *in a sense* after all, but we get into a position to see this only once we have freed ourselves of the blinders imposed by large-scale position-formulating polemics. Indeed, what we might then see would be suitably particularized to the individuals in question, and respectful of their idiosyncratic experience and its multiple and complex resonances within that life span (true to Larkin's observation), which itself would be a lesson on a larger scale about self-understanding. But it would not take the form of a generic, philosophical theory that might be named as an "ism." Literature so often sets out to show such self-constitutive language in action with the fine contextual detail necessary to truly understand the words used in the transaction; philosophy so often sets out with presuppositions on both sides of the polemicized debate (and often where both sides share one heretofore unexamined presumption[18]) that, directly contrary to its clarificatory ambitions, in fact prevents a clear view of this most-human process.

Rorty, in short, runs the risk of occluding the distinction between life and art in such a way that the content and structure of autobiographical understanding seems nothing more than a whimsical construction, rendered in a free-form manner independent of any epistemic constraints. And that would fail to acknowledge important – in some cases life-defining – distinctions we make between right and wrong, acceptable and unacceptable, illuminating or un-illuminating, plausible and implausible, self-descriptions.[19] But he believes – and this is another place where he takes one essentially significant feature of the way we make sense of our lives and then quickly ascends far above the life-giving particularities that motivated this entire line of thinking in the first place – that such distinctions need to be grouped together and (sounding rather like a post-modern Schiller) then replaced, wholesale, by a heightened sense of *play*:

> This playfulness [of metaphorical[20] self-construction] is the product of their shared ability to appreciate the power of redescribing, the power of language to make new and different things possible and important – an appreciation which becomes possible only when one's aim becomes an expanding repertoire of alternative descriptions rather than The One Right Description. Such a shift in aim is possible only to the extent that both the world and the self have been de-divinized. To say that both are de-divinized is to say that one no longer thinks of either as speaking to us, as having a language of its own, as a rival poet. Neither are quasi-persons, neither wants to be expressed or represented in a certain way. (39–40)

But if it were *all* a matter of simply working to expand, without end or limit in sight, our repertoire of alternative descriptions as instruments for understanding ourselves, we would lose not only the distinctions we make between the right and the wrong, the plausible and the implausible, and so forth as mentioned above. We would lose a set of highly significant distinctions we make *about the descriptions themselves*, e.g. the apt, the fitting, the concise, the resonant, the revealing, the intriguing, the suggestive, the just, the fair, the inverses of all of these, and countless others that, again, an Austinian linguistic investigation (and the kind that literature, along the course of its narrative path, so often undertakes) would detail.

What Rorty perhaps needed to put together was not his Heraclitean view with Davidson's conception of metaphor (where metaphors do "not *express* something which previously existed," 36), but rather his sense of freedom from the picture of the One Right Description with the views of Davidson's that we saw above. Davidson, giving his most rudimentary definition of interpretation, said that it is "a redescribing of certain events in a revealing way." Those redescriptions are not cut loose from the moorings of our deeply embedded intuitions concerning rightness,[21] wrongness, the apt, the inapt, the fair, the unfair, and all the rest in the Austinian catalogue of distinctions that are used as descriptions of utterances. But we see those distinctions, and we use those descriptions of utterances, only within the expanded frame, the indefinitely limited web of beliefs, associations, connotations, expectations, intimations, and so forth that, as we saw above, both show us what the words used in an utterance mean and more fundamentally make those utterances so much as possible in the first place. The distinctions between the kinds of utterances we make, the descriptions we employ of those utterances, and the ultimate acceptance or rejection of them are not – here Rorty is right – measured in any simple one-to-one way against the One Right Description to gauge their veracity. But it does not follow from this that they are thereby put forward, like or as mere articles of play or whimsy, without constraints, without measures, without the standards and justifications of rationality. That these constraints and measures are not reducible to One does not make them any less real (quite the reverse), nor does the Rortyan shattering of the myth of the One Right Description preclude objectivity in such distinctions and descriptions, ushering in an epistemologically undifferentiated play of subjectivity. Such distinctions and descriptions, like distinctions and descriptions concerning selfhood and self-identity, are made possible within that expanded web, indeed *within language*. Only a grand picture of language as being utterly separate from, and posterior to – rather than indissolubly wound together with, and indeed constitutive of – the world would make us falsely believe that, because such distinctions and descriptions take place in language, they are thus always relative, always adventitious, always secondary to what really matters.

They aren't. We can indeed entertain (in the foregoing literary-imaginative sense) possible selves: we can construct, by focusing on a coherent collection of described characteristics to the exclusion of others, what we might call imaginary identities[22] within the larger mental act of absorbed literary reading, asking ourselves as we proceed as readers to what extent, and in what precise ways, we are similar to and different from them. This process yields, for reasons we have begun to see above, self-knowledge. And in autobiographical reflection we can, having rehearsed this process in literary reading, construct similarly entertained versions of ourselves, in one case (with generosity-to-self to the fore) emphasizing and collecting together instances of kindness, in another case (with past-felt negative emotion at the fore) emphasizing and collecting together causes for regret and self-recrimination. And so with a thousand other cases of inward self-portrayal. Where we judge – in the particularized, intricately contextualized Austinian way – an entertained self-description positively, i.e. as having a sufficient verisimilitude but where this verisimilitude is not measured simply and mono-dimensionally against the (mythical) One Right Description, we take it on as a part of who and what we are. The portrayal-description, far from merely adventitious and hardly detached from what really matters, becomes the very substance of selfhood. And that selfhood displays aspects both of fluidity and of fixity that are ungeneralizeable, unsimplifiable. Literature, as we will see, in a special double-focused way both shows this within the imaginary world of the narrative and occasions it within the real world of the reader.

The Textually Cultivated "I": Making up One's Mind

Private or self-directed soliloquy, or silent thought to oneself, often exhibits a public, or public-like, dimension that its image of metaphysically enclosed solitude would belie. Such self-directed thinking obviously takes place in autobiographical reflection, but it also takes place within, and in an important sense alongside, as we have now begun to see, absorbed literary reading. Goethe captures this in a remarkable passage in his autobiographical writings; the passage casts light on Goethe, on his compositional process, on the similarity of such thought to epistolary (and hence relationally intertwined) exchange, on the tellingly *dialogical* character of inward reflection (as we have seen it in Augustine, in Kierkegaard, in Wittgenstein, and in many others), and more generally on the public dimension of self-directed soliloquy that I am pursuing presently. Goethe, having referred to his "peculiar habit of recasting even soliloquy as dialogue,"[23] writes (instructively, in the third person):

> Being accustomed to spend his time preferably in company, he transformed even solitary thinking into social conversation, and in the following way: namely, when he found himself alone, he would summon up in spirit some person of his acquaintance. He would ask this person to be seated, pace up and down by him, stand in front of him, and discuss whatever subject he had in mind. The person would occasionally answer him and indicate, with the customary gestures, his agreement or disagreement; and everyone has a particular way of doing this. Then the speaker would continue, and expand on whatever seemed to please his guest; or he would qualify what the latter disapproved of, and define it more clearly, and even finally be willing to abandon his thesis. The most curious aspect of this was that he never chose persons of his closer acquaintanceship, but those he saw only rarely, nay, often some who lived in far-off places and with whom he had merely a passing relationship. But usually they were persons more receptive than communicative in nature, open-minded and prepared to be calmly interested in matters within their ken, although sometimes he would also summon contentious spirits to these dialectical

exercises. Persons of both sexes, and of every age and condition, submitted to this and proved agreeable and charming, because the conversation was only about subjects they liked and understood. Yet many of them would have been greatly amazed had they been able to find out how often they were summoned to those imaginary conversations, since they would hardly have come to a real one.

It is quite clear that such thought-conversations are closely related to correspondence, except that the latter responds to an established familiarity, while the former creates a new, ever-changing familiarity for itself, with no reply.

This passage paints a portrait of a thinker engaged in the process of making up his mind by speculatively reflecting on possible beliefs. This involves both (1) recognizing what Rorty called the contingency of our views, our stances, and our positions as they take on greater specificity when compared to other possible positions, and (2) working through an expanding and deepening awareness of what it means to hold these possible beliefs. This also describes the character of autobiographical reflection, just as it describes the special kind of literary absorption of which I am pursuing a fuller account throughout this chapter. To identify some of this passage's elements: (1) To so quickly turn "solitary thinking into social conversation" just is in a sense to recognize, with Wittgenstein (on the topic of privacy and private language[24]) that, to put the point strongly, there *is* no solitary thinking in the profoundly solitary (i.e. utterly non-dialogical) sense.[25] (2) To have the imagined interlocutor answering and indicating with gestures just is to situate the initial remark being answered into an expanded web of (possible) belief, and to embody that belief (with gestures) in a manner that preserves a mindfulness of the fact that *persons* make remarks and hold, discuss, and debate views, positions, stances, and beliefs – they are not abstract incorporeal propositions, but are entertained and held by contextually situated people. (3) Following on the last element, if we truly imagine a possible belief, we imagine an individual person holding that belief (which, again, is precisely what literature shows with the requisite detail), and our capacity to imagine our holding it (if that belief is deeply different or, in Goethe's phrase, "far-off" from views we do hold) is not only to imagine human difference, but to become able – and here we answer, in a differently articulated way, Rorty's call to recognize our contingency – to imagine ourselves as a different person (where, again, belief-webs are in considerable part what differentiates persons, Rorty's I and all the other I's, as we conceive of them both in life and in literature).[26] (4) When a speaker exhibits a capacity to "continue, and expand," or "qualify," or "define more clearly," that speaker thereby shows a facility and ease of movement within the interwoven and indeterminately bounded web of which we saw Davidson speak, and where a speaker is "willing to abandon his thesis," that speaker is shifting, however large, however small, a part of belief-constituted selfhood. Indeed that person will, in this imaginary dialogical engagement, through the process of more clearly defining his or her thesis as a result of a very close scrutiny and patient comparing and contrasting of views, positions, stances, and beliefs taken or held, more clearly define herself or himself. (5) The very capacity to change our mind is itself a precondition for the possibility of self-creation, and it is accomplished not prior to, but here again rather *in*, language. The dialogical structure of self-directed reflection in part shows that. Thus it is *within* such reflection that we entertain beliefs, and it is here that we decide to take them on or not, to become the person whose self is constituted by – whose mind is made up by – such movements and settlements of thought. (It is also important to see here that the holding of a given belief or position – in politics, say – is not uniform across all cases of persons who hold it; i.e. to have held a very different view initially, and then to have worked through intricate issues in order to arrive at the present one, is very different from having simply held from the outset the present view unproblematically. This is a fact that is much easier for literature than for philosophy to capture, given the high-resolution focus literature can offer on what we might here call epistemological psychology.) To the extent to which we are "open-minded and prepared to be calmly interested" in Goethe's sense, we are – to precisely the degree of intellectual openness that is shown – mindful in a serious way of circumstantial mind-making contingency. (6) To be, as we revealing say, *conversant* in a subject is to be able to imagine a multiplicity of perspectives ("persons of both sexes, and of every age and condition"), and this, I am suggesting, is to be able to imagine in a full sense the sentences, the words, the language, that articulate them. That self-defining capacity (and this is the point most central to this entire chapter) is not only shown in literature, but (at the third level described above) *occasioned* by it. To learn to be conversant with a subject is at least in part to learn to imagine, and those acts of imagining rest upon – indeed they reside within – language. (7) Lastly, while it is right to emphasize and draw out the dialogical-linguistic character of the process Goethe has captured in this passage, it is not by any means thereby wrong to keep in mind that it *is* still a kind of self-reflective soliloquy we are discussing; it is still, in a sense, a private activity of mind – in precisely the sense that absorbed literary engagement is a private experience (within the expanded frame of a public language[27]). It is, despite the public and dialogical character of reflection, still *self*-constitutive reading we are discussing.

There are many places throughout Goethe's autobiographical writings where the themes he captures in the above passages are given full and detailed examples: in writing of his early student years in Leipzig, he refers to "intolerable demands" (192) that were intolerable precisely for the reason that they suppressed what he felt, at that stage of his development (or within the belief-web of that self), naturally disposed to say. He was "prohibited from alluding to pithy Bible passages and from using naïve expressions out of the chronicles;" he had – important for our present concerns – to forget that he had read certain authors and to "dispense with everything [his] youthful enthusiasm had embraced." In short, he was being in a perhaps more than metaphorical sense "edited" and then "recast" into a different (linguistically constituted) person. While at the early stage of this self-transition he felt himself a lost soul ("I felt paralyzed in the core of my being"), and he felt himself anything but conversant as described in his passage above ("so that I could scarcely talk about the most ordinary things"), we see along the lengthy course of this gradual and not always easy process a person, to put it most bluntly, *working out who he is*. He shapes his identity, his moral, aesthetic, and linguistic sensibility, just as a sculptor begins by carving overall contours and then refines, feature-by-feature, from there. And then as we as readers see this process, we also, alongside of our outward-directed reading of Goethe's self-defining narrative, work on, and work out ourselves – through the above-mentioned process of inward-directed identification, comparison, contrast, differentiation, and all the other elements of imaginary interlocutorship.

The short story "The Book of Sand" by Jorge Luis Borges[28] can function as a remarkably adept allegory of the kind of self-constitutive reading we are presently pursuing. In the story Borges describes a stranger who appears at his (or the protagonist's – although as Borges has repeatedly called attention to the autobiographical content of his writing this is an unclear distinction) door eager to sell a strange and eerie book. The unnamed protagonist opens the book "at random" (118) – indeed just as we always hear details, episodes, or encounters of a person's experience *in medias res*, and never in any complete way from a pure beginning – only to find that (1) the book's contents never appear on the same page again, i.e. he closely scrutinizes an illustration, then closes the book, and on re-opening it to that page finds utterly different content there (and never sees that same illustration again), and (2) he could never, despite repeated attempts, get to the first or last page (every effort invariably yielded still a few more pages between the pages he was on and the cover binding). The webs of interwoven belief, the webs that serve to make us who we are, as Davidson observed, are of indeterminate reach – whenever we reach what we might take as the end of an inferential link from the entertained belief in question, we find that we can follow numerous individual strands still further. And the contingent (cautiously described) nature of our own present selfhood and the relationally enmeshed character of that self's experience always reconfigure experience;[29] they always weave it into a pattern generating a set of present and subsequent echoes or reverberations distinctive to *that* pattern that not only significantly change, through these echoes and reverberations, its linked associations and connotations in its presentations to the self, but more importantly they change *it itself* – the content of experience is never the same, because the context, strictly speaking, is never the same.

And just so, the reader's experience is never, in this sense, the same – the mind that comes to the text is always altered upon return to it, so the associative webs, the sometimes explicitly articulated, sometimes only dimly sensed linkages to the past, differ time to time. Thus what we might call "the same diagram," the same content, is never exactly, or in a very fine-tuned sense, findable again, just as the self that turns to the text comes to it not without a beginning that much precedes it (in terms of the past associations and the reflections it awakens or occasions), nor does that self close its story at the end of the book – its resonance, its impact, its sense, continue beyond that textual closing.[30] (One might call it an apparent narrative closing that is in truth by its nature incompatible with genuine closure.) Just as we can become haunted by the past, or by aspects or episodes of it, Borges's protagonist becomes haunted by the book whose contents, like sand, always shift, are always elsewhere upon return. He contemplates burning it – just as one can try to repudiate or even obliterate the past – but he fears that (like fearing the continuing and indeed increasingly haunting influence upon the future of that past) "the burning of an infinite book might likewise prove infinite and suffocate the planet with smoke" (122). In the end, the protagonist – for us an image of the resolute denial or repudiation of all self-reflection, an image of attempting to close and flee from what is by its nature perennially open – abandons the wondrous but threatening book in the basement (the subconscious?) of a library, where in addition to books, maps (charting out and understanding a life in cartographic terms?[31]) and periodicals (continually updating and reweaving the past into the present and future?[32]) were kept. It was surreptitiously deposited on one of the basement's musty shelves and abandoned there.

Now, to stand back a bit, why should a willingness to embrace a reflective life, rather than to turn away from it, be a virtue? Why should this allegory of a reader's experience seem to deserve the words "denial," "repudiation" and "flee from"? At least in part, Davidson and Rorty, when woven together, have already answered the question. To fully and seriously imagine what it is to believe things other than we presently believe is, as I am suggesting, a way of coming to know ourselves and our self-constitutive beliefs fully, with far greater exactitude and refinement than we would have had without these literary occasions for reflection. To be made, through literary engagement, mindful of what is contingent about ourselves is to be made broader and more capacious in our human understanding. To turn from that process is to turn away from growth, from openness, to the narrow, to the familiar, to the – indeed like the finite book we cannot truly find (Borges's wondrous book is also a metaphor for all books) – closed. Rorty himself wrote that our self-narratives, themselves always implicitly evocative of Nabokov's line concerning life as "an unfinished poem,"[33] "cannot get completed because there is nothing to complete, there was only a web of relations to be rewoven, a web which time lengthens every day."[34] And it is literature that affords an opportunity to reflect upon, to extend, to reweave, and – in the belief-as-entertained to belief-as-held process of self-directed epistemic acquisition described above – to create those self-constitutive relations of psychological association and meaning-contributing connotation.[35] But it is time to sum up where we are within a rather extended discussion and then to move ahead.

I said above that the kind of literary absorption of which I am pursuing a fuller understanding in this chapter functions on three levels, with the third, more psychologically complex level itself dividing into three.[36] With the themes we have covered in the foregoing now explicitly in play, we are in a position to see this three-tiered experience with much greater clarity. First, and simplest, we had characters as agents whose range of possible actions is itself made possible by the explicit and implicit belief-webs within which they reside. To put to work in this context a resonant line from Emily Dickinson, they dwell in possibility, where the reach of the possible coextends with the reach of that indeterminately bounded web. And, as in life (but as we will see below with a reflective-contemplative distance that life doesn't in its ordinary course allow) we comprehend (also as in life) their actions to the extent that we comprehend the particularities of the contexts within which they act. That understanding depends on our cultivating a real sense of the scope, the reach, of possibility, but – to avoid Rorty's overstatement of freedom – also a sense of the limits, the constraints. Edward Said has drawn attention to precisely this kind of double-aspectual understanding of human action through reference to the philosopher often thought to have most strongly emphasized unrestrained volitional freedom. Said writes:

Let us return to Sartre. At the very moment that he seems to be advocating the idea that man (no mention of woman) is free to choose his own destiny, he also says that the situation – one of Sartre's favorite words – may prevent the full exercise of such freedom. And yet, Sartre adds, it is wrong to say that milieu and situation unilaterally determine the writer or intellectual: rather there is a constant movement back and forth between them.[37]

The character-constitutive beliefs that we see represented in fiction function in precisely this way, where to genuinely and truly understand, to fathom, what it means to hold a belief involves understanding what interwoven, and sometimes epistemologically interlocking, beliefs can and cannot be held or entertained by that character at that time of his or her development in that context. (It is for this reason that we can find a character – just as we may in life – morally blameworthy for not having had a thought he or she should have had, or not having thought harder about the ramifications of a belief upon which he or she has acted; such moral evaluations of mental action and inaction are made possible just by the scope of what indeed is, for that character, possible.)

So the first level of this kind of self-constitutive reader's experience, is simply (or perhaps not so simply, as we shall see in a moment) to see a character acting, in word and deed, upon a belief that is for this moment, for this particular action, prominent (having emerged on this occasion from that extensively webbed background or from Wittgenstein's scaffolding). Examples of this in literature truly are too numerous to mention: we see them in psychologically refined descriptions in Homer, Greek tragedy, Virgil, Dante, Shakespeare, George Eliot, Tolstoy, Dostoevsky, Proust, Iris Murdoch, and obviously countless others. But then, given an awareness of the psychological astuteness of these authors, one wants to add that this matter indeed is perhaps not so simple: to *understand* the strength of the suppressed and concealed reaction of the old woman recognizing by his scar Odysseus dressed as a beggar just before he reveals his identity is to know more than a little about (1) her past with Odysseus as a boy, (2) the power of her instantaneously awakened recollection of all of that by the scar, (3) her thoughts and feelings concerning the present state of Penelope, (4) her seeing the courage of the father suddenly manifest in the son Telemachus in what immediately follows upon that moment of memory-web-activating recognition, (5) her almost Proustian sense of time past (specifically, the sense of time and what was a possible future made real by Odysseus's presence, thought to be irretrievably lost in the past) being suddenly and dramatically regained as Odysseus slays Penelope's increasingly impatient suitors, and surely many other things (extending as webs reaching out from those themes). To know the true content of her reaction at the recognition scene is to know a very great deal about humane content that extends vastly beyond what any philosophical picture or simplifying template of localized and immediately given experiential content (essentially, the reductive picture of experience given to us by British empiricism[38]) could account for. Humane understanding – the kind of awareness cultivated within this kind of reader's absorption – is anything but atomistic or experientially isolable or narrowly determinately bounded. What we would, with respect for the term, be able to call an *understanding* of Medea's terrible acts,[39] or the filial piety shown to Orestes,[40] or Dante's description of the place and condition of Ugolino,[41] or

Casaubon's inwardly vacuous and aesthetically posturing ability to say the right thing (actually if we understand the case not that, but rather to parrot what sound like the right words),[42] involve an extensive grasp of humane content far beyond what an anemic description, or what we might initially think of as the brute facts alone, would capture. (And any attempt to state the brute facts quickly generates the sense that one does not at all know where to stop tracing out the webs in describing the act in question – think of the psychological complexity of Medea's act.) Examples of what it takes for such understanding, layered and intricate in all their complexity, are – if taken with the patient case-by-case attention that true understanding requires – everywhere throughout the history of literature. That gradually acquired sense of complexity carries over to our self-descriptions and self-definitions as well.

At the second level, we had the literary depiction of entertained belief, where that entertained belief stands against the backdrop of a network of related and settled, accepted, or held beliefs – in short, the body of beliefs to which, we might say, the entertained belief aspires and by which it is being considered as a candidate. Examples here are naturally legion as well, but perhaps one may stand for the many.

In Iris Murdoch's *The Sea, The Sea*,[43] Charles Arrowby, retired and now reflecting back on his earlier life in the ever-engaging world of the theatre in London (where he was actor, director, and playwright), later in the novel is "in a sick trance" of mourning and self-recrimination at the drowning death of his friend Hartley's son Titus. Arrowby in these pages reflects on: (1) whether or not people to whom he tells things believe him; (2) to what extent he is right to blame himself (for not sufficiently watching over Titus and for not sufficiently warning him of the power of the sea in the first place); (3) to what extent the view of stone cottages, willows, butterflies, box hedges, rambler roses, and so forth have been transfigured, by association to the tragic loss, from images giving great pleasure to "the very images of sorrow," and to what extent (in terms of which entertained beliefs concerning his responsibility and the correlated extent to which these beliefs, once taken on board and interwoven as part of himself, profoundly and forever change his relations to the others and what one might call his moral relation to himself) he will ever be able to see them in what we call the same way again; and (4) what it is to now see the world and its inhabitants "through a black veil of misery and remorse and indecision [where the indecision is indeed about which self-constitutive beliefs to hold and which to reject] and fear" – where the object of the fear is precisely the set of consequences of those entertained beliefs once they are hardened into a part of who and what he is, where he realizes that his emotions of self-assessment will follow from these beliefs once settled. Murdoch captures the emotive potency of Arrowby's reflections in an unforgettable description of deep sadness: she has him say "and there was a feeling as if I carried a small leaden coffin in the place of my heart." Arrowby also (5) reflects on the meaning of silences, the very concept of which (let alone the nuanced particularities of) the philosophy of language could well learn from literature. Arrowby says

> We spoke little as we walked and I could see Lizzie looking at me now and then and she was thinking to herself: it is a relief to him to walk with me thus in silence. My presence, my silence is healing him.

Murdoch here has Arrowby inwardly articulating his silent-interlocutor's thoughts on the meaning of their companioned silence, showing that in this case he sees perfectly well what she is thinking.[44] And then adding a further layer of entertained belief (showing that the phenomenology of self-constitutive belief-acquisition does not proceed one item at a time), Murdoch gives us (6) Arrowby reflecting upon the justifiability of the preceding thought, the preceding interpretation of silence (here Arrowby has become a somewhat complex interpreter of another's thought in Davidson's sense above), by adding to the previous the parenthetic reflection "(This last belief was probably justified)," where the meta-reflection implied by the word "probably" indicates its status as a candidate-belief. Arrowby reflects ("I went over and over these things in my mind") upon why he failed to warn Titus, provisionally settling (and thus showing within the fiction that we have in life a stage of intermediate or provisional settling on what and what not to believe where these beliefs are strongly self-determining vis-à-vis who and what we are, and who and what we may or may not then become) on the view that he turned away from prudence in order to preserve reciprocally his sense of Titus and – this is especially important to his estimation of self-blame – Titus's sense of him. (He wanted to show the boy that he was indeed, like the boy himself, "strong and fearless"; warning him would have "spoilt the charm of that moment." Or, if he knew that he was not in this sense strong and fearless, he wanted to preserve the false appearance of this to the boy – which would in this case be all the more morally blameworthy.) Arrowby considers, going over in his mind, the very sentences he might have uttered to voice that suppressed (and what would have been lifesaving) prudence: "It's not that easy to get out" or "I don't think I will swim here"; such sentences, like those of less psychologically mimetic complexity from the *Odyssey* or *Medea* above, have a meaning as they roll into and out of his mind that is not only inflected by (that is to put the point too weakly), but in truth given content by, the circumstances of their contemplation.[45] To understand (again, in the fuller sense of understanding that warrants the term) those words is to understand these circumstances and the psychologically dire condition of the person who entertains them. And like the first level, all of this as well carries over to inform and refine our processes of self-description and self-definition.

The third level of the literary experience it is my purpose in this chapter to characterize is one to which we now return, but now here too with a good deal more of the web (i.e. all of the foregoing discussion) surrounding the sentences that articulate this experience explicitly in place and in view. I said above that when identifying with a literary character we must first – in order for that identification to be psychologically possible – comprehend the context of that character's action, the web of belief (of settled, entertained, and, as Murdoch has shown, half-settled kinds) that makes the real and possible action intelligible. To clarify that (and in review), in so identifying, within this autobiographically engaged mode of literary absorption, we: (1) grasp what it is, and what it means, to perform the actions that evince the action-determining belief held by the character; (2) grasp what it is like to be a character who chooses to act on such a belief in this particular way (*we* might choose very different actions, indirect or secondary actions, or inactions to express those beliefs according to the patterns of action that constitute our character); and (3) see the situation of the character with whom we vicariously identify as a metaphor for our life-circumstances real or possible (knowing "what we would do if . . ." is as important to self-knowledge as knowing "what we did do when . . ." or "what we will do when . . ."). And coming to see what we would do is often a function of resolving (in the very act of reflecting upon such possibilities or Rortyan contingencies that literature affords) what we would do; i.e. the reflection-via-vicarious-identification becomes, through settling a disposition to react in this or that way or according to this or that pattern of reactions, self-constitutive. In most succinct form: reading in this way – given an imaginative scope that yields the kind of genuine understanding described above – in significant part determines the content of selfhood. But if articulating this distinctively reflexive mode of aesthetic experience in these compact terms is just to say it, where in literature is it more fully shown?

At the close of the *Aeneid*,[46] in mortal hand-to-hand combat with his nemesis Turnus, murderer of his most beloved comrade and dear friend Pallas, Aeneas hurls a spear with a force that "like a black whirlwind bringing devastation" "passed clear through/The middle of Turnus' thigh" (401). This blow "Brought the huge man to earth, his knees buckling." With a groan expressing a dire expectation of the worst from his on-looking supporters echoing from all sides, there follows a perfectly turned literary portrayal of (1) a moment of reflection, (2) a near-settlement on a belief, (3) a profound re-minding occasioned by the sudden perception of a meaningful artifact, (4) a correspondingly sudden reversal to the contrary belief, (5) a deep conviction or resolution taken on in the name of another (and yet – or even all the more because of this – one that makes Aeneas who he is), and (6) an irreversible and irreversibly character-defining action that follows as the consequence-in-action of all the preceding reflection. But, tellingly, a precondition for understanding this sequence is to first gain an awareness of the content of the plea uttered by the fallen Turnus with Aeneas's sword at his chest, that (in terms of meaning-determinants) again not only inflects, but substantively contributes to, the sequence's content. Turnus, on his back and wounded beyond continuing to fight, "held his right hand out to make his plea" (402):

> Clearly I earned this, and I ask no quarter.
> Make the most of your good fortune here.
> If you can feel a father's grief – and you, too,
> Had such a father in Anchises – then
> Let me bespeak your mercy for old age
> In Daunus, and return me, or my body,
> Stripped, if you will, of life, to my own kin.
> You have defeated me. The Ausonians
> Have seen me in defeat, spreading my hands.
> Lavinia is your bride. But go no further
> Out of hatred.

Turnus does a great deal with these words: he acknowledges what he has done, what he deserves, and what it would be unjustifiable and dishonorable to ask. He appeals to an element of our common humanity – he entreats Aeneas to remember both any father's grief at the loss of a child and to remember his own father – in this case a thought,

LITERATURE AND THE CONSTITUTION OF PERSONHOOD

an act of remembrance, capable of awakening powerful sentiment. Turnus speaks of the doubled or extended consequence if Aeneas does kill him, and then, once he is deceased, refuses the honorable return of his body. His words make Aeneas mindful of the contingency of his victory on this occasion, reminding him that he could easily have been in Turnus's position here (Turnus's massive strength uncharacteristically failed him in his attempt to hurl a great stone at Aeneas in the preceding passage), that there was no necessity to this outcome. But he acknowledges his defeat, acknowledges the disgrace of having been publicly seen in this defeat, and acknowledges the humiliation of his having non-heroically gestured, while fallen, for mercy. And in exchange for this multiple and layered acknowledgement, the web of associations he has strung powered by the emotive fuel of the reference to a father's, and *his* father's, suffering (i.e. weaving together his acknowledgement with the set of self-constitutive beliefs Aeneas has about his own father), Turnus implores Aeneas to save him the post-mortem indignity of an unreturned corpse and to save his family the added suffering of a burial and mourning denied.

All of this (and, in the fullest sense, the entire book that precedes it) is what gives content to the unforgettable sequence of events we see next:

> Fierce under arms, Aeneas
> Looked to and fro, and towered, and stayed his hand
> Upon the sword hilt.

We see fierceness calmed by reflection: we see a hand stayed, and to look to and fro is both an external and internal description, both literal and metaphorical. Aeneas, towering, looks about him as he pauses in indecision, the emotion of fierce battle now cooling; and one sees him looking to the past and its claims, and then to the future and its possibilities, and then for moderation, for reduced severity – Turnus's words have awakened the reality of that possibility, that future contingency. And it appears that Aeneas, still wavering in indecision but now leaning in favor of Turnus's plea, is settling on a kind of self, resolving to be the kind of self, sensitive to and positively disposed toward such pleas from the vanquished, however despicable their previous deeds:

> Moment by moment now
> What Turnus said began to bring him round
> From indecision.

But at this moment – a moment that shows Aeneas for who he is in his thought, and that resolves who he is in terms of his immediately subsequent action – Aeneas sees the belt of Pallas that Turnus is wearing as a morally grotesque token of that previous murderous victory:

> Then to his glance appeared
> The accurst swordbelt surmounting Turnus' shoulder,
> Shining with its familiar studs – the strap

141

> Young Pallas wore when Turnus wounded him
> And left him dead upon the field; now Turnus
> Bore that enemy token on his shoulder –
> Enemy still.

It is at precisely the instant of this perception (another recognition scene) that Aeneas, now turning swiftly back to the claims of the past and away from even partial conciliation, in a very real sense simultaneously discovers, and yet decides, who and what he is. Because the circumstances, in all their detailed and occasion-specific subtlety, give rise to an experience, a sudden perception, that strongly aligns episodes and human connections from his past and thus delivers a clear and forceful trajectory from the past through the present and into the future, Aeneas both (1) volitionally comes out of indecision into unwavering resolution, and in the act, in doing so, simultaneously also (2) reveals himself to himself, thus discovering, and then as quickly staying true to, who he is, the kind of person, the kind of character, he is. (This is precisely the interaction between self and context that we saw intimated in Said's mention of Sartre's view above.) One can say this is in part volition – he decides. And yet that decision, the moral phenomenology of which is exquisitely captured by Virgil, is determined by character – it is thus not wholly decided, but to an extent discovered, by a most pressing emergent circumstance. It is in fact instructive that the dichotomized language of decision versus discovery, of making up one's mind versus disclosing one's mind, does not sit comfortably in this self-defining field. As a hardened dichotomy-template it has repeatedly been forced upon, but does not naturally emerge from, this region of self-confrontational human experience. Virgil's words show this:

> For when the sight came home to him,
> Aeneas raged at the relic of his anguish
> Worn by this man as trophy. Blazing up
> And terrible in his anger, he called out:
>
> "You in your plunder, torn from one of mine,
> Shall I be robbed of you? This wound will come
> From Pallas: Pallas makes this offering
> And from your criminal blood exacts his due."

"The relic of his anguish, worn by this man as trophy." I believe that the words "this man" should be heard in the tone of a profoundly invidious comparison to Pallas and extreme derision (as though the word "this" points contemptuously): "*this* man." It would be folly to attempt to separate off into distinct categories these words' power from their meaning – and their power comes from all that has come before that shows us the person, Turnus, as described by Aeneas's words. And it is Aeneas, the person as holder of beliefs and as life-and-death-determining actor upon them, who utters them and who gives them their point, indeed their life. Understanding the "web" within which those words function and have their point and power as linguistic actions is, I want to say, to understand the meaning.

Most of us know what it is to be suspended in a state of "crossroads" indecision, what it is to emerge resolute in a future-determining way from that state, what it is to have eyes fall on a relic of our anguish, what it is to evince strong belief in the form of irreversible action. But to know these things is not an all-or-nothing affair, not a matter of *simply* knowing or not knowing, like knowing or not knowing the name of a dog or the temperature outside presently. Humane knowledge is severely miscast in these brutish scientistic terms (scientistic because scientific terms do not, against a false image of directly corresponding brute-fact language or what used to be called observation sentences, function in any such simple way either), and to know what it is like[47] to hold a view (in a suitably particularized context) amounts to much more than knowing the minimal decontextualized content of that belief. (I want to suggest that the very idea of the determinate minimal content of context-independent belief is a philosophical myth, or at the most an extremely reductive term of art – and literature helps us advance to a stage of linguistic sensitivity from which we can, against some sometimes-prevalent methodological presuppositions in the philosophy of language, see that and keep it in focus.)

The first two of the subdivided parts of the third layer of the reader's experience (see p. 126), then, are fairly evident in a reading of Virgil's lines: we (a) see what it *means* to perform those life-and-self-determining actions; and we (b) grasp to an extent what it would be *like* to perform them. But what of (c) seeing the situation or complex circumstances of the character into whose life we imaginatively project as a metaphor for our own lives? Concerning Turnus, the extent to which we identify (and thus possibly gain or confirm self-knowledge from this identification) with him is the extent to which we are able to see his multiple eleventh-hour acknowledgement as sincere: in his last words he at least summons the decency to unambiguously state in a clear-eyed way what he has done and what, by virtue of this late clarity, he recognizes (where the scope of this recognition is calibrated within the ethos of his world, to remind us of the Rortyan elements in play here) he deserves. We as readers may take a lesson from that, resolving to be better, and more clear-eyed (and not at the eleventh hour), about acknowledging our misdeeds. And in seeing the appeal to fatherhood (to the extent we take this as sincere and not manipulative) we see a flash of humanity, and this glimpse may well solidify our resolve to look for the humanity in others we find to be cold, alien, detached, indifferent, or even in the extreme case devoid of a sense of humane presence.[48] So in this fairly straightforward way, once we are positioned to see it, literary-characterological reflection on him doubles as a morally self-constitutive act for us. So we do see in this passage about Turnus, if briefly, the third subdivision of the third layer. The case of Aeneas, however, is more nuanced, and instructively so.

We know what it is to emerge from a conflict with the upper hand, and we know what it is to act impulsively, thoughtlessly, imperiously, unilaterally, single-mindedly, unreflectively, self-aggrandizingly, and so forth. First, in seeing Aeneas *towering*, we see – to articulate some strands of the web surrounding that positioning, that circumstance, or in Sartre's sense, situation – the possibility of all of these types of action. That recognition of possibility – of multiple routes into morally blameworthy acts from this pre-decision moment in time – can itself instill (or re-instill) in us as readers, or remind us of the value of, a laudable moral caution, where such re-minding leads us to greater awareness, and thus to better choices, at just such decision-points of our own. Second, in seeing Aeneas looking to and fro, we as readers are made to recall – we are, while following that unfolding narrative, here as well reminded[49] of – the value of taking stock, of looking around us, of remembering to *actively* look to see just where we are, to try to be (in Henry James's phrase) a person on whom nothing is lost. Third, in witnessing in our reader's imagination the staying of the hand, we are again in this doubled way reminded of deliberation, reflectiveness, the value of taking a moment to let cool the immediately felt impulse to act precipitously, to keep our wits about us. Fourth, in seeing a person brought round from indecision by taking the human measure of an appeal to fatherhood and kinship, we are – within the self-directed part of our imaginative world that parallels the literary narrative – reminded of the need to cultivate and strengthen such forms of responsiveness (and reminded of the virtue of patience and listening[50] upon which such responsiveness depends) in ourselves. All of this is relatively straightforward. But it is in seeing, fifth, the close of the epic story of Aeneas that the reader's relation to the text gets more complicated. After having made his speech for Pallas, and just after the above line "And from your criminal blood exacts his due," we have the final act of the narrative described:

> He sank his blade in fury in Turnus' chest.
> Then all the body slackened in death's chill,
> And with a groan for that indignity
> His spirit fled into the gloom below.

Does this exemplify reflection-borne compassion? Is it to assess and respond to Turnus's vanquished appeal and to respond to the flash of humanity we see shining through the brutal exterior? Is it to expand the mind so that it capaciously encompasses an awareness of his good fortune and the contingency of his victory? Is it to cool impassioned impulses that would motivate and, unchecked, lead to perhaps ultimately undesirable irreversible action?

The picture of moral psychology that Virgil's text paints is not in any clear sense any of these. But it is an act that in an important sense *includes* (given what we have seen in the foregoing passages) all of these: the final act of Aeneas is one of considerable moral complexity, and it reminds us of the fact that moral actions are often of a complex kind with a particularized intricacy that simplifying reductive (i.e. motive-unifying) utilitarian (consequence-identifying) or deontological (duty-identifying) moral systems fail to capture. The moral psychology of Aeneas does, as we see in the foregoing passages, include reflection upon those reductive elements: both consequence-calculation and duty-consideration are in play. But *then*, with that reflection behind him, he moves to a resolute self-definition that here again is both chosen and yet in another sense determined by who and what he is – where who and what he is, and who he is to himself, is then immediately reinforced by the action. This "bootstrapping" process, when seen through our doubled literary experience, reminds us of the Aristotelian[51] character of moral action that, becoming engrained through repetition and through self-defining moments (as I want to discuss Aeneas's final act here) of resolution, makes us who we are. Such occasions, as mimetically represented in Aeneas's act, are like (i.e. have the same structure as) the beliefs that we first entertain and then, after a process of epistemic acquisition of the kind described above, take on as part of us. Aeneas reflects, is aware, is responsive, and is fully alive to where he is, but then in seeing the relic of his anguish, he also sees beyond this that his sense of who he is, interwoven with his sense of who Pallas was, together make one course of action impossible, and the other course of action – for him, within the ethos of his world – necessary. And, in seeing that, we as readers are reminded – made mindful of the self-individuating fact – that there are for us limits: there are things we simply will not abide, and outrages we cannot forgive. To recklessly or whimsically or arbitrarily (in Rorty's overstated and over-generalized sense above) dispense forgiveness would, in the sense that the case of Aeneas portrays with such precision, be to take the "we" out of play, or to diminish, to erode, or in an extreme case of a violation of self-integrity, to begin to eradicate the selves that we are – selves of which we have an abiding sense (which literary experience cultivates) and to which we have an ongoing responsibility (which literary experience occasions).

But before closing this chapter, more still needs to be said, and now with greater specificity, about what I have repeatedly called the "doubling" of the reader's experience, the process by which we make the textual narrative a metaphor for our own lives (the third strand of the third layer of the reader's experience as schematically described above), and the process of aesthetic-to-moral "bootstrapping," i.e. the self-constitutive power of this variety of reading that is at the very least autobiographically informative, and at most, nothing less than self-creative.

Metaphorical Identification and Self-Individuation

Arthur Danto has described the relation between the reader and the literary text as metaphorical in structure, and this proves to be an extraordinarily illuminating way of articulating one part of the distinctive experience I am pursuing throughout this chapter.[52] Danto's position, stated in its most succinct form, is that literature is "about each reader who experiences it."[53] He is quick to set aside the obviously false claim that, for example, the primary subject matter of *Paradise Lost* is the story of the life of the person who reads it. But it is about that reader in the way, as Danto presents it, that Hegel said the work of art

> reveals its purpose as existing *for* the subject, for the spectator, and not on its own account. The spectator is, at it were, in it from the beginning, is counted in with it, and the work exists only for this point, i.e. for the individual apprehending it.[54]

And for Danto, in a way that is uniquely particularized to the individual reader, the literary work nevertheless exhibits a kind of universality:

> The universality of literary reference is only that it is about each individual that reads the text at the moment that individual reads it, and [here we connect explicitly to present

> concerns] it contains an implied indexical: each work is about the "I" that reads the text, identifying himself not with the implied reader for whom the implied narrator writes, but with the actual subject of the text in such a way that each work becomes a metaphor for each reader: perhaps the same metaphor for each.[55]

Part of what makes metaphor an attractive concept to bring in to describe the reader–text parallel relation is precisely that it possesses (Danto does not put it exactly this way) the "doubled" structure described above – it is clearly literally false to say that the *Odyssey* is about reader A rather than about the trials and tribulations of Odysseus; it is clearly false to say that *The Sea, The Sea* is about reader B rather than about the later-life autobiographical reflections and reconsiderations of retired thespian Charles Arrowby; it is clearly false to say that the *Aeneid* is about reader C and not about the inward and outward travails and triumphs of Aeneas. Juliet is not the sun; and yet, in a sense far too important, and far too illuminating to allow any residue of positivism to crush, she is. And in *that* sense, Danto rightly insists, "for each reader I, I is the subject of the story. The work finds its subject only when read."[56] Thus it is in a simple (too simple) sense clearly false to say these things about these texts and the readers A, B, and C, and yet, like the claim about Juliet, in another distinct sense – indeed a sense closely related to the literary cultivation of our sense of self – they are not at all clearly false. As they read of Odysseus, Arrowby, and Aeneas they – with a doubled consciousness, a bi-focal concentration – read of themselves. This way of putting it would suggest (and Danto sees this danger and steers clear of it) that, as the lives, outward and inward, of the protagonists are mimetically depicted in the text, and we as readers clearly are not authorially empowered to change that text (i.e. we can't through an act of will, manifested as a kind of reader-as-writer psycho-kinesis, change the words on the page), then the doubled narrative of our lives, to the extent that the works are in this metaphorically structured way about us, will be fixed in their mimetic content as well. We would, in that case, look into the text and – bi-focally doubled – simultaneously look into ourselves, therein seeing, like the fixed printed words of the text, the fixed representation of ourselves.[57] This, as Danto rightly insists, is too passive a way of picturing the reader's psychology here: the truth, as I also have been suggesting from various avenues of entry (T. S. Eliot, Davidson, Rorty, Goethe, Borges, Murdoch, and Virgil) into the topic throughout this chapter, is far more active – and far more interesting. The content of the reflection in a mirror is wholly fixed by the features of the real object or person that is reflected in it; this is strict mimesis. It is a mirror held up to a *pre-existent* reality. But the reflection we see in literature is – rather strikingly (and this was the point I called "rather unexpected" in the introduction to this chapter) once we stop to think of it – in part of our own making. Juliet is not the sun – and yet she is. We do not have authorial or psycho-kinetic powers over the text – and yet, if in a way we must quite cautiously describe, we do. Danto writes "Because of this immediacy of identification, it is natural to think, as theorists from Hamlet upward have done, of literature as a kind of mirror."[58] But he continues with what is most important for present concerns:

not simply in the sense of rendering up an external reality, but as giving me to myself for each self peering into it, showing each of us something inaccessible without mirrors, namely that each has an external aspect and what that external aspect is. Each work of literature shows in this sense an aspect we would not know was ours without benefit of that mirror: each discovers – in the eighteenth-century meaning of the term – an unguessed dimension of the self. It is a mirror less in passively returning an image than in transforming the self-consciousness of the reader who in virtue of identifying with the image recognizes what he is. Literature is in this sense transfigurative, and in a way which cuts across the distinction between fiction and truth. There are metaphors for every life in Herodotus and Gibbon.[59]

Danto does not here go into just what precisely is that "something inaccessible without mirrors," or what precisely is "the aspect that one would not know is ours" without this kind of experience of literary absorption. (Although the blunt answer "We know it when we see it" would not, as anyone who has gained some self-knowledge through this kind of literary absorption probably implicitly knows, be an entirely bad one.[60]) I want to suggest that such otherwise-inaccessible (or at least otherwise difficult to obtain – Danto may have overstated the case) content of the indexical "I" is the kind of thing described throughout the preceding two sections of this chapter: it is, through vicarious identification, coming to see ourselves as one contingent self realized from a matrix of other, web-interrelated possible selves, where we ever more finely chisel (and in this sense we are co-authors of the text) the portrayals of ourselves along with, or in subtle contrast to, the other side of our doubled concentration, the protagonist with whom we experience the immediate identification of which Danto writes. We see here again that we gain knowledge not only of who and what we are in a passive sense (although the simpler side of the experience, where we recognize telling similarities to the protagonist, will work in this fairly simple way), but as a function of the active process, the self-constitutive process of thinking through (as we saw in – or actually parallel to or bi-focally with – the case of Aeneas's final choice above) the "what-we-would-do-when" questions that take as many particularized formulations as there are imaginary literary worlds. And again (going back to the Davidsonian element in play here), we understand the words that describe those scenarios just to the extent that we – in the fuller and deeper sense of the word "understand" employed above – understand the webs of belief, and the possible and actual action and interaction upon those beliefs, that give those words sense. An unguessed dimension of the self becomes through this process a known one, but in ways where, like Aeneas, we nevertheless volitionally make up our minds in a self-constitutive way that makes us who we are. It is indeed, as Danto describes it, a process that transforms the self-consciousness of the reader. A metaphor, as we have seen briefly, cuts with a fine epistemological disregard[61] across the distinction between truth and falsity, as does (as Danto also puts it) this kind of transfigurative literature. The occasion for this reflexive contemplation, the fiction, is (in a narrow or strict sense) false by definition. But the other half of the doubled experience, where we gain self-knowledge often by making constitutive self-resolutions, much like the claim about Juliet, is not.

But there is still another dimension, also deserving of fuller elucidation, concerning the image of ourselves that we create and then identify with (Danto's words were "who in virtue of identifying with the image recognizes what he is"). Much has been written about the problem of moral improvement through fiction.[62] The appeal to metaphor offers a fairly concise way (a way that does not run afoul of the many difficulties that beset conceptions of literary didacticism[63]) of schematically picturing this process (where the details of the literary case are then positioned into the schematic). If, as Danto suggests, we are active, self-transforming agents in making the portrayal (through something like the intricate comparative and then self-determining process I have described in the preceding sections of this chapter, where again a certain circumstantially limited flexibility of self, of possible and actual belief, and of possible and actual self-description comes into play), then there is no reason why we would not be able, in being reminded of particular aspects of our selfhood and possible selfhood, to cast those aspects in higher relief in our self-picture. And this would accentuate the characteristics we, in our ideal (or closer-to-ideal) realizations of ourselves, want exemplified in us as persons. Like Aristotle, who in the course of his aesthetic thinking said that an artist can portray us better, as, or worse than we in fact are, so, as "co-authors" of the reflexive side of our doubled attention, we as readers could (parallel to the work of the literary authors considered in the previous sections) arrive at a finely chiseled (i.e. exactingly described) self-image. This, it is true, would in part reflect only what we want to become, not what we are (although such an image serving as an internal regulative ideal toward which we aspire is no small moral matter). And indeed, if the image we sculpt is far removed from the cold truth about the subject of the portrayal, i.e. us, then this process could, it would seem, become an instrument for self-deception. But then recall what we saw in the doubled reading of Aeneas's moral psychology above. To the extent that we take on, and resolve to hold, characteristics that are us at our best (e.g. most attentive, most sympathetically imaginative, most generous-minded, most kind, most mindful of the material or psychological constraints under which others we might too-easily criticize have acted, most aware of subtlety in human affairs, most discerning of motives behind appearances, most sensitive to what can for a particular person mobilize insecurities, etc.) in precisely the way we saw entertained beliefs become held beliefs and thus become part of who and what we are, we can self-constitutively resolve to be that person (or to a fuller extent approximate that person). And thus, as Danto expresses it, we can indeed transfigure ourselves through the experience of literature.[64] Or, to re-employ Davidson's phrase, we enact through this absorbed literary reading a layered auto-dialogical process where we grow into the ability – with all the serious linguistic understanding upon which this depends – to "redescribe certain events [in this case the events of our lives that are selected as episodes in a life-narrative] in a revealing way."

Still, the characterization of this process as a kind of inward dialogical *negotiation* can seem counterintuitive, and before concluding we should pause to reflect on the reasons for this. In initially coming to the subject of autobiographical reflection we may well expect an extremely simple dichotomy to keep in order, or in a sense undergird, all of the rest of the proceedings. We might expect that there are statements concerning how things are in the world external to my mind (these would on this simple scheme be classified objective descriptions) and those concerning how things are within my mind, independent of the world (these would, by contrast, be classified subjective descriptions). And in a manner corresponding to a simplified picture or model of the mind that is complicit with this oversimplifying dichotomy, we might intuitively believe that any question of the first world-describing type can always be judged *against* an external measure of veracity, i.e. how the world actually is. For such statements, we too-easily think (and, given the richness and complexity of both outward and inward descriptive life, this in truth is an appalling oversimplification), skepticism is always, indeed ineliminably at home, because even our greatest degree of felt certitude ("Obviously the earth is flat"; "Obviously we will never travel to the moon") is and will remain open to falsification or correction. And a place, so we think, for skepticism is reserved even in cases of presently verified simple assertions ("I am now standing on a sandy beach gazing at the surf") by maneuvers such as Descartes's dream argument. It appears, given these too-simple reflections and the undergirding upon which they stand, that self-descriptive, or internally reflexive statements are invariably closed to skepticism; this is really nothing more than the classic picture of privileged access to our own mental contents applied to self-descriptive sentences. Our knowledge that Jones is gullible requires that we make a distinction between what is the case and what Jones believes (and the kind of thing he is habitually willing to believe); no such wedge can, we think too quickly on this model, be driven in the first-person case, because the contents therein described are immediately given to the self-describer. This is not the place to pursue this matter at length,[65] but it perhaps is the place to say that this picture, this conceptual model, illicitly presumes from the outset that the function of autobiographical language is essentially and invariably mimetic; i.e. it provides a representation after and apart from the inward facts of the first-person case. The power of Danto's point, following Hegel's, is to redirect us away from this embedded presumption, and in his remarks we can begin to see the active power of self-descriptive language in shaping, giving content to, again no less than *constituting*, the reality it allegedly describes. To express the point in a formula, one might say: Such language is in truth more self-defining than self-describing. Or (cautiously): more self-creative than self-reflective.

One of the evident great gifts of literature to humane self-understanding is that it can provide the exacting language within which questions concerning selfhood are asked, where the articulation of such questions generates in turn the language in which the self-constitutive answers are given. What this chapter has offered is one way of articulating the special place where beliefs about the self (understood through reference to Davidson, Rorty, and now Danto as well) co-mingle with that self and thus provide – forming a kind of virtuous circle, or functioning in a way that is virtuously a self-fulfilling prophecy – the referential content of the indexical that that self-descriptive belief is about. To take one final (misleadingly simple) case of this – autobiographical writing is full of far more extensive and intricate cases – asking a question voiced in tandem with the travails of a protagonist concerning our own courage and then, upon reflection, answering it positively through reflection upon a set of possible-contingency "What if . . . ?" questions can itself, in subsequent cases where courage is called for, make us more courageous. Thus (1) the state of courageousness is not invariably there prior to this self-negotiating process; (2) the language we use to discuss that courageousness is not invariably secondary to it, not invariably mimetic; and (3) our self-understanding concerning it will be made available in, and not (as we are inclined to think of it in accordance with the over-simple dichotomy between the objective and the subjective fields described above that shapes our preliminary intuitions against the active process of self-negotiation) prior to and separable from, language.

Now, it might be argued (if the embedded misleading presumptions concerning fundamental objectivity and subjectivity considered above are especially difficult to dislodge) that the distinctive self-creative reader's process that I have been pursuing throughout this chapter is, however matters may appear when all the foregoing considerations concerning self, belief, and self-determining resolution are brought together, not *genuinely* self-constitutive; resolutions of this self-reflective kind yielding reflexive belief are made – and, here is the argument – broken all the time, and anyone with a sufficient grasp of the distinctively human side of human nature knows that. Thus the self-believer may take on any reflexive belief he or she likes; this will not (returning to the threat of self-deception mentioned above) be a reliable guide to the truth about the settled or abiding content of that person, nor will such a belief serve as a criterion for what it is or will be true to say of that person. First, I would say that this fails to sufficiently acknowledge the considerable extent to which, as covered above, our belief-constellations actually do make us who we are (e.g. the person who is *proud* to be the kind of person who would never believe in the holocaust). The person who makes this objection is simply not looking at a sufficiently broad and detailed range of cases. Beliefs about the self undeniably are (once we clear away the blinding over-simple categories and dislodge the simplified conceptual pictures that put them in place) in many cases constitutive of that self. But there is more to say to the anti-constitutive argument than this blunt – if factually forceful – head-on repudiation. It is possible that we resolve and re-resolve frequently, but never succeed in avoiding the revocation of the resolution, never get the chosen action or group of actions repeated, or performed in such a way that it hardens into an Aristotelian character trait. On this topic Richard Moran has made some particularly helpful remarks. Moran writes that this line of argument about this kind of self-reflector

> suggests that his reflection on his best reasons for belief or reasons for action still leaves it an open question what he will actually end up believing or doing. This is not a stable position one can occupy and continue to conceive of oneself as a practical and theoretical deliberator. One must see one's deliberation as the *expression and development* of one's belief and will, not as an activity one pursues in the *hope* that it will have some influence on one's eventual belief and will. Were it generally the case (for Sartre's gambler, say) [who upon considered reflection seriously resolves to stop going to the gaming tables] that the conclusion of his deliberation about what to think about something left it still open for him what he does in fact now think about it, it would be quite unclear what he takes himself to be *doing* in deliberating. It would be unclear what reason was left to *call* it deliberation if its conclusion did not count as his making up his mind; or as we sometimes say, if it didn't count as his coming to know his mind about the matter.[66]

Another way to put this galvanizing point would be say that, if the self-reflecting gambler proceeds as he does, then this is in fact not a case of considered and serious reflection leading to a self-constitutive resolution, not genuine deliberation *of the kind in question*. It is not such a case because that quite flatly is not, in their intertwining and indeterminate webs of significance, implication, and connotation, what the words "self-constitutive resolution" and words like them mean. And with this observation concerning how we use the words like "deliberation" and perhaps "resolution" in place, we can now put it very briefly: the skeptics can argue that a given case of belief-settling resolution may be disguised irresolution and so not truly self-constitutive, and one can reply that yes, there can be such cases – but those are then cases we might group together under the heading of *akrasia* or weakness of will, or, if differently described psychologically, indeed under the heading of self-deception. But they are, by virtue of the hardly small matter of the usage of our words, not the cases we are presently talking about. As one would thus expect, *they* – by contrast with the real cases they superficially resemble – are not instructive vis-à-vis our self-creative engagement with literature: they undermine nothing of relevance here. Questions concerning self-deception and the construction of a false self-image will arise in very specific, and very particular, circumstances: a *general* skepticism concerning self-constitutive self-deception is not at home here.

The picture of mental privacy, of the hermetically sealed Cartesian mind, suggests unmediated non-inferential access to our inner world – where that world would have its fixed stability and determinate content prior to our describing it. Thus it would, by virtue of this hermetic priority, have a metaphysically ensured immunity to the power of language. But the actual inner world, the one we inhabit as absorbed readers, is as we have seen in this chapter not at all like that. The reader's inner world does not conform to that metaphysical picture, and we should neither wittingly nor unwittingly force our understanding of personally engaged reading to conform to that false model (just as Ryle taught us not to unreflectively presume that the inner world must be modeled upon the outer[67]). Nor, I am suggesting, should our conception of autobiographical or self-descriptive language be modeled upon a too-easily-adapted picture of world-to-language correspondence, or of invariably mimetic, *ex post facto* language. The interwoven and possibility engendering webs of belief of the kind we discussed with Davidson, the kind of moderate, realistic, or non-overstated (i.e. limited by the Sartrean "situation") contingency of selfhood we discussed with Rorty, and the kind of self-transfiguring metaphorical relation between text and self we discussed with Danto, are anything but out of place in our articulation of the reader's role as a special kind of textually doubling co-author of a self-image. In fact, what we might call our stance toward ourselves when engaged to this self-constitutive degree in literary experience is deeply reminiscent of Hegel's remark about our stance toward art more generally: we come to it and find, in a distinctive reflexive way that shows its dependence on the mind of the beholder, that we are and were already there.

T. S. Eliot painted the competing pictures of on the one hand the fixity of the referent of the first-person pronoun and on the other the Heraclitean fluidity of the "I". We, as Eliot's travelers in literary worlds, as imaginative readers, do not, as he said, really escape from the past into different lives, but nor are we exactly the same people who left the station. The truth of the matter, as we saw Eliot intimate, escapes this oversimple dichotomy – and his literary words now resonate with both greater volume and greater extension in their philosophical significance. Earlier in that poem, Eliot wrote "You must go through the way in which you are not" (29), a line now for us linked to Danto's remarks about the literal falsity of the instructive metaphor. And Eliot wrote, in a way now interwoven with the subtle comparative and belief-acquiring process of doubled attention through which we define ourselves, "And where you are is where you are not" (29): we are not these protagonists, and yet we are. Our situations are not theirs – and yet, in a way I have tried to help articulate throughout this chapter, they are. But most importantly in connection with present purposes, Eliot wrote that words "reach into the silence" (19) – for us, the transformational process through which a self's words reach into what, in the language-game[68] of selfhood (one that is founded on spatial metaphors) we call its own interior. And they are words that do so with a self-constitutive power that immediately falsifies any conception of literature as mere diversion or escape; in truth, they give voice to what was, and may otherwise have remained, inarticulate, and they have the power to help create what we can too-easily believe they merely describe. Of such words, Eliot wrote that they "will not stay in place,/Will not stay still" (19). For reasons we have seen, for the profoundly transfigurative service such words can perform when in motion or when in the serious aesthetic play of reflexive negotiation, we should not want them to. "I" is central among them.

Notes

1 T. S. Eliot, *Four Quartets* (San Diego: Harcourt Brace Jovanovich, 1988), 140.
2 I discuss the competing pictures of the closed versus the open past (and the sense in which the past can intelligibly be thought to be open) in *Describing Ourselves: Wittgenstein and Autobiographical Consciousness* (Oxford: Clarendon Press, 2008), chapter 6, §3, "Iris Murdoch, the 'Unfrozen Past,' and Seeing in a New Light," 202–22. The subject of the attempt to escape the past wholly, followed by the discovery that this is impossible within the confines of self-identity, has been a frequent literary theme. Lydia Davis explores this within the fictional setting of a short-term affair and its complex (and instructively inescapable) aftermath in her novel *The End of the Story* (New York: Farrar, Straus, Giroux, 1995); Julian Barnes examines the gradual mental erosion of a person increasingly obsessed with another's past in the setting of an historian discovering unsettling facts about his new lover (and his increasingly ruinous search for clues about that past in their present) in his novel *Before She Met Me* (London: Jonathan Cape, 1982). The titles themselves are telling.
3 Donald Davidson, "Thought and Talk," in *Inquiries into Truth and Interpretation* (Oxford: Clarendon Press, 1984), 155–70. For a particularly helpful discussion of Davidson in connection with the issues that follow, see Samuel C. Wheeler III, "Language and Literature," in Kirk Ludwig, ed., *Donald Davidson* (Cambridge: Cambridge University Press, 2003), 183–206.
4 I have examined the deep and powerful misleading force this linguistic picture exerts on our thinking about artistic meaning in *Art as Language: Wittgenstein, Meaning, and Aesthetic Theory* (Ithaca, NY: Cornell University Press, 1995), passim.

5 This presumption became entrenched as a given fact of the human condition, and thus as a kind of methodological axiom, in the structuralist and semiotic traditions, and appears in differing manifestations in the writings of Saussure, Barthes, Lacan, and many others. And Sartre's autobiography, after all, is titled *The Words*, trans. Bernard Frechtman (New York: George Braziller, 1964). Sartre provides a useful illustration of the distinction I will discuss in what follows in this chapter between a superficial acquaintance with a familiar string of words and a deeper and fuller understanding of their content as used by a particular person in a particular context for a particular purpose or intertwined set of purposes. Sartre writes "I reread the last pages of *Madame Bovary* twenty times and ended by knowing whole paragraphs by heart without understanding any more about the poor widower's behavior."

6 I treat what I call here this irreducible complexity much more fully in *Describing Ourselves: Wittgenstein and Autobiographical Consciousness*: chapter 3, "The Self Speaking," 76–118; chapter 6, "The Uniqueness of Person-Perception," 185–222; and the third section of chapter 7, "On Philosophy as Therapy: Wittgenstein, Cavell, and Autobiographical Writing," 240–57.

7 See W. V. O. Quine, *The Web of Belief* (New York: Random House, 1970).

8 For a morally insightful discussion of a real case of such denial and its self-defining power, see Raimond Gaita, *A Common Humanity: Thinking about Love and Truth and Justice* (London: Routledge, 2000), 157ff.

9 I offer a discussion of how such retrospective meaning-determinations are made, and how such changes are possible, in *Describing Ourselves*, chapter 5, "The Question of True Self-Interpretation," particularly §1, "Meaning in Retrospect," 154–84, especially 154–62.

10 Arthur C. Danto, in "Philosophy as/and/of Literature," in *The Philosophical Disenfranchisement of Art* (New York: Columbia University Press, 1986), 135–61, has pointed out some extremely promising directions on this point, directions to which I will return in the final section of this chapter. Danto's essay is reprinted in this volume (chapter 4, PHILOSOPHY AS/AND/OF LITERATURE).

11 I pursue one non-dualistically-entrenched way of characterizing such cases of self-investigative resistance and self-deception in *Describing Ourselves*, chapter 3, §3, "Real Introspection (and Kierkegaard's Seducer)," 97–118.

12 Richard Rorty, *Contingency, Irony, and Solidarity* (Cambridge: Cambridge University Press, 1989), chapter 2, "The Contingency of Selfhood," 23–43.

13 Richard Rorty, *Philosophy and the Mirror of Nature* (Princeton, NJ: Princeton University Press, 1979), passim.

14 Friedrich Nietzsche, *Twilight of the Idols*, trans. R. J. Hollingdale (Harmondsworth: Penguin, 1990 [1889]).

15 *Twilight of the Idols*, "The Problem of Socrates," 39–44. My following remarks concern also the section "How the 'Real World' at last Became a Myth," 50–51.

16 For helpful discussions of Rorty on the presuppositions of traditional epistemology, see Gary Gutting, "Rorty's Critique of Epistemology," in Charles Guignon and David R. Hiley, eds., *Richard Rorty* (Cambridge: Cambridge University Press, 2003), 41–60, and Michael Williams, "Rorty on Knowledge and Truth," in the same collection, 61–80.

17 For an exemplary awareness of the all-important subtleties of the descriptions of actions (and the significance of those very subtleties for the dismantling of overarching general questions concerning action-description), see Frank B. Ebersole, "The Analysis of Human Actions," in his *Language and Perception: Essays in the Philosophy of Language* (Washington, DC: University Press of America, 1979), 199–222.

18 I am alluding here to the methodological insight that has come to be known as "Ramsey's Maxim"; I discuss this, particularly in connection with self-constitutive literary experience, in "Imagined Identities: Autobiography at One Remove," *New Literary History* 38:1 (Winter 2007): 163–81.
19 I discuss this range of life-defining possibilities in *Describing Ourselves*, chapter 5, "The Question of True Self-Interpretation," 154–84.
20 For an insightful discussion of the powerful role metaphor plays in human understanding, see Ted Cohen, *Thinking of Others: On the Talent for Metaphor* (Princeton, NJ: Princeton University Press, 2008), and his essay in this volume, of particular relevance here (see chapter 27, AT PLAY IN THE FIELDS OF METAPHOR).
21 For a most acute discussion of the sense of rightness and its (too often underappreciated) role in our interpretative and creative practices, see Michael Krausz, *Rightness and Reasons: Interpretation in Cultural Practices* (Ithaca, NY: Cornell University Press, 1993). I pursue the topic of rightness as Krausz has demarcated it in "Rightness Reconsidered: Krausz, Wittgenstein, and the Question of Interpretive Understanding," in A. Deciu and G. L. Pandit, eds., *Interpretation and Ontology: Studies in the Philosophy of Michael Krausz* (Amsterdam: Rodopi, 2003), 25–37.
22 This is the process described, but in relation to the relational conception of selfhood adumbrated in American pragmatism, in my "Imagined Identities: Autobiography at One Remove," cited in note 18 above.
23 Johann Wolfgang von Goethe, in *From My Life: Poetry and Truth*, trans. Robert R. Heitner, ed. Thomas P. Saine and Jeffrey L. Sammons (Princeton, NJ: Princeton University Press, 1994), 424.
24 The topic of Wittgenstein on privacy and private language is one with a long and much-debated history; for a recent discussion of the terrain see Stephen Mulhall, *Wittgenstein's Private Language* (Oxford: Oxford University Press, 2006). I offer a brief discussion of the impact the notion of private language can have on our thinking in aesthetics in *Art as Language*, chapter 6, "The Silence of Aesthetic Solipsism," 118–35.
25 It is in this connection revealing that even a figure we might think of as private to the point of being near-solipsistic, i.e. Werther (in Goethe, *The Sorrows of Young Werther*), as he describes his interior world in his letters, nevertheless and indeed necessarily describes that interior world publicly, or in what we might call "public" language. In fact, Goethe writes,

> The letters of Werther ... probably owe their manifold appeal to the fact that their various contents were first rehearsed in imaginary dialogues with several individuals, whereas in the composition itself they seem to be directed to only *one* friend and sympathizer. (Goethe, *From My Life*, 425)

To put it one way, the kind of deep privacy that we understand Werther to exemplify actually depends for its intelligibility on Goethe's public, dialogical imagination, just as our understanding of the words Werther uses to express himself in his letters are words we understand as tools for use in a larger public or relationally intertwined dialogical forum.
26 Goethe, previously in this autobiographical writing (*From My Life*), describes the process through which he himself becomes increasingly able to imagine himself, and then become, in this sense, a different person. It comes through his first imagining, then contemplating, and then finally resolving, in a self-constitutive way, to oppose his father's plans for him:

> Now I really began to regard it as legitimate self-defense to resolve on the adoption of my own way of life and study, against his will and sentiments. My father's obstinacy in unknowingly opposing my plans encouraged me in my impiety, and it did not hurt my conscience to listen to him for hours while he told and retold me about the course of life and study I would have to pursue at the university and in the world. (Ibid., 185)

This, in short, is a dialogical (in this case contra-paternal) process of self-redefinition via resolution.

27 I offer a fuller discussion of some ways in which our understanding of the words we use to describe privacy is situated within a public context in *Describing Ourselves*, chapter 1, §3, "Real Privacy (and Hidden Content)," 33–43.

28 Jorge Luis Borges, *The Book of Sand*, trans. Norman Thomas di Giovanni (New York: Dutton, 1977), 117–22. In connection with present issues it is worth having a look at his early essay, "The Nothingness of Personality," in Jorge Luis Borges, *Selected Non-Fictions*, ed. Eliot Weinberger (New York: Viking, 1999), 3–9. He begins a number of paragraphs, each developing a separate line of thought, with the sentence "There is no whole self." It is fitting to the theme of this chapter that the words Borges uses concerning the problems of selfhood can be much more fully understood by considering the biographical setting in which he wrote that essay; see Edwin Williamson, *Borges: A Life* (New York Viking, 2004), 98ff. For an interesting contrast, one that agrees with the centrality to human life of the question of the possibility and nature of "whole selfhood" but that gives it a different answer, see Milan Kundera, *Identity*, trans. Linda Asher (New York: HarperCollins, 1998). See especially p. 45:

> He reminded me of what I must have said when I was sixteen. When he did that, I understood the sole meaning of friendship as it's practiced today. Friendship is indispensable to man for the proper function of his memory. Remembering our past, carrying it with us always, may be the necessary requirement for maintaining, as they say, the wholeness of the self. To ensure that the self doesn't shrink, to see that it holds on to its volume.

29 This reconfiguration of experience as its relational meshing changes is, to my mind, helpfully understood in connection with the non-atomistic conception of experience articulated in American pragmatism and the writings of William James on perception; I offer a discussion of this in Hagberg, "Imagined Identities."

30 Indeed see, in this connection, Borges's own words closing the afterword he wrote for the collection in which this story appears: "I hope that these hasty notes I have just dictated do not exhaust this book and that its dreams go on branching out in the hospitable imagination of those who now close it" (Borges, *The Book of Sand*, 125).

31 Cartographic and architectural metaphors are used very frequently in our language-games of self-description; I examine some of these, and the life-structuring frameworks they offer, in "The Thinker and the Draughtsman: Architecture and Philosophy as 'Work on Oneself,'" in Clare Carlisle, ed., *Philosophy as Therapeia*, Royal Institute of Philosophy supplementary volume (forthcoming, 2009).

32 This is precisely the sense of the openness of the past of which Iris Murdoch wrote; see note 2 above.

33 Rorty, *Contingency, Irony, and Solidarity*, 42.

34 Ibid., 42–3.

35 We are initially inclined to think of such relations in too-simple terms as invariably and wholly either discovered or created; I discuss this misleading dichotomy in *Describing Ourselves*, chapter 5, §2, "The Pain and the Piano," 163–75.

36 I offer this, it should be noted, as a rough schematic of one kind of aesthetic experience; I would welcome what could initially seem counterexamples that would in fact further reveal the complexity, and the intricacy, of these mind–text relations.
37 Edward W. Said, *Representations of the Intellectual* (New York: Random House, 1994), 74.
38 I refer here to the picture of sensory experience put forward in Locke's *Essay Concerning Human Understanding* and subsequent writings on perception in that tradition. One might briefly characterize that as a kind of perceptual "snapshot" model, where each of the five sensory modalities continually takes in its atomistically isolated blocks of experience. The distortions brought in by this picture become especially visible when brought up against the intricacies of our perceptions of persons. I offer a discussion that attempts to diagnose, and then counter, this trend in *Describing Ourselves*, chapter 6, "The Uniqueness of Person-Perception," 185–222.
39 Euripides, *The Medea*, trans. Rex Warner, in David Grene and Richard Lattimore, eds., *The Complete Greek Tragedies, Euripides I* (Chicago, IL: University of Chicago Press, 1955), 55–108.
40 Aeschylus, *Oresteia*, trans. Richard Lattimore, in David Grene and Richard Lattimore, eds., *The Complete Greek Tragedies, Aeschylus I* (Chicago, IL: University of Chicago Press, 1955), 33–171.
41 Dante Alighieri, *The Divine Comedy*, trans. Charles S. Singleton (Princeton: Princeton University Press, 1970). Ugolino is placed in the ninth circle of hell in quite inventive morally retributive circumstances; *Inferno*, cantos 32 and 33, 339–59.
42 George Eliot, *Middlemarch* (New York: New American Library, 1964).
43 Iris Murdoch, *The Sea, The Sea* (Harmondsworth: Penguin, 1978), 400–03.
44 For a helpful discussion of our knowing another's thoughts (against the misleading picture of hermetic or unbridgeable mental enclosure), see Ray Monk's essay in this volume (chapter 24, GETTING INSIDE HEISENBERG'S HEAD). See also in this connection Frank Kermode's discussion of *Middlemarch* in his afterword to that volume, specifically seeing the novel as (as Eliot herself puts it) a project of discovering "how ideas lie in minds other than my own" (p. 814 of the New American Library, 1964, edition).
45 For helpful discussions of the determination of what is often called (although this is in fact an interestingly dangerous metaphor) propositional content by precisely this kind of context-embeddedness, see Charles Travis, *Occasion-Sensitivity: Selected Essays* (Oxford: Oxford University Press, 2008).
46 Virgil, *The Aeneid*, trans. Robert Fitzgerald (New York: Random House, 1983).
47 I allude here to the fine and directly related anti-reductionist essay of Thomas Nagel's, "What is it Like to Be a Bat?" *Philosophical Review* 83 (1974): 435–50.
48 The close study of the morally grotesque absence of such a sense shows us, I believe, a good deal about what its presence amounts to; I examine such a case in "Leporello's Question: *Don Giovanni* as a Tragedy of the Unexamined Life," *Philosophy and Literature* 29:1 (April 2005): 180–99.
49 I mean "reminded" in a broadly Wittgensteinian sense here, that is, the reorienting experience of being reawakened to sets or networks of connotations that connect the case before us to other cases previously known but until now forgotten or overlooked, and that thus bring out features of the case before us that were, prior to this recontextualization in memory, obscured.
50 What this suggests – rightly, I believe – is that listening is a far more important matter than has been generally acknowledged in moral philosophy. I describe what I take to be an exemplary case of such listening within artistic creativity and as it mimetically reflects moral

engagement in "Jazz Improvisation and Ethical Interaction: A Sketch of the Connections," in Garry L. Hagberg, ed., *Art and Ethical Criticism* (Oxford: Blackwell, 2008), 259–85.

51 Aristotle, *Nicomachean Ethics*, in Jonathan Barnes, ed., *The Complete Works of Aristotle* (Princeton: Princeton University Press, 1984).

52 Arthur C. Danto, "Philosophy and/as/of Literature," cited in note 10 above. See also his illuminating interview "Why We Need Fiction: An Interview with Arthur C. Danto," *The Henry James Review* 18:3 (Fall 1997): 213–16. Although this is not the place to pursue the matter, it is worth noting that there are informative parallels between the self-reflective and self-finding process Danto is describing in literature and the painting of a self-portrait. For an insightful discussion, see Jodi Cranston, *The Poetics of Portraiture in the Italian Renaissance* (Cambridge: Cambridge University Press, 2000); see especially p. 98:

> A category of portraiture explicitly devoted to representing oneself, self-portraits claim to present the "I," the maker, through the circumstances of their making. . . . The process and the product contribute toward presenting some aspect of the artist's self, that part beyond the physical, with the act of painting constituting and generating as much of the artist's self as the completed representation.

53 Danto, "Philosophy as/and/of Literature," in *The Philosophical Disenfranchisement of Art*, 154. Also in this volume, chapter 4, PHILOSOPHY AS/AND/OF LITERATURE, 63.

54 Hegel, *Werke*, 15:28; translated as *Aesthetics: Lectures on Fine Art*, trans. T. M. Knox (Oxford: Oxford University Press, 1975), p. 806.

55 Danto, "Philosophy as/and/of Literature," in *The Philosophical Disenfranchisement of Art*, 155. Also in this volume, chapter 4, PHILOSOPHY AS/AND/OF LITERATURE, 64.

56 Ibid.

57 The metaphorical picture of the self as a text, one that we look into and read pre-written content that is fixed prior to the act of reading, is one that has been presumed as unproblematically helpful by many. I suggest otherwise in "Wittgenstein's Voice: Reading, Self-Understanding, and the Genre of *Philosophical Investigations*," *Poetics Today* 28:3 (Fall 2007): 499–526.

58 Danto, "Philosophy as/and/of Literature," in *The Philosophical Disenfranchisement of Art*, 156. Also in this volume, chapter 4, PHILOSOPHY AS/AND/OF LITERATURE, 64.

59 Ibid.

60 The experienced idiosyncratic content of the moment of self-recognition as the criterion for, or definition of, such experience need not be viciously circular in the way it may to a superficial glance seem; there is much discussion of the "ah-ha" experience in psychoanalysis that casts light on this phenomenon, and these experiences can, in some cases, assume the authority of a legitimation or confirmation. Yet they are by no means intrinsically verifying: the criteria for their credibility will emerge in the expanded contexts where the words in which such experiences are expressed have their life. This particular issue is examined in a literary setting in James Joyce, *A Portrait of the Artist as a Young Man* (New York: Viking, 1972). See, for example, the problem as it is illustrated on p. 153:

> A restless feeling of guilt would always be present with him: he would confess and repent and be absolved, confess and repent again and be absolved again, fruitlessly. Perhaps that first hasty confession wrung from him by the fear of hell had not been good? Perhaps, concerned only for his imminent doom, he had not had sincere sorrow for his sin? But the surest sign that his confession had been good and that he had had sincere sorrow for his sin was, he knew, the amendment of his life. – I have amended my life, have I not? he asked himself.

The answer to this last question will take form within the expanded context of his life and working out, and through, the ramifications of the self-directed belief, and not by consulting exclusively what we call the inner experience.

61 I perhaps should say that my allusion here to Kirk Varnedoe's *A Fine Disregard: What Makes Modern Art Modern* (New York: Abrams, 1990) is I think apt. In both cases (i.e. in artistic creation and self-description – Varnedoe of course discusses the artistic side of the comparison implied by the allusion) the full awareness of the rules being broken in the act of breaking them opens the way into further creative work that would otherwise have remained beyond the bounds of the possible.

62 For a helpful orientation see Noel Carroll, "Art, Narrative, and Moral Understanding," in Jerrold Levinson, ed., *Aesthetics and Ethics: Essays at the Intersection* (Cambridge: Cambridge University Press, 1998), 126–60.

63 See, for a particularly discerning discussion, Joshua Landy, "A Nation of Madame Bovarys: On the Possibility and Desirability of Moral Improvement through Fiction," in Hagberg, *Art and Ethical Criticism*, 63–94.

64 See in this connection Iris Murdoch's journal entry: "Man is a creature who makes pictures of himself, and then comes to resemble the picture," quoted in Peter J. Conradi, *Iris Murdoch: A Life* (New York: W. W. Norton, 2001), 272.

65 I offer a fuller discussion in *Describing Ourselves*, chapter 5, "The Question of True Self-Interpretation," 154–84.

66 Richard Moran, "Self-Knowledge: Discovery, Resolution, and Undoing," in Brie Gertler, ed., *Privileged Access: Philosophical Accounts of Self-Knowledge* (Aldershot: Ashgate, 2003), 173.

67 Gilbert Ryle, *The Concept of Mind* (New York: Barnes and Noble, 1949).

68 The concept of a language-game as it is developed, and variously used, in Wittgenstein's philosophy is not, despite the frequently unexplained use of the term, transparent; I examine Wittgenstein's uses of the term and its significance for aesthetics in *Meaning and Interpretation: Wittgenstein, Henry James, and Literary Knowledge* (Ithaca: Cornell University Press, 1994), chapter 1, "Language-Games and Artistic Styles," 9–44.

Part III

Philosophy, Tragedy, and Literary Form

9

Tragedy and Philosophy

ANTHONY J. CASCARDI

In a famous passage of the *Republic*, Plato refers to an "ancient quarrel" between literature and philosophy. More specifically, it is epic poetry and its close relative, tragedy, that concerns Plato, and tragedy because it is perceived as posing a threat to the integrity of the polis. If Plato's critique of tragedy is embedded in a theory of politics, this is because tragedy is itself political, although not necessarily in the ways that have often been imagined. To say this is hardly to deny that tragedy's implications go well beyond any narrow definition of politics, or that Plato's *Republic* deals with matters that bear on nearly every aspect of philosophy. At least one important line of interpretation argues that philosophy's response to tragedy turns on questions of ethical and existential concern. Indeed, philosophy may help rule out the fear, uncertainty, and vulnerability to accident and misfortune on which tragedy seems to insist.

Such things affect individual human lives as well as the life of the polis. Plato himself seems to argue for a form of self-sufficiency, one that is consistent with the Enlightenment's later interest in autonomy. "The good man's life," Plato says in *Republic* 3, is "the most complete in itself and the least dependent on others."[1] Justice itself, Plato says, is concerned "with a man's inward self," which ought to comprise "a single controlled and orderly whole." The just individual will be insulated against any great emotional upheavals and unexpected changes in fortune and so will be "ready for action of any kind, whether personal, financial, political or commercial" (*Republic*, 443, pp. 196–7). So too with the state. Parts of the *Republic* are conceived as an extended analogy in which character and polis serve as figures for one another. Constructing a stable platform for the soul helps insure a stable platform for the state, and vice versa, such that, in Plato's words "there will be no difference between a just man and a just city" (*Republic*, 435, p. 185).

The best-known features of Plato's critique of tragedy can all be understood in relation to this schematic theory of soul and state. They are consistent with what Plato believed was at work in the tragedies that preceded him, though not necessarily with what I would argue is central to the genre, or with what lies at stake in tragedy's political import. Thanks nonetheless to Plato's enormous influence, his vision of tragedy

---

A Companion to the Philosophy of Literature, First Edition. Edited by Garry L. Hagberg and Walter Jost.
© 2010 John Wiley & Sons Ltd. Published 2015 by John Wiley & Sons, Ltd.

became a central part of subsequent philosophical engagements with it, including for philosophers and critics who would oppose Plato on some fundamental points. The relatively recent work of Bernard Williams in *Shame and Necessity* and, more emphatically, Martha Nussbaum in *The Fragility of Goodness*, are good examples of this.[2] The central elements of the Platonic critique to which they are responding are both thematic and formal: some have to do with the plots and characters of ancient tragedies, while others have to do with the nature of tragedy as a form of dramatic poetry, as representation or "imitation." They comprise four elements, and since most of these are familiar I simply note them here so as to be able to address what this picture leaves out.

The first element of the critique concerns *poiēsis* as the production of inferior or degraded artifacts that are distanced from the truth of ideas, which by contrast are stable and eternal; tragedy is a form of mimesis and is faulty because it proliferates unreliable and untruthful entities. Second, and related to this, mimesis in tragic drama falters because it involves what early modern writers called "personation." Tragedy is dangerous (as all drama is) because in it characters speak in the voice of others and not as themselves (*Republic*, 398, p. 137). The third of Plato's objections to tragedy involves the way in which it presents the gods. Because tragedy shows the gods as having imperfections, as involved in sometimes irreconcilable disputes, and as the source of unhappiness and injustice, Plato argues that it ought to be rejected.[3] For Plato, the true and just thing is to affirm that the gods insure the possibility of perfection and underwrite the good: without them – without the "metaphysical comfort" they provide – there could be no possibility of human happiness. The fourth component of Plato's objection to tragedy involves the passions that tragedy arouses, which encourage an unstable disposition and cultivate "unmanly" responses. (One wonders what Plato might have thought about the defiance of Antigone.) Tragedy indulges our vulnerability to forces beyond our control. In Plato's ideal state poetry would be bereft of pitiful laments; the fear-inspiring names of underworld places would be erased, or changed to more euphemistic ones; even the laughter that comedy provokes would be silenced. Moreover, the suffering that comes with tragic grief, which cultivates a "womanish" character, would be suppressed; if and when it arises, it would be borne by the virtuous man in stoic silence.[4]

I am interested in the alignment of all the points just mentioned with the larger goals of the *Republic*, an alignment that works, in fact, toward a synthesis of justice and happiness. Indeed, there is in Plato's view something terribly wrong about the very premises that spark tragic grief, for it seems that the tragic poets would have us believe that just human beings may be unhappy even while those who are unjust can live in bliss. In Nussbaum's plausible account in *The Fragility of Goodness*, Plato aims to immunize the individual and the state against the kinds of turmoil and injustice to which tragedy exposes us, and hopes to set in place a framework for ethics that will avoid both inner and outer forms of strife. Plato's *Republic* is a "theory" in this respect: it presents an idea of the individual and the state which, while not guaranteeing goodness or virtue, nonetheless imagines them as co-conditions of happiness and the state. "Perhaps," he says, this state is laid up as a pattern in heaven, where those who wish can see it and found it in their own hearts. But it doesn't matter whether it exists or ever will exist; it's the only state in whose politics [the intelligent man] can take part. (*Republic*, 592, p. 369)

Philosophers beginning immediately after Plato, with Aristotle, have responded to some of the shortcomings of Plato's views on tragedy. Nussbaum's own recent work has helped articulate a stance that shifts emphasis from Plato's conception of the good toward the more sympathetic view of the virtues of tragedy developed in the *Poetics* and, along with it, toward the more flexible vision of practical reasoning elaborated in Aristotle's *Nicomachean Ethics*. While I concur with Nussbaum that Plato's view of character and polis fall especially short when measured against the insights that tragedy can provide, my agreement with her ends roughly where my reservations about Aristotle begin. Her aesthetic defense of tragedy as a source of ethical insight rests largely on the belief that tragedy, unlike philosophy, gives us "complex characters" and tells "whole stories" about vulnerable individuals.[5] If this is true it would seem better said of the novel than of tragedy.[6] To claim in addition to this that tragedy shows human life as beautiful *because* it is vulnerable seems, moreover, to place an aestheticized and romantic "overlayment" on top of what is a very un-romantic genre. Characters like Oedipus or Philoctetes, to take but two examples, hardly strike us as beautiful, least of all in their suffering. There is horror in Oedipus' fate, and the wound from which Philoctetes' suffers is irreducibly stinking and ugly. Something has gone awry, I would suggest, in the ethical aestheticizing of tragic pity and fear.

These differences of opinion about tragedy reflect a series of doubts about whether Plato's and Aristotle's philosophical "responses" to tragedy in fact reflect a genuine hearing and seeing of it, or whether they are, rather, avoidances of it. Indeed, I would suggest that these views preclude a reading of tragedy as responding to philosophy and likewise that they tend to obscure the fact that philosophy's counter-tragic impulse is rooted in the methodological commitments philosophy makes. The counter-tragic impulse of philosophy is embedded in the very procedures and presuppositions endemic to its self-understanding, which in turn have implications in the political and ethical domains. Indeed, Plato's methodological commitments are at least as deep as his ethical and political ones, though in a work like the *Republic* they may be somewhat concealed. This counter-tragic impulse becomes especially salient when viewed against the backdrop of a play like *Oedipus Tyrannus*, for the method of Socratic dialogue and the procedures of open inquiry to which Plato is committed are opposed in a nearly systematic way to what we see in Sophocles' play.

First, Plato's conception of philosophy is inextricable from a particular *way of speaking*. The principle (or at least the pretense) of the dialogues is that of free and open speech, in which the participants can attend to the stimulating and difficult questions that Socrates typically poses and in which they are unconstrained in their response. To say "unconstrained" means that the interlocutors consent to be led wherever the pursuit of the truth along any given line of questioning may take them. Notwithstanding the sometimes rather forceful "leading" that Socrates engages in, the idea is that the powers of articulation and utterance, of criticism, agreement, objection, insight, and judgment, are to be vested in the interlocutors themselves and in their capacity to recognize the truth. The prior condition for this procedure is an agreement among the participants in the dialogues to free themselves from all pre-determining utterances. It is not inconsistent with Plato's more general interest in un-encumbering the interlocutors in the dialogues. In this vein Heidegger, for instance, notes that the turn away from the world of appearances is not just a conclusion of Plato's dialectic but a procedural means by which the interlocutors in the dialogues can unfetter themselves from substantive knowledge: "dialectic runs best when unencumbered by substantive knowledge."[7] As for language, the premise of the dialogues is that there is no *prior* form of speech that ought to constrain whatever responses the interlocutors might give.

We can appreciate the degree to which Plato's *Republic* is a counter-tragic text if we focus on the question of speech in *Oedipus Tyrannus*. Sophocles' play hinges in part on what might be called the "conditions of enunciation," which is to say, on the fundamental constraints that govern all language: in this case, the fact that any given utterance is dependent upon prior enunciations, and that the very possibility of speech itself depends upon what has already been said.[8] Indeed, one of the chief insights of *Oedipus Tyrannus* has do with the force of an oracular utterance that exists *prior* to all inner-worldly forms of speech. Within these circumstances are set the various speech-acts of the play, including the acts by which speech is forced from various interlocutors – as Oedipus tries to force Tiresias to speak the truth, for instance, and later as he forces the herdsman to render up whatever he might know about his origins. "If you do not talk to gratify me, you will talk with pain to urge you," he says to the old shepherd; "here, one of you, twist his hands behind him"[9] (cf. Oedipus to Tiresias: "You would provoke a stone [to anger]! Tell us, you villain, tell us, and do not sit there unmoved and balking at the issue," 5.335–7). In spite of these forceful, even violent, articulations of authority, none of the speech-acts within the play is able to be effected from a standpoint as powerful or encompassing as that which is claimed by the prior speech of the oracle. This includes the speech-acts that are crucial to the founding and governing of a state: commanding, promising, ordering, establishing laws, making decrees, pursuing inquests, punishing criminals, and the like. *Oedipus Tyrannus* reveals itself as a political play in the more or less ordinary sense from the very start, where Oedipus the Tyrant (or "King" – both terms are inadequate) is confronted with what seems to be a practical matter: how to bring an end to the plague afflicting Thebes. But Sophocles' interest in politics ultimately revolves around the tragically structured conflict between the force of an utterance (a law) that precedes all inner-worldly speech and the institutionally grounded utterances through which a legislator attempts to bring health and order to the polis.

Plato's attempt to avoid such potentially tragic circumstances is rooted in a commitment that underlies the dialogues both conceptually and methodologically: the principle of unconstrained speech. As a matter of political theory, free speech is intrinsic to the operations of the dialectic, which can be characterized as the comprehensive "science of free men."[10] To be sure, the dialectic implies quite a bit more than this principle suggests. In Plato's words, the dialectic is "the only activity whose method is to challenge its own assumptions so that it may rest firmly on first principles" (*Republic*,

533, p. 302). Dialectic rests on a commitment to the critical self-questioning of a free mind as well as on what Plato describes as the ability "to give an account of the essential nature of each particular thing" (*Republic*, 533, pp. 302–3). The dialectic requires, in other words, that the interlocutors say not only freely and openly but also *specifically and positively* what any particular thing *is*. The principal conceptual instruments for this task are *diarēsis*, or the separation of kinds according to their likenesses and differences, and definition, which involves delimiting the scope over which particular concepts hold sway. Both of these instruments have implications that are deeply counter-tragic.

In the *Sophist*, *diarēsis* is characterized (oddly, it first seems) as a method of hunting; incidentally, it is not unlike Oedipus' hunt for the murderer of Laius in Sophocles' play. (And recall in this regard that in the *Republic*, book 4, the characters say that they are searching for justice like hunters going after quarry.) But if we look at the *Sophist*, it is clear that *diarēsis* is a very special variety of hunting, one that proceeds by sorting and separating. For Plato it involves the division and collection of beings according to kinds. The word itself is part of a family that means "to cleave," "to take apart," and "to split." As Heidegger commented in his lectures from 1924–5, the process of *diarēsis* is linked to dichotomization, cutting, and dissecting.[11] *Diarēsis* serves as a method of purification, notably one less bloody than the ritual purification associated with the elimination of the criminal from the midst of the city in *Oedipus Tyrannus*.[12] It performs tragedy's work of eliminating confusion and contamination, but by "clean," intellectual means. At stake in this process of intellectual purification is the identity of the true philosopher, which is established by clarifying the difference between the philosopher and the sophist. Since these two – philosopher and sophist – so closely resemble one another, this process necessarily involves distinguishing like from like, or, perhaps more accurately, establishing difference where there is an *appearance* of likeness.

It is nonetheless difficult to predict the success of this attempt to eliminate the confusing conflation of identities. We have a method and no guarantees. This may be one of philosophy's concessions to tragedy. Moreover, it could be said of Plato's writings *überhaupt* that nowhere does he offer a non-metaphorical account of *diarēsis* as the *essential* method of philosophy.[13] And *this* might well be one of philosophy's concessions to literature at large were it not for the fact that *diarēsis* and dialectic are linked with the more "positive" ambitions of definition: not merely to distinguish one thing as a function of its difference from another, or to eliminate false semblances, but to say concretely and positively what a *thing essentially is*.

> You agree that dialectic ability can only be acquired after the course of study we have described, and in no other way? . . . And it can't be denied that it's the only activity which systematically sets out the definition of the essential nature of things. Of other activities some are concerned with human opinions or desires, or with growing or making things and looking after them. . . . Dialectic, in fact, is the only activity to challenge its own assumptions so that it may rest firmly on first principles. . . . So you agree in calling the ability to give an account of the essential nature of each particular thing Dialectic; and in saying

that anyone who is unable to give such an account of things either to himself or to other people has to that extent failed to understand them. (*Republic*, 533, pp. 302–3)

A long and involved philosophical dispute has evolved around the question of whether in saying these things Plato pursues a form of "fundamental ontology" that is anything like the modern conception of that term. Suffice it to say that Plato's interest in definition was considerably expanded by Aristotle, and that it was, not surprisingly, a strategy of Aristotle's *Poetics* to deal with the complex question of tragedy by the procedure of definition. (In fact, Stephen Booth has cogently argued that the pursuit over the centuries of a definition of tragedy has been more assiduously undertaken than any other non-religious quests for definition – being outranked in all categories only by the quest for a definition of God![14]) The point is that the effort to define, and in Aristotle's case to define *tragedy*, is one of the principal means by which the *Poetics* is able to *contain* the terrible insights that tragedy presents. Recall that the centerpiece of the *Poetics* is in fact a definition, one that Aristotle repeats, once in chapter 6 and again in chapter 7. I quote the second of these passages because it elaborates on the components of action as Aristotle understands it:

> Tragedy is an imitation of an action that is complete, whole, and of a certain magnitude. ... A whole is that which has a beginning, a middle and an end. A beginning is that which does not itself follow anything by causal necessity, but after which something naturally is or comes to be. An end, on the contrary, is that which itself naturally follows some other thing, either by necessity, or as a rule, but has nothing following it. A middle is that which follows something as some other thing follows it.[15]

If, however, one in fact looks at dramatic tragedies, including the tragedy that Aristotle himself chooses to exemplify the genre, *Oedipus Tyrannus*, it turns out that things are hardly so neat and well-defined. Indeed, it seems that in tragedy there is no category that will stay firmly fixed around any object, at least not for long.[16] Whereas definition for Aristotle is closely bound up with the clear and unequivocal assignation of predicates to subjects – and even a cursory glance at his work, the *Categories*, suggests that it is – there is a crossing of categories that affects (one wants to say "afflicts") *Oedipus Tyrannus*. That is, Oedipus is both king and criminal; he is both son of and husband to Jocasta; he is the one entrusted to save Thebes and the source of the pollution in the city. Oedipus is the one who issues the command to seek out the murderer of Laius and also the object of that search. He is both the speaker and the addressee of his own utterances. Moreover, the plot in *Oedipus Tyrannus* turns on certain "grammatical" questions that can hardly be answered in the way that Aristotelian logic would lead us to desire, if not expect. For example, the question "Who is the murderer of Laius?" understood by Oedipus as a question asked about a third person, some "he" or a "she," turns out to be answerable only in and by the *first* person, not the *third*. The answer redounds to the one asking the question and can only be phrased in the form of a grammatical contradiction: "he is I," or "I am he." Oedipus' identity is revealed only as a function of a question that seems to be about *something or someone else*. Thus, for Oedipus to say that "I am the murderer of Laius" means effectively just what Iago says in act I of Shakespeare's *Othello* – namely "I am not what I am" (*Othello*, 1.1.64).[17] Moreover, it turns out that in *Oedipus Tyrannus* the question of self-knowledge on which philosophy insists is accessible only in indirect terms, as the pursuit of a question about someone or something else and moreover, that comes too late. Before the action of the play itself, Oedipus had famously solved the riddle of the Sphinx, which presents itself as an encrypted definition of man. But to identify and define Oedipus as "the murderer of Laius" misses the point that Oedipus does not fully coincide with the definition of himself until he able to *recognize* who he is; a true identification of Oedipus would have to account for this widening scope of awareness, and of the tragic implications that follow from it.

As if to deny these very things – not to mention the horror of their consequences – the pursuit of definition in its positive, direct, and simply "assertive" forms is the means by which two of the fundamental principles of Aristotle's *Metaphysics* bear on his theory of tragedy: by saying *what* tragedy is ("the imitation of an action . . ."), and by defining its central component, action, as an integrated whole. The principles I am referring to are the law of the excluded middle and the rule of non-contradiction. Recall that the rule of non-contradiction has it that opposing statements cannot be true at the same time and in the same respect, that contradictories cannot both at the same time be said of a given thing. Likewise, the law of the excluded middle requires that it is necessary either to affirm or deny in asserting one thing about another, that we cannot stand, as it were, *between* affirming and denying.[18] These are Aristotle's "logical" transpositions of the still more fundamental metaphysical assertion of the priority of being over non-being.

Stephen Booth's work on definition mentioned above presents a host of examples of the ways in which Shakespearean tragedy – *Macbeth* and *King Lear* in particular – relentlessly resists definition, confounding and confusing categories in such a way as to render the very notion of a "clear and distinct concept" untenable. The work of definition, which derives both lexically and conceptually from the notion of end (*finis*) implies placing limits. What Booth doesn't explain is the degree to which the counter-Aristotelian strategies of *Macbeth* and *Lear* in fact continue the work of *Oedipus Tyrannus* – in confusing fair and foul, for instance, or in the sustained ambiguity that, in *Macbeth*, surrounds the witches themselves: whether they are natural or supernatural, and if they are natural are they are male or female – all of which is further complicated by the theatrical conditions of Shakespeare's stage. As Booth notes, the actors that Shakespeare's audience saw play the parts of the witches were indisputably male, but what of the bearded women those actors play?[19] ("You should be women, / And yet your beards forbid me to interpret / That you are so," 1.3.45–7).

One might well object that a work like Aristotle's *Categories* can handle the problem of definition in (and of) tragedy perfectly well, and that Oedipus can be "defined" as the King of Thebes who has also murdered Laius, as the ruler who is also the source of the miasma afflicting Thebes, as both son of and husband to Jocasta, and so on. But no degree of definition will be able to portray the tragic consequences these contradictions have – tragic for Oedipus. That is, it will not adequately define him as a tragic subject. Nor will it explain the terrible irony of the fact that, while Oedipus has solved the riddle of the Sphinx and attempts to find out everything he can about the murder of Laius, he makes no inquiry into the oddness of his own name. As Jonathan Lear remarked, "Suppose your name were Abandoned Smith. Would you be able to get through life treating your name as just a name, without a serious wonder whether it had descriptive import for you?"[20]

One might likewise argue that Aristotle's account of "peripety," as elaborated in the *Poetics*, is perfectly able to explain the fact that Oedipus suffers because he experiences a "reversal of fortune." But the theory of peripety is bound to Aristotle's notion of action, and in Sophocles' play the principal change of fortune has to do not with action but with what Oedipus comes to realize about what he has *already* done. Aristotle's conception of the form of tragic action as bounded, integral, and, in his words, "complete," is designed to place bounds around connected events, to delimit them as a relational whole (the parts of which – beginning, middle, end – are defined strictly in terms of one another). This concept of action allows for the analysis of tragedy as a well-contained form, but tragedies themselves tend to present actions that are messy and unbounded, that spill over their limits. In *Oedipus Tyrannus* scarcely anything happens that is contained within the bounds of the play. The crucial action, the murder of Laius, takes place before the play begins, and the consequences of the events we see reach well beyond the borders of this play to affect Oedipus' children (especially the daughters, less clearly the sons). The dramatized events are situated very much in the middle of some other action; the play occurs both before and after the fact, one might say. Indeed, there is an overarching story, a *mythos* about Oedipus that is widely known and in circulation, so that the dramatic action itself has very much the character of a twice-told tale.

Likewise, one might cite the references to Lady Macbeth's mysteriously missing children and the allusion to a time ominously, unknowably, and yet undeniably before the "beginning" in the case of Shakespeare's play.[21] Doubling and repetition pervade tragedy and help further explain why tragedy was a literary thorn in Plato's philosophical side. Aristotle, by contrast, explained mimesis by naturalizing and instrumentalizing it:

> The instinct of imitation is implanted in man from childhood, one difference between him and other animals being that he is the most imitative of living creatures, and through imitation learns his earliest lessons. (*Poetics*, 6, p. 55)

The problem of the copy, which greatly worried Plato, was of relatively little concern to Aristotle, at least in aesthetic and dramatic terms. Moreover, the *Poetics* theorized how it is that the emotions tragedy leaves uncompensated, which tend to provoke the greatest suffering among the characters on stage, can be marshaled to productive ends for the audience: the work of tragic drama is affective and theatrical, and theatre is for Aristotle a place where something worthwhile can be made of suffering, a place where the powerful emotions of pity and fear can be summoned up and purified of their harmful effects. For the tragic hero or heroine, however, suffering is literally "to no end."

Antigone is, of course, a continuation of the messiness begun in *Oedipus* in spite of the fact that it pre-dates *Oedipus Tyrannus*. The play opens with a reminder of the suffering that Oedipus' daughters will have to bear. Dramatically, however, this play is quite different. The action of *Antigone* turns on a deed that is minimally performed: it is a mater of just the handful of dirt that Antigone throws over the body of her dead brother Polynices. The deed is important enough, nonetheless, for Antigone to reinforce and repeat it when it is undone, and likewise for her to make a public proclamation of it. When Ismene urges her not to speak of the act to anyone and to bury Polynices in secret, Antigone replies "Oh, no! Shout it out. I will hate you still worse / for silence – should you not proclaim it / to everyone."[22] The public assertion that follows her action, her "yes, *I did this*," is set starkly against the force of Creon's injunction, his official "thou shalt not."

The first point that Sophocles makes through Antigone involves the irreducible fact that action involves something external, that it implies some material change, however minimal, in the world. It would not be enough for Antigone simply to mourn her brother in silence. Something must be done. Moreover, action, *human* action, implies responsibility. It is integral to Antigone's act that she also accept responsibility for it.[23] Hegel cites *Antigone* in the translation by Hölderlin that had been published just a few years before the *Phenomenology of Spirit*: " 'Because we suffer we acknowledge we have erred' " (par. 470). Moreover, Antigone's action is unlike Oedipus' in that it follows from a choice made deliberately and directly, in light of Creon's prohibition, and not in ignorance or by mistake. Hegel is again insightful in pointing out that, in a figure like Antigone,

> the ethical consciousness is more complete, its guilt more inexcusable, [since] it knows *beforehand* the law and the power which it opposes, it takes them to be violence and wrong, to be ethical merely by accident, and, like Antigone, knowingly commits the crime. (Par. 470)

For Hegel, this form of commitment and choosing epitomize the "ethical order." "The ethical consciousness . . . knows what it has to do, and has indeed already decided whether to belong to the divine or the human law" (par. 465).

And yet there is tragic conflict, which Hegel hopes to see resolved in his further account of the ethical order. The conflict stems from the fact that a resolute decision acknowledges only one law and excludes or opposes others. *Characters* are established through their adherence to a given law, and these oppose one another as do the *dramatis personae* of a tragic drama:

> the ethical order essentially consists in this immediate firmness of decision, and for that reason there is for consciousness essentially only one law, while, on the other hand, the ethical powers are real and effective in the *self*-consciousness, these powers acquire the significance of excluding and opposing one another. . . . The ethical consciousness, because it is *decisively* for one of the two powers, is essentially character. (Par. 466)

The central tragic conflict that is played out through the characters has its roots in the irreconcilability of two spheres of value, and it pits two forms of obligation and their associated spheres – family, state; divine law, human legislation – against one another:

> If both powers are taken according to their specific content and its individualization, we are presented with the picture of the conflict between them in their individual forms. . . . On the side of content, it is the clash between divine and human law. (Par. 473)

And yet for Hegel these tragic conditions provide the ingredients for reconciliation within the ethical order. He acknowledges that "we do indeed see [the ethical realm] divide itself into two essences and their reality," but he goes on to say that

> their antithesis is rather the authentication of one through the other, and where they come into direct contact with each other as real opposites, their middle term and common element is their immediate inter-penetration. (Par. 463)

I will explain below how Hegel envisions this reconciliation through the "inter-penetration" of elements. But first I would note that, if we consider *Antigone* more closely, what we see is not so much a struggle between two sets of laws, or between two conflicting sets of claims (family, state), but a tragedy that revolves around a political question, namely Creon's attempt to extend the laws of the polis in such a way that they apply *universally*. One could of course understand Creon's efforts as the marks of hubris and pride, but "hubris" here indicates an attempt to reach too widely and to equate the polis with the whole, rather than an attempt to attempt reach too "high." *Antigone* is a tragedy that is rooted in the temptation to take the polis not as an *image* of the whole but as the whole *itself*.

Antigone's commitments bring this to light. Were it not for her, there would be every reason to think that the polis is indeed the whole.[24] And already in Plato it might seem as though the polis is not just *figured by* the soul or a figure *for* it, but that it is encompassing and integrated, that it *is* indeed the, *whole*. (If it is, then the crucial question is how we might gain knowledge of the whole.) But in the political context that Hegel was addressing, which he saw presaged in Creon's rule, the polis has a more specific set of connotations and historical references; it refers to an order in which the commands of government have "a universal, public meaning open to the light of day." Antigone's duty to her brother would seem to stand outside of it. Indeed, Hegel characterizes the force of her obligations to the dead as deriving from "the darkness of the nether regions" (par. 466). It may well be that the weakness of Antigone's position stems from the fact that, in contrast to the power and authority of publicly manifest law, it has only what Hegel calls "the bloodless shade to help it in actually carrying out *its* law" (par. 474). Therefore it succumbs to "the powerful law of the upper world, for the power of the former is effective in the underworld, not on earth" (par. 474).

What, more specifically, must be given up in order for the state to fashion itself as a totality, with laws that pretend to apply to one and all alike? The answer for Hegel is clear. The "*living* spirits" perish in a community whose "simple universality" seems soulless and dead:

> The *universal* unity into which the living immediate unity of individuality and substance withdraws is the soulless community which has ceased to be the substance ... of individuals, and in which they now have the value of selves and substances.... The universal being is thus split up into a mere multiplicity of individuals, this lifeless Spirit is an equality, in which all count the same, i.e. as *persons*. What in the world of the ethical order was called the hidden divine law has in fact emerged from its inward state into actuality; in the former state the individual was actual, and counted merely as such, merely as a blood-relation of the family. As *this* particular individual, he was the departed spirit devoid of a self; now, however, he has emerged from his unreal existence. (Par. 477)

With this, Hegel leads us out of tragedy and into the realm where persons have what he calls "legal status." Here, the possibility of tragedy is denied by the equality of individuals; tragedy is likewise averted by the transformation of ethical "characters," who deeply adhere to well-defined values, into legal "persons," who are to be treated as identical under the law. With this *political* institution of the principle of identity – call it the "regime" of identity – tragedy is defeated. And yet even Hegel recognizes that there is a price to pay for this, insofar as the legal order produces a community bereft of life and soul; the universal state is, furthermore, unstable for reasons intrinsic to its formation. This publicly manifest, "official" form of Spirit has not completely severed its ties to the "nether world" that it had hoped to exclude. The problem is that the dead remain with us, while there is no longer any effective form, once tragedy is overcome, by which to honor their claims. Plato objects to plays that encourage us to weep for the dead, but Hegel warns that the dead in turn find "instruments of vengeance" through "*other communities whose altars the dogs or birds defiled with the corpse; [the corpse] ... remains above ground in the realm of outer reality*" (par. 474).

Tragedy, for its part, tries to make a place for the dead among the living, and not only for the work of revenge, by denying the impulse to divide the states of human being categorically between "living" and "dead." I think of three particular instances where Shakespeare's characters seem as if to oscillate between these two states. The first is in *Romeo and Juliet*, and helps make the point that some of what tragedy knows was learned from comedy. At the end of the play, Juliet drinks a potion given to her by an apothecary and falls into a death-like sleep. This sleeping appearance of death is enough to drive Romeo to take his own life. Whereupon Juliet awakes and dies again, this time for "real," (or for as "real" as the conventions of drama, which keep "real" death from happening in any final way, will allow). The second instance is in *Othello*, where Desdemona seems to die not once but twice. First, Othello smothers her but she seems, in his words, "Not dead? Not quite dead?" (5.2.86). She then appears to lie as "still as the grave" (5.2.95). But Desdemona is in fact not yet dead, or if she is she comes to life again just long enough to give Othello an alibi and say that it was not he who killed her. Whereupon she dies (dies again?) and Othello brands her as "a liar gone to burning hell" (5.2.130). The final instance is from *King Lear*. The example is, again, from the end of a play that seems not to want to end. Cordelia appears as dead, and Lear is carrying her in his arms, as if to suggest the image of an inverted *pietà*: instead of a mother bearing her son we see a dead or dying daughter in her father's arms. And although Cordelia may be dead, the power of Lear's wishing it otherwise is so strong that she is imagined by him as brought back to life:

> I know when one is dead, and when one lives;
> She's dead as earth. Lend me a looking glass;
> If that her breath will mist or stain the stone,
> Why, then she lives. . . .
> This feather stirs; she lives! If it be so,
> It is a chance which does redeem all sorrows
> That ever I have felt. (5.2.259–65)[25]

We should not miss the degree to which all of these examples draw out the powerful ambiguity that is frozen in Antigone's fate, which is to be entombed alive. But what to say about this ambiguity in light of philosophy's hope, that the difference between the living and the dead could be settled as if it were a matter of definition? Insofar as philosophy seeks to overcome tragedy, or to deny it, to refuse its preconditions and to guard against its outcomes, it will always be faced with the problem of the unmourned. It will be at a loss about what to do about the dead. But this suggests that tragedy ought to be regarded as an *indispensable* element in the construction of the state, and that excluding tragedy (and, by extension, poetry too) in the interests of sustaining a polis that is integral and whole, in fact produces a deficient idea of the state, one that is, furthermore, liable to forget just what it has lost in the course of imagining itself as invulnerably whole.

Notes

1. Plato, *Republic*, trans. H. D. P. Lee (Harmondsworth: Penguin, 1955), 387, p. 124. Numerals here and parenthetically refer first to the standard citation of Plato's texts and, second, to page numbers in the Lee edition.
2. Bernard Williams, *Shame and Necessity* (Berkeley, CA: University of California Press, 1993); Martha Nussbaum, *The Fragility of Goodness* (Cambridge: Cambridge University Press, 1986).
3. See, for example, *Republic*, 380, p. 118.
4. See *Republic*, 387 (p. 124) and 605 (p. 383).
5. See Nussbaum, *Fragility*, 13.
6. Not surprisingly, Nussbaum takes this tack in *Love's Knowledge* (New York: Oxford University Press, 1990).
7. See Heidegger *Plato's "Sophist,"* trans. Richard Rojcewicz and André Schuwer (Bloomington, IN: Indiana University Press, 1997), 137.
8. What appears to be the condition of "free speech," and the possibility of speaking freely on the part of the (tragic) subject, is rather a function of what Althusser calls "interpellation." See "Ideology and Ideological State Apparatuses," in *Lenin and Philosophy and Other Essays*, trans. Ben Brewster (London: NLB, 1971). Oedipus fails, or learns too late, to recognize the truth of the fact that he is his linguistic interpellation.
9. Sophocles, *Oedipus the King*, trans. David Grene (Chicago, IL: University of Chicago Press, 1991), 5.1152–4.

10 Plato, *Sophist*, trans. Seth Benardette (Chicago, IL: University of Chicago Press, 1984), 253c. See also Stanley Rosen, *Plato's Sophist* (New Haven, CT: Yale University Press, 1983), 258.
11 Heidegger, *Plato's "Sophist,"* 196–7.
12 Plato, *Sophist*, 226d-e.
13 Rosen, *Plato's "Sophist,"* 261; see Plato, *Republic*, 507a and 533a.
14 Stephen Booth, *"King Lear," "Macbeth," Indefinition and Tragedy* (New Haven, CT: Yale University Press, 1983).
15 Aristotle, *Poetics*, trans. S. H. Butcher, ed. Francis Fergusson (New York: Hill and Wang), 65.
16 See Booth, *"King Lear," "Macbeth,"* 96.
17 Shakespeare, *Othello*, ed. Russ McDonald (Harmondsworth: Penguin Putnam, 2001).
18 Aristotle, *Metaphysics*, trans. Richard Hope (Ann Arbor, MI: University of Michigan Press, 1952), Book Gamma, 7 (1011b–1012a) and Book Gamma, 6 (1011a–1011b).
19 Booth, *"King Lear," "Macbeth,"* 101–2.
20 Jonathan Lear, *Open Minded* (Cambridge, MA: Harvard University Press, 1998), 49. He goes on to say:

> And when Oedipus, as a young man on the run, arrives in Thebes, he is remarkably incurious about the missing king. . . . Does it make sense that Oedipus should be asking this question about twenty years after the event? (49)

21 Booth, *"King Lear," "Macbeth,"* 94.
22 Sophocles, *Antigone*, trans. David Grene (Chicago, IL: University of Chicago Press, 1991), 5.86.
23 Hegel is especially accurate in his account of these things when he says that an action, when complete, alters the consciousness of the agent, that the act in completion turns its powers back on the agent and transforms his or her consciousness: it "completely alters the point of view [of the ethical consciousness]." In the case of wrongs done, the ethical consciousness is forced, on account of its deed, to acknowledge that something which would seem to be antithetical to its nature is in fact part of it. In his view, "the ethical consciousness must, on account of this actuality and on account of its deed, acknowledge its opposite as its own actuality, must acknowledge its guilt" (*Phenomenology of Spirit*, trans. A. V. Miller, Oxford: Oxford University Press, 1977, paragraph 470).
24 In our own times we tend to believe this, at least insofar as politics and the economy, and increasingly the media as well, seem to leave no other space. Here I am put in mind of an essay by Stanley Cavell: "Politics as Opposed to What?" *Critical Inquiry* 9:1 (1982): 157–78.
25 Shakespeare, *King Lear*, ed. Kenneth Muir (London: Methuen, 1975).

10

Iago's Elenchus: Shakespeare, *Othello*, and the Platonic Inheritance

M. W. ROWE

Several writers have sensed philosophical issues in *Othello* (1604),[1] and wished to locate it within a discussion of epistemological scepticism.[2] In this essay, however, my focus is both more particular and more general: more particular because I want to concentrate on act 3, scene 3 (which I shall call the "temptation scene");[3] more general because I want to argue that the philosophical issues are grounded less in the content of the scene than in its dramatic form, and that the scene is at once an enactment, parody, and critique of the elenctic method. This is the technique used in Plato's early dialogues, where Socrates tries to gain wisdom by cross-examining interlocutors who claim to have knowledge. In the first part of the essay, therefore, I consider the case for thinking that Shakespeare was influenced by Plato and Socrates in the years prior to 1604. In the second, I show how the temptation scene assimilates and transmutes the dramatic motivation of the dialogues Shakespeare had been reading.

Platonic Influences on Shakespeare's Pre-1604 Work

The first line of the inscription on Shakespeare's Stratford monument reads: "Iudicio Pylium, Genio Socratem, Arte Maronem" (In judgment a Nestor, in genius a Socrates, in art a Virgil). The monument was in place by 1623, seven years after Shakespeare's death, and the inscription was probably written by his son-in-law, Dr John Hall. Clearly the figures mentioned in the inscription are primarily designed to illustrate the magnitude of Shakespeare's achievement, but it would be fitting and natural for Hall to choose exemplary men who meant a good deal to his father-in-law. This is borne out when we turn to Shakespeare's works, and discover that Nestor and the works of Virgil (in which Nestor also appears) play a consistently prominent role in them. Accordingly, it comes as something of a surprise to discover that Shakespeare's works contain no direct mention of Plato and only one of Socrates. The latter occurs in an early play, *The Taming of the Shrew* (c.1592), and is more concerned with Socrates' wife than Socrates himself: Petruchio, outlining the characteristics he seeks in a spouse, says he does not care if she is "as curst and shrewd / As Socrates' Xanthippe, or a worse . . ."

A Companion to the Philosophy of Literature, First Edition. Edited by Garry L. Hagberg and Walter Jost.
© 2010 John Wiley & Sons Ltd. Published 2015 by John Wiley & Sons, Ltd.

(1.2.69–70).⁴ This cannot refer to Plato. Xanthippe is mentioned briefly in the *Phaedo*, but her behavior in this dialogue is far from "curst and shrewd" (60a, 116a–b), and Shakespeare's information is much more likely to derive from Xenophon's *Memorabilia* and *Symposium*, or Diogenes Laertius's third-century biography of Socrates. Both of these were available to Shakespeare,⁵ both dwell at length on Xanthippe's shrewish characteristics, but there is no reason to suppose he read either of them first-hand.

However, the ideas that Socrates and Plato meant something to Shakespeare, and that he did read some Plato, receive support when we listen for literary echoes rather than names, and there is a small but telling cluster of such echoes around the year 1600. The first occurs when the Hostess recounts Falstaff's death in *Henry V* (1599):

> **Hostess:** 'A made a finer end, and went a way an' it had been any christom child . . . 'a bade me lay more clothes on his feet. I put my hand into the bed and felt them, and they were as cold as any stone. Then I felt to his knees, and so up'ard and up'ard, and all was as cold as any stone. (2.3.9–25)

If we compare this with the account of Socrates' death at the end of the *Phaedo*, then we can note a number of striking parallels:

> **Phaedo:** The man – he was the same one who had administered the poison – kept his hand upon Socrates, and after a little while examined his feet and legs, then pinched his foot hard and asked if he felt it. Socrates said no. Then he did the same to his legs, and moving gradually upwards in this way let us see that he was getting cold and numb. Presently he felt him again and said that when it reached his heart, Socrates would be gone. (117e–118)⁶

Like Falstaff's, Socrates' death is not shown directly but reported by a friend and witness. Its first symptoms are coldness and numbness which begin in his feet and move upwards, and their ascent is followed by someone pressing progressively higher points on his legs. We can hear an echo of Plato's "moving gradually upwards" in Shakespeare's "up'ard and up'ard," and when the protagonist dies, it is reported that his death would have gratified the prevailing deities: Crito says that Socrates made his death exceedingly well and that he has gone to live with the gods; while the Hostess reports, "Nay, sure, [Falstaff's] not in hell; he's in Arthur's bosom" (2.3.9–10), and that he departed as if he had been a Christian child.⁷

The gradually ascending paralysis from which Falstaff appears to have died is now known as Guillain-Barré Syndrome. Besides hemlock poisoning, it is caused by botulism, diphtheria, poliomyelitis, thallium or arsenic poisoning, and several other diseases and conditions.⁸ Shakespeare could have heard about or witnessed such a death in real life, but the literary similarities of his and Plato's account suggest that the *Phaedo* is much the most probable source.⁹

This naturally raises the questions: why did Shakespeare decide to have Falstaff die in the same way as Socrates? In what way are the two figures analogous? At first there seem to be no connections at all, and then one recalls that both were portly men past middle age, foot soldiers, and famous drinkers. More importantly, both were given to asking "What is . . . ?" questions ("What is honour?" asks Falstaff in *1 Henry IV* [5.1.133–4]); neither is conventionally attractive, but both attract young men; both are held to be corrupters of youth ("That villainous abominable misleader of youth, Falstaff..." [*1 Henry IV* 2.4.456–7; *Ap.* 24c]); and both are accused of sophistry: "wrenching the true cause the false way," in Falstaff's case (*2 Henry IV* 2.1.110–11), and "making the weaker argument [appear] the stronger," in Socrates'. (*Ap.* 19b)[10]

This leaves the problem that Falstaff seems an essentially comic figure in a way that Socrates does not, but this is easily resolved when we realize that during the Renaissance Socrates was often thought of as a clown: Erasmus, for example, writes: "his eternal jesting gave him the air of a clown," and "it was not unjust that . . . this jester alone should have been declared by the oracle to be wise . . .".[11] "Jester," of course, is the term the newly crowned Henry V applies to Falstaff at the end of *2 Henry IV*: "How ill white hairs becomes a fool and jester!" (5.5.48.)

The Platonic elements in *Julius Caesar* (1600) have been the object of much recent scholarly attention. Barbara Parker draws attention to the way Plato's *Republic* seems to have influenced the play's interest in the relations between a tyrant and the mob, the structure of the state and the human soul, and particularly the analogy between social classes and metals.[12] The last of these is much to the fore in Cassius's soliloquy beginning: "Well, Brutus, thou art noble. Yet I see / Thy honourable metal may be wrought / From that it is dispos'd. Therefore it is meet / That noble minds keep ever with their likes . . ." (1.2.308–10) This shows a number of striking parallels with Socrates' statement: "[The] diviner metal is within [the Guardians], and they . . . ought not to pollute the divine by any such earthly admixture; for the commoner metal has been the source of many unholy deeds . . . But should . . . [pollution occur], they will become . . . enemies and tyrants instead of allies of the other citizens . . . plotting and being plotted against . . ." (*Rep.* 3:416–7)[13]

In *Hamlet* (1600), as in *Henry V*, we find a close textual correspondence that seems most unlikely to have come to Shakespeare second-hand. It occurs in one of Hamlet's most famous soliloquies, after the First Player has just performed his speech about the Queen of Troy:

> **Hamlet:** O what a rogue and peasant slave am I!
> Is it not monstrous, that this player here,
> But in a fiction, in a dream of passion,
> Could force his soul so to his own conceit,
> That from her working all his visage wann'd,
> Tears in his eyes, distraction in his aspect,
> A broken voice, and his whole function suiting
> With forms to his conceit? And all for nothing!
> For Hecuba!
> What's Hecuba to him, or he to Hecuba
> That he should weep for her? What would he do,
> Had he the motive and cue for passion
> That I have? He would drown the stage with tears,
> And cleave the general ear with horrid speech,

>   Make mad the guilty and appal the free,
>   Confound the ignorant, and amaze indeed,
>   The very faculties of eyes and ears. (2.2.550–66)

If we now turn to Plato's *Ion*, we discover the following conversation between Socrates and the ageing rhapsode:

> **Socrates:** Wait now, Ion; tell me this. And answer frankly what I ask you. Suppose you are reciting epic poetry well, and thrill the spectators most deeply. You are chanting, say, the story of Odysseus as he leaped up to the dais, unmasked himself to the suitors, and poured the arrows out before his feet, or of Achilles rushing upon Hector, or one of the pitiful passages, about Andromache, or Hecuba or Priam. When you chant these, are you in your senses? Or are you carried out of yourself, and does not your soul in an ecstasy conceive herself to be in the actions you relate, whether they are in Ithaca, or Troy, or wherever the story puts them?
>
> **Ion:** . . . I will tell you frankly that whenever I recite a tale of pity, my eyes are filled with tears, and when it is one of horror or dismay, my hair stands up on end with fear, and my heart goes leaping.
>
> **Socrates:** Well now, Ion, what are we to say of a man like that? . . . [Who] weeps, though he has lost nothing of his finery. Or he recoils with fear, standing in the presence of more than twenty thousand friendly people, though nobody is stripping him or doing him damage? Shall we say that the man is in his senses?
>
> **Ion:** Never, Socrates, upon my word. That is strictly true.
>
> **Socrates:** Now then, are you aware that you produce the same effect in most of the spectators too?
>
> **Ion:** Yes, indeed, I know it very well. As I look down at them from the stage above, I see them, every time, weeping, casting terrible glances, stricken with amazement at the deeds recounted. (535b–e)

Hamlet uses one of Socrates' examples (Hecuba), and he has just watched the First Player use two (Priam and Hecuba); in both passages the absence of normal causes for rage and misery are noted, while the presence of one of their normal symptoms (tears) is dwelt upon; in both, the power of art to drive someone out of his senses is emphasized; in both, the soul is referred to as "her"; the subject is a solo recitation by a mature man; and in Plato and Shakespeare the discussion passes from passion's effect on the actor to its effect on the spectators.

Troilus and Cressida (1602), like *Julius Caesar*, draws analogies between the city and the soul. Compare Brutus's, "The genius and the mortal instruments / Are then in council, and the state of man, / Like to a little kingdom, suffers then / The nature of an insurrection" (*JC* 2.1.66–9), with Ulysses': "Kingdomed Achilles in commotion rages / And batters down himself" (*TC* 2.3.174–5). The genius mentioned at the beginning of the quotation from Brutus, whose job it is to ensure that we do not escape the life-plan we have chosen, is also found in *Troilus* ("Hark, You are called. Some say the Genius so / Cries 'Come!' to him that instantly must die" [4.4.49–50]), and this peculiar use of the word again derives from the *Republic*: "And [Lachesis] sent with each, as the

guardian of his life and the fulfiller of his choice, the genius that he had chosen . . ."
(*Rep.* 10:620e).[14]

It is clear that Shakespeare intended *Troilus and Cressida* to be a self-consciously philosophical play, and unlike his two previous plays with classical settings – *Titus Andronicus* (c.1592) and *Julius Caesar* – it is very much a play of debates: the Greek debate about their lack of success (which includes Ulysses' speech on degree), the Trojan debate about whether they should return Helen to the Greeks, and the discussion between Ulysses and Achilles about the need publicly to demonstrate one's qualities. It seems highly likely that, before sitting down to write a philosophical play involving the ancient Greeks, Shakespeare made an effort to read some Greek philosophy. Aristotle's name appears in the play (2.2.166), and echoes of the *Nicomachean Ethics* are so frequent as to suggest first-hand and recent acquaintance.[15] In addition, the discussion about whether personal qualities should be publicly demonstrated seems to come from Plato's – possibly spurious – *Alcibiades I*, where the doctrine is first stated. (Ulysses is shown to come across the idea from reading [3.3.94–104])[16] But the most obvious echoes of Plato occur when the Trojans debate whether they should keep Helen. Consider the following exchange:

> **Hector:** Brother, she is not worth what she doth cost
> The holding.
> **Troilus:** What's aught but as 'tis valued?
> **Hector:** But value dwells not in particular will;
> It holds his estimate and dignity
> As well wherein 'tis precious of itself
> As in the prizer. 'Tis mad idolatry
> To make the service greater than the god . . . (2.2.53–7)

This seems to compress several pages of the *Euthyphro*.[17] First, there is the discussion of whether something has a value because it is valued, or whether it is valued because it is valuable. As in the debate about Helen, Socrates first takes the case of what is loved, and then moves on to what is regarded as holy:

> **Socrates:** It is not because a thing is loved that they who love it love it, but it is loved because they love it.
> **Euthyphro:** Necessarily.
> **Socrates:** Then what are we to say about the holy, Euthyphro? According to your arguments, is it not loved by all the gods?
> **Euthyphro:** Yes.
> **Socrates:** Because it is holy, or for some other reason?
> **Euthyphro:** No, it is for that reason.
> **Socrates:** And so it is because it is holy that it is loved; it is not holy because it is loved. (10d)

Second, there is Hector's notion of *service* to a god. The notion is introduced by Euthyphro, and Socrates, like us, finds it puzzling:

Euthyphro: I think that the part of justice which is religious and is holy is the part that has to do with the service of the gods . . .
Socrates: . . . I am not yet clear about the thing which you call "service." (12e–13)

Socrates explores the notion and defines it – with Euthyphro's assent – as "a kind of waiting on the gods" (13d). He then argues that service must be of benefit to the person or persons served, and asks what possible advantage the gods could gain from this service. Euthyphro, like Hector, finds the idea that we can benefit the gods impious and absurd: our services have no value when set against their overwhelming power and greatness:

Socrates: [What] advantage could come to the gods from the gifts which they receive from us? . . .
Euthyphro: What! Socrates. Do you suppose that the gods gain anything by what they get from us? (15)

How can the Platonic influence on Shakespeare during the period 1599–1604 be explained? I suspect there are three reasons. First, in 1599, the company had physically moved its theatre to Bankside and renamed it "The Globe." Access, finance, and conditions of rehearsal were now much improved, and paved the way for far more ambitious plays. Second, in *Julius Caesar* and *Hamlet*, he must have been conscious that his art had acquired vastly greater power and amplitude, and that it could now absorb and transform ideas which had traditionally been the preserve of philosophy alone. Third, by 1598, when Shakespeare is mentioned on the cast list of *Every Man in his Humour*, he had come to know Ben Jonson. Although the basic tenor of their relationship was friendly, there was also considerable competition between the two men. Jonson set tremendous store by his classical learning, and Shakespeare may well have felt a need to raise his intellectual game to compete on equal terms with a formidable new rival.[18]

Shakespeare's knowledge of Latin and Greek is, of course, disputed, but it would be hard to pass through an Elizabethan grammar school education without acquiring some fluency in Latin, and Latin editions of Plato's dialogues by Ficino (1484) and Serranus (1578) were widely available.[19] Indeed, Ben Jonson owned Serranus's edition (it is now in Chetham Library, Manchester); and a 1590 printing of Ficino's edition in the British Library contains the penciled note: "Ben Jonson's own copy with 219 Annotations in his hand 33 Trefoil marks in his hand." In the first flower of their friendship, Jonson may well have lent Shakespeare these very copies.[20]

The dialogue which appears first in both Serranus's and Ficino's edition is the *Euthyphro*, and Stephen Medcalf suggests that this dialogue could have had a temporary effect on Shakespeare's vocabulary.[21] The Latin word Ficino uses for "holiness," "piety," and "service" is "sanctum" and in his edition the word is associated with vows: thus Socrates' account of sanctum, "a science of sacrifice and prayer," is rendered "scientiam quandam vovendi atque sacrificandi" (14c). The closest English word in both sound and meaning to Ficino's "sanctum" is "sanctimony." This is a word that Shakespeare only uses on three occasions: all of these occur in plays written in the period 1602–4, and two of them, like Ficino, link the word with the idea of vows. In *Troilus and Cressida*, "sanctimony" is used twice in Troilus's horrified speech after he has just seen his beloved betraying him with the Greek, Diomedes. The passage is also noteworthy because it again raises the peculiar question of whether the gods are pleased by our services:

> This she? No, this is Diomed's Cressida.
> If beauty have a soul, this is not she;
> If souls guide vows, if vows be sanctimonies,
> If sanctimony be the gods' delight,
> If there be rule in unity itself,
> This is not she. (5.2.144–9)

"Sanctimony" occurs once more in *All's Well that Ends Well* (c.1603) when Helena's pilgrimage is described as a "holy undertaking [which] with most austere sanctimony she accomplished" (4.3.47–8). And it occurs finally, again associated with vows, in *Othello*, when Iago dismisses the marriage of Othello and Desdemona as: "sanctimony and a frail vow betwixt an erring barbarian and a supersubtle Venetian" (1.3.356–8).

After 1604, I have only been able to discover one direct echo of Plato in Shakespeare. In the *Symposium*, Alcibiades ends one section of his speech with the phrase "like the poor fool in the adage" (222b). Shakespeare clearly remembered these words, and, in *Macbeth* (1606), has Lady Macbeth virtually quote them at end of one of her speeches: "Like the poor cat i' th' adage" (1.7.45).

But this lack of later parallels does not indicate that Plato had ceased to be influential. We can see why this might be so by considering Aristotle's influence on Shakespeare. Aristotle's name first occurs in the *Taming of the Shrew* in a context which does not suggest close acquaintance with the philosopher's works (1.1.32). The second mention occurs in *Troilus and Cressida*, but here the surrounding text, as I mentioned above, shows wide familiarity at least with the *Nicomachean Ethics*. But *Troilus and Cressida* has never been one of Shakespeare's more popular plays. There are no records of a performance in Shakespeare's lifetime; it was not produced for nearly 300 years after his death; and even now, performances are rare. This can partly be explained by the inconclusive nature of its action, and the sour, rancid flavor of its atmosphere, but the main reason for its failure is the undigested philosophical content: static debates on abstract issues do not make for lively entertainment. Shakespeare may well have felt that if he wished to write another philosophical play then including extended dialogues on philosophical topics was not the way to go about it.

In one of his next plays – *Measure for Measure* (1604) – he discovers a much more successful way of assimilating philosophical issues, and produces his most Aristotelian work. This is not because the play contains more mentions of Aristotle's name and doctrines than previous works, but because the entire structure and plot indicate a profound understanding of Aristotle's ethical outlook, especially of temperance or *sophrosyne*. Aristotle's name and doctrines no longer sit on the surface of the text: the philosopher's abstract thoughts are enacted and particularized; his *êthos* has been absorbed into the whole structure of Shakespeare's ethical thinking.[22]

We can discern a similar pattern in Shakespeare's assimilation of Plato. Socrates is mentioned in the *Taming of the Shrew* but this reference must ultimately derive from a non-Platonic source. In *Henry V*, *Julius Caesar*, and *Hamlet*, we find no mentions of Plato's name, but there are several passages which suggest close acquaintanceship with two Socratic dialogues (the *Ion* and *Phaedo*) and a middle-period work (the *Republic*). In *Troilus and Cressida*, several sections are modeled on debates in the *Euthyphro* and there are further allusions to the *Republic*, but these do no more than the ideas from Aristotle's *Ethics* to enhance the play's dramatic effectiveness. In the next section, I shall argue that, in the temptation scene of *Othello*, Shakespeare discovers how to make theatrical use of the Platonic inheritance. He does not enact Socrates' philosophical ideas in his plot; Socrates, after all, has very few positive ideas (perhaps the unity of virtue, the impossibility of weakness of the will, and the benefits of the moral life for the agent). But what Socrates does have is a technique of cross-examination which issues in a certain kind of dramatic structure, and it is this which Shakespeare assimilates into the texture of his play. Consequently, this scene of *Othello* stands to Plato, as *Measure for Measure* stands to Aristotle.

There are several other significant patterns in Shakespeare's absorption of Plato. As well as making the philosopher's work more concrete and overtly emotional, Shakespeare tends to introduce a touch of mockery. In 1599, the classical dignity of Socrates' death is transmuted into the death of an old, fat, hard-hearted reprobate in an inn's back room. Again, in 1600, the performances of one of Greece's most famous rhapsodes, accustomed to declaiming before 20,000 people, is taken downmarket. Ion's recitals become a single performance by a provincial touring actor in front of four men, and his style is now shown up as touchingly rhetorical and old fashioned. Accordingly, in *Othello*, Shakespeare not only assimilates the movement and motivation of the dialogues, but holds the elenchus up to parody and critique.

Othello's "Temptation Scene" as a Parody of the Elenchus

In what ways does this scene – where Iago persuades Othello of Desdemona's unfaithfulness – show the influence of the Socratic dialogues? In each of the early dialogues, Socrates investigates a general moral issue. In the *Euthyphro* it is piety, in the *Charmides* temperance, in the *Laches* courage, and so on. The elenctic method these exemplify usually operates as follows. Socrates invites someone to state a basic belief *A*. Some time later, Socrates persuades him to agree to another belief (or cluster of beliefs) *B*, and Socrates then shows that *B* is incompatible with *A*. The interlocutor sees this, and withdraws or modifies his earlier belief.[23] Thus, in the *Gorgias*, Polus argues that it is worse to suffer than to do wrong (469b and 473). This is belief *A*. Socrates then asks him: "[Is] it more shameful to do or to suffer wrong?" to which Polus replies: "To do wrong" (474c). This is belief *B*. Socrates soon gets Polus to agree that "to inflict wrong is worse than to suffer it through excess of evil" (475c), and this section of the dialogue reaches its elenctic climax in the following exchange:

Socrates: And would you choose the more evil and shameful in preference to the less?
. . .
Polus: No, I would not prefer it, Socrates . . .
Socrates: Then I spoke the truth when I said that neither I nor any man whatever would rather do than suffer wrong, for to do it is worse.
Polus: Evidently (475e).

Polus has admitted that *A* and *B* are incompatible, and now feels under pressure to withdraw *A*.

In the temptation scene, Iago and Othello also investigate a moral issue, but in accordance with what Shakespeare had learnt from *Troilus and Cressida*, the issue is now made more concrete, emotional, and dramatic. The discussion is not about faithfulness or unfaithfulness in general, but the faithfulness or unfaithfulness of Desdemona in particular. Nonetheless, we can see that the scene exhibits the same underlying pattern of argument. Othello's opening position, his implicit belief in his wife's faithfulness, is expressed in act 1 as, "My life upon her faith" (1.3.296). This is belief *A*. Iago then makes Othello accept a cluster of propositions that he uses to undermine *A*. Under pressure from this second set of beliefs *B*, Othello moves to a position of doubt and uncertainty: "I think my wife is honest, and I think she is not, / I think that thou [Iago] art just, and I think thou art not" (387–8). Eventually, he becomes utterly convinced of what Iago tells him: "Damn her, lewd minx! O, damn her!" (478.)

There is a puzzle about this kind of argument. Why should *A* be the belief which is withdrawn or modified?[24] This happens in every early elenctic dialogue, and also in the temptation scene, but it is not at all clear why *B* should not be the belief given up or amended. Indeed, from the epistemological point of view, *A* should be harder to give up. First, it is usually a conscious belief (unlike *B*, which Socrates frequently presses the interlocutor to acknowledge). Second, as the topic and starting point of the dialogue, it is usually more important than *B*. To reject *A* is to reject a conscious belief on which many other beliefs rest; to reject *B* may simply be to reject one hitherto unconscious belief on which few other beliefs rely. But from the dramatic and psychological point of view, the consequences of giving up *A* are much more spectacular, and rejecting *A* often entails massive mental restructuring.[25] As Alcibiades, who was frequently on the receiving end of Socrates' questions, asserts: "[He] turned my whole soul upside down and left me feeling as if I were the lowest of the low" (*Symp.* 215e). It was surely the dramatic potential of this move which Shakespeare sensed in the dialogues.

At one point early in the temptation scene, Othello comes dangerously close to simply rejecting what Iago tells him:

> Why? Why is this?
> Think'st thou I'd make a life of jealousy,
> To follow still the changes of the moon
> With fresh suspicions. No! To be once in doubt
> Is once to be resolved. . . .
> . . . No, Iago.

I'll see before I doubt; when I doubt, prove;
And on the proof there is no more but this:
Away at once with love or jealousy. (179–95)

If Othello had continued in this vein, he would simply have dismissed Iago's alleged suspicions, given up his belief in Iago's honesty, and possibly dismissed him from his service. That would have been an end of the matter. But Iago counters brilliantly and the virus he implants rampages with increasing vehemence through Othello's belief-system: the general reflects gloomily on his age, race, past history (262–78); he feels that the employment from which he derives his identity is no longer possible ("Farewell the plumed troops, and the big wars / That make ambition virtue! . . . Othello's occupation's gone!" [352–60]); and finally he collapses into complete incoherence and unconsciousness (4.1.35–44).

Socrates does not simply state what he thinks (because he claims to know nothing) but questions those who claim to know; he does not pass on information but prompts his interlocutors into discovering truths for themselves. In the *Seventh Letter*, Plato argues that this method is far superior to straightforward instruction. Anyone, he says, can pick up a smattering of philosophical doctrines (340d), and texts can be read by all and sundry, but true philosophy can only be taught to the "few who are capable of discovering the truth for themselves with a little guidance" (341e). They must study the subject for an extended period, enjoy close companionship and verbal dialogue, and then "suddenly, like a blaze kindled by a leaping spark, it is generated in the soul and at once becomes self-sustaining" (341d).

Iago knows this truth, and in this scene, he rarely tells or states what he thinks, but proceeds by indirections. In 137 lines of dialogue, from the beginning of Iago's assault ("Ha! I like not that" [34]) to the first sign of Othello's despair ("O misery!" [173]), Iago produces not a single piece of evidence that Desdemona is unfaithful. Instead, he asks questions, he drops hints, he makes Othello question him, he echoes Othello, he feigns reluctance, he makes Othello reflect, and so on.[26] In this way, Othello's mind is made to engage in the inquiry, so he feels he has discovered the horrifying fact of Desdemona's treachery for himself (with a little guidance). It is only late in the scene (413–42) that Iago tells some straightforward lies about Cassio's dream and the handkerchief, but by this stage the important damage has already been done.

Socrates' method causes him to seek out people with pretentions to wisdom, and thus he frequently questions older men, landowners, aristocrats, and generals. Othello is an aristocrat ("I fetch my life and being / From men of royal siege" [1.2.21–2]); he is a general in the Venetian army; and he is, according to his own – admittedly depressed – self-description, "declined / Into the vale of years" (269–70). Many of Socrates' older interlocutors, like Ion, Euthyphro, and Gorgias are supremely self-confident, and this can make the result of the method agreeably unsettling. "Confident" hardly captures the aura of massive invulnerability which Othello conveys in the play's opening act, and this, of course, makes the effect of Iago's poison all the more obvious and devastating.

Even when the subject of moral inquiry is general and abstract, as in the Socratic dialogues, the method produces remarkable and distinctive results. In the *Seventh*

Letter, Plato describes its effect as like a spark leaping from one person to another. The spark sets the other person "on fire with philosophy" (340b), and the fire is "self-sustaining." In the *Symposium*, Alcibiades adopts a different metaphor:

> People say, you know, that when a man's been bitten by a snake he won't tell anybody what it feels like except a fellow sufferer, because no one else would sympathize with him if the pain drove him into making a fool of himself. Well, that's just how I feel, only I've been bitten by something much more poisonous than a snake; in fact, mine is the most painful kind of bite there is. I've been bitten in the heart, or the mind, or whatever you like to call it, by Socrates' philosophy, which clings like an adder to any young and gifted mind it can get hold of, and does exactly what it likes with it. (217e–218)

Like poison, the Socratic effect lingers in the system, and is just as effective when Socrates is not there as when he is. The poison produces a "philosophical frenzy," (218b) "a kind of sacred rage . . . and the tears start into my eyes . . . and left me feeling as if I were the lowest of the low" (215d–e).

When, as in the temptation scene, the object of discussion is concrete, personal, and mortifying, the content serves to enhance and exacerbate the method's effects. Iago illustrates the effect of his remarks on Othello with his own example of a self-sustaining fire: "dangerous conceits," he says, "burn like mines of sulphur" (329–32). The analogy of the internal snakebite (as if in "the heart, or the mind"), and the lingering effect of its poison, is developed at greater length. "Swell, bosom," says Othello, "with thy fraught, / For 'tis full of aspics' tongues!" (452–7.) And at several points in the play, Iago's words are likened to a "medicine" (a word which Shakespeare often uses to mean "poison") that continues to act on Othello even, perhaps especially, when Iago is not speaking to him. When Othello is out of the room, Iago reflects: "The Moor already changes with my poison: / Dangerous conceits are in their nature poisons" (328–9). When he is unconscious from a fit, Iago exults: "Work on, / My medicine, work!" (4.1.44–5.) Finally, Iago suggests that no drug exists to counter the effect of his own: "Not poppy nor mandragora, / Nor all the drowsy syrups of the world / Shall ever medicine thee to that sweet sleep / Which thou owedst yesterday" (332–6). Like Socrates' poison, Iago's provokes frenzy, rage, tears, and an overwhelming sense of shame.

Alcibiades explicitly contrasts the intensity and intimacy of this effect with that of the most eloquent rhetoricians of his day: "Yes, I've heard Pericles and all the other great orators, and very eloquent I thought they were, but they never affected me [as Socrates affected me]; they never turned my whole soul upside down . . ." (*Symp.* 215e) And, of course, in works like the *Gorgias* and *Republic*, Socrates explicitly defines himself and his philosophical method against the mere routines and knacks of the rhetoricians who aim just to sway crowds and win public debates (*Gorg.* 463b). Shakespeare too had moved away from the rhetorical training he had received at school. In the early plays (the *Henry VI* trilogy or *Titus Andronicus*, for example) one can hear the powerful influences of writers like Seneca, and can go through the text identifying examples of *epistrophe* (repeating words at the end of a series of clauses), *antanaclesis* (a type of pun which repeats a word with a shifting sense), and other formal rhetorical devices.[27] But during the mid- and late 1590s, Shakespeare had developed a much more fluid, freer, naturalistic style, and by the time of *Hamlet*, the public style had become an object of irony. The intimacy of the temptation scene is as remote from formal rhetoric as the *Phaedo* is from the style of Gorgias.

The Socratic method, where a thought begun in one mind is finished in another, and where one's whole personality can be reconstructed by another's promptings, encourages companionship and intimacy, and it is thus not surprising that both Socrates and Alcibiades cannot separate their love for one another from their joint love of philosophy (*Gorg.* 481d). Accordingly, it is significant that several commentators have suggested that a form of homosexual relationship begins to develop between Iago and Othello.[28] Initially, the idea seems implausible because there are no signs of physical attraction, and neither Othello nor Iago are particularly sexual men, but critics are certainly right to sense that the temptation scene is a kind of *seduction*. However, it is a form of *mental* seduction, and this carries its own intimate and erotic charge. Indeed, for Socrates, a seduction of the mind is both deeper and more sexual than the physical variety. In *Charmides* 153d–154e, for example, the elenctic method is presented as a method of pleasurably stripping the beloved's soul, just as a lover would pleasurably strip the beloved's body. Socrates agrees that the youthful Charmides has a beautiful face and form, but expresses himself more interested in his nobility of soul: "Then, before we see his body, should we not ask him to strip and show us his soul?" (154e), and it is at this point that Charmides' interrogation on the topic of temperance begins.[29]

Socrates' relationships with many of his interlocutors were intensified by a shared experience of battle, and all of the dialogues in which Socrates appears as an adult are set against a background of war (either imminent, actual, or recently ended). It is returning from the battle of Potidaea that Socrates makes his inquiry "about the present state of philosophy, and about the youth" (*Charm.* 153d), and his relationships with both Alcibiades and Laches are shaped and strengthened by shared military hardships and dangers. After the battle of Potidaea, Alcibiades received a medal and recommended the same honor for Socrates (*Symp.* 220e); and Alcibiades reports that during the battle of Delium: "You could see from half a mile away that if you tackled *him* [Socrates] you'd get as good as you gave – with the result that he and Laches got clean away. For you're generally pretty safe if that's the way you look when you're in action" (*Symp.* 221b).

Othello too is set against a background of Mediterranean war (which like the Peloponnesian War would eventually end in defeat) and the play itself has a specifically military context. Iago's relationship with Othello was also tempered and proven in battle: Othello's eyes, he says, have seen "the proof [of Iago's military ability] / At Rhodes, at Cyprus, and on other grounds / Christian and heathen" (1.1.27–9); while Iago has seen Othello remain calm "When [the cannon] hath blown his ranks into the air / And, like the devil, from his very arm / Puffed his own brother" (3.4.136–8). These, of course, are only Iago's words, but presumably there would be witnesses to confirm his reports.

Like Socrates, Iago is more intellectually able than his interlocutor. There is something of the philosopher about him. He is one of the few characters in Shakespeare with a worked-out philosophy (1.1.40–64), and he loves the language of logic: "Therefore, put money in thy purse" (1.3.354); "Therefore, make money" (1.3.359–60); "Now sir, this granted – as it is a most pregnant and unforced position" (2.1.233–4); "And this may help to thicken other proofs / That do demonstrate thinly" (432–3). He also relishes a pose of epistemic caution: "I speak not yet of proof. / Look to your wife . . . / Wear your eyes thus: not jealous nor secure" (199–201); "one that so imperfectly conceits . . . / Out of his scattering and unsure observance" (152–4); "If imputation and strong circumstances / Which lead directly to the truth / Will give you satisfaction" (409–11). When he argues Roderigo out of drowning himself, he shows himself as adept with an extended horticultural metaphor as any ancient philosopher:

> ['Tis] in ourselves that we are thus, or thus. Our bodies are gardens, to which our wills are gardeners. So that if we will plant nettles or sow lettuce, set hyssop and weed up thyme, supply it with one gender of herbs or distract it with many, either to have it sterile with idleness or manured with industry – why, the power and corrigible authority of this lies in our wills. If the balance of our lives had not one scale of reason to poise another of sensuality, the blood and baseness of our natures would conduct us to most preposterous conclusions. But we have reason to cool our raging motions, our carnal stings or unbitted lusts; whereof I take this, that you call love, to be a sect or scion. (1.3.321–34)

The argument probably derives from Aristotle's *Nicomachean Ethics*, where Aristotle demonstrates that we can be blamed not only for actions, but for mental and bodily states and dispositions – such as obesity, dipsomania, and gluttony – that we have allowed ourselves to develop over the course of time:

> For in an irrational being the appetite for what gives it pleasure is insatiable and indiscriminate, and the exercise of the desire increases its innate tendency; and if these appetites are strong and violent, they actually drive out reason. . . . Thus the desiderative element of the temperate man ought to be in harmony with the rational principle. (1119b5–10)[30]

Passion and desire's ability to overthrow reason was clearly a topic Shakespeare thought hard about, and it is during a discussion of this very issue that he mentions Aristotle's name in *Troilus and Cressida*. Hector accuses Paris and Troilus of arguing superficially:

>   not much
> Unlike young men, whom Aristotle thought
> Unfit to hear moral philosophy.
> The reasons you allege do more conduce
> To the hot passion of the distempered blood
> Than to make a free determination
> 'Twixt right and wrong; for pleasure and revenge
> Have ears more deaf than adders to the voice
> Of any true decision. (2.2.166–73)

But at least two of Iago's philosophical traits are specifically reminiscent of Socrates' practice. First, he exhibits the quick wit, resourcefulness, and ability to improvise so necessary in Socratic discussion. Second, although Socrates has a few positive views, the vast majority of his intellectual activity is *negative*: he shows that others do not know what they think they know; a task often accompanied by a mild and mocking humor. Iago too is possessed by the spirit of negation: his intelligence is entirely at the service of destruction (including the destruction of genuine knowledge); and he also goes about his work with humor – in his case, a dark, malicious glee.

It is the philosophical nature, argues Socrates in book 6 of the *Republic*, that is the most easily corrupted, and the very qualities necessary for the philosopher ("quickness in learning, memory, courage . . ." [*Rep.* 6:494b]) are those which make him most dangerous to society when corruption sets in:

> The most surprising fact of all is that each of the gifts of nature which we praise tends to corrupt the soul of its possessor and divert it from philosophy. I am speaking of bravery, sobriety, and the entire list. (*Rep.* 6:491b)

> [Do] you suppose that great crimes and unmixed wickedness spring from a slight nature and not from a vigorous one corrupted by its nurture . . . ? (*Rep.* 6:491e)

> Such, my good friend . . . is the destruction and corruption of the [philosophical character], which is rare enough in any case, as we affirm. And it is from men of this type that those spring who do the greatest harm to communities and individuals. (*Rep.* 6:495b)

There is good evidence that Shakespeare knew at least some sections of the *Republic*, and there is thus some likelihood that the character of Iago is influenced by Plato's account of the philosophical character gone to the bad.

This may be the reason why Iago exhibits debased versions of Socrates' manner and motive. Both men wear a mask and frequently do not say what they mean: one is a liar, the other an ironist, and the two roles are interestingly interlinked. Indeed, if we return to the original root of the word "irony," we discover that it comes from a form of Greek dialogue where an *eiron* (a dissembler) uses understatement to overcome an *alazon* (a braggart).[31] This could be Iago's description of his relationship with Othello: Iago, after all, prides himself on his own powers of dissimulation ("I am not what I am" [1.1.64]), and claims that Othello made Desdemona fall in love with him "but for bragging and telling her fantastical lies" (2.1.221).

Othello also accuses Iago of saying less than he knows, and the latter uses this telegraphed pose of ignorance to inveigle Othello into his snare (133–6). In fact, of course, Iago's pose of ignorance is genuine insofar as his "knowledge" of Desdemona's unfaithfulness is entirely fraudulent. Similarly, Thrasymachus says to Socrates:

> Ye gods! Here we have the well-known irony of Socrates, and I knew it and predicted that when it came to replying you would refuse and dissemble and do anything rather than answer any question that anyone asked you. (*Rep.* 1:337a)

Most philosophers have followed Thrasymachus in thinking that Socrates' profession of ignorance is a pose, but the idea that Socrates' disavowal of knowledge is entirely genuine now looks much more plausible.[32] Each man's show of ignorance is taken as a sign they know more, but Iago certainly knows less than he hints, and Socrates probably knows no more than he claims.

Socrates and Iago are, in a sense, disinterested: neither is motivated by straightforward *gain*. Socrates refused to accept any money, office, power, or other direct advantage from his teaching; Iago does not intend his plot to produce money (except indirectly by duping Roderigo) and he does not love or lust after Desdemona (his occasional remarks to this effect notwithstanding [e.g., 2.2.288–91]). This does not imply that they lack motives. Socrates says his reason for engaging in dialogues is his desire to discover the truth, and Iago is certainly motivated by racism, class resentment, and a profound hatred for people who can experience emotions which are out of his reach. Moreover, intellectual vanity is clearly central to both their characters. Disguised under a meek mildness, it is one of the most provoking elements in Socrates' personality, and Iago prides himself on the excellence and destructive power of his own intellect.

The central difficulty with the elenctic method is that it is not at all clear why it should lead to truth, as all the method can obviously achieve is consistency.[33] If it shows that someone's beliefs are incompatible then this will show that the system contains at least one false belief – although we do not know, of course, which one it is. If the method proves that someone's belief-system is consistent then, unless we have some independent reason for thinking the majority of his beliefs true, we have no more reason for thinking that the majority of someone's beliefs are consistently false rather than consistently true. Indeed, the elenctic method could be used to make someone's beliefs consistently false. Now, if Iago is an example of the philosophical nature corrupted, what could be more satisfying than showing that the elenctic method – the very method Socrates uses to seek general truth and virtue – can just as easily be shown to lead to particular falsehood and vice?

In order to do this, Shakespeare exaggerates – or perhaps extrapolates from – three aspects of the Socratic dialogues. First, in all of these dialogues, the initial assumptions or beliefs are rejected, but no general and agreed conclusion is reached at their end. Iago's elenchus, however, is wholly successful, and Othello, by the end, is utterly convinced of Iago's assumed position.

Second, although Alcibiades implies that the elenctic method in Socrates' hands can produce a kind of love, none of the early dialogues actually shows this happening. The characters seem as far from one another at the end as they were at the beginning. In the temptation scene, however, we do see a kind of perverse bond spring up between Othello and Iago: they swear to a common purpose and even begin to take on one another's vocabularies and tricks of speech.

Third, in the dialogues, Socrates succeeds in eliciting a second belief B from his interlocutor which he shows is incompatible with his initial belief A. But it would be true to say that Othello harbors no doubts, not even unconscious doubts, about Desdemona. All his beliefs are utterly consistent: she is a model of virtue. What he does have are certain insecurities about his age, race, not being a native Venetian, and lack of experience with women. Iago encourages him to review the behavior of Desdemona and

Cassio in the light of these insecurities, and produces first hesitation and doubt, and then utter conviction that Desdemona is unfaithful. Socrates leads his interlocutors from one inconsistent set of beliefs to another (although at least they now know they hold inconsistent beliefs); Iago guides Othello from consistent truth to consistent falsehood.

In Shakespeare's parody of a Socratic dialogue, the elenctic method works much better than it does in any of the originals, and for this very reason its capacity to cause harm is made all the clearer.

Probably for some of the reasons given above, Plato evidently became dissatisfied with the elenchus and attempted to replace or supplement it with another method. His first thought was the theory of recollection – *anamnesis*.[34] This is the idea that the soul has knowledge before it is born, but loses its knowledge at the moment of birth. However, it can be recovered and brought to recollection by certain kinds of reminding (*Phaedo* 75e), and Plato demonstrates the latter with the slave boy's construction of the visual proof in the *Meno* (81d–86). Othello too, feels that mere talk is insufficient to decide the issue of Desdemona's guilt, and demands more information from outside his current belief-system; in fact, like Plato, he demands a visual proof: "Villain, be sure thou prove my love a whore! / Be sure of it; give me the ocular proof" (362–3).

In Shakespeare's oeuvre, the temptation scene is unique. He has shown plotters and Machiavels before (Aaron, Richard III, Don John), and he has written short scenes where people, by being given false information, are persuaded out of deeply held beliefs. But prior to 1604, he had not written a protracted scene where a character is induced to persuade himself out of his own most fundamental convictions, nor a scene of such coruscating philosophical brilliance. As there are reasons for thinking that Shakespeare had read a good deal of Plato over the previous five years, and as the early Socratic dialogues prefigure so many aspects of the scene, it is hard to resist the thought that the Platonic inheritance was a vital source of inspiration.

Notes

Several discussions with Marie McGinn were vital in formulating the ideas for this paper, and an early version benefited considerably from being read to the Birkbeck philosophy department in May 2007. Here, comments by Sue James, Ian Rumfitt, Sam Guttenplan, and Barry Smith helped me formulate what I wanted to say more clearly. Dolores Iorizzo gave me much useful information about early editions of Xenophon; Anthony Price placed his expert knowledge of Greek at my disposal; and Garry Hagberg's comments on a late draft were extremely helpful.

1 I give an approximate date for each play the first time I mention it.
2 See Stanley Cavell, "Othello and the Stake of the Other," in *Disowning Knowledge in Seven Plays of Shakespeare* (Cambridge: Cambridge University Press, 2003), 125–42; and Colin McGinn, "Othello," in *Shakespeare's Philosophy: Discovering the Meaning Behind the Plays* (New York: HarperCollins, 2006), 61–89.
3 In all references to the "temptation scene," *Othello*, act 3, scene 3, I use line numbers only.
4 All Shakespeare references, unless otherwise stated, are taken from Richard Proudfoot, Ann Thompson, and David Scott Kastan, eds., *The Arden Shakespeare: The Complete Works*, rev. edn. (London: Thomson Learning, 2001). All Plato references are to Edith Hamilton and

Huntingdon Cairns, eds., *The Collected Dialogues of Plato* (Princeton, NJ: Princeton University Press, 1973). Where the text being referred to is not obvious, I use the following abbreviations for Plato: *Ap.* – *Apology*; *Charm.* – *Charmides*; *Gorg.* – *Gorgias*; *Rep.* – *Republic*; *Symp.* – *Symposium*. And the following for Shakespeare: *1 Henry IV* – *King Henry IV, Part 1*; *2 Henry IV* – *King Henry IV, Part 2*; *JC* – *Julius Caesar*; *TC* – *Troilus and Cressida*; *TS* – *The Taming of the Shrew*.

5 Nicholas Jenson's Latin edition of Diogenes Laertius had appeared in 1475; an Aldine edition of Xenophon's complete works in 1525.

6 This paragraph is from Tredennick's translation. In the same passage, Jowett uses "pressed" for Tredennick's "pinched," and "upwards and upwards" for Tredennick's "moving gradually upwards," thus bringing it even closer to the Shakespeare. (*The Dialogues of Plato*, trans. Benjamin Jowett, 4th edn., Oxford: Clarendon Press, 1953, 1:477.) It is quite possible that Jowett had the scene from *Henry V* at the back of his mind as he worked. I use Tredennick's translation (in Hamilton and Cairns, *The Collected Dialogues*) for the sake of consistency, and to avoid any implication that I have simply chosen a version to resemble the Shakespeare passage. Classicists of my acquaintance generally prefer the translation by G. M. A. Grube, which can be found in *Plato: Five Dialogues* (Indianapolis, IN: Hackett, 1981), 93–155.

7 Similarities between the deaths of Falstaff and Socrates are discussed by Emrys Jones in *The Origins of Shakespeare* (Oxford: Clarendon Press, 1977), 20–21. Jones's views are helpfully supplemented and amplified in Leon H. Craig, *Of Philosophers and Kings* (Toronto: Toronto University Press, 2001) 266–7, 390–91; Michael Platt, "Falstaff in the Valley of the Shadow of Death," *Interpretation* 8:1 (January 1979): 12–13; and John Barker, "Falstaff's Debt to Socrates' Death," http://www2.localaccess.com/Marlowe/Greek.htm, accessed November 2, 2007.

8 On Guillain-Barré Syndrome see Jean D. Wilson et al., eds., *Harrison's Principles of Internal Medicine*, 12th edn., *Companion Handbook* (New York: McGraw-Hill, 1991), 675–8.

9 Christopher Gill and William Ober have argued for the thesis that death by hemlock poisoning is violent and unpleasant, and that Plato's description must be at least partly mythical: an allegorical portrayal of the philosopher's soul leaving his body, retreating first from the feet, and later from the higher seats of feeling and reason. See Christopher Gill, "The Death of Socrates," *Classical Quarterly* 23 (1973): 25–8; and William Ober, "Did Socrates Die of Hemlock Poisoning?" *New York State Journal of Medicine* 77:1 (February 1977): 254–8. Their view would be very convenient for my thesis; unfortunately, it seems to have been conclusively refuted by Enid Bloch in "Hemlock Poisoning and the Death of Socrates: Did Plato Tell the Truth?" *Journal of the International Plato Society*, http://www.nd.edu/~plato/bloch.htm, accessed May 29, 2008.

10 For analogies between the characters of Falstaff and Socrates see Craig, *Of Philosophers and Kings*, 266–7, 390–91; Michael Platt, "Falstaff in the Valley of the Shadow of Death," 12–13; and Barker, "Falstaff's Debt to Socrates."

11 From M. M. Philips, *The "Adages" of Erasmus* (Cambridge: Cambridge University Press, 1964), 270–71, quoted in Jones, *The Origins of Shakespeare*, 20–21.

12 Barbara L. Parker, "'A Thing Unfirm': Plato's *Republic* and Shakespeare's *Julius Caesar*," *Shakespeare Quarterly* 44:1–4 (1993): 30–43. In this paragraph, the quotation from *Julius Caesar* is taken from the edition Parker uses: David Bevington, ed., *The Complete Works of Shakespeare*, 3rd edn. (Glenview, IL: Scott, Foreman and Co., 1980). The Arden edition has "mettle" in line 309.

13 The translation of the *Republic* is taken from Parker, "'A Thing Unfirm,'" 33. She uses *The Dialogues of Plato*, trans. Benjamin Jowett, 3rd edn. (Oxford: Clarendon Press, 1892), vol. 3.

14 The information in this paragraph is taken from I. A. Richards, "Troilus and Cressida and Plato," in his *Speculative Instruments* (London: Routledge and Kegan Paul, 1955), 198–213; and Stephen Medcalf, "Shakespeare on Beauty, Truth and Transcendence," in Anna Baldwin and Sarah Hutton, eds., *Platonism and the English Imagination* (Cambridge: Cambridge University Press, 1994), 117–25.

15 The parallels between *Troilus and Cressida* and the *Nicomachean Ethics* are spelt out in my "The Dissolution of Goodness: *Measure for Measure* and Classical Ethics," collected in M. W. Rowe, *Philosophy and Literature: A Book of Essays* (Aldershot: Ashgate, 2004), 92–125, especially 102–3. This essay also considers the role of Montaigne as a source for Shakespeare's knowledge of Socrates; see especially 104–5.

16 See Richards, "Troilus," 205–6; and Medcalf, "Shakespeare on Beauty," 122–5.

17 The similarities between *Troilus* and the *Euthyphro* are explored in Richards, "Troilus," 209–13; and Medcalf, "Shakespeare on Beauty," 122–5.

18 In 1592, Shakespeare was singled out for disparagement by Robert Greene on the grounds that he was a mere jack-of-all-trades with no university education. *The Taming of the Shrew*, probably written shortly before the death of the Cambridge-educated Marlowe in 1593, may well try to deflect this charge by making more references to formal philosophy than any other Shakespeare play: it contains his only reference to Socrates; one of his two references to Aristotle; and his only uses of "metaphysics," "logic," and "stoic." Act 1, scene 1 of Marlowe's play, *Dr Faustus* (c.1588–92), begins with a tremendously learned list of academic subjects which Faustus will ultimately reject for necromancy ("Settle thy studies, Faustus, and begin / . . . /And live and die in Aristotle's works. / Sweet *Analytics*, 'tis thou hast ravished me," etc. [*Dr Faustus* 1.1.1–6]) and Shakespeare could well be showing that he is not intimidated by learning of this kind. Indeed, "To such the sweets of sweet philosophy" (*TS* 1.1.318), which also occurs in act 1, scene 1, of *The Shrew*, can be seen as deliberately trying to outsweet Marlowe's lines. The early deaths of many of the leading university writers may explain why formal philosophy drops out of Shakespeare's work between 1592 and 1598–9. The emergence of Jonson represents a new challenge in that, formidable classicist though he was, he seems to have had no more formal education than Shakespeare.

19 See Sarah Hutton, "Introduction to the Renaissance and Seventeenth Century," in Baldwin and Hutton, eds., *Platonism and the English Imagination*, 67–75, especially 69–70.

20 There are many uncertainties here. Jonson's library suffered from at least one fire, and he had to sell portions of it at various times to pay off debts. In addition, it is not clear whether the penciled comment in the British Library copy was written on good authority. See Medcalf, "Shakespeare on Beauty," 118.

21 See Medcalf, "Shakespeare on Beauty," 123–5.

22 This case is argued in detail in my "The Dissolution of Goodness."

23 The difficulties and structure of elenctic argument are brilliantly discussed in Gregory Vlastos, "The Socratic Elenchus: Method is All," in his *Socratic Studies*, ed. Myles Burnyeat (Cambridge: Cambridge University Press, 1994), 1–38; and Donald Davidson, "Plato's Philosopher," and "The Socratic Concept of Truth," in his *Truth, Language, and History* (Oxford: Clarendon Press, 2005), 223–50. I have drawn freely on insights in all these papers.

24 For a different explanation of why *B* should be given up, see Vlastos, "The Socratic Elenchus," 21–3.

25 The greater drama of giving up *A* is mentioned in Davidson, "Plato's Philosopher," 227–8.
26 My characterization of the beliefs Iago inculcates, and the methods he uses to inculcate them, are necessarily sketchy through lack of space. I hope shortly to complete a separate essay which examines both topics in detail.
27 For a discussion of the declining influence of formal rhetoric on Shakespeare's work, see Frank Kermode, *Shakespeare's Language* (Harmondsworth: Allen Lane, 2000), 3–34. The decline of the old rhetoric in drama parallels, with good reason, the rise of a new naturalistic mode of acting referred to by contemporaries as "personation." On this, see Frank Kermode, *The Age of Shakespeare* (London: Weidenfeld and Nicolson, 2004), 53–4, 99, 108.
28 See, for example, René Weis, *Shakespeare Revealed: A Biography* (London: John Murray, 2007), 287–8. It is important that both Iago and Socrates have prosaic marriages; their more intense erotic pleasures have to be found elsewhere.
29 For a more extended discussion of the connections between sexuality and the intimacy of the Socratic method, see my "Wittgenstein, Plato, and the Historical Socrates," *Philosophy* 82 (January 2007): 45–85, especially, 75–9.
30 Aristotle, *Nicomachean Ethics*, ed. Jonathan Barnes (Harmondsworth: Penguin, 2004), 68–9.
31 See M. H. Abrams, *A Glossary of Literary Terms*, 6th edn. (Fort Worth, TX: Harcourt Brace, 1993), 97.
32 The case is argued in Gregory Vlastos, "Socrates' Disavowal of Knowledge," in Vlastos, *Socratic Studies*, 39–66.
33 This problem is discussed in Vlastos, "The Socratic Elenchus," 21; and Davidson, "Plato's Philosopher," 224, 230–40.
34 For the methodological importance of the theory of recollection, see Vlastos, "The Socratic Elenchus," 28–9.

11

Catharsis

JONATHAN LEAR

Tragedy, says Aristotle, is a mimesis of a serious and complete action, having magnitude, which through pity and fear brings about a catharsis of such emotions.[1] But what Aristotle meant by what he said – in particular, what he meant in claiming that tragedy produces a catharsis – is a question which has dominated Western philosophy and literary criticism since the Renaissance.[2] In the last hundred years it has been widely accepted that by catharsis Aristotle meant a purgation of the emotions.[3] Now, there is a sense in which the interpretation of catharsis as purgation is unexceptionable: having aroused the emotions of pity and fear, tragedy does leave us with a feeling of relief; and it is natural for humans to conceive of this emotional process in corporeal terms: as having got rid of or expelled the emotions.[4] But at this level of generality, the interpretation is as unhelpful as it is unexceptionable. For what we wish to know is how Aristotle conceived of the process of catharsis as it occurs in the performance of a tragedy. Even if we accept that Aristotle drew on the metaphor of purgation in naming this emotional process "catharsis," what we want to know is: did he really think that this process was an emotional purgation or did he merely use the metaphor to name a process which he understood in some different way? At the level of metaphor there seems little reason to choose between the medical metaphor of purgation and its traditional religious competitor, purification, not to mention more general meanings of "cleansing," "separation," and so on.[5] In fact, Aristotle's preponderant use of the word is as a term for menstrual discharge.[6] As far as I know, no one in the extended debate about tragic catharsis has suggested the model of menstruation. But why not? Is it not more compelling to think of a natural process of discharge of the emotions than of their purging?

It is only when we shift from the question of what metaphors Aristotle might have been drawing on to the question of what he took the process of catharsis in tragedy to be that there is any point in choosing among the various models. Of course, the task of figuring out what Aristotle meant by catharsis is made all the more alluring, as well as frustrating, by a passing remark which he makes in the *Politics* while discussing the catharsis which music produces: "the word 'catharsis' we use at present without explanation, but when later we speak of poetry we will treat the subject with more

---

A Companion to the Philosophy of Literature, First Edition. Edited by Garry L. Hagberg and Walter Jost.
© 2010 John Wiley & Sons Ltd. Published 2015 by John Wiley & Sons, Ltd.

precision."[7] We seem to be missing the section of the *Poetics* in which Aristotle explicitly set out what he meant.[8]

Here I will first isolate a series of constraints which any adequate interpretation of catharsis must satisfy. These constraints will be derived from a consideration of Aristotle's extended discussion of the emotions, of the effect of tragedy, and of how tragedy produces this effect. The constraints may not be tight enough to delimit a single acceptable interpretation, but I shall argue that they are strong enough to eliminate all the traditional interpretations. Second, I will offer an interpretation of tragic catharsis which satisfies all the constraints.

Let us begin with the suggestion that a catharsis is a purgation of the emotions. To take this suggestion seriously one must think that, for Aristotle, catharsis is a cure for an emotionally pathological condition: tragedy helps one to expel or get rid of unhealthily pent-up emotions or noxious emotional elements.[9] The only significant evidence for this interpretation comes from Aristotle's discussion in the *Politics* of the catharsis which music produces:[10]

> We accept the division of melodies proposed by certain philosophers into ethical melodies, melodies of action, and passionate or inspiring melodies, each having, as they say, a mode corresponding to it. But we maintain further that music should be studied, not for the sake of one, but of many benefits, that is to say, with a view to education, to catharsis (the word catharsis we use at present without explanation, but when hereafter we speak of poetry we will treat the subject with more precision) – music may also serve for intellectual enjoyment, for relaxation and for recreation after exertion. It is clear, therefore, that all the modes must be employed by us, but not all of them in the same manner. In education the most ethical modes are to be preferred, but in listening to the performances of others we may admit the modes of action and passion also. For emotions such as pity and fear, or again enthusiasm, exist very strongly in some souls, and have more or less influence over all. Some persons fall into a religious frenzy, whom we see as a result of the sacred melodies – when they have used the melodies that excite the soul to mystic frenzy – restored as though they had found healing and catharsis. Those who are influenced by pity or fear, and every emotional nature, must have a like experience, and others in so far as each is susceptible to such emotions, and all receive a sort of catharsis and are relieved with pleasure. The cathartic melodies likewise give an innocent pleasure to men. Such are the modes and melodies in which those who perform music at the theater should be invited to compete.[11]

It does seem that Aristotle distinguishes cathartic melodies from those "ethical melodies" which help to train and reinforce character – and thus that the point of catharsis cannot in any straightforward way be ethical education.[12] But the only reason for thinking that catharsis is a cure for a pathological condition is that Aristotle's primary example of catharsis is as a cure for religious ecstasy.[13] However, even if we accept that religious ecstasy is a pathological condition, the idea that catharsis is meant to apply to a pathological condition can be sustained only by ignoring an important claim which Aristotle makes in the quoted text. Having begun his discussion of catharsis with the example of those who are particularly susceptible to religious frenzy, Aristotle goes on to say that the same thing holds for anyone who is influenced by pity and fear and, more generally, anyone who is emotionally influenced by events.[14] In case there should be any doubt that Aristotle means to include us all under that category, he continues: "and a certain catharsis and lightening with pleasure occurs for everyone."[15] But "everyone" includes virtuous people, and it is absurd to suppose that, for Aristotle, virtuous people were in any kind of pathological condition.

Nor does the idea of a purgation seem a plausible analogue for tragic catharsis. In a medical purge, as the Aristotelian author of the *Problems* says, "drugs are not concocted – they make their way out carrying with them anything which gets in their way: this is called purging."[16] The idea of a purgation seems to be that of the introduction of a foreign substance, a drug, which later gets expelled from the body untransformed along with the noxious substances. But the idea of a purgation as it is suggested by the commentators is of a homeopathic cure: we introduce pity and fear in order to purge the soul of these emotions.[17] The problem is that though the idea of a homeopathic cure was available in Aristotle's time, there is no evidence that he was aware of it and lots of evidence that he thought that medical cure was effected by introducing contraries.[18] But once we abandon the idea that for Aristotle a medical purgation was a homeopathic cure, there seems to be little to recommend the medical analogy. What foreign substance is introduced to expel what contrary noxious substance in the soul? Why should one think that the virtuous man has any noxious elements in his soul which need purging?

Indeed, if we look to Aristotle's account of the emotions, they do not seem to be the sort of things which are readily conceived as purgeable. Fear, for example, is defined as a pain or disturbance due to imagining some destructive or painful evil in the future.[19] That is, the emotion of fear is not exhausted by the feeling one has when one feels fear. In addition to the feeling, the emotion of fear also requires the belief that one is in danger and a state of mind which treats the danger as worthy of fear. All three conditions are required to constitute the emotion of fear.[20] If, for example, one believes one is in danger but one's state of mind is confidence in being able to overcome it, one will not feel fear.[21] An emotion, then, is not merely a feeling; it is an orientation to the world. But if an emotion requires not merely a feeling, but also a belief about the world one is in and an attitude toward it, then it is hard to know what could be meant by purging an emotion. An emotion is too complex and world-directed an item for the purgation model to be of significant value.

I do not wish to spend time on the idea that tragic catharsis effects a purification of the emotions, for though this view has had proponents since the Renaissance, it is not seriously held today.[22] The major problems with the idea of purification are, first, that virtuous people will experience a certain catharsis in the theater, but their emotional responses are not impure; second, it is not clear what is meant by purifying the emotions. One possibility was suggested by Eduard Muller: "Who can any longer doubt that the purification of pity, fear, and other passions consists in, or at least is very closely connected with, the transformation of the pain that engendered them into pleasure?"[23] The fact that we do derive a certain pleasure from the pitiable and fearful events which are portrayed in tragedy is, I think, of the greatest importance in coming to understand tragic catharsis. However, it is a mistake to think that, in tragedy, pain is transformed into pleasure. Pity and fear are not abolished by the tragedy; it is just that in addition to the pity and fear one feels in response to the tragic events, one is also capable of experiencing a certain pleasure. Moreover, even if there were a transformation, to conceive of it as a purification is to assume that the original emotional response of pity and fear is somehow polluted or unclean. But this isn't so. Aristotle makes it abundantly clear that pity and fear are the appropriate responses to a good tragic plot.[24] The pain of pity and fear is not an impurity which needs to be removed; it is the emotional response which a virtuous man will and ought to feel.

Perhaps the most sophisticated view of catharsis, which has been argued for in recent years, is the idea that catharsis provides an education of the emotions.[25] The central task of an ethical education is to train youths to experience pleasure and pain in the right sort of ways: to feel pleasure in acting nobly and pain at the prospect of acting ignobly.[26] This is accomplished by a process of habituation: by repeatedly encouraging youths to perform noble acts they come to take pleasure in so acting. Virtue, for Aristotle, partially consists in having the right emotional response to any given set of circumstances.[27]

Tragedy, it is argued, provides us with the appropriate objects toward which to feel pity and fear. Tragedy, one might say, trains us or habituates us in feeling pity and fear in response to events which are worthy of those emotions. Since our emotions are being evoked in the proper circumstances, they are also being educated, refined, or clarified. By being given repeated opportunities to feel pity and fear in the right sort of circumstances, we are less likely to experience such emotions inappropriately: namely, in response to circumstances which do not merit pity and fear. Since virtue partially consists in having the appropriate emotional responses to circumstances, tragedy can be considered part of an ethical education.

There are two overwhelming advantages to this interpretation, which, I think, any adequate account of catharsis ought to preserve. First, this interpretation relies on a sophisticated, and genuinely Aristotelian, conception of the emotions. Tragedy provides (a mimesis of) certain objects toward which it is appropriate to form certain beliefs and evaluative attitudes as well as to feel certain pains. Second, this interpretation offers an account of the peculiar pleasure we derive from a performance of tragedy.[28] Aristotle, as is well known, believes in an innate desire to understand, and a special pleasure attends the satisfaction of that desire.[29] If tragedy helps to provide an ethical education, then in experiencing it we come better to understand the world, as fit object of our emotional responses, and better to understand ourselves, in particular, the emotional responses of which we are capable and which the events portrayed require. It is because we gain a deeper insight into the human condition that we derive a special cognitive pleasure from tragedy.

This interpretation does have a genuinely Aristotelian ring to it: it is a position which is consonant with much that Aristotle believed, and it is a position he might have adopted. But I don't think he did. First, as we have seen, a virtuous person will experience a certain catharsis when he sees or hears a tragedy performed; but he is in no need of education.[30] Second, the *Politics*' discussion of music clearly distinguishes music which is educative of the emotions and should be employed in ethical training from music which produces catharsis.[31] The best attempt I have seen to meet this problem is an argument that the type of catharsis which Aristotle is contrasting with ethical education is only an extreme form derived from orgiastic music:

> Once attention is shifted to types of katharsis connected with more common emotions and with those who do not experience them to a morbidly abnormal degree (and both these conditions are true of the tragic variety), it is possible to discern that katharsis may after all be in some cases compatible with the process which Aristotle characterizes in *Politics* 8 as a matter of habituation in feeling the emotions in the right way and towards the right objects (1340a16–18) . . . Simply to identify tragic katharsis with a process of ethical exercise and habituation for the emotions through art would be speculative and more than the evidence justifies. But to suggest that these two things ought to stand in an intelligible relation to one another (as the phrase "for education and katharsis" at *Pol.* 1341b38 encourages us to see them) is only to argue that tragic katharsis should be capable of integration into Aristotle's general philosophy of the emotions, and of their cognitive and moral importance, as well as into the framework of his theory of tragedy as a whole.[32]

Of course, tragic catharsis and ethical education might stand in an "intelligible" relation to each other even if they served completely different purposes; but when one sees the phrase "for education and catharsis" quoted out of context, it is tempting to suppose that education and catharsis are part of a single project. Unfortunately, the text will not support this supposition. Aristotle explicitly says that although one should use all the different types of melodies, one should not use them for the same function.[33] And when he says that music may be used "for the sake of education and of catharsis,"[34] he is unambiguously listing different benefits which may be derived from music.[35] Nor is it true that in this passage Aristotle is only contrasting education with an extreme, orgiastic form of catharsis. For although, as we have seen, he begins by talking about the catharsis of religious frenzy, he very quickly goes on to mention a certain catharsis had by everyone, and the fact that two lines before he explicitly mentions those who are susceptible to pity and fear suggests that he had tragic catharsis in mind.[36] Thus the contrast which Aristotle draws between ethical education and catharsis cannot easily be brushed aside.

Moreover, Aristotle continues by saying that vulgar audiences will have vulgar tastes and that professional musicians ought to cater to those tastes, since even vulgar people need relaxation.[37] But if even some melodies are ethically educative, why doesn't Aristotle insist that the vulgar be confined to such uplifting tunes? The answer, I think, is that it's too late. Aristotle contrasts two types of audience: the vulgar crowd composed of artisans and laborers on the one hand, and those who are free and have already been educated on the other.[38] In each case the characters of the audience have been formed, and ethical education would be either futile or superfluous.

Aristotle clearly thinks that tragedy is among the highest of art forms. Aside from the fact that tragedy is the culmination of a teleological development of art forms which began with dithyrambs and phallic songs,[39] and aside from the fact that Aristotle explicitly holds it in higher regard than epic, notwithstanding his enormous respect for Homer, Aristotle criticizes certain forms of inferior plots as due to the demands of a vulgar audience. For example, Aristotle criticizes those allegedly tragic plots which end with the good being rewarded and the bad being punished: "It is ranked first only through the weakness of the audiences; the poets merely follow their public, writing as its wishes dictate. But the pleasure here is not that of tragedy."[40] The implication seems to be that a proper tragic plot would be appreciated and enjoyed above all by a cultivated person. It is hard to escape the conclusion that, for Aristotle, education is for youths, and tragic catharsis is for educated, cultivated adults.

The third reason why the education interpretation of catharsis ought to be rejected is that there is a fundamental sense in which tragedy is not evoking the proper responses to events portrayed. Should we be spectators to tragic events which occur not in the theater but in real life to those who are close to us, or to those who are like us, the proper emotional response would be (the right amount of) pity and fear. To take any kind of pleasure from these events would be a thoroughly inappropriate response. Thus there is a sense in which tragedy provides a poor training for the emotional responses of real life: first, we should not be trained to seek out tragedy in real life, as we do seek it in the theater; second, we should not be trained to find any pleasure in real-life tragic events, as we do find pleasure in the tragic portrayals of the poets. Although a mimesis of pitiable and fearful events must to a certain extent be like the real-life events which they represent, the mimesis must, for Aristotle, also be in an important respect unlike those same events. For it is precisely because the mimesis is a mimesis that a certain type of pleasure is an appropriate response to it. Were it not for the fact that Aristotle recognized a salient difference between mimesis and the real-life events it portrays, Aristotle would have had to agree with Plato that poetry should be banned from the ideal state. Aristotle disagrees with Plato not over whether tragedy can be used as part of an ethical education in the appropriate emotional responses, but over whether a mimesis is easily confused with the real thing. Aristotle's point is that although the proper emotional response to a mimesis would be inappropriate to the real event, a mimesis is sufficiently unlike the real event that there is no danger of its having an improper educational effect on the audience. From the point of view of ethical education alone, poetry is allowed into the republic not because it has any positive educational value, but because it can be shown to lack any detrimental effects. If poetry has positive value, it must lie outside the realm of ethical education.

"There is not the same kind of correctness in poetry," Aristotle says, "as in politics, or indeed any other art."[41] The constraints on the poet differ considerably from the constraints on the politician. The politician is constrained to legislate an education in which youths will be trained to react appropriately to real-life events; in particular, to feel the right amount of pity and fear in response to genuinely pitiable and fearful events. The tragedian is constrained to evoke pity and fear through a mimesis of such events, but he is also constrained to provide a catharsis of those very emotions. It is in the catharsis of those emotions that the emotional response appropriate to poetry goes beyond that which is appropriate to the corresponding real-life events. Thus in coming to understand what catharsis is, we will be approaching an understanding of the special contribution poetry makes to life.

The final reason why the education interpretation of catharsis ought to be rejected is that in the end it does not explain the peculiar pleasure of tragedy.[42] Of course, a proper appreciation of tragedy does require a finely tuned cognitive appreciation of the structure of the plot, and there is no doubt that the exercise of one's cognitive faculties in the appreciation of tragedy does afford a certain pleasure. But the pleasure we derive from tragedy is not primarily that which comes from satisfying the desire to understand.

In fact there is little textual support in the *Poetics* for the hypothesis that the peculiar pleasure of tragedy is a cognitive pleasure. The main support comes from *Poetics* 4, where Aristotle explains the origins of poetry:

> It is clear that the general origin of poetry was due to two causes, each of them part of human nature. Imitation [*mimesis*] is natural to man from childhood, one of his advantages over the lower animals being this, that he is the most imitative creature in the world, and learns at first by imitation. And it is also natural for all to delight in works of imitation. The truth of this second point is shown by experience; though the objects themselves may be painful to see, we delight to view the most realistic representations of them in art, the forms for example of the lowest animals and of dead bodies. The explanation is to be found in a further fact: to be learning something is the greatest of pleasures not only to the philosopher, but also to the rest of mankind, however small their capacity for it; the reason of the delight in seeing the picture is that one is at the same time learning and reasoning what each thing is, e.g., that this is that; for if one has not seen the thing before, one's pleasure will not be in the picture as an imitation of it, but will be due to the execution or coloring or some similar cause.[43]

Aristotle is here concerned with the origins of a process which culminates in the development of tragedy. Children begin learning by their early imitations of the adults around them, and in learning they derive a rudimentary form of cognitive pleasure; but this is only an explanation of how elementary forms of imitation naturally arise among humans. It is not an explanation of the peculiar pleasure of tragedy.

One must also be cautious in interpreting Aristotle's claim about the pleasure in learning. Aristotle is trying to explain why we take pleasure in viewing imitations of objects which are themselves painful to look at. Now, it is tempting to assimilate this passage with Aristotle's admonition in *Parts of Animals* that one should not shy away "with childish aversion" from studying blood and guts and even the humblest of animals: for the study of even the lowest of animals yields a pleasure which derives from discovering the intelligible causes of its functioning and the absence of chance.[44] For Aristotle there contrasts the cognitive pleasure derived from coming to understand causes from the pleasure derived from an imitation:

> For even if some [animals] are not pleasing to the sense of sight, nevertheless, creating nature provides extraordinary pleasures for those who are capable of understanding causes and who are by nature philosophical. Indeed, it would be unreasonable and strange if mimetic representations of them were attractive, because they disclose the mimetic skill of the painter or sculptor, and the original realities themselves were not

more interesting, to all at any rate who have eyes to discern the reasons that determined their formation.[45]

Aristotle is saying that there are two distinct pleasures to be derived from animals which are in themselves unpleasant to look at: a cognitive pleasure in understanding their causes, and a "mimetic pleasure" in appreciating an artist's skill in accurately portraying these ugly creatures. It is this distinctively "mimetic pleasure" which Aristotle is concentrating on in *Poetics* 4. The reason he focuses on the artistic representation of an ugly animal is that he wants to be sure he is isolating the pleasure derived from the mimesis, rather than the pleasure one might derive from the beauty of the animal itself. In explaining this "mimetic pleasure," Aristotle does allude to the pleasure derived from learning. But that Aristotle has only the most rudimentary form of "learning" in mind is made clear by his claim that this pleasure in learning is available not only to the philosophically minded, but to all of mankind, however small their capacity for it. What one is "learning" is that this is that: that this (picture of a dead mouse) is (an accurate representation of) that ([a] dead mouse). The "reasoning" one is doing is confined to realizing that one thing (an artistic representation) is an instance of another. The pleasure, Aristotle says, is precisely that which would be unavailable to someone incapable of formulating this elementary realization: that is, to someone who had never seen a mouse or someone who, for whatever reason, was not able to recognize representation as a representation.[46] Thus it is a mistake to interpret this passage as suggesting that the reasoning is a reasoning about causes. *Poetics* 4, then, is about the most elementary pleasures which can be derived from the most elementary forms of mimesis. Although this is a first step toward an understanding of tragic pleasure, it does not lend support to the thesis that tragic pleasure is a species of cognitive pleasure.

Now, Aristotle does repeatedly insist that a good tragedy must have an intelligible plot structure. There must be a reason why the tragedy occurs: thus Aristotle says that the events must occur plausibly or necessarily,[47] that the events must occur on account of one another rather than in mere temporal succession,[48] and that the protagonist must make a certain mistake or error (*hamartia*) which is responsible for and explains his downfall.[49] And I think there is no doubt that the proper effect of tragedy on an audience is brought about via the audience's cognitive appreciation of the intelligible plot structure. The question, then, is not whether an audience must exercise its cognitive faculties, nor whether it may find pleasure in so doing; the question is whether this cognitive exercise and its attendant pleasure is the proper effect of tragedy. Is this cognitive pleasure the pleasure appropriate and peculiar to tragedy? To see that the answer is no, consider one of Aristotle's classic statements of the demand for intelligibility:

> Tragedy is a mimesis not only of a complete action, but also of fearful and pitiable events. But such events occur in the strongest form when they occur unexpectedly but in consequence of one another. For the events are more marvelous [*thaumaston*] when they occur thus than if they occur by chance.[50]

Aristotle's point is that a plot structure in which the events do not merely succeed each other in time, but stand in the relation of intelligible cause to intelligible effect, albeit a relation in which the intelligibility comes to light only with a reversal and recognition, is the best plot structure for portraying truly pitiable and fearful events. What it is to be a pitiable and fearful event is to be an event capable of inducing pity and fear in the audience. But pity and fear is clearly not the proper effect of tragedy: it is merely a necessary step along the route toward the proper effect. For Aristotle says that it is from pity and fear that tragedy produces a catharsis of these emotions.[51] Therefore, the audience's cognitive appreciation of the plot's intelligible structure and attendant pleasure is important, but they are causal antecedents of the proper effect and proper pleasure of tragedy.

Aristotle does say that events are more marvelous when they occur unexpectedly but in an intelligible relation to each other. And this fact is invoked by those who wish to argue that tragic pleasure is a cognitive pleasure. For in the *Metaphysics* and *Rhetoric*, Aristotle links the wondrous or marvelous with our desire to understand.[52] It is owing to wonder, Aristotle says, that man first began to philosophize: the rising and setting of the sun, for example, provokes man's wonder, and this wonder sets him on a journey to explain why this phenomenon occurs.[53] Thus it is suggested that the wonder that is produced in a tragedy provokes the audience to try to understand the events portrayed, and the pleasure which attends coming to understand is tragic pleasure.[54]

If there were already a strong case for thinking that tragic pleasure was cognitive pleasure, then the link between the marvelous and tragedy, on the one hand, and the desire to understand, on the other, would be suggestive. However, in the absence of a strong case, there are three reasons why Aristotle's remarks on the marvelous cannot be used to lend any significant support to the idea that tragic pleasure is cognitive. First, in the *Poetics* passage just quoted Aristotle seems to be suggesting that the relation between wonder and understanding is precisely the opposite of that suggested by the *Metaphysics*: it is by cognitively grasping that the events, though unexpected, are intelligibly linked to one another that wonder is produced in us. So whereas in the *Metaphysics* wonder provokes us to understand, in the *Poetics* understanding provokes us to experience wonder. Second, although in the quoted passage Aristotle associates intelligibility with wonder, toward the end of the *Poetics* Aristotle also associates wonder with irrationality.[55] One advantage of epic over tragedy, he says there, is that it is better suited to portraying irrational events (*to alogon*). For since the audience of an epic narrative does not actually have to see the irrationality acted out onstage, it is less likely to notice it as irrational. However, Aristotle says, it is the irrational which chiefly produces wonder. And he says that the experience of wonder itself is pleasant.[56] So in this case it cannot be that wonder provokes understanding which is pleasant – for irrationality ultimately resists understanding. And at the end of the *Poetics* Aristotle suggests that the pleasure proper to epic and the pleasure proper to tragedy are of the same type,[57] even though tragedy is a higher form of art. Yet if the pleasure proper to epic can be derived from a plot containing irrationalities, it hardly seems that this pleasure can be cognitive. Finally, even granting a link between wonder and cognitive pleasure in itself does nothing to support the thesis that tragic pleasure is cognitive.

For an anti-cognitivist like myself does not believe that there is no role for cognition and its attendant pleasure in the appreciation of a tragedy; he only denies that cognitive pleasure is to be identified with tragic pleasure. For the anti-cognitivist, cognitive pleasure is a step which occurs en route to the production of the proper pleasure of tragedy.

The final text cited in support of the cognitivist thesis is Aristotle's claim that poetry is "more philosophical" than history:

> Poetry is more philosophical and more serious than history: for poetry speaks more about universals, while history speaks of particulars. By universal is meant what sort of thing such a sort of person would plausibly or necessarily say or do – which is the aim of poetry though it affixes proper names to characters; by a particular, what Alcibiades did or had done to him.[58]

Of course, philosophy is an exercise of man's cognitive faculties, and, as is well known, Aristotle repeatedly insists that it is universals which man understands.[59] However, even if we interpret this passage just as cognitivists would like us to – as suggesting an intimate link between the appreciation of tragedy and the exercise of our cognitive abilities – nothing in this passage would help us decide between the cognitivist and the anti-cognitivist theses. For, as we have seen, the anti-cognitivist does not deny that a cognitive understanding of the plot is essential to the proper appreciation of a tragedy; he only denies that tragic pleasure can be identified with the pleasure which attends understanding.

But, more importantly, I don't think we should interpret this passage as the cognitivists would like us to. There is a certain plasticity in the idea of a universal which facilitates the transition from poetry to cognition. The true objects of knowledge, for Aristotle, are essences, and these essences are "universal" in the sense that two healthy human beings will instantiate the same essence: human soul. But the reason that essences are linked with knowledge is that in coming to understand a thing's essence we come to understand what that thing is really like. In coming to understand human essence, we come to understand what it is to be a human being. Now, when Aristotle says that poetry is "more philosophical" than history because it deals with universals, it is tempting to read him as saying that poetry provides us with deeper insights into the human condition. This is a temptation which ought to be resisted.[60] If we look to what Aristotle means by "universal" in the passage under discussion, it is clear that he does not mean "universal which expresses the essence of the human condition," but something much less grandiose: that poetry should refrain from describing the particular events of particular people and instead portray the sorts of things a given type of person might say or do. Aristotle later gives an example of what he means by the universal element in poetry:

> The following will show how the universal element in *Iphigenia*, for instance, may be viewed: a certain maiden having been offered in sacrifice, and spirited away from her sacrificers into another land, where the custom was to sacrifice all strangers to the Goddess, she was

made there the priestess of his rite. Long after that the brother of the priestess happened to come: the fact, however, of the oracle having bidden him go there, and his object in going, are outside the plot of the play. On his coming he was arrested, and about to be sacrificed, when he revealed who he was – either as Euripides puts it or (as suggested by Polyidus) by the not improbable exclamation, "so I too am doomed to be sacrificed as my sister was"; and the disclosure led to his salvation. This done, the next thing, after the proper names have been fixed as a basis for the story, is to turn to the episodes.[61]

Aristotle's point is simply that poetry deals with types of actions and type of persons, even though the poet, after having constructed the "universal" plot, later assigns names to the characters.[62] Aristotle does say that such a universal plot is "more philosophical" than history, but by this he did not mean that poetry gives us ultimate understanding of humanity. Rather, he meant that it has emerged from the mire of particularity in which history is trapped and thus has taken a step along the way toward philosophy. Whether fairly or unfairly, Aristotle had a very low opinion of history (he seemed to hold history in the same regard as we hold newspapers), and thus something doesn't have to be very philosophical to be more philosophical than history.[63]

What then is the point of Aristotle's requirement that poetry deal with universals, if it is not to insist upon poetry's ultimate cognitive value? If we read *Poetics* 9 through to the end it becomes clear that Aristotle's overall concern is with the formation of a plot which effectively produces pity and fear in the audience.[64] But in order to feel pity and fear the audience must believe that there is a certain similarity between themselves and the character in the tragedy: and the reason they must believe in this similarity is that they must believe that the events portrayed in the tragedy might happen to them. For a person to feel pity and fear, he must believe that he himself is vulnerable to the events he is witnessing. That is why Aristotle says that the poet's function is to portray not events which have happened, but events which might happen – and that these possible occurrences must seem plausible or even necessary.[65] The point of portraying events which might plausibly happen is that the audience will naturally come to believe that these events might happen to them. And this is a crucial step in the production of pity and fear in their souls. Poetry uses universals for the same purpose. Because poetry is not mired in particularity, but concerns itself with types of events which occur to certain sorts of people, it is possible for the audience to appreciate that they are the sort of people to whom this sort of event could, just possibly, occur. The universality Aristotle has in mind when he talks about the universality of poetry is not as such aiming at the depth of the human condition; it is aiming at the universality of the human condition.[66]

The education of interpretation, however attractive it is, must be rejected as an account of what Aristotle meant by tragic catharsis. But having already rejected the purgation and purification interpretations, we have abandoned all the important traditional accounts. What then did Aristotle mean by tragic catharsis? It is to this question that I now turn.

Although the work so far has been largely critical, I think something of positive value has emerged. For in seeing how previous interpretations fall short, we have isolated a series of constraints which any acceptable interpretation of catharsis must satisfy. These constraints may not be so narrow as to isolate a single, definitive interpretation, but they at least set out a field in which the truth must lie. In this section I would like to state the constraints on any acceptable interpretation of catharsis and to offer an interpretation which fits those constraints.

One of the major constraints on any interpretation is:

1. There is reason for a virtuous person to experience the performance of a tragedy: he too will experience a catharsis of pity and fear.[67]

Precisely because of (1), it follows that

2. Tragic catharsis cannot be a process which is essentially and crucially corrective: that is, it cannot be a purgation, insofar as purgation is of something pathological or noxious; it cannot be a purification of some pollution; it cannot be an education of the emotions.

This is not to deny that a cathartic experience may be corrective. Aristotle, as we have already seen, thought that cathartic melodies can help to restore those who are particularly susceptible to religious frenzy; and one might similarly suppose that a tragic catharsis could restore those who are particularly susceptible to the tragic emotions of pity and fear. Nor do I mean to deny that a virtuous person may experience relief in a cathartic experience – a relief which it is natural to conceive of in terms of the release of pent-up emotions. However, the virtuous person is not in a pathological condition, nor is he polluted with some impure element which needs to be removed. Nor is he in need of any further training of the emotions: indeed, it is because he is already disposed to respond appropriately to the situations of life, in judgment, in action, and in emotion, that he is virtuous. The idea that catharsis provides an education of the emotions suffers further from the fact that

3. What one feels at the performance of a tragedy is not what one would or should feel in the real-life counterpart.

For although tragedy provokes pity and fear in the audience, it also elicits an appropriate pleasure. This pleasure would be thoroughly inappropriate to real-life tragic situations. But the fact that a good person (at least) feels pleasure in the performance of a tragedy, but would not do so in real life, suggests that

4. A proper audience does not lose sight of the fact that it is enjoying the performance of a tragedy.

Although the audience may identify emotionally with the characters in the tragedy, this identification must remain partial. Throughout its emotional involvement, the audience keeps track of the fact that it is an audience. For in a real-life tragedy a person would feel fear and, if he stood in the right relation to the tragic event, pity, but he would derive no pleasure from the tragic event. This implies that

5   The mere expression or release of emotions is not in itself pleasurable.

For Aristotle, pity and fear are unadulterated pains.[68] The mere opportunity to feel these painful emotions does not in itself provide relief: everything depends on the conditions in which these painful emotions are to be felt. Those who have assumed that a catharsis, for Aristotle, was a release or discharge of pent-up or unexpressed emotions have also assumed that the mere experience of emotions, even painful ones, has a pleasurable aspect to it. There is pleasure to be had in a good cry. Such an idea may have a certain plausibility to it, but it is foreign to Aristotle. For him, it depends on what one is crying about. If one is crying in the theater, a certain pleasure may ensue, but there is, for Aristotle, no pleasure to be had in crying over real-life tragic events. This is the problem with taking catharsis to be the mere release of emotion. For Aristotle there is nothing pleasurable *per se* about experiencing pity and fear.

These conditions under which we can derive pleasure from pity and fear and the conditions under which a catharsis of pity and fear occurs are intimately linked, for

6   Catharsis provides a relief: it is either itself pleasurable or it helps to explain the proper pleasure which is derived from tragedy.[69]

Constraints (3)–(6) together suggest that if we are to understand tragic catharsis, we should look to the special ways in which tragedy produces its emotional effects.

Aristotle, as we have seen, defines tragedy in part by the effect it has on its audience: it is a mimesis of an action which by arousing pity and fear produces a catharsis of those emotions.[70] It might seem odd to a modern reader to see Aristotle define tragedy in terms of its effect, for in a modern climate we tend to think that a work of art should be definable in its own terms, independently of whatever effect it might have on its audience. But it would be anachronistic to insist that Aristotle could not have been defining tragedy in terms of its effect on the audience. Poetry, for Aristotle, is a type of making, and the activity of any making occurs in the person or thing toward which the making is directed.[71] For example, the activity of the teacher teaching is occurring, not in the teacher, but in the students who are learning; the activity of the builder building is occurring, not in the builder, but in the house being built. It stands to reason that, for Aristotle, the activity of the poet creating his tragedy occurs ultimately in an audience actively appreciating a performance of the play.[72]

Not only does Aristotle define tragedy in terms of its effect; he thinks that various tragic plots can be evaluated in terms of their effects on an audience.

> We assume that, for the finest form of tragedy, the plot must be not simple but complex; and further, that it must imitate actions arousing fear and pity, since that is the distinctive function of this kind of imitation. It follows, therefore, that there are three forms of plot to be avoided. A good man must not be seen passing from good fortune to bad, or

> a bad man from bad fortune to good. The first situation is not fear-inspiring or piteous, but simply disgusting. The second is the most untragic that can be: it has no one of the requisites of tragedy; it does not appeal either to the human feeling in us, or to our pity, or to our fears. Nor, on the other hand, should an extremely bad man be seen falling from good fortune into bad. Such a story may arouse the human feeling in us, but it will not move us to either pity or fear; pity is occasioned by undeserved misfortune, and fear by that of one like ourselves; so that there will be nothing either piteous or fear-inspiring in the situation.[73]

The important point to note about this passage is that Aristotle is evaluating plots not on the basis of feelings, but on the basis of the emotions. The reason we do not feel pity and fear in witnessing the fall of a bad man from good to bad fortune is that pity requires the belief that the misfortune is undeserved, and fear requires the belief that the man who has suffered the misfortune is like ourselves.[74] (Presumably Aristotle assumed that the proper audience of tragedy would not believe themselves to be sufficiently like a bad person to believe that the things which befall him – most likely as a consequence of his badness – might befall them.)

Similarly with the disgust we feel when watching a good man fall from good to bad fortune: such disgust isn't a pure feeling which can be identified on the basis of its phenomenological properties alone. Disgust requires the belief that there is no reason at all for this good man's fall. It is sometimes thought that Aristotle contradicts himself, for he elsewhere seems to suggest that tragedy is paradigmatically about admirable men falling to bad fortune.[75] But if we take the rest of chapter 13 as explicating what Aristotle means when he denies that the fall of a good man can be the basis of a properly tragic plot, I think we can see a consistent point emerging. In tragedy, Aristotle insists, the central character must make some mistake or error which leads to his fall.[76] The *hamartia* is a mistake which rationalizes the fall. So what Aristotle is excluding when he prohibits the fall of a good man is a totally irrational fall: one which occurs through no fault of the good man at all. Aristotle certainly does allow the fall of a good man to be the subject matter of tragedy, but not of a man who is so good that he has made no mistakes which would rationalize his fall. This distinction illuminates what is meant by disgust: disgust is an emotion which is partially constituted by the belief that there is no reason at all for the misfortune. Disgust is something we feel in response to what we take to be a total absence of rationality.

Aristotle thinks that the mere fact that tragedy must arouse pity and fear in the audience justifies him in severely restricting the range of tragic plots.

> It is not necessary to search for every pleasure from tragedy, but only the appropriate pleasure. But since it is necessary for the poet to produce the pleasure from pity and fear through a mimesis, it is evident that he must do this in the events in the plot. We should investigate, then, what sorts of events appear to be horrible or pitiable. In respect to such actions, it is necessary that the people involved be either friends with each other or enemies or neither of these. But if enemy acts on enemy, there is nothing pitiable about this – neither in the doing of the deed, nor in intending to do it – except in relation to the terrible event itself [*kat' auto to pathos*]. The same is true when the people stand in neither

relation. But whenever the terrible events occur among loved ones [friends, kin], for example if a brother should kill or intend to kill or do some other such thing to a brother, or a son to a father, or a mother to a son, or a son to a mother: we should search for these things.[77]

Aristotle is clear that the peculiar pleasure of tragedy is produced by evoking pity and fear in the audience and that this is accomplished by constructing a mimesis of a special type of terrible event (*pathos*). Aristotle uses the same word, *pathos*, both to signify a terrible event, catastrophe, or serious misfortune and to signify emotion. When, for example, Aristotle cites *pathos* as one of the three ingredients needed in a plot, along with reversal and recognition, in order to produce pity and fear, he is not requiring a certain emotion to be portrayed onstage; he is requiring that there be a destructive act.[78] So one might say that, for Aristotle, there is an objective *pathos* and a subjective *pathos*; and the two are related. For what Aristotle is trying to do in this passage is delimit the precise type of objective *pathos* which is adequate to bring about a particular type of subjective *pathos* – pity and fear – in response.[79]

The objective *pathos* required to produce the tragic emotions is a terrible deed done between kin or loved ones. That is why the great tragedians have correctly focused on just a few families which have been ripped apart by terrible deeds.[80] But what is it about the portrayal of a terrible deed done among kin which makes it particularly well suited to evoking pity and fear?

Perhaps a start may be made in answering this question by recognizing that at least a necessary condition for the audience to feel pity and fear in response to such terrible deeds is that they believe that such events could happen to them. For fear, this is obvious. Aristotle, as we have seen, defines fear as a pain due to imagining some painful or destructive event befalling one. And he further requires that the fearful event be both imminent and capable of causing great pain.[81] For we do not fear distant pains, for example death, nor do we fear imminent but minor pains: "From the definition it will follow that fear is caused by whatever we feel has great power of destroying us, or of harming us in ways that tend to cause us great pain."[82] Aristotle is explicit that we feel fear only when we believe that we are ourselves vulnerable to an imminent and grave danger: "we shall not fear things that we believe cannot happen to us."[83] A further condition on fear is that we must believe that there is at least a faint possibility of escape from the danger.[84]

At first sight, it appears that pity is the paradigm of an other-regarding emotion. We feel pity for others when they suffer what we believe to be undeserved pain.[85] However, Aristotle makes it clear that in order to feel pity for others we must also believe that the terrible event which has befallen them might befall us or our loved ones and, moreover, might befall us soon. Thus in order for us to feel pity for others, we must believe that the others' situation is significantly similar to our own. One might at first think that pity can be felt for those who are in some relevant respect like us – in either social standing, or character, or age – even though we do not believe we could end up in their situation; but Aristotle denies this. We do feel pity for those who are like us, but the reason we do, Aristotle thinks, is that in such cases we think it more likely that the misfortune which has befallen them can befall us.[86] This likelihood explains Aristotle's otherwise puzzling remark in the *Poetics* that we fear for someone who is similar to us.[87] Why not simply pity him? Aristotle's point is that fear is an appropriate emotion to feel in response to a similar person's misfortune: for through his similarity we recognize that we stand in the same danger he did.

Likewise with pity. Aristotle's only caveat is that the perceived danger cannot be too immediate, for in that case fear (for oneself) will drive out pity (for others).[88] Pity will also be driven out of the souls of those who, already ruined, believe that no ill can further harm them, and of those who believe themselves omnipotent and impervious to harm.[89]

> Those who think they may suffer are those who have already suffered and have safely escaped from it: elderly men, owing to their good sense and their experience; weak men, especially men inclined to cowardice; and also educated people, for they are able to reason well.[90]

Aristotle clearly recognizes pity as a reasonable emotion for an educated and thoughtful person: and since good tragedy is ideally for an educated audience, it follows that, for Aristotle, the pity which good tragedy evokes is a reasonable emotional response to the events portrayed.

It follows that a normal, educated audience, going to a performance of a good tragedy, believes that the terrible events portrayed – infanticide, parricide, matricide, the tearing apart of the most primordial bonds of family and society – could happen to them. If they lacked that belief they would, in Aristotle's eyes, be incapable of experiencing the tragic emotions. This shared belief allows us to impose a further constraint, at least upon the emotions from which a tragic catharsis is produced:

7   The events which in a tragedy properly provoke the pity and fear from which a tragic catharsis occurs must be such that the audience believes that such events could happen to them.

First I would like to dispose of two objections which might be raised against this conclusion. The most serious objection is that the audience need not believe that the terrible events could happen to them: they are able to experience the tragic emotions because they are able to identify imaginatively with the central character and thus empathically feel what he feels. Within Aristotle's world, it is clear that the objection has the situation the wrong way around: for Aristotle, it is only because we think ourselves to be sufficiently like another that we can identify with him.[91] On Aristotle's view, we cannot identify with the very bad or with the gods: it is precisely because we are so distant from such beings that our emotions must retain a similar distance from theirs. That is why, for Aristotle, there is no important distinction to be made between our feeling our fear and our feeling Oedipus' fear. The very possibility of our imaginatively feeling Oedipus' fear is grounded in the recognition that we are like him: that is, it is grounded in the possibility of our fearing for ourselves.[92] Moreover, this objection does not take seriously the emotion of pity. We cannot feel pity in imaginatively identifying with Oedipus: part of what makes Oedipus such a remarkable and admirable figure is his lack of self-pity. But if our pity isn't an imaginative reenactment of Oedipus' self-pity, then it must, as we have seen, be grounded in the belief that his fate could be ours.[93]

The less serious objection is that the audience doesn't come to the performance believing that the terrible events portrayed in the tragedy could happen to them: they are persuaded that this is so by the performance itself. The shortest answer to this objection is also the best: tragedy is not rhetoric; it is poetry. Because fear sets us thinking about how to escape from the perceived danger, an orator may wish to persuade his audience that they are in danger;[94] but a tragedy doesn't try to persuade its audience of anything. The only effect on the audience which a tragedy aims to produce is a certain emotional response (the content of which we are trying to uncover). Of course, if tragedy is to succeed in this, it must portray events which are convincing, plausible – events which plausibly could occur.[95] But Aristotle's point in insisting that the poet construct plausible, convincing plots is not so that the poet may persuade the audience of anything but so that he may portray an event which the audience can recognize as one which could, just possibly, happen to them.

Now, if a normal, educated audience attending the performance of a good tragedy believes that the terrible events to be portrayed could, just possibly, happen before they enter and after they leave the theater: they seem to have the beliefs which would justify the experience of pity and fear, but they are not experiencing those emotions.[96]

A misleading way of putting an important truth is this: that when a normal, educated person experiences a performance of a good tragedy, he is able to unify certain beliefs he has with feelings which are appropriate to those beliefs. He came to the theater believing that he could commit or suffer terrible deeds. In the theater he is able to feel those beliefs. But before we jump to the conclusion that catharsis is a unification of belief and feeling, a unification of the tragic emotions, let us stop to consider why this mode of expression is misleading. It is misleading because it suggests that what we feel in the theater is what we ought to feel in real life: that in real life the appropriate feelings are somehow kept at bay from the beliefs which would rationalize them.

But this cannot be right. For constraint (1) requires that the virtuous person experience a catharsis in the performance of a tragedy, but his emotional reactions are already appropriate to the real-life situations in which he lives; and constraint (3) requires that our emotional response to tragedy is not what we would or should feel in response to real-life counterparts. Tragic pleasure depends crucially on the belief that one is emotionally responding to a mimesis of tragic events. Without this belief, tragic pleasure is impossible. Therefore, constraint (7) – that the audience believe that tragic events could happen to them – must be interpreted in a way which does not suggest that the virtuous person, in not feeling pity and fear in ordinary life, is somehow cut off from a proper emotional response to his situation. It is completely un-Aristotelian to suppose that what we feel in the theater is what we ought to feel in real life, but for some reason do not. In real life the virtuous man feels just what he ought to feel. But then, how could he believe that terrible, tragic deeds could, just possibly, befall him and not feel fear and dread?

Everything depends on the strength of the modal operator. The virtuous man believes that terrible, tragic events could happen to him, true, but the possibility that those things will happen is, in his opinion, too remote for the actual feeling of fear to be warranted.[97] Although a tragic breakdown of the primordial ties of human life is possible, the virtuous man also recognizes that this is less likely to happen to him than almost anything else. That is why it is misleading to say that tragedy restores the appropriate feelings to our already existing beliefs. Our belief that tragic events could, just possibly, befall us already has the appropriate feeling attached to it outside the theater. No unification is needed, for, at least in the case of the virtuous person, there is no split which needs to be overcome.

And yet the belief that tragic events could, just possibly, happen to us does exert some pressure on our souls – even on the souls of us virtuous people. This is precisely the pressure which takes us to the theater. For in the theater we can imaginatively bring what we take to be a remote possibility closer to home. As Aristotle himself said:

> those who heighten the effect of their words with suitable gestures, tones, appearance, and dramatic action generally are especially successful in exciting pity: they thus put the disasters before our eyes, and make them seem close to us, just coming or just past.[98]

The tragic poet, for Aristotle, plays a role in the world of emotions somewhat similar to the role of the skeptic in the world of beliefs. The skeptic awakens us to the fact that we ourselves believe in certain epistemic possibilities which in ordinary life we ignore: for example, that we could be asleep, dreaming, or perhaps deceived by an evil demon. On the one hand, these possibilities are extremely remote, so we are justified in ignoring them in ordinary life; on the other hand, they lend content to the idea that in ordinary life we are living "inside the plain": and they fuel our desire to get outside the plain of everyday life and see how things really are, absolutely.[99]

The tragic poet awakens us to the fact that there are certain emotional possibilities which we ignore in ordinary life. On the one hand, these possibilities are remote, so it is not completely unreasonable to ignore them in ordinary life; on the other hand, they lend content to the idea that in ordinary life we are living "inside the plain": and they fuel our desire imaginatively to experience life outside the plain. Even if tragedy does not befall us, it goes to the root of the human condition that it is a possibility we must live with. And even if remote, the possibility of tragedy is not only much more imminent than the skeptical possibilities; it is much more threatening. For while skeptical possibilities are so designed that they make no difference to the experience of our lives, in tragedy our lives are ripped asunder.

But there is a genuine problem about how to experience tragic possibility. On the one hand, the possibility of tragedy in ordinary life is too remote to justify real fear; on the other hand, it is too important and too close to ignore. Tragic poetry provides an arena in which one can imaginatively experience the tragic emotions: the performance of a play "captures our souls."[100] However, it is crucial to the pleasure we derive from tragedy, that we never lose sight of the fact that we are an audience, enjoying a work of art. Otherwise the pleasurable catharsis of pity and fear would collapse into the merely painful experience of those emotions. Aristotle is keenly aware of the important difference between a mimesis of a serious action and the serious action of which it is a mimesis. The emotional response which is appropriate to a mimesis – tragic pleasure and catharsis – would be thoroughly inappropriate to the real event.

It is this experience of the tragic emotions in an appropriately inappropriate environment which, I think, helps to explain our experience of relief in the theater. We imaginatively live life to the full, but we risk nothing. The relief is thus not that of "releasing pent-up emotions" *per se*; it is the relief of "releasing" these emotions in a safe environment. But to say that it is this experience of relief to which Aristotle gave the name "catharsis" is not to characterize it fully: one needs also to know the content of our relief, what our relief is about.

Here I will only mention briefly certain consolations which are integral to Aristotle's conception of tragedy. The world of tragic events must, Aristotle repeatedly insists, be rational. The subject of tragedy may be a good man, but he must make a mistake which rationalizes his fall.[101] The mere fall of a good man from good fortune to bad fortune for no reason at all isn't tragic, but disgusting. The events in a tragedy must be necessary or plausible, and they must occur on account of one another. Insofar as we do fear that tragic events could occur in our lives, what we fear is chaos: the breakdown of the primordial bonds which link person to person. For Aristotle, a good tragedy offers us this consolation: that even when the breakdown of the primordial bonds occurs, it does not occur in a world which is in itself ultimately chaotic and meaningless.

It is significant that, for Aristotle, *Oedipus Tyrannus* is the paradigm tragedy rather than, say, *Antigone*.[102] For the point of tragedy, in Aristotle's eyes, is not to portray a world in which a person through no fault of her own may be subject to fundamentally irreconcilable and destructive demands. In Aristotle's conception of tragedy, the individual actor takes on the burden of badness, and the world as a whole is absolved.[103] And there is further consolation is recognizing that even when they are responsible for their misfortunes, humans remain capable of conducting themselves with dignity and nobility.[104] Even in his humiliation and shame, Oedipus inspires our awe and admiration.

In the *Rhetoric* Aristotle says that those who have already experienced great disasters no longer feel fear, for they feel they have already experienced every kind of horror.[105] In tragedy, we are able to put ourselves imaginatively in a position in which there is nothing further to fear. There is further consolation in recognizing that one has experienced the worst, there is nothing further to fear, and yet the world remains a rational, meaningful place in which a person can conduct himself with dignity. For Aristotle, even in tragedy the fundamental goodness of man and world is reaffirmed.[106]

Notes

1. See Aristotle, *Poetics* 6.1449b22–28.
2. See Baxter Hathaway, *The Age of Criticism: The Late Renaissance in Italy* (Ithaca: Cornell University Press, 1962), 205–300.
3. This is due largely to Jacob Bernays' influential *Zwei Abhandlungen uber die aristotelische Theorie des Drama* (1857; reprint, Berlin, 1880). A chapter of this book has been translated as "Aristotle on the Effect of Tragedy" by Jonathan and Jennifer Barnes, in

J. Barnes, M. Schofield, and R. Sorabji, ed., *Articles on Aristotle*, vol. 4, (London: Duckworth, 1979). Bernays' interpretation had a wider influence than on Aristotelian scholarship alone; for Bernays was Freud's wife's uncle, and it seems that Freud and Breuer were aware of the interpretation and relied on it when formulating his conception of catharsis in the early stages of the formation of psychoanalytic theory. (See Bennett Simon, *Mind and Madness in Ancient Greece* [Ithaca: Cornell University Press, 1978], 140–3.) The catharsis-as-purge metaphor is used by Plato in the *Sophist* (230c–231e), where Socrates' elenchic method is represented as purging one of false beliefs.

4   See, e.g., Sigmund Freud, "Notes upon a Case of Obsessional Neurosis," *Standard Edition* 10: 233–4; "Formulations on the Two Principles of Mental Functioning," *Standard Edition* 12: 218–26; *Totem and Taboo, Standard Edition* 13: 78–90; "On Narcissicm: An Introduction," *Standard Edition* 14: 73–102; "Negation," *Standard Edition* 19: 235–9; Wilfrid Bion, *Learning from Experience* (London: Maresfield, 1984) and *Second Thoughts* (London: Maresfield, 1984); Melanie Klein, *Narrative of a Child Analysis* (London: Hogarth Press, 1961) 31ff.; *Contributions to Psycho-Analysis* (London: Hogarth Press, 1948), 140–51, 303; *Developments in Psycho-Analysis* (London: Hogarth Press, 1952); W. R. D. Fairburn, "Schizoid Factors in the Personality," in *Psychoanalytic Studies of the Personality* (London: 1984); Richard Wollheim, "The Mind and the Mind's Image of Itself," in *On Art and the Mind* (Cambridge, MA: Harvard University Press, 1974); "Wish-Fulfilment," in Ross Harrison, ed., *Rational Action* (Cambridge: Cambridge University Press, 1979); and *The Thread of Life* (Cambridge: Cambridge University Press, 1984).

5   The idea that purgation and purification need not be treated as contraries *is* argued by Humphry House, *Aristotle's Poetics* (London: R. Hart-Davis, 1956), 104–11; and by Stephen Halliwell, *Aristotle's Poetics* (Chapel Hill: University of North Carolina Press, 1986), 184–201.

6   See, e.g., Aristotle, *Generation of Animals* I.20.728b3, 14; IV.5.773b1, IV.6.775b5; *History of Animals* VI.18.573a2, a7; VI.28.578b18; VII.2.582b7, 30; VII.4.584a8; VIII.11.587b2, b30–33, 588a1. For the use of *katharsis* to describe seminal discharge: *Generation of Animals* II.7.747a19; for the discharge of urine: *History of Animals* VI.18.573a23; for birth discharge: *History of Animals* VI.20.574b4.

7   Aristotle, *Politics* VII.7.13411337–9.

8   Aristotle uses the word *katharsis* only twice in *Poetics*: once, as we have seen, in the definition of tragedy, and once to refer to the ritual of purification at which Orestes is recognized by his sister, Iphigenia; *Poetics* 17.1455b15.

9   Bernays is explicit that catharsis is a cure for a pathological condition.

10 See *Politics* VIII.5–7. Bernays emphasizes the importance of this passage; though, as we shall see, he is less persuasive in his interpretation of that discussion. G. R. Else and, following him, Leon Golden have argued that one should not look outside the *Poetics* for the meaning of tragic catharsis (G. F. Else, *Aristotle's Poetics: The Argument* [Cambridge, MA: Harvard University Press, 1957], 439ff.; Leon Golden, "Catharsis," *Transactions and Proceedings of the American Philological Association* 93 [1962]: 51–60; and "Mimesis and Catharsis," *Classical Philology* 64 [1969]: 145–53). This, I believe, is a misapplication of a principle from new criticism. The *Poetics* was not meant to be a self-contained universe; it was an integral part of Aristotle's philosophy. If, for example, we were trying to determine what Aristotle meant by art *(techne)* or poetry *(poiesis)* in the *Poetics*, there would be no plausibility to claiming that we should completely restrict ourselves to the *Poetics'* discussion. Of course, Aristotle does use *poiesis* in a special way in the *Poetics*: it is to be

translated as "poetry" rather than as a "making," which is the appropriate translation in the *Metaphysics*. However, if we ignore all other Aristotelian works we remain blind to the philosophically important fact that, for Aristotle, poetry is a special type of making. There is no doubt that we must approach other texts with care, for, to return to our current concern, Aristotle's use of "catharsis" when discussing medical purging may be different in significant respects from his use of the term when discussing tragedy. But such interpretive difficulties are not sufficient grounds for ignoring other texts altogether. (Indeed, Else's and Golden's strictures led them to formulate a highly implausible account of catharsis, in which catharsis is not an effect on the audience of tragedy, but a resolution of the events in the play. This implausible interpretation depends upon an even more implausible translation of Aristotle's definition of tragedy. For an excellent criticism of this interpretation, see Halliwell, *Aristotle's Poetics*, app. 5, especially 354–6.)

11   *Politics* VIII.7.1341b32–42a18. Here I have made a few changes in the revised Oxford translation: I use "ethical melodies" rather than "melodies of character" for *to ethika*; I use "catharsis" rather than translating it as "purgation"; I translate *pathos* as "emotion" rather than as "feeling"; and I translate *kouphidzesthai meth' hedones* as "relieved with pleasure" rather than as "lightened and delighted."

12   Bernays makes this point. Halliwell interprets this passage so as to diminish Aristotle's apparent contrast between education and catharsis. For a criticism of this interpretation, see pages 206–13, later in this chapter.

13   See especially *Politics* VIII.7.1342a4–11. Bernays takes religious ecstasy to be a pathological condition.

14   1342a11–13: *tauto de touto anagkaion paschein kai tous eleemonas kai tous phobetikous kai tous olos pathetikous*.

15   *Kai pasi gignesthai tina katharsin kai kouphidzesthai meth' hedones*: 1342a14–15 (my translation and emphasis). This statement seems to me to provide absolutely conclusive evidence against House's claim that, for Aristotle, a *phronimos* at the theater would experience no catharsis; *Aristotle's Poetics*, chapter 8.

16   Aristotle, *Problems* 42.864a34.

17   See, e.g., Franz Susemihl and R. D. Hicks, *The Politics of Aristotle* (London, 1894), p. 651, n. 1, who, along with House, *Aristotle's Poetics*, p. 110, quotes Milton's preface to *Samson Agonistes*. Cf. Halliwell, *Aristotle's Poetics*, 192–4.

18   Halliwell is aware of this; *Aristotle's Poetics*, p. 193, n. 37. See *Nicomachean Ethics* 1104b17–18, *Eudemian Ethics* 1220a36.

19   *Rhetoric* 11.5, 1382a21 ff.

20   See *Rhetoric* II.1 and II.5. In addition, Aristotle believes there are certain physiological changes which accompany an emotion; *On the Soul* 403a16–19.

21   *Rhetoric* II.5.1382b30 ff.

22   See Hathaway, *The Age of Criticism*.

23   Eduard Muller, *Theorie der Kunst bei den Alten*, 2: 62, 377–88, quoted by Bernays, *Zwei Abhandlung*, p. 156.

24   See, e.g., *Poetics* 13–14, where plots are evaluated on the basis of the type of emotional response they tend to evoke in an audience. Those which do not produce pity and fear but, for example, disgust are rejected as inadequate for tragedy.

25   See House, *Aristotle's Poetics*; Halliwell, *Aristotle's Poetics*; Golden, "Catharsis"; and Martha C. Nussbaum, *The Fragility of Goodness* (Cambridge: Cambridge University Press, 1986). Golden and Nussbaum speak of a "clarification" of the emotions.

26 *Nicomachean Ethics* II.
27 Ibid., II.6.1106b6–28. This is Aristotle's famous doctrine of the mean.
28 Aristotle is clear that one need not actually see a performance onstage in order to experience the effect of tragedy; simply hearing it read out loud is sufficient. See *Poetics* 14.1453b4–7; 6.1450b18–19; 26.1462a11–12. For Aristotle's mention of the peculiar and appropriate pleasure of tragedy, see *Poetics* 14.1453b10–14; 23.1459a17–24; 26.14652b12–14; cf. 1462a15–17.
29 Aristotle, *Metaphysics*, I.1.
30 Nor, *contra* Golden and Nussbaum, do his emotions need to be clarified.
31 *Politics* VIII.7.1341b32–1342a18 (quoted above).
32 Halliwell, *Aristotle's Poetics*, 195–6.
33 *Politics* VIII.7.1342a1–2.
34 My translation of 1341b38.
35 This is made clear by 1341b36–38: *ou mias heneken opheleias tei mousikei dein alla kai pleionon charin (kai gar paideias heneken kai katharseos)*. But in case there is any doubt, it is settled by *triton* at 1341b40: clearly, education, catharsis, and intellectual enjoyment are being listed as three distinct benefits obtainable from music.
36 Ibid., 1342b11–15.
37 Ibid., 1342b18–29. This passage is also cited by Bernays as part of his argument that catharsis is not meant by Aristotle to be morally educative.
38 *Ho men eleutheros kai pepaideumenos*: 1342b19. Cf. also *Poetics* 26 (especially 1461b27–8), which suggests that tragedy will be appreciated by a better sort of audience.
39 *Poetics* 4.1449a10–15.
40 Ibid., 13.1453a33–6.
41 Ibid., 25.1460b13–15.
42 Here I am particularly indebted to Giovanni Ferrari.
43 *Poetics* 4.1448b4–19. I have altered the revised Oxford translation of 1448b14–15: *sullogidzesthai ti hekaston, hoion hoti houtos ekeinos*, which is rendered there as "gathering the meaning of things, e.g. that the man there is so-and-so." My translation is more literal, which I think is important to the interpretation of this passage.
44 *Parts of Animals* I.5.645a4–37.
45 Ibid., 645a8–15.
46 *Poetics* 4.1448b17–19. Such a person, presumably, would not have heard a sufficient description to recognize a mouse: the person Aristotle has in mind, I think, is someone who has no idea of a mouse: so he is in no position to recognize of any painting that it is a painting of a mouse.
47 See, e.g., *Poetics* 9.1451a37–8; 10.1452a17–21; 15.1454a33–6; 16.1455a16–19; 25.1461b11–12.
48 E.g., ibid., 9.1452a3–4; 10.1452a20–21.
49 Ibid., 13.1453a8–30. Nussbaum argues that the point of a *hamartia* is to render the protagonist sufficiently like us that we can identify with him to the extent required to experience the tragic emotions of pity and fear (*The Fragility of Goodness*, 382ff.). Her reasoning is based on her more general interpretation that, for Aristotle, the point of tragedy is to explore the gap which inevitably exists between being good and living well. I do not think that the general interpretation can be correct. Although Aristotle does accept that being virtuous is not sufficient for happiness and that external misfortune can ruin a thoroughly good man (*Nicomachean Ethics* I.10), it is quite clear that Aristotle does not

think that such an event could be the basis for a tragedy. Consider *Poetics* 13.1452b30–36, where Aristotle says that tragedy cannot portray the fall of a good man from good to bad fortune, for such an event does not arouse the tragic emotions of pity and fear but a thoroughly non-tragic emotion of disgust. Aristotle does reluctantly admit that a virtuous man can be destroyed for no reason at all, that is, through misfortune, but he denies that this is the stuff of tragedy. Tragic events always occur for a reason.

50   *Poetics* 9.1452a1–6 (my translation except for two phrases from Oxford).
51   Ibid., 6.1449b27–8. Literally, Aristotle says a "catharsis of such emotions" *(ton toiouton pathematon)*, but Bernays has argued convincingly that "such" should be understood demonstratively, as referring exclusively to pity and fear.
52   *Metaphysics* I.982b12–25, 983a12 ff.; *Rhetoric* I.1371a31–b1.
53   *Metaphysics* I.982b12N25. I discuss this at some length in *Aristotle: The Desire to Understand* (Cambridge: Cambridge University Press, 1988).
54   See, e.g., Halliwell, *Aristotle's Poetics*, 70–74.
55   *Poetics* 24.1460a11–17.
56   Ibid., 24.1460a17.
57   Ibid., 26.1462b13–14. See the note on the passage in D. W. Lucas, *Aristotle's Poetics* (Oxford: Clarendon Press, 1968), p. 257.
58   *Poetics* 9.1451b5–11.
59   At *Metaphysics* XIII.10.1087a10–25, Aristotle does qualify his claim that episteme is of universals. See Jonathan Lear, "Active Episteme," in A. Graeser, ed., *Mathematics and Metaphysics in Aristotle: Proceedings of the Xth Symposium Aristotelicum* (Bern, 1986), for an analysis of this passage.
60   Although I am certainly willing to accept that Aristotle thought that tragedy provides deeper insight into the human condition than history does, I don't think that is the immediate point he is making in the passage under discussion.
61   *Poetics* 17.1455b2–13 (Oxford trans.). See also Aristotle's description of the plot of the *Odyssey* at 1455b16–23.
62   Ibid., 17.1455b, 12–13; cf. 9.1451b8–16.
63   Aristotle does not seem to have been familiar with Thucydides. One cannot but wonder how Aristotle would have changed his mind about history if he had carefully read the History of the Peloponnesian War.
64   As we have seen, that is why Aristotle says at the end of chapter 9 that the events in a tragedy should occur unexpectedly but on account of one another.
65   *Poetics* 9.1451a36–38, repeated at 1451b4–5, just before Aristotle claims that poetry is more philosophical than history because it deals with universals (1451b5–7).
66   Among humans, that is.
67   See *Politics* VIII.7.1342b14 and the numerous references in the *Poetics* in which the plot of a good tragedy is distinguished from that which will appeal to a vulgar audience, e.g., 13.1453a30–36 (cf. 9.1451b33–1452a1 and 6.1450b16–19) and chapter 26, in which Aristotle seems to accept the principle that tragedy is a higher art form than epic precisely because it appeals to a better audience.
68   See *Rhetoric* II.5.8; cf. the account of anger as a composite of pain and pleasure; *Rhetoric* II.2.
69   Aristotle, as we have seen, says that everyone undergoes a "certain catharsis and lightening with pleasure"; *Politics* VIII.7.1342b14–15.
70   *Poetics* 6.1449b24–8.

71 *Physics* III.3.
72 I say "ultimately" because there is a two-step process involved: the poet's creating the plot and writing the play, and the performance of the play before an audience. I am using the word "performance" widely to cover both the enactment of the play onstage by actors and the simple reading or recital of the play out loud. Aristotle is explicit that a tragedy can have its proper effect even when it is not acted out on stage: a person who merely hears the tragedy read out loud will experience pity and fear. See *Poetics* 14.1453b3–7; 6.1450b18–19; 26.62a11–12, a17–18.
73 Ibid., 13.1452b30–1453a8 (Oxford trans. except that I use "disgusting" for *miaron* rather than Oxford's "odious").
74 Ibid., 13.1453a4–6.
75 See ibid., 15.1454b8–13.
76 Ibid., 13.1453a8–17.
77 Ibid., 14.1453b10–22 (my translation).
78 Ibid., 11.1452b10–11. For other objective uses of *pathos* in the *Poetics*, see, e.g., 13.1453b18, b19–20, b39, 1454a13. See also *Rhetoric* II.5.1382b30; *Metaphysics* V.21.1022b20–21; *Nicomachean Ethics* I.11.1101a31.
79 It is tempting to speculate that, for Aristotle, there is an objective as well as a subjective catharsis. For the catharsis referred to in the definition of tragedy is clearly subjective – i.e., something which goes on within the souls of the members of the audience; while the catharsis at which Orestes is saved (*Poetics* 17.1455b14–15) is clearly objective: viz. a ritual sacrifice. It goes beyond the evidence of the texts to construct a theory of the relation of objective to subjective catharsis. But it is worth noting in passing that if Aristotle believed that a subjective catharsis occurs in response to an objective catharsis, then the entire debate over where the catharsis is occurring, within the play itself or in the audience, would be idle. It would be occurring in both places (albeit in different forms).
80 Ibid., 13, especially 1453a17–22; 14.1454a9–13.
81 *Rhetoric* II.5.1382a22–30.
82 Ibid., 1382a28–30.
83 Ibid., 1382b31–31; cf. b28–1383a12.
84 Ibid., 1383a5–8. Those who have lost all hope of escape grow resigned and callous.
85 *Poetics* 13,1453a5; *Rhetoric* II.8.1385b14 ff.
86 *Rhetoric* II.8.1386a2.4–27.
87 *Poetics* 13.1453a5–6.
88 *Rhetoric* II.8.1386a24–5.
89 Ibid., 1385b19ff.
90 Ibid., 1385b23–7. Cf. *Politics* VIII.7.1342b19, where an educated audience *(hoi pepaideumenoi)* is contrasted with a vulgar one.
91 Since it is an incredibly complicated subject, I would like to reserve for another occasion a discussion of the general conditions required for emotional identification.
92 *Poetics* 13.1453a5–6; *Rhetoric* II.5.1383a10–13.
93 One might lamely try to keep the objection alive by saying that when we feel pity we are identifying with the chorus. But then the question arises: why should we identify with the chorus? The only plausible answer is that the chorus is in some way expressing our views. And if that is so, we are again led back to the conclusion that we believe that what happened to Oedipus could happen to us.
94 *Rhetoric* II.5.1383a7–12.

95 E.g., *Poetics* 9.1452a36–8, b5–7, b15–19.
96 I use "outside the theater" in the widest possible way: even the oral recitation of a tragedy counts for the purposes of this essay as going on "inside the theater."
97 If I may for a moment indulge my desire to be droll, let me put this in the language of modal semantics: In the virtuous man's opinion (and thus: in truth) the worlds in which he kills his mother, is killed by his mother, etc. are possible worlds and thus stand in an accessibility relation to the real world. All tragic worlds are possible worlds. However, all such tragic worlds are sufficiently removed from the actual work of a virtuous person (in ordinary circumstances) that they do not fall within the set of legitimately feared worlds.
98 *Rhetoric* II.8.1386a32–5. Of course, Aristotle is here talking within the context of rhetorical persuasion, but his point obviously carries over to the theater.
99 See Thompson Clarke, "The Legacy of Skepticism," *Journal of Philosophy* 69 (1972): 754–69.
100 *Psychagogei*: cf. *Poetics* 6.1450a33–6.
101 *Poetics* 13.1453a7–17; 15.1454b8–13.
102 Which was, of course, Hegel's choice.
103 See W. R. D. Fairbairn's account of "the moral defense" in "The Repression and the Return of Bad Objects," in *Psychoanalytic Studies of the Personality* (London, 1984).
104 Aristotle makes a related (though different) point at *Nicomachean Ethics* I.10: he reluctantly admits that even a virtuous person can suffer great misfortune; however, he offers the consolation that the virtuous person will at least bear his misfortunes nobly and with greatness of soul.
105 *Rhetoric* II.5.1383a3–5.
106 For another treatment of skepticism and its relationship to tragedy see, of course, Stanley Cavell, *The Claim of Reason* (Oxford: Clarendon Press, 1979).

12

Passion, Counter-Passion, Catharsis: Flaubert (and Beckett) on Feeling Nothing

JOSHUA LANDY

The plot of *Madame Bovary* can be stated in a single sentence: a young woman reads too many romances, finds no satisfaction in her marriage to a mediocre husband, has two affairs, finds no more satisfaction in either, accumulates huge debts to her clothing supplier, and finally, when the bill comes due, swallows arsenic and dies. This, I imagine, is how most of us remember the work, when we are merely *remembering* it, rather than looking at it up close. This is the shape it comes to occupy in our minds: a single road which seemed for a moment as though it might lead to marital happiness but which quickly forks into the parallel paths of adultery and acquisition, before reconverging in apparently inevitable catastrophe. As we recall it, the novel begins in a convent, where Emma first reads dangerous literature handed to her by an old maid, and ends in a bedroom, where she breathes her last to the sound of a blind man's salacious song. (At most perhaps we recollect the galling triumph of Homais, the pharmacist with an excessively high opinion of his own abilities who winds up receiving France's highest honor.)

But the novel does not, as it happens, start and end with Emma. In fact, it would be closer to say that it starts and ends with Charles.[1] We follow him from youth, in the opening chapter, to death, in the final chapter, almost as though this were the story of *his* life, the story of a simple but well-meaning man who makes a bad choice in marriage. And if that is the case, then why do we so often relegate him to the periphery? Why does Flaubert devote the all-important overture and finale to Charles, if he also plans to make him so eminently forgettable? Who is Charles really: an interchangeable bit-player, good only, as Prufrock would say, for swelling a progress and starting a scene or two, or the (co-)protagonist of the entire tragic tale?

Three Coffins

Matters in *Madame Bovary* are, as it happens, more complicated still, when we consider not just the quantity of space Charles occupies in the opening and closing

---

A Companion to the Philosophy of Literature, First Edition. Edited by Garry L. Hagberg and Walter Jost.
© 2010 John Wiley & Sons Ltd. Published 2015 by John Wiley & Sons, Ltd.

sections of the book but also the quality of his actions. Almost immediately after his wife's death, he issues elaborate and peremptory instructions for her funeral:

> I want her buried in her bridal dress, with white shoes and a wreath and her hair spread over her shoulders. Three coffins – one oak, one mahogany, one lead. No one has to say anything to me: I'll have the strength to go through with it. Cover her with a large piece of green velvet. I want this done. Do it.[2]

Homais the pharmacist and Bournisien the priest react as one: they are "much taken aback by Bovary's romantic ideas" (386) ("ces messieurs s'étonnèrent beaucoup des idées romanesques de Bovary," 403). They are quite right to be stunned, but, I would like to suggest, they are surprised about the wrong thing. From their point of view, the shock is that Charles's ideas do not conform to ordinary standards of burial practice. From ours, however, it is that Charles is in any way capable of such outlandish flights of fantasy. Three coffins, one inside the other? White dress, white shoes, green velvet? Since when did Charles pay such attention to the details of décor?

Perhaps one wants to say that Charles has learnt this from Emma, been influenced by her over the years they have spent together; perhaps he intuits that the only way to do justice to her memory is to give her the funeral she would herself have wanted, which is to say, an absurdly overinflated caricature of grief.[3] But one would still have to ask: where do his *specific* ideas come from? Even if he has heard that Napoleon (interred in 1821, but exhumed as recently as 1840) was buried in coffins of iron, lead, and mahogany, and even if (as is less likely) he has heard that Emma, on the death of her mother, expressed the wish to be laid to rest in the same tomb, Charles's imagination is nonetheless still at work, selecting materials and accoutrements.[4] Charles may well be capable of understanding that his wife had bizarre and baroque ideas, but is he really capable – are any of us capable – of learning, all of a sudden, to have an imagination?

Still more perplexing, perhaps, is what happens next. After discovering a stack of loveletters from Léon and a portrait of Rodolphe among Emma's effects, and after running into Rodolphe at a market, Charles collapses and dies in Emma's bower, suffocated, the narrator says, by "vague romantic vapours."[5] Summoned to perform an autopsy, Dr Canivet "l'ouvrit et ne trouva rien" (424).[6] Charles, that is, has died of nothing. Or rather, Charles has accomplished a feat that, within the Flaubertian fictional world, is almost inconceivable: whereas his wife succumbed to the most brutally material causes imaginable – the ravaging of her insides from arsenic poisoning – Charles has actually managed to die of grief.[7] It is not, then, just his ideas that have become romantic: his very *being* has, too.

How is *this* Charles imaginable on the basis of the man we have seen, the bovine ruminant barely capable of articulate speech, the incompetent surgeon, hopeless husband, and overall lump? Or if you prefer: what happened to this Charles during the middle portion of the novel, this man who had begun by laying claim at least in part to our sympathy, who had been capable of a little eloquence when the occasion demanded,[8] who touchingly blushed when he so much as thought of asking for Emma's hand? Where did that man go?

The Charges Against Charles

At a first approximation, the answer is actually straightforward. It suffices to read carefully the charges against Charles:

> Charles's conversation was flat as a sidewalk, a place of passage for the ideas of everyman; they wore drab everyday clothes, and they inspired neither laughter nor dreams. When he had lived in Rouen, he said, he had never had any interest in going to the theatre to see the Parisian company that was acting there. He couldn't swim or fence or fire a pistol; one day he couldn't tell her the meaning of a riding term she had come upon in a novel.
>
> Wasn't it a man's role, though, to know everything? Shouldn't he be expert at all kinds of things, able to initiate you into the intensities of passion, the refinements of life, all the mysteries? (48)[9]

"Charles's conversation was flat as a sidewalk." Fair enough; that's more or less how it seems to us, judging from the snippets we overhear. "He had never had any interest in going to the theatre." That too appears to be correct, judging from his complete incomprehension, in part 3, of *Lucia di Lammermoor* (293–4). But now, "he couldn't swim or fence or fire a pistol"? Very likely so, but are we to judge him utterly incapable, on this basis, of inspiring love? And then – the final nail in the velvet-covered coffin – "he couldn't tell her the meaning of a riding term she had come upon in a novel." Again, I am entirely ready to believe that accurate, all the more so as I myself could probably not tell you the meaning of a riding term you found in a novel (or, to adjust for temporal inflation, the meaning of a motorcycle term you heard at the cinema). I have no idea what a crupper is, let alone a surcingle, a shabrack, or a bradoon. What are lauffer reins and chambons? What does it mean to "longe" a horse?

I'm not sure we're supposed to judge Charles too harshly for not knowing, any more than we do, the answer to such questions. Which is to say, I'm not sure we're supposed to judge Charles the way Emma does. For we are, of course, inside Emma's head here; in typically Flaubertian fashion, the paragraph gives us what appears to be objective description but what turns out to be a set of tendentiously selective, tendentiously evaluative, perhaps even tendentiously distorted details. Sliding imperceptibly from objective reportage to character assassination, it forces us to pull ourselves up when we suddenly notice that at some juncture along the way – and we cannot quite be sure where – Emma's voice has taken over. (Such, needless to say, is the power of free indirect speech.) It is *Emma* who considers it indispensable to know every single riding term. It is *Emma* who considers it impermissible not to be able to fence. (*Because* he cannot fence, *therefore* I cannot possibly love him: Mikhail Bakhtin would call this "pseudo-objective motivation."[10]) It is *Emma* who decides that Charles must be written off because his conversation is not interesting. And it is *Emma* who decides that Charles is responsible for every single one of her woes, "the cause of all her wretchedness."[11] Flaubert does not agree, and neither should we.[12]

The Cracked Kettle

In case we remain in any doubt, we receive explicit confirmation a bare three pages later. "Having thus failed to produce the slightest spark of love in herself," notes the narrator, "and since she was incapable of understanding what she didn't experience, or of recognizing anything that wasn't expressed in conventional terms, she reached the conclusion that Charles's desire for her was nothing very extraordinary" (51).[13] Uncommonly forthright here, the narrator is chastising Emma for her crashing obtuseness, for deciding not only that Charles is unworthy of her but also that he does not even love her very much, and for doing so solely on the basis of his failure to express his feelings in the manner of Orlando Furioso or Amadis of Gaul. If Charles's affection appears mediocre, it is merely because Emma is incapable of imagining that anyone could feel differently from her and of recognizing love except when expressed in the form of romantic clichés. Fascinatingly, this is the mirror image of the mistake that Rodolphe will make in relation to *her*, perhaps a rare instance of poetic justice in Flaubert's almost Schopenhauerian universe. For where Emma wrongly assumes that only someone who speaks like a book can have genuine passion, Rodolphe wrongly assumes exactly the opposite:

> He had had such things said to him so many times that none of them had any freshness for him. Emma was like all his other mistresses; and as the charm of novelty gradually slipped from her like a piece of her clothing, he saw revealed in all its nakedness the eternal monotony of passion, which always assumes the same forms and always speaks the same language. He had no perception – this man of such vast experience – of the dissimilarity of feeling that might underlie similarities of expression. Since he had heard those words uttered by loose women or prostitutes, he had little belief in their sincerity when he heard them now; the more flowery a person's speech, he thought, the more suspect the feelings, or lack of feelings, it concealed. Whereas the truth is that fullness of soul can sometimes overflow in utter vapidity of language, for none of us can ever express the exact measure of his needs or his thoughts or his sorrows; and human speech is like a cracked kettle on which we tap crude rhythms for bears to dance to, while we long to make music that will melt the stars. (223–4)[14]

The above paragraph is, of course, widely quoted, and it seems to lend credence to Emma's position: she has great depths in her heart, and she therefore (there's that "therefore" again) deserves better than the clumsy oaf she somehow ended up married to, as well as the libertine oaf, blind to her unique charms, with whom she is having an ill-considered affair. Perhaps it does lend a certain amount of credence to Emma – indeed, for reasons I shall come back to, it is important that it does – but like all maxims, it applies universally if it applies at all, and that means that it applies also to Charles, another individual who is incapable of "giving the exact measure of his needs, his conceptions, his sorrows," and whose fullness of soul may perhaps be overflowing in the conversation as flat as a sidewalk.[15] Endlessly sincere, devoted to the last,[16] and with emotional depths at which we can only guess, Charles Bovary has every right to the concern we accord him in the opening and closing sections of the book. We are justified, early on, in wanting him to marry Emma, so that he may for the first time have something good in his life[17] – we may later regret having wished for this, but that will be my point – and then, in the final chapter, we are justified in wanting him not to find Léon's letters or Rodolphe's portrait, justified in wanting him to go on living. His death, there are no two ways around it, is genuinely and deeply moving.[18] *Charles Bovary, c'est moi.*

Behind Emma's Eyes

In short, Emma misjudges Charles disastrously. And since the majority of the novel is filtered through her point of view, we too misjudge Charles disastrously. Granted, Charles is not the world's greatest surgeon: he does indeed botch the operation on the clubfoot.[19] He lacks the talent of a Léon or a Rodolphe for stringing together romantic clichés. And he doesn't know his equestrian terminology. But is Emma that much more eloquent herself? (" 'There's nothing I love as much as sunsets,' she said. 'But my favorite place for them is the seashore,'" 97.[20]) That much more self-aware? More capable of genuine passion?[21] Does Emma, as one might say colloquially, really deserve better than Charles?

My purpose here is not to defend a literary character against calumny by another literary character; the exercise would of course be highly questionable. Instead I am simply suggesting, along with Graham Falconer and others,[22] that the reason we remember Charles Bovary as so unremittingly dismal, as irremediably inferior to Emma, is that most of the story is told from her perspective. Where does the romantic, imaginative Charles disappear to in the middle section of the novel? Answer: *behind Emma's eyes.* No wonder he is suddenly a different person once she's dead; her gaze is no longer there to refract his image for us.

We are still left, however, with the need for a higher-level explanation. Why, if Charles is worthy of some caring attention, do his virtues suddenly find themselves buried for most of the novel? Or to put it the other way around: why, in a novel that largely concerns the hopes and dreams of its eponymous heroine, should a relatively sympathetic husband bookend the tale?[23] What does Flaubert have to gain from thus stirring our emotional investment? What is such empathy actually *for*?

The Trouble With Catharsis

It might be tempting to seek assistance here from Aristotle, for whom empathy (in tragedies at least) appears to be justified as a means to *katharsis*, which is to say "the purgation, by means of pity and fear, of these and similar emotions."[24] The problem, of course, is that this famous definition leaves us, equally famously, with more questions than answers. In the first place, it's not clear that we can extrapolate from fear and pity to anything about empathy *per se*, since we fear for *ourselves*, not for the character,[25] and we *pity* the character, rather than directly sharing his or her pain. Secondly, it's not clear what Aristotle actually means by "purgation." It might very well mean cleaning out, but it might, quite the contrary, mean cleaning *up*. Does Aristotle think pity and fear are prized possessions, so wonderful that they need to be polished from time to time, like one's best silver; or does he think instead that they are ugly accretions, to be washed away in the soapy water of Attic tragedy? (To put it another way, if tragedy is laundry day, are emotions the clothes or the stubborn stains?) While the cleaning out view, first advanced by Jakob Bernays in 1857, continues to be the dominant one, the cleaning up view – on which the function of tragedy is to refine the emotions, training them to aim reliably at the proper objects – has, thanks to the work of Nussbaum, Halliwell, and others, become an important rival in recent years.[26]

Rather surprisingly, the likelihood is that Aristotle subscribed to neither of them. In his seminal article of 1988 (reprinted in this volume, chapter 11, CATHARSIS), Jonathan Lear demonstrated (contra Bernays) that Aristotle could not have been advocating the wholesale removal of fear and pity, since these emotions are an entirely appropriate response under many circumstances; that even if he had desired such an outcome, he would not have proposed a homeopathic remedy (curing emotion with emotion) as its means; and that even if he had believed in homeopathic treatment, he would not have seen it as operative in tragic catharsis, since according to him, cathartic poetry is not the improving kind.[27] Nor can Aristotle have been advocating the *clarification* of fear and pity (contra Nussbaum), since catharsis is supposed to benefit everyone in the audience, virtuous people included, and the emotions of virtuous people by definition require no such improvement. (Not to mention that watching a tragedy is poor practice for everyday reactions: in real life, we are hardly supposed to seek out and take pleasure in the suffering of others.[28]) In short, Aristotelian catharsis does not make us virtuous and it does not make us calm; its benefits, which must be inferred from a massively enigmatic pair of passages, remain highly uncertain.[29]

The Limits of Empathy

We may appear to be no further advanced – in trying to get to the bottom of these difficult matters, one risks ending up not so much using Aristotle to clarify tragic emotion as using tragic emotion to clarify Aristotle – but I think we may usefully hang on to two points from the discussion. First, the now standard understanding of the word catharsis (the rather sloppy usage of Bernays, which Aristotle clearly did *not* mean) may nonetheless be of help to us. Second, we can also keep on hand the idea, emphasized by the proponents of the clarification theory, that one aspect of virtue consists in *failing to feel certain emotions*. Not all emotion all the time, to be sure, but some emotion some of the time. And this places Aristotle in stark opposition to modern theorists of readerly emotion. For on the contemporary consensus, fictional empathy serves the function of increasing real-world empathy, and real-world empathy is what we need above all things; there is simply no such thing as too much *Mitgefühl*.

The argument for this position – which is more or less that held by Lynn Hunt, William Roche, Richard Rorty, and others[30] – falls, as I see it, into three parts. First, we hold it to be self-evident that treating other people well is a good thing. (There are shades here, perhaps, of Adam Smith's theory of moral sentiments: in commercial and egalitarian societies, Smith argues, honor plays a smaller role than before, and sympathy takes over as the predominant endorsed mode of interpersonal relations.) Second, we assume that the desire to treat other people well is strengthened, if not generated, by an ability to put oneself in their position.[31] And third, we posit that such real-world empathy is strengthened, if not generated, by empathy toward fictional entities. Ostensibly, empathy for fictional characters guarantees more charitable treatment of one's neighbors, those at least whose representatives feature in our imaginative reading.

The empathist approach, while attractive for various reasons, nevertheless faces a number of serious difficulties. For one thing, it's not a given that understanding will lead to *compassion*. It's entirely possible that from an evolutionary point of view, our capacity to assess the brain states of others is designed not just to help us cooperate with them but also to help us *defeat* them, to trick them out of food, find their weak spots, and so on.[32] (Evolutionary psychologists, who claim to have detected just this behavior in monkeys and apes, refer to it as Machiavellian intelligence.[33]) Some will use their knowledge of your preferences in order to buy you the perfect gift; others will use it, like O'Brien in *1984*, to extract what they need from you. For every Amélie Poulain, there is an Iago; for every Mrs Dalloway, there is a Mlle Vinteuil.[34]

For another thing, it's not a given that imaginative identification with those who are not like us is an absolute good, such that its presence automatically enhances, and its absence automatically lowers, the moral status of any given situation. Moral behavior is not just a matter of making benevolent, broad-minded judgments (for example, "people from a different country may be just as nice as people from my country"); it is also a matter of making the appropriate *negative* judgments (for example, "murderers are not nice people"). This means that if fictions really do train me to be compassionate towards all others, then I may actually start becoming *less* moral.

In order to see this, it is sufficient to imagine someone who reads Vladimir Nabokov's *Lolita* and concludes that abduction and sexual abuse are really not so terrible after all. This would be not only a disastrous reading of the text but, I think, also a disastrous event in that person's moral life. In *Lolita*, the ideal reader is not one who gives herself over lovingly to the character but, on the contrary, one who continually *stands back* from her empathy. Indeed, the peculiar power of the work derives from the perpetual feeling of unease generated by the oscillation between disgust, connivance, and disgust at our connivance. Moralists will of course tell us that this is quite right, since that is how *Lolita* teaches us that pedophilia is to be avoided and condemned, and that, in general, we should pay attention to the desires of other people before selfishly using them as mere means.[35] But how many readers do not *already* think this before picking up the book? We don't *learn* this from *Lolita*; on the contrary, a healthy moral compass is the price of admission, the price of entry into that vertiginous affective space.[36] And if we *did* learn that, then this would rather give the lie to the idea that we automatically empathize with novelistic heroes, gradually expanding the category "we" until it encompasses all of "them." We don't, and we shouldn't. It is dangerous to empathize indiscriminately. It is almost as though Nabokov wrote *Lolita* with no other purpose than to provide a ready example with which to defeat the simplistic view of realist fiction as caritas-based savior of the world.[37]

Multifocal Empathy

There is one final objection to the empathist view, an objection which will bring us back to *Madame Bovary*. The objection is this: if the aim of fiction is to invite imaginative identification with those who are not like us, then why do so many novels offer us *multiple* targets for our empathy? It is, I think, telling that the examples standardly deployed by the empathists focus our attention on a single character: Maggie Verver, Philoctetes, Pamela, Clarissa, Rousseau's Julie, Ellison's "invisible man." But what about the multifocal text? How does the empathist view explain the fact that so many realist fictions shift focus from one character to another, indeed among characters whose temperaments are powerfully antithetical? There is no particular reason why stories, in order to increase our capacity for compassion, would need to give access to more than one mind at a time; on the contrary, one might worry that the reader's compassion might become dangerously dispersed and thus, in each case, diluted.

Now in Flaubert, not only are we invited to empathize with two separate characters; not only is it the case that the interests of the two are violently opposed; but empathy for the one positively *precludes* empathy for the other. As long as we are imaginatively projecting ourselves, with emotion, into Emma's predicament, we can only see Charles as a buffoon, an oaf, an obstacle; and as long as we are imaginatively projecting ourselves, with emotion, into Charles's predicament, we can only see Emma as a monster of heartless narcissism and blind superficiality. Charles is pitiable because he has a soul to be wounded; Emma is pitiable because her husband lacks a soul. Charles's pain is meaningful *if and only if Emma's is meaningless*, and vice versa. We pity her at his expense, and the other way around.

The situation here bears some comparison to that of Sophocles' *Antigone*. There, too, we are asked to empathize with a pair of characters – Creon and Antigone – each of whom stands for a value diametrically opposed to that of the other, such that we cannot endorse both at once; hence the full force of tragedy, in Hegel's view, as a situation in which no good solution is (yet) available, since the two "ethical powers" in question are "opposite but equally justified."[38] But the difference is that here the collision of claims is entirely implicit, and, more importantly, that it is not the case that both sides are right. Flaubert is not, I think, hinting at a dialectical resolution of the predicament, or even drawing our attention to the existence, in life, of irreconcilable tragic conflicts. Nor is he merely offering us the opportunity to witness, from a (Leibnizian) God's eye view, the perspectival nature of human experience. I wish to suggest, rather tentatively and in full awareness of the necessarily speculative nature of my hypothesis, as well as of the uses to which multifocal empathy may be put in other narratives,[39] a different rationale for Flaubert's procedure, one which we may best understand by taking a detour through Beckett.

Beckett and the Abdication of Intellect

> [W]e would seem to know for certain ... that it has not yet been our good fortune to establish with any degree of accuracy ... if it's I who seek, what exactly it is I seek, find, lose, find again, throw away, seek again, find again, throw away again, no, I never threw anything away, never threw anything away of all the things I found, never found anything that I didn't lose, never lost anything that I mightn't as well have thrown away, if it's I who seek, find, lose, find again, lose again, seek in vain, seek no more. (*The Unnamable* 388–9)[40]

What is going on here? What is going on, in general, in Beckett's Trilogy? The question here is not what Beckett's words *mean*, but rather what they are *for*. What are they supposed to *do* for us? Many critics appear to assume, as though it goes without saying, that Beckett is simply trying to *inform* us of something: that free will is an illusion, for example, that the self is in language, that Descartes is wrong, or that there is no ground for epistemological certainty.[41] Others, anchoring themselves unsteadily on the shifting sands of the *Three Dialogues*, inform us that his aim is expression, the paradoxical expression of an inability to express. But both of these approaches take it for granted that the what-for question can and need only be answered with relation to the writer. Whereas it must also be answered, as Beckett is well aware, with relation to the reader.[42] What do Beckett's texts do for *us*? Why do we, some of us at least, willingly put ourselves through them?

The answer can only be, I think, that readers of Beckett are suffering from the same disease as Beckett's characters, in search of the same recovered health, and eager to undergo the same treatment. (Incidentally, this may also explain why many do *not* take pleasure in Beckett's texts: these are presumably the healthy, or at least those suffering from *different* afflictions.) Now health here, let me add, means peace of mind; the disease, here, is philosophy;[43] and the treatment, here, is nothing other than the trilogy itself. "To know nothing is nothing, not to want to know anything likewise, but to be beyond knowing anything, to know you are beyond knowing anything, that is when peace enters in" (64). Molloy could not be any clearer: the ultimate *telos* of the Beckettian quest, whether or not such a *telos* may in practice ever be attained, is *peace*. And this means that Molloy, like most of Beckett's heroes, is not just a skeptic but an *ancient* skeptic, indeed a *Pyrrhonian* skeptic.[44] For him, that is, epistemological questions, questions about what can and cannot be known, and with what degree of certainty, are *secondary*, merely instrumental to the primary goal, which is *ataraxia*, freedom from disturbance, enduring peace of mind.[45]

The problem, of course, is that peace of mind is precarious. In particular, it is liable to be disturbed by philosophical questions – Who am I? Is free will an illusion? Is there a God? What is the relationship between mind and body? – which tempt us both by their genuine importance and by their apparent susceptibility to resolution. Once down this path, we lose all hope of tranquility. And once down this path, as Aristotle was happy to point out, we cannot be cured by philosophy. "If one must philosophize," he explains, "then one must philosophize; and if one must not philosophize, then one must philosophize; in any case, therefore, one must philosophize."[46] No-one can *argue* herself out of philosophy, for argument is merely a continuation of philosophy. Further, it's not enough to have a particular approach to, say, the mind–body problem demolished; it is always possible to switch to a new approach. Nor will mere ignorance suffice, since the temptation to address the unanswered questions, the dim intuition that certainty is somewhere to be had, will never cease being a danger. *There is no way to make an end-run around intellect*: once we are started on the game of ruminating, we cannot simply will ourselves to stop. The intellect refuses to take orders from the intuition and the emotions. The only person it takes orders from is itself.

The sole remaining solution, at this point, is to convince the intellect to abdicate (as Proust would say) of its own accord, out of sheer despair. It must somehow be convinced not only that it *does* not know, but also that it *cannot* know; it must be convinced, as Molloy puts it, that it is "beyond knowing anything." And in order to bring about this blissful condition, one must bring before it *opposite hypotheses* in answer to every question that arises, the equal plausibility of which is sure to leave the intellect in the appropriate state of *epoché* (suspension of judgment).[47] Silence and resignation are not givens, but require to be *made*; nothingness is not a state that pre-exists objects and beliefs but is, instead, a state that results from their mutual cancellation.[48] Or again in Molloy's words, one must indulge the "two fools" within oneself, until both of them give up.[49]

All this, of course, is straight out of the skeptical playbook. "Skepticism," writes Sextus Empiricus, "is an ability . . . which opposes appearances to judgments in any way whatsoever, with the result that, owing to the equipollence of the objects and reasons thus opposed, we are brought firstly to a state of mental suspense and next to a state of 'unperturbedness' or quietude."[50] *Antilogoi, epoché, ataraxia*; in Beckettian terms, "find again, lose again, seek in vain, seek no more." Or again: "You announce, then you renounce, so it is, that helps you on, that helps the end to come" (406).[51]

Beckett does depart from the ancient skeptics in one important way. The quotation from which we started speaks, to be sure, of the abdication of the intellect; but the self-correction here yields not uncertainty but *certainty*, to such an extent indeed that the sentence continues to build on the newly acquired foundation. In a way that is actually typical of Beckett at this stage of his career, epanorthosis (revision) repeatedly gives way to anadiplosis (a new clause opening with the last word of the previous).[52] Beckett's text is constantly moving in two directions at once, forward into corollaries of premises already posited, backward to test or reject those premises. Regressing as much as it advances, it relentlessly pares away to the essential, builds another layer upon that foundation, finds that layer flimsy, knocks it down, builds another, and so on and on. At the end, every question has either been solved or dissolved (some issues, in Beckett, *are* actually settled, in spite of what many might say). At the end, we can hope at least to know what can be known, and to know of everything else that it cannot; to know, in other words, the limits of our knowledge.

In all of this, what Beckett is offering us is not a reservoir of information but a spiritual exercise, one that has powerful affinities with those offered by the ancient skeptics, and as therapy for precisely the same disease.[53] We are not supposed to be edified by the "claims" presented in the texts, or to treat their protagonists as positive or negative models; instead we are to look to the *structure* of the text, and to look to it as a *formal model for the dissolution of philosophical questions* in circumstances of our own. What we stand to learn is not facts or arguments but a *method*, one by which philosophy can bring itself to an end.

Feeling Nothing

Recall, now, what Flaubert does to his reader. He makes us empathize first with Charles (we hope this kind-hearted man wins the hand of young Emma), then with Emma (she deserves so much better than this vapid non-entity), and then again with Charles (a soul tender enough, after all, to die of grief at a love betrayed).[54] And yet each of the empathies is, strictly speaking, incompatible with the other. We cannot simply extend our compassion to encompass both at once – let alone all of God's creatures, as the empathists would like.[55] To feel for Emma is to feel for her *because* she is tormented by a non-entity. And to feel for Charles is to feel for him *because* his wife is a narcissist, incapable of perceiving the depth of his love for her. We are not supposed to empathize with both. On the contrary, we are supposed to empathize with neither.

But let's be clear about this: empathizing with neither does not mean remaining aloof from each, and never feeling anything for anyone. It means, instead, allowing the two empathies to *cancel each other out*, like a force and a counter-force in physical equilibrium. We are *supposed* to feel pain for Emma, and we are *supposed* to feel pain for Charles, and it is only *after* we have felt pain for both that we can end up, on the other side, free of all feeling and at peace. This is how readers of Flaubert may achieve on the affective level what readers of Beckett may achieve on the cognitive. For human beings do not start out as passionless entities, emotional blank slates; rather, they constantly trail affective tendrils around with them, just waiting to attach to an object. We do not begin from nothing, but only *end* there, if we are lucky. (Emotional) nothingness is not a given; it is something that needs to be made.

And so it turns out that in this instance at least, and in one understanding of the term at least, empathy really does have the goal of catharsis. Just as the priest and the scientist cancel each other out with their equally fanatical claims on the eve of Emma's death,[56] and just as, in Flaubert's *Bouvard et Pécuchet*, one theory relentlessly collides with its antithesis in an orgy of mutually destroyed beliefs, so here the goal of "loving nothing,"[57] the goal of being at last outside of desire, is achieved not by stopping *en deça* but by proceeding *au-delà*. There is no stopping short of involvement, only *ex post facto* extrication from it. And it is the *method* of such extrication that Flaubert seeks, I would argue, to offer us, in the fibers of his novel. We may learn to see our own lives, too, "au point de vue d'une blague supérieure," just as long as we seek out those perspectives from which our greatest desires are the greatest obstacle, live into them empathetically, and let ourselves be cured by them.

One last scene from Flaubert. Emma and Charles are preparing for the ball at the Vaubyessard estate. "Emma devoted herself to her toilette with the meticulous care of an actress the night of her debut . . . Charles's trousers were too tight at the waist." (57) ("Emma fit sa toilette avec la conscience méticuleuse d'une actrice à son début . . . Le pantalon de Charles le serrait au ventre," 109.) Charles is, of course, ridiculous, bathetic; failing to appreciate the magnitude of what is in store, all he can think about is his trousers. We share Emma's frustration at being trapped with such an earthbound simpleton. Yet at the same time, do we really share Emma's view that the ultimate goal of life is to be able to attend such events? Isn't she, ultimately, just as ridiculous for failing to stay earthbound at all? And if so, isn't Charles a little to be pitied for being dragged off the ground in the direction of a cliff? To take this passage right is to feel excitement for Emma, superiority over Charles, distaste for Emma, and pity for Charles, all in succession – and then, as a result, to feel, with the hard-bitten, hard-won resignation of the ancient skeptics, the perfect calm of absolutely nothing.

Notes

This chapter was originally given as a talk at the University of Chicago's Committee on Social Thought. I am grateful to all my interlocutors there, including Paul Friedrich, Jonathan Lear, Robert Morrissey, Thomas Pavel, and Robert Pippin, as well as to Andrea Nightingale for her very helpful insights on the subject of catharsis.

1. To be sure, it opens a split second before Charles's arrival in the narrator's classroom, and lingers on for a couple of paragraphs after his death; but these concluding paragraphs are mostly there to explain what happens to Charles's successors (driven away, one after the other, by the fearsome Homais) and to Charles's daughter (condemned to factory work).
2. Gustave Flaubert, *Madame Bovary*, trans. Francis Steegmuller (New York: Random House, 1992), 386. Subsequent parenthetical page citations for English-language quotations from *Madame Bovary* refer to this edition. "Je veux qu'on l'enterre dans sa robe de noces, avec des souliers blancs, une couronne. On lui étalera ses cheveux sur les épaules; trois cercueils, un de chêne, un d'acajou, un de plomb. Qu'on ne me dise rien, j'aurai de la force. On lui mettra par-dessus tout une grande pièce de velours vert. Je le veux. Faites-le." Gustave Flaubert, *Madame Bovary* (Paris: Garnier-Flammarion, 1986), 403. Subsequent parenthetical page citations for French-language quotations from *Madame Bovary* refer to this edition.
3. It is true that Charles consciously begins emulating his late wife: "Pour lui plaire, comme si elle vivait encore, il adopta ses prédilections, ses idées; il s'acheta des bottes vernies, il prit l'usage des cravates blanches. Il mettait du cosmétique à ses moustaches, il souscrivit comme elle des billets à ordre. Elle le corrompait par delà le tombeau." (417–8; "To please her, as though she were still alive, he adopted her tastes, her ideas: he bought himself patent leather shoes, took to wearing white cravats. He waxed his mustache, and signed – just as she had – more promissory notes. She was corrupting him from beyond the grave," 403.) But this is some time after the funeral.

4   As Jane Kairet notes, putting the velvet on the outside is itself a strikingly original gesture. My reading departs from Kairet's, and also that of Roberto Speziale-Bagliacca, in stopping short of symbolic readings (Kairet views the three coffins as standing for the three Madame Bovarys; Speziale-Bagliacca claims they testify to Charles's fear of Emma's ghost). See Jane E. Kairet, "Sur La Signification Mytho-Poétique Des 'Trois Cercueils' De Madame Bovary," *French Review* 70.5 (1997): 676–86, pp. 682, 677; Roberto Speziale-Bagliacca, *The King and the Adultress: A Psychoanalytic and Literary Reinterpretation of Madame Bovary and King Lear*, Durham, NC: Duke University Press, 1998, 49. For Emma's wish to be buried in the same tomb as her mother, see *Madame Bovary* 98 (45 in the Steegmuller translation).

5   "Le lendemain, Charles alla s'asseoir sur le banc, dans la tonnelle. Des jours passaient par le treillis; les feuilles de vigne dessinaient leurs ombres sur le sable, le jasmin embaumait, le ciel était bleu, des cantharides bourdonnaient autour des lis en fleur, et Charles suffoquait comme un adolescent sous les vagues effluves amoureux qui gonflaient son coeur chagrin" (424). In Steegmuller's translation, "The next day Charles sat down on the bench in the arbor. Rays of light came through the trellis, grape leaves traced their shadow on the gravel, the jasmine was fragrant under the blue sky, beetles buzzed about the flowering lilies. A vaporous flood of love-memories swelled in his sorrowing heart, and he was overcome with emotion, like an adolescent" (410–11).

6   "He performed an autopsy, but found nothing" (411).

7   Some have argued that if Canivet opens Charles up and "finds nothing," this is simply because the latter is vacuous (see Tony Tanner, *Adultery in the Novel: Contract and Transgression*, Baltimore, MD: Johns Hopkins University Press, 1979, 252; Jean Améry, *Charles Bovary, Landarzt: Portrait eines einfachen Mannes*, Stuttgart: Klett-Cotta, 1978, 151; Speziale-Bagliacca, *The King and the Adultress*, 54). I follow Ulrich Schulz-Buschhaus ("Charles Bovary: Probleme Der Sympathiesteuerung Und Der Figurenkohärenz in Einem Flaubertschen Roman," in Wolfgang Riehle Herbert Foltinek and Waldemar Zacharasiewicz, eds., *Tales and "Their Telling Difference": Zur Theorie und Geschichte der Narrativik (Festschrift zum 70. Geburtstag von Franz K. Stanzel)*, Heidelberg: Universitätsverlag C. Winter, 1993, 243–62, p. 257) and Enid Starkie (*Flaubert: The Making of the Master*, New York: Atheneum, 1967, 318) in departing from this view.

Fascinatingly, Flaubert's very first work of fiction ends with a death that the narrator explicitly deems fantastical: "At length, last December, he died . . . solely by the force of thought, without any organic malady, as one dies of sorrow – which may seem incredible to those who have greatly suffered, but must be tolerated in a novel, for the sake of our love of the marvelous." ("Enfin, au mois de décembre dernier, il mourut . . . par la seule force de la pensée, sans qu'aucun organe fût malade, comme on meurt de tristesse, ce qui paraîtra difficile aux gens qui ont beaucoup souffert, mais ce qu'il faut bien tolérer dans un roman, par amour du merveilleux.") Gustave Flaubert, *November*, trans. Francis Steegmuller, (New York: Serendipity Press, 1967), 163–4; *Novembre* (Neuchâtel, Switzerland: Ides et Calendes, 1961), 177.

8   "Words came to them both" (27); "les phrases leur vinrent" (82).

9   "La conversation de Charles était plate comme un trottoir de rue, et les idées de tout le monde y défilaient dans leur costume ordinaire, sans exciter d'émotion, de rire ou de rêverie. Il n'avait jamais été curieux, disait-il, pendant qu'il habitait Rouen, d'aller voir au théâtre les acteurs de Paris. Il ne savait ni nager, ni faire des armes, ni tirer le pistolet, et il ne put, un jour, lui expliquer un terme d'équitation qu'elle avait rencontré dans un roman.

Un homme, au contraire, ne devait-il pas tout connaître, exceller en des activités multiples, vous initier aux énergies de la passion, aux raffinements de la vie, à tous les mystères?" (101)

10   Bakhtin: "the logic motivating the sentence seems to belong to the author, i.e. he is formally at one with it; but in actual fact, the motivation lies with the subjective belief system of his characters, or of general opinion." M. M. Bakhtin, *The Dialogic Imagination*, trans. Caryl Emerson and Michael Holquist (Austin and London: University of Texas Press, 1981), 305.

11   "N'était-il pas, lui, l'obstacle à toute félicité, la cause de toute misère . . . ? Donc, elle reporta sur lui seul la haine nombreuse qui résultait de ses ennuis" (173). "Wasn't he the obstacle to every kind of happiness, the cause of all her wretchedness . . . ? So he became the sole object of her resentment" (128).

12   Critical response to Charles Bovary has gone through two main stages. With the notable exception of Jules Sénard, Flaubert's trial lawyer – who noted that the novel's conclusion treats Charles with admiring tenderness and Emma with unmitigated contempt – readers agreed in emphasizing Charles's mediocrity, if they bothered to mention him at all. (No doubt they dismissed Sénard's remarks as rhetorical, as indeed they were.) Thus Charles Baudelaire, also writing in 1857, noted simply the "infériorité spirituelle" of his namesake; Albert Thibaudet, in 1935, went so far as to say that "Flaubert a donné à Charles tous les caractères qui lui étaient odieux chez les bourgeois"; Erich Auerbach spoke of "his stupid philistine self-complacency"; "Charles Bovary . . . concretely oozes boredom and greyness," agreed Jean-Pierre Richard in 1954; so too Anthony Thorlby, in his 1956 study, presented the novel's dénouement as a potentially moving ending "reduced to the level of Charles' mediocre intelligence and Rodolphe's cheap sensitivity."

Starting in the 1960s, however, Charles underwent something of a rehabilitation, beginning with Harry Levin's declaration in *The Gates of Horn* (1963) that "for all his shortcomings . . . Dr. Bovary is the neglected protagonist" and culminating in 2006 with a novel actually presenting itself as a biography of Charles (Antoine Billot's *Monsieur Bovary*). In between, favorable comments have been heard from Victor Brombert, Maurice Bardèche ("only in the astonishing figure of Charles Bovary, to whom little justice has been done, does Flaubert allow us a glimpse of the unplumbed depths of the soul"), Dominick LaCapra ("Charles's devotion to Emma . . . bear[s] the closest of resemblances to Flaubert's own paradoxical dream"), Gérard Gengembre, Ulrich Schulz-Buschhaus, Michèle Breut, Dacia Maraini, and to some extent Jean-Marie Privat.

This has not prevented a number of critics from offering rather self-contradictory assessments. Enid Starkie, for instance, feels both that "the main characters – Charles and Emma – are drawn . . . always with compassion" *and* that "Charles is all the things most abhorred by Flaubert"; similarly, Eugene Gray suggests that while "Charles does have his good qualities, a point often overlooked," still his fidelity to Emma's memory is simply "foolish." (Compare Lowe, Nadeau, Turnell, and Williams.) Nor indeed has it prevented the periodic return of out-and-out dismissal, which one sees in Neefs and Mouchard, in Collas, in Berg and Martin, in Lattre ("la bêtise . . . le suivra jusque dans son engourdissement définitif, sous la tonnelle, dans le fond du jardin"), in Zenkine ("Charles Bovary est un grand enfant incapable de se mettre au niveau des exigences de la vie adulte"), and, most prominently, in Claude Chabrol's 1991 film adaptation.

See Jules Sénard, "Plaidoirie," in *Madame Bovary*, 461–515, p. 486; Charles Baudelaire, *Oeuvres Complètes* (Paris: Robert Laffont, 1980), 481; Albert Thibaudet, *Gustave Flaubert* (Paris: Gallimard, 1935), 108; Erich Auerbach, *Mimesis*, trans. Willard R. Trask

(Princeton, NJ: Princeton University Press, 1953), 489; Jean-Pierre Richard, "The Creation of Form in Flaubert," trans. Raymond Giraud, in Raymond Giraud, ed., *Flaubert: A Collection of Critical Essays* (Englewood Cliffs, NJ: Prentice-Hall, 1964), 36–56, p. 47; Anthony Thorlby, *Gustave Flaubert and the Art of Realism* (London: Bowes & Bowes, 1956), 44; Harry Levin, *The Gates of Horn: A Study of Five French Realists* (New York: Oxford University Press, 1963), 269; Antoine Billot, *Monsieur Bovary* (Paris: Gallimard, 2006); Victor Brombert, *The Novels of Flaubert: A Study of Themes and Techniques* (Princeton, NJ: Princeton University Press, 1966), 42; Maurice Bardèche, in *Madame Bovary* (Paris: Librairie Générale Française), 516 (quoted by Speziale-Bagliacca, *The King and the Adultress*, 8); Dominick LaCapra, *Madame Bovary on Trial* (Ithaca, New York: Cornell University Press, 1982), 113; Gérard Gengembre, *Gustave Flaubert: Madame Bovary*, Paris: PUF, 1990), 93–6; Schulz-Buschhaus, "Charles Bovary: Probleme Der Sympathiesteuerung Und Der Figurenkohärenz in Einem Flaubertschen Roman," 259; Michèle Breut, *Le Haut et le Bas: Essai sur le Grotesque dans Madame Bovary de Gustave Flaubert* (Amsterdam: Rodopi, 1994), 239; Dacia Maraini, *Searching for Emma*, trans. Vincent J. Bertolini (Chicago, IL: University of Chicago Press, 1993), 79, 137–8; Jean-Marie Privat, *Bovary Charivari: Essai d'ethno-critique* (Paris: CNRS, 1994), 123, 140; Enid Starkie, *Flaubert: The Making of the Master*, 1:315–6; Eugene F. Gray, "Bovary, Charles," in Laurence M. Porter, ed., *A Gustave Flaubert Encyclopedia* (Westport, CT: Greenwood Press, 2001), 38–9, p. 39; Margaret Lowe, *Towards the Real Flaubert: A Study of Madame Bovary* (Oxford: Clarendon Press, 1984), 33; Maurice Nadeau, *The Greatness of Flaubert*, trans. Barbara Bray (New York: The Library Press, 1972), 138; Martin Turnell, *The Rise of the French Novel* (New York: New Directions, 1978), 189; D. A. Williams, *Psychological Determinism in Madame Bovary* (Hull: University of Hull Publications, 1973), 68, 72; Jacques Neefs and Claude Mouchard, *Flaubert* (Paris: Balland, 1986), 149; Ion Collas, *Madame Bovary: A Psychoanalytic Reading* (Geneva: Droz, 1985), 74, 113; William Berg and Laurey Martin, *Gustave Flaubert* (New York: Twayne Publishers, 1997), 59; Alain de Lattre, *La Bêtise d'Emma Bovary* (Paris: José Corti, 1980), 9; Serge Zenkine, *Madame Bovary et l'Oppression réaliste* (Clermont-Ferrand: Association des publications de la Faculté des Lettres et Sciences Humaines de Clermont-Ferrand, 1996), 115.

13 "Quand elle eut ainsi un peu battu le briquet sur son coeur sans en faire jaillir une étincelle, incapable, du reste, de comprendre ce qu'elle n'éprouvait pas, comme de croire à tout ce qui ne se manifestait point par des formes convenues, elle se persuada sans peine que la passion de Charles n'avait rien d'exorbitant" (103).

14 "Il s'était tant de fois entendu dire ces choses, qu'elles n'avaient pour lui rien d'original. Emma ressemblait à toutes les maîtresses; et le charme de la nouveauté, peu à peu tombant comme un vêtement, laissait voir à nu l'éternelle monotonie de la passion, qui a toujours les mêmes formes et le même langage. Il ne distinguait pas, cet homme si plein de pratique, la dissemblance des sentiments sous la parité des expressions. Parce que des lèvres libertines ou vénales lui avaient murmuré des phrases pareilles, il ne croyait que faiblement à la candeur de celles-là; on en devait rabattre, pensait-il, les discours exagérés cachant les affections médiocres: comme si la plénitude de l'âme ne débordait pas quelquefois par les métaphores les plus vides, puisque personne, jamais, ne peut donner l'exacte mesure de ses besoins, ni de ses conceptions ni de ses douleurs, et que la parole humaine est comme un chaudron fêlé où nous battons des mélodies à faire danser les ours, quand on voudrait attendrir les étoiles" (259).

15 Complaining to Louise Colet about women, Flaubert wrote: "Ce que je leur reproche surtout, c'est leur besoin de poétisation. Un homme aimera sa lingère, et il saura qu'elle est

bête et n'en jouira pas moins. Mais si une femme aime un goujat, c'est un génie méconnu, une âme d'élite, etc., si bien que . . . elles ne voient pas le vrai quand il se rencontre, ni la beauté là où elle se trouve." ("What I most blame them for is their need for poeticization. A man can love his laundry maid, and know that she is stupid, and be no less happy for it. But if a woman loves an oaf, he is an unrecognized genius, an elite soul, etc., so much so that . . . they do not see the real when it presents itself, nor beauty where it is to be found.") Gustave Flaubert, *Correspondance*, Paris: Nizet, 2001, 2.61 (April 24, 1852). Subsequent references to this edition will be cited parenthetically in the text under the abbreviation *Corr*.

16 In his notebook, Flaubert wrote of Charles that he "ADORES his wife, and of the three men who sleep with her, is certainly the one who loves her most." ("ADORE sa femme et des trois hommes qui couchent avec elle, est certainement celui qui l'aime le plus.") Claudine Gothot-Mersch, *La genèse de Madame Bovary* (Paris: Corti, 1966), 136 (quoted in Brombert, *The Novels of Flaubert*, 9). This is borne out by the novel, with Charles being the only one of Emma's three lovers to be profoundly affected by her death: "Charles lay awake, thinking ceaselessly of *her*. Rodolphe, who had spent all day roaming the woods to keep his mind off things, was peacefully asleep in his chateau; and Léon was sleeping, too, in the distant city" (400). ("Charles, éveillé, pensait toujours à elle. Rodolphe, qui, pour se distraire, avait battu le bois toute la journée, dormait tranquillement dans son château; et Léon, là-bas, dormait aussi" 415.)

17 "Up until now, had there ever been a happy time in his life? His years at the lycée, where he had lived shut in behind high walls, lonely among richer, cleverer schoolmates who laughed at his country accent and made fun of his clothes and whose mothers brought them cookies in their muffs on visiting days? Or later, when he was studying medicine and hadn't enough in his purse to go dancing with some little working girl who might have become his mistress? After that he had lived fourteen months with the widow, whose feet in bed had been like icicles. But now he possessed, and for always, this pretty wife whom he so loved" (40). ("Jusqu'à présent, qu'avait-il eu de bon dans l'existence[?] Etait-ce son temps de collège, où il restait enfermé entre ces hauts murs, seul au milieu de ses camarades plus riches ou plus forts que lui dans leurs classes, qu'il faisait rire par son accent, qui se moquaient de ses habits, et dont les mères venaient au parloir avec des pâtisseries dans leur manchon? Etait-ce plus tard, lorsqu'il étudiait la médecine et n'avait jamais la bourse assez ronde pour payer la contredanse à quelque petite ouvrière qui fût devenue sa maîtresse? Ensuite il avait vécu pendant quatorze mois avec la veuve, dont les pieds, dans le lit, étaient froids comme des glaçons. Mais, à présent, il possédait pour la vie cette jolie femme qu'il adorait" 93–4.)

18 "Il faut," Flaubert told Louise Colet, "que mon bonhomme . . . vous émeuve pour tous les veufs" ("my fellow must move you on behalf of all widowers"). To Louise Colet, June 7, 1853, *Corr.* 2.339.

19 Even here, one could argue that he is talked into it, against his better judgment (242 / 205; cf. Gray, "Bovary, Charles," *A Gustave Flaubert Encyclopedia*, 38); he is otherwise a reasonably competent and well-liked doctor (Speziale-Bagliacca, *The King and the Adultress*, 22; Marc Girard, *La passion de Charles Bovary*, Paris: Imago, 1995, 8).

20 " – Je ne trouve rien d'admirable comme les soleils couchants, reprit-elle, mais au bord de la mer, surtout" (146). The entirety of Emma's first conversation with Léon (144–8 / 96–100) is in fact one long stream of clichés, some of them later reprinted in Flaubert's *Dictionnaire des idées reçues*.

21 Emma's strikingly cold-blooded treatment of her daughter, Berthe, may well imply the contrary. See 136 / 181, 262 / 227, and 265–6 / 231.

22 See Gray, "Bovary, Charles," *A Gustave Flaubert Encyclopedia*, 39; Breut, *Le Haut et le Bas*, 227; Marc Girard, *La Passion De Charles Bovary*, 9; Schulz-Buschhaus, "Charles Bovary: Probleme Der Sympathiesteuerung Und Der Figurenkohärenz in Einem Flaubertschen Roman," 258; and Graham Falconer, "Flaubert Assassin De Charles," in Michael Issacharoff, ed., *Langages de Flaubert: Actes du Colloque de London* (Paris: Minard, 1976), 115–41, pp. 121–3.

23 For Falconer, the character shift is just a mistake, "tout à fait gratuit," indeed "un défaut esthétique" ("Flaubert assassin de Charles," 140, 132). For Speziale-Bagliacca, it is evidence of Flaubert being mistaken about his own character (who is, incidentally, a sadomasochist (*The King and the Adultress*, p. 18) with latent homosexual tendencies (*The King and the Adultress*, 53)). More compellingly, Marc Girard suggests that the point is to force the reader to choose a side, in an act of existential self-determination (*La passion de Charles Bovary*, 167–8). As will be apparent, I am offering a different hypothesis.

24 Aristotle, *On Poetics*, trans. Seth Benardete and Michael Davis (South Bend, IN: St Augustine's Press, 2002), 1449b.

25 Alexander Nehamas, "Pity and Fear in the *Rhetoric* and the *Poetics*," in Amélie Oksenberg Rorty, ed., *Essays on Aristotle's Poetics* (Princeton: Princeton University Press, 1992), 291–314, p. 301.

26 See Stephen Halliwell, *Aristotle's Poetics* (Chicago: University Of Chicago Press, 1998); Martha Nussbaum, *The Fragility of Goodness* (Cambridge: Cambridge University Press, 1986). For a full history of catharsis theories, see Andrew Ford, "Katharsis: The Ancient Problem," in Andrew Parker and Eve Kosofsky Sedgwick, eds., *Performativity and Performance* (New York and London: Routledge, 1995), 109–32, pp. 111–3.

27 Jonathan Lear, "Katharsis," *Phronesis* 33 (1988): 297–326, pp. 303, 301, 300. In *Politics* 8.5–7, Aristotle distinguishes between cathartic music and ethical music, strongly implying that the cathartic variety does not improve character (Lear 300). On the homeopathy point, cf. Nehamas, "Pity and Fear in the *Rhetoric* and the *Poetics*," 304.

28 Lear, "Katharsis," 301 (again with *Politics* 8.5–7); cf. Arthur C. Danto, *The Transfiguration of the Commonplace* (Cambridge, MA: Harvard University Press, 1981), 22; James Harold, "On Judging the Moral Value of Narrative Artworks," *The Journal of Aesthetics and Art Criticism* 64.2 (2006): 259–70, p. 267.

29 For Lear's positive view, see Lear, "Katharsis," 323–6; for an even more deflationary hypothesis, see Nehamas, "Pity and Fear in the *Rhetoric* and the *Poetics*," 306.

30 Thus Lynn Hunt argues that the theory of human rights, though it had multiple causes, could not have succeeded without an explosion of novel-reading. "In the eighteenth century, readers of novels learned to extend their purview of empathy," she writes. "As a consequence, they came to see others – people they did not know personally – as like them, as having the same kinds of inner emotions. Without this learning process, 'equality' could have no deep meaning and in particular no political consequence." (*Inventing Human Rights: A History*, New York: Norton, 2007, 40; cf. 32 and chapter 1 *passim*.) Similarly, Richard Rorty considers novels of the self-improving type not only "appeals to fellow feeling" but *indispensable* appeals to fellow feeling, since philosophy, religion, and science are unable to persuade people that others are like them, whereas novels, along with non-fictional "sad stories," are able to do so. (Richard Rorty, *Critical Dialogues*, ed. Matthew Festenstein and Simon Thompson, Oxford: Blackwell, 2001, 133, 132; see also *Truth and Progress: Philosophical Papers III*, Cambridge: Cambridge University Press, 1998, 185.) Martha Nussbaum, whose view is sometimes that fiction gives us practice in handling complicated moral

predicaments, at other times agrees with Rorty that "the literary imagination . . . seems to me an essential ingredient of an ethical stance that asks us to concern ourselves with the good of other people whose lives are distant from our own." (*Poetic Justice: The Literary Imagination and Public Life*, Boston, MA: Beacon Press, 1995, xvi; cf. "Invisibility and Recognition: Sophocles' *Philoctetes* and Ellison's *Invisible Man*," Philosophy and Literature 23 (1999): 257–83, p. 265.) For a recent restatement of this view, see Mark William Roche, *Why Literature Matters in the Twenty-First Century*, New Haven: Yale University Press, 2004, 26.

31 Martha Nussbaum, for one, believes that altruism is generated by empathy: "Civic love comes before, and nourishes, civic justice." ("'Finely Aware and Richly Responsible': Literature and the Moral Imagination," in Anthony J. Cascardi, ed., *Literature and the Question of Philosophy*, Baltimore: Johns Hopkins University Press, 1987, 167–91, p. 184.)

32 Cf. Gregory Currie: "In order to defeat my enemy I may need to simulate his mental operations, so as to know what he will do. That need not make me like him any better." ("The Moral Psychology of Fiction," *Australasian Journal of Philosophy* 73.2: 250–9, p. 257.)

33 See e.g. Richard W. Byrne and Andrew Whiten, eds., *Machiavellian Intelligence: Social Expertise And The Evolution Of Intellect In Monkeys, Apes, And Humans* (New York: Oxford University Press, 1988). For connections to literature, see Lisa Zunshine, *Why We Read Fiction: Theory of Mind and the Novel* (Columbus, OH: Ohio State University Press, 2006) and Blakey Vermeule, *Why We Care About Literary Characters* (Baltimore, MD: Johns Hopkins University Press, forthcoming).

34 Part of the issue here has to do with a deficit of historicity. It appears to be assumed by some of the theorists in question that fictional empathy has always been marshaled in the service of real-world compassion toward "those who are not like us." But as we have just seen, it is entirely possible for a culture to place a premium on *limits* to real-world compassion; and this very fact may well have influenced the way in which contemporary spectators of Sophocles and Aeschylus experienced their tragedies. For the self-understanding of a culture will very likely have an effect – not an absolutely determining effect, but an effect nonetheless – on the way in which its individual members opt to situate themselves in relation to artworks.

35 Richard Rorty reads *Lolita* as a cautionary tale, one which ostensibly fills the reader with remorse for his or her moral failings (*Contingency, Irony, and Solidarity*, Cambridge: Cambridge University Press, 1989, 164). But he does not explain how this is consistent with his standard account on which fictions that describe lives different from our own have the effect of bringing people once thought of under the designation "them" under the designation "us." One would presumably not want this to happen for real-life counterparts of Humbert Humbert.

36 Cf. Noël Carroll, "Art, Narrative, and Moral Understanding," in Jerrold Levinson, ed., *Aesthetics and Ethics: Essays at the Intersection* (Cambridge: Cambridge University Press, 1998), 126–60, p. 130.

37 I develop some of these ideas further in "A Nation of Madame Bovarys: On the Possibility and Desirability of Moral Improvement through Fiction," in Garry L. Hagberg, ed., *Art and Ethical Criticism* (Oxford: Blackwell, 2008), 63–94.

38 Hegel: "the heroes of Greek classical tragedy are confronted by circumstances in which, after firmly identifying themselves with the one ethical 'pathos' which alone corresponds to their own already established nature, they necessarily come into conflict with the opposite but equally justified ethical power." (*Aesthetics*, trans. T. M. Knox, Oxford: Oxford University Press, 1975, 2.1226.)

39 In the novels of Jane Austen, for example, multifocal empathy may well – as Lisa Zunshine suggests – serve the function of allowing the reader to practice his or her skills of nested "mind-reading," with a view to increasing his or her capacity for social dominance. In other cases (such, for example, as Toni Morrison's *Song of Solomon*, or W. M. Thackeray's *Vanity Fair*) the array of generally empathetic characters invites us, in Bakhtinian fashion, to define our own stance in relation and/or contradistinction to theirs. In Dostoevsky, it may be (here *pace* Bakhtin) that the situation is even more complex. If *The Brothers Karamazov* gives such eloquent voice to Ivan as well as to Alyosha, it is not because we are simply being offered a choice between faith and doubt but because the ideal stance is a *combination* of doubt and faith, an almost Kierkegaardian faith *sustained* by doubt; here, then, our empathetic engagement with antithetical characters becomes, surprisingly enough, a formal model for the attitude we are supposed to take to life. Ivan is necessary not as a foil to Alyosha, nor as a rejected position, nor yet as a Bakhtinian option, but instead as part of an accurate picture of a soul with the right kind of faith, and hence a blueprint for the reader of the shape his or her own soul could one day possess.

40 Samuel Beckett, *Three Novels: Molloy, Malone Dies, the Unnamable* (London: Grove, 1994). Subsequent references to this edition will be cited parenthetically in the text.

41 The paradigmatic case is perhaps John Calder's *The Philosophy of Samuel Beckett*, which more or less opens with the claim that "What future generations can expect to find in his [Beckett's] work is above all an ethical and philosophical message; the novels and plays will increasingly be seen as the wrapping for that message." So too the Hamiltons also invoke "Beckett's message about man"; John Fletcher speaks of Beckett's works pointing a moral; in David Hayman, they shed light on existence; in Hugh Kenner, they affirm some general truth; in Thomas Cousineau, they seek to convince; in Maurice Blanchot, they make evident something that is merely implicit in other literary works; and in Georges Bataille, they are "telling us" about reality. John Calder, *The Philosophy of Samuel Beckett* (Edison, NJ: Riverrun Press, 2001), 1; Kenneth and Alice Hamilton, *Condemned to Life: The World of Samuel Beckett* (Grand Rapids, MI: Wm. B. Eerdmans Publ. Company, 1976), 11; John Fletcher, *The Novels of Samuel Beckett* (New York: Barnes and Noble, 1970), 176; David Hayman, "*Molloy* or the Quest for Meaninglessness: A Global Interpretation," in Melvin J. Friedman, ed., *Samuel Beckett Now: Critical Approaches to His Novels, Poetry and Plays* (Chicago: Chicago University Press, 1970), 129–56, p. 156; Hugh Kenner, *Samuel Beckett: A Critical Study* (Berkeley: University of California Press, 1974), 10; Thomas J. Cousineau, *After the Final No: Samuel Beckett's Trilogy* (Newark: University of Delaware Press, 1999), 120; Maurice Blanchot, "Where Now? Who Now?" trans. Richard Howard, in S. E. Gontarski, *On Beckett: Essays and Criticism*, New York: Grove Press, 1986, 141–9, pp. 147–8; Georges Bataille, "Molloy's Silence," trans. John Pilling, in Gontarski, ed., *On Beckett: Essays and Criticism*, 131–9, p. 131.

42 Thus the Unnamable speculates as to why exactly "they" have told him a particular story: "there's a story for you, that was to teach me the nature of emotion, that's called emotion, what emotion can do, given favourable conditions, what love can do, well well, so that's emotion, that's love, and trains, the nature of trains . . . , it was to teach me how to reason, it was to tempt me to go, to the place where you can come to an end" (407). Notice that there are three separate hypotheses here – instruction, training, manipulation – and that the instruction theory is bathetically undermined by the rather hilarious "trains."

43 There is an important parallel here with the work of the late Wittgenstein (at least on one reading of the latter). "Thoughts that are at peace. That is what someone who philosophizes

yearns for," Wittgenstein famously claims (*Culture and Value*, trans. Peter Winch, Oxford: Blackwell, 1994, 43); and again, equally famously, "The real discovery is the one that makes me capable of stopping doing philosophy when I want to. – The one that gives philosophy peace, so that it is no longer tormented by questions which bring *itself* in question." (Ludwig Wittgenstein, *Philosophical Investigations*, trans. D. F. Pears and B. F. McGuinness, New York: Prentice Hall, 1999, §133.) On Wittgensteinian "therapy," cf. Garry L. Hagberg, "On Philosophy as Therapy: Wittgenstein, Cavell, and Autobiographical Writing," *Philosophy and Literature* 27 (2003): 196–210.

44 On Beckett and ancient skepticism, see David H. Hesla, *The Shape of Chaos: An Interpretation of the Art of Samuel Beckett* (Minneapolis: University of Minnesota Press, 1971), 121; and Steven J. Rosen, *Samuel Beckett and the Pessimistic Tradition* (New Brunswick, NJ: Rutgers University Press, 1976), 53–4. To cast Beckett as a Stoic, as does Calder (*The Philosophy of Samuel Beckett*, p. 1), is to miss the force of the carefully opposed claims.

45 "I grew calm again and was restored," Molloy writes at one point, "to my old ataraxy" (42).

46 From the *Protrepticus*, in *Aristotelis Fragmenta Selecta*, ed. W. D. Ross (Oxford: Clarendon Press, 1955), vii, 27–8.

47 "What am I to do, what shall I do, what should I do, in my situation, how proceed? By aporia pure and simple? Or by affirmations and negations invalidated as uttered, or sooner or later? . . . I say aporia without knowing what it means. Can one be ephectic otherwise than unawares? I don't know" (291). ("Ephexis," like "epoché," means suspension of judgment.)

48 Cf. *The Calmative*: "All I say cancels out, I'll have said nothing" (*The Complete Short Prose, 1929–1989*, ed. S. E. Gontarski, New York: Grove Press, 1995, 100–54, p. 62).

49 "For in me there have always been two fools, among others, one asking nothing better than to stay where he is and the other imagining that life might be slightly less horrible a little further on. . . . And these inseparable fools I indulged turn about, that they might understand their foolishness" (*Molloy* 48).

50 Sextus Empiricus, *Outlines of Pyrrhonism*, trans. R. G. Bury, London: Heinemann, 1933, 1.8 (p. 7). See also 1.31 (p. 23) and 1.232 (p. 143).

51 This continues into the *Texts for Nothing*: "And it's still the same road I'm trudging, *up yes and down no*, towards one yet to be named, *so that he may leave me in peace*, be in peace, be no more, never have been . . . *believing this, then that, then nothing more*" (*The Complete Short Prose*, pp. 144–5; my emphasis).

52 See Bruno Clément, "A Rhetoric of Ill-Saying," trans. Thomas Cousineau, *Journal of Beckett Studies* 4.1 (1994): 35–53, pp. 41, 36.

53 Sextus: "The Sceptic, being a lover of his kind [i.e. humanity], desires to cure . . . the Dogmatists" (*Outlines of Pyrrhonism*, 3:280, p. 511).

54 It is not the case, I think, that we are entirely prevented from empathizing with Emma. On the contrary, many readers view her as the rather appealing victim of a bad marriage, an unfair society, misleading fictions, and so on. Witness the plot summary recently provided by the online journal Salon.com: "Flaubert brings to life a hopeless romantic who believes that true love should strike with the blinding intensity of a thunderbolt that 'plunges the entire heart into an abyss.' Unfortunately, she is married to a dull clod of a man." And compare the more measured Wayne Booth who, without going quite so far, nonetheless feels that Flaubert "takes sides" in Emma's favor: "*Madame Bovary* is unfair to almost everyone but Emma" (Wayne Booth, *The Rhetoric Of Fiction*, Chicago: University of Chicago Press, 1983, p. 78;http://www.salon.com/promo/97/09/08.classic_bovary.html.)

55 One might imagine the empathists arguing that the ideal would be to remain *neutral* between Emma and Charles, caring fully about both. I would contend, first, that this cannot be Flaubert's intention, and also, second, that this would not actually count as *caring*. Where viewpoints are incommensurable, it is impossible to adopt both in the manner required for genuine *Mitgefühl*.

56 See René Girard, *Deceit, Desire and the Novel: Self and Other in Literary Structure*, trans. Yvonne Freccero (Baltimore: Johns Hopkins University Press, 1965), 152. In Flaubert, writes Girard, "false oppositions . . . confront each other symmetrically and then fall back into the void; this impassive juxtaposition reveals the absurdity" (151).

57 "Je crois donc qu'il ne faut «*rien aimer*», c'est-à-dire qu'il faut planer impartialement au-dessus de tous les objectifs": "I believe then that one must '*love nothing*' – that is, that one must glide impartially above all objectives" (to Ernest Feydeau, end July 1857, *Corr.* 2.770). Flaubert has his moments of mystical detachment, as when he notes that "c'est une délicieuse chose que d'écrire! que de ne plus être *soi*, mais de circuler dans toute la création dont on parle. Aujourd'hui par exemple, homme et femme tout ensemble, amant et maîtresse à la fois, je me suis promené à cheval dans une forêt, par un après-midi d'automne sous des feuilles jaunes, et j'étais les chevaux, les feuilles, le vent, les paroles qu'ils se disaient et le soleil rouge qui faisait s'entrefermer leurs paupières noyées d'amour." ("Writing is a delicious thing! no longer to be *oneself*, but to circulate in the whole creation of which one speaks. Today for example, man and woman together, lover and mistress at once, I rode around a forest on horseback, in an autumn afternoon under yellow leaves, and I was the horses, the leaves, the wind, the words they said to each other and the red sun which half-closed their eyelids drowned in love.") (To Louise Colet, December 24, 1853, *Corr.* 2.487.)

Part IV

Literature and the Moral Life

13

Perceptive Equilibrium: Literary Theory and Ethical Theory

MARTHA C. NUSSBAUM

> Mrs Newsome's dress was never in any degree "cut down," and she never wore round her throat a broad red *velvet* band; if she had, moreover, would it ever have served so to carry on and complicate, as he now almost felt, his vision?[1]
>
> Henry James, *The Ambassadors*

Speaking to Little Bilham about Chad Newsome's surprising development, Strether describes his own viewpoint and his interest:

> I'm speaking – in connexion with her – of his manners and morals, his character and life. I'm speaking of him as a person to deal with and talk with and live with – speaking of him as a social animal. (1.283)

The speech of literary theory, especially in recent years, has not often shared Strether's concerns and connections. I believe that it has an impoverished future without them. I imagine, instead, a future in which our talk about literature will return, increasingly, to a concern with the practical – to the ethical and social questions that give literature its high importance in our lives. A future in which these interests, like Strether's here, will find themselves connected to an interest in Mme de Vionnet – in, that is, those emotions and desires that do not reside harmoniously within the domain of ethical judgment. In which a literary-philosophical inquiry, with something like Strether's "candour of fancy" (1.52) and his "conscientious wonder" (1.49), will ask what literary works express about these matters – express in virtue of their "content," but also, and inseparably, in virtue of their forms and structures, their ways of describing, since those ways are "at all times" (as Strether "philosophized") "the very conditions of perception, the terms of thought" (2.49). In short, a future in which literary theory (while not forgetting its many other pursuits) will also join with ethical theory in pursuit of the question, "How should one live?"

The Absence of the Ethical

Recent literary theory has taken a keen interest in philosophy. In fact, it is hard to distinguish it from philosophy, either by the nature of its questions or by the names to which it turns for illumination. Questions about realism, relativism, and subjectivism; about skepticism and justification; about the nature of language – these are now common ground between the two professions. And in pursuit of these questions literary theory discusses and teaches not only the work of philosophers who write directly about literary matters (e.g., Nietzsche, Heidegger, Hans-Georg Gadamer, Stanley Cavell, Nelson Goodman, Hilary Putnam), but also the ideas of many (e.g., W. V. O. Quine, Paul Feyerabend, S. A. Kripke, Thomas Kuhn, Jürgen Habermas) who do not. (These lists, intentionally eclectic, show, too, the diversity of the philosophical styles and methods that have influenced the current literary scene.) Indeed, with several prominent contemporary figures – above all Jacques Derrida and Richard Rorty – there is no clear answer to the question, to which profession do they belong? The question, indeed, loses its interest, since the professions share so many issues, and since differences about method are internal to each group, rather than divided simply along disciplinary lines.

But when we turn from epistemology to ethics, the situation is very different. This is a rich and wonderful time in moral philosophy.[2] One cannot find for generations – since the time of John Stuart Mill, if not earlier – an era in which there has been so much excellent, adventurous, and varied work on the central ethical and political questions of human life. Questions about justice, about well-being and social distribution, about moral realism and relativism, about the nature of rationality, about the concept of the person, about the emotions and desires, about the role of luck in human life – all these and others are debated from many sides with considerable excitement and even urgency. These philosophical debates have frequently become interdisciplinary, touching as they do on human issues that are central to more than one field of study. On the emotions, for example, moral philosophers have a lively dialogue with psychologists; on moral relativism, with cultural anthropologists; on rationality and well-being, with economists. One would certainly expect that literature and theory about literature would play a role in these debates. For literature offers us insight on all of these questions, and in a way that is inextricable from literary forms. So one would expect that the people whose profession it is to think in general about literature and its forms would speak to these issues and join in these public debates.

This, we know, has not happened. Literary criticism dealing with particular texts and authors continues, of course, to speak about the ethical and social concerns that are central to those authors. But even this sort of concern has been constrained by pressure of the current thought that to discuss a text's ethical or social content is somehow to neglect "textuality," the complex relationships of that text with other texts; and of the related, though more extreme, thought that texts do not refer to human life at all, but only to other texts and to themselves.[3] And if one turns from criticism to more general and theoretical writing about literature, the ethical vanishes more or less altogether. One way we perceive this is by considering the philosophical references.

Philosophers' names constantly appear. But the names of the leading moral and political philosophers of our day – of John Rawls, Bernard Williams, Thomas Nagel, Derek Parfit, Judith Jarvis Thomson, and many others – and also the names of the great moral philosophers of the past – of Mill, Bentham, Henry Sidgwick, Rousseau, of the ethical sides of Plato, Aristotle, Hume, and Kant – do not appear, more or less, at all. (This is strikingly true even of those recent moral philosophers, such as Bernard Williams, Hilary Putnam, and Iris Murdoch, who have criticized systematic ethical theory in ways that lead them to ally themselves with literature.) These writers about ethics are not studied in literary theory programs, as their epistemological and metaphysical companions are; those among them (past and present) who write on both ethics and epistemology are studied one-sidedly. In short, these diverse and excellent analyses of human social experience are usually not taken to have any interesting bearing on the activity of the theorist.

Literary theory could neglect moral philosophy and still show a keen interest in the ethical – though I shall later offer, tentatively, some reasons why a turn to philosophy can offer valuable illumination here. But in the midst of all this busy concern with other types of philosophy, the absence of moral philosophy seems a significant sign. And in fact it signals a further striking absence: the absence, from literary theory, of the organizing questions of moral philosophy, and of moral philosophy's sense of urgency about these questions. The sense that we are social beings puzzling out, in times of great moral difficulty, what might be, for us, the best way to live – this sense of practical importance, which animates contemporary ethical theory and has always animated much of great literature, is absent from the writings of many of our leading literary theorists. One can have no clearer single measure of this absence than to have the experience of reading Jacques Derrida's *Éperons*[4] after reading Nietzsche. Once one has worked through and been suitably (I think) impressed by Derrida's perceptive and witty analysis of Nietzsche's style, one feels, at the end of all the urbanity, an empty longing amounting to a hunger, a longing for the sense of difficulty and risk and practical urgency that are inseparable from Zarathustra's dance. A longing for some acknowledgment of the fact that Nietzsche saw a crisis at hand for Europe, for all of human life; that he thought it mattered deeply whether one lived as a Christian or in some other as yet unspecified way; and that he dedicated his career to imagining that way. Nietzsche's work is profoundly critical of existing ethical theory, clearly; but it is, inter alia, a response to the original Socratic question, "How should one live?" Derrida does not touch on that question. "Of all that is written," says Zarathustra, "I love only what a man has written with his blood."[5] After reading Derrida, and not Derrida alone, I feel a certain hunger for blood; for, that is, writing about literature that talks of human lives and choices as if they matter to us all.[6]

This is, after all, the spirit in which much of great literature has been and is written and read. We do approach literature for play and for delight, for the exhilaration of following the dance of form and unraveling webs of textual connection. (Though even here I would not be quick to grant that there is any coherence to an account of aesthetic pleasure that abstracts altogether from our practical human interests and desires.) But one of the things that makes literature something deeper and more central for us than a complex game, deeper even than those games, for example chess and tennis, that move us to wonder by their complex beauty, is that it speaks like Strether. It speaks *about us*, about our lives and choices and emotions, about our social existence and the totality of our connections.[7] As Aristotle observed, it is deep, and conducive to our inquiry about how to live, because it does not simply (as history does) record that this or that event happened; it searches for patterns of possibility – of choice, and circumstance, and the interaction between choice and circumstance – that turn up in human lives with such a persistence that they must be regarded as *our* possibilities. And so our interest in literature becomes (like Strether's in Chad) cognitive: an interest in finding out (by seeing and feeling the otherwise perceiving) what possibilities (and tragic impossibilities) life offers to us, what hopes and fears for ourselves it underwrites or subverts.[8]

To explain how literary theory lost this practical dimension would be a long story. This story would include the influence of Kant's aesthetics; of early twentieth-century formalism; of the New Criticism. It would include the influence of several prevailing trends in ethical theory as well – above all that of Kantianism and of utilitarianism, ethical views that in their different ways were so inhospitable to any possible relation with imaginative literature that dialogue was cut off from the side of ethics as well.[9] It would include, too, a critical look at some writing about literature that did, during this long period, keep ethical concerns in view. For much of this writing has understandably given ethical writing about literature a bad name, by its neglect of literary form and its reductive moralizing manner. It has been easy enough to feel that ethical writing must do violence to the literary work. Of course it should have been obvious that to concentrate on form to the neglect of the work's sense of life and choice is not a solution, only violence of a different sort. It should have been recognized that neither sort of violence is required: that we grasp the practical content of a literary text adequately only when we attentively study the forms in which it is embodied and expressed; and that, in turn, we have not correctly described the literary form of, say, a James novel if we have not asked what sense of life it expresses. But, with certain striking exceptions,[10] this was on the whole not acknowledged; and we can see the historical reasons why.

One important task for a future literary theory, as I see it, will be to write out this history in detail. I shall not attempt that task here. I shall instead begin on a different part of the enterprise that I imagine. By bringing one example forward in a certain amount of detail, I shall try to illustrate this idea of a literary theory that works together with ethical theory, sketching out some of the concerns this theory might have; and I shall suggest ways in which a dialogue with moral philosophers might help us develop them. It will be no surprise by this point in the argument that I shall talk about James's *The Ambassadors*, which I take to be a major work in moral philosophy – talking about what it is to be assailed by a perception, about how the character of Mrs Newsome's gown points to a deficiency in some accounts of ethical rationality that even now influence our daily lives.

Reflective Equilibrium

But before we can begin to talk of Strether we need some story, however sketchy and incomplete, about the enterprise in which I propose to join literary theory with ethical theory.[11] For some enterprises, and some descriptions of this one, will demote one or the other party to the partnership. The very difficulty of discovering a non-prejudicial description of the task of ethical inquiry will itself illuminate our problem; and the concealed prejudices in some prominent contemporary philosophical descriptions of the task will begin to show us what moral philosophy has lost through the absence of dialogue with literary thought.

I have said that the question with which my projected literary–ethical inquiry begins is the question, "How should one live?"[12] This choice of starting point is significant. This question does not (like the Kantian question, "What is my moral duty?") assume that there is a sphere of "moral" values that can be separated off from all the other practical values that figure in a human life. Nor does it assume, as does the utilitarian's focus on the question, "How shall I maximize utility?" that the value of all choices and actions is to be assessed in terms of a certain sort of consequence that they tend to promote. It does not assume the denial of these claims either. So far it is neutral, leaving them for investigation inside the inquiry. The point is to state the opening question in a general and inclusive way, excluding at the start no major story about the good life for human beings.

The inquiry asks, then, what it is for a human being to live well. This investigation as I imagine it, is both empirical and practical. Empirical in that it is based on and responsible to actual human experience; it aims to elicit an "intelligent report," as James puts it, of that experience – that is, of "our apprehension and our measure of what happens to us as social beings."[13] (It is not, as Kant thought, *a priori*.) Practical in that it is conducted by people who are themselves involved in acting and choosing and who see the inquiry as having a bearing on their own practical ends. They do not inquire in a "pure" or detached manner, asking what the truth about ethical value might be as if they were asking for a description of some separately existing Platonic reality. They are looking for something in human life, something, in fact that they themselves are going to try to bring about in their lives. What they are asking is not what is the good "out there," but what can we best live by, and live together as social beings? Their results are constrained, and appropriately constrained, by their hopes and fears for themselves, their sense of value, what they think they can live with. This does not mean that inquiry cannot substantially modify their antecedent conception of their "target," specifying goals that were vague before and even convincing them to revise in substantial ways their conception of their goal. But their end is practice, not just theory. And inquiry is valuable because it contributes to practice in two ways: by promoting individual clarification and self-understanding, and by moving individuals toward communal atonement.[14] By now this view of procedure should be recognizable as Aristotle's; it has been endorsed and used by later thinkers, such as Henry Sidgwick and, recently and influentially, by John Rawls, in *A Theory of Justice*.[15] It has a good deal in common with Henry James's remarks about his purpose as a novelist.

The central procedural idea is that we work through the major alternative views about the good life, holding them up, in each case, against our own experience and our intuitions. The first step will be to get a perspicuous description of these alternatives (though we should bear in mind that these descriptions will already contain an element of evaluation and response). Prominent among these views will be views embodied in texts of many kinds, both recent and older. Next we notice and clearly describe the conflicts and tensions among the views that we find. Where there is inconsistency or irreconcilable tension – and where this tension corresponds to something that we notice in our own experience and thought (individually or communally) – we aim to revise the overall picture so as to bring it into harmony with itself, preserving, as Aristotle says, "the greatest number and the most basic" of the original judgments and perceptions. There is no rule about how to do this.[16] Individuals simply ask what looks deepest, what they can least live without – guided by their sense of life, and by their standing interest in consistency and in community. That is, they want to arrive at a view that is internally coherent, and also at one that is broadly shared and shareable. (Thus frequently they will move away from a personal claim, even when narrow consistency does not require it, in order to find one on which more of them can agree.) Nothing else is non-negotiable, not even the precise interpretation of these regulative principles themselves. The procedure is holistic:[17] it holds nothing unrevisable, but seeks for coherence and "fit" in the system as a whole.

So far, notice, we have said nothing about what faculties of the person (intellect, imagination, emotion) we trust, or trust most, inside the procedure; nothing, again, about which judgments we would tend to trust more than others; and nothing very concrete about how, and in what result, the procedure comes to an end. This is appropriate, since norms of good (or rational) judgment and appropriate sorting – of the intelligent "reading" of life – are themselves up for debate inside the procedure. But in preparing the way for Henry James's contribution (which I believe to be closely related to Aristotle's), I want to describe a prominent and influential version of the Aristotelian procedure that does add at this point some further (and very un-Aristotelian) specifications. What is interesting for us is that these are added as if they were about as non-controversial as anything could possibly be; and indeed, within the tradition of modern moral philosophy, this is pretty well true. In *A Theory of Justice*, then, describing the task of moral theory, John Rawls adopts a procedure that he traces explicitly to Aristotle; but he makes three significant additions to the general outline I have reported.[18] First, Rawls gives a name to the desired end of the procedure: it is "reflective equilibrium." This is the condition at which we arrive when we have gone through the procedure; the name suggests balance, an absence of inconsistency or tension, and the dominance of intellectual judgment. Second, he provides an account of "considered judgment" that tells us which judgments to trust and mistrust during the procedure. (He seems to assume from the start that we are using only standing judgments of varying degrees of concreteness, and not immersed situational perceptions.)[19] Mistrusted will be "those judgments made with hesitation, or in which we have little confidence. Similarly, those given when we are upset or frightened, or when we stand to gain one way or another can be left aside."[20] This is taken to give us the conditions "in which our moral capacities are most likely to be displayed without distortion."[21] Finally, Rawls later adds five constraints that must be met by any ethical theory that will even be seriously considered during the procedure of scrutiny. These conditions are that its principles should be *general* in form and *universal* in application; that they should be *public* and available to all; that they should impose a general ordering on conflicting claims; and that these principles should be regarded as final and conclusive – "the final court of appeal in practical reasoning." In short,

> if we think in terms of the fully general theory which has principles for all the virtues, then such a theory specifies the totality of relevant considerations and their appropriate weights, and its requirements are decisive.[22]

I have said that Rawls regards these requirements, including the final five, as relatively uncontroversial. And so, indeed, they have been, in contemporary debates about his (otherwise controversial) theory. Strether's relation to them is no simple one, as we shall see; much of our work on his story will consist in articulating this (sometimes tragic) relation. And in general we might expect that ethical thought that begins from literature – which, if it shares anything at all, would seem to share a commitment to the ethical relevance of particularity and to the epistemological value of feeling – would not find these limits at all trivial or uncontroversial. Should we indeed aim at a condition of balance or equilibrium? Should this equilibrium indeed be "reflective" – that is, presumably (as Rawls uses the word), a condition that is detached from powerful feeling and from particular situational immersion? Should we in fact exclude our bewilderment and our hesitation from the deliberative process? Should we automatically mistrust the information given us by our fear, or grief, or love? (For being in love would surely count as a case of "being upset.") Should we in fact go for theories that embody generality and universality – rather than saying, with Aristotle, that "the discrimination lies in perception"?[23] Do we believe that a general (rather than a particular) ordering *can* be imposed, and imposed in advance, upon conflicting claims? Above all, do we feel that a general system of principles can and should be a court of last appeal in practical reasoning, determining standards all in advance of life itself? In these conditions we begin to sense the austere presence of Mrs Newsome, "all fine cold thought," impervious to surprise, idealistic and exceptionless in her justice.

Straightness and Surprise

> "That's just her difficulty – that she doesn't admit surprises. It's a fact that, I think, describes and represents her; and it falls in with what I tell you – that she's all, as I've called it, fine cold thought. She had, to her own mind, worked the whole thing out in advance, and worked it out for me as well as for herself. Whenever she has done that, you see, there's no room left; no margin, as it were, for any alteration. She's filled as full, packed as tight, as she'll hold, and if you wish to get anything more or different either out or in – "
>
> "You've got to make over altogether the woman herself?"
>
> "What it comes to," said Strether, "is that you've got morally and intellectually to get rid of her." (2.239)

James's richly comic portrait of Mrs Newsome lies at the center of his story of Strether's adventure. Present vividly in her absence, she articulates, by contrast, Strether's moral movement. He begins as her ambassador, the agent of her antecedently fixed moral purpose; he ends as a child "toddling" alone, a diver in depths, a hearer of strange and crowded voices, a floater upon inexorable tides of light. To understand Strether's struggle we must understand *her* – and with a certain sympathy: asking how, for example, her refusal of surprise "falls in" with the fact that she is all fine cold thought; asking, too, why her vision of life appeals to our friend and stirs, as it continually does, his moral imagination.

We notice first and most obviously her moralism, her preoccupation with questions of moral right and wrong, with criticism of offense, with judgment upon vice. "Essentially all moral pressure" (2.198), as Strether describes her, she motivates his own obsession with discipline and punishment, his determination "always, where Lambert Strether was concerned, to know the worst" (2.69). Indeed he is attracted to her, perhaps, just because of

> his old tradition, the one he had been brought up on and which even so many years of life had but little worn away; the notion that the state of the wrongdoer, or at least this person's happiness, presented some special difficulty. (2.272)

It is no accident that her principles are, for him, embodied in the dream figure of a judging mother who "loom(s) at him larger than life" until "he already felt her come down on him, already burned, under her reprobation, with the blush of guilt. . . . He saw himself, under her direction, recommitted to Woollen as juvenile offenders are committed to reformatories" (2.61).[24] To her obsession with the priority of moral right, which fills, it seems, the entirety of her exalted consciousness (the presence of moral pressure is "almost identical with her own presence" [2.198]), we may add rigorism in her conception of principles. Everything in her world must be "straight" (Strether, later, calls her "the whole moral and intellectual being or block"); and her rules of right admit of no softening in the light of the present circumstance, the individual case. "She was the only woman he had known, even at Woollett, as to whom his conviction was positive that to lie was beyond her art": she "refused to human commerce that mitigation of rigor" (1.95). Strether links his thought of her with the idea of an exceptionless justice that dwells outside "in the hard light" (2.5). This moral rigorism, together with the ubiquity of moral assessment, permits her two attitudes only, when confronted with a new occurrence: approval or disapproval. "From the moment they're not delighted," Strether says of her and her new Ambassador Sarah, "they can only be – well what I admit she was" (2.218).

If universal and general principles of right take precedence over (and indeed swallow up) all other elements of life, there are three aspects of human experience that Mrs Newsome especially dislikes and avoids: emotion, passivity, and the perception of particularity. These items are connected in an interesting and, in a certain sense, profoundly appealing way. Strether describes her as a person who "won't be touched" (2.239); when he imagines her his eyes "might have been fixing some particularly large iceberg in a cool blue northern sea" (2.240); and, as we have seen, he refers to her, in her "tightly packed" fullness, as a "block." Her emotional coldness is seen by him, in these images, as an aspect of her larger impassivity, her resistance to any modification by worldly circumstance. This is why her being all "fine cold thought" "falls in" so well with her resistance to surprises. Solid and purely active as she is (essentially all *pressure* without response), life cannot leave a mark on her. It is not *permitted* to enter in, or to pull anything out. She is, Strether muses, the sort of meal that can be "served cold" (represented by an ambassador) "without its really losing anything" (2.237) of its essential flavor – so little does its character consist in responsiveness to what is at hand.

This connection between absence of emotion and absence of passivity is made long before on behalf of Woollett as a whole, when Strether tells Maria Gostrey, "Woollett isn't sure it ought to enjoy. If it were, it would" (1.16). The first half of this remark is frequently quoted by critics; the second is, I think, even more significant. For it informs us that Woollen conceives of everything valuable in life as activity that can be morally willed. If it *were* sure that enjoyment was its duty, it would set itself to do that duty, it would simply will itself to enjoy. The oddness of this idea reminds us that some of the valuable things in life have more to do with passivity and responsiveness than with active willing; and their connection with "ought" is therefore to be viewed with deep suspicion.

What all this comes to is that the people of Woollett cannot, will not, live in the present moment, confronting the things that life brings their way in all their newness and particularity. They come to a situation determined that it should not touch them, holding their general and rather abstract principles fixed and firm. These principles, the court of last appeal in practical reason, even govern what they may *see* and consider relevant in the new. Particularity of vision brings surprise, surprise passivity and a loss of moral control. Chad is therefore "the youth," Mme de Vionnet "the Person"; it is already clear beforehand what principles will govern Woollett's dealings with then. Any more personal encounter is made impossible by the nature of the view itself. It comes to what Strether, speaking for the Woollett in himself, calls "the obsession of the other thing": "I'm always considering something else; something else, I mean, than the thing of the moment" (1.19). And this tendency, which strikes Strether with perplexity and even with "terror," is Mrs Newsome's fineness and her exaltation.

For Mrs Newsome is "exalted." Behind her coldness and her blocklike hardness, Strether permits us to understand the deep sense of dignity that motivates her assault on life. "Pure and by the vulgar estimate 'cold,'" she is not, he reflects, coarse or hard, but, rather, "deep devoted delicate sensitive noble" (2.47). We see her underlying motivation nowhere more revealingly than in the one verbatim quotation we are given:

> Sarah's answer came so straight, so "pat," as might have been said, that he felt on the instant its origin. "She has confided to my judgment and my tenderness the expression of her personal sense of everything, and the assertion of her personal dignity."
>
> They were the very words of the lady of Woollett – he would have known them in a thousand; her parting charge to her child. (2.203)

This surprises us at first; for we may have been encouraged by some of Strether's remarks to think of this woman as a hard insensitive being, whose utterances would

249

be icy imperatives. Her words, which we are told to see as exemplary, suggest, I think, a more complex understanding. We have here the expression of a keen sense of human dignity – of an idea of our worth as agents that is the basis of Kantian morality (and through this of Rawls's Kantianism). It is the idea that we do not need to go through the world as the plaything of its forces, living "from hand to mouth," merely "floating" with its currents. We are dignified moral beings; and it is in virtue of our moral powers of will and judgment that we can be dignified, making rather than being made, agents rather than victims or dependents. Strether recognizes Mrs Newsome by the assertion of her dignity; and he knows that what the vulgar see as coldness is really a kind of nobility. What this comes to, I think, is that he sees her moralism as based on an idea of the dignity of agency. To the noble and autonomous moral agent, nature has, and should have, no power to jolt or to surprise, and also no power to inspire delight and passionate wonder. Such an agent will seem cold to the vulgar; but any other relation to the world surrenders dignity, inviting violation or at least seduction.

Such an agent will treat others with an equal respect, attending to their own dignity as moral beings. For Mrs Newsome, we remember, would never wear her dress cut down, encouraging Strether to perceive her as a surprisingly particular physical being and so to surrender his own dignity before her. (In her actual black ruched dress she reminds him of Queen Elizabeth, virginal out of a commitment to autonomy, preserver of the dignity of a nation [1.51].) What seems like insensibility in the women of Woollett is, from their point of view, the high determination to treat each other person as an autonomous moral will, relating to them through the moral faculties and judging them with a stringency that shows respect for their freedom. Any note of tenderness would compromise this moral relation. When Strether yields to the gentle voice of Marie de Vionnet the Woollett in him observes, "She really had tones to make justice weep" (1.275).

It is because Mrs Newsome is no mere caricature, but a brilliantly comic rendering of some of the deepest and most appealing features of Kantian morality, that the novel has the balance and power that it does. We see the Kantian attitude as one that gives us a special dignity and exaltation; we see it, too, as a deep part of our culture. We see that the women of Woollett, unlike Marie de Vionnet in her love of an irreplaceable particular person, are able to triumph over life and to avoid becoming its victims. But that's just it: they triumph over life, they don't *live*. What is absent from the speech of the lady of Woollett? Particularity; the names of Chad and of Strether, the injunction to look and see; a sense of personal vulnerability; a fear of loss. Strether says that no trivial alteration will make this woman admit surprises, and we feel that he is correct. But is there another way to be rational and moral, a way that is more hospitable to life?

Strether begins the novel with a question. (The first sentence is: "Strether's first question, when he reached the hotel, was about his friend" [1.3].) That's already a departure. From the beginning we sense in him a curiosity about the actual situation before him, an openness and a lack of self-sufficiency, that make him a dubious ambassador of Mrs Newsome's will. In the style of Woollett, the interrogative, we feel, must play a small role. Strether is still closely linked, at this point, to his past, but:

> He was burdened, poor Strether – it had better be confessed at the outset – with the oddity of a double consciousness. There was detachment in his zeal and curiosity in his indifference. (1.5)

In his moral purpose as ambassador is an independence of purpose; in his lack of interested engagement with the new is an eager desire to *see* it. His initial steps into the new world that confronts him are marked by a child's fresh delight in seeing and an undirected openness to the new concrete thing. He has "the idlest eye" (1.36) for the sights and sounds of the garden; the "smallest things so arrested and amused him" (1.39). He finds himself "given over to uncontrolled perceptions" – among them the perception of Maria Gostrey's complicating neckband; and he takes this surprising piece of red velvet as "a starting-point for fresh backward, fresh forward, fresh lateral flights" (1.51). His relation to his situation is dominated, above all, by the sense of freshness and susceptibility to adventure; and he sees this susceptibility as connected with a new sharpness of perception:

> Nothing could have been odder than Strether's sense of himself as at that moment launched in something of which the sense would be quite disconnected from the sense of his past and which was literally beginning there and then. It had begun in fact already, ... begun with a sharper survey of the elements of Appearance than he had for a long time been moved to make. (1.9)

This sense that life is an adventure, and that part of its joy precisely is the confrontation with the new – this is a sense of life already far removed from that of Woollett, where dignity is preserved by keeping down the new, acknowledging it only insofar as it exemplifies some law whose sense is already understood. Mrs Newsome is about as far removed from the childlike as a human being can be. (In comparing her to Queen Elizabeth – who never even mothered children and seems to the reader of history to have been always adult, always self-sufficient – Strether depicts her as heroically untouched by any horrible or wonderful aspect of life.) But Strether, as he embarks on his adventure, becomes no longer a controlling adult; he is a child learning to "toddle" (2.48), eyes wide open, vulnerable, wondering at each new thing.

In his growing awareness of the world we discover the three elements of judgment that Mrs Newsome above all avoids, significantly linked in his affirmation as they were in her denial. Most emphasized in the text is Strether's willingness to be passive, surrendering the invulnerable agency of the Kantian self. He speaks of "letting go" (2.64), of "taking things as they come" (1.83), of living "from hand to mouth" (2.3); perceptions bear in or "press" (1.276) upon him, acting on him rather than being made or impressed upon the world. He even feels himself to be like a person who has "been tripped up and had a fall" (1.276), so sharply does life make itself felt. But passivity is more often joyous. A sharp "assault of images," in Gloriani's garden, makes him have "the consciousness of opening . . . for the happy instant, all the windows of his mind, of letting this rather grey interior drink in for once the sun of a clime not marked in his old geography" (1.196–7). In the novel's continual emphasis on this feature, we are made to feel that it is somehow a key to all the rest that a willingness to surrender invulnerability, to take up a posture of agency that is porous and susceptible of influence, is of the highest importance in getting an accurate perception of particular things in the world.

For Strether's vision of particularity involves a willingness to be incomplete, to be surprised by the new, to see that and how our "actual adventure" (1.176) transcends our "personal experience." And so, by being able to grant the incompleteness of past experience, which he calls "this last queer quantity" (1.176), Strether allows himself to emerge as (in Maria's words) a person for whom "nothing . . . will ever come to the same thing as anything else" (1.70). Part of this vision of the particular lies in his sharp concrete perceptions of particular objects and people; part, too, in a new willingness to see a composite situation as so connected together, so complex in its relations, that as a whole it is like no other. Just as Maria's neckband is permitted to complicate his vision, so in general new elements constitute new relations. "All voices had grown thicker and meant more things; they crowded on him as he moved about – it was the way they sounded together that wouldn't let him be still" (2.210).

And this vision of particularity is shaped (as Woollett's view could not be) by the responsive activity of the emotions and the imagination, working closely together. From the beginning, Strether is surprised by "how much there had been in him of response" (1.6); and Maria correctly observes, "No one feels so much as you. No – not any one" (2.126).

All of this comes together in the sense of happy though perplexed immersion in the adventure of living[25] that makes it possible for Strether to make such simple statements as, "The Sunday of the new week was a wonderful day" (1.193) – a chapter opening that could never have been written by the lady of Woollett; in the way, too, that he is with people, "looking kindly from one to the other and wondering at many things" (1.222); in the hesitation with which he searches for names (1.49), gropes after the right description for the strange things that confront him. Hesitation and bewilderment are a part of his sense of life, *and* part of its accuracy:

> "It isn't playing the game to turn on the uncanny. All one's energy goes to facing it, to tracking it. One wants, confound it, don't you see?" he confessed with a queer face – "one wants to enjoy anything so rare. Call it then life" – he puzzled it out – "call it poor dear old life simply that springs the surprise. Nothing alters the fact that the surprise is paralyzing, or at any rate engrossing – all, practically, hang it, that one sees, that one *can* see." (1.167–8)

The life of perception feels perplexed, difficult, unsafe. (Strether's sentences here have the awkwardness and riskiness of which he speaks.) But this life also seems to Strether – and to us – to be richer, fuller of enjoyment, fuller too of whatever is worth calling knowledge of the world. In one of the novel's most famous passages, he connects immersion in impressions with being really alive, having one's life; and he passionately urges Little Bilham not to miss that adventure:

> Live all you can; it's a mistake not to. It doesn't so much matter what you do in particular, so long as you have your life. If you haven't had that what *have* you had? This place and

these impressions – mild as you may find them to wind a man up so; all my impressions of Chad and of people I've seen at *his* place – well, have had their abundant message for me, have just dropped *that* into my mind. I see it now. I haven't done so enough before – and now I'm old; too old at any rate for what I see. Oh, I *do* see, at least; and more than you'd believe or I can express.... Don't at any rate miss things out of stupidity.... Live! (1.217–18)

(And we notice, once again, that the novel connects this new sense of life with a certain literary style: for Strether delivers this speech "slowly and sociably, with full pauses and straight dashes" (1.218), writing his own response to life in the style of a Henry James novel.)

Strether's consciousness finds vivid metaphors to express this new moral attitude – images of improvisatory game-playing; of complex connectedness and the absence of Woollett "straightness"; of childhood, of flying; above all, images of water, and of water and light together – signaling that illumination is now seen as inseparable from a risky passivity before the physical being of things. (To Sarah's protest against his new view, he replies that he can hardly help the way he has come to see: "an inexorable tide of light seems to have floated us into our perhaps still queerer knowledge" [2.201].) We notice, too, how he and Maria Gostrey, in conversation about what they have seen, will arrive at a new perception and, struck by it as if by finding themselves suddenly in a place where they have never been and to which they have not realized they were going, exclaim, "So there we are," – or, "Then there we are" (2.138, 143, 327). (The novel, which began with a question, ends on just such a moment of surprised arrival.)

In the new norm of perception, unlike the norm of Woollett, there is a bewildering problem about authority. For if the ethical norm consists not in obeying certain antecedently established general rules, but in improvising resourcefully in response to the new perceived thing, then it is always going to remain unclear, in the case of any particular choice or vision, whether it is or is not correctly done. This does not mean that there are no criteria and anything goes. But it does mean that the standard will ultimately be nothing harder or clearer than the conformity of this choice or description to those of agents on whom we can rely for competent judgment – just as, in Aristotle's very similar view, the norm of good perception is the judgment of a certain type of person, the person of practical wisdom.[26] In this very way, when Strether wonders whether he has not "only been silly," his recourse can only be to think of the company he keeps:

He glanced at such a contingency, but it failed to hold him long when once he had reflected that he would have been silly, in this case, with Maria Gostrey and Little Bilham, with Madame de Vionnet and little Jeanne, with Lambert Strether, in fine, and above all with Chad Newsome himself. Wouldn't it be found to have made more for reality to be silly with these persons than sane with Sarah and Jim? (2.81)

And we ourselves, in asking how right Strether is, can only do the same – wondering, for example about whether Chad Newsome's judgment is, after all, such a very fine thing, and wondering about the part of Lambert Strether's imagination that holds

Chad in such great esteem. There is no sure guarantee, either for the judge or for our judgment about him. As Aristotle says in just this context, "The discrimination lies in perception."

This is an ethical norm to rival the norms of Woollen.[27] It deserves to be taken seriously as a picture of rationality and correct choice. And insofar as it captures our imagination and answers to our sense of life, it calls into question those elements of the pictures of judgment and agency in our moral theories that are motivated by the concerns of Woollett and resemble Woollett in their structure. Holding Strether up against Rawls's idea of considered judgment and his constraints upon admissible theories, we want to object that emotions may after all in many cases be an invaluable guide to correct judgment; that general and universal formulations may be inadequate to the complexity of particular situations; that immersed particular judgments may have a moral value that reflective and general judgments cannot capture. We want to suggest that bewilderment and hesitation may actually be marks of fine attention. As Strether summarizes the matter, "There's all the indescribable – what one gets only on the spot" (2.126) – and all of this appears to be omitted from the data that lead to reflective equilibrium. Indeed, his experience suggests a rival story about the end of the ethical process itself. There is still a search for equilibrium here, as Strether tries to make it all "hang beautifully together" (2.172). But his equilibrium, dealing, as it does, with impressions, emotions, and, in general, with particulars, had better be called by a different name. We would do better, perhaps, to call it "perceptive equilibrium": and with the agent's general principles; an equilibrium that is always ready to reconstitute itself in response to the new.

Can we view this new norm as simply an extension of the old one – so that we *supplement* Rawls's general theories with the immersed judgments of experience? This idea has been persuasively argued, with reference to Aristotle and Rawls's Aristotelianism, in some very interesting recent writing by Henry Richardson, who coins the name "extended reflective equilibrium" to designate the end of an ethical procedure that takes in all of this.[28] Strether had, we recall, a different view about Mrs Newsome – that one cannot touch her, put any of life into her, fully packed as she is; that it's fundamental to her entire being and her basic motivation not to *be* touched by the immersed perceptions of life. (We supported this in our analysis of her Kantian conception of agency; for we said that it was fundamental to her whole project not to be passive toward the world.) So what one must do, if one chooses to value perceiving, is to get rid of "the whole moral and intellectual being or block." (To put it differently, you cannot add Maria Gostrey's red velvet band to Mrs Newsome's ruche: she would not wear such a garment, she would view it as a desecration of her dignity.) This does not mean that the way of perceiving cannot make use of rules and universal principles; plainly it does, and it would be an important part of an extended inquiry into Strether's standards to ask how and when.[29] But it cannot use them in the way and for the reasons that Mrs Newsome would recommend; and it must give a central place to elements of judgment that she would, for consistency and dignity, insist on leaving out.

What prepares Strether to see this way? Why, among all those who come out from America to Paris, does he alone "come out" in fact,[30] opening himself to the influences of perception? We are given several clues. One, certainly, is his low sense of his own dignity. So far is he from asserting it that he permits himself to be treated, persistently, as an agent of the purposes of others. His name (in the Woollett Revue) is "on the green cover, where he had put it for Mrs Newsome" (1.84); and his willingness to serve as her ambassador shows a not altogether robust sense of Kantian autonomy. It is an unsettling thought, and one on which James insists,[31] that this very weakness in him (from the point of view of our interest in our dignity) may be a necessary preparation for this other sort of strength.

But James points even more insistently to another sort of preparation. For from the beginning Strether has a deep connection with literature. An editor and writer himself, he has a serious love of all the arts, but especially of the literary art, and the novel above all. The imagination of the reader and the writer are shown as abilities that have prepared him to see and to respond in a non-Kantian way. His concern with novels is an old one; and Paris recalls it to him, reminding him of the "lemon-colored volumes" he brought back from Europe and of "the sharp initiation they represented" (1.86–7). These volumes have been sitting "stale," "soiled," even unbound, in Woollett – but their memory "throbs again" for him in Paris until his conscience reacts with alarm, "amusing itself for the forty-eight hours by forbidding him the purchase of a book" (1.87).

It does no good: for the early love of stories floods back, animating his desire to wait and see, his tendency to attend to new people and events with the novelist's "vision kindly adjusted,"[32] a loving non-judgmental attention to their particularity. References to his favorite authors grow increasingly dense until, floating finally in the current of new sights and sounds, he notices that

> it was the way of nine tenths of his current impressions to act as recalls of things imagined – of some fine firm concentrated heroine of an old story, something he had heard, read, something that, had he a hand for drama, he might himself have written. (2.6–7)

And writing too (narrative, however, and not dramatic)[33] expresses increasingly his determination not to fall short, not to miss anything that is there to be seen and cared for "When anything new struck him as coming up, or anything already noted as reappearing, he always immediately wrote, as if for fear that if he didn't he would miss something" (1.257). It is the narrative character of his letters (quite different, we must suppose, from her own) that so alarms Mrs Newsome. Writing this way, seeing this way, he is no longer her ambassador. His style gives him away.

Here James shows us that there is a complicity between the consciousness of the reader (and the writer) of stories and the consciousness, the morality, of perception. For stories cultivate our ability to see and care for particulars, not as representatives of a law, but as what they themselves are: to respond vigorously with senses and emotions before the new; to care deeply about chance happenings in the world, rather than to fortify ourselves against them; to wait for the outcome, and to be bewildered – to wait and float and be actively passive. We are so accustomed to the novel that we tend to forget how morally controversial a form it has been in the eyes of various sorts of religious and secular moralisms. (Even as I write this, fundamentalist parents in the state of Tennessee are seeking a ban on stories that freely exercise the imagination, holding that the law laid down in the Bible is truth enough.) Questionable with very good reason: for the novel acknowledges a wonder before worldly sensuous particulars that Mrs Newsome would never feel or approve; and they attach a dangerous importance to outcomes that lie beyond the control of the moral will. By showing us the novel's world (more or less) through Strether's eyes, indeed by making it next to impossible to distinguish those eyes from the author's eyes – and by showing us at the same time how different the story would look (or the events and people would, as a non-story, look) to the women of Woollett – by letting us know enough of what they see to discover that they do not perceive and could not describe the same reality – James makes a case for the moral significance of the novelist's (and the reader's) "sense of life," for the vigilant and responsive imagination that cares for everyone in the situation and refuses the injunction of Woollett to "simplify" for the sake of purity and safety. The very sentences are Strether's, straining toward perceptual rightness in the midst of wonderful puzzling mysteries.[34] The sentences of Woollett are crisp, "straight," and, as Strether says, "pat." And the fullness, the density, of the narrative style is itself the fitting expression of a certain sort of moral imagination. Indeed, James recalls to us that even the novel, with all its richness, can actually express but a fraction of the crowded consciousness of someone who is really making an effort to *see*. For at one point he remarks,

> If we should go into all that occupied our friend in the watches of the night we should have to mend our pen; but an instance or two may mark for us the vividness with which he could remember. (1.139)

The novel has its own simplifications – but it is the genre, among the available forms of writing – that most appropriately exemplifies what James calls the "projected morality."[35]

Perception and Method

We begin to see two opposing conceptions of practical reason, together with some of the motivations for and consequences of each. The morality of perception is put before us in a textual form that fittingly expresses its claim on our imaginations. What now would be the next step in the proposed interchange between literary and ethical theory? Here nothing can be said in depth; but I can sketch out some of the pieces that I think this larger project might include.

First, I believe, we would need, in pursuing our goals of understanding and attunement, to get a much richer and deeper understanding of the Kantian conception and of its modern continuations (Rawls's above all). This novel is Strether's story. Mrs Newsome does not do full justice to the power of Kant's arguments in the way that Strether does justice to his own way (and to Aristotle's related conception). If we are correct about the close relationship between content and form this is no accident.

No narrative dealing in empirical particulars *could* see Kant's conception in a fully sympathetic way. This does not mean that there isn't a special interest, too, in seeing just what sort of character in a story (in our lives) a thoroughgoing Kantian would be: for this certainly helps us see how Kant matches (or fails to) our own active sense of life. But we would want to look at the arguments of Kantian philosophers directly and seriously in their own right; otherwise this inquiry could too easily get corrupted, get used to treat complex philosophical positions as straw men. The same applies to other leading ethical conceptions with which Strether's perception might fruitfully be contrasted – above all, the morality of classical utilitarianism.[36]

Having started on this sort of investigation, we would now, I think, want to look very carefully at the different elements of Strether's conception (and their relatives in the contrasting conceptions) asking how they are connected and interrelated, how each one is supported and defended. How the perception of particularity is connected with an openness to surprise; how both are connected with a commitment to the cognitive guidance of emotion. Of particular importance here will be to ask what role rules and universal principles *can* and should play inside the morality of perception, and in general what sort of systematic theoretical approach to practice would be compatible with Strether's insights. This needs to be carefully considered, if we want to defend this conception as normative, especially for our public life. I imagine that by confronting Strether (and his philosophical relatives) with challenges from the Kantian and utilitarian positions, we will arrive at a deeper understanding of this position and of the connection all the positions have with our own sympathies.

At this point many fruitful and interesting projects suggest themselves. We need to pursue in much greater depth and detail the stylistic portion of my argument, saying a great deal more, in connection with many more authors and many different genres and styles, about the practical and human expressive content of structural choices at all levels of specificity. And we would want to look at philosophical authors as makers of stylistic choices, asking what ethical commitments their own literary choices express. (I suspect that we will often discover that some of these choices are not supported by the argument in the "content" of the work, and that some may even be in tension with the content – as when an article about the crucial cognitive role of the emotions is written in a style that seems to assume that the intellect is the only part of the reader worth addressing. It is not clear that there are no good reasons for this discrepancy; but we need to ask hard questions about it.)

We would also want to turn to our own lives, both private and public, examining the conceptions of rationality (of the person, etc.) that we discover there, and asking how all this fits with what we have so far puzzled out. It would be an especially useful exercise, for example, to work through the contemporary economic literature on rationality, in which there is much pertinent debate about commensurability, about ordering, about universality, and to see what elements of Strether's "position" are incorporated in these debates; to ask, too, what workable social science could be built on what Strether offers us. Many other related projects can be imagined.

Throughout this open-ended inquiry, we will need to maintain as much self-consciousness as possible about our own methods and our implicit ends, asking what evaluative content they themselves express. Perceptive equilibrium is not the same end as reflective equilibrium; it does not use the same judgments or the same faculties. This does not mean that there can be no objectivity in the ethical inquiry; it does not mean that all choices of method are subjective.[37] But it does mean that procedures themselves are value-laden, and thus part and parcel of the holistic enterprise they organize; replaceable, like any other part, to the end of deeper and more inclusive attunement. So we must examine them at each stage, asking whether they are capable of doing full justice to everything that our sense of life wants to include.

Perception and Love

At this point, however, we are brought back again to *The Ambassadors*. For we have given, so far, too simple a story about Strether's imagination.[38] And part of the longer story of perceptive equilibrium is surely to discover the ways in which James's novel itself complicates our admiration for Strether, causing us to see that the perception of life may not have, in the end, an equilibrium – that the keen sight of the writer and reader of life is in a standing tension with the "sight" of passion. We have thought of Strether as yielding to the impressions of life as they unfold themselves before him – as allowing himself to be seduced. We must now think, also, of his inability to see, and later to accept, the sexual love of Chad and Marie de Vionnet; his inability to see Maria Gostrey's deepening feeling for him; his failure to examine and to acknowledge his own complicated feelings for Marie de Vionnet, and his jealousy of Chad. We must think of his blush of shame, when he realizes how he had concealed from himself their intimacy, "dressed the possibility in vagueness, as a little girl might have dressed her doll" (2.266). He too has simplified life; and by refusing himself feelings and ways of living that he could not reconcile with his personal demand for perceptual clarity and unselfish general concern, he has prevented himself, in the end, from perceiving a crucial fact about the situation around him. ("'It's beautiful,' he said to Miss Barrace, 'the way you all can simplify when you will.' But she gave it to him back. 'It's nothing to the way *you* will when you must'" [2.180].) When he does confront Marie de Vionnet in his newly gained knowledge, he cannot achieve, in this one case, a particular perception; she becomes, distanced by his own inner refusal of passion, a mere abstraction.

> It was actually moreover as if he didn't think of her at all, as if he could think of nothing but the passion, mature, abysmal, pitiful, she represented, and the possibilities she betrayed. (2.286)

From her wonderful variegated self she becomes, for him, merely "a creature so exploited," "a maid servant crying for her young man." Distant watcher, pitying judge, he is in the end, in his way, the ambassador of Woollen; for his sharp eye will not turn aside in tenderness before the intimacy of others, and his spirit will not moderate its ubiquitous demand for rightness and for judgment. He too resists; he too refuses to allow his vision to be complicated by the band of broad red velvet.

And now we see, too, that the earlier remark about Strether's "double consciousness" can have another reading. There *is* a curious "detachment in his zeal" – in his zeal to see there is a detachment from strong emotion. And in his "indifference" – his perceiver's impartiality, the equipoise of the body drawn strongly to no extreme – there is an almost voyeuristic "curiosity," the curiosity of the uninvolved gaze.

And this incompleteness in Strether is unmistakably linked to his interest in literature: for we are shown repeatedly that the stance of the reader and writer of life is a stance that achieves a certain clarity of vision at the expense of a certain emotional depth; one that forgoes, or even scorns, immersion in the darker, messier passion, one that "reduces" them all to a simplified generic story, read with only a reader's interest (to what Strether calls "the convenient terms of Victor Hugo" [2.7]). The outing during which Strether makes his upsetting discovery has been seen by him, up until that moment, as if it were the exploration of a Lambinet painting that he remembers: his life, to that point, "continued in the picture . . . and had meanwhile not once overstepped the oblong gilt frame" (2.251–2). Even the loving couple in their boat can be held in the "picture" (or the story, since the picture has, for Strether, a marked narrative quality) – so long as he doesn't have to acknowledge them as the very individuals he cares about and has to deal with in his own personal life, so long as he doesn't have to acknowledge his own personal feelings of jealousy and longing. Then the story is no longer just a story, then it is threat to equilibrium.

James reminds us here that before a work of art we are detached perceivers, free to explore all fine perceptions, but liberated (or cut off) from the tumultuous perceptions of personal passion, freed also – as we enjoy its delicious half-expected surprises – from the hard jolting shocks of the real surprises that mark our actual personal relations. Reading is a preparation for a life that is lived at one remove from life, a life that gains fineness and clarity by warding off certain risks and dangers. Is this good, or is it bad? When Strether sits, later, in Maria Gostrey's dining room, he reflects:

> To sit there was, as he had told his hostess before, to see life reflected for the time in ideally kept pewter; which was somehow becoming, improving to life, so that one's eyes were held and comforted. (2.319)[39]

Art does not simply perceive life; it also comforts us by keeping us at a distance from life's violence and arbitrariness. (For even when its content deals with violent passion, our own relation to it is not violent; the terms of Victor Hugo are indeed so much more "convenient" than those of our own loves and jealousies and fears and angers.) The novelist stands apart from some of the confusing complexity of the human scene; he owes his clarity to that "improving" absence of immersion. And yet, doesn't this make him, as a human being, somehow incomplete, somehow lacking in humanity? Reassuring Strether, who fears that Waymarsh may talk about him behind his back, Maria says, "'For what do you take people, that they're able to say words about anything, able remorselessly to analyze? There are not many like you and me'" (1.44). The novelist is a third; as reader we follow. Is this, in fact, a good or full way to live?

259

Do we put such problems down to Strether's own idiosyncrasy, and to his regretful sense that he is too old for what he sees, or are they the faults of the morality of perception? One of his reflections is, I think, significant. What he dislikes about the revealed intimacy is that it was, before, concealed: it went on between two people apart from perception and description. "Intimacy, at such a point, was *like* that – and what in the world else would one have wished it to be like? It was all very well for him to feel the pity of its being so much like lying" (2.266). What Strether senses is that what he calls the "deep deep truth" of sexual love is at odds with the morality of perception, in two ways. It asks for the privacy, for others to avert their gaze; and on the inside it asks that focus be averted from around and about them. That vision excludes general attention and care, at least at that moment. And this intimacy is a part of the world that demands *not* to be in the eyes of the perceiving, recording novelist – at least not in all of its particularity. But to the person who is dedicated to perceiving (to novel-writing), that looks like a bad way to be; bad both because it impedes the subject's moral vision of the whole and because it asks not to be included as an object in that vision. To be sure, these ruminations emerge from Strether's loneliness, But he is convinced that loneliness is the condition of luminous perception; and his fear of intimacy is at the same time a fear for his moral being.

We need to take this seriously. Perception as a morality enjoins trust in responsive feeling; but its feelings are the feelings of the friend. (Strether's first question was about his friend; and the novelist's vision of him is a vision "*kindly* adjusted.") There is reason to suppose that the exclusivity and intensity of personal love would in fact impede the just and general responsiveness that these gentler feelings assist. And if they impede that, they impede the perceiver's contribution to our moral project, to our communal effort to arrive at perceptive equilibrium. But the recognition that there is a view of the world from passion's point of view, and that this view is closed to the perceiver, shows us that perception is, even by its own lights, incomplete. The perceiver as perceiver cannot see it all; to get the whole he must at times stop being the sort of person who cares for wholeness. As a perceiver he is morally admirable, both wonderful and quite lovable. Yet just that commitment that Maria loves (not just admires, but loves) in Strether, just that is the reason why he not only cannot love her, but cannot in any way understand or see her love or any love. She "can't resist" him when he tells her the reasons for his refusal; this is their comedy and their tragedy. Maria's "all comically, all tragically" (2.327) is a response to the moral impossibility of human love. For so long as our eyes are open, we are wonderful and lovable and finely responsive; but when we immerse ourselves in the most powerful responses, entering silence, closing our eyes, are we then capable at all of asking questions about our friends, of thinking of the good of the community? And if we are not capable of this, are we worthy of the deepest feelings and commitments of others? James once wrote about his mother that, swallowed up in her intense love of her husband and family, she had nothing "acutely to offer."[40] Does any lover do better? Without this depth life seems incomplete and perception itself seems blind; but it cannot itself be ordered inside the equilibrium of perception or seen by its fine-tuned vision of the complete life.

This complicates still further our idea of what might be the practical goal of ethical inquiry. It would be simple if Strether's perceptive equilibrium were simply undercut, shown not to be a high human goal. But perceptive equilibrium is loved and affirmed, "all comically, all tragically," at the novel's end. It is what makes him fine and lovable, even while it is what makes him incapable of love. It would be simple, again, if we were shown a way in which Strether's incompleteness could be completed and filled up, by love, in some harmonious manner. (A way in which the novelist could have an intimate personal life and still see for us all.) Neither of these easy exits is offered us. And if there is for us any prospect held out for a life that combines fine perception with the silence and the hidden vision of love, it would only be in a condition that is not itself "equilibrium" at all, but an unsteady oscillation between blindness and openness, exclusivity and general concern, fine reading of life and the immersion of love.

Here we find another way in which the novel can make a contribution to ethical theory. So far it has (or this one novel has) shown the way from a narrow Kantian understanding of the question, "How should one live?" to a wider and richer understanding. Now it asks us to see the limits of that ethical question itself. It gestures toward the limits of ethical consciousness, making us aware of the deep elements in our ethical life that in their violence or intensity lead us outside of the ethical attitude altogether, outside of the quest for balanced vision and perfect rightness. It can include, or at least indicate, the silence into which its own responsive prose has no entry.

Literary Theory and Ethical Theory

I have imagined a literary theory that works in conversation with ethical theory. I have imagined this partnership as a practical one, in which we search for images of life by which we might possibly live together, and ask what conceptions and images best match the full range of our perceptions and convictions, as we work toward "perceptive equilibrium." (And now we have, too, the thought that the goal might not be equilibrium at all, but a dynamic tension between two possible irreconcilable visions.) I have imagined that literary theory will make a creative and rather radical contribution to this enterprise – as we see from the fact that the very end and methods of the enterprise have been called into question by Strether's achievement, and his tragedy.

Why, however, *should* literary theory engage itself with ethical theory here? For we might acknowledge the practical dimension of literature and insist on restoring that dimension to theoretical writing, without taking the further step proposed here. Why can't the literary theorist simply say about Henry James what it is lucid and helpful to say, without studying and teaching Kant and Aristotle, Bentham and Rawls, and drawing these figures into the account he or she gives of James's novels? This question arises all the more since major figures of past theory with whom I implicitly link my proposal – F. R. Leavis, say, and Lionel Trilling – seem to have been perfectly able to speak of the ethical content of literature and the ethical expressiveness of literary forms without bringing moral philosophy into the picture.

The explicit and deep study of ethical theory will, first of all, clarify to us just what it is that works of literature offer to our sense of life. We grasp by contrasting; we sense what something *is* by bounding it off against something different. If it should prove true that novels share certain ethical commitments (to particularity, to the moral relevance of surprise) just in virtue of their form, we will grasp these shared commitments better by seeing on what grounds some philosophers have denied or refined them. We grasp the force of James's account of perception more clearly when we see how it goes against norms of considered judgment that prevail in almost all of the Western ethical tradition. And we have to do this by reading the philosophers in a serious way, not, as I say, by using them polemically, as straw men. Our understanding is enhanced in a different way when we encounter inside philosophy several friends of perception and of literary insight, whose explicit arguments against much of the prevailing tradition clarify for us the elements of Strether's accomplishment. (I think here, in different ways, of Aristotle, of Iris Murdoch, of Bernard Williams – and, also, of William James.)[41] And if we look more closely now at the examples of Leavis and Trilling, I think we will discover that they do not go against these claims. For Leavis's denigration of the late novels of James[42] is, I believe, superficial in a way that most of his work is not, precisely *because* he does not make these reflective philosophical contrasts and so demarcate for himself what it is that James is opposing and putting forward. Trilling's wide and deep knowledge of political and ethical and psychological thought, though displayed with understated grace and elegance, does, I think, consistently inform his most memorable and characteristic writings – not least his writing on James in *The Liberal Tradition*.[43]

Then, too, ethical theory, just because of its systematic and inclusive disciplinary character, can contribute to our understanding of a literary work by raising questions that this work may or may not explicitly ask itself concerning the relationship of its ethical views to other issues on which we have to make up our mind – issues about social structure, about economic distribution, about the self and personal identity. My imagined theoretical dialogue will, for example, lead us to ask what political structures are compatible with Strether's moral norm, whether in opting for that norm we would have to forgo some or all of our democratic traditions. We will have understood James more deeply if we can answer this question. And the answer will emerge not only out of a deeper reflection about novels such as *The Ambassadors* and *The Princess Casamassima*, but also out of a more general reflection about the connections between a conception of personal rationality and a political conception.

These are some reasons why literary theory needs ethical theory. (And this close connection with theory would be one way of distinguishing literary theory, should we want to, from good criticism – to which it should always remain almost inseparably close.) On the other side a similar and equally strong argument can be made. It is reasonably clear by now what that argument is: that literary theory can improve the self-understanding of ethical theory by confronting it with a distinctive conception or conceptions of various aspects of human ethical life, realized in a form that is the most appropriate one for their expression. Insofar as great literature has moved and engaged the hearts and minds of its readers, it has established already its claim to be taken seriously when we work through the alternative conceptions.

These alternatives could be described and investigated by the ethical theorist; sometimes they are. But this too often results in a criticism that simply mines the work for a set of propositional claims – rather than what I am calling for, an investigation of that which is expressed and "claimed" by the shape of the sentences themselves, by images and cadences and pauses themselves, by the forms of the traditional genres, by narrativity, themselves. It seems unlikely that this richer ethical task can be carried out by someone who is not in the habit of attending to these things.

But why should we *care* about describing literary alternatives to ethical theory? Suppose there is a task in (or side by side of) ethical theory that literary people are best equipped to perform: why should anyone want to take on that task, rather than some other one of the many interesting tasks that literary theory might and does perform? If moral philosophers (or political theorists or economists) have gotten themselves into difficulty, why should we bail them out? Here I come back to my idea of the practical goal of ethical inquiry – which involves self-understanding and communal attunement. These goals matter. Each of us is not only a professional, but a human being who is trying to live well; and not simply a human being, but also a citizen of some town, some country, above all a world of human beings, in which attunement and understanding are extremely urgent matters. Now certainly we can promote these goals in indefinitely many ways, apart from our professional lives: by raising children, by engaging in some form of political action, by using our money generously, by seeing and conversing and feeling. And yet, when a person happens to have a professional activity that is or becomes relevant to major ends of human life – how exhilarating that activity then is, and how deep, I think, the obligations it then imposes.

All around us other intellectual disciplines are shaping the private and public life of our culture, telling us how to imagine or think about ourselves. Economic theory forges conceptions of human rationality that govern public policy decisions, decisions about the distribution of food, about social well-being. Legal theorists and jurists search for understanding of basic rights (for example, the right to privacy) and the role that they play in our lives with one another. Psychology and anthropology describe our emotional lives, our experience of gender, our forms of communal interaction. Moral philosophy attempts to arbitrate disputes concerning medical care, abortion, basic freedoms. Literary theory has been too silent too long in these debates. And yet it has a distinctive speaking role to play – a first part of which might be to confront reigning models of political and economic rationality with the consciousness of Strether. Silence, in these matters, is a kind of capitulation. If these alternatives are not brought forward and described, we will go on being governed from day to day by conceptions of rationality that seem impoverished next to the ones we know well and care about in novels that we love. Worse, most people will not perceive, and therefore not really have, the choice among conceptions. The hungry will be fed (or not fed) according to some idea of the person; patients will be treated; laws and policies will be made – all according to some conception or conceptions of human personhood and human rationality. If we do not take a hand in these choices, they will be made by default without us.

I propose an apparently thankless task. Is there any reason at all to suppose that entrenched conceptions (of rationality, of value) that currently govern our daily lives through their reception in economic theory and public policy will be modified by contact with Lambert Strether, or that the holders of these conceptions will pay any attention at all to Henry James and related authors at any time? Can any possible practicable goal be achieved by subtle precise writing about books that most people in public life do not read anyway? Those of us who are Americans might also ask: can *any* writing that is Strether's, that is responsive and delicate and committed to perception, impose itself upon the form of our American culture, concerning which we sometimes have good reason to think (as Strether of Mrs Newsome) that it "won't *be* touched," that it can only come to a question of dislodging "the whole moral and intellectual being or block" that looms up before us, with its strange combination of utilitarianism and religious moralism, like some particularly large blue iceberg in a cool blue northern sea. (The same question may of course be asked about the practical value of ethical theory itself, with whose collaboration we proposed to "touch" her – though theory's colder hand may less quickly be felt as a threatening assault.)

Well, what can we do but try? Some major choices affecting our lives – say, Supreme Court decisions – made in effect by one or two complex reflective processes in the minds of one or two reading, thinking, feeling beings. An eloquent piece of writing (say, about James on the moral value of privacy) might possibly alter the course of that reflection. Do we know such things before attempting? James once wrote that the task of the literary imagination, face to face with social obtuseness and general failure of perception, would be:

> to *create* the record, in default of any other enjoyment of it; to imagine, in a word, the honourable, the producible case. What better example than this of the high and the helpful public and, as it were, civic use of the imagination?[44]

We could aim, for a future, at that degree of love. (Though bewildered, increasingly, about the nature of that love and its relation to other loves, to life itself.) His plain gravestone, in the Cambridge Cemetery, on an open bright hill (where one can sit and read all morning alone in the still sun, vaguely hearing children's voices reflected up, as it were, from the school below) bears the inscription: "Henry James, novelist, citizen of two countries, interpreter of his generation on both sides of the sea." So – as Strether observes – there we are.

Notes

This paper was first read at the conference on Virtue and Agency at Santa Clara University, February 1987. I am grateful to David Fisher for his stimulating comments delivered on the occasion. I am also grateful to Paul Seabright and Amartya Sen, whose questions and comments led to numerous revisions, and to audiences at Oxford University, the University of York, Yale University, the University of London, Harvard University, and the Rhode Island Humanities Forum.

1 Henry James, *The Ambassadors*, New York Edition (New York: Charles Scribner's Sons, 1907–9), 1.50. All page references will be to this (two-volume) edition.

2   Throughout this essay, I tend to use the term "ethical theory" rather than "moral theory," since the former does not suggest a division of human values into two distinct groups, the moral and the non-moral. On this division and some reasons for questioning it, see Bernard Williams, *Ethics and the Limits of Philosophy* (Cambridge, MA: Harvard University Press, 1985), and Martha C. Nussbaum, *The Fragility of Goodness: Luck and Ethics in Greek Tragedy and Philosophy* (Cambridge: Cambridge University Press, 1986), chapters 1 and 2. I use the term "moral philosophy" here simply because no corresponding term "ethical philosophy" is in use (as both ethical theory and moral theory are). My use of the distinction between ethical theory and moral philosophy is closely related to Rawls's use of a distinction between moral theory and moral philosophy: see John Rawls, *A Theory of Justice* (Cambridge, MA: Harvard University Press, 1971), 46ff. Moral philosophy is a general and inclusive rubric covering, in principle, many different types of ethical investigations, of which one sort is the theoretical study of substantive ethical positions, or ethical (moral) theory. A consequence of this distinction for my project is that an ethical investigation that is not systematic and theoretical, and therefore not ethical theory, might still lie within moral philosophy. It was with this broad understanding of moral philosophy that I argued that certain works of literature are part of moral philosophy: see "Flawed Crystals: James's *The Golden Bowl* and Literature as Moral Philosophy," in Martha C. Nussbaum, *Love's Knowledge: Essays in Philosophy and Literature* (New York: Oxford University Press, 1992), 125–47; see also "Introduction: Form and Content, Philosophy and Literature," in *Love's Knowledge*.

3   See Arthur C. Danto, "PHILOSOPHY AS/AND/OF LITERATURE," chapter 4 in this volume. Originally published in the *Proceedings and Addresses of the American Philosophical Association* 58 (1984): 5–20.

4   Jacques Derrida, *Spurs: Nietzsche's Style*, trans. B. Harlow (Chicago, IL: University of Chicago Press, 1979).

5   Friedrich Nietzsche, *Thus Spoke Zarathustra*, trans. W. Kaufmann (New York: Vintage, 1966), part 1, "On Reading and Writing."

6   Clearly, feminist criticism and Marxist criticism are major exceptions to the situation described here. But they are, in their difference from and frequent opposition to what surrounds them, exceptions that prove the rule.

7   See Danto, "Philosophy."

8   See Nussbaum, *Fragility*, Interlude 2; also Hilary Putnam, "Literature, Science, and Reflection," in *Meaning and the Moral Sciences* (London: Routledge and Kegan Paul, 1979), 83–96.

9   On this see "The Discernment of Perception: An Aristotelian Conception of Private and Public Rationality," in Nussbaum, *Love's Knowledge*, 54–105.

10 I think, first, of F. R. Leavis and Lionel Trilling (see nn. 42, 43); see also, more recently, Peter Brooks *Reading for the Plot* (New York: Knopf, 1984); Martin Price, *Forms of Life: Character and the Moral Imagination in the Novel* (New Haven., CN: Yale University Press, 1983); and especially Wayne Booth, *The Company We Keep: An Ethics of Fiction* (Berkeley: University of California Press, 1984).

11 Compare my sketch of an ethical inquiry in "Flawed Crystals," and also *Fragility*, chapters 1 and 8; and see also my "Introduction," in *Love's Knowledge*. A related picture is developed, with greater skepticism, in Cora Diamond, "Having a Rough Story About What Moral Philosophy Is," *New Literary History* 15 (1983): 155–70.

12 On this question and its relation to the moral/non-moral distinction, see Williams, *Ethics*, and Nussbaum, *Fragility*, chapter 1.

13 Henry James, preface to *The Princess Casamassima* – see "Flawed Crystals" and "Perception and Revolution," in Nusbaum, *Love's Knowledge*.
14 I discuss this further in "Therapeutic Arguments: Epicurus and Aristotle," in M. Schofield and G. Striker, eds., *The Norms of Nature* (Cambridge: Cambridge University Press, 1986) 31–74; and also in Martha C. Nussbaum, *The Therapy of Desire: Theory and Practice in Hellenistic Ethics* (Princeton, NJ: Princeton University Press, 1996).
15 Rawls, *A Theory*. 46ff. Rawls's discussion refers both to Aristotle and to Henry Sidgwick's *The Methods of Ethics*, 7th edn. (London, 1907).
16 See Nussbaum, *Fragility*, chapter 8; and Nussbaum, "The Discernment of Perception"; also Rawls, *A Theory*, 46ff.
17 See Rawls; also the excellent discussion of Rawls's method in Henry Richardson, "Deliberation Is of Ends," PhD thesis, Harvard University, 1986.
18 Pages 46–53 and 130–35; see also Rawls's Dewey Lectures, "Kantian Constructivism in Ethical Theory," *Journal of Philosophy* 77 (1980).
19 This is not explicitly stated by Rawls, but is implied in his discussion; it is argued convincingly by Richardson, in a way that seems to have met with Rawls's agreement.
20 Rawls, *A Theory*, 47.
21 Ibid., 47–8.
22 Ibid., 135. Since this discussion is not part of the discussion of reflective equilibrium, there is some unclarity as to whether it is supposed to be a part of the general method that we use to consider all theories or is to be understood as a part of the specific account of the moral point of view that is contained in the (Kantian) original position. But since its restrictions are said to "hold for the choice of all ethical principles and not only for those of justice" (130), and since they govern the choice of the theories that the parties are even permitted to consider, it seems likely that Rawls regards them as reasonable moral constraints to impose on all practical reasoning, not only the reasoning of the specifically Kantian conception. There is, in any case, some difficulty in disentangling these two levels of Rawls's project, since even the account of "considered judgments" that is explicitly made a part of the general method that we use to consider all alternative conceptions – that that should therefore be fair not only to the Kantian conception but to its rivals as well – has strong affinities with Kantianism. This problem is further discussed in the Dewey Lectures, with no definitive resolution.
23 *Nicomachean Ethics* 1109b18–23 and 1126b2–4; see also Nussbaum, "The Discernment of Perception."
24 The figure in the dream is actually identified as Sarah Pocock, but she figures here as Mrs Newsome's ambassador.
25 See "'Finely Aware and Richly Responsible': Literature and the Moral Imagination," in Nussbaum, *Love's Knowledge*. At the original American Philosophical Association symposium where I presented that paper, I had the benefit of excellent comments by Cora Diamond, entitled "Missing the Adventure," and abstracted in *Journal of Philosophy* 82 (1985): 529ff; these have shaped my views on these questions.
26 The charge that the view has no standards was forcefully made (against the Jamesian view of Nussbaum, "Flawed Crystals") by Hilary Putnam, in "Taking Rules Seriously: A Response to Martha Nussbaum," *New Literary History* 15 (1983): 193–200. For my reply, see "The Discernment of Perception," "'Finely Aware,'" "Perception and Revolution," and "Introduction," in Nussbaum, *Love's Knowledge*.
27 See "The Discernment of Perception" and "'Finely Aware,'" in Nussbaum, *Love's Knowledge*.

28 Richardson, "Deliberation is of Ends." I am very grateful to Richardson for discussion of these issues. A new paper of his, "The Emotions of Reflective Equilibrium," carries the issue further, in a manner that is close to the argument of this essay, and especially close to the argument of "Steerforth's Arm: Love and the Moral Point of View," in Nussbaum, *Love's Knowledge*.
29 See Nussbaum, "The Discernment of Perception."
30 Compare *The Ambassadors*. 1.200, 209, 213, etc.
31 See 1.209: "Our poor friend, conscious and passive . . ."
32 1.8; the description of Strether that follows is a result of this vision.
33 The negative reference to dramatic writing encourages, clearly, our connection of Strether with Henry James himself.
34 There is a fine account of the novel's style in Ian Watt "The First Paragraph of *The Ambassadors:* An Explication" in *Essays in Criticism* 10 (1960): 254–68; a revised version appears in A. E. Stone, Jr., ed., *Twentieth-Century Interpretations of "The Ambassadors"* (Englewood Cliffs, NJ: Prentice-Hall, 1969), 75–87.
35 The phrase is used by James in the preface to *Portrait of a Lady*; see Henry James, *The Art of the Novel* (New York, 1907), 45.
36 For some elements in that contrast, see "The Discernment of Perception" and "Plato on Commensurability and Desire," in Nussbaum, *Love's Knowledge*.
37 On this, see Nussbaum, "Therapeutic Arguments," above, n. 14.
38 These aspects of the novel are well discussed by Philip Weinstein in *Henry James and the Requirements of the Imagination* (Cambridge, MA: Harvard University Press, 1971), 121–64.
39 This passage and others using the word "life" are well discussed in Joan Bennett, "The Art of Henry James: *The Ambassadors*," *Chicago Review* 9 (1956): 16–26, reprinted in Stone, *Twentieth-Century Interpretations*, 57–65.
40 From a letter quoted in Leon Edel, *Henry James: The Untried Years* (New York, 1953), 49.
41 I am particularly thinking of the essay "The Moral Philosopher and the Moral Life," in William James, *Essays on Faith and Morals* (New York, 1962), 184–215.
42 F. R. Leavis, *The Great Tradition* (London: Chatto & Windus, 1948), 154–72.
43 Lionel Trilling, *The Liberal Imagination: Essays on Literature and Society* (New York, 1950), especially the essays, "The Princess Casamassima," "Manners, Morals, and the Novel," and "The Meaning of a Literary Idea."
44 James, *The Art of the Novel*, 223–24.

14

Henry James, Moral Philosophers, Moralism

CORA DIAMOND

> The theorizing mind tends always to the oversimplification of its materials.
> William James, *The Varieties of Religious Experience*

Henry James wrote no book *The Varieties of Moral Experience*, but he was a great observer and painter of that variety, and philosophers, who often miss the variety, can learn much from him. In this essay I am concerned with the variousness of moral disagreement and with the place of moralism in these forms of disagreement.

Philosophers tend to see ethics in terms of a background idea of the primary importance of judgment. Moral thinking is a type of evaluative thinking, and in evaluative thought one has in mind something or other – act, person, character trait – and considers the application to it of some evaluative term. The picture supports a philosophical conception of moral disagreement: moral disagreement will be disagreement whether a term of moral evaluation applies to such-and-such. We may also recognize a further possible kind of disagreement, over the acceptance or rejection of an evaluative concept (*blasphemous*, say, or *chaste*) or a set of such concepts.

For Henry James, the characterization of the distances there may be between human beings in their moral life and understanding proceeds altogether differently; judgment has not got the central position it has for philosophers. The immense difference between James and philosophers in approach to the description of moral life is tied to a difference in *which* concepts are salient. For philosophers: right and wrong, good and bad, duties, rights and obligations, notions of virtue and of particular virtues. These hardly drop out of the picture for James: consider, for example, his interest in the very particular kind of courage shown by his cousin Minny Temple, and how he turns and returns to the representation of forms of courage like Minny's. James, though, isn't interested in the judgment that someone or some action is courageous but in the exhibition and appreciation of this or that particular striking form. Among the concepts salient for James are some to which philosophers pay relatively little attention. Thus, for example, the opening of *The Tragic Muse*, displays before us forms of philistinism,

---

A Companion to the Philosophy of Literature, First Edition. Edited by Garry L. Hagberg and Walter Jost.
© 2010 John Wiley & Sons Ltd. Published 2015 by John Wiley & Sons, Ltd.

moralism, and aestheticism. We are indeed also warned that *responsibility* will count for something in this story, but we are warned too that what is to be understood *as* responsibility will itself not be separable from the very different lives we are just at that stage glimpsing. I focus on *moralism* as a notion that has or can have an interesting and deeply suggestive role in moral thought, too little reflected on by philosophers (Nietzsche being the most important exception), in large part because responsiveness to moralism isn't so much a matter of judgment as of appreciation and of what we make the appreciation count for. I shall interweave discussion of what moralism is for James with discussion of some philosophical views of it.

Whatever the ambiguities and complexities of Henry James's relation to his father, one thing they share is an interest in moralism. In the case of Henry James, Sr., the interest is entirely hostile; moralism, for him, is *the* spiritual evil. What he means by moralism is a kind of pride in the possession of moral goodness, but not only that. Moralism involves giving to the sphere of the moral a fundamental human importance which it lacks; it involves also a kind of fear of natural instincts and desires:

> Leading me as it does to regard my inward self as corrupt, to distrust my heart's affections as the deadliest enmity to God, it logically prompts the crucifixion of those affections as especially well pleasing to Him . . . (James, Sr., 1850, 160)

His son wasn't given to theorizing about spiritual evil, and moralism as he saw it was not an unmitigated evil: it had its varieties, some of them even admirable. Although he doesn't theorize about moralism, James does think about it: characters and forms of living which one could describe as moralistic have, throughout his life, a conspicuous role in his fiction. Further, in his understanding of art – his own and its contrasts and similarities with that of his predecessors and contemporaries – the presence or absence of moralism is important. And a concern with moralism was, further, forced on him by the moralistic criticism of his day.

The term "moralism" is almost always used pejoratively – but not by James. Although he rejected from the start a moralistic conception of art, he could write this of Henry Fielding:

> we see [Tom Jones] through the mellow air of Fielding's fine old moralism, fine old humour and fine old style, which somehow really enlarge, make every one and every thing important. (*CM* 503)[1]

The complexity of James's response to Fielding's moralism comes out in the contrast he drew between Walter Scott and Fielding. Fielding's novels, like those of Smollett and Richardson, aim, James says, to instruct and edify. Of *Tom Jones* in particular he writes,

> The story is like a vast episode in a sermon preached by a grandly humorous divine; and however we may be entertained by the way, we must not forget that our ultimate duty is to be instructed. With the minister's week-day life we have no concern: for the present he is awful, impersonal Morality. (*CM* 21)

James goes on to make clear the contrast with *Waverley*, the first "self-forgetful" novel. "It proposed simply to amuse the reader, as an old English ballad amused him. It undertook to prove nothing but facts. It was the novel irresponsible" (*CM* 21).

The term "irresponsible" is not used wholly ironically, but I am interested in what the passage suggests about James's view of moralism and how that view may be connected with some remarks of twentieth-century philosophers. D. A. J. Richards has argued that it is rational to accept a moral principle about mutual love,

> requiring that people should not show personal affection and love to others on the basis of arbitrary physical characteristics alone, but rather on the basis of traits of personality and character related to acting on moral principles. (Richards 1971, 94)

Bernard Williams refers to Richards's principle as "this righteous absurdity," and the account of which it is part as "richly moralistic" (Williams 1981, 16); Rai Gaita describes the same passage as involving the moralistic devaluing of what in human life makes possible our sense of the preciousness and irreplaceability of persons (Gaita 1991, 156).[2]

What kind of criticism is made by the term "moralistic"? Williams suggests that the source of the "righteous absurdity" is "a feeling that love, even love based on 'arbitrary physical characteristics,' is something which has enough power and even authority to conflict badly with morality unless it can be brought within it from the beginning," and he adds that the feeling is a sound feeling (Williams 1981, 16). That is, the criticism that Richards's account is *moralistic* does not rest on a judgment that Richards is mistaken about the possibility of such conflict; the idea is rather that Richards's moralism, taken to be a disabling distortion of thought, lies in his way of conceiving the conflict as well as his response to it.

Williams's description of Richards's proposal as moralistic needs to be understood in the context of his more general criticism of the treatment by contemporary moral theories of a broadly Kantian type of the relation between the *moral* and the *non-moral*, and especially their treatment of possible conflicts between morality and what lies outside it. When Williams describes as moralistic Richards's response to the possibility of conflict between love and morality, what he takes to be moralistic is not just Richards's proposal of a moral principle intended to prevent such conflict, but also, and at least as significantly, his understanding of the character of the conflict, involving as it does a Kantian conception of human nature and of the role in our thought of the moral and the non-moral. The moralism of Richards's *proposal* is inseparable from a moralistic understanding of the nature of the conflict which the proposal aims to head off.[3] Although Williams uses the term "moralistic" only in his criticism of Richards, the term could have been used in expressing one of the essay's main criticisms of much contemporary moral theory, namely, that such theories are moralistic in their characteristic way of dealing with *all* the relations between "the moral" and "the non-moral": in their way of dealing with possible conflict, and in their way of dealing with what "morality" *allows* to go on outside its own realm, allows to go on in the realm of personal relations and personal projects.

What then is the connection between Williams's description of Richards's moralism and James's description of Fielding's? Williams describes Richards's feeling that love has power and authority enough to conflict badly with morality unless it is *brought within it from the beginning*. And James, in describing the eighteenth-century moralistic storyteller, tells us that he brings the entirety of the story into the sphere of the moral, from beginning to end. That is, Fielding's moralism is described by James as a mode of story-telling in which conflict of the sort Williams mentions cannot arise. The implied author, telling us of human love, human acts, human relations, does not allow us to enter sympathetically into these relations except in so far as that care is subject to the authority of awful, impersonal Morality. What is being thought of as "moralism" in the case of Fielding is not just the imposition of the authority of Morality, but also Fielding's conception of the point of view of Morality. We may contrast James on Turgenev: the seriousness of a human subject is in what it reveals of human life to the caring mind. Turgenev's object is "that of finding an incident, a person, a situation, *morally* interesting," but finding a subject morally interesting is not a matter of finding in it what Morality would find. The eye for all of human passion, the "deeply sympathetic sense of the wonderful complexity of our souls," makes the moral interest; what can be of moral interest is discovered in the writing or in the reading (CM 82–84, 205). There is no idea here of a "moral point of view" *set over against* other sorts of attention to the human soul. If there is such a thing as a "moral point of view" exemplified by a writer like Turgenev, it is simply the point of view from which we see and attend with warmth and sympathy to the complex reality of human life: what is "moral" here emerges from the intelligence and fineness of the consciousness.

In remarking Turgenev's "deeply sympathetic sense of the wonderful complexity of our souls," James expresses a view of the relation between morality and art which is in several interconnected ways offensive to moralism. It suggests that the sympathy and interest of the artist may appropriately go wherever they go, independently of any prior considerations of moral desert. But the description with sympathetic interest of someone whom morality condemns, someone who is taken not to deserve our sympathy, arouses moral outrage. The artist's sense of what is humanly interesting is like love in its capacity to conflict with and even to subvert morality, and it may seem thereby to constitute a possible threat to morality, if not subjected to its authority.

James's view further implies that no subject matter, no "sharp reality" (see *WM* 12), is out of bounds. Nor is an artist committed, in his treatment of a subject he finds of interest, either to making the judgments Morality would make or to inviting or inducing his readers to make those judgments. Fielding's reader may be amused and entertained by the way, but his ultimate duty is to be instructed. James's rejection of a moralistic conception of the role of judgment is really the same point, seen from another angle, as the point about the artist's sympathy not being subjected to Morality: the stance of sympathetic interest and that of judgment are opposed, as is illustrated by the contrast in *The Ambassadors* between Lambert Strether and Mrs Pocock in relation to the immoral but highly interesting couple in Paris.

The term "moralistic" frequently indicates an insistence on moral judging or the habit of moral judging, in contexts which only some would see as calling for such judgment.

But the relation between moralism and the place and character of moral judging in human life is complex, as comes out in Annette Baier's discussion of Hume and Kant.

In "Moralism and Cruelty: Reflections on Hume and Kant," Baier several times describes Kant's account as moralistic[4] (Baier 1993, 443, 450–51) and explains why:

> Kant's is an overtly moralistic morality, holding us to account for all failures in which our faulty will has played a role, encouraging us to anticipate a just judgment by an all-seeing God. . . . Human conscience is to be a stand-in for the just divine judge, but not for the merciful pardoner, so forgiving ourselves is not encouraged. We are to demand moral perfection of ourselves, as God demands it of us. We are to be punctilious about leaving it to magistrates to punish people for breaches of their perfect obligations, and leaving it to others to demand, each of herself, her own perfection. We are to show some concern for the happiness of our fellows, but only as far as the moral law allows room for that concern. . . . The Kantian conscience accuses, recognizes that punishment is deserved, but leaves it to God or the magistrate to inflict it. (443–4)

Here what makes an account moralistic is not the idea that people should be forever acting as moral judges of *others*; it is rather the modeling of one's relation to one's own actions and character in terms of a kind of internal moral courtroom. Thus Baier later makes the contrast with Hume's *non*-moralistic account by referring to Kant's as "moral law enforcement" (451).

Baier's contrast between Hume's non-moralism and Kant's moralism turns also on the *content* of their accounts. She describes Humean morality as "[boasting] of its non-moralistic avoidance of 'useless austerities, rigors and self denials' and [promising] 'nothing but gentleness, humanity, beneficence, affability; nay even, at proper intervals play, frolic and gaiety' ";[5] the contrast between Hume and Kant is that between *epicureanism* and *moralism* (450–51). This contrast in content suggests something further. For a morality to be moralistic is not merely for it to prescribe what from a Humean point of view look like useless austerities, rigors, and self-denials. Such prescriptions have their source in a conception of human nature and of the significance in our lives of morality – and thus also of what needs to be strengthened in us, what we may need to be protected from. Any human good independent of morality, any interest or desire, might on occasion give rise to conflict with morality, hence (from the point of view we are characterizing as moralistic) should be brought under morality from the beginning, and tendencies to indulge such interests or desires should be regarded with suspicion. That conception of human nature was a great theme of Henry James's (as it had been of his father). For James it was associated in particular with New England. The New England character "takes things hard": wants always to know what its duty is, and is unwilling to *enjoy* unless it is certain it ought to. (See *The Bostonians*, chapter 2; *The Europeans*, chapter 3; compare also *The Ambassadors*, chapter 1: "Woollett [the New England town] isn't sure it ought to enjoy. If it were it would" [13].)[6] For James, what is to be contrasted with the New England subjection of life to "ought" is, most frequently, Europe; those of his characters who are New Englanders through and through hate Europe (Olive Chancellor, for example, in *The Bostonians* and Waymarsh in *The Ambassadors*). There are a number of reasons for their disliking Europe, and one is that

Europe does not want to be improved. The New Englander feels the iniquity of the world and in Europe is painfully aware of iniquity ignored. Another thing hated in Europe is its "discrimination of types and tones," its interest in, tolerance of, shades and ambiguities.[7] Europe is seductive, something to be resisted, to be on one's guard against.[8] New England places under suspicion whatever might elude the authority of morality. That habit of suspicion (that form of the habit of judging) is an essential element in what James calls "taking things hard" (*BO* 7; *EU* 33).

In discussing James on moralism and puritanism in *The Ambassadors*, Martha Nussbaum notes his portrayal of the moralistic character as "all moral pressure" (Nussbaum 1990, 176; see also chapter 13, PERCEPTIVE EQUILIBRIUM: LITERARY THEORY AND ETHICAL THEORY): there is in that character an essential opposition to *passivity* and to (non-moralized) emotion. This, I think, leads us back to the issues which lie just under the surface of James's remarks about Turgenev and the "deeply sympathetic sense of the wonderful complexity of our souls." What is objectionable there, from the point of view of moralism, is precisely that we may *yield* to sympathy, find ourselves enticed by it, when it is morally appropriate to resist. Nussbaum describes the hero of *The Ambassadors* as "yielding to the impressions of life as they unfold themselves before him – as allowing himself to be seduced" (Nussbaum 1990, 187).

The level of specificity of content at which there is a tie between the content of a morality and the morality's being moralistic goes below the level alluded to by Baier in her quotation of Hume's "useless austerity" passage. Certain vices and virtues, certain principles, have particular significance in characterizing a morality as moralistic – lying, for example. Nussbaum mentions the importance James attaches to hatred of lying, as a characteristic of New England moralism in *The Ambassadors*. The attitude towards lying also has great significance in his other treatments of moralism: in *The Europeans*, Europeans fib and lie (and are thus contrasted with New Englanders);[9] and again, in *The Bostonians*, Boston itself is "this unprevaricating city" (*BO* 1), while Southerners and people from New York not only fib but (more significantly still) joke about it. The moral character of places is intensely felt by James. The contrast between America (or New England) and Europe is for James not just the contrast between moralism and aestheticism but often the more specific contrast between *rigor as to truth* and *enjoyment of appearance*. Another important connection between the content of a morality and its being moralistic concerns the significance attached to sexual morality and the particular character of the sexual morality itself;[10] yet another connection lies between the role given to retributive punishment and the morality's being moralistic. This latter tie is indeed central in Baier's account of Kant's morality as moralistic.

Some, at least, of the resentment occasioned by what is now labeled "political correctness" is a response to moralism on the left, moralism of a sort already present in the feminists and reformers sketched by James in *The Bostonians* and attacked by George Orwell in "The Art of Donald McGill" and other essays. No better example can be found of an element of human nature capable of clashing with morality, or what we take to be morality, than our sense of what is funny. Jokes, especially vulgar ones, depend heavily on stereotypes and on topics taken to be intrinsically funny, like sex and drunkenness; they thus have enormous potential for moral offensiveness and are frequently cruel.

Hence the familiar use of "That's not funny" to mean not that something is not funny but that we ought not to find it so. But how far should the jokey side of us, what Orwell called the Sancho Panza in us, be squashed into the space which morality (conceived in this or that particular way) is willing to allow it? If some answers to such questions are felt to be puritanical or moralistic, that feeling is a response to underlying ideas about human life and human good. Under cover, as it were, of "the authority of Morality," something with its own rights is being denied them: *that* is the feeling.[11]

These metaphors of territory, rights, authority, insubordination, and possible subversion are important; the figures of speech turn literal when poetry, the enemy of moral order, is banned from the territory of the Republic, as by Plato. I cannot here discuss Plato, but I want simply to note the connection between his treatment of art and what is being responded *to*, when someone's mode of thought is taken to be moralistic, namely, ideas about the distinctions between kinds of good and about possible conflicts between them, ideas within which the moral interests of the soul, which can be understood in a wide sense, are identified with one type of good or one group of goods (see Goldberg 1993, *passim*, especially 27–9, 234–8). Perhaps it is worth noting here that Henry James was educated on principles very distant indeed from Plato's. Henry James, Sr., believed, says Leon Edel, that "there was Divine Truth in the world and this the children were bound to discover for themselves under Divine Guidance" (Edel 1978, 115). In other words, the principles of the education to which the younger Henry James was subject involved the very opposite of the idea that morality dictates the exclusion from education of those elements of life which might subvert or conflict with morality.

I want now to look at the faults and failings to which those who reject moralism may be thought to be subject, starting with Hume as he might be seen by Kant. Baier states that "We know what Kantians should think about Hume's version of morality, since Kant more or less told us that" (Baier 1993, 436). What she has in mind may include the opening section of part 1 of the *Groundwork of the Metaphysics of Morals*. Kant says there that a being endowed with all sorts of good qualities or with riches, power and so on, but without a good will, will not give pleasure to a rational impartial observer; whereas Hume holds that what gives us pleasure has nothing to do with reason. There is no "ought" about it. A good will (in Kant's sense) is not, on Hume's view, a condition for some special sort of approval or pleasure significantly distinguishable from other sorts of response to people's qualities. This is not just a contradiction between two reflective accounts of morality. The contradiction at that level reflects a great difference in temperament and in the way temperament enters our conception of morality and of its place in our life.

The opening section of part 1 of the *Groundwork* provides also an account of what may be found troubling in the attitude to art expressed by James not just in the remarks I have already discussed but also, for example, in his review of *Hedda Gabler* (CM 295–302). There is a strong current of life in Hedda, but there is (or so Kant would tell us) nothing good or admirable about such strength of life without a good will, which would direct that strength and make it conform to universal ends. Without the principle of a good will, the strength of life in Hedda makes her more dangerous and more abominable.[12] And what is the matter with *Hedda Gabler* from the Kantian point of view is that, in inviting us to view Hedda with sympathy and interest, to see her as complex and even attractive, the play corrupts moral thinking. James was all too aware of the fact that art as he understood it would be seen as likely to corrupt judgment. Mrs Ambient, in James's "The Author of 'Beltraffio,'" finds the writings of her husband immoral and fears them as *contagiously* so. The object of this fear is his representation of life, the "distillation of the actual" (56), *not* brought under morality.

We have so far seen only part of the range of response that I am looking for. When Hume or others who reject what they call moralism (or what they think of in similar terms) are considered by those whom they would think of as moralistic, what does *their* mode of thinking look like? Dorothea Krook describes Hume's approach to morality as shallow, trivial, low, frivolous, unserious, unsolid, unreal, lacking any sense of the higher, lacking any genuine sense of evil. Hume's cheerfulness is the complacent comfortableness of the eighteenth-century clubman; reading Hume is like "being asphyxiated in an ocean of cotton wool." There is nothing in Hume for "the poor, the wretched, the deprived and dispossessed," no place to be found for "those who are weary and heavy-laden" (Krook 1959, chapter 6, especially 173–7). What Krook sees in Hume is a profound *irresponsibility*.[13]

The passage to which Krook especially draws attention (as justifying the epithets she uses) is exactly the passage quoted by Baier in her contrast between Hume's non-moralism and Kant's moralism – a passage (see note 5) in which Hume himself attacks moralistic writers as enemies of joy and pleasure. Krook's sense of being asphyxiated is tied to what she feels as the difficulty of objecting to Hume: "There is nothing solid [in that passage] to resist, nothing real to protest against" (174–5).[14] Her sense of Hume's thought about morality as *unsolid* is in part a response – very far from Baier's – to features of Hume's voice, "features of tone, emphasis, personal accent" (9). Krook and Kant differ in their responses to Hume, but both can be read as seeing in the Humean approach a denial of the *reality* of morality, and this is a source of Krook's perception of Hume as unserious, frivolous.

I want to pursue the idea that a feature of at least some of the approaches to morality which reject what they take to be moralism, when viewed by those who are seen as moralistic, is *frivolousness*, failure of (due) seriousness. One form which this idea takes is opposition to aestheticism. "Aestheticism," as a term of criticism, is no easier to pin down than is "moralism." An aestheticized version of morality does not allow morality to be itself; the seriousness of morality is gone.

In Henry James's fiction, Europe, Paris, and Europeanized Americans or Englishmen frequently represent aestheticized conceptions of life and of morality. Gabriel Nash in *The Tragic Muse* is one example; Paris in *The Ambassadors* is another, as in this passage:

> "You've all of you here so much visual sense that you've somehow all 'run' to it. There are moments when it strikes one that you haven't any other."
> "Any moral," little Bilham explained, watching serenely, across the garden, the several *femmes du monde*. . . .
> "I daresay, moreover," [Miss Barrace] pursued . . . "that I do, that we all do here, run too much to mere eye." (127–8)

James treats moralism and aestheticism, New England and Paris, as – both of them – distorted modes of thought and response to life.[15] And *frivolousness, lack of seriousness* are important notions not just in articulating the response of the *moralistic* to something they see or think they see in others, but also in articulating a possible non-moralistic understanding of what is the matter with aestheticism. New England may hate Paris, may not see what is splendid about Paris, but it is responding to unseriousness, failure of responsibility: various forms of failure of responsibility run through "aestheticized" thought. James, though, does not equate responsibility with what moralism makes of it. Genuine responsibility takes forms which moralism will not recognize, and moralism involves its own kinds of evasions. A great question for James is, then, the possibility of responsibility without moralism, the possibility of the quickened life of reflection and observation, in which neither the "visual" sense nor the sense of responsibility is scanted.[16] *The Tragic Muse* and *The Ambassadors* are especially interesting in this connection. Thus, for example, in the latter we see Strether's development, and the kind of moral thinking he reaches, in a complex contrasting relation not just to the moralism of New England but also to the aestheticism associated with Paris. To understand his moral journey, we must see it with the genuine attractiveness and the genuine limitations of *both* Paris and Woollett; we need also an account of the relation between the inadequacies of Paris and those of Woollett.[17]

Our *particular* moral views emerge from a more general background of thought and response. We differ in how we let (or do not let) moral concepts order our life and our relations to others, in how such concepts structure the stories we tell of what we have done or gone through. I have been focusing on the ways we respond to modes of moral thought which we do not share and which may appear to us as distortions of thought.[18] If it is indeed our forms of responsiveness that give rise to explicit moral thought and particular decisions, if it is indeed clashes in mode of responsiveness that underlie much moral disagreement, then it seems that moral philosophers and (more generally) people reflecting on ethics should attend to texture of life, to modes of responsiveness, and to the relation between texture of life and particular acts, thoughts, responses. That is indeed explicitly argued for by Iris Murdoch (1956), and similar arguments are developed by Nussbaum. But the conclusion may be resisted; the kind of approach to morality that gets called *moralistic* can lead to a rejection of the argument that we should attend to modes of responsiveness to life. Here I want to turn to *What Maisie Knew* and the moralistic criticism it inspired.

In *What Maisie Knew*, James portrays the freshness of Maisie's view and how she remarkably maintains that freshness within the morally corrupt world of her parents and their shifting sexual partners. From the point of view of good moral people (whom James refers to elsewhere as *bonnes gens*), this was an inappropriate subject for a novel. The world of the adults was morally disgusting, and the "mixing-up" of the child with that world aggravated the inappropriateness of subject: "nothing could well be more disgusting than to attribute to Maisie so intimate an 'acquaintance' with the gross immoralities surrounding her" (*WM* 12). One part of James's response to this criticism (and to similar criticism of other writers, like Zola and Ibsen) is that the value of any subject cannot be seen in advance of its treatment, of what that treatment may have in it of responsiveness to life. Let us say that there is in the treatment a sense of the infinitude of character, a care for *that*; let us say that there is in the account we are given perhaps unexpected intensity of life: there is not then anything else that needs to be demanded of it. We cannot write off in advance, on the grounds that a *sympathetic* picture will be corrupting, the sympathetic treatment of (say) a wicked, diseased, disagreeable woman: of a Hedda Gabler.[19]

We might describe the clash between James and moralistic critics of his own work and that of others as a clash between views of life, or alternatively as a clash between James – taken as believing in the possible appropriateness and importance of representing any subject, the representation itself reflecting a responsiveness to life – and people who have a sort of meta-view about views of life, who hold that *whether* it is appropriate or decent or useful to attend to a mode of responsiveness to life or to put a treatment of a particular subject before the public are questions to be judged on external moral grounds. On James's view the ground for such a judgment does not exist in advance of the treatment and what it has in it of the "quality of mind of the producer." On the fineness of that intelligence depends the achieving of "rightness" of discrimination (including moral discrimination) (CM 204–6).[20] The view of life of James's critics was that views of life are judgeable by morality; James rejects the "grotesque finality" (WM 12) of the characterizations appealed to by those critics and their underlying, blinkered conception of morality. He takes moralism itself to be a human phenomenon (like any other), judgeable only when we take it up in our thought, represent it, and understand it to whatever degree, at whatever depth. Our thought about moralism, or any judgment of it, grows out of a mode of responsiveness to life. *That* responsiveness has its moral character: is morally alive, or dead, or obtuse, or shallow, or whatever it may be.

Henry James believed that the moralistic critics of such novels as *What Maisie Knew* failed to understand it. But then they did not want what he would regard as understanding; the effort to achieve such understanding they would take to be misplaced. Compare the idea, characteristic of moralism, that it is out of place to try to see the sinner or criminal in the light of a sympathetic understanding. The invitation to take up such an understanding is conceived as an invitation to feel sorry for such a person, and to avoid making the judgment on him that he deserves. The route leading towards understanding seems (to the moralistically inclined) a route leading away from appropriate judgment, judgment depending on moral firmness that sympathetic understanding might soften. For James, in contrast, a consciousness that takes (as Lambert Strether's does), in all its difficulty and windingness, the route towards understanding is exercising a vital kind of responsibility. The disagreements I have been describing are disagreements in understanding, but also in the desire for understanding, the conception of its use, its place, its limits. These disagreements are then reflected also within moral philosophy. Thus, some contemporary followers of Kant take Kantian moral philosophy to be distinctively "agent-centered," but an essential element in their conception of "agency" is that a Jamesian appreciation of the actions and changing character, the passions and endurings of others, would be *contrasted* with the exercise of moral agency and not a fine and central case of it. To emphasize such appreciation would be to direct attention away from the "problems we have to face," but this is to hold that the real problems we have as moral beings, responsible agents, do not include those of achieving the kind of understanding which James sought. Moral agency is there tied by moral philosophy to principled choice; within such philosophy, the achieving of a Jamesian kind of understanding of things is described in a vocabulary which cuts it off from genuine exercise of moral responsibility in the face of real problems.[21] The Lambert Strethers, the Henry Jameses, go in for what is in these terms mere "moral connoisseurship," i.e., a kind of spectatorship unconnected with the hardships of choice and dependent on the kind of leisure that would free one for mere appreciation. Here, we are back *within* the issues explored in *The Ambassadors* and elsewhere in James's fiction and criticism; we haven't reached some neutral philosophical standpoint where inclinations towards or away from moralism no longer count.[22]

James's characters respond to moral things in life in an immense variety of ways; they find themselves at odds about everything from relatively simple, straightforward propositions (whether, for example, Morris Townsend, in *Washington Square*, is a decent young man) to life in general (Olive Chancellor and Basil Ransom, in *The Bostonians*). Philosophers, in their thought about moral disagreement, have focused almost exclusively on cases like the first. Because the judgments about which we disagree in such cases resemble ordinary factual judgments, philosophers have endlessly debated *how far* the resemblance to factual judgment goes. In this essay, I have looked at clashes in people's response to life, in their way of using moral concepts in understanding their own life and their relations to others. We may react very strongly to other people's mode of moral thought. What is being responded to is not this or that particular judgment. If we differ from others in *this* way, the disagreement does not resemble disagreements over admittedly factual matters. So the kind of philosophical question that arises about particular moral judgments – whether they are as much like factual judgments as they appear – does not arise in connection with *these* disagreements.

The idea that, phenomenologically, ethical thought resembles thought in which we judge how the facts stand is a starting point for much philosophical work. But the belief that that *is* the phenomenology of ethical thought is the result of ignoring much ethical thought – much ordinary unreflective, as well as reflective, thought. Ethical thought includes a variety of complex responses to what seem to us distorted or bad modes of moral thinking, modes of thinking which we may take (with greater or lesser awareness) to challenge or threaten our own sense of what is important. Although we may regard those from whom we feel thus distant as making false judgments about moral facts, the difference about those particular matters is not the heart of the disagreement, nor is it usually taken to be. The *character* of a mode of thought has great interest for us, not just as a matter of a disposition to reach or to miss accurate judgments. To call someone's mode of moral thought moralistic, or to call it on the other hand unsolid, evasive, frivolous, irresponsible, immoral, is in neither case to be claiming that the other person has got some moral facts wrong. The phenomenology here is different; we need to be much more suspicious of philosophical remarks about *the* phenomenology of moral thought.

If James describes for us the varieties of forms which can be taken by our disagreements with each other on moral matters, philosophers should learn more from this than just that they had had an inadequate idea of the phenomenology of moral disagreement. Where did the apparent self-evidence of that initial philosophical reading of the phenomenology of moral life come from? It is hardly innocent of all connections with a moralistic inheritance. So what we need from James is also his portrayal of what these differences between us mean in our lives, what their significance is. His own complex response to the inheritance of moralism is in that complex portrayal of importances. It's all in the shades! – as some of his unmoralistic characters might say. But a dislike for shades is what marks us as philosophers.

I quoted William James at the beginning of this essay about our tendency as theorizers to oversimplify our material. He was thinking in particular of theories of religion and warning of the danger of taking there to be some essence of religion tied to the nature of religious experience *as such*. The will thus to oversimplify leads, he says, to "all that absolutism and one-sided dogmatism by which both philosophy and religion have been infested" (William James 1960, 46). So too there is a need for philosophy not to oversimplify the phenomena of moral life and thought, not to look for some single basic characterization of moral experience. But in ethics the theorizing mind is not the only source of the tendency to oversimplify. A moralistic conception of morality – not just a theorizing mind – can lead us to say: *this* (whatever it may be) is what moral thinking in essence is; all else is not *really* moral thinking. The requirements of morality, not just the requirements of theory, may seem to lead us away from any recognition of genuine variety within moral experience.

Notes

I am very glad to have had the chance to present an earlier version of some parts of this essay at the Inter-Nordic Symposium on Ethics and Understanding, in Turku in 1993. An expanded version of the conference paper, overlapping this present essay, has been published under the title "Moral Differences and Distances: Some Questions" in *Commonality and Particularity in Ethics*. I am grateful to Macmillan Press for permission to include portions of that essay. I was much helped by the discussion at the conference, and by comments and suggestions afterwards from Lars Hertzberg, Harald Johannessen, Kurt Baier, and Annette Baier. I am also very grateful to A. D. Woozley and to James Conant for their helpful comments on various versions of the essay.

1   The following abbreviations are used for parenthetical citations of works by Henry James: CM – Henry James, *The Critical Muse*; WM – *What Maisie Knew*; BO – *The Bostonians*; EU – *The Europeans*.
2   Gaita's phrase is actually "philosophical and moralistic devaluing."
3   For a valuable detailed account of how just such a moralistic conception of the relation between love and morality can distort moral thought, see Goldberg 1993, chapter 5 ("Moral Thinking in *The Mill on the Floss*"). That detailed account is part of the book's more general criticism of what it explicitly takes to be a moralistic understanding of moral value (see 250); see also Goldberg's discussion of Williams's views (274–8).
4   I am not concerned with the question whether her account of Kant is fair but rather with the question what is involved in the characterization of a view, whether Kant's or not, as

moralistic. It should, however, be noted that some defenses of Kant as not moralistic or even anti-moralistic appeal to a very narrow conception of what it is to be moralistic. Being moralistic may be identified with making or encouraging the making of moral judgments about other people and with failing to respect their choices; it may then seem easy to show that Kant is not moralistic. See, e.g., Baron 1988 (98, 102).

5   I shall refer again to the passage which Baier quotes, from part 2 of the conclusion to Hume's *Enquiry Concerning the Principles of Morals*. Here is the passage:

> But what philosophical truths can be more advantageous to society than those here delivered, which represent virtue in all her genuine and most engaging charms, and make us approach her with ease, familiarity, and affection? The dismal dress falls off, with which many divines, and some philosophers have covered her; and nothing appears but gentleness, humanity, beneficence, affability; nay even, at proper intervals, play, frolic, and gaiety. She talks not of useless austerities and rigors, suffering and self-denial. She declares, that her sole purpose is, to make her votaries and all mankind, during every instant of their existence, if possible, cheerful and happy; nor does she ever willingly part with any pleasure but in hopes of ample compensation in some other period of their lives. The sole trouble, which she demands, is that of just calculation, and a steady preference of the greater happiness. And if any austere pretenders approach her, enemies to joy and pleasure, she either rejects them as hypocrites and deceivers; or if she admit them in her train, they are ranked, however, among the least favoured of her votaries. (279–80)

6   On the New England character taking things hard, see also the final chapter of *The Ambassadors*. See Nussbaum's discussion of the quotation from *The Ambassadors* and, more generally, of James's treatment of moralism in that work (Nusbaum 1990, chapter 6; reprinted in this volume, chapter 13, PERCEPTIVE EQUILIBRIUM: LITERARY THEORY AND ETHICAL THEORY). See also Baier's discussion of the Kantian duty to enjoy doing one's duty (1993, 444–5). Compare also James's view of Woollett's self-distrust with his father's view of moralism (quoted above) as leading one to distrust the heart's affections.

7   The New Englander's intolerance of shades and ambiguities, of moral mixture, marks an important connection with Kant. Kant insists on the enormous importance of avoiding so far as possible in ethics the admission of anything "morally intermediate," any real (as opposed to merely apparent) mix of good and bad, in actions or human character: ambiguity undermines the precision and stability of moral maxims (Kant 1960, 18). For more about Henry James on shades and ambiguities, see Nussbaum 1990, especially chapter 4, "Flawed Crystals: James's *The Golden Bowl* and Literature as Moral Philosophy"; see also Nussbaum's discussions of a related topic, the incommensurability of valuable things, in, e.g., Nussbaum 1990, chapter 2, "The Discernment of Perception: An Aristotelian Conception of Private and Public Rationality."

8   See especially chapter 3 of *The Ambassadors*. The complexity of James's use of "Europe" allows Chester to belong to Europe in one work, and Europe to be contrasted with England in others, thus demonstrating that Europe is a place in the American (or English) consciousness, not identical with any place on a map. The relation between Europe and England in *The Tragic Muse* allows James to make contrasts between philistinism and aestheticism that overlap but do not duplicate the contrasts between New England moralism and aestheticism. (Philistinism can, though, be tied quite directly to moralism, as in the character of Lady Agnes in *The Tragic Muse*, and even more clearly in the character of Mrs Ambient in "The Author of 'Beltraffio.'") The hatred of art in the political/English characters

is tied to a dislike of "discrimination of tones" just as is the hatred of Europe in James's moralistic/New England characters. The English liberal and the New Englander are equally appalled by iniquity, equally committed to active reform and improvement, equally suspicious of the aesthete's lack of commitment to reform, his willingness instead simply to "feel," his utter lack of responsibility. For a similar use of "place" in relation to the criticism of moralism, see Ibsen's *Ghosts*, and the use of Norway/Paris in it; also Ibsen's *Pillars of Society*, and the use of Norway/America.

9 See Krook on the role of lying in *The Europeans* (Krook 1967, 293n).

10 In "The Author of 'Beltraffio,'" James tells us nothing about what it is that the moralistic Mrs Ambient objects to in "Beltraffio" and the other writings of her husband, but we are expected to recognize that what she objects to is the treatment of sex.

11 I am grateful to Julie Diamond for discussion of the issues in this paragraph.

12 We should note here the connection of Kant's idea that an otherwise admirable trait becomes abominable in the absence of a good will with his view (see note 7 above) that we must in ethics avoid so far as possible the very idea of a *mix* of good and bad in human character: if the absence of a good will makes an otherwise admirable trait *not* good, the presence of such traits in the absence of a good will cannot create a "morally mixed" character. Here we can see further the contrast with Henry James: what interests him not just as author but also as critic, as for example in considering Hedda, is precisely the possibility of complex moral "mixtures" (*CM* 301).

13 Krook's response to Hume contains many of the elements that may be found in the responses of those described as "moralistic" to the thought of someone like Hume (which is the reason for choosing her as an example) although her own approach to morality might be seen by those rejecting it not as moralistic, I think, but perhaps as religiose.

14 The passage to which Krook objects so strongly is also one that Kant would condemn, although in different terms. In *Religion within the Limits of Reason Alone*, Kant tells us that our relation to morality is properly awe and not familiarity; he rejects the idea of morality as having "charm" for us. Hume's words for our relation to morality: "engaging charm ... ease, familiarity, affection" (see note 5 above) would be seen by Kant as suggesting in two ways a kind of moral corruption: in their implicit rejection of the centrality of duty (duty tied to the moral law as having majesty) and in their consequent denial of the *sublimity* of our own destiny as moral beings. There is, though, a limited agreement between Kant and Hume in rejecting "monkish" self-immolation.

15 See, for example, the entirety of chapter 10, from which the quoted passage comes. I should note that, within the context of James's fiction, it is oversimple to identify moralism with "New England," as I have been doing. In two of his most interesting treatments of art in relation to a hatred of art tied to a sense of its immorality (*The Tragic Muse*, "The Author of 'Beltraffio'"), it is not New England but England that is the place associated with moralism/philistinism.

16 My phrasing draws on the first two chapters of *The Tragic Muse*. James's remarks, quoted above, about the novels of Scott and Fielding reflect related ideas: Scott is "irresponsible," Fielding a didactic, though amusing, moralizer. The possibility of responsibility without moralism is then important in James's understanding of his own aims as a novelist.

17 Nussbaum's discussion of *The Ambassadors* differs sharply from mine (see especially Nussbaum 1990, 182, 185); it is framed in terms of *two* rival norms, two opposing conceptions of practical reason, Strether's and Woollett's. See also Barbara Hardy's description of the slow, complex, "eddying" process of moral transformation in which Strether rejects

two moral cultures (Hardy 1970, 27–31); and see Michael Levenson's illuminating account of the three "moral attitudes" in *The Ambassadors* (Levenson 1991, 1–77). Levenson makes clear the possibility of a critical perspective on "Paris" distinct from that of Woollett, and essential to the novel's conception; he gives a detailed account of the "matching" failings of the two attitudes contrasted with Strether's. I am grateful to James Conant for discussion of these issues.

18 It is important to note that the disagreements of which I have been speaking can be found within the mind of a single person. Two examples: fru Alving, in *Ghosts*, has still within herself the woman, or the ghost of the woman, who refused, years ago, to see how her moralism was destroying her husband's life and her own. Her struggle during the period leading up to that of the play, and during the play, is to free herself from that woman's mode of thought. In Tolstoy the relation goes in the opposite direction: it is the inner moralizer who, in Tolstoy's later life, wants to put himself at a distance from the author of *Anna Karenina*, now seen as irresponsible, immoral, elitist.

19 We should note that, in James's defense of Hedda as subject, he defends Ibsen's choice of subject in exactly the terms that the moralistic would take to constitute a condemnation: Hedda, well-acted, will no longer appear the wicked, disagreeable woman we may at first take her to be. We will become unsure of her wickedness, and will indeed find her complicated, various, graceful; she suffers, she struggles, she is human; she is exposed to a dozen interpretations (*CM* 301). This description, from the point of view of Kant, would constitute all the justification needed for treating Ibsen's art as corrupt and corrupting. (The complicated, various, graceful bad woman who suffers, struggles, is human: this would also describe Kate Croy, in *The Wings of the Dove*.)

20 See "The Art of Fiction" in *CM*. I have in mind also Levenson's use of "rightness" as a term which, for James, "stands at the place where moral and aesthetic judgments meet" (Levenson 1991, 63). My discussion is meant to suggest that Levenson's treatment of "rightness" in *The Ambassadors* brings out the continuing significance to James of finding a way of thinking about ethics which resists moralism but does not give over the moral to the aesthetic, does not give it away.

21 Various passages in O'Neill 1989 would provide examples (see especially 176); see also Korsgaard 1996 (186 note 21).

22 Much of Nussbaum bears on the issues of this paragraph (see, e.g., Nussbaum 1990, 26 and the whole of chapter 6; reprinted in this volume, chapter 13, PERCEPTIVE EQUILIBRIUM: LITERARY THEORY AND ETHICAL THEORY). Conant's account of the misunderstandings to which Nietzsche's perfectionism has been subject, as seen from a point of view which Nietzsche would have taken to be that of the moralism of moral philosophy, is relevant to all the questions I have examined. It is particularly relevant, too, to an important distinction made by O'Neill between the exercise of moral agency on the one hand, and moral development and moral education on the other (O'Neill 1989, 176). Her understanding of that distinction is precisely what is called into question by perfectionism as described in Conant's essay. The relevance of this issue to James's understanding of moral life cannot be underestimated. See Hardy's description of *The Ambassadors* as a kind of *Bildungsroman* (Hardy 1970, 28). Any attempt to separate Strether's real doings as a moral agent from his moral education and development (taking his enhanced capacity to appreciate and understand to belong to the latter) would again impose the point of view associated with moralism. Cf. also Murdoch's description of M's inner progress (Murdoch 1970, 21–3).

Bibliography

Baier, Annette (1993). "Moralism and Cruelty: Reflections on Hume and Kant," *Ethics* 103: 436–57.

Baron, Marcia (1988). "Was Effi Briest a Victim of Kantian Morality?" *Philosophy and Literature* 12: 95–113.

Conant, James (2001). "Nietzsche's Perfectionism: A Reading of Schopenhauer as Educator," in Richard Schacht, ed., *Nietzsche's Postmoralism* (Cambridge: Cambridge University Press).

Diamond, Cora (1997). "Moral Difference and Distances: Some Questions," in Lilli Alanen, Sara Heiämaa, and Thomas Wallgren, eds., *Commonality and Particularity in Ethics* (Basingstoke: Macmillan), 197–234.

Edel, Leon (1978). *Henry James: The Untried Years, 1843–1870* (New York: Avon).

Gaita, Rai (1991). "The Moralization of Good and Evil," in Alanen, Heinämaa, and Wallgren, *Commonality and Particularity in Ethics*.

Goldberg, S. L. (1993). *Agents and Lives: Moral Thinking in Literature* (Cambridge: Cambridge University Press).

Hardy, Barbara (1970). *The Moral Art of Dickens* (New York: Oxford University Press).

Hume, David (1902). *Enquiry Concerning the Principles of Morals* (Oxford: Clarendon Press).

Ibsen, Henrik (1961). *Pillars of Society. Hedda Gabler and Three Other Plays*, trans. Michael Meyer (Garden City: Anchor), 15–124.

Ibsen, Henrik (1964). *Ghosts and Other Plays*, trans. Peter Watts (Harmondsworth: Penguin), 19–102.

James, Henry (*CM*) (1987). *Henry James, The Critical Muse*, ed. Roger Gard (Harmondsworth: Penguin).

James, Henry (1960). *The Ambassadors* (New York: New American Library).

James, Henry (*EU*) (1964). *The Europeans* (Harmondsworth: Penguin).

James, Henry (*WM*) (1966). *What Maisie Knew* (Harmondsworth: Penguin).

James, Henry (1969). "The Author of 'Beltraffio,' " in Morton Danwen Zabel, ed., *Eight Tales from the Major Phase: "In the Cage" and Others* (New York: Norton), 29–78.

James, Henry (1978). *The Tragic Muse* (Harmondsworth: Penguin).

James, Henry (*BO*) (1980). *The Bostonians* (New York: New American Library).

James, Henry (1986). *The Wings of the Dove* (Harmondsworth: Penguin).

James, Henry, Sr. (1850). *Moralism and Christianity: Or, Man's Experience and Destiny* (New York: Redfield).

James, William (1960). *Varieties of Religious Experience* (London: Collins).

Kant, Immanuel (1956). *Groundwork of the Metaphysics of Morals*, trans. H. J. Paton (London: Hutchison).

Kant, Immanuel (1960). *Religion Within the Limits of Reason Alone* (New York: Harper).

Korsgaard, Christine M. (1996). *Creating the Kingdom of Ends* (Cambridge: Cambridge University Press).

Krook, Dorothea (1967). *The Ordeal of Consciousness in Henry James* (Cambridge: Cambridge University Press).

Krook, Dorothea (1959). *Three Traditions of Moral Thought* (Cambridge: Cambridge University Press).

Levenson, Michael (1991). *Modernism and the Fate of Individuality: Character and Novelistic Form from Conrad to Woolf* (Cambridge: Cambridge University Press).

Murdoch, Iris (1956). "Vision and Choice in Morality," *Proceedings of the Aristotelian Society* supp. vol. 30: 32–58.

Murdoch, Iris (1970). *The Sovereignty of Good* (London: Routledge).
Nussbaum, Martha (1990). *Love's Knowledge: Essays on Philosophy and Literature* (New York: Oxford University Press).
O'Neill, Onora (1989). *Constructions of Reason: Explorations of Kant's Practical Philosophy* (Cambridge: Cambridge University Press).
Orwell, George (1954). "The Art of Donald McGill," in *A Collection of Essays* (Garden City: Doubleday), 111–23.
Richards, D. A. J. (1971). *A Theory of Reasons for Action* (Oxford: Clarendon Press).
Williams, Bernard (1981). *Moral Luck: Philosophical Papers, 1973–1980* (Cambridge: Cambridge University Press).

15

Literature and the Idea of Morality

EILEEN JOHN

When philosophers bring literature and morality together, it is often to ask, roughly, how morally charged content has an impact on literary value. Would morally good or morally reprehensible content have the power to make a literary work better or worse?[1] I don't think there is a general answer to that kind of question, though it is worth asking with respect to each work whether its moral status matters to its literary value, and if so, how.[2] In thinking about that kind of impact, either generally or in particular cases, we are thinking about the literary value of moral value, that is, how the latter feeds into the former. I note that, on this approach, moral value is in some sense left alone, treated as something that contributes morally, and the question then is to see if that moral contribution makes a difference to a literary project. I am interested here in bringing literature and morality together by asking a somewhat different question concerning the literary role of morality itself – does the moral domain have non-moral or not-merely-moral features that are artistically relevant to literary projects?[3] That is, my focus is not on the moral value of a work that emerges from its content and that then may contribute to a work's literary value, but on whether and how the presence and presentation of morality can be exploited, as it were, for literary purposes. What is the literary potential of the moral domain, aside from the specifically moral contribution that may be made by the content of a work?

Approaching the literary import of morality in this way opens up the possibility that literature does not just "leave morality alone," but shapes or presents the moral domain with literary goals in mind. If that kind of artistically motivated shaping happens, as seems likely, it suggests complications for views of literature as a prompter or vehicle of moral illumination or education. Rather, morality in literature may sometimes need to be acknowledged as morality-serving-the-needs-of-literature. The significance of that recognition is not straightforward. If we take the loosely Nietzschean idea that morality is a matter of variously driven human conceptions in every context in which it plays a role, there is no immediate reason to think that the literary context is an unusually problematic context. We may, in fact, have better resources in the literary context for recognizing the pressures on construal and presentation of morality, and perhaps we can temper what we make of morality in literature accordingly.

A Companion to the Philosophy of Literature, First Edition. Edited by Garry L. Hagberg and Walter Jost.
© 2010 John Wiley & Sons Ltd. Published 2015 by John Wiley & Sons, Ltd.

And there are a number of other possibilities that complicate what might be said on this issue: literary shapings of morality may not be substantive enough to have much impact, or literary goals that affect the presentation of morality may tend to coincide with morally educative goals, or we might take a literarily shaped conception of morality to be educative because it is flawed (e.g., as an exaggeration or caricature can be illuminating).

In general, taking literary goals to affect the presentation of morality does not directly support any particular objections against viewing literature as morally educative. At the end of the chapter, I will return briefly to this issue to sketch how we might recognize problematic kinds of literary shaping of morality. My hope, however, is that thinking along these lines will not lead to dismissal of literature as a source of morally significant experience, but will add complexity to the way we understand the moral interest of literature. We can see literary practice as having something at stake in conceptions of morality and as interestingly immersed in how morality is experienced and understood. We can also look at morality from a funny angle – e.g., why does moral import help to make a story exciting? – where I think this angle has some philosophical relevance. Philosophers in recent decades, following out some of Nietzsche's concerns, have taken an interest in what might be called the "personality" and presence of morality, as in questions of how stern and pure it is, how encompassing and relentless its demands.[4] The suggestion in this philosophical work is that these aspects of morality are as important to the worth and legitimacy of morality as whether it can provide substantive guidance in a life. Thinking about the literary potential of morality leads us into ideas about the presence and "personality" of morality, and once these are on the table I will return to consider them in light of some of these philosophical ideas about morality.

Let me begin with some very basic thoughts about why literary practice would be able to work to advantage with the moral domain. We could say that literature and morality share their central stuff, the lives of human beings, so there is at the least a convenient overlap of subject matter. This makes morality more promising for literature than, say, the domains of astronomy and horticulture. However, if we try to follow out this thought either to explain why literature does not take the behavior of stars and planets, or the life of plants, as its central stuff, or to explain why morality is more promising for literature than domains such as medicine and sports, which do centrally concern human life, we may end up with an unhelpful or circular collapsing of the concerns of the literary and the moral – "planets and plants, and sports and medicine, just don't have enough of the morally interesting significance that matters to literature."

One possibility is that there is indeed a collapsing of literary and moral concerns – perhaps literature is constitutively engaged with moral attention to human life. Does literature need the moral domain? I do not think that literature as a whole does, though it is plausible that specific forms and corresponding interpretive practices do.[5] Roughly, I think literature springs from a more general impulse – to explore the possibilities for categorization and evaluation of experience – and that makes moral categorization and evaluation just one approach of many that literature can explore.

But I would also say that there is a challenging kind of closeness between literature and the moral domain, and I want to consider why, even though literature does *not* need the moral domain, there are nonetheless reasons for literature to gravitate toward moral concerns.

Remaining at the very basic level, the facts that (1) morality is indeed an evaluative domain, and that (2) it in various ways makes perspective important, provide two overarching reasons why morality has literary potential. The evaluative aspect of morality matters in part for the fairly brute reason that evaluation is interesting to us. It takes us out of the business of just registering things and into the potentially controversial, more challenging business of having evaluative criteria and of appreciating how well or badly things fare on them. Evaluation can of course be rather standardized and automatic, but it can also be something we actively, thoughtfully do. If literary works generate moral concerns, then they can take advantage of the potential for evaluative controversy and engagement. Involving evaluation does not distinguish morality from many other domains, such as sports and medicine, so more would need to be said to explain the particular literary value of morality on this score (a few points made below are relevant to this). The fact that morality makes perspective important means roughly that the moral domain foregrounds questions of "where to stand" in relation to human life, and questions of which informational, conceptual, emotional resources to bring to bear. Answers to those questions are often controversial (e.g., should I be impartial and fully informed? emotionally sensitive and attentive to particulars?), but a common assumption is that morality asks us to take up a perspective that requires some training or switching from perspectives that come, it seems, more naturally to us. I take the centrality of perspective to morality to be especially congenial for an art form like literature that has so much capacity for representation and change of perspective, and that aims to make questions of perspective – what are the possible places to stand in experience – have weight and interest for an audience. Briefly, then, we can set up the literary promise of morality by pointing to it as an evaluative and perspectivally sensitive domain.

To move beyond these basic ideas means plunging into the mass of idiosyncratic, historically and culturally diverse ways in which morality is presented and functions in literary works. I cannot say that I have a respectable methodology in approaching this territory, since my approach depends primarily on the happenstance of my own experience with literature, but I can illustrate my ideas with examples from fairly well-known authors and works from the late nineteenth- and twentieth-century Western literary tradition, and I am thus thinking about how morality is presented, and how it serves literary concerns, in that particular cultural tradition. Three ideas explained below are offered as routes into the phenomena and not as providing an exhaustive and settled account: (1) morality demands an evaluative "double take," (2) morality is not a game, and (3) morality is pragmatic about imperfection. The general goal is to see how these conceptions of morality can further literary goals.

The idea that morality asks for an evaluative "double take" gestures at the way in which literary works set up moral judgment as a form of complex judgment, one that asks for more than one perspective to be taken on situations or persons. Readers may, for instance, be led to a painfully acute awareness of a character's failings, so that we have grounds for judging the character negatively, for allotting blame. But often we are not allowed to leave it at that, as the work also gives us the resources to see the failings as understandable, perhaps as reflecting a social and psychological context in which some human tendencies are encouraged and some discouraged, or in which human nature is put under severe pressures. Or the failings may not be made exactly understandable, but they may appear to call for acknowledgment as human and to deserve some form of compassion. This second take often won't eliminate the bases for blame and negative moral judgment, but it will add another layer of non-judgmental response. So moral matters show up in literature as calling both for appraisal and for non-appraising understanding and acknowledgment. This presents moral matters as having the scope for this double take, as involving both the character traits and responsibilities of individuals *and* the larger context of human tendencies and social constraints that influences desires and character and generally provides the conditions for human development. It also presents moral judgment as putting pressure on the judge, in this case the reader, not to be a mere issuer of condemnation. Someone else's moral failings are not things I can fully distance myself from, but should view as possibly shared by me, or as influenced by a social world that I help to sustain, or as making manifest the possibilities of my human kind.

Consider, for instance, Forster's character Henry Wilcox in *Howards End*, who receives a fierce and well-deserved moral rebuke, and yet whose hypocrisy and self-serving obtuseness are made understandable and are framed in a larger context that allows us to step back from the morally critical stance. Or consider Chekhov's *The Seagull*, which works simultaneously to expose moral flaws and to expose the unsatisfying, stultifying conditions of life that promote cruelty, jealousy, and self-absorption. Let me illustrate the double take with one small example that I offer as paradigmatic of the phenomenon, using a brief scene in Edith Wharton's novel *The House of Mirth*. The protagonist, society belle Lily Bart, is leaving a young man's apartment, where she has done nothing but have tea and conversation, and yet from which she would rather not be seen leaving.

> There was no one in sight, however, but a charwoman who was scrubbing the stairs. Her own stout person and its surrounding implements took up so much room that Lily, to pass her, had to gather up her skirts and brush against the wall. As she did so, the woman paused in her work and looked up curiously, resting her clenched red fists on the wet cloth she had just drawn from her pail. She had a broad sallow face, slightly pitted with small-pox, and thin straw-coloured hair through which her scalp shone unpleasantly.
>
> "I beg your pardon," said Lily, intending by her politeness to convey a criticism of the other's manner. (Wharton 1969/1905, 13)

Here we have an encounter that has minor, incidental status within the plot. It is a momentary exchange early on in the story, but it has some weight for the reader partly because it is one of the first indications of the protagonist's limitations – she is not able to avoid defensiveness and uses a marker of social status to assert her superiority. We might have a slight bristle of distaste for Lily, as she insinuates that the other woman has no right to stare at her and as she uses polite words insincerely. The brief interaction has certain kinds of potential that we experience as morally significant: there could be sincerity, respect across social class lines, or appreciation of each other's vulnerability. In this example, none of this is achieved, and, while this is also due to the charwoman, whose curiosity probably is aggressive in this context, the focus of our interest in the novel is Lily, and it seems we gather a small bit of morally critical data about her – she could not react in the moment without an effort to claim superiority.

The reader is set up for a double take on this in at least three ways. Two of them work through taking up Lily's point of view on the cleaning woman. I may have a brief encounter with my own desire not to be humanly accessible to the person with bucket and wet rag on the stairs. If I experience that distaste, in the description of the clenched fists, shining scalp, and so on, then the passage has caught me in a morally vulnerable position as well as Lily – I experience my own momentary recoil and cannot feel comfortable or superior about my own impulses. Second, the reader is likely to be attached enough to Lily at this point to feel anxiety for her sake about being seen coming from a man's apartment – we have an empathetic experience of the pressures on her not to diverge, even quite innocently, from rigid social norms of respectability. Third, we also have a view of Lily that is not fully hers and that takes into account precisely those circumstances that encourage her to behave ungraciously in this encounter. She has a precarious perch in a very restrictive, unforgiving social world, and it makes sense that her first instinct is likely to be to defend her status. It would be quite impressive if she had the kind of flexibility that would allow her to know herself as a vulnerable member of her social class in one moment, and to feel some comradeship, kindness, or openness to the charwoman the next. In that moment she cannot imagine how far she herself could (and will) sink, and she cannot find a footing with the woman that would allow her to be genuinely polite. But we can easily see why she is unable to find that footing – her social context only gives her reason to isolate herself and to fear the woman's stare. So I think we are steered very carefully by the novel toward the understanding, acknowledging response to the scene as well.

Two examples of a somewhat different type, in which the double take is called for even though we may not reach understanding, involve the central criminal figures in Graham Greene's *Brighton Rock* and Flannery O'Connor's "A Good Man Is Hard to Find." Each of these works presents a shockingly brutal character who doesn't repent or redeem himself, and for whom I don't think we can say that the brutality makes sense, in the way that Lily's bit of rudeness makes sense in her situation. Nonetheless, I think these works make it hard to appraise these characters from a safe distance and to reject them as inhuman monsters. This is partly made possible by the fact that characters within the stories attempt some closeness with the killers, and their efforts, though doomed, appear to show strength and possibly even wisdom – they are not dismissed as unworthy or deluded efforts. But there is also the force of seeing that the brutal characters have suffered and have struggled to fit into the world – we are able at least to acknowledge how hard it would be for them to fit in (as is signaled by the killer's nickname, the "Misfit," in the O'Connor story).

I hope the literary potential of this is clear. If moral judgment is presented in this way, as involving both clear-headed appraisal and non-critical understanding or acknowledgment, then its complex substance will support various kinds of complexity of representation and response. The work will be able to bind together different layers of description and explanation in asking us to see the circumstances from different perspectives and with different categories and questions in mind (e.g., what kind of person would do this, and what kind of world would make this possible?). We can be engaged in an interesting way if we are asked to take up the different perspectives and are led to keep our own moral vulnerability in view. Here perhaps we can see a way of distinguishing the evaluative practices of sports and medicine, which seem to offer less scope for this kind of complexity: evaluations of athletic performance and health can take many factors into account, but they tend to feed into a unified judgment or perhaps a contested judgment involving factors at the same level of evaluation. They are less likely to leave us with perspectives that temper each other as the differing perspectives invoked by literary moral judgment do. The literary presentation of the moral "double (or multiple) take" projects the sense that moral judgment is not a safely distant seeking of verdicts, but a plumbing of human circumstances that will issue both in praise and blame and in a non-righteous understanding of our praiseworthy and blameworthy lives. The question of whether this is a coherent approach to moral judgment is not necessarily broached or worried about within the literary context; it seems rather that the double take is presented as morally called for, even if it does not allow us to settle clearly on a reconciliation of the perspectives. That unclarity and the possible failure of reconciliation might look like defects in a philosophical theory of moral judgment, but they are not literarily negative, to the extent that they allow for experiences of unfolding, deepening, and reversal as Aristotle might put it.

I will sum up the second idea about how the moral domain is presented in literature by saying that, in the literary context, morality is not a game. Various things might be suggested by this, but I want to focus on the notion of morality as non-game-like in the following sense: morality is not an optional, bounded activity whose constraints apply only to those who have knowingly committed themselves to engaging in the activity. On this construal, we know when we are and are not playing a game, there are identifiable intentions and actions that mark that one is playing the game, and certain circumstances count as doing well in the game. If we choose to stay in the non-game-playing conditions, then we will never count as playing the game. The idea is that morality in literature is presented as contrasting with this game-paradigm because there is no way to contain or demarcate moral relevance. There is a kind of ever-present possibility that a person's intentions, actions, dispositions, and traits will be morally relevant and morally assessable. The people involved in a situation may not be in the best position to notice or understand the moral significance of their involvement, and they might even be actively hoping to reject moral concerns. But that is no protection against the possibility of moral significance emerging and providing a basis for moral challenge and assessment. So, while not everything will have moral significance, you cannot predict confidently what will and will not have it.[6]

One might wonder whether it is plausible that morality should have this ever-present possibility of application: does the literary context suggest any explanation for this? I am not sure, but one might think that the literary context points to human beings' prodigious ability to attach value to things and to interpret things in creative ways. If moral concerns to some degree track what matters and is meaningful to people, and what can count as a harm and a benefit to us, and we are prodigious and creative in determining harms, benefits, and significance, then there is no reliable way to limit moral concerns. One can read the Lily Bart scene mentioned above, for instance, as manifesting this conception of morality as non-game-like. Passing someone on the stair would not seem like an obvious locus of moral significance, so it has a quality of coming out of nowhere, of not being part of a recognized moral activity, yet nonetheless presenting a moral challenge. Certainly the agents involved do not choose to participate in it as a morally testing moment. Lily would like to dismiss it as negligible, a briefly worrying and irritating moment in her day, and while we don't have enough evidence of the charwoman's perspective, it could be that she notes it mainly as breaking the tedium of cleaning the stairs and doesn't consider herself as having been hostile or threatening to Lily. Lily's effort to deal strategically with the situation, using polite words to convey criticism, signals her participation in what could be called a social game, where etiquette can be used to position oneself socially and to defend one's status. And that defensive move contrasts with whatever might be a morally more acceptable way to address the woman on the stair. This hinted-at contrast (the strategic social game versus the unforeseen moral demand) illustrates a way in which works of literature convey and take advantage of the view of morality as not a game; morality shows up as an interesting counterweight to our game-like commitments. I'll refer to two examples that illustrate this use of morality rather explicitly.

One is the Hemingway story, "Hills Like White Elephants," which presents a conversation between a man and a woman who are waiting for a train to take them to the city, so that the woman can have an unnamed "operation," presumably an abortion. The woman alternates between trying to keep up normal social chatter and pressing the man to think about whether the abortion will make any difference to them. In this passage, the man speaks first.

> Well, let's try and have a fine time.
> All right, I was trying. I said the mountains looked like white elephants. Wasn't that bright?
> That was bright.
> I wanted to try this new drink. That's all we do, isn't it – look at things and try new drinks?
> I guess so.
> The girl looked across at the hills.
> They're lovely hills, she said. They don't really look like white elephants. I just meant the coloring of their skin through the trees. (Hemingway 1938/1927, 274)

The story sets up the life of looking at things, trying new drinks, and making bright remarks as something like a game with clear boundaries and goals, and with a wonderful shallowness of concern. She retracts and reinterprets her remark about the hills, as if in an attempt to speak outside their game. The abortion decision prompts this character, if not the other, to feel that, while they appear to have no serious commitments, a serious consequence is accruing anyway. The story does not appear to be about the abortion being wrong but rather about the characters' ability to experience things as having moral weight at all. The woman now implicitly claims to know that they have such weight, which in the story is highlighted via the contrast with the life of mere looking-drinking-talking. The moral domain is there as a persistent challenge, undermining their assumed freedom and ownership of the world, whether or not they acknowledge its force.

A second example comes from the Borges story, "Tlön, Uqbar, Orbis Tertius." On a first reading I myself did not take this story as having much or any moral import. It involves a nicely mysterious Borgesian, bibliographic quest that leads to exposure of a grand conspiracy and experiment in philosophical idealism. In the "Postscript" at the end of the story, we find out that the experiment has won over the world; the mentally sustained realm of Tlön has carried the day. The story is intellectually playful, with the tone of a true-life scholarly espionage tale. The interest seems to lie in the imaginative and funny exploration of what it would be like to experiment with idealism (how would grammar be affected, what would count as a paradox, would the past be malleable), with the beautifully absurd consequence that people thoroughly abandon their attachment to the real. The passages that signal a further kind of reading of the story are primarily those that date the events. The "Postscript" is dated 1947, and it includes a passage mentioning, for instance, that an aristocrat had her valuables shipped from France to Argentina in 1942. The following passage is dated 1944:

> Almost immediately, reality "caved in" at more than one point. The truth is, it wanted to cave in. Ten years ago, any symmetry, any system with an appearance of order – dialectical materialism, anti-Semitism, Nazism – could spellbind and hypnotize mankind. How could the world not fall under the sway of Tlön, how could it not yield to the vast and minutely detailed evidence of an ordered planet? . . . Contact with Tlön, the *habit* of Tlön, has disintegrated this world. Spellbound by Tlön's rigor, humanity has forgotten, and continues to forget, that it is the rigor of chess masters, not of angels. (Borges 1998/1941, 81)

First, let me note that the reader will thus have the years of World War II and the Holocaust in mind as the time in which the "caving in" of reality occurred, but the world-absorbing war is not mentioned in the story. At a basic interpretive level, it is unclear how to take this: is it a story about the war not happening because people got caught up in a philosophically extreme fantasy, perhaps precisely to avoid facing the reality that was leading to war? Or a story in which the war happened (and, for instance, led aristocrats to flee to Argentina) but wasn't counted as worth mentioning by the narrator? Would the war be not worth mentioning because it was too obvious and overwhelming to need mention? Or because, ironically, something more dangerous – the embrace of idealism – was going on? Or is the story a kind of fable in which the war *is* an escapist fantasy that disintegrates real history? Without settling on a reading, we can say that the story offers the embrace of Tlön's alternative to reality as either a fully entwined companion to or a parallel evasion of war. One way or another, turning to fascism or Tlön or both, something massively destructive occurs, and the story asks us to understand the destruction as partly a matter of philosophical tendencies (e.g., a carelessness about language and history; wanting order and rigor, no matter what the substance of the order is; wanting to sidestep material constraints). The quotation above ties the philosophical impulse to a game, to the rigor of chess, and thus sets up that contrast between the morally demanding reality and a game that can give us something relatively limited, simple, and controllable. This contrast can also be enacted, in a sense, by readers like me who are caught up in the philosophical fantasy and lose contact with an important reality. As with the case of passing someone on the stair, I did not expect that adopting philosophical idealism could count as morally significant. The story lets me revel in the pleasures of an intricate, inventive tale, not expecting it to turn into a story about humankind's delusory, destructive, humanity-denying tendencies. Moral evaluation shows up here as asking something of me beyond curiosity for story and intellectual playfulness, so the story gets me to experience my own impulses toward game-like order and control, and frames those impulses as distractions from moral concern.

I have pointed to a few examples in which I think the moral domain is presented in part via a contrast with something game-like. This means that it functions, in that contrast, as a kind of inescapable horizon, an ongoing possibility for challenge and assessment that cannot be limited and predicted. What might be the literary value of such a horizon? One might think that an inescapable possibility of moral relevance would be a drag on an imaginative work – why wouldn't it be a sobering, relentless, boring element? Certainly appeals to the moral domain can have that dreary kind of literary impact. But that would have to do with the details of how the moral domain was used in a given work. In fact, I think that having morality show up as not a game is an invaluable dramatic device in many works of literature. It is needed so that there is something to be reckoned with, some evaluatively substantive project that won't go away just because characters (or readers) want it to. This does not mean that the moral project has to be given priority within the work, but if it has a kind of implacable presence, then it can serve to play off of and highlight the meaning of other evaluative schemes; for example, pursuits of hedonistic pleasure, social control, aesthetic devotion, blithe egoism, and even nihilism show up as interesting choices or commitments with this other evaluative possibility in the background. If every evaluative scheme were presented as optional, its relevance hanging on whether anyone committed themselves to it, the literary work would have a harder time sustaining some of the tensions that drive many stories. If morality is presented in contrast to preoccupying games of various kinds, then it also can involve us in a shifting of perspective: we try to understand the game but also try to understand moral perspectives that don't fit within the framework of the game. The element of unpredictability – that moral relevance can emerge in unexpected contexts – is a further literary advantage, for it can support characters' having morally revelatory experiences and can help readers be surprised with moral meaning.

Allow me, then, briefly to consider one last idea, which is that, in literary presentation, morality is shown as pragmatic about imperfection. This means roughly that morality as an evaluative and guiding practice is presented as being at home with imperfection and working with it constructively. Given imperfect people and conditions, there needs to be a great deal of flexibility about what can count as a morally acceptable path through life. This can work as a sort of softening companion to the notion that morality is not a game, since the persistent possibility of moral relevance is not tied to rigid expectations about how to fare well in moral terms. The embrace of the imperfect allows for a contrast between that kind of pragmatic morality and a morality of rigid expectations that appears unrealistic and insensitive by contrast. Such a dogmatic morality (e.g., a morality dictated by strict religious or social conventions or abstract principles) can be played off against what appears as the more sensitive, intuitive moral practice that adapts itself to the unpromising human material at hand. We might think, for instance, of the plot of Hawthorne's *The Scarlet Letter*, or of an anti-hero such as Yossarian in *Catch-22*.

I will illustrate this more fully by referring to Ibsen's *The Wild Duck*, which takes this kind of contrast as an explicit theme. One character, Gregers Werle, presses the others to accept the "claim of the ideal," which is a stern, unbending claim on us to live by principles, with perfect honesty being the principle that Gregers pushes most adamantly. Various other characters discuss and criticize his ideal, and the progress of the play itself portrays it as deeply culpable folly to orient one's life around such an ideal.

> **Relling:** Listen, Mr Werle Junior. I've a strong suspicion you're still carrying that "claim of the ideal" unabridged in your back pocket.
> **Gregers:** I carry it in my heart.
> **Relling:** Well, wherever you have the bloody thing I'm damned if I'll let you blackmail anyone with it as long as I'm in this house. (Ibsen 1961, 3.84)

The world of the play is populated with highly imperfect people, but some of them appear to counter the claim of the ideal through the ways they have found to make an imperfect life work as well as possible. Hjalmar, the man who falls briefly and tragically under the sway of the ideal, is at his best when he is avoiding work, playing the flute for his family, and helping his father escape into a fantasy world. Hjalmar's wife Gina sustains a number of lies successfully, pretending that her husband is the breadwinner, that he is a promising inventor, and that he is the father of her child, and it is essential to the viability and lovingness of her family that she maintains these lies. Of the models on offer in the play, it is plausible to say that Gina is the most morally admirable, as she has made a home and nurtured loving relations, despite pressures that lead to her various pretences.

Now, her efforts might be considered too compromised, too imperfect, to count as morally admirable. They certainly do not seem to work toward a kingdom of ends, in which people are respected as free to exercise their rational wills (consider Gina's treating her husband more like a child than as a responsible agent, and meanwhile subordinating herself, disguising her own talents). Or one might say rather that the play, in rendering her as admirable, is endorsing ideals, say, ideals of home and of love, and thus endorsing some form of moral perfectionism. However, I think we can see the play finding middle ground here in showing the moral achievement of a character like Gina to be embedded in, and infected by, the compromised, imperfect conditions of human nature and her social world. Gina figures out what will work well enough, where doing that depends on meeting emotional and social goals that are not endorsable from the point of view of an "ideal" (treating one's spouse as a child cannot be an ideal but it may be worth doing). Love and home in this view are valued, but they are not ideals, I would say, because they have to come to life in these imperfect conditions.[7]

Returning again to the question of literary value, how would this way of conceiving of moral achievement, as embedded in compromised, imperfect conditions, lend itself to literary aims? One answer is that it allows moral evaluation to show up as sensitive to the complex conditions of life, and it makes moral achievement something that can be found, surprisingly, in lives that might not look morally pleasing on superficial inspection. To the extent that literature aims to show the evaluative possibilities of life in an interesting way, this moral complexity, the way in which opportunities for moral value emerge from messy conditions, has literary potential. The scope for messiness and exploration of compromised conditions that is available in a form like the novel suggests that this conception of morality is especially promising for that form. Conceiving of morality as a matter of clear, unbending imposition of principles would, arguably, mean that morality was less congenial as substance for literary works engaged with portraying problematic complexity.

I have here tried to articulate some ideas about morality that play a role in literary experience and have made some suggestions about their literary value. Although the discussion thus far has framed these ideas as belonging in the literary context, I take them to be part of the culture in which we experience and reflect on the nature of morality more broadly. Their literary context does not give these ideas special authority, as representing what morality is for us or how we should conceive of it, but to the extent that they have some compelling power in literary representation, they seem not to be negligible either. I think they are worth considering in relation to philosophical claims about morality; so I will make a few connections and comparisons here. Richard Wollheim makes the point that philosophical practice tends to seek unity and cohesion, even with respect to something like the moral domain that might, in reality, resist unified understanding (Wollheim 1984, 197, 199). On that basis, one might think it worthwhile for philosophers to take stock of how morality is represented in unsystematic sources such as literature, to get a sense of the possible variety of conceptions of morality.

The notion of morality as not a game, but as offering an ever-present possibility of challenge and assessment, is related to Bernard Williams's critical view of morality as inescapable (Williams 2006/1985). Williams characterizes what he calls "the morality system" as putting obligation at the center of an "intimidating structure." In this system, moral obligation is inescapable: it applies universally, obligating people no matter what their desires and commitments might be. "[T]here is nowhere outside the system" (178), and there is a tendency for moral obligation "to dominate life altogether" (182). Morality makes it hard to find "room for morally indifferent actions" (181). The notion that I have tried to isolate from literary works is a form of inescapability, but it is a weaker notion. It coincides with Williams's notion that morality "applies to people even if they don't want it to" (178), but it does not mean that, from the moral perspective, we are constantly to be assessed as meeting or failing to meet moral obligations. For one thing, there is no assumption built in that moral concern must take the form of moral obligation, but further, it allows that many or most aspects of human life will be morally insignificant. The inescapability comes in rather in the idea that one must regard moral significance as a live possibility; one cannot be fully confident of not being morally engaged in some way. Williams also emphasizes that morality embodies an ideal of *purity*, as it isolates itself from empirical influences in order to seek a pure basis for allotting praise and blame. On this view it works with extremes and stark contrasts. "The attitude that leads it to emphasize all these contrasts can be labeled its *purity*" (195). I think the notions of morality as asking for a double take involving both appraisal and understanding, and as having a pragmatic approach to imperfection, suggest conceptions of morality that do not embody ideals of purity. Gina's achievement in *The Wild Duck*, for instance, does not seem well captured by saying that she has met her obligations and thereby deserves praise. It's not clear what someone in her situation could be obligated to do at all; none of the choices seems obviously a matter of duty, so our admiration for her seems to rest on some other basis. None of this is to say that Williams is wrong about how morality is construed within the philosophical tradition, following Kant in particular; it is just to suggest that there are other conceptions of morality at work in our culture that would not call for quite the same criticisms that he lodges against "the morality system."

Martha Nussbaum, largely in agreement with Williams about the problematic nature of the philosophically entrenched conception of morality, has offered the notion of the moral *adventure* as a corrective. Her concern with this idea in *Love's Knowledge* is entwined with her argument for acknowledging the limitations of traditional philosophical activity, as in the following:

> It is this idea that human deliberation is constantly an *adventure* of the personality, undertaken against terrific odds and among frightening mysteries, *and* that this is, in fact, the source of much of its beauty and richness, that texts written in a traditional philosophical style have the most insuperable difficulty conveying to us. If our moral lives are "stories" in which mystery and risk play a central and a valuable role, then it may well seem that the "intelligent report" of those lives requires the abilities and techniques of the teller of stories. (Nussbaum 1990, 142)

Some of the ideas and values associated with the moral adventure in her discussion are curiosity, surprise, mystery, risk, improvisation, creativity, and heroism. On this view, the moral domain offers challenges that we meet in the right spirit if we embrace them as helping to frame our lives as adventures and as asking for risk-taking, openness to the unknown, and creative improvisation under pressure. The idea of morality as not a game relates to the idea of the moral adventure in a complicated way. The ever-present risk of moral entanglement that characterizes morality-as-not-a-game seems to be another way of saying that morality engages us in a risky, surprising project. Should we call that an adventure? I'm not sure. I stop short of calling it an adventure because of the tension between being an adventure and not being a game. The moral adventure notion introduces an element of enjoyment of risk, surprise, and good stories that would link the moral domain with domains that we choose to participate in at our pleasure. However, the notion of morality as an adventure seems to be another conception of morality that would have good literary potential (albeit, I think, interestingly different literary potential than the notion of morality as not a game). In any case, in linking the ideas grounded in literary works to those offered by philosophers, my aim is not to show that the ones found in literature are right or philosophically superior. But I think that the ideas found in literature are relevant to how people who soak up this literary tradition experience and understand morality, and for that reason these ideas are worth exploring. We should not assume that explicit philosophical theorizing about morality exhausts our conceptions of morality and we should be open to the complications that may result from consulting literature as a resource.

This leads me to a few concluding thoughts about attending to literature for purposes of reflecting on morality. We can note, first, that works of literature such as *The Wild Duck* are often quite interested in exploring the dangers of conceptions of morality, as are philosophers like Williams, Nietzsche, and others. Literature is one of the sites in which ideas about morality are exposed as problematic, as forming evaluative schemes that are very easy for us to misuse. I have been arguing here, however, that literary practice also takes great advantage of morality as a resource for creating compelling, complex, dramatic, engaging works. With that in mind, it's clear that literary practice has goals and values that could motivate certain kinds of attention to and representation of morality, while screening out others. Very crudely, if the basic artistic goal of literature is to be interesting, then that is some pressure on literary artists to portray the moral domain as an interesting one. Now, what would make morality show up as interesting? As the above discussion suggests, it seems, for instance, that a systematic moral code, setting up a starkly clear form of moral judgment, issuing neatly in praise and blame, would not necessarily be all that interesting. Just as philosophers have goals that might lead them to gravitate toward simpler, more unified accounts of morality, the practice of literature has pressures on it that are likely to influence how it lets morality show up in literary forms. One possible example of influence is suggested by the idea of morality as requiring a double take. The literary cases I mentioned illustrated the phenomena of readers being encouraged not to stop with judgment of moral failing, but to pursue a broader understanding of the conditions that may explain the failing. It seems that if morality asks for a double take, it should ask for it with respect to moral approval as well, but it is not obvious to me that literary works encourage a double take with respect to moral praise as commonly as they do for moral blame. That is, characters' morally admirable lives are often experienced as those individuals' moral achievements rather than as achievements that emerge from some broader explanatory context. If that asymmetry is indeed a pattern, it might be explained more by a literary interest in portraying individual achievement against the odds than by a consistent view of the complexity of moral understanding. Or, more broadly, we could expect literature to present morality as rooted in the intimate, personal level of affairs, rather than giving it an institutional, societal, impersonal basis, if the latter basis does not lend itself as well to compelling literary portrayal. So, while my view is that literary presentations of morality are a valuable resource for understanding what morality can and does mean for us, it is also important to consider this resource with the literary context and its distinctive goals and values in mind.

Notes

This paper benefited from comments at the Universities of Bergen, Hull, York, and Sussex, and at the London Aesthetics Forum. I especially thank Paul Davies, Katerina Deligiorgi, Tom Hall, Peter Lamarque, Kathleen Lennon, Marie McGinn, Julia Peters, Ole Martin Skilleas, David Smith, Kathleen Stock, and Hong Yu Wong.

1 See Carroll 1996; Devereaux 1998; Gaut 1998; Jacobson 1997.
2 See Jacobson 2006; John 2006.
3 Roman Bonzon (2003) is also interested in how moral content works aesthetically; see his discussion for attention to how specific moral content is experienced aesthetically in a way that allows it to contribute to artistic value.
4 See Williams 2006/1985; Wollheim 1984; Taylor 1995.
5 With respect specifically to the category of narrative art, Noel Carroll has argued for a pervasive, and possibly constitutive engagement with moral concerns: "Reading a novel . . . is itself generally a moral activity insofar as reading narrative literature typically involves us in a continuous process of moral judgment" (Carroll 1998, 145). Iris Murdoch said, "Life is soaked in the moral, literature is soaked in the moral. . . . The author's moral judgement is in the air which the reader breathes" (Carroll 1998, 27). Various examples have been suggested to me, some narrative but others not, to contest the claim for literature overall: love poetry, imagist poetry, Greek tragedy (with *Antigone* as a possible exception).
6 Compare Robert Pippin's delimiting claims in discussing the purview of morality within Henry James's fiction: "The distinctive moral failure is, roughly, egoism," because "Moral issues arise distinctly in respect to actions by people, which can affect . . . the actions of others," and so "The great, paradigmatic moral phenomenon . . . is the promise and the subsequent keeping of trust; the moral question always: Why keep such trust apart from my own interest or fear of consequences?" (Pippin 2000, 25, 27.) Without trying to argue the claim about James, my point is that much fiction makes it hopeless to settle on a paradigmatic moral phenomenon, as moral concern can attach to nearly anything people do.
7 Here's a scene with Gina and Hjalmar.

> **Gina:** Do you regret the fifteen years we have lived together?
> **Hjalmar:** Have you not every day, every moment, regretted the web of concealment and deceit that you've spun around me like a spider? Answer me that! Do you mean to tell me that all this time you haven't been living in anguish and remorse?
> **Gina:** Oh, my dear Hjalmar, I've had enough to think about trying to run the house without –
> **Hjalmar:** Then you never probe your past with a questioning eye?
> **Gina:** You know, I'd almost forgotten the whole dirty business. (Ibsen 1961, 4.94)

So yes, perhaps there is dirty business here, but the project of squaring it away and seeking a clean starting point is here presented as naïve, even ridiculous, and destructive.

Bibliography

Bonzon, Roman (2003). "Fiction and Value," in M. Kieran and D. Lopes, eds., *Imagination, Philosophy, and the Arts* (London: Routledge).

Borges, Jorge Luis (1998/1941). "Tlön, Uqbar, Orbis Tertius," in *Collected Fictions*, trans. Andrew Hurley (New York: Viking).

Carroll, Noel (1996). "Moderate Moralism," *British Journal of Aesthetics* 36: 223–238.

Carroll, Noel (1998). "Art, Narrative, and Moral Understanding," in J. Levinson, ed., *Aesthetics and Ethics* (Cambridge: Cambridge University Press).

Devereaux, Mary (1998). "Beauty and Evil: The Case of Leni Riefenstahl's *Triumph of the Will*," in J. Levinson, ed., *Aesthetics and Ethics* (Cambridge: Cambridge University Press).

Gaut, Berys (1998). "The Ethical Criticism of Art," in J. Levinson, ed., *Aesthetics and Ethics* (Cambridge: Cambridge University Press).

Hemingway, Ernest (1938/1927). "Hills Like White Elephants," in *The Short Stories of Ernest Hemingway* (New York: Charles Scribner's).

Ibsen, Henrik (1961). *The Wild Duck/Hedda Gabler*, trans. Michael Meyer (New York: Norton). (*The Wild Duck* first published 1884.)

Jacobson, Daniel (1997). "In Praise of Immoral Art," *Philosophical Topics* 25: 155–99.

Jacobson, Daniel (2006). "Ethical Criticism and the Vice of Moderation," in M. Kieran, ed., *Aesthetics and the Philosophy of Art* (Oxford: Blackwell).

John, Eileen (2006). "Artistic Value and Opportunistic Moralism," in M. Kieran, ed., *Aesthetics and the Philosophy of Art* (Oxford: Blackwell).

Nussbaum, Martha (1990). *Love's Knowledge* (New York: Oxford University Press).

Pippin, Robert (2000). *Henry James and Modern Moral Life* (Cambridge: Cambridge University Press).

Taylor, Charles (1995). "A Most Peculiar Institution," in J. Altham and R. Harrison, eds., *World, Mind, and Ethics* (Cambridge: Cambridge University Press).

Wharton, Edith (1969/1905). *The House of Mirth* (New York: Charles Scribner's).

Williams, Bernard (2006/1985). *Ethics and the Limits of Philosophy* (London: Routledge).

Wollheim, Richard (1984). *The Thread of Life* (Cambridge: Cambridge University Press).

16

Styles of Self-Absorption

DANIEL BRUDNEY

> Ah, you are a strange fellow, one moment a child, the next an old man; one moment you are thinking most earnestly about the most important scholarly problems, how you will devote your life to them, and the next you are a lovesick fool.
>
> Kierkegaard, *Either/Or*[1]

> For good people are just good, while bad people are bad in all sorts of ways.
>
> Aristotle, *Nicomachean Ethics*[2]

In "Against Dryness," Iris Murdoch notes that "Simone Weil said that morality was a matter of attention, not of will. We need a new vocabulary of attention."[3] Actually, more useful might be a vocabulary of *inattention*. All morality may not be alike but immorality is surely quite varied.

This is clear enough if we look at Murdoch's own examples. Speaking generally, the attentive person registers the morally relevant features of a situation. She overlooks neither the presence of a moral demand, e.g., someone is in pain and could be helped, nor the relevant facts, e.g., no one is helping him.[4] The inattentive person fails to notice such things. She is lost in herself, self-absorbed. But consider Murdoch's famous example of a mother-in-law describing a daughter-in-law, at first harshly and, we are led to suppose, inaccurately. As the mother-in-law herself says, "I am old-fashioned and conventional. I may be prejudiced and narrow-minded. I may be snobbish. I am certainly jealous. Let me look again."[5] At a second, and presumably more accurate look, she finds the positive: now the daughter-in-law "is discovered to be not vulgar but refreshingly simple, not undignified but spontaneous, not noisy but gay, not tiresomely juvenile but delightfully youthful, and so on."[6] Here, the idea is that if I shed not merely my self-absorption but my tendency to see things as I want them to be, the way things actually are can become manifest. The mother-in-law is more than self-absorbed. Her distorted perception is largely a function of her prejudice, narrow-mindedness, etc. The proper metaphor for self-absorption in general is blinders,

---

A Companion to the Philosophy of Literature, First Edition. Edited by Garry L. Hagberg and Walter Jost.
© 2010 John Wiley & Sons Ltd. Published 2015 by John Wiley & Sons, Ltd.

something that narrows my vision; with the mother-in-law, the proper metaphor is a distorting lens.[7]

Inattention thus comes in different forms. In this essay, I examine two further forms, as depicted in J. M. Coetzee's *Disgrace* and Saul Bellow's *Herzog*.[8] Each is a distinctive form of self-absorption, each is different from those Murdoch presents. Still, like those, each involves a failure to get beyond the self, a failure, as Murdoch puts it, "to pierce the veil of selfish consciousness and join the world as it really is."[9]

Among the tasks of the moral philosopher is to describe the moral life but not necessarily as a whole. Often the bits and pieces are instructive. Here, literature is useful, holding the elements up to scrutiny. The point is not to find a counterexample to this or that general moral theory. Stories do get invoked for this purpose – Ursula LeGuin's "The Ones Who Walk Away from Omelas" against the utilitarian or Theodor Fontane's *Effi Briest* against the Kantian[10] – but these are rarely decisive. In most cases, the utilitarian or Kantian can present a more sophisticated variant of her theory to handle the story in question.[11]

My goal is different. It is to use the two novels to bring into focus an element of our moral psychology, taking this category broadly, so that it includes forms of perception and responsiveness, indeed one's general stance toward the world. Several philosophers have discussed something like the element I am after. Murdoch refers to a person's "vision of life," Martha Nussbaum talks of "views of the world and how one should live in it," Cora Diamond of a "general picture," Alice Crary of a "practical orientation toward the world."[12] I take such phrases to be deliberately vague, a concession to the fact that the element at issue manifests itself in multiple and subtle ways. It would be a basic mistake to see it on the model of a determinate mental item, as with, say, a faculty or a drive. Nevertheless, I think we can give it some substance. That is where reading the novels comes in. I want to show the visions of life or, as I will simply call them, the *orientations*, of two literary characters.

Murdoch, Nussbaum, Diamond, and Crary have all urged that the moral life includes more than what one chooses to do[13] and more than how one operates with respect to a limited set of moral concepts.[14] My readings of the novels are intended to show such claims at work. The subsequent reflections on the category of orientation are intended to point to some features of this element of our moral psychology, broadly construed. Unfortunately, these reflections will be brief. They are intended merely to flag topics for further inquiry.

Literature and the Moral Life

(1) Examining an element of the moral life seems a respectable enough enterprise. Still, why pursue it via novels? Are there specific advantages to doing so? The quick answer is that it is largely through a narrative, through seeing the development of a life, that the element I am after appears most compellingly.[15] A narrative that presents a life's details provides a picture within which we can identify a range of phenomena, including the one I am after.

But this is in fact too quick. In particular, it omits two claims – one phenomenological, one concerning textual authority – about the special status of a fictional narrative. These point to further reasons to use literature to explore moral psychology.

The first, the phenomenological claim, is that a fictional narrative can facilitate a distinctive and powerful relationship between the reader and a character, more powerful than with, say, a psychological case study. It is common to talk of "identifying" with a literary character in a way that goes especially deep. The thought seems to be that we do not experience things vicariously *through* the character (as parents might through their children) but, rather, have experiences *along with* the character. I take this to be Arthur Danto's claim when he says that, for the reader, "each work is about the 'I' that reads the text, identifying himself not with the implied reader for whom the implied narrator writes, but with the actual subject of the text"[16] (see chapter 4, PHILOSOPHY AND/AS/OF LITERATURE, 64). Somehow, my relation to the character is so close that I can respond to her in all her dimensions (including dimensions in which I had thought I was *unlike* her). I can get a feel for her vision of life.[17]

Of course, this is merely to state not to argue for the claim that a novel can foster a distinctive form of identification. I don't see how to make a conclusive argument for that claim but maybe I can make the claim plausible by noting two formal features of narrative fiction.

To begin with, in a novel there is *nothing but* the narrative, the words of the text. Contrast this with a psychological case study. There, we find a real person whose existence transcends the words of the study. So far as my claims are about her (and not about the being depicted by the words of the study), new data could falsify them. Moreover, there is a built-in limit to how far I can identify with the subject of the study. The subject is a real person with a distinct existence, emotions, relationships, etc. She exists and is very much not me. A fictional character, however, is constituted solely by the words of the text. The character has no other existence. No further data can be decisive about her (this is the truth in the New Critical piety toward the text). Anything there is to be known about a literary character can only be inferred from the text. If you ask about the color of a character's eyes or what she is thinking or would do in some counterfactual set of circumstances, any answer is, in the end, a textual claim, a claim entirely about this particular set of words; not so with the subject of a case study.[18] A consequence is that there isn't, we might say, the same epistemic limit to identification with the fictional character. The character's separateness is different from that of the real person, and in some way significantly less. No doubt, the reader cannot literally affirm, "Madame Bovary, c'est moi," but the limits of my identification with Emma Bovary are different from the limits of my identification with Flaubert. With Flaubert, part of that limit comes from the fact that I can know and respond to only a small part of who Gustave Flaubert was. I can know and respond to everything that Emma Bovary is.[19]

Second, Emma Bovary and every other fictional character always *is*. She may die but she never vanishes. In the famous ode, Keats mistakes art's preservative power for a point about what the Grecian urn does and does not show: "For ever wilt thou love, and she be fair!" – as if the lady would not have been forever fair had the urn's other side shown her old and gray. Actually, what makes her forever fair is that she is a figure on an urn. Suppose the urn had been different, on the other side shown the lady old and gray; nevertheless, turn it to the fair side and there she would be in her youthful loveliness. Emma Bovary is young again, comes into being again, every time I read the novel.[20]

Jointly, these formal features point to the lesser resistance a character opposes to the reader. There is neither epistemic nor ontological resistance. Two limits on losing oneself in an actual human being (on what Danto calls the "immediacy of identification") are missing.[21]

It should be kept in mind here that, even granting the above claims about identification, a crucial step is missing. The general thesis about novels is that they can reveal human psychology in an especially informative way. The claim just developed is that a reader can identify with a literary character in a distinctively close manner. The connecting claim that would have to be established is that through such close identification the reader can come to see human psychology in an especially informative – say, an especially subtle and complex – way. This strikes me as a plausible claim but, once again, an argument is needed.[22]

(2) There is something further to note. For millennia, philosophers have quoted literature. Seemingly, they have believed that poets, novelists, etc. have been onto something, that in some way their texts are authoritative. Two points should be made about this philosophical use of literary texts.

First, when used as a philosophical example, a novel – that is, a reading of a novel – is different from the usual off-the-rack examples for testing philosophical theories. It draws on the reader's sensibility. An off-the-rack example presents a scenario whose meaning is supposed to be transparent. The example is poorly done if Jack sees it as incompatible with theory T but Jill does not. By contrast, as an example, a reading of a novel might convince Jill – but it also might not. She might read the novel differently from Jack, i.e., as compatible with T.[23] Without distorting the novel, appealing to it could as easily deepen as resolve the disagreement between Jack and Jill.[24]

Second, works of relatively high aesthetic quality are hardly the only kind that can teach the reader, develop her moral understanding. *Uncle Tom's Cabin* may have changed the way many white people thought of black people. Such a real and profound change was infinitely more important than, say, the development of sensibility fostered by Henry James's last novels.[25]

Nevertheless, most people have the intuition that works of high aesthetic quality are morally relevant – morally revelatory – in a way that lesser works are not.[26] Attempts to justify the intuition tend simply to restate it. The great work's greater "complexity" is often invoked but bad novels can be extremely "complicated" (have intricate plots and characters with multiple traits), and to explicate the complex/complicated distinction would be, in effect, to explicate what high aesthetic quality here comes to. Or one might invoke the great work's greater "plausibility" or "believability," but these moves come to grief when one tries to pin down just what makes the high-quality work more plausible, believable, etc. Taken flatly, such criteria amount to things like "presenting characters not too different from you or me," or "presenting people you might meet in real life." Such criteria could easily be satisfied by poor-quality works. Moreover, they are far too narrow: who has met Don Quixote or Pantagruel? But taken more broadly – e.g., "captures the essence of a certain kind of person" – they are uninformative. That a character satisfies this standard just is part of what makes the work a good one. How it does so is the question, and while a careful critic might show different writers' masterly techniques work by work, a general account is almost certainly not going to be forthcoming. (Incidentally, Aristotle's claim that poetry, especially tragedy, is more universal than history also won't do. That is a claim about genre that applies equally to good and bad instances.[27])

I have no defense of this intuition about literary authority but I share it. Maybe you do as well. Imagine that you are a defense attorney arguing an appeal against a capital punishment statute. You want the judges to see the possibility for redemption in even the worst offender. You consider citing a recent television adaptation of *Crime and Punishment*. Still, although the storyline was the same as Dostoyevsky's, the script was badly written and the acting horrendous. So you decide instead to cite the actual novel. Opposing counsel then gets up. She first points out that the recent television program supports your view. Then she delivers a brilliant and what you concede is a completely convincing reading of the novel itself, showing that, contrary to the standard view, it is thoroughly ironic and Raskolnikov is not the least bit redeemed. After this reading, you won't be able to read the novel in the old way. If you feel that this new reading of *Crime and Punishment* at all undermines your claims with respect to capital punishment – to put matters more precisely, if you wish that the great novel rather than the fourth-rate television program supported your claims – then you, too, have the sense that something of import goes on in great works of literature and that at least part of our understanding of the moral life hangs on how we read them.[28]

On now to Coetzee and Bellow.

David Lurie

> Although he may have forfeited the reader's moral sympathy early in the novel, he is far from being a dismissible figure at the end.
> Derek Attridge, *J. M. Coetzee and the Ethics of Reading*[29]

(1) Most commentators on *Disgrace* cast it as a political novel.[30] The story takes place in post-apartheid South Africa and the events reflect that fact: from the rechristening of Cape Town University College as Cape Technical University and the official change of the protagonist, David Lurie, from professor of modern languages to adjunct professor of communication, to the profound lawlessness in the country and, when Lurie returns to Cape Town, in the city as well, to the explicit declaration that white suffering will be part of the atonement for centuries of black oppression. So the novel is very

much of its time and place, and it is perfectly proper to see it in political terms. My focus, however, is different. It is on the character growth, what seems most properly described as the spiritual growth, of David Lurie.

What we are given first is Lurie with Soraya, a prostitute. He sees her Thursdays at two. "He has been on her books for over a year; he finds her entirely satisfactory" (*D* 1). So we start with self-satisfaction and commodification ("For a man of his age, fifty-two, divorced, he has, to his mind, solved the problem of sex rather well," *D* 1). But there is also something more. When Soraya asks if Lurie misses her, he answers, "I miss you all the time" (*D* 1), and it is true, he does. There is a hole in Lurie's life, something missing. And so when he runs into Soraya outside working hours he tries to approach her. Predictably, this drives her away. Having no longer solved the problem of sex, Lurie then begins an affair with Melanie, one of his undergraduate students. This triggers the novel's events: Lurie is hauled up on charges of sexual harassment; he is found lacking in sincere repentance and refuses to abase himself (as he thinks of it) before the politically correct disciplinary tribunal; he is fired, deprived of all benefits, including his pension; he goes to the country to stay with his daughter, Lucy, on her subsistence farm; Lucy is raped and Lurie nearly murdered by three young black men, one not much more than a boy and who turns out to be connected to Petrus, the neighbor on whom Lucy is dependent (a true Balzacian peasant: no scruples and an overwhelming determination to acquire land); Lurie begins a chamber opera on the theme of Byron's mistress, Teresa; he works at the local animal clinic, helping to put to sleep stray dogs; he drives to Melanie's parents' home and apologizes (rather bizarrely) for the pain he has caused them; and the book ends with Lurie living alone near Lucy, and spending his time working again at the animal clinic. So much for the novel's bare bones.

The book also finishes with Lurie with a woman, Bev Shaw, with whom, midway through the novel, he has had a brief affair. She runs the animal clinic, and, by the novel's end, has become what Lurie seems never to have had, a friend. She has also taught him the one thing needful.

> He has learned by now, from her, to concentrate all his attention on the animal they are killing, giving it what he no longer has difficulty in calling by its proper name: love. (*D* 219)

So Lurie changes. He does so against his own insistence that he cannot and will not do so. "His temperament," he thinks at the start, "is not going to change, he is too old for that. His temperament is fixed, set" (*D* 2). When he agrees to help Bev Shaw at the animal clinic it is "only as long as I don't have to become a better person. I am not prepared to be reformed" (*D* 77). Yet he cannot remain as he has been. "Do I have to change, he thinks" (*D* 126; see also *D* 172). Finally, he does resolve on change. Lucy, pregnant by one of her rapists, declares, "I am determined to be a good mother, David. A good mother and a good person. You should try to be a good person too." With Lurie, there is, as always, the sardonic surface. "I suspect it is too late for me. I'm just an old lag serving out my sentence. But you go ahead. You are well on the way." Now, though, this seems merely surface. His next thought is, "A good person. Not a bad resolution to make, in dark times" (*D* 216).

What has changed?

(2) Coetzee is a skillful novelist and a learned man. His tale is rife with references. Some are no doubt merely playful but others situate Lurie on a moral map. Many are minor, e.g., the gesture at Dostoyevsky's *Crime and Punishment* (the intellectual commits a crime and is punished, complete with exile to the provinces) or naming Lurie's daughter "Lucy", as in Wordsworth's poems.[31] Others are more sustained. For instance, there is, I think, an ongoing play with the first half of Kierkegaard's *Either/Or*, especially with the part called, "The Seducer's Diary."[32] In a central sense, that is what *Disgrace* is.

The first half of *Either/Or* is the "aesthetic" and the second the "ethical." One way to think of Lurie's trajectory is from the aesthetic to something else – though whether he ends in the ethical and what, with him, that amounts to is precisely the question. For Kierkegaard, there is a step after the ethical, the religious, but Lurie surely does not end there, at least not as that category is conventionally understood. When I say that Lurie's growth is "spiritual," I intend the term as a placeholder, leaving open the kind of growth he achieves.

The writer of "The Seducer's Diary" sees the world under the category of the aesthetic, that is, in terms of his own attainment and enjoyment of complex pleasures. Now, this is not quite right for Lurie. His focus is not merely on arousing and gratifying his desires. He is invariably a professor and critic of desire as much as – sometimes, more than – a sensualist. The aesthetic is, for him, mostly what it is in its usual meaning: the sphere of music, painting, literature, of artistic activity of various kinds.

Here, I introduce the category of *orientation*. I hope it will gain its meaning from its application to the two novels. As a first cut, though, one's orientation is the way one filters the world, sifts it so that it shapes itself in a certain manner. One's orientation involves what one notices and puts stress on in the world, finds salient.[33] It involves the descriptions under which one perceives things. The pattern of those descriptions says a good deal about who one is.

I don't want to make the category merely epistemic, merely a way of recording the world. An orientation is a way of living, a basic stance or attitude toward the world. Compare two incidents in Joseph Conrad's *Lord Jim*. Here is the character Stein, when set upon in the jungle to be murdered: "I see it all in a minute, and I think – This wants a little management." And here is Jim, facing a storm:

> The next gust seemed to blow all this away. The air was full of flying water. There was a fierce purpose in the gale, a furious earnestness in the screech of the wind, in the brutal tumult of earth and sky, that seemed directed at him, and made him hold his breath in awe. He stood still. It seemed to him he was whirled around.[34]

Each character is presented with a crisis, each describes the crisis in a manner that both expresses a way of living in the world and frames the possibilities of action (or their absence). The filter I have in mind constitutes both a constraint on how the world is described and a fundamental way of being in it.

Most of us filter the world in different ways at different times (though there are usually important continuities). Among the advantages of literary characters is that they tend to highlight a specific orientation. A character's filter may be complex and may shift, as in these novels, but at a given moment we can get a pretty good handle on it.

For Lurie to have an *aesthetic orientation* is for him to have a pervasive tendency to register and catalogue people under literary or other artistic descriptions (sometimes positive, often not), and to have a penchant for assessing people and conduct in aesthetic terms. Upon finishing sex with Melanie, he looks at her. "*After the storm*, he thinks: straight out of George Grosz" (*D* 19). After sex with Bev Shaw, he recalls Emma Bovary "strutting before the mirror after her first big afternoon. *I have a lover! I have a lover!* sings Emma to herself. Well, let poor Bev Shaw go home and do some singing too" (*D* 150). Even later, when apologizing to Melanie's father, Lurie casts his seduction in aesthetic terms:

> "One word more, then I am finished. It could have turned out differently, I believe, between the two of us, despite our ages. But there was something I failed to supply, something" – he hunts for the word – "lyrical. I lack the lyrical. I manage love too well. Even when I burn I don't sing, if you understand me. For which I am sorry. I am sorry for what I took your daughter through. You have a wonderful family. I apologize for the grief I have caused you and Mrs Isaacs. I ask for your pardon." (*D* 171)

A strange apology, apologizing literally for an aesthetic incapacity (note that the "lyrical" is an important category from the aesthetic half of *Either/Or*). Even the self-criticism – that he manages too well something that shouldn't be managed at all – sounds as if what makes it problematic are the aesthetic consequences. And Lurie's apology is followed quickly by an internal aesthetic critique of his description of the Isaacs family: "*Wonderful* is not right. Better would be *exemplary*" (*D* 171).

Right to the end, these associations are triggered like a psychic tic. Watching his daughter working on her farm, Lurie thinks, "*das ewig Weibliche*, lightly pregnant, in a straw sunhat. A scene ready-made for a Sargent or a Bonnnard" (*D* 218). He reflects that "he has never had much of an eye for rural life, despite all his reading in Wordsworth" (*D* 218). Yet at the end something is different. In the same passage Lurie also says of Lucy, "but even city boys can recognize beauty when they see it, can have their breath taken away" (*D* 218). Here, he is aware of beauty but with no aestheticizing associations.

In a more profound way Lurie's attitude toward Bev Shaw changes. Even from the start he knew he was being unfair. After comparing Shaw to Emma Bovary he immediately thinks, "And let him stop calling her poor Bev Shaw. If she is poor, he is bankrupt" (*D* 150). But this is just a beginning. Early on, Lucy remarks of Shaw,

> "You underestimate her. She is a more interesting person than you think. Even in your own terms." His own terms: what are they? That dumpy little women with ugly voices deserve to be ignored? (*D* 79)

Now, "interesting" is a key term for Kierkegaard's seducer. To find that which is interesting is his persistent goal.[35] So we have Lurie's initial aesthetic contempt expressed via the seducer's category. However, at the end we find Lurie struggling to write a chamber opera on the theme of Byron's mistress, Teresa, in her middle age – not the young Teresa, but "a dumpy, little widow . . . [w]ith her heavy bust, her stocky trunk, her abbreviated legs, [who] looks more like a peasant, a *contadina*, than an aristocrat" (D 181). It is hard to miss the transition from Melanie to Bev Shaw. True, Lurie wonders whether he can love the dumpy Teresa sufficiently to generate music for her, whether she will "engage his heart as his heart is now" (D 181): "Can he find it in his heart to love this plain, ordinary woman? Can he love her enough to write a music for her?" (D 182). Still, whether or not Lurie loves Shaw – and with what sort of love – he clearly now sees her as "interesting," just as Lucy had said, but that category is no longer an aesthetic one.

Even early on, Lurie is not without some self-awareness. He knows he should not follow Soraya or call her at home (D 9), he knows his affair with Melanie is wrong (D 20), and he is capable of self-criticism. Nevertheless, he succumbs to temptation. More accurately, he not only yields to but affirms what he calls "the rights of desire" (D 89). It is not precisely that he exhibits weakness of will, at least not in the straightforward sense of having a desire overcome his better judgment. Nor is it precisely that he has a set of principles (about the rights of desire) on which he acts and that he eventually sees are inadequate. Rather, the appeal to desire is really an appeal to an aesthetic category. *That* he appeals to desire is an expression of his way of registering the world. What I am designating as an "orientation" involves not just conative elements but also beliefs (e.g., about the value of the aesthetic); centrally, though, it functions as a kind of perception.[36] Lurie sees Melanie under the description "an object of the rights of desire." That Lurie also has the seeds of change is shown by the fact that he also sees Melanie under a different description: "*A child!* he thinks: *No more than a child! What am I doing?*" (D 20).

(3) On the surface, Lurie's moral growth goes through conventional stations. There is baptism simultaneously by liquid and fire, a kind of double purification (the men who rape Lucy splash him with methylated spirits and set him alight, D 96), and repentance or at least its outward form, apology (D 171, 173). There is even punishment, a sentence to be served (D 216), and, as noted, Lurie ends by being able to give another being what he has hitherto been unable to give, namely, love.

Still, it remains unclear what sort of growth Lurie has attained. He starts by being plunged into disgrace. He describes himself to Bev Shaw as "[n]ot just in trouble. In what I suppose one would call disgrace" (D 85), and later to Melanie's father: "I am sunk into a state of disgrace from which it will not be easy to lift myself" (D 172). For a while Lurie takes up residence with his daughter Lucy, replacing an absent roommate who at one point, with some heaviness, is mistakenly referred to as "Grace" (D 187).[37] So if there is growth, it is somehow growth away from disgrace. In some way his character's "state" – not his status but his spiritual condition – improves. In what way?

STYLES OF SELF-ABSORPTION

We should go back to Lurie's sin/crime/misdeed. He has had an affair with one of his students. He has abused the power he held over her. But this understates things. Lurie was wrong to have sex with his student, but suppose he had not been Melanie's teacher. Given who she is, i.e., given how vulnerable she seems in Lurie's own depiction, his conduct would still have been wrong. Melanie is, technically, an adult, and Lurie does not literally force himself on her. The sex is not wanted but it is acquiesced in. In some sense Melanie exerts her agency, yet it is the agency of someone not wholly mature, a fact Lurie senses but ignores.[38]

Vulnerability is pervasive in this novel. Melanie is vulnerable to Lurie; Lucy and Lurie are vulnerable to their attackers; Lurie is vulnerable to students who jeer him; his city house to those who ransack it; the various animals to the desires of humans. In all these cases, persons, animals, things are vulnerable to the (often cruel) unchecked human will.

Toward the story's close, we find Lurie devoting his life to caring for a subset of the vulnerable but it is an odd sort of caring. On the one hand, his ability to love is expressed in the way he helps to "put down" (a strange phrase, as if they are rebels) unwanted animals, mostly dogs, who would otherwise starve. Most oddly, he has taken on the task of dealing with the dogs' corpses. He hauls them to a local incinerator, handling the dogs himself so that they will be slid into the furnace with a modicum of gentleness rather than having their stiffened bodies pounded and smashed until they fit the opening to the flames. Lurie wonders why he does this. "For himself. For his idea of the world, a world in which men do not use shovels to beat corpses into a more convenient shape for processing" (*D* 146). He reflects further.

> Curious that a man as selfish as he should be offering himself to the service of dead dogs. There must be other, more productive ways of giving oneself to the world, or to an idea of the world. One could for instance work longer hours at the clinic. One could try to persuade the children at the dump not to fill their bodies with poisons. Even sitting down more purposefully with the Byron libretto might, at a pinch, be construed as a service to mankind.
>
> But there are other people to do these things – the animal welfare thing, the social rehabilitation thing, even the Byron thing. He saves the honour of corpses because there is no one else stupid enough to do it. That is what he is becoming: stupid, daft, wrongheaded. (*D* 146)

The theme of dogs runs throughout the novel. Petrus refers to himself as a "dog-man" and perhaps that is what Lurie is now. The point about these dogs is that they are superfluous. There are many dogs in the novel who have a social role (e.g., Lucy's) and so are fed and cared for. The ones at the clinic have no such role and so must die, either starved or euthanized. (No doubt, some readers will see a political point here.) And here is Lucy's decision to remain on the land in complete vulnerability, to make herself completely vulnerable:

> "Yes, I agree, it is humiliating. But perhaps that is a good point to start from again. Perhaps that is what I must learn to accept. To start at ground level. With nothing. Not with nothing but. With nothing. No cards, no weapons, no property, no rights, no dignity."
> "Like a dog."
> "Yes, like a dog." (*D* 205)

Coetzee has written extensively on Kafka so it is not a stretch to note that the final words of *The Trial*, a book detailing everyone's vulnerability, coming as K. is being executed are, "'Like a dog!' he said: it was as if the shame of it must outlive him."[39] What Lurie does is to try to ensure that dogs die without fear and are consumed in a manner not shameful.

Lurie feels this duty deeply. It seems not to have limits. He takes a trip back to Cape Town, is away for some time.

> As for the dogs, he does not want to think about them. From Monday onward the dogs released from life within the walls of the clinic will be tossed into the fire unmarked, unmourned. For that betrayal, will he ever be forgiven? (D 178)

It is easy to mock where Lurie has come to. His disgrace flows from his maltreatment of a human being yet his redemptive focus is on his "betrayal" of dead dogs. Where he ends is difficult to justify in either consequentialist or Kantian terms. His service to superfluous and dead dogs is hardly the best way to promote the general welfare. (Are there really enough others to do "the social rehabilitation thing"?) Moreover, what Derek Attridge calls Lurie's "life of toil in the service of others" is not only not in the service of rational beings but for the most part not even in the service of currently sentient beings.[40] Attridge writes:

> These activities of Lurie's are not presented, I would argue, as the achievement of redemption or as a prescription for ethical behaviour, but rather as an instance of a commitment that signals, in its very irrelevance to larger programmes and practices, its integrity in a world of calculation and accumulation. It is a commitment above all to the singularity of the other – even if that other is an invented character in an opera or a dead dog being conveyed into an incinerator – that obeys no logic and offers no comfort.[41]

The idea seems to be that protection of the other, in all its vulnerability, is important and involves no requirement to triage within that category. But this is difficult to accept. There is nothing wrong with protecting the honor of dead dogs but there are surely more pressing demands. Herbert Simon taught us that good managers satisfice rather than maximize, and the insistence on what Samuel Scheffler calls an "agent-centered prerogative" is something like the moral philosophical analogue: we need only do enough rather than maximize the good.[42] The problem is that Lurie's new conduct, harmless though it may be, surely doesn't do remotely enough, at least not judged by the usual standards.

We could try to make excuses. Lurie claims to be striving for "a world in which men do not use shovels to beat corpses into a more convenient shape for processing." One might say (a) this is a general protest against the administered world, and (b) a world in which corpses aren't beaten is likely to be a world in which humans aren't beaten (a variant on the zero-tolerance for graffiti strategy). But (b) is at best tenuously true and (a) attributes to Lurie too abstract, too academic, an attitude. In a review of Coetzee's next novel, *Slow Man*, John Lanchester writes that the thread that runs through Coetzee's recent work . . . is close to being a mystical idea, about the primacy of feeling, of our basic impulses of empathy and sympathy and solidarity and . . . kindness, over reason.[43]

This is not inaccurate; it also doesn't resolve the problem.

We should give Coetzee's character credit. Lurie is puzzled by himself. "[H]e is becoming: stupid, daft, wrongheaded" (D 146). This is not irony. What he does *is* puzzling. If it makes sense, if it is worth a person's time and effort given all there is to do in the world, it must be because protecting the vulnerable in any way is worthwhile. But this hardly helps since the category of "the vulnerable" is itself obscure. Consider that a thing is always vulnerable in some particular way but that these ways seem to have little to do with one another. Melanie was emotionally vulnerable; Lurie and Lucy were vulnerable to physical violence; the excess dogs were vulnerable to starvation; their corpses were vulnerable to dishonor. Seeing things under the category of the vulnerable doesn't tell us much.[44] In the end, the meaning of Lurie's change remains unclear. There is in fact change. The aesthetic orientation is shed. What remains unclear is whether what we see is, in the end, spiritual growth (of what sort?) or merely a peculiar form of self-indulgence.

Moses Herzog

> . . . but sad, unable to take what his heart really desired, a man tempted by God, longing for grace, but escaping headlong from his salvation, often close at hand. This Herzog . . .
>
> Saul Bellow, *Herzog*[45]

(1) True to its focus on an intellectual and his angst, in *Herzog* very little happens. The eponymous hero is met inhabiting his tumbledown Berkshire retreat. Through flashbacks we see a bit of childhood, two failed marriages (mostly the second), a moment of flight to Martha's Vineyard, and an ostensibly murderous romp to Chicago's Hyde Park neighborhood, the *idée fixe* being to kill both the second wife (Madeleine) and her lover/Herzog-friend (Gersbach). But though there is travel and even trauma (a minor car wreck) the novel essentially takes place in Herzog's head or out of his pen, in the endless letters he endlessly writes to the world's great and near-greats.

Disgrace makes use of a Christian model of moral development. Neither in deed nor thought does *Herzog* instantiate any model of *Bildung*, and so it is hard to tie what happens to a pattern, e.g., sin and repentance, that spreads a sheen of intelligibility over the character development. This may be why some reviewers found the slightly upbeat finale unearned: it triggers no standard image of redemption.

(2) We begin near the end, with Herzog on his country property, glancing back over the past. "Considering his entire life, he realized that he had mismanaged everything

– everything. His life was, as the phrase goes, ruined" (*H* 3). How so? Moses Herzog is a defrocked, middle-aged academic. He has resigned a position and failed to finish a book. He has had murder (seemingly) in his heart and a gun in his pocket. Still, what has he actually *done*? Married poorly and been betrayed by wife and friend, been a victim.

> He had more enemies and hatreds than anyone could easily guess from his thoughtful expression . . . They mustn't think they can get away with it – make such a fool of me, put me on. (*H* 18 and 34)

Such thoughts – his self-description as victim – are a central symptom of what ails him.

Maybe the question should be put in the negative. What has he not done, failed to do? First, be a good enough father to his children. He is twice-divorced, twice a father, and rarely sees either child. Intermittently he recognizes the issue. "It was painful to his instincts, his Jewish family feelings, that his children should be growing up without him. But what could he do about that?" (*H* 23; see also *H* 27). Second, get on with his unfinished book or find something else to do but stop wallowing in his own *tsuris*. Here, too, there is recognition. "This confusion was ugly, and he despised himself for creating it. Was this all the work a man could find to do?" (*H* 104). So he knows he has a problem, knows he has to change his life, hopes he may in fact be "going through a change of outlook" (*H* 188), longs for such a thing: "Oh, for a change of heart, a change of heart – a true change of heart!" (*H* 201).

All this is deeply felt. It is also in large part a role, a piece of theater. The novel is rife with Herzog's comments on his own and others' role-playing. Indeed, he minimizes his bit of murderousness in these terms, his role-playing quickly punctured by the vision of the humanity of his intended target, his wife's lover, Valentine Gersbach, as he bathes Herzog's child.

> The man washed her tenderly . . . But see how he was with June, scooping the water on her playfully, kindly . . . As soon as Herzog saw the actual person giving an actual bath, the reality of it, the tenderness of such a buffoon to a little child, his intended violence turned into *theater*, into something ludicrous. (*H* 257 and 258)

I want to note several things about Herzog's *theatricality*, which I will take to be his distinctive orientation.[46] First, it is not just about playing roles but about an awareness of oneself and others *as* role players:

> He knew that Ramona [the woman he's involved with who would like to be his wife] was keen about scholarship, his books and encyclopedia articles, Ph.D., University of Chicago, and would want to be Frau Professor Herzog. Amused, he saw how they would arrive at white-tie parties at the Hotel Pierre, Ramona in long gloves and introducing Moses with her charming, lifted voice: "This is my husband, Professor Herzog." And he himself, Moses, a different man, radiating well-being, swimming in dignity, affable to one and all. Giving his back hair a touch. What a precious pair they'd make, she with her tics and he with his! What a vaudeville show! (*H* 202)

He is amused at the image, aware it is born of *ressentiment*. "Ramona would get revenge on people who had once given her a hard time. And he? He too would get back at his enemies" (*H* 202). Most important, he would be "a different man" – the attraction and impossibility.

Second, Herzog's own contrast to theatricality is what he calls "ordinary" life. He remarks on its importance:

> No philosopher knows what the ordinary is, has not fallen into it deeply enough. The question of ordinary human experience is the principal question of these modern centuries, as Montaigne and Pascal, otherwise in disagreement, both clearly saw. – The strength of a man's virtue or spiritual capacity measured by his ordinary life. (*H* 106)

Even in 1963 this thought was hackneyed.[47] Still, what draws the reader to Herzog is not his intellectual originality but precisely this aspiration: to attain, though he never quite does, ordinary life. "The more Madeleine and Gersbach lectured me, the more I thought that my only purpose was to lead a quiet, regular life" (*H* 192). The novel's beginning and end are gestures toward pastoral, the country life, decent and simple, the fantasy of the ordinary, the best of all roles.

Third, on the whole we don't take Herzog's murder fantasy seriously. He is a Chekhovian actor, complete with an ancient, heavy, Russian pistol (which we know will *not* be fired in the last act), playing at being the vengeful lover, and the point is that he is, in sufficient part, merely playing a role.

Fourth, and perhaps most interesting, Herzog's theatricality is tied to his intellectualism, something about which Bellow, himself, seems ambivalent. Herzog's focus is wide. Nothing is beyond his ken. The novel is filled with his intellectual ramblings, and of course there are his letters, his pontifications to all and sundry. Why is this problematic? Here, I quote from a Bellow lecture.

> So it comes down to this: the living man is preoccupied with such questions as who he is, what he lives for, what he is so keenly and interminably yearning for, what his human essence is, and instead of the bread of thought he is offered conceptual stones and fashionable non-ideas. And so, immensely needy, people are engaged in thought or with the products of thought, taking attitudes that presuppose thought – attitudes toward public responsibility, or personal adjustment, or crime, morality, punishment, abortion, child care, education, love, race relations. This is what people, aided or misled by advisers, teachers, experts, therapists, social scientists, newspaper columnists, television writers, actors, and political leaders, are attempting to work out.[48]

Bellow's thought seems to be that preoccupation with such questions is right and proper, and the only problem is the answers offered by the gabbling pundits. Buzzwords and phrases, Bellow says, "are distracting, and distraction is the word by which I designate the main difficulty."[49] Unfortunately, Herzog takes it to be vitally important to respond to the pundits, to get the theory right – and this is itself a distraction. Here, again, is Bellow: "I have said enough to bring us fully to the heart of distraction – the subject of my seemingly endless sermon. Can our distraction . . . be induced to yield to attention?"[50]

Herzog is endlessly distracted, endlessly thinking that he must nail intellectual theses to a wall. But this is to take oneself too seriously, to see one's allotted tasks in a grandiose light – theatrically – to be attentive not to others but only to a vision of oneself. So Herzog must, as he finally does, stop writing letters.

(3) What about those letters? Should we take their content seriously, i.e., not merely as expressive of a character in a book? Hardly. Frank Kermode remarks of Herzog's letters that they are "the kind of letter you might frenetically compose, if you had enough in your head, in the early stages of a sleepless night."[51] This points not to the problem with their content but to the problem with the letters themselves: they are an expression of Herzog's despair, and the idea that the way out of despair is through gaining some new remarkable *thought* is wondrously absurd.

Nevertheless, several critics have suggested just that. The novel is supposed to be a novel of ideas and so the hero, at the end, is supposed to get not the girl but the right idea. And certainly the novel's less savory characters berate Herzog for failing to learn some sort of life lesson. In part, apparently, what he is supposed to learn about is evil.

> A man in years he then was, but in years only ... stubbornly un-European, that is, innocent by deliberate choice. Moses refused to know evil. But he could not refuse to experience it. And therefore others were appointed to do it to him, and then to be accused (by him) of wickedness. (H 245)

Theodore Solotaroff describes the lesson.

> Thus, though Herzog lives in the world, he has been able to spare himself real understanding of the vast range of human experience that exists outside his self-regarding categories. Similarly, his morality has remained one based on evasion and repression. It is only when he strays into a criminal courtroom and suddenly comes up against genuine sordidness and evil that he begins to realize how insulated he has been ...
>
> The jolt in the New York courtroom is followed by an automobile accident in Chicago in which Herzog almost kills himself and his little girl and is apprehended by the police for carrying his useless gun. These are the blows by which truth generally comes in Bellow's fiction. The first sharply teaches Herzog the limits and shallowness of his "essential humanity" in the face of what is merely another routine day for a criminal judge. The second brings him back from his dangerous preoccupations with his indignities, his rights, his need for justice.[52]

What appears to be learned about is the existence of everyday, even if often ghastly, evil, a sordid dimension of that ordinary life Herzog yearns for. Yet what sort of learning is this? Alfred Kazin says of Bellow, "The key belief was that right thinking is virtue and can leave you in charge of the life that is so outrageous to live."[53] One might imagine that this is Herzog's code as well, some final right thought being the goal of his ceaseless cerebration. But of course in the sense of affirming a proposition Herzog knows all he needs to know long before his learning experiences. He lives

STYLES OF SELF-ABSORPTION

in New York City. He doesn't need a criminal court to know there is murder and mayhem around him. Presumably, Solotaroff has a deeper form of learning in mind. What might that be?

Among the trite yet profound things we try to teach our children is to have "perspective" on their lives. We tend to mean that our children should step back from their own lives in order to register others' lives, aspirations, and miseries, in effect, to attend to – pay attention to – others. Not only is this the right thing to do, but against such a backdrop, or so parents claim, one will take one's own troubles less seriously and, indeed, see how modest they are in the grand scheme of things.

According to Solotaroff, Herzog gains some such perspective by his visit to the criminal court. So what does this amount to if it goes beyond affirming a proposition? Let's ask the same question about the scene where Herzog recognizes Gersbach's humanity. There is a bit of information gleaned here – that Gersbach is capable of tenderness – but the point of the gleaning is to convey what? That Gersbach is human? In what way was this *not* known? Again, knowledge is not the issue but rather some way of relating to what is known.

Herzog's change is not simply a change of mind, say, of his beliefs. It is also not simply a change of feelings, anyway not toward Madeleine and Gersbach. Perhaps he no longer hates them, at least not so obsessively, but his feelings toward them are hardly positive. There is, though, a lightening of his obsession. Herzog won't again be heading to Hyde Park packing.

What changes or is in the process of change is Herzog's orientation. His particular orientation has involved the tendency to see himself and others under theatricalized role descriptions and so to have his life's meaning inflected this way and that, role by role. The primary thing that is to ease away is not beliefs or feelings but Herzog's theatricalizing ("Herzog smiled at this earlier avatar of his life, at Herzog the victim, at Herzog the would-be lover, Herzog the man on whom the world depended for certain intellectual work, to change history, to influence the development of civilization," H 104–5). Herzog longs for a change of heart (H 201) but this is best understood as a change in the way one is disposed to see and to respond to others. Because by the end he is, finally, not theatricalizing everything and everyone, his heart can be open (say, to an appreciation of Gersbach's tenderness), i.e., is changed.

(4) Seeing the world aright is connected to the knowledge that Herzog is said to lack. "What the fuck does *he* know what it is to face facts. All he wants is everybody should love him. If not, he's going to scream and holler" (H 83). This from the sleazy lawyer, Sandor Himmelstein, scarcely an unbiased source. But there is something Herzog doesn't know. What he doesn't know is not facts but "facing" facts, i.e., he has shirked registering the facts. Why? Because he wants love. But what kind of love? "Moses felt the potato love. Amorphous, swelling, hungry, indiscriminate, cowardly potato love." (H 91) This is a feeling projectable onto almost anyone or anything, a love that is not person-specific and so not about the object but only about the subject, namely, Moses Herzog. Thus the diagnosis: Herzog shirks facts, sees the world wrong, because of an overriding narcissism.

Does Herzog have any real – person-specific – feelings? Yes: for his children, his parents, his siblings. The most touching, the least theatrical, interaction is between Herzog and his brother Will (significantly, it comes toward the novel's end). There is a straightforward quality to it because, whatever Herzog's internal maunderings about their different lives ("[T]here's a strange division of functions that I sense, in which I am the specialist in ... in spiritual self-awareness; or emotionalism; or ideas; or nonsense," *H* 307), this is a relationship in which he loves and feels himself loved. It is perhaps the one piece of ordinary life we see. Moreover, perhaps because here the emotional claims are stable, the only thing Herzog wants from Will is something simple that Will can in fact provide, a bit of money.

From others, Herzog wants much more. "[A]ll he asked, it seemed to him, was a bit of cooperation in his effort, benefiting everyone, to work toward a meaningful life" (*H* 123). How will others, e.g., Madeleine, benefit? Depicted as the harpiest of harpies, one still feels some sympathy for her. After all, it takes two to ruin a marriage, and it is unlikely she could ever compete with Herzog's grand self-narrative that pushes everyone else to the wings. Bellow's notorious lack of sympathy with his female characters comes out at times in the portrayal of Ramona, but it is indicative of Herzog's slow tacking toward a "quiet, regular life" (*H* 192) that she is a woman who has had and will have her own story and who wants his cooperation, too, in the search for a meaningful life (and maybe the cooperative search *is* the meaningful life). Inch by inch Herzog begins to get the point. "And anyway he was growing tired of his obsession. Besides, she had troubles of her own" (*H* 189). Herzog is worth caring about because by the end he is edging toward the kind of attentiveness to and engagement with others that constitutes caring for them.

Letters are addressed *to* someone. One way to think of Herzog's problem is less that he has to stop writing letters than that he has to become ready to receive them, to accept that he is being addressed by someone, i.e., to listen to, pay attention to, someone, and to be ready to receive affection, love.

At the novel's end, for the first time, we do see him receive someone in his space. All previous encounters happen in others' houses or apartments but at the end Herzog receives Will in his Berkshire house, and the final scene shows him getting the place ready to receive Ramona. It is fitting that from Will, there, in his own house, Herzog can accept and express love, i.e., person-specific, not mere potato, love. So we end with a decent omen concerning Ramona.

(5) Lurie and Herzog are importantly different. True, each is an academic who has lost his professional slot, each is twice-divorced, each has fled to the country to heal, and each goes through and (in some sense) comes out from a bout of despair. However, they are different in that, while each is self-absorbed, Lurie is not but Herzog is narcissistic. Lurie's aestheticizing pins people into aesthetic categories but the categories don't inevitably refer back to him. Herzog's theatricalizing pins people into roles and those roles are inevitably in a drama in which Herzog is the protagonist. In developing a vocabulary of inattention it is important for the self-absorption it usually involves to have diverse manifestations, in particular not to be limited to the

narcissist. Lurie has great difficulty getting out of himself but he is not always focused *on* himself. This is a very modest compliment. For much of *Disgrace* he is thoroughly selfish and blinkered. That his failing is not precisely the same as Herzog's merely shows, as Aristotle points out in one of this chapter's epigraphs, that vice is various.

The Category of Orientation

(1)   So much, then, for the readings of the two novels. It is time to discuss orientation as a philosophical category. Now, it might seem that what these novels give us is some psychological data that any moral theory must take into account. And that is surely correct. However, the data is about how human beings live in the world. I have presented two (problematic) ways of relating to others, two (problematic) forms of being in the world with others. At issue is not just bits of data about human psychology as with, say, Hume's point that human generosity is limited.[54] At issue is the fact that there are basic ways in which people comport themselves to others. This is a familiar feature of our lives. The novels don't reveal anything we don't already know. On the other hand, though pervasive, important, and familiar, this feature of our lives is extremely difficult to pin down. That also makes it difficult to pin down the philosophical issues it prompts. Here, there is not space to do more than sketch these issues; however, a few things can be said.

Right off, I should sideline the thought that what is at issue is a person's "temperament." Clearly, an orientation is among the *patterning* features of human psychology, those elements that foster patterns of perception, feeling, belief, and conduct. The same is true of temperament, and I don't want to deny that theatricality and aestheticizing fit into its general landscape. At the beginning of *Disgrace*, Lurie even remarks, "His temperament is not going to change, he is too old for that. His temperament is fixed, set" (*D* 2), and of course it is precisely what he calls his "temperament" that does change. I have avoided the term because these days psychologists use it in a restricted fashion, as referring to such things as anxiety or confidence, particularly in children. In earlier eras, temperament's subdivisions were certain allegedly biologically-based ways of classifying people, such as into the bilious, phlegmatic, sanguine or melancholic.[55] Lurie and Herzog are not usefully identified by any of these categories. Their orientations are about their relations to others, about their failure to shed their forms of self-absorption.[56]

In some ways, an orientation is akin to the sort of thing one finds in Theophrastus, with his discussion of the boor, the ill-tempered man, the hero.[57] There, too, one finds the filtering aspect of character, the taking in of and responding to the world according to a pattern. But Theophrastus gives us caricatures, beings who are locked in with respect to some quite simple trait. The interest of Lurie and Herzog comes from their greater complexity and especially from the way they resist and eventually change their orientations.

(2)   An orientation is not reducible to a set of beliefs. Any orientation O surely involves beliefs but the beliefs don't entail the orientation. Take Herzog. One could believe

that one is a victim and yet not have a theatrical orientation. In his stories and novels Conrad presents a range of officers from the British merchant service. With few exceptions all hold the same basic beliefs about proper conduct and an officer's proper attitudes, yet their orientations are often radically different (e.g., compare Marlow and Jim in *Lord Jim*; or compare both to Captain Mitchell in *Nostromo*). These characters do have different as well as shared beliefs, but against the background of so much that is shared it is unlikely that their differences in orientation reduce to the differences in their remaining beliefs. I suspect that, for any set of beliefs, more than one orientation will fit; and for any orientation, more than one set of beliefs.[58]

We can return to the fact that Lurie has some self-awareness about what he is doing with Soraya and Melanie, and that Herzog is not merely laboring under false beliefs, not merely missing the right ideas. Their orientations do involve specific beliefs (e.g., Lurie about the rights of desire, Herzog about his victimhood) but what is at stake is not evidence and arguments pro or con these beliefs but rather a way of being in the world. Only a change in orientation would allow evidence and arguments to change their beliefs.[59]

An orientation is also not reducible to a set of desires. Again, orientation O will tend to involve some set of desires, and a given O will set parameters on desires (the desire to be overlooked will not fit with Herzog's theatricality). Still, this will leave a wide array of desires that might fit a given orientation: sets of desires S or S* or S** might each be compatible with O. Conversely, having a specific set of desires is likely to be compatible with more than one orientation. Lurie's initial desires probably overlap with many men's, say, with Byron's, but Byron's orientation was hardly similar.

(3)   One thing an orientation might seem to resemble is an emotion. A number of philosophers have stressed that emotions filter the world.[60] Peter Goldie writes of how an emotion can "skew the epistemic landscape";[61] and Ronald de Sousa of how an emotion can "influence decisions . . . by orienting attention toward this or that among the plethora of considerations that might be thought relevant at any particular juncture."[62]

The emotions are a large area of philosophical inquiry in which there is large disagreement, even about what an emotion is and about which phenomena count as emotions. However, the following seem to be differences between emotions and an orientation.

(a)   Compared to an orientation most emotions have a relatively brief lifespan. There are fits of anger and spasms of hatred. Of course, some emotions can be quite long-lasting, e.g., love. Still, Herzog's theatricality and Lurie's aestheticizing are significantly longer-lasting than most emotions. It is *characteristic* of an orientation to be quite long-lasting. Emotions can be long-lasting but they are not characteristically so.[63]

(b)   One is sometimes unaware that one has emotion E, and one can become aware that one has orientation O. Yet, once again, it is characteristic of an emotion that one is or can fairly easily become aware of it while the contrary seems true of an orientation. The latter is sufficiently pervasive that its output seems normal, the way things are.

(c) Although feelings are generally agreed not to be required for emotions, they do often accompany them. There is, I think, no feeling that goes with Herzog's theatricality or Lurie's aestheticizing.

(4) I should also say a little about how an orientation relates to the virtues and vices.

(a) A virtue or a vice is a disposition, among other things, to act and to feel, and there is a sense in which an orientation is a disposition to act and to feel (even though an orientation does not *itself* involve a feeling).[64] The way that Herzog sees the world profoundly affects how he acts and feels. But the relation to the virtues is complicated. Herzog's orientation is often a cognitive distortion on the exercise of particular virtues. An orientation O might keep the agent from perceiving a situation for what it is, for instance, a time to risk your life to save another, i.e., a time for courage. Suppose we accept something like John McDowell's account of virtue. McDowell claims that the virtuous person has a "single sensitivity ... an ability to recognize requirements that situations impose on one's behaviour."[65] Now, a virtuous person, one equipped with a properly operating sensitivity, always does the right thing for the right reason and with the right feelings. This seems to exclude from the completely virtuous person any orientation that blocks the operation of the sensitivity. Thus any such blocking orientation counts as a failing. It is a hindrance to being completely virtuous. A proper orientation seems to be a form of human excellence, an improper one a form of human defect. Maybe having a proper orientation should count as a part of excellence in practical deliberation, as among the intellectual excellences of the practical realm.[66] Or perhaps Lurie's and Herzog's orientations simply provide robust illustrations of the virtue theorist's claim that having a good character crucially involves having proper perceptions, involves seeing the world aright.

(b) If an agent has all the virtues, she will have a proper set of desires; and if she has a proper set of desires, she is likely to have a proper orientation. Suppose that temperance involves desiring only a modest degree of social attention and praise. It is hard, then, to see how a temperate person could have Herzog's theatrical orientation. Still, the orientation/desire connection is far from clear. For instance, might a distorting orientation spawn problematic desires even in a person who is, for the most part, quite virtuous? Imagine that I am constantly filled with self-doubt. I might interpret many conversations as involving contempt from others or failures on my part. This might lead me to act as I shouldn't, e.g., to respond harshly to imagined insults or to hide myself and not use my talents. Yet there is nothing vicious about having self-doubt, and the central contents of my desires could well be those of the virtuous person. It might be only a very particular desire – here and now to respond harshly to Joe or to run to my room – that would be problematic. Or would my self-doubt tend to elicit something more worrisome, say, an excessive and pervasive desire for reassurance upon reassurance that would tend to be at odds with proper desires and, in general, with a good and useful life?[67] Will a distorting orientation almost inevitably lead to desires that in one way or another take one away from virtue?

(c) I have noted that any orientation could be consistent with a range of particular desires. Yet might a given individual's problematic orientation be the output of some basic and underlying problematic desire, say, with Herzog, the underlying desire always to be seen in the central role, always to be seen as the leading man? If it is, the virtue theorist can say that Herzog merely needs to get rid of this underlying problematic desire. On this picture, change the underlying desire and the problematic orientation will vanish. In some cases that might be possible (though to change this kind of desire would be no small trick). However, I suspect that many problematic orientations (including many involving a problematic underlying desire) arise as a consequence of some kind of developmental damage to the individual, damage linked to profound but unsatisfied and altogether *unproblematic* childhood desires. And if that is an orientation's origin, then it might seem that, rather than eliminating these earlier unproblematic desires, one must somehow deal with them as a condition for changing the agent's orientation.[68]

The above remarks are hardly sufficient; how the concept of orientation relates to the virtues is an area that needs much more investigation.

(5) Lurie's and Herzog's orientations are moral disorders, flawed forms of living with others, and it is tempting to blame them for this way of living. Yet is one's orientation subject to one's will? Can one simply decide to alter it? (Especially if, psychologically, its origin goes far back and deep?) Moreover, orientations function as cognitive filters. They present the world in such a way that the agent's (possibly false) beliefs about, say, particular others, are confirmed.[69] But then the agent doesn't seem to be in a position to see that these very beliefs (a) do not track the world and (b) are a symptom of her orientation. At its most seamless, an orientation is a classic form of false consciousness, constantly validating itself to those within.[70] However, we don't fault people for being subject to false consciousness. Of course, with a problematic orientation the fault is not in one's local stars (i.e., background social institutions) but in oneself – though apparently in a feature of oneself that is as unreachable as background social institutions.

Still, and even in the teeth of the above considerations, I suspect that most of us do fault Lurie and Herzog. One reason might be that, whatever its background workings, we think that at least sometimes an agent can come to see that he has a certain orientation, that is, can come to see that he is constantly distorting the world – and that at least sometimes he can adjust his beliefs and so his actions accordingly. There might be a kind of deliberative continence available here. If I come to accept that I am (frequently) subject to a distorting filter, there are (sometimes) things that I can do – or fail to do – to compensate for this distortion. The idea is that it is possible both to misperceive and to know this, and so in my deliberations to substitute (even if not necessarily to have) the right perceptions and thus to attain the right beliefs and to do the right actions. At least to some degree this seems a real possibility.

More generally, I suspect that we simply believe that Lurie and Herzog ought not to see people the way they do. Lurie's orientation does change, as does Herzog's, and if they are to be praised for achieving change, they should also be blamed for needing it. It seems as if in some way, and to some degree, we believe that they are responsible for their orientations, could in fact alter them.

We come, then, to the issue of character change. However, if we look at the novels and ask how character change comes about, we will be puzzled. With Herzog, we have three ostensibly epiphanic events: the morning in criminal court, the car crash in Chicago, the vision of Gersbach bathing June. Do they cause character change? That seems unlikely. Are they unrelated to that change? Equally unlikely. But as the old joke about psychiatrists goes, the light bulb has to want to change. Herzog's epiphanic moments are such only because he can now read the world a certain way. He could have been merely outraged that Gersbach was bathing his daughter, utterly missed the tenderness. Apparently, change has to precede the events that precipitate change.

As for Lurie, Attridge notes that

> There is no conscious change of heart; without warning, events and feelings simply overtake him . . . Although Lurie's motives for doing what he does seem as obscure to him as they are to us, something leads him in his "'state of disgrace'" to undertake a life of toil in the service of others.[71]

Here is the sort of thing Attridge has in mind. A pair of Petrus's sheep that have been grazing on Lucy's land will be the central meal at a party. Lurie finds, to his surprise, that he wants them not to die. He knows that there is nothing to be done, nothing to be done with them, the sheep, even if he were to buy them out of slaughter. There is no other role for them in the world they are in. Yet their plight bothers him.

> A bond seems to have come into existence between himself and the two Persians, he does not know how. The bond is not one of affection. It is not even a bond with these two in particular, whom he could not pick out from a mob in a field. Nevertheless, suddenly and without reason, their lot has become important to him. (D 126)

This scene comes long before Lurie acknowledges that becoming good might be the thing to do (D 216). No doubt, this early bit of change in Lurie is a precondition for that later moment. So what, we need to ask, brought about this early bit?

Character change is not easy to understand. This is partly because it comes in many forms. There is the dramatic redemption of the evil man turned saint, as well as the growth in kindness and consideration of the teenager turned adult. When philosophers focus on character change they tend to think of the first, and so we get such things as Kant's idea of the choice of a new "ground" maxim.[72] In the current world, twelve-step programs are a less abstract attempt to revise one's character, though these, too, tend to look for the big switch, e.g., from addiction to sobriety. However, the modest form of character change is not only far more frequent but, I suspect, more interesting – the change of the ordinary person who must struggle with his ordinary sins and ordinary despair: toned-down and law-abiding Raskolnikovs and Mersaults.[73]

Here, there is space to note only one thing about character change. If one's model of character and character change is Kant's, literature will not be enlightening. That is because the Kantian model involves a choice not in space and time, and so not capable of being revealed by a narrative restricted, as all are, to space and, certainly, to time. Kant puts it that moral change involves a "revolution . . . in the mode of thought," and by "mode of thought" here he means the noumenal realm, not the workings of an individual's empirical psychology.[74] Thus there can be no literary evidence that this is or is not how character change works. Nothing literature shows could bear on what is involved in Kantian character change. I leave to another day the question of whether this should be considered a problem for Kant.

Literature can bear on moral philosophy in several ways. One is through presenting a picture of human psychology, broadly construed, a picture of what it is or could be like to be a human being. Any moral theory presupposes such a picture. I have pressed that *Disgrace* and *Herzog* show that a human being lives in a world that is already patterned by one's character, that one's way of being with others is a fundamental feature of human life, a feature that does not reduce to one's beliefs, desires and actions. Any moral theory ought to deal with this fact.

Notes

I am grateful to Kristin Boyce, Ted Cohen, Alice Crary, Garry Hagberg, Gabriel Richardson Lear, Martha Nussbaum, and Uri Pasovsky for their very helpful comments on earlier drafts of this essay.

1 Søren Kierkegaard, *Either/Or*, trans. Howard V. Hong and Edna H. Hong (Princeton, NJ: Princeton University Press, 1987), 2.7–8.
2 Aristotle, *Nicomachean Ethics*, 1106b, trans. Roger Crisp (Cambridge: Cambridge University Press, 2000), 31. The words are not Aristotle's. He is quoting an unnamed and unknown source.
3 Iris Murdoch, "Against Dryness," in Murdoch, *Existentialists and Mystics* (New York: Penguin Putnam, Inc., 1998), 293.
4 See Lawrence A. Blum, *Moral Perception and Particularity* (Cambridge: Cambridge University Press, 1994); and Barbara Herman, "The Practice of Moral Judgment," in Herman, *The Practice of Moral Judgment* (Cambridge, MA: Harvard University Press, 1993).
5 Iris Murdoch, *The Sovereignty of Good* (Oxford: Oxford University Press, 1985), 17; reprinted in Murdoch, *Existentialists and Mystics*, 313.
6 Murdoch, *The Sovereignty of Good*, 17–18; *Existentialists and Mystics*, 313; emphasis in original.
7 A third variant of inattention comes out in the following Murdoch passage.

> I am looking out of my window in an anxious and resentful state of mind, oblivious of my surroundings, brooding perhaps on some damage done to my prestige. Then suddenly I observe a hovering kestrel. In a moment everything is altered. The brooding self with its hurt vanity has disappeared. There is nothing now but kestrel. And when I return to thinking of the other matter it seems less important. (*Sovereignty of Good*, 84; *Existentialists and Mystics*, 369)

Here, Murdoch's self-absorption has *herself* as its content, is doubly problematic in being a focus purely on the self. Moreover, this example's phenomenology differs from that of the others. Those called upon an active focus. One is to look broadly and carefully; one pays attention. By contrast, the kestrel example involves an achievement of passivity; one makes oneself open to the beauty of the kestrel.

The example, incidentally, also suggests something else: a link between attaining perspective on one's narrow concerns and gaining contact with something transcendent. The kestrel is an image of beauty and value unconnected to human concerns. It takes one away not just from one's particular concerns but from human concerns altogether. It is clearly intended to evoke Gerard Manley Hopkins's falcon in "The Windhover."

8   J. M. Coetzee, *Disgrace* (New York: Penguin Books, 2000) and Saul Bellow, *Herzog* (New York: Viking Press, 1964).
9   Murdoch, *Sovereignty of Good*, 93; *Existentialists and Mystics*, 376–7.
10 For such a reading of *Effi Briest*, see Julia Annas, "Personal Love and Kantian Ethics in *Effi Briest*," *Philosophy and Literature* 8:1 (1984): 15–31.
11 Against Annas on *Effi Briest*, see Marcia Baron, "Was *Effi Briest* a Victim of Kantian Morality?" *Philosophy and Literature* 12:1 (1988): 95–113.
12 See Iris Murdoch, "Vision and Choice in Morality," *Proceedings of the Aristotelian Society*, supp. vol. 30 (1956), 38, reprinted in *Existentialists and Mystics*, 79; Martha Nussbaum, *Love's Knowledge* (Oxford: Oxford University Press, 1990), 3; Cora Diamond, "Martha Nussbaum and the Need for Novels," *Philosophical Investigations* 16:2 (1993), 134; Alice Crary, *Beyond Moral Judgment* (Cambridge, MA: Harvard University Press, 2007), 43.
13 See, for instance, Murdoch, "Vision and Choice in Morality," 40; *Existentialists and Mystics*, 82.
14 See, for instance, Diamond, "Martha Nussbaum and the Need for Novels," 134:

> The making of particular moral judgments is decisively *placed* within the more general picture, which includes an idea of the workings of the soul, a conception of fullness of life, and a contrast between the world as it appears to a dead habitual kind of perception and the "active" universe (emphasis in original).

See also Crary, *Beyond Moral Judgment*, chapters 1 and 4.

15 See Martha Nussbaum, *Love's Knowledge*, 5: "[C]ertain truths about human life can only be fittingly and accurately stated in the language and forms characteristic of the narrative artist."
16 Arthur Danto, "Philosophy as/and/of Literature," *Proceedings and Addresses of the American Philosophical Association* 58:1 (1984), 16. Reprinted in this volume, chapter 4, PHILOSOPHY AND/AS/OF LITERATURE.
17 Gabriel Lear has suggested to me that this kind of identification may be more suited to modern novels than to other genres, say, ancient epic. Of course, readers and auditors were surely moved by the ancient stories but it is not clear that this amounted to that losing oneself in the character which identification seems to involve. For my purposes, this question can remain open. It is sufficient if reading (many) modern novels works in the way I describe.
18 I thank Ted Cohen for pressing me to make this point.
19 I suspect that the absence of constraining external data provides the reader with more leeway to project herself onto the character, that such projection is easier when there is less that is and can be directly known about the character.
20 On the constant presentness of fictional characters, see Stanley Cavell's remarks on how rushing the stage cannot affect the characters in a play: "Quiet the house, pick up the thread again, and Othello will reappear." See Stanley Cavell, "The Avoidance of Love," in Cavell,

Must We Mean What We Say? (Cambridge: Cambridge University Press, 1976), 326–331. The quoted passage is from 330.

21 Arthur Danto, "Philosophy as/and/of Literature," *Proceedings and Addresses of the American Philosophical Association* 58:1 (1984), 16. See also this volume, chapter 4, PHILOSOPHY AND/AS/OF LITERATURE, 64.

22 While I don't have space to discuss it, this is the place at least to note the recent claim that, through reading a novel, we can become sufficiently emotionally engaged that we can have experiences that, in Alice Crary's words, "are capable of qualifying as developments of our moral outlooks" (Crary, *Beyond Moral Judgment*, 128; this is also a central theme of Nussbaum's work on literature). Reading can be not a purely passive activity but an active one in which I feel something of myself at stake in the story and so I develop in the process of reading it, of being engaged with it. Perhaps if one accepts Danto's thesis that, in the end, the text is about "the 'I' that reads the text," it should be unsurprising that this "I" finds herself affected by the process of reading, i.e., of being read. And perhaps a fictional character's lack of epistemic or ontological resistance helps facilitate the emotional engagement that Crary discusses. On this topic, see also, Gary L. Hagberg, "Imagined Identities: Autobiography at One Remove," *New Literary History* 38 (2007); see especially 168–70.

23 Of course, a philosopher might invoke an incident from a novel as a shortcut to what is, in effect, an off-the-rack example. This is usually done without invoking the actual words of the text (about whose meaning there could be disagreement) and invariably without providing the detail and discussion that amounts to a *reading*.

24 There has been much discussion about the differences between philosophical and literary examples. Good places to start are R. W. Beardsmore, "Literary Examples and Philosophical Confusion," in A. Phillips Griffiths ed., *Philosophy and Literature* (Cambridge: Cambridge University Press, 1984); Nussbaum, *Love's Knowledge*, 46ff; Onora O'Neill, "The Power of Example," *Philosophy* 61:235 (1986); and Cora Diamond, "Anything but Argument?" *Philosophical Investigations* 5:1 (1982), reprinted in Diamond, *The Realistic Spirit* (Cambridge, MA: MIT Press, 1991); see also Diamond, "Wittgenstein and Metaphysics," in *The Realistic Spirit*.

25 If it is worried that popular works often endorse contemporary prejudices, well (a) that is not necessarily true (again, consider *Uncle Tom's Cabin*) and (b) it can surely be true of works of high aesthetic quality.

26 See, for instance, R. W. Beardsmore, "Literary Examples and Philosophical Confusion."

27 Aristotle, *Poetics*, 1451b. In the Leon Golden translation (Tallahassee, FL: University Presses of Florida, 1981), the key sentence reads: "Poetry, therefore, is more philosophical and more significant than history, for poetry is more concerned with the universal, and history more with the individual."

28 Many people clearly share this intuition. Here, for instance, Russell Hardin discusses the role of examples in moral philosophy:

> An artificial example should be especially suspect. It may serve a role in clarifying the structure of an argument or in helping us discover a class of problem. But if there is a point of persuasion in using it, we should be able to find real or literary instances to illustrate our point.

Interestingly, literary instances are placed on the same side as real instances and are opposed to the artificial examples of moral philosophers. See Russell Hardin, *Morality Within the Limits of Reason* (Chicago: University of Chicago Press, 1988), 27. I have dealt elsewhere at greater length with the intuition discussed here. See my "*Lord Jim* and Moral Judgment: Literature and Moral Philosophy," *The Journal of Aesthetics and Art Criticism* 56:3 (1998): 265–81.

29 Derek Attridge, *J. M. Coetzee and the Ethics of Reading* (Chicago: University of Chicago Press, 2004), 183.

30 Citations to *Disgrace* and *Herzog* are in the text and employ the abbreviations *D* and *H*. As mentioned above, the editions used are J. M. Coetzee, *Disgrace* (New York: Penguin Books, 2000) and Saul Bellow, *Herzog* (New York: Viking Press, 1964). All emphases are in the originals.

31 Perhaps Lurie named his daughter for those poems. She has certainly become someone who dwells among what seem to be untrodden ways, but she is not in the usual sense a lyrical figure. She is heavy and somewhat stolid and works a farm in heavy peasant boots. She has become a peasant, Lurie thinks. And yet when he can see her properly, she is beautiful, in fact rightly named (*D* 218).

32 See Kierkegaard, *Either/Or*, 1:301–445.

33 The registering of things as salient or not is something Alice Crary stresses about what she calls a person's "moral outlook." See Crary, *Beyond Moral Judgment*, 43.

34 Joseph Conrad, *Lord Jim*, chapter 20 and chapter 1.

35 For instance, see Kierkegaard, *Either/Or*, 1. 345–6.

36 A different theme might be broached here, one tied to Kierkegaard's seducer. Garry Hagberg argues that the seducer is engaged in systematic self-deception, conceals himself from himself, is subject to what Hagberg terms, "willful blindness." Lurie might also be thought of in these terms (see below, §5 in the discussion of Moses Herzog), although how to understand the relation of an orientation to the will is among the crucial questions. See Garry L. Hagberg, *Describing Ourselves: Wittgenstein and Autobiographical Consciousness* (Oxford: Oxford University Press, 2008), chapter 3, §3. The quoted phrase is from p. 114.

37 The Christian category is juxtaposed with a Greek or, in this case, an aesthetic one. The missing roommate's actual name is that of the embodiment of mortal beauty, "Helen."

38 For a subtle discussion of complications in the concept of agency, see Sarah Buss, "Valuing Autonomy and Respecting Persons: Manipulation, Seduction, and the Basis of Moral Constraints," *Ethics* 115: 2 (2005). See also Sarah Conly, "Seduction, Rape, and Coercion," *Ethics* 115:1 (2004).

39 Franz Kafka, *The Trial*, trans. Willa Muir and Edwin Muir (New York: Modern Library, 1964), 286. For Coetzee on Kafka, see J. M. Coetzee, "Kafka: Translators on Trial," *The New York Review of Books* 45:8 (May 14, 1998) and the section titled "Kafka," in J. M. Coetzee, *Doubling the Point* (Cambridge, MA: Harvard University Press, 1992).

40 Attridge, *J. M. Coetzee and the Ethics of Reading*, 181.

41 Derek Attridge, "J. M. Coetzee's *Disgrace*: Introduction," *Interventions: International Journal of Postcolonial Studies* 4:3 (2002): 318.

42 See Samuel Scheffler, *The Rejection of Consequentialism* (Oxford: Oxford University Press, 1982).

43 John Lanchester, "A Will of His Own," *The New York Review of Books* 52:18 (November 17, 2005).

44 Note also that being vulnerable is not the same as being fragile. A china demitasse is fragile but not necessarily vulnerable; stiffened canine corpses are vulnerable but hardly fragile.

45 Bellow, *Herzog*, 184.

46 Herzog's "theatricality" is not quite the same as what Michael Fried means by the term. In Fried's use what is crucial is an awareness of being viewed. To the extent that this is true

of Herzog, the one who does the viewing is usually himself. More important, for Herzog the key to being viewed is the playing of this or that role. Fried does not make much of this latter element. See Michael Fried, *Absorption and Theatricality: Painting and Beholder in the Age of Diderot* (Berkeley, CA: University of California Press, 1980).

47 But the passage is also prescient. It antedates by just a few years the work of a philosopher who has tried to go "deeply enough" into the ordinary, namely, Stanley Cavell.
48 Saul Bellow, "The Distracted Public" (1990), in Bellow, *It All Adds Up* (New York: Viking Press, 1994), 129.
49 Bellow, "The Distracted Public," 155.
50 Bellow, "The Distracted Public," 167.
51 Frank Kermode, "Herzog," in Irving Howe ed., *Herzog: Text and Criticism* (New York: Viking Press, 1976), 468–9.
52 Theodore Solotaroff, "Napoleon Street," in Howe ed., *Herzog: Text and Criticism*, 478.
53 Alfred Kazin, "The Earthly City of the Jews," in Howe ed., *Herzog: Text and Criticism*, 485.
54 See David Hume, *A Treatise of Human Nature*, book 3, part 2, section 2.
55 See Jerome Kagan, *Galen's Prophecy: Temperament in Human Nature* (New York: Basic Books, 1994).
56 No doubt, certain kinds of self-absorption could count as personality disorders. Lurie and Herzog may be on this continuum; still, neither goes that far. They are not, for instance, borderline personalities. Their disorders are, I want to say, garden-variety moral disorders.
57 See Theophrastus, *The Characters*, trans. Philip Vellacott (Baltimore, MD: Penguin, 1967).
58 An orientation is also not expressive of or constituted by a global belief, e.g. "everyone is against me." If a belief were at issue, contrary evidence would undermine it but orientations are notoriously resistant to evidence. They are better understood as *behind* the global belief rather than as its expression.
59 I thank Alice Crary for pressing me to discuss this issue.
60 For good anthologies concerning current debates, see Amélie Oksenberg Rorty ed., *Explaining Emotions* (Berkeley: University of California Press, 1980); and Robert C. Solomon ed., *Thinking about Feeling* (Oxford: Oxford University Press, 2004).
61 Peter Goldie, "Emotion, Feeling, and Knowledge of the Word," in Solomon ed., *Thinking about Feeling*, 99.
62 Ronald de Sousa, "Emotions: What I Know, What I'd Like to Think I Know, and What I'd Like to Think," in Solomon ed., *Thinking about Feeling*, 65.
63 Is an orientation a character trait? Amélie Rorty claims that some "emotions come close to being dispositional character traits: we speak of vengeful or affectionate persons." See Rorty, "Explaining Emotions," in Rorty ed., *Explaining Emotions*, 105. However, Lurie's and Herzog's orientations go considerably beyond, are more pervasive and all-distorting than what Rorty has in mind.

One of the foremost writers on emotions, Robert Solomon, writes that

> I am interested . . . not in those brief "irruptive" reactions or responses but in the long-term narratives of Othello, Iago, Lily Bart, and those of my less drama-ridden but nevertheless very emotional friends. I am interested in the meanings of life, not short term neurological arousal.

See Robert C. Solomon, "Emotions, Thoughts, and Feelings: Emotions as Engagements with the World," in Solomon ed., *Thinking about Feeling*, 78–9. The characters he is talking about seem either dominated by a single emotion (jealousy, envy) or in fact to have what I would call a problematic orientation (Lily Bart). On the whole, Solomon's concerns here are very close to my own. However, I think that, in this respect, the phenomena on which Solomon focuses are not the usual ones for theorists of the emotions.

64 In this way, an orientation is not like a virtue or a vice. To be virtuous is usually said to involve taking pleasure in the right things, but one does not take or fail to take pleasure in an orientation.

65 John McDowell, "Virtue and Reason," in McDowell, *Mind, Value, & Reality* (Cambridge, MA: Harvard University Press, 1998), 53.

66 I have focused on forms of defect. This is the place to note that there can probably be more than one "proper" orientation. The requirement is to see the world as it is. That seems a standard that could be satisfied by more than one way of living in it.

67 I owe this point to Kristin Boyce.

68 I have benefited greatly from a conversation with Gabriel Lear about the issues in this subsection.

69 Here, too, there is overlap with the way some emotions work. This is de Sousa's point when he invokes the way emotions orient us. See de Sousa, "Emotions: What I Know, What I'd Like to Think I Know, and What I'd Like to Think," in Solomon ed., *Thinking about Feeling*, 65.

70 George Sher has recently investigated the issue of responsibility with respect to cases of inadvertence, forgetfulness, and other traits for which we might seem responsible but which seem not directly and immediately under the control of the will. See George Sher, "Out of Control," *Ethics* 116:2 (2006).

71 Attridge, *J. M. Coetzee and the Ethics of Reading*, 175 and 181.

72 See Immanuel Kant, *Religion within the Boundaries of Mere Reason* (Cambridge: Cambridge University Press, 1998), part 1.

73 See Fyodor Dostoyevsky, *Crime and Punishment*, and Albert Camus, *The Stranger*.

74 Kant, *Religion within the Boundaries of Mere Reason*, 68. Kant goes on to say that character change involves "a gradual transformation in the mode of sense," something that can be seen and so could be literarily depicted. But Kant is clear that the noumenal change is the key to the phenomenal. It is the fundamental and morally laudable form of change.

Part V

Narrative and the Question of Literary Truth

17

Narration, Imitation, and Point of View

GREGORY CURRIE

In some narratives a character tells the story; he or she inhabits its world, knowing of its events first hand or by the testimony of other characters. In other tales we have the impersonal, anonymous narration that comes from outside the story-world, yet mysteriously unlimited in its access to information about that world. There are questions to be asked about both these kinds of narration, but the greater difficulty for narrative theory comes with forms that fit neither model, while they seem to deploy elements of both. I am concerned here with the case of narration which is not narration *by* a character but which is – it is claimed – narration *from the character's point of view*. Before surveying attempts to account for this, I'll indicate the direction of my own thinking, and how it will structure the essay.

I say the idea of narration by one agent from the point of view of another is incoherent if taken literally; I'll also reject a tempting non-literal interpretation of it. So it's perhaps unfortunate that we are now comfortable with this way of speaking. But labeling is the least of our worries, and I'm content to go on using the phrase "point of view narration" and its relatives; what I hope to show is that current theories of what goes by this label are badly wrong.

They are wrong for a reason. Narrative theory has long been a taxonomic project, apt to provide labels such as "mood" and "voice," but reluctant to explain them except by vague analogies; it is notably distant from testable theories of thought and action. Its priorities, unsurprisingly, are wrong. The formal distinctions on which it thrives, such as those between narrators at different levels, are just the book-keeping part of narrative theory; the substantive problem is to say what narrators do, and how readers respond to what they do, when some distinctive and important mode of narration is in play.[1] If this is declared to be not narrative theory but something else – psychology of narrative, say – then so much the worse for narrative theory.

What's the key to the reorientation I propose? Something from Jowett's version of the *Republic* nicely summarizes it: "[W]hen the poet speaks in the person of another . . . the narrative of the poet may be said to proceed by way of imitation."[2] Imitation, in more or less the ordinary, current sense, is the key to understanding what theorists of narrative call point of view narration. But I will call as well on ideas not part of the

---

A Companion to the Philosophy of Literature, First Edition. Edited by Garry L. Hagberg and Walter Jost.
© 2010 John Wiley & Sons Ltd. Published 2015 by John Wiley & Sons, Ltd.

folk concept of imitation; social psychology is teaching us how extraordinarily prone to imitation we are, in ways that reach far down into the psyche. The self-conscious and sustained imitation of the actor will not be our model; we will be more concerned with fleeting and internalized movements of the body and mind which mirror the responses of a person before us or in our thoughts.

In the first section of this chapter, I begin with a general account of point of view, and an important constraint that any theory of point of view in narrative ought to meet. The next section catalogues some ways in which theories of point of view have failed to meet the constraint. The third section begins the task of developing a new, more naturalistically inclined theory. The final two sections narrow the focus, examining some subtly distinct ways in which authors use imitative techniques so as to make salient to readers a character's way of responding to the world of the story.

Agency and Access to the World

Narrative theorists most often reach for a visual model when summarizing the notion of point of view.[3] But understanding a subject's point of view is a much larger project than cataloguing what is seen. To say that we have points of view is an expression of our limited access to the world, across modalities of perception, feeling, thought, and action. It is partly a matter of perceptual orientation, which means that only some things can be seen, or heard, or otherwise perceptually encountered, at a given moment. And position in space and time makes certain events and objects available for direct manipulation and others not. We need also to accommodate *cognitive* aspects of point of view so as to allow for both the reflection in thought of our access to the world (thinking: the hammer is near by) and the limitations thought imposes on that access, as when a train of ideas makes some options more accessible than others, and some not accessible at all. At the limit, the agent may simply not possess the relevant concept of that which is otherwise available to be grasped, as with Henry James's Maisie, and hence be compromised in both thought and action. And there are non-cognitive limitations imposed on our access to the world, as when our preferences and interests make unavailable to us what are, from other perspectives, adequate characterizations of things and events as interesting or dull, valuable or worthless.[4]

All these are important aspects of point of view, though not all are stable or emblematic of a subject's identity; Marcel's highly contingent physical position at various points in Proust's narrative crucially restricts his access to information, and hence the shape of his narrative. And what is crucial to me at one moment may be of no importance at the next. But there are differences in point of view which are more robust: *dispositional* aspects, to be contrasted with the *state* aspects just illustrated. Iago manipulates Othello's perceptual point of view, ensuring that he sees and hears crucial things, and he does so knowing much about how Othello is disposed to respond to these things: how he will be emotionally engaged by certain ideas, will pursue certain questions, ignoring questions that for others would seem urgent. Most of us have similarly stable if less arresting dispositions: we reason in a certain way, give special weight to certain kinds of factors, attend to certain facts or possibilities more than to others; we have general beliefs and preferences which are resistant to revision and which affect our practical and theoretical reasoning; we have emotional sensitivities which highlight some options and obscure others. These patterns of response are slow to change, if they change at all.

Together, state and dispositional aspects of point of view constitute a person's way of responding to the world. Whether any given description of point of view is dominated by state or by dispositional aspects depends on the narrative choices of the author: a conventional way to start is with the broad dispositional picture, thereafter focusing on state aspects as events unfold; in other forms the dispositional aspects are left to be inferred from descriptions, often minimal ones, of particular states. We don't need to hear much of the speech of the two entrants to Henry's lunchroom in *The Killers* to infer dispositional aspects of their points of view.

So much for what point of view is. Now for a necessary truth about it.

1   Whatever we do, we do from our own point of view. We cannot act on – or perceive, or think about, or respond in any way to – the world from a point of view other than our own.

And as a special case of this:

2   We cannot narrate from any point of view other than our own.

Yet it's a commonplace of narrative theory that a narrator can narrate *from a point of view other than his or her own*. If (2) is true, the commonplace is false. I believe we ought to reject the commonplace; in doing so we will better understand what narrators actually do.

I will come to the argument for this shortly, but note now that (2) is consistent with what we know about the manipulation and restriction of our own points of view, and about the comprehension of points of view not our own. I can arrange for my field of vision to be adjusted or restricted so that I see pretty much what you see; that is altering my (visual) point of view, not swapping mine for yours. After all, my point of view then has a property that yours lacks: being manipulated or restricted. Nor does the principle deny that the points of view of others are accessible; we can take them into account, we can think about how the world seems from that point of view, we can understand another's thoughts or actions in the light of what we know about their point of view; we may – to come to the topic – convey something about another's point of view in the act of narrating a story. But only the most deluded subject would believe they occupy a point of view not their own.

Speaking and Seeing

It may seem irritatingly pedantic to insist on the truth of (1) and (2). Who would deny these things? While writers on narrative do not directly challenge these propositions, there has, since Henry James, been a slide towards doctrines which contradict them. Of *The Ambassadors*, James wrote that "Strether's sense of these things, and Strether's only, should avail me for showing them."[5] More generally, "there is no economy of treatment without an adopted, a related point of view."[6] Beach and Lubbock quickly distilled from the later Jamesian canon, and from the armory of commentary which James put around it, the rule that action is to be shown, not told. Their emphases are slightly different: Beach contrasts the intrusive "impudence" of an omniscient narrator moving from psyche to psyche with the "close-woven psychological tissue" of James, arguing that James's commitment to illusion required "consistency in the point of view," which he achieved most completely in *The Ambassadors*;[7] Lubbock focuses on the decision not to make Strether the narrator, for that would weaken the desired sense of an immediate connection between the reader and Strether's state of mind. While Lubbock is sensitive to the variation of effect in James, his summary, unanalyzed judgment is always that the story is told from Strether's point of view.[8]

The implication, a little clearer in Lubbock than in Beach, is that the story is narrated, not by Strether, but from Strether's point of view. Writing somewhat later, Gerard Genette claimed to see some backsliding in other commentators, who suggest that Strether narrates his own story.[9] We must, he says, distinguish the point of view of narration and the identity of the narrator. While there are cases where these things coincide (as with Ishmael in *Moby Dick*), this is not so with *The Ambassadors*: Strether is not the narrator, though the point of view of narration is his.[10]

We need not ask whether James consistently adopts the kind of character-focused narration which the formulations of Lubbock, Genette, and others are intended to capture.[11] If James's narrator consistently restricted himself to perceptions and knowledge had by Strether at the relevant time, I would still deny that the narrator has thereby got into the position of narrating from Strether's point of view. As long as there is textual evidence enough for us to say that the narrator is not Strether, Maisie, or any other character within the world of the action, there is evidence enough for us to say that the point of view of narration is not that of Strether, Maisie, or any such character.[12] The point of view of the narration is the point of view of the narrator, and Genette's breakthrough is simply a road to further confusion.[13]

This follows immediately from (2) above, according to which a narrator narrates only from her own point of view. And as I indicated at the announcement of (2), it is not an argument for distinguishing the identity of the narrator and the identity of the point of view to say, as one sometimes can, that the narrator restricts herself to what is known or seen by a character. The nature of a point of view is not exhausted in what the person with that point of view does know, or see, or hear, or tell, or do, but in what he or she *can* know, or see, etc. Point of view is an intentional notion, inseparable from questions about possibility. Othello knows various things, and falsely believes others. But there are things he *should* know, *could* disbelieve, *would* be questioning about if he were not so easily led down certain paths; all this is constitutive of his point of view. Two people may see or hear or tell the same things (they may both see or hear or tell nothing) without their points of view being the same. If their points of view are distinct, then there must be at least one thing which one of them could see or hear or tell which the other could not. To understand a narrator's point of view fully is to understand what resources for knowing, sensing, telling, and doing that point of view makes available, and knowing that means a great deal more than knowing simply what the person with that point of view knows.

These are not the only differences between points of view. Two people may know and tell the same thing, but given their different points of view it may be surprising in the case of the one that she knows it and not surprising in the case of the other. Given A's point of view, it took insight to know that P, and courage to tell it, while B's point of view made P obvious and unproblematic. B cannot make it difficult for himself to know something that is in fact obvious to him, cannot make it an act of courage to tell that which for him has no consequences. But these are the sorts of things that would be required if one person were to narrate from another's point of view.

These general observations about points of view can be restated in more narrative-relevant terms as claims about an audience's experience of engaging with narrative. Being aware of the point of view from which a narration is given involves having a sense of what sorts of things *might* fall within the narrative, whether or not they do so. If the narrator in a story happens to be a character, it does not follow that we will learn all that the character knows – much of it would be irrelevant and some that is highly relevant is withheld from us for dramatic purposes.[14] But we do recognize that anything that is known by the character-narrator is potentially available to us in the narrative; that is why we sometimes feel cheated by artful withholdings of information. And if the narrator is not a character, then we know that the restriction of information to that which is available to a character is at best a convenience – something adopted by the narrator for certain purposes, and able to be put aside at will.[15] A useful analogy here is the difference between a still photographic image of a motionless object, and a cinematic image of one. The object is seen as motionless in both cases, but in the case of the cinematic image and not in the case of the photographic one, there is a possibility of motion; if the object had moved during the taking of the image, the cinematic image would register the movement. And this difference with regard to what is possible makes for different experiences for the viewer in the two cases; one experiences a possibility in the one case which is absent in the other.

Nothing depends on claiming that two people never share the same point of view. Sameness of point of view is a loose notion, and we are sometimes happy to count two people as having a single point of view. If two people share a point of view then each can narrate from the point of view of the other by narrating from his own. But points of view are not shared in the case of narrator-character pairs as we find them in *The Ambassadors* or other Jamesian and James-like fictional works. For the narrator does not occupy a place in the world of the fiction that would allow him to share the point of view of the characters. The narrator occupies a status with respect to the events of the story quite different from that of any character caught up in the action. Indeed, this is common ground with those who claim that the narrator can narrate from the point of view of a character.[16] We all agree that the point of view of the character is not that of the narrator; we disagree about whether the narrator can narrate from a point of view other than his own.

335

Narratologists are apt now to speak more of focalization than of point of view, and we should ask whether the new term reflects a conceptual shift that might avoid the problems thus far encountered. "Focalization" was introduced by Genette himself, as an alternative to "point of view" without, he claims, the latter's "specifically visual connotation."[17] But there is one way in which "focalization" is asked to do extra work, and that is to mark a distinction between internally and externally focalized narratives. While the former are narratives from the point of view of one or more characters, the latter are narratives, like *The Maltese Falcon*, in which "the hero performs in front of us without our ever being allowed to know his thoughts or feelings."[18] As a distinction this is baffling; thus defined, an externally focalized narrative might also be an internally focalized one, as would be the case where we are told what the character sees, but not what he thinks or feels, since it is no part of the concept of focalization that every aspect of the character's point of view be presented. But we need not struggle with this, for the concept *externally focalized narrative* is irrelevant to our concerns. *Narrative from the point of view of a character* is equivalent to *internally focalized narrative*, and our worry has been that a narrative cannot be narrated by one person and told from the point of view of another. The worry is reformulable as the thought that an internally focalized narrative cannot be narrated by a non-character narrator. Talk of focalization, whatever it is helpful for, will not help us out of the difficulty posed by (2).[19]

Imitation

A natural idea to reach for at this point is this: narrators do not really narrate from any point of view other than their own, but they may pretend to do so, and we, participating in the pretence they create, may imagine that it is so. There are occasions, rather unusual ones, when this is an apt description, and I'll present one later on. But in general this idea has limited capacity to illuminate the sorts of cases people have in mind when they speak of "shifts of point of view." James's narrator in *The Ambassadors* does not pretend to narrate from Strether's point of view, nor does the reader imagine that he does. Somehow, the narrator's engagement with that point of view does affect the imaginings of the reader and may encourage, at various points, a form of imagining of the character "from the inside." Somehow, the narrator is allowing us imaginative glimpses – brief and partial ones – of what it is like for that character to sense, contemplate, and respond to the actions and events of the story. But these character-focused imaginings do not generally arise because the narrator is pretending that the point of view of the character is his or her own.[20]

How, then, do they arise? I'm not sure there is a fully general characterization that answers this question; I at any rate don't have one. But a good many central cases – those which are apt to come up in literary discussions – get some illumination from the idea of imitation or (a term we shall meet later) enactment. Of course imitation is a notion close to pretence and to imagination. A good deal of pretence involves imitation, and as we shall see, it is possible to imitate merely imagined people. Perhaps capacities for pretence and imagination evolved from older, imitative capacities. In some of the cases I shall describe, imitative behaviors amount to a kind of pretending, and may provide the impetus for certain kinds of imaginative, empathic explorations of character.[21] But imitation is the most generally applicable tool I have for understanding the kinds of cases I shall describe.

I'll now summarize the relation, as I see it, between imitation and point of view narration in two claims. First, in the sorts of cases where we are inclined to say that the narrator takes the point of view of some character, what actually happens is that the narrator imitates that character. This imitation is generally very partial and temporary: much more so than in the case where, say, an actor imitates the voice, mannerisms, and other aspects of the persona of Churchill or some other historical character. Secondly, this imitative mode of narration is effective in making the character's point of view salient for us readers if it encourages us to imitate the character. Putting these two ideas together we can say: narrators give us insight into a character's point of view by imitating aspects of that character's response to the world, and thereby encouraging us to do the same.

This is not the only way for a narrator to give salience to a character's point of view. At one extreme, the narration may be given over, temporarily, to that character; in such a case the narration really is *from* that character's point of view, because the character *is* (now) the narrator. And a narrator may make a character's point of view salient while retaining the *opacity* of the point of view; simply by telling us what the character says and does, the narrator makes it plain that the character has a vividly inhabited perspective on things, without it being at all clear to the audience what having that perspective is like.[22] And narrators can simply describe a point of view, or significant parts of it, telling us general facts about how the character tends to respond to the world. But these devices are ones we can ignore because they are not among the narratorial tropes it is tempting to describe as "narrating from the character's point of view." What I am suggesting is that we can get much (perhaps not all) that we would want from a theory of "character-focused narration" from a theory that foregrounds the role of imitation. The rest of this essay is devoted to exploring the resources of this idea.

How does one imitate a point of view? There is a tendency to announce the subjectivity of point of view, and so we are pushed towards saying that what is being imitated is goings on within a private sphere of consciousness, the inner mental life of the agent whose point of view this is. It is unclear how this could be achieved.[23] But there is no purely phenomenological approach to point of view which brackets the world and focuses on the subjectivity of the point of view itself. We do better – as I have been insisting – to think of point of view as a way of responding to the world. And the narrator who tells us about things and events in the world of the story, may tell us in ways which imitate the responses to that world which are characteristic of the point of view in question. Some of these ways involve specialized tropes of language which have long been associated with the manipulation of point of view. With the most noted of these, free indirect discourse (FID), the narrator uses language in ways which, very selectively and rarely for sustained periods, imitate the spoken language, or sometimes the thought-in-language, of a character, as with

(a) Tomorrow was Monday, Monday, the beginning of another school week.[24]

The narrator is not understood as offering a complex time-travel scenario, but as mimicking the character's own expression of, or tendency to express, her feelings about the imminence of the unwanted new school week.[25] He does not do this by quoting a whole sentence or more which did or might issue from the character. But imitation need not be systematic and sustained; one might imitate a friend's tone by placing a certain emphasis on a single word. Here the narrator's repetition ("Monday, Monday") is understood to mirror the character's own, expressive of her dismay at the closeness of the school week.[26]

Linguists have accounted for the peculiarity of FID by saying that it involves two distinct contexts with respect to which semantic values for different sorts of expressions are evaluated. Suppose that (a) is uttered by Albert, indirectly reporting what Bernard has said: "Tomorrow is Monday, Monday, the beginning of another school week." Then the values of pronouns and tenses in (a) depend on the context of Albert's utterance, while the values of other indexicals in (a) (demonstratives such as *this*, *that*, *here*, *there*, *now*, and, as in this case, *tomorrow*) depend on the context of Bernard's utterance.[27] It is tempting to infer from this that the narrator who uses FID speaks in a way which somehow combines or compromises between these two points of view.[28] But the utterance would not be intelligible in the way that it is if that were so; it must be seen as issuing squarely from the narrator, speaking, as always, with his own voice, but using thereby one of the devices of imitation. In this case the device is one which draws on aspects of Bernard's point of view so as to allow us to evaluate "tomorrow" correctly. And by its uncomfortable repetition of the word, it raises the salience of that point of view. But that point of view is not to be understood as, or as a constituent of, the point of view of utterance.

Isn't there a much more obvious and systematic – and hence more effective – form of imitation that narrator's have available, namely the direct (word for word) reporting of speech (DRS)? If so, it would be hard to claim that FID is valued because it is a powerful imitative device. But while FID is much less a *replication* of the character's speech/thought than is DRS, it is much more an imitation, at least in cases where DRS occurs in a written and not a spoken context.[29] Suppose my job is to look out for semaphore signals from someone on the next hill, and pass them on. What I do is replicate (more or less) the movements I see from the other hill; it would seem odd to say that I was imitating the person on that hill.[30] Suppose, however, I was giving you a verbal account of the semaphore-encoded message, but every now and again performed little movements notably like the movements of the flag-waver; in that case you would (if you understood what was going on at all) see highly salient evidence of imitation in my movements, wondering perhaps whether I was making some ironic comment on his odd flag-waving style. Where someone sets themselves to report, in writing, the language of a message directly, the closeness between what the two people do does not count as imitation on anyone's part. But when someone uses an indirect method of reporting which does not *require* sameness of words and word order, any salient resemblance between the report and what is being reported on strikes us very naturally as imitative.

It is noted that we are especially (though not invariably) apt to empathize with a character whose point of view is made salient through the narrator's use of FID, while the direct reporting of speech is generally less empathy inducing.[31] What explains this? When we recognize that the narrator is imitating the character, as he or she is with FID but not with DRS, there is tendency for us as readers to do the same. We tend – to a degree only of course, and very selectively – to imitate that way of responding to the world, and come thereby to feel some of the emotional and other effects of responding in that way.

I expect a skeptical response to the idea that we imitate the character because we imitate the imitation of the narrator. Is it not simpler and more plausible to say that we imitate the character, and leave the narrator out of it? I don't say that it is always the lead of the narrator that brings us to imitate the character; this can occur in other ways. But the narrator's example is often a powerful one and one we are inclined to follow, because the narrator plays such a central role in orienting us to the story. The narrator is our source, the one on whom we depend for all our information about the story, the one whose choice of words and their order sets the emotional and evaluative tone of the work and the episodes it contains. Finding a narrative to be worth engaging with is in large part a matter of finding the narrator's outlook to be one we find sympathetic, or at least interesting. If we are engaged by the narrative, we are likely to be engaged by the narrator, and hence likely to follow him or her in our exploration of the character.

Some Resources of Narration

It's time to reflect a little on the kinds of imitation available to a narrator. Imitation of speech and, by extension, of thought, is unproblematically within the scope of the narrator's activity. But what of other aspects of a character's ways of responding which go to constitute point of view? How does a narrator imitate hesitancy, or pessimism, or a tendency to colorful reinterpretation of the facts? We might insist on a very narrow reading of "imitation" according to which we can imitate only that which is directly manifest in behavior. This would rule out the imitation of those dispositions just now listed. On the other hand, there is plenty of good evidence that we are as prone to model (I am trying to find a neutral word here) aspects of other people's personalities and relatively stable cognitive "set" when we think about them, as we are to model their outward behavior. Ap Dijksterhuis, who has done much experimental work in this area, says that "we not only imitate the observable behaviour of others, . . . we adopt multiple, sometimes rather complex aspects of others' psychological functioning."[32] Some of the experimental basis for this claim is worth summarizing. Merely by being exposed to aggression- or rudeness- or politeness-related words we are apt to become more aggressive or rude or polite.[33] Youthful subjects primed with words related to the elderly tended both to walk more slowly and to remember less well than controls.[34] Subjects asked to imagine a "typical professor" turned out to do better on Trivial Pursuit questions than did subjects who had not been asked to engage in any imaginative task; subjects who had been asked instead to imagine soccer hooligans did worse.[35]

It is not likely that the people in these experiments are consciously imitating a stereotypical elderly person's tendency to walk slowly or to misremember, or a rude person's tendency to interrupt – that would require much more calculation in imitation than we can credit these subjects with; in none of these cases are the subjects aware of the modifications in their behavior. Rather it seems that they are captured by a picture of a certain type of person with salient mental and physical characteristics, and tend to take on, temporarily, those characteristics.

The participants in these experiments did not become more intelligent while imagining a professor, or less intelligent when imagining a soccer hooligan. Dijksterhuis and his colleague Ad van Knippenberg suggest the following mechanism for these temporary transformations: intelligence is likely to be linked in the minds of participants with such traits as concentration, the use of varied strategies, confidence in one's abilities, and careful and rational thoughts. These are likely, therefore, to be prominent elements within a mental model built up through the act of imagining a professor, since professors are generally thought of as intelligent. The effect of the task, then, is to cause participants to call up their knowledge of intelligence and its more obvious facets, and then to cause them to exercise (for them) untypical levels of epistemic effort by way of an attempt to imitate the levels exemplified by the model, much as the vivid example of an athletic triumph might make you run that little bit harder during your daily exercise. The mind is, without your conscious awareness, adjusting its level of activity in various areas as a result of your contemplation of an imaginary mind in which those levels are habitually high. You are unconsciously imitating the characteristics of a mind you imaginatively construct, much as you unconsciously imitate the bodily movements and posture of those around you.

I see no reason, therefore, to restrict the use of the term "imitation" to a narrowly behavioral class of cases.[36] Certainly, whatever term we use, the modeling of cognitive processes and reactions and the modeling of behavior seem to be elicitable under the same conditions and via the same mechanisms, so we are not violating natural distinctions with the more extended usage.

The Varieties of Narrative Imitation

How may a narrator imitate, in my now fully mentalistic sense, aspects of a character's non-verbal ways of responding to or dealing with the world? In a literary narrative the narrator has only language, and whatever is imitated must be imitated by using language in certain ways. But we may speak in a certain way, intending to imitate characteristics which lie behind speech and of which speech may be expressive, as we may imitate a person's hesitant or angry frame of mind by speaking in a hesitant or angry way. We may not be speaking quite as they have spoken, and the words uttered may bear on matters distant from their own current concern. But if the style of speech is right, it may communicate the frame of mind, or the disposition to approach the world, which we suppose them to have. This is one of the things James is very apt to do in making salient a character's point of view. Ian Watt, describing the opening of *The Ambassadors*, notes that

> There are 6 "noes" or "nots" in the first 4 sentences; four implied negatives – "postpone"; "without disappointment"; "at the worst"; "there was little fear": and two qualifications that modify positiveness of affirmation – "not wholly," and "to that extent." This abundance of negatives . . . enacts Strether's tendency to hesitation and qualification.[37]

And when "the consoling reflection that 'they [Strether and Waymarsh] would dine together at the worst' " is followed by "there was little fear that in the sequel they shouldn't see enough of each other" we find James imitating a style of thought (Strether's own) that demands that "open statement be veiled in the obscurity of formal negation."[38]

Two other brief points concerning Watt's analysis. To make out the case for an imitative effect here, we need not assume that the narrator's constructions correspond to precise articulations in Strether's thoughts. The idea that the delay in meeting Waymarsh is "not insupportable" need not be a thought had by Strether; it may signal a tendency to think such thoughts, or be an explicit formulation of an affective response that remains, with him, unconceptualized. Giving us imaginative access to Strether's point of view is a matter of making available to us ways of responding to the world (the world, in this case, of the story) that are saliently those of Strether himself; it is not a matter of having us walk through the narrative in lock-step with Strether himself, having just the thoughts he has at the point he has them. Secondly, Watt's analysis also makes clear how unrealistic is any presumption that James's narration is from the point of view of a character (even granting coherence to this notion). In complex ways James's "enactment" of aspects of the point of view of Strether is enmeshed with his own point of view. Watt shows, for example, how, in the same paragraph, "elegant variation and the grammatical subordination of physical events" express "the general Jamesian tendency to present characters and actions on a plane of abstract categorization."[39] Indeed, we might say that the narrator's tendency to imitate his character in the ways he does is merely one facet of his own point of view.

I said that empathy may be generated by such acts of imitatitive narrating. Empathy with someone involves coming to think or feel or in other ways respond to the world as they do, but within the confines of an imaginative project which does not require you to take on their beliefs, desires, values, and emotion which, for reasons already indicated, we could not anyway do. If I empathize with your fear I may come to have feelings that resonate with your fear and which may drive my thoughts in the same fearful direction as your own. But my thoughts will be imaginings, not affirmations, and my feelings will not amount to genuine fear of something I perceive to be a danger, since what threatens you probably does not threaten me. Empathy may come about spontaneously and can be provoked by people's facial expressions or other aspects of bodily comportment. But it may also arise through a conscious effort to think myself, in imagination, into your situation – to take on your point of view. In doing that I set myself to imitate aspects of your mental life; to imagine things being for me as they actually are for you, and to respond (imaginatively) to them as you really do respond.[40]

But empathy needs to be distinguished both from sympathy and from identification. We may place ourselves, or be placed by the narrator, in the shoes of a character without coming to have much or any sympathy for that character, though there is a general tendency for empathy to make sympathy a more likely response. And empathizing with a character is consistent with retaining a significant distance from that character, recognizing, in the very act of empathizing, some of the limitations of the point of view we are empathizing with. Empathy need not, and anyway could not, amount to the wholesale taking on of the subject's point of view.

To underline this point, consider a case where the narrator's limited but telling imitation of a character opens the door for us to imagine things from the character's point of view, while at the same time a certain ironic tone makes it transparent that this point of view is out of step with reality.[41] The example is from James – M. R. James this time. Mr Dennistoun is at work in the church:

> It was nearly five o'clock; the short day was drawing in, and the church began to fill with shadows, while the curious noises – the muffled footfalls and distant talking voices that had been perceptible all day – seemed, no doubt because of the fading light and the consequently quickened sense of hearing, to become more frequent and insistent.[42]

The reader will not suppose that the narrator's remarks on the noises and their relation to fading light represent his own opinion; there is too much reason to think the true explanation more sinister. But the explanation in terms of fading light and quickening sense is one that would appeal to Mr Dennistoun, a typically Jamesian academic, nervously completing his examination of the building and its decoration. James's narrator imitates, just for a moment, the manner of thinking of Mr Dennistoun, who thinks (and how obviously wrong he is to think it) that the apparent increase in these disturbing noises might be innocently caused. The narrator could have said, flatfootedly, that Mr Dennistoun convinced himself that this was so, but he would not have so vividly conveyed the pressures on Mr Dennistoun's thinking, or encouraged us to imagine ourselves in Mr Dennistoun's position, comforted by this unrealistic thought. The irony here is sympathetic; Mr Dennistoun's point of view is presented as defective, but understandably so, and we are not prevented from empathizing with him. But it is remarkable how robust in their encouragement of empathy are those devices which provide imitation-based access to the point of view of a character, even when irony is used to indicate real personal and moral failings. As Dorrit Cohn notes of an excoriatingly unsympathetic exercise in FID from Sartre,

> no matter how devastating the picture, the attempted empathy implied in this narrative situation is not entirely cancelled, and the story leaves one with a feeling of having understood the type "from within."[43]

Here is another case from M. R. James. This time the narrator gives the exact words spoken by the character, but not by the conventional method of DRS. Instead,

NARRATIVE, IMITATION, AND POINT OF VIEW

the narrator suddenly and without any warning starts to speak in the voice of the character; perhaps we could say that in this case the narrator pretends, briefly, to *be* the character. In this story, the narrator is once again a conventional educated and literary figure who seems to know about the events he describes, without having participated in them. Yet in the long sentence below, summarizing the conclusion to some unpleasant events, there is a shift from the voice we have become used to – cultured, distanced from the events he describes – to another more participatory voice, and that of a less educated person:

> People still remembered last year at Belchamp St Paul how a strange gentleman came one evening in August years back; and how the next morning but one he was found dead, and there was an inquest; and the jury that viewed the body fainted, seven of 'em did, and none of 'em would speak to what they see, and the verdict was visitation of God; and how the people as kept the 'ouse moved out that same week, and went away from that part.[44]

"Years back" and "the jury that viewed the body" do not sound quite like the narrator we have come to know, and by the time aitches are dropping we realize that the narrator has taken on the persona of an artisan-witness recollecting events in his own community; by the next sentence, we are firmly back with our familiar narrator. Here the pretence does not involve FID, for the speech (following the introductory phrase "people still remembered last year at Belchamp St Paul") can be reasonably taken to be an exact replication of words spoken by the witness. But it is not directly reported speech either. By dropping into the voice of the witness the narrator manages to emphasize that person's point of view in a way that simply displaying his words, as in DRS, would not achieve. Here, the purpose of the imitation is especially complex. It serves partly, as before, to ironize the perspective of the witness: the uneducated speech, compounded by the somewhat conventional emphases in the exposition of the horrors, raises a slight doubt as to the veracity of the account. At the same time a vivid, eyewitness feel is given to the recounting of events which the narrator himself could not plausibly describe from a first-person perspective. These two effects are in tension with one another, and a very rational thinking through of the issues might result in each reducing the effect of the other. But James can count on our not responding so reflectively.

This, at least, seems to me a plausible account of what we are intended to imagine in the course of this narration. An alternative would be to say that, for the same brief space, the identity of the narrator has changed, as it changes in many fictional narratives such as *Dracula* and other epistolary novels. But the extreme brevity of the period for which we could identify this distinct narrator argues against this hypothesis.

Finally, and to illustrate the variety of uses to which an imitative style such as FID can be put, consider one other example from M. R. James. Here the narrator describes a meeting between Mr Humphreys, newly in possession of an estate, and Mr Cooper, his dependable but slightly tiresome manager. The narrator tells us: "He was very breezy this morning, Mr Cooper was."[45] We can assume that Mr Cooper would not have said, of himself, that he was breezy that morning; the narrator is not reporting, even indirectly, anything that Mr Cooper said or thought. He is telling us, using elements characteristic of Mr Cooper's verbal style, something about Mr Cooper of which that person himself was perhaps unaware, but of which (the narrator manages to suggest) Mr Humphreys was very aware. By using the resources of FID, the narrator manages to imitate the style of one character, and gives us thereby an empathic glimpse of how that character is perceived by *another* character.[46]

These are some of the ways that narrators have of making a character's point of view vivid, without their making that point of view the directly described subject of the narration, and certainly without their giving their narrations from that point of view. I've contrasted this rich budget of narrative devices with the very blunt instruments available within narrative theory for describing all this. Should we resolve to be less theoretical? Course-grained theory need not worry us if it is amenable to refinement that progressively models the distinctions out there in the real world of narratives. Standard approaches to narrative theory are poor candidates for this refinement; they are constructed in determined isolation from anything we know or might want to know about how we respond to narrative. A theory of how light comes in minutely variable wavelengths is not yet a theory of color, since it tells us nothing about how humans respond to certain regions of the wavelength spectrum as being distinct shades of the same in color. We don't all respond to narratives in the same way, but there are certain basic human capacities, such as those I have discussed in connection with imitation, which underlie our responses to narrative; understanding them will help us see why certain ways of making salient a point of view are successful and widely reproduced.

Notes

I am grateful to Andrew Kania and Jenefer Robinson for their comments on an earlier version of this chapter. Work on this chapter was conducted while the author was a British Academy Leverhulme Trust Senior Research Fellow. A similar treatment of imitative narration is developed by Daniel Gunn ("Free Indirect Discourse and Narrative Authority in *Emma*," *Narrative* 12:1 (2004): 35–54). I did not come across this essay until late in the writing of the present piece. Gunn's treatment is especially valuable in its analysis of ways in which a narrator may subtly modulate between imitative and non-imitative narration within the space of a sentence.

1 Recent work in what is called "cognitive theory of narrative" has not, I think, shed much light on these questions.
2 *Republic*, book 3. "Imitation" is now thought an unsatisfactory translation of *mimesis*. See Stephen Halliwell, *The Aesthetics of Mimesis: Ancient Texts and Modern Problems* (Princeton, NJ: Princeton University Press, 2002).
3 Genette speaks of " 'vision' or 'point of view' " (Gerard Genette, *Narrative Discourse: An Essay in Method*, Ithaca, NY: Cornell University Press, 1980, 162); Mieke Bal says that "whenever events are presented, they are always presented from within a certain vision" (*Narratology*, 2nd edn., Toronto: University of Toronto Press, 1997, 142). Some writers even insist that narrators, while not within the story-space, still perceive the events they report

(James Phelan, "Why Narrators Can Be Focalizers," in W. van Peer and S. Chatman, eds., *New Perspectives on Narrative Perspective*, Albany: State University of new York Press, 2001). The emphasis on the visual is not confined to any particular school; Ian Watt, discussing the opening of *The Ambassadors*, speaks of "the characters' awareness of events: the narrator's seeing of them" ("The First Paragraph of The Ambassadors," *Essays in Criticism* 10 (1960): 250–74). Later I shall make positive use of Watt's analysis.

4   See Adrian Moore's *Points of View* (Oxford: Oxford University Press, 1997), especially chapter 1.
5   Preface to *The Ambassadors*.
6   Preface to *The Wings of the Dove*.
7   Joseph Warren Beach, *The Method of Henry James* (New Haven, CT: Yale University Press, 1918), chapter 5.
8   See *The Craft of Fiction* (London: Jonathan Cape, 1921) especially 161 ("the point of view is primarily Strether's"), 165 ("Strether's point of view still reigns"), 167 ("our point of view is his").
9   See Genette, *Narrative Discourse*, 188. Genette quotes Wayne Booth, who certainly has a profligate attitude to narrators: "Any sustained inside view, of whatever depth, temporarily turns the character whose mind is shown into a narrator" (*The Rhetoric of Fiction*, 2nd edn., Chicago, IL: University of Chicago Press, 1983, 164); Lubbock occasionally falls into this way of speaking: "Strether is apparently in the position of a narrator throughout" (Lubbock, *The Craft of Fiction*, 169). See also Donald Ross, Jr, "Who's Talking? How Characters Become Narrators in Fiction," *Modern Language Notes* 91 (1976): 1222–42:

> Attributing the [first] paragraph (and most of the novel [*The Ambassadors*]) to Strether as a source greatly simplifies the explanation and removes the need to search for a ghostly narrator who is somehow external to the events and characters. (1232)

10 Genette, *Narrative Discourse*, 187.
11 See John E. Tilford, Jr., "James the Old Intruder," *Modern Fiction Studies* 4 (1958): 157–64. The prescriptivism of Beach and Lubbock has also been criticized, notably by E. M. Forster (*Aspects of the Novel*, New York, 1927, 118–28), and by Wayne Booth (*The Rhetoric of Fiction*).
12 With *What Maisie Knew*, Genette tells us "we almost never leave the point of view of the little girl whose 'restriction of field' is particularly dramatic in . . . a story whose significance escapes her" (*Narrative Discourse*, 189). If the story is told from her point of view, it ought to be told using concepts available only to her; yet the story is so conceptualized as to make manifest to us many aspects of its significance which escape her, though many of these are a matter of implicature rather than outright statement. If the implicature is there in the narrative, as I believe it is, the narration cannot be from her point of view; she has not the resources to intend the implicature.
13 For the purposes of this argument, I need not take sides on the question whether every narration has a narrator, since I need not take sides on the question whether every narration has a point of view. The issue is whether, for those narratives which have a point of view, that point of view can be anything other than that of the narrator. I say that it can't.
14 As Genette concedes (*Narrative Discourse*, 195).
15 Genette seems to recognize this, though his position requires him to state the matter in paradoxical terms: "The narrator almost always 'knows' more than the hero, even if he himself is the hero" (*Narrative Discourse*, 194).

16 Though I think there is considerable disagreement – and some confusion – about exactly what the situation of such a narrator is. It would be a distraction to pursue this here.
17 *Narrative Discourse*, 189. Genette refers (*Narrative Discourse*, 186) to Brooks and Warren's earlier use of "focus of narration."
18 Genette, *Narrative Discourse*, 190.
19 Focalization has been taken up by others whose treatment has made it more and more distant from our present concerns. We now have focalization whenever someone tells us what someone else has seen; the seeing character is then the focalizer (Bal, *Narratology*, 143; Shlomith Rimmon-Kenan, *Narrative Fiction*, London: Routledge, 1983, 72). And the narrator may also focalize, as the older Pip focalizes the "ideology" of *Great Expectations* (Rimmon-Kenan, *Narrative Fiction*, 82). With Bal, any statement of a "perceptible" fact involves focalization, with an external focalizer stipulated to be doing the perceiving (*Narratology*, 157). All seeing is focalization, and so presumably are all forms of sensory and cognitive contact with anything. What is explained by any of this is unclear, but these progressive weakenings of the notion suggest no way to resolve the problem of narration from a point of view.
20 The idea of someone pretending to take on a point of view is of relevance to some other kinds of cases. I have not here taken up the issue of the relation between the narrator and the author, but in many cases we can say that the author creates a narrator by pretending to be that narrator. Perhaps James pretends to be the narrator of *The Ambassadors*. But the boundaries between this and a variety of other cases are vague and hardly yet explored: an author might simply narrate from his or her own point of view, but with elements of irony in the narration; the author may invent a character whose role it is to narrate. This issue deserves separate treatment. I will not pursue it here.
21 Then there is the looming fact that narrators are generally themselves fictional constructions whose activities we have to imagine, knowing as we do that the person who really created the work is the author. Taking one thing at a time, I ignore this for present purposes.
22 As with Lady Dedlock in *Bleak House* (I am indebted here to Steven Cohan, "Figures beyond the Text: A Theory of Readable Character in the Novel," *Novel* 17 (1983): 5–27, especially 14).
23 Writers on narrative sometimes endorse a peculiarly spatial notion of inner consciousness, as a place where the narrator may take us to observe a projection, or examine a repository, of experience, or from whence we may view the world as through a window; as Sartre says "we depicted consciousness as a place peopled with small imitations" (*The Imaginary*, London: Routledge, 2004; first published in French, 1940, 5). Of Christopher Newman in *The American*, Henry James says that "at the window of his wide, quite sufficiently wide, consciousness we are seated" (preface to *The American*, *The Art of the Novel*, 37); According to Ian Watt "we and the narrator are inside Strether's mind" ("First Paragraph," 266); Chatman, describing the "mediating function of a character's consciousness" says that "The story is narrated *as if* the narrator sat somewhere inside or just this side of a character's consciousness and strained all events through that character's sense of them" (Seymour Chatman, *Coming to Terms*, Ithaca: Cornell University Press, 1990, 144, emphasis in the original); Norman Friedman says that "the reader ostensibly listens to no one; the story comes directly through the minds of the characters as it leaves its mark there ("Point of View in Fiction: The Development of a Critical Concept," *PMLA* 70:5 (1955): 1160–84, 1176).

24 From *Women in Love*. Cited in Anne Banfield, *Unspeakable Sentences: Narration and Representation in the Language of Fiction* (London: Routledge and Kegan Paul, 1982), 98. Dorrit Cohn's account of the development of the style (which she proposed to label "narrated monologue") and of its critical reception remains useful ("Narrated Monologue: Definition of a Fictional Style," *Comparative Literature* 18:2 (Spring 1966): 97–112).

25 On the imitative use of FID see the treatment in Meir Sternberg "Proteus in Quotation-Land: Mimesis and the Forms of Reported Discourse," *Poetics Today* 3:2 (1982): 107–56, especially 115ff. I am indebted to this essay. Best of all is the essay by Gunn referred to in the acknowledgment note above.

26 See Graham Hough, "Narrative and Dialogue in Jane Austen," *Critical Quarterly* 12 (1970): 201–29, on the subtle and constant shifting between different forms of narration in *Emma* (Hough calls them "continual slight shifts in the point of view," 210).

27 See Edit Doron, "Point of view as a factor of content," in S. M. Moore and A. Z. Wyner, eds., *Proceedings of SALT 1* (Ithaca: CLC Publications). Thus construed, FID is the mirror image of a way of speaking appropriate if you were describing the imaginings you have when picturing yourself doing something from a distance. Thus with FID one would say "Here she was, with the scene before her . . ."; whereas in self-imagining mode: "There I am, with the scene before me. . . ." Dickens uses this latter form of speech in *Our Mutual Friend* when Lizzie Hexham, imagining the future, says "There am I, continuing with father and holding to father because father loves me . . ." (*Our Mutual Friend*, chapter 3). But a rigidly grammatical delineation of the category of FID is of limited use; there is plenty of narration which, intuitively, counts as FID without displaying this dual evaluative structure. See Brian McHale, "Free Indirect Discourse: A Survey of Recent Accounts," *PTL* 3:2 (1978): 249–87. The idea, exemplified in Banfield's work, that modes of narration can be individuated syntactically rather than by appeal to pragmatics is, thankfully, disappearing (see Monika Fludernik, *The Fictions of Language and the Languages of Fiction*, London and New York: Routledge, 1993).

28 Genette speaks of the merging of voices (*Narrative Discourse*, 174). For critical discussion of, and reference to sources for, this view, which she calls "dual voice theory," see Banfield, *Unspeakable Sentences*, 185. But Banfield proposes to abolish the role of the narrator altogether in such contexts and assign the role of speaker to the character – the opposite of my proposal.

29 See Genette, *Narrative Discourse*, 169. François Recanti (*Oratio Obliqua, Oratio Recta*, Cambridge, MA: MIT Press, 2000, 172) is inclined, following Herb Clark and others, to see direct quotation as a form of "play-acting" in which we "simulate" the person whose words we quote. I don't quarrel with this classification, but I think we need to keep in mind, at least for present purposes, the distinction between the rather routine, unremarkable, and psychologically unengaging pretence involved here and the more saliently imitative actions involved in, say, uttering "I want to be alone" complete with Garboesque voice and posture (Clark's example, *Using Language*, Cambridge: Cambridge University Press, 1996, 175). We might call this the distinction between formulaic and sustained pretence. But even direct reproduction of a character's words can, given the right context, become saliently imitative; see discussion of a passage from M. R. James's "Count Magnus," below. (Recanati's book is, by the way, a careful reflection on topics relevant here such as FID, quotation, and pretence, but there is not space for me to take up any of his important and controversial claims directly.) Also, I don't deny that, in many ways, the use of quoted speech in a narrative transforms our understanding of that speech, as Meir Sternberg subtly

demonstrates in his "Proteus in Quotation-Land." And the contrast between FID and DRS is much less when we consider verbal reports, exactly because the maker of a verbal report, even when committed to an exact reproduction of the speaker's words, is (normally) able to exercise a degree of freedom in choosing whether to imitate tone, inflection, etc. And so even a direct verbal report may take on a significantly imitative aspect.

30 Unless, say, I did not actually know how to convey messages in semaphore and so relied on being able to imitate the movements of the other person. It is stipulated that in the present scenario this is not so.

31 Rimmon-Kenan says that FID has a tendency to "promote an empathic identification on the part of the reader" (*Narrative Fiction*, 114). Steinberg neatly summarizes the grounds for denying a special tendency for DRS to promote empathy: "direct speech itself exhibits the widest and most flexible variability in that it bestrides the whole scale of response, from identification to caricature and condemnation" ("Proteus in Quotation-Land," 115).

32 Ap Dijksterhuis, "Why we are social animals," in Susan Hurley and Nick Chater, *Perspectives on Imitation*, vol. 2, *Imitation, Human Development and Culture* (Cambridge, MA: MIT Press, 2005). I am grateful to Tamar Gendler who first alerted me to the existence of this body of research. See her "Imaginative Contagion," *Metaphilosophy* 37:2 (2006): 183–203, for analysis of research in this area.

33 See C. Carver, R. Ganellen, W. Froming, and W. Chambers, "Modelling: An Analysis in Terms of Category Accessibility," *Journal of Experimental Social Psychology* 19 (1983): 403–21; J. Bargh, M. Chen, and L. Burrows, "The Automaticity of Social Behaviour: Direct Effects of Trait Concept and Stereotype Activation on Action," *Journal of Personality and Social Psychology* 71 (1996): 230–44.

34 Bargh, Chen, and Burrows, "The Automaticity of Social Behaviour"; A. Dijksterhuis, H. Aarts, J. Bargh, and A. van Knippenberg, "On the Relation Between Associative Strength and Automatic Behaviour," *Journal of Experimental Social Psychology* 36 (2000): 531–44.

35 A. Dijksterhuis, A. van Knippenberg, "The Relation Between Perception and Behavior, or How to Win a Game of Trivial Pursuit," *Journal of Personal and Social Psychology* 74 (1998): 865–77, who drew on suggestive earlier work by Bargh, Chen, and Burrows, "The Automaticity of Social Behaviour."

36 Those who have seen imitation as important for explaining human social relations have generally had a mentalistic conception of imitation; the social thinker Gabriel Tarde was very clear that imitation is fundamentally a matter of conforming one's state of mind to that of another (*The Laws of Imitation*, trans. E. C. Parsons with introduction by F. Giddings, New York: Henry, Holt and Co., 1903).

37 Watt, "First Paragraph," 259.

38 Ibid., 265. In the same spirit we may point to the "massed block[s] of portentous qualifications" (263) that James provides.

39 Ibid., 259. Indeed, the points of view are not always distinguishable. Watt notes that

> in the later novels ... we do not quite know whether the awareness implied in a given passage is the narrator's or that of his character. [B]ecause the narrator's consciousness and Strether's are both present, we often don't know whose mental operations and evaluative judgments are involved in particular cases. (261)

The narrator's own point of view is dominant in the second paragraph.

40 For more on the role of imitation in allowing narrators (and the authors who guide them) to influence the responses of the reader, see my "Narrative Frameworks," in Daniel D. Hutto, ed., *Narrative and Understanding Persons* (Cambridge: Cambridge University Press, 2007).
41 On irony as pretending to adopt a defective point of view see my "Why Irony is Pretence," in Shaun Nichols, ed., *The Architecture of the Imagination* (Oxford: Oxford University Press, 2006).
42 "Canon Alberic's Scrapbook," *Collected Ghost Stories* (Harmondsworth: Penguin, 1984).
43 "Narrated Monologue," 112.
44 "Count Magnus," *Collected Ghost Stories*, 64. The narrator's voice reverts to its normal style directly after this sentence, and in the same paragraph.
45 "Mr Humphreys and his inheritance," *Collected Ghost Stories*.
46 See Dorrit Cohn's discussion of stylistic contagion in her *Transparent Minds: Narrative Modes for Presenting Consciousness in Fiction* (Princeton, NJ: Princeton University Press, 1978), especially 33.

18

How and What We Can Learn from Fiction

MITCHELL GREEN

Literature, Fiction, and Truth

When someone looks out the window and tells me about the weather as they can perceive it, I tend to assume that what they say is true or at least in the ballpark of the truth. We rely every day on the accuracy and sincerity of one another's reports, at least as they pertain to observable or otherwise feasibly decidable states of affairs. One reason for this is that the sentences we utter in such cases we put forth *as true*:[1] such utterances come with the understanding that they aim to be accurate representations of the world. What's more, speakers tend to put forth as true only those propositions they can back up: I'll lose my reputation for reliability if too often I am challenged and can't substantiate my claims, or if my claims too often turn out to have been based on inadequate evidence. On the assumption that we care to protect our reputations, and have some success in doing so, this is good reason to think that, on the whole, we can take someone's word at face value as accurately representing the world.[2]

Matters seem different with literature, at least when the literature in question is a work of fiction. First of all, as Berys Gaut (2007) observes, literature and fiction are not the same: some literary works are not fictional, and some fictional works are not works of literature. Edward Gibbon's *Decline and Fall of the Roman Empire* and Anne Frank's *Diary of a Young Girl* are widely considered works of literature but are not fiction; some fiction, for instance some erotic fantasy writing, is not literature. I will use the term "literary fiction" to refer to those works of literature that are also fictional.

In literary fiction, the bulk of propositions expressed are not put forth as true, or at least as true beyond the world of the work of fiction. If someone challenges my claim about the impending storm with the question, "How do you know?" I might reply by throwing open the curtains or at least switching on the Weather Band radio. By contrast, if someone were to challenge George Eliot's claim that Rosie Vincy craned her neck on a certain occasion, Ms Eliot would, I take it, be nonplussed. Her reply might go like this: "I know what Rosie did because I simply decide what she did. She's my creation after all. Perhaps I *shouldn't* have had her do all the things she did in *Middlemarch*, but that's another question." That Rosie craned her neck on the occasion in question is true in the world of *Middlemarch*, but outside the world of the work, the question does not even seem to arise.

No doubt, many works of literature are, or contain sentences that are, largely true in a way not likely to raise any hard questions. For instance, many works are historical or journalistic while having been "fictionalized" in order to protect identities of the characters discussed. A reporter might for instance go undercover posing as an addict in an American city for an article about the methadone trade. She might then change the names of her informants to protect their identity. In that case, we take what she writes as a memoir rather than a novel or short story with the understanding that minor parts have, in effect, been redacted.

More germane for our purposes are cases in which an author will intersperse her novel with observations on city life, marriage, jealousy, political intrigue, and the like that she puts forth as straightforward assertions. In some cases what then occurs in the novel is meant to support one or more of those claims. Jane Hamilton begins her novel, *A Map of the World*, with one of her characters saying:

> I used to think if you fell from grace it was more likely than not the result of one stupendous error, or else an unfortunate accident. I hadn't learned that it can happen so gradually you don't lose your stomach or hurt yourself in the landing. You don't necessarily sense the motion. I've found it takes at least two and generally three things to alter the course of a life: You slip around the truth once, and then again, and one more time, and there you are, feeling, for a moment, that it was sudden, your arrival at the bottom of the heap. (Hamilton 1994, 1)

Whether or not this view represents that of Ms Hamilton, we might ask, "Is it true?" If we are not already sure that it is, does Hamilton's novel give us any reason to believe it to be? Alternatively, are we supposed to rely on the author's, or character's testimony in the way that I rely on a friend's meteorological pronouncements?

Another important way in which literature may be thought to impart knowledge is not by what the author puts forth directly, but by what she conveys by more indirect means. Something might happen in a work of fiction that suggests an implicit claim about how things are. For instance, after Susie Salmon in Alice Sebold's *The Lovely Bones* is raped and murdered, she finds herself in Heaven. However, Heaven as characterized by this novel is not perfect: its citizens have case workers, who help their "clients" with such issues as longing to be back with loved ones on Earth, regret for things not done, etc. If one believes in Heaven, is this a plausible picture of how things might work there? If so, we also need to keep in mind that some literary genres self-consciously depart from reality: people in Márquez's *One Hundred Years of Solitude* do things like subsist on dirt, see into the future, or are born with the tail of a pig. Here there is no implicit claim as to how things are. The genre of a work brings with it certain norms as to what is supposed to be real. I return this point below.

We do sometimes turn to fictional literature with the feeling that we can learn something, and indeed something important about the world outside the work, including ourselves, by reading what's between the covers. Those who feel this way approach literature for reasons other than the desire to escape the pain or banality of daily life.³ What sense can we make of the idea that one can learn from a work of literary fiction?

Literary Cognitivism

In an attempt to make sense of that idea, we may crystallize the thought of the foregoing paragraphs with a thesis I shall term Literary Cognitivism.

> *Literary Cognitivism*: Literary fiction can be a source of knowledge in a way that depends crucially on its being fictional.⁴

This thesis builds in a crucial dependence on fictionality in order to accommodate our observation in this chapter's opening section that many essentially journalistic works are fictional in name only. Our ability to learn from such works doesn't depend crucially on their being fictional. Further, a work of literary fiction's being a source of knowledge does not imply that it was intended to be, by the author, editor, or anyone else. The author may have had a didactic aim in writing the work that she did, or she may just have been in the grip of a narrative welling up inside her that she felt compelled to write down. In the latter case our ability to learn from her product is a happy, if unintended consequence of her writing what she has.

The knowledge invoked in the thesis of Literary Cognitivism may, strictly speaking, come in any of a variety of forms. Here are some of them: (a) propositional knowledge – knowledge that such and such is the case; (b) phenomenal knowledge – knowledge of what an experience is like, or how an emotion or mood feels; (c) knowledge how to do something, where the doing in question may include not only bodily actions, but those involving use of the imagination. Good works of literary fiction often contain a mixture of all three kinds of knowledge.

Literary Cognitivism is stronger than the claim that literature can be a source of belief. The belief in question must be *supported* by the work itself in such a way as to produce, or at least enable, justification. Just as a bumper sticker might express a slogan without providing any support for it, so too it is easy to think of literary works that express beliefs without justifying them. Such works would fall outside the purview of the doctrine of Literary Cognitivism. Similarly, the purview of Literary Cognitivism is not meant to include such cases as a work's simply reminding me of something I already knew. The name of a character in a short story might remind me of an old friend with whom I've lost touch and entirely forgotten. I might be grateful for having read the story because it prompts me to revisit a friendship, but it wouldn't be plausible to credit the work with having justified any of my beliefs. So too, Literary Cognitivism is also meant to exclude such cases as a work's espousing or endorsing what is in fact a reasonable view, but on bad grounds: a novel might offer a cautionary tale against the corrupting influence of money, but in so doing make implausible assumptions about human psychology. Even if I for some reason find independent justification for the view that the novel endorses, it would be a mistake to describe such a work as a source of knowledge.

In contrast to other authors, I also mean to exclude from Literary Cognitivism such cases as a work's formulating a thought that the reader substantiates elsewhere. Suppose a literary work expresses a thought about human character that it gives no, or bad, reasons for. I then find after perusal of recent issues of the journal *Psychological Science* that the view is indeed correct. I don't know whether in such a case the work is a source of knowledge. If it is, however, its ability to be such a source is relatively uninteresting: the interesting epistemic work is done by the research that went into the psychology article, not the novel, which of course might be excellent and informative for other reasons.[5]

All this is consistent with the fact that it can often be hard to discern what message, if any, a literary work might be trying to convey. We often have to peel away layers of irony, ambivalence, and insinuation before finding reason to think of a work, or some part of it, as presenting a point of view. What is more, that point of view need not be something that the author herself espouses: she might for instance present a point of view that she only tentatively, or ambivalently endorses. The work might nevertheless express that point of view relatively clearly, and in that case we may still ask with what cogency it does this.[6]

Again, one can espouse Literary Cognitivism without being committed to the view that every person who exposes herself to a work having the capacity to engender knowledge will in fact acquire such knowledge. A person might read a work of literary fiction while missing its point entirely. That shows nothing at all about the ability of a such a work to produce knowledge. Good or even great literature doesn't force anyone to cotton on.

Common sense generally admits a distinction between having *some* justification for a belief, and having sufficient justification requisite for knowledge. Exploring in the woods I come across a mushroom that looks just like a portabella. In spite of being an amateur mushroom enthusiast, I have some justification for thinking it to be a portabella. However, there are plenty of other toxic fungi about that look similar, and I can't be sure that this isn't one of those imposters. Most of us would conclude that in spite of my having some justification for believing this one to be a portabella, I don't know it to be. That would be so even if it is in fact a portabella, and I believe it is. What is evidently missing is an adequate level of justification: only if I have a sufficiently high degree of justification do I know this to be a portabella.

A fictional work providing non-trivial, but perhaps not knowledge-enabling justification for a belief should nevertheless interest us. We might value it because of the justification that it does provide, and it might spur us to investigate its suggestions further. The work's ability to do these things is an achievement in itself. Accordingly, I shall take Literary Cognitivism to include works that are a source of knowledge by virtue of providing *some* justification for a belief.

Having clarified Literary Cognitivism, we may formulate our problem. How can we learn from fiction in a way that this thesis suggests? In my opening section, an imaginary conversation with George Eliot seemed to show that she can make up what she wants to in her novels. As a result, it is hard to see how we can learn from what goes on in them (other, perhaps, than about Eliot's psychological profile) just as it hard to see how someone can learn from my daydreams anything other than my own psychological profile. Unlike someone reporting on the weather or today's stock market fluctuations, Eliot is under no obligation to tell the truth, so why should we expect to get any from her novels?

Thought Experiments

It is sometimes suggested that we can learn from literature by virtue of its ability to get us to imagine things. David Lewis, for instance, holds that one can learn from a literary work that it is possible to be a dignified pauper.[7] Presumably that is because the work in question depicts an impoverished person with a dignified character. Others have suggested that I can learn about myself by imagining what I would do in certain situations. Perhaps, it might be suggested, I can learn about my own attitudes and propensities by imagining what I'd do if I were an impoverished, pregnant teenager locked into an abusive relationship with a boyfriend.

Such claims need to be approached with care. It is well known, first of all, that something's being conceivable does not show that it is genuinely possible. We can easily conceive of traveling backwards in time, and many works of science fiction ask us to imagine just this. That, however, would be a facile way of establishing the possibility of time travel. For all that such novels reveal, time travel might harbor hidden contradictions showing it to be impossible after all. Similarly, we can conceive of a jilted lover feeling no regret, anger, or resentment toward the person who rejected her. That, however, would be in such violation of basic facts of human psychology that a narrative describing her as accepting her fate with no turmoil whatsoever would do nothing to establish that such a reaction is possible.

We don't resolve this issue of what we can learn from something's being conceivable by suggesting that if we carefully examine the story and fail to detect a contradiction, then it must be possible. I can carefully examine and find no contradiction in a story in which gold has a different atomic number from the one it actually has. However, if widespread consensus among current philosophers is correct, that doesn't show that such a scenario is possible: most philosophers would agree that it is "metaphysically impossible" for gold to have a different atomic number from the one it actually has. While more controversial, it has also been argued with some force that some emotions have an essential nature that cannot be discerned by mere reflection: only empirical inquiry can determine the characteristic causes and effects of, say, anger (Griffiths 1997). So too for the other so-called basic emotions: fear, surprise, disgust, happiness, sadness.[8]

Should we conclude that conceivability never shows us anything about what is possible? That would be rash. Rather than thinking of cases in which an author asks us to imagine a situation, perhaps outlandish, and then puzzling over whether such a case is possible, we do well to consider scenarios that ask us to draw on what we already know of the world. Consider a famous example of Galileo's aimed to refute the ancient Aristotelian doctrine that the heavier a body the faster it falls. Suppose two objects are falling toward the ground. Imagine now that they happen by accident to hook onto each other, perhaps because of some slight wind and a chance combination of a hook on one and a thing to latch onto on the other. Then they will start falling together, and you can see intuitively that the new composite object will not fall any faster than did either of its components before their union. This thought experiment makes clear that, contrary to the Aristotelian tradition, it is not the case that the heavier an object the faster it falls. Further, you don't need to drop cannonballs off towers to establish the thesis: drawing upon one's knowledge of the everyday behavior of objects, one can see intuitively that Aristotle was mistaken.

This example sheds light on how knowledge can be generated through thought experiments, including those that authors of literary fiction ask us to engage in. First of all, the example relies upon our background knowledge: although it can be contemplated in an armchair, when contemplating it there we draw upon our knowledge of the world gained either from experience or known innately.[9] It is not by conceptual analysis alone that we reach the anti-Aristotelian conclusion. Second, in spite of the example's drawing out implications of what we already know, it can well happen that we come upon surprising conclusions, even conclusions that contradict some of our other beliefs. As a result, we can learn something new from a thought experiment even if we do so just by discovering implications of already held beliefs.

Thought experiments do not always offer such a straightforward "Aha!" experience as that devised by Galileo. Some such experiments invite us to consider cases in which our concepts lack clear conditions of application. One character finds much to love in a woman who, unbeknownst to him, two decades earlier as a Nazi prison-guard allowed 200 inmates to burn to their deaths (Schlink, *The Reader*). In another case (Le Guin's *The Left Hand of Darkness*) we are asked to consider what long-term relationships would be like among people who regularly, and as a matter of course, change their genders.

Here we have cases that do more than ask us to consider the consequences of our implicit beliefs. They also require us to apply our concepts in ways that might not be easily inferred from their previous applications. One might have thought that a person's being lovable was not compatible with her having been a mass murderer; one might have thought that being chronically gendered was a condition of long-term intimacy, and so on. *The Reader*, and *The Left Hand of Darkness* challenge these presumptions, respectively, forcing us to reconsider our habits of mind and heart.

In such cases, it's plausible that the authors intend us to examine our views about, for instance, evil or gender, and if we see fit, revise them. However, while this process of revision is valuable, perhaps even indispensable, to becoming a reflective person, it would be optimistic at best to describe our resulting opinions as knowledge. These matters – evil, gender, and so on – are too often ones on which the most we can often hope for is *some* justification rather than a level of justification adequate for knowledge. Given our liberal reading of Literary Cognitivism, however, that will not prevent such cases from falling under its purview. So long as a literary work leads me to a somewhat justified opinion, that will still allow it to fall within the scope of that principle.

What about those thought experiments prompting me to ask what I would do under certain conditions (as opposed to asking what would happen in a more general way)?

355

After reading a short story about such a case, I might think that if I were a teenage girl in an abusive relationship, I would – unlike the girl in the story – take immediate measures to protect myself and my unborn child from the perpetrator. Yet in so doing I might be overestimating myself. Perhaps in that situation I would believe that my relationship with my boyfriend could be improved with time, or perhaps I would feel that in spite of his problems he is one of the few people who truly know and appreciate me. Notoriously, women in abusive relationships go back to their abuser not long after leaving them. What makes me think I would do any different?

How, then, may the imagination be used reliably in such a way as to justify beliefs? Galileo's example shows that it sometimes can, yet we have also seen many pitfalls to its use. How can we tell the reliable uses of imagination from those that are not? One beginning is to notice that literary fiction often comes in the form of a genre, which carries its own norms. It is to these genres that I now turn.

Genres

The very act of imagining something to be so permits a departure from how things are. However, we participate in a great many types of imagining, all the way from daydreaming about a fishing expedition in a trackless wilderness to considering what would be the case were the oceans to rise in temperature by two degrees. While the fishing daydream permits flights of fancy – the size of the fish, the ferocity of the grizzly avoided, etc. – in a way that the oceanographic one does not, both are subject to norms: you're simply not daydreaming about fishing if your consciousness is replete with images of space travel or bread baking.

The same holds of genres of fiction. Many such genres mandate certain standards of veracity. A detective novel requires rough accuracy about the ways of criminals and detectives. A political thriller needs to attain ballpark plausibility about governments and politicians, and so forth. It is, however, in the nature of certain genres to be deliberately liberal about certain issues. Magical realism (exemplified in the works of Gabriel García Márquez, Gunter Grass, Mikhail Bulgakov, Toni Morrison, and Salmon Rushdie) permits violations of laws of human physiology. Science fiction permits violation of current technological limitations. However, that does not mean that such literature is sheer fantasy. Even in these genres the author must adhere to a plausible human psychology. That means that if a character in such a work is feeling jealous, she will behave in ways that jealous people tend to, and if another character is overbearing he will behave in a way that overbearing people tend to. So far as I know there is no genre in which jealous people act generously and in which overbearing people are solicitous. When a genre permits departures from how things are, it does so in fairly circumscribed ways. More generally, I suggest that it is part of the definition of a given genre to imply norms as to which departures from reality are permissible and which are not. (This does not mean that these norms are always assiduously followed: you can easily imagine a detective novel that naïvely treats cops as impervious to the temptations of bribery. Here we would have a detective novel that is, to this extent at least, mediocre, since it does not conform to the standards of the genre.)

Experienced readers are sensitive to clues, often subtle, as to the genre of the work at hand. Discerning the genre then enables them to form expectations as to the standards of veracity to which the work should conform. In one genre we read, without blinking an eye, of characters conversing with ghosts; in another those same events would provoke disdain. In one genre the use of a magic spell seems a *deus ex machina*, in another it just comes with the territory. Insofar as we are habituated to characteristic departures from reality that accompany various genres, those genres differ from *counterfactual reasoning* as we find it in everyday life and scientific inquiry. This is, roughly, reasoning that tries to answer questions of the form, "If A were to be the case, would B be the case also?" For instance, if I were to strike this dry, well-made match, would it light? Or, If the seas were to rise in temperature by a few degrees, would hurricanes become more common? It is generally accepted that in answering question like these, *conservatism* reigns: in the match case, I am to make the minimal changes to the current situation required to accommodate the lighting of the match. That is why if there is currently oxygen in the room, we keep that fact fixed while supposing the match to be struck.

By contrast with everyday counterfactual reasoning, literary genres are often permitted to transgress conservatism. The noir tendency of detective novels protects the author from questions of the form: Are people really that corrupt/deceptive/carnivorous, etc.? The magical tendency of magical realism protects the author from questions of the form: Can a person really subsist on dirt or be born with the tail of a pig? Historical fiction and New Journalism are, similarly, permitted to fill in the gaps in our historical knowledge. We are not allowed to ask how Truman Capote knows the last words of the murdered family members as described in *In Cold Blood*.

That is not to say that all fictional literature will violate conservatism. Counterfactual history may not do so. A novel that imagines a nuclear confrontation resulting from the Cuban Missile Crisis of 1962 would keep as much fixed as is compatible with the assumption that one or both of Kennedy and Khrushchev push the button. Notice that it may be difficult to tell whether such a work should count as fictional literature rather than historical scholarship, albeit of a somewhat speculative sort. That is suggestive, for I want to argue that the difference between counterfactual reasoning and fictional literature is one of degree rather than of kind.

Return to the example of the political thriller. Imagine one in which a terrorist has planted explosives all around London set to go off simultaneously in the middle of a business day. The mayor is made aware of this fact, and her advisors also inform her that there is no way to defuse them before evacuating the city. Any attempt to evacuate the city sooner will cause panic and at least as much carnage as the explosives would. Also, the mayor's advisors inform her that the terrorist is known to the authorities, and has a daughter who can be apprehended. If apprehended, the daughter, who is entirely innocent of any wrongdoing, can perhaps be used as a bargaining tool: we know that if we make the terrorist aware that she is being tortured, he will very likely crack and tell us how to defuse the explosives.

The novel asks us to consider our own moral convictions, and forces us to see that whether we take a consequentialist or deontological approach to ethics, that approach will have disturbing consequences. The novel may also help us to come to grips with what we believe about the nature of morality in a way that we had not been aware of before: up until that novel you may have thought that nothing could possibly justify torturing an innocent child. Now perhaps you think otherwise. The political thriller, note, asked the same question as did the counterfactual history: What if a situation such as the former describes were to occur in a major city? That question, if it activates any genre at all, does not license any departures from reality other than the following: the characters, political institutions, technological limitations, and the like need to be relevantly similar to those that we find in major, contemporary first-world cities. The author will likely add romantic or other kinds of intrigue in order to increase the appeal of the story, but from our point of view that is an essentially decorative, albeit unobjectionable, maneuver.

Learning by Supposing

Many defenders of the idea that knowledge can be gleaned from works of literary fiction think of the process along the following lines. The work in question either implicitly or explicitly suggests a proposition – about freedom of will, the nature of fate, romance, death, what have you. The reader is then invited to reflect on that proposition and then draw her own conclusions, whether they be in agreement or disagreement with any suggestions by the author. Thus for instance Berys Gaut writes,

> reasoning plays little explicit role in most artworks – exceptions being those works of literature that are also works of philosophy, such as Plato's dialogues, or in those works of literature, such as Thomas Mann's *The Magic Mountain*, that have philosophical aspirations. In the case of most works, audiences "draw their own conclusions," as we say, and the reasoning going on lies in the audience's response to the work. (Gaut, 2007, 142)

Similarly, Kivy imagines what he terms a "laboratory of fictional truth." On this proposal, the author floats a proposition by means of some aspect of her literary work, and then each reader is invited to contemplate it:

> Intelligent readers of the canon often have proposed to them live hypotheses of a religious, metaphysical or moral content that they continue to think about and try, thereby, to evaluate during and after the reading process. (Kivy 1997, 127)

The set of contemplating readers for a work constitutes, for Kivy, a "laboratory" for that work in which, presumably, the hypotheses in question will be decided (126).

Gaut's and Kivy's suggestions are reasonable descriptions of some cases, but I will argue that they fail to appreciate the full knowledge-enabling capacity of fictional literature. As the plot of a good work of literary fiction develops, we often find ourselves pulled along, having the sense that this is a natural, if not entirely inevitable way for things to go. Returning to Hamilton's *A Map of the World*, a young mother is distracted with a map she made as a child while her and a neighbor's children play outside; during that time the neighbor's child drowns in a nearby pond. Crushing guilt, ostracism, marital stress, all ensue. This is not to say that when you pause over a relic of your childhood, tragedy must result. However, our background knowledge enables us to see that this *could very well happen*: many parents can vividly recall occasions when tragedy brushed very near to their own children or those for whom they were caring. We may accordingly think of Hamilton's novel as a plausible account of what would have ensued had the event been more than a brush.

Let us unpack the mechanism at play here a bit further. One widely used technique in reasoning involves suppositions for the sake of argument. It is often of interest to interlocutors as well as to agents reasoning on their own to settle a question, and to do so we often seek an answer to that question that will be acceptable to all parties to the discussion. Sometimes the wanted answer is conditional in form; in other instances a good route to establishing that answer is an indirect one showing an alternative to be unacceptable. To either such end one may invoke a practice permitting a proposition P to be put forth as a supposition rather than as an assertion. Doing so entitles the reasoner to draw inferences from P, together with other propositions already established or accepted, in order to infer a proposition Q still under the scope of the supposition P. Having reached Q, the reasoner is entitled to put forth "If P, then Q" no longer under the scope of P, and if no other suppositions are in force she is entitled to put forth that conditional as an assertion rather than as a supposition. Ideally, with the aid of other propositions established or accepted the assertion justified by this procedure will settle the question at issue.

An analogous style of reasoning works for so-called *reductio ad absurdum* argumentation, in which one assumes a proposition for the sake of argument in order to debunk it. One such might be the proposition that the heavier the body, the faster it falls. After we assume this, our reasoning under the scope of this supposition shows that it would contradict other things we know from our everyday experience with objects in free fall. That, in turn, justifies us in rejecting the original supposition outright: no longer supposing anything, we can see that it isn't true that the heavier the body, the faster it falls.

Suppositions can also nest within one another. Within the scope of a supposition of a proposition P, one can add a new supposition, Q. What is established under Q's scope can then, once the supposition Q is discharged, be added to the things that have been established under the scope of P. This process has no finite upper bound, so that within the scope of Q one can also suppose a third proposition, R, and so on. Such recherché cases are not likely to be analogous to much in literature, but when a Q is supposed within the scope of a larger supposition, P, we may well see analogies with cases of "plays within plays." Observe also that one making a supposition of P must do so in such a way as to be entitled to reason under its scope without being answerable to objections to P's truth, and in such a way as to be entitled to infer a proposition no longer under the scope of P that either has P as its antecedent, or is P's negation. Further, these norms distinguish supposition from other acts significant for inquiry such as assertion, conjecture, presumption and presupposition. To take just one difference, a speaker performing any of these acts is, unlike the supposer, answerable to objections to the truth of the content forwarded. By contrast, if I ask you to suppose P for the sake of argument, and you reply by pointing out that P is not true, I'll feel you've missed my point.

How does this relate to literary fiction? An author of a literary fiction who implicitly or explicitly imagines that something is so is, I am now suggesting, often supposing those things to determine what consequences will plausibly follow. "Determine" may be misleading here, since the author might already have a clear idea of what will ensue from her supposition. Further, as we have mentioned, the author may just be in the grip of a narrative rather than being guided by any didactic aim. Even so, return to the story of the terrorist. We may think of this novel as asking, "What if this were to happen?" In the process it employs counterfactual reasoning under the scope of this supposition, often, perhaps not coincidentally, described as the "premise" of the story. The behavior of the main actors in the drama must then be plausible given what we know about human psychology; the technological facts about explosives, crowd control, and so forth, must be accurate, and so on. So far we don't have a crucial departure from cases such as that of the warming oceans.

Some fictional literature can plausibly be construed as taking the form of a *reductio ad absurdum*. Some dystopian literature is a clear instance of this kind. Huxley's *Brave New World* asks what would be the case were a society to exist based on principles associated with hedonic utilitarianism. We may think of Huxley as asking, What if a society were set up along these lines? We are then led through a working out of the implications of that supposition by being shown the various things that would ensue: the state would support an orgiastic religion and drug-induced anaesthetization of its citizens, it would suppress all independent inquiry, and so forth. The reader is then justifiably expected to recoil with horror at such a world. As a result, the structure of the "argument" implicit in Huxley is:

1. Suppose a society were organized along the lines dictated by hedonic utilitarianism.
2. In such a world, people would lack freedom of thought, freedom of expression, and the ability to cultivate the capacities for critical reflection on their surroundings.
3. Therefore, in such a world, life would be intolerable to all but those who have lost the capacity for the activities mentioned in premise (2).
4. Therefore, such a world would be unacceptable.
5. Therefore, hedonic utilitarianism is an incorrect theory of how to achieve happiness.

Line (5), our conclusion, is no longer under the scope of supposition (1). It stands as justified by premises (1)–(4). So far the "logic" of the novel is strikingly similar to that of the Galileo thought experiment.

Background knowledge is nearly always in play in suppositional reasoning. In the meteorological reasoning concerning the heating of the oceans, I will only be able to follow the scientist's line of thought if I have some familiarity with how oceans work, the water cycle, major currents, and so forth. This does not imply that the scientist is just telling me what I already know. I can realize something new by drawing out consequences from information I already possess, say for instance about how bodies fall through space. So too, the meteorologist might produce surprising results by asking me to combine disparate pieces of information already available to me and/or draw out some unexpected consequences of that information. The same goes for the example of the political thriller: here I will be able to assess the veracity of the plot's unfolding only if I have relevant background knowledge. So here again we do not find a crucial disanalogy between counterfactual reasoning and fictional literature.

The aforementioned novel about the Cuban Missile Crisis might go the same way. So long as the author remains within the bounds of political, technological, and psychological plausibility, her novel may well justify some such conclusion as: If Khrushchev had not backed down, much of Russia and central Europe would have been devastated by nuclear fallout. We have said that genres imply various kinds of violation of conservatism. Does this imply that literary genres, other perhaps than counterfactual history, cannot generate justification? I suggest it does not. Consider so-called hard science fiction (examples of which are James Blish's *Surface Tension*, 1952, and Frederik Pohl's *Day Million*, 1971). This is a subgenre of science fiction in which adherence to the laws of physics is required: no superluminal travel, teleportation, etc. Here too, however, it is accepted that facts about human psychology are to be kept fixed. In these novels, people who get angry, scared, surprised, and so forth behave pretty much as you would expect them to do. As a result, in a hard sci-fi novel you might, for instance, imagine a world in which we have begun to mine the Moon for minerals. What social formations would result from this? If the novel justifies its conclusions, it can produce knowledge of a conditional statement that is no longer under the scope of any assumptions.[10]

So far we have found significant similarities between non-fiction when it engages in counterfactual reasoning, and much fictional literature, particularly when it has a didactic capacity; indeed, the two cases are not different in kind. The point also applies to genres that permit a dramatic departure from veracity. In fantasy literature such as the *Harry Potter* series or the *Inheritance* trilogy, violations of physics and biology are abundant. One can nevertheless learn new truths without taking the author's word for anything.

A natural concern here is this: It might be suggested that while counterfactual reasoning in science tends to proceed in such a way that each step must follow from the previous; by contrast, a plot, even in a quite realistic genre, rarely proceeds by means of necessity. "Could very well happen" is far weaker than "must happen." However, much scientific reasoning proceeds by plausible steps rather than by necessity. Returning to the case of meteorological prediction as it pertains to the heating of the oceans, no scientist could expect to make more than plausible claims about what would ensue. The reason is that there are simply too many factors interacting in stunningly complex ways. The same may be said of human affairs. Whether or not universal determinism is true, we are far from a rigorous science of human behavior. Instead, we may make use not just of everyday knowledge about matters of the heart and mind, but also of the findings of psychology and neuroscience as we construct a plot.

De se Suppositions

Loosely following a tripartition offered by Lewis (1979), let us call supposing what would happen were a proposition true, *de dicto supposition*. Then, supposing, of a certain object, that it were to be different from how it in fact is, we may call *de re supposition*. Then a special case of this will be *de se supposition*, in which I suppose, concerning myself, that I am in some way different from the way I in fact am. Considering how I would feel if I won a lucrative lottery, lost a child, or learned that I was suffering from a terminal illness, are all cases of *de se* supposition.[11]

De se suppositions are treacherous. I might have a view about how I would fare under conditions of extreme deprivation, danger, or some other forms of duress, and that view might be activated by my engagement with a fictional work. So too, I might think I know what I'd do if I were a pregnant teenage girl with an abusive boyfriend. The trouble with these views is that they fly in the face of a large body of current research concerning our limited self-knowledge. Under the rubric of affective forecasting, research suggests that we vastly overestimate, for instance, how happy we'd be if we won a large sum of money, or acquired a luxury item such as a fancy home or sports car. We also tend to overestimate how devastated we'd be by tragedy such as the loss of a loved one. Forecasts about our future are not the same as *de se* suppositions, which need make no commitment about what will actually befall us. However, the relevance of forecasting to supposition should be clear: my views about how I'd feel if A *were* to happen to me are typically drawn from the same source as those about how I *will* feel if A happens to me.[12]

Given these pitfalls, we should consider whether fictional literature can really provide substantial justification for a view I acquire by means of *de se* supposition. It is here that the author's role as more than a story-teller is crucial. I mentioned at the start of this chapter that we often take someone's word for what they say on the default assumption that they know whereof they speak. Most of us can be relied upon to speak accurately about the nearby weather. Some of us can be relied upon to speak accurately about tomorrow's weather, and so forth. It is no accident, I suggest, that aspiring writers are often counseled to know their subject matter well, be it bullfighting, seafaring, hairdressing, or space exploration. A writer who draws on her expertise can be a source of testimonial knowledge not only in a factual way – an author with nautical experience can be depended upon to speak reliably on maritime matters – but also in a more personal way. She can do the latter by showing how a certain experience, feeling, or emotion feels, drawing, typically but not exclusively, on first-hand knowledge.[13]

Alice Sebold was beaten and raped while walking across campus as a college student. She draws on that experience in her account of Susie Salmon, the fictional teenager who is raped and murdered in *The Lovely Bones*. Her ability to do this adds to the power of the story, precisely by showing some dimension or dimensions of how that must have felt to the victim. By showing us how that experience felt, Sebold provides us with the tools for a *disciplined* use of our imagination: she guides us toward a proper understanding of what, or some portion of what, Susie Salmon must have felt while being raped and before her murder.

Some authors attempt to enable *de se* imaginings for what might seem impenetrable cases. In *The Curious Incident of the Dog in the Night-Time*, the author Mark Haddon tells a story from the point of view of an autistic boy, Christopher Boone. In some cases, you can imagine Christopher doing something but may find it hard to imagine yourself in his shoes: for instance, when upset he will calm himself with a repetitive activity, whereas I have no idea what it would be like to scrape a coin against a radiator for over three hours in order to calm myself down. In such a case we may engage in a *de dicto*, and perhaps also a *de re* supposition, but not a *de se* supposition. In other cases we do get some glimpse of what it would be like to walk in the boy's shoes. Like me, you probably can discern another's emotion by the look on their face, without however having consciously to reflect what their facial expression means. Most of us determine affect through facial expression rapidly and unconsciously. Not Christopher Boone. However, his teacher Siobhan has helped him over the years to connect faces with emotions:

> I got Siobhan to draw lots of these faces and then write down next to them exactly what they meant. I kept the piece of paper in my pocket and took it out when I didn't understand what someone was saying. But it was very difficult to decide which of the diagrams was most like the face they were making because people's faces move very quickly. (Haddon 2003, 3)

It is no accident, I suggest, that the dust jacket of Haddon's book mentions that he worked with autistic individuals before trying his hand as an author. This makes it plausible that he speaks with some authority about what autists experience. It is that authority, and Haddon's talent in giving it voice, that enables us not only to engage in *de se* supposition, but to do so in a sufficiently disciplined way as reasonably to expect to learn something from the exercise.

De se suppositions, then, can as easily be the source of illusion as knowledge. However, one important role for authors as the source of testimony is in guiding such suppositions in the right way. Most of us need knowledgeable guidance in trying to understand the world from an autistic boy's point of view, just as, thankfully, most of us need guidance in trying to understand what it is to be raped. Talented, informed authors can do just this.

The authors of works that guide disciplined *de se* imagining go beyond reportage-with-the-names-changed such as we considered in our example of a journalist doing a story about the methadone trade. On one hand authors of fiction are not beholden to factual detail in the way that a journalist is. On the other hand, the author of fiction does well to show how the situations of the characters she discusses feel "from the inside."

Literary fiction, then, is more closely associated with and bound by the real than might at first glance appear. Our imaginary discussion with George Eliot suggested that adherence to the truth is no standard for the writer. However, this is only superficially the case. At a deeper level, we have seen that, intentionally or inadvertently, many authors use their fiction to show how things are, and our characterization of many works as having a suppositional structure helps to explain how this is so. First, an author can show how things are by drawing out conclusions from things we already know with the aid of suppositional reasoning, typically *de dicto* suppositions. Second, an author can show how an experience, emotion, or mood feels by inviting the reader into a *de se* imagining. In this case, however, it is crucial that the author knows her subject matter, either by personal experience or careful study. The qualified author can then provide her reader knowledge of what an experience is like by serving, in effect, as a source of testimony.

Notes

My thanks to the editors for comments on an earlier draft of this paper.

1. I use "true" in the everyday usage of that term. On this usage, it's true that gasoline is flammable and that Richard Nixon died in 1991. Use of "true" in this everyday sense commits me neither to the claim that there is a unique, God's-eye, view of the world, nor to the claim that all truths that there are must be accessible to us.
2. The phenomenon of testimony has become a topic of considerable interest in recent epistemology. Essays by influential figures in that discussion are collected in Lackey and Sosa 2006.
3. Many also feel that literature can give us knowledge that either cannot, or can only with great difficulty, be acquired from non-literary works. What we might call the thesis of Literary Cognitive Uniqueness (literary fiction can be a source of knowledge of a kind that cannot be had from other sources) is an important thesis outside the scope of the present essay. Also, this essay will not investigate the question whether the ability of a literary work to cultivate knowledge in its audiences is relevant to its appreciation as a literary work. Instead, see Lamarque's chapter in this volume (19, LITERATURE AND TRUTH) for an investigation of this issue.
4. As with "truth," I use "knowledge" in the most quotidian way possible. On this everyday usage, it is doubtful that knowledge requires certainty: I can know something without being certain that it is so. Similarly, it is doubtful that knowing something requires that you know you know it. Also, compare Literary Cognitivism with a similar thesis propounded by Kivy: "Some fictional works contain or imply general thematic statements about the world that the reader, as part of an appreciation of the work, has to assess as true or false" (Kivy 1997, 122). Following Larmarque and Olsen, Kivy characterizes general thematic statements as those expressing generalizations. (These are distinguished from subject descriptions, which refer to particular situations, events, characters, and so on.)
5. My approach is thus different from that of Gaut, who writes, "one can confirm the implicit psychological or moral tenets advanced even by fictional artworks in the light of one's earlier experience, and also by one's later experience, successfully applying them to the world (Gaut 2007, 142). Gaut gives this as a reason for supposing that literature can be a source of knowledge, whereas I see the knowledge thus generated as adventitious at best.
6. A fuller discussion of how it is possible and on what basis we might impute "messages" to works of art may be found in Levinson 1995.

7   Lewis writes,

> I find it very hard to tell whether there could possibly be such a thing as a dignified beggar. If there could be, a story could prove it. The author of a story in which it is true that there is a dignified beggar would both discover and demonstrate that there does exist such a possibility. An actor or painter might accomplish the same. (Lewis 1983, 278)

8   Yablo 1993 provides a fuller discussion of the relation of conceivability and possibility.
9   My knowing something innately does not mean that I know it *a priori*. That innate knowledge might be inherited through my parents' genes, and acquired through the evolution of my species. Such knowledge would then be known by experience, but not by *my* experience.
10 A fuller treatment of subgenres within science fiction may be found in Clute and Nichols 1995.
11 *De se* imaginings (of which *de se* suppositions are a special case) are discussed at further length in Walton 1990, and in Currie 1995.
12 A survey of the relevant literature may be found in Wilson 2002.
13 I develop an account of the various means by which one can show what's within – be it emotional, cognitive, or affective states – in Green 2007.

Bibliography

Clute, J., and Nichols, P. (eds.) (1995). *The Encyclopedia of Science Fiction* (New York: St Martins).
Currie, G. (1995). "The Moral Psychology of Fiction," *Australasian Journal of Philosophy* 73: 250–9.
Diffey, T. J. (1997). "What Can We learn from Art?" in S. Davies, ed., *Art and its Messages: Meaning, Morality, and Society* (University Park: Penn State Press).
Freeland, C. (1997). Art and Moral Knowledge, *Philosophical Topics* 25: 11–36.
Gaut, B. (2007). *Art, Emotion, and Ethics* (Oxford: Oxford University Press).
Green, M. (2007). *Self-Expression* (Oxford: Clarendon Press).
Griffiths, P. (1997). *What Emotions Really Are: The Problem of Psychological Categories* (Chicago, IL: University of Chicago Press).
Haddon, M. (2003). *The Curious Incident of the Dog in the Night-Time* (Doubleday).
Hamilton, J. (1994). *A Map of The World* (Doubleday).
John, E. (2001). "Art and Knowledge," in B. Gaut and D. Lopes, eds., *The Routledge Companion to Aesthetics* (London: Routledge), 329–40.
Kivy, P. (1997). "The Laboratory of Fictional Truth," in P. Kivy, *Philosophies of Arts: An Essay on Differences* (Cambridge: Cambridge University Press), 120–39.
Lackey, J., and Sosa, E. (eds.) (2006). *The Epistemology of Testimony* (Oxford: Oxford University Press).
Lamarque, P., and Olsen, S. (1994). *Truth, Fiction and Literature* (Oxford: Oxford University Press).
Le Guin, U. K. (1969). *The Left Hand of Darkness* (New York: Walker).
Levinson, J. (1995). "Messages in Art," *Australasian Journal of Philosophy* 73: 184–98.
Lewis, D. (1978). "Truth in Fiction," *American Philosophical Quarterly* 15: 37–46. Reprinted, with postscript, in Lewis, *Philosophical Papers*, vol. 1 (Oxford: Oxford University Press, 1983), 261–80.
Lewis, D. (1979). "Attitudes De Dicto and De Se," *Philosophical Review* 88: 513–43.

Schlink, B. (1999). *The Reader* (New York: Vintage).

Sebold, A. (2002). *The Lovely Bones* (Little, Brown, and Co.).

Stolnitz, J. (1992). "On the Cognitive Triviality of Art," *British Journal of Aesthetics* 32: 191–200.

Swirski, Peter (2007). *Of Literature and Knowledge: Explorations in Narrative Thought Experiments, Evolution and Game Theory* (London and New York: Routledge).

Walton, K. (1970). "Categories of Art." Reprinted in Walton 2008.

Walton, K. (1990). *Mimesis as Make-Believe* (Cambridge, MA: Harvard University Press).

Walton, K. (1997). "Spelunking, Simulation, and Slime: On Being Moved by Fiction," in M. Hjort and S. Laver, eds., *Emotion and the Arts* (New York: Oxford University Press).

Walton, K. (2008). *Marvelous Images: On Values and the Arts* (Oxford: Oxford University Press).

Wilson, T. (2002). *Strangers to Ourselves: Discovering the Adaptive Unconscious* (Cambridge, MA: Harvard University Press).

Yablo, S. (1993). "Is Conceivability a Guide to Possibility?" *Philosophy and Phenomenological Research* 53: 1–42.

Zemach, E. (1995). "Truth in Art," in D. Cooper, ed., *The Blackwell Companion to Aesthetics* (Oxford: Blackwell), 434–8.

19

Literature and Truth

PETER LAMARQUE

One problem with the truth debate about literature is pinning down substantial points of contention so as to identify precise claims and counter-claims. Does truth have *some* connection with literature? Of course. On that there is no disagreement. A multiplicity of connections will emerge as we proceed. Can works of fiction convey truth? Can readers learn from works of fiction? Undoubtedly so. Examples are readily at hand. Readers of Trollope can learn about rural deans in nineteenth-century England. (It is another matter whether Trollope always gets it right.) Is it the aim of literature to convey truth? In some cases – so-called didactic literature – the answer is obviously Yes, even if there is not a clear Yes in every case. Do we value literary works that convey truth? To the extent that truth is better than falsehood and learning better than ignorance then conveying truth is valuable and works that convey truth have value in that regard. But does truth contribute to *literary* value? Not until here does an issue of genuine controversy arise. Other issues flow from it. If we value literature for its truth is that because there is a special kind of truth involved? Do works of literature make any distinctive contribution to truth, in a way that enhances their value? The proper focus for the truth debate must rest with the question of value rather than the question of fact and not so much with the value of truth, which is not controversial, but the value of literature, which is.

No Easy Answers

Is truth a criterion of literary value? Is truth part of what makes great literature "great"? The questions might seem straightforward but as we examine claims and counter-claims in the debate it becomes apparent that a range of different opinions can underlie positive and negative responses. It is not reasonable, in so intractable a debate, to expect an *obvious* Yes or *obvious* No to our key questions, although there are some pressures in that direction.

A Companion to the Philosophy of Literature, First Edition. Edited by Garry L. Hagberg and Walter Jost.
© 2010 John Wiley & Sons Ltd. Published 2015 by John Wiley & Sons, Ltd.

Against an obvious Yes

Two considerations, at least, might initially suggest an obvious Yes. The first is the vagueness or generality of the idea of "literature." There is a generic sense of "literature" which encompasses the great works of philosophy, history, and biography. Are not David Hume's *Treatise on Human Nature* and Thomas Macaulay's *History of England* works of literature? Yet surely they aspire to truth and should be judged at least partially on that criterion? Thus philosophical acumen and historical accuracy seem to be obvious and recognizable criteria for the value of some works of literature. It might be tempting to forestall this response by delimiting the relevant class to *fictional* works of literature. But that is not helpful. For one thing, it threatens to exclude a literary paradigm, lyric poetry, which is not straightforwardly classifiable as fictional, and also the boundaries of fiction and non-fiction are far from clear. Of course our primary interest will be in poems, novels, and dramas of a recognizable kind but it would hopelessly beg the question to characterize such works, in contrast to the broader species, by postulating a line between works that aspire to truth and those that do not. A better move is to take a relaxed view of the extension of "literature" and focus instead on the idea of distinctively *literary* values or judging a work *from a literary perspective*. There might not be agreement on exactly what this entails but it is at least not obvious that it must involve truth-assessment even in those instances where the assertive mode is paramount. Arguably what gives Hume's *Treatise* literary value, in a strict sense, is not its philosophical insight but the way it is written.

Further pressure to grant an obvious Yes to our key questions comes from the time-honored tradition, dating at least from Aristotle, that recognizes an instructive as well as pleasure-yielding function for poetry. Its early manifestation in *Ars Poetica* by the Roman poet Horace in the dichotomy between *utile* (usefulness) and *dulce* (sweetness) is echoed over and over, as when Dr Johnson writes that "the end of poetry is to instruct by pleasing."[1] The idiom of "truth" is never far behind; indeed Johnson himself uses it in an often-quoted formula "Poetry is the art of uniting pleasure with truth." Johnson goes on: "Epick poetry undertakes to teach the most important truths by the most pleasing precepts."[2] This weight of tradition might make it seem futile to resist the obvious Yes. However, it is far from obvious that the "instructive" element of poetry, Horace's *utile*, demands an explanation in terms of truth or even that when the truth idiom is used, as by Johnson, the notion of truth is anything like that familiar to philosophers. What Horace, and probably Johnson too, seem to have had in mind was something more like the *seriousness* of poetry. Poetry, they thought, surely rightly, could offer more than just a passing or sensuous pleasure, often inviting serious reflection, opening the mind to new possibilities, or stretching the imagination. At an early stage of the argument it should not be assumed that the seriousness of poetry must automatically be associated with truth.

Against an obvious No

On the other side of the debate it is equally important to resist an obvious No to our questions. Those inclined to a swift No might stress the fictiveness of imaginative literature. It is not, and could not be, *truth*, they say, that gives literature its value but rather inventiveness, imagination, clever plots, or engaging characters. Fiction, surely, is the very opposite of truth! Truth is the province of science or history, poetry resides in creativity and make-believe. Literature lifts us beyond the mundane world of fact and verification. But again this is too swift. Fiction and truth are much more closely intertwined, as Shakespeare recognized in observing that "the truest poetry is the most feigning."[3] Fiction is an apt vehicle for teaching truths, as in parables, or moral tales told to children, or philosophers' thought experiments, even police profiles. Also works of fiction are usually set in the real world, often referring to real places, events, or famous people, and drawing on familiar facts about how humans behave, what clothes they wear, the sorts of things they say. It is no wonder that readers can learn from novels out of this background: about history, geography, etiquette, customs, modes of speech. Whether all this is a source of *literary* value is yet to be determined but it cannot be ruled out without argument.

Another tendency towards an obvious No comes from those who either deny the existence of truth altogether or play down its significance. Truth cannot be a value of literature if it is of no value itself. Radical skepticism of this kind, associated with the further reaches of post-structuralism, is sometimes attributed to Friedrich Nietzsche, who famously wrote: "truths are illusions of which one has forgotten that they *are* illusions" and truth is only "a mobile army of metaphors, metonyms, and anthropomorphisms."[4] Even when not strictly denying the existence of truth, post-structuralists sometimes see language as *self-reflexive*, pointing not outwards at the world (truth) but inwards at itself, an idea nicely captured in Roland Barthes's essay title "To Write: An Intransitive Verb." For Barthes, "*writing* can no longer designate an operation of recording, notation, representation, 'depiction' . . . ; rather, it designates . . . a performative . . . in which the enunciation has no other content . . . than the act by which it is uttered."[5] Paul de Man applies a similar thought to literature: "It is . . . not *a priori* certain that literature is a reliable source of information about anything but its own language."[6] But skepticism about truth is no less controversial than issues about literature's value so it cannot provide any easy solution on its own.

The Classical Background

It is common in the truth debate to pit Aristotle against Plato as the first systematic proponents of the pro-truth and anti-truth lines of argument. Indeed their positions have served to lay down the parameters for subsequent debate. However, they did not disagree at all points; both accepted, for example, that poetry (a generic term for imaginative literature) is a kind of "imitation" (mimesis) but also, notably for our purposes, that truth (especially moral truth) is indeed a criterion for judging poetry. They differ in that Plato thought that poetry must always fall short on this criterion, by the very fact of relying on mimesis, whereas Aristotle felt that poetry could make an important and distinctive contribution, precisely through mimesis.

Plato's challenge

Plato put an entirely negative gloss on "imitation" – more like "mimicry" – and saw poets as mere tricksters who pretend to knowledge they do not possess, using the charms of poetry to seduce a gullible audience into thinking they speak with real authority. As a purveyor of truth, poetry comes at the lowest level of cognition. Poets rely on inspiration (a kind of madness) rather than reason, they "imitate" appearance rather than reality, they are mostly ignorant of what they speak, they put pleasure before truth, and they stir up emotion which must always cloud judgment. However, Plato offers one last chance to poets, or those who "champion poetry because they like it," to make a case that "there's more to poetry than mere pleasure – that it also has a beneficial effect on society and on human life in general"; "we won't listen in a hostile frame of mind," he says, "because we'll be the winners if poetry turns out to be beneficial as well as enjoyable."[7] So began two deeply entrenched lines of thought: that poetry is deceptive and potentially dangerous, and that poetry's legitimacy can only be defended in terms of its "usefulness."

Aristotle's response

Aristotle mounted one of the first "defenses," conceding the terms of Plato's assault and in effect arguing for poetry's usefulness especially in living up to the criterion of truth. Aristotle presented a more positive account of mimesis allowing for different objects of "imitation": "as they were or are, or as they are said or thought to be or to have been, or as they ought to be."[8] Poetry can aspire to truth by describing not mere facts but "a kind of thing that might be." This, he argued, made poetry "more philosophic and of graver import than history, since its statements are of the nature rather of universals, whereas those of history are singulars." He goes on: "By a universal statement I mean one as to what such or such a kind of man will probably or necessarily say or do."[9] Aristotle also gave a more positive account of poetic form and diction, not, as with Plato, seeing these as devices of charm and trickery but finding for them an integral role in the presentation of a plausible plot out of which the universal truths can develop.

So it is that Aristotle, like Plato, initiated a stream of thought about poetry that resonated down the centuries. The positive idea of mimesis became the established "classical" conception of poetry, re-emerging most notably in the eighteenth century, again with Dr Johnson, who remarks in his "Preface to Shakespeare" (1765) that "Nothing can please many, and please long, but just representations of general nature." The "universal" statements that Aristotle associated with poetry became the touchstone both of neo-classical theory and of certain strands of Romanticism. There is a striking similarity between Dr Johnson's assertion that "The business of a poet . . . is to examine, not the individual, but the species; to remark general properties and large appearances" and that of Wordsworth: "Its [poetry's] object is truth, not individual and local, but general and operative."

Conceptions of Poetic Truth

The idea that poetry affords a species of general or universal truth needs to be pursued more carefully, not least because any precise claim to that effect is hard to pin down. However, it is by no means the only conception of truth in this debate.

Acceptability and "ringing true"

The critic I. A. Richards in *Principles of Literary Criticism* (1924) identified two other senses of "truth" relevant to criticism: "acceptability" and "sincerity." Richards explains acceptability as equivalent to "internal necessity" or "rightness." So, "the falsity of happy endings to *Lear* or *Don Quixote*, is their failure to be acceptable to those who have fully responded to the rest of the work."[10] The idea might connect with that of "ringing true." A work fails to "ring true" if it seems unconvincing, exaggerated, implausible, or contrived.

Sincerity, authenticity and clarity

Truth as sincerity is different again. The operative idea is truthfulness or honesty, its opposite sentimentality or affectation. A work is "true" in this sense if it does not attempt to deceive or flatter or charm or soften the edges, if it confronts unpalatable facts with an unblinking eye, be they about the author's own hidden secrets or about worldly affairs. The idea of "authenticity" is related, as is the idea of "clarity" or seeing things clearly, without illusion. This latter notion is prominent in Iris Murdoch's philosophical writing:

> Truth is not a simple or easy concept. Critical terminology imputes falsehood to an artist by using terms such as fantastic, sentimental, self-indulgent, banal, grotesque, tendentious, unclarified, wilfully obscure and so on. The positive aspect of the avoidance of these faults is a kind of transcendence: the ability to see other non-self things clearly and to criticise and celebrate them freely and justly.
>
> "Truth" is something we recognize in good art when we are led to a juster, clearer, more detailed, more refined understanding. Good art "explains" truth itself, by *manifesting* deep conceptual connections. Truth is clarification, justice, compassion.[11]

Iris Murdoch's conception of artistic truth is of special interest both intrinsically and because as a novelist herself she presumably saw as one aspiration in her own fiction the pursuit of a kind of truth found, she argues, in all great literature:

> what we learn from contemplating the characters of Shakespeare or Tolstoy ... is something about the real quality of human nature, when it is envisaged, in the artist's just and compassionate vision, with a clarity which does not belong to the self-centred rush of ordinary life.... [T]he greatest art ... shows us the world ... with a clarity which startles and delights us simply because we are not used to looking at the real world at all.[12]

Truth here becomes clear vision.

True to, verisimilitude

There are other notions to take into account as well. One is that of being "true to": true to life, true to oneself, true to human nature. To be true to life a fiction must offer recognizable characters and situations, must avoid implausibility in plot structure (a point emphasized by Aristotle), and must conform to norms of action and motivation. The idea is similar to that of "ringing true." It also connects to "verisimilitude," a conception of truth implying resemblance to fact or "realistic" description. There are further conceptions still. Cecil Day Lewis speaks of "poetic truth [as] . . . unverifiable . . . but operative,"[13] William Wimsatt of the "concrete universal,"[14] Morris Weitz of "depth meaning,"[15] and Colin Falck of "ontological truth."[16]

Beauty and truth

A perhaps over-literal reading of Keats's line "Beauty is truth, truth beauty" (from his "Ode on a Grecian Urn") might suggest yet another notion: that beauty is sufficient for truth, that nothing could be beautiful and false. Although it would be contentious to attribute that conception to Keats from the evidence of the poem alone, it is often pointed out that he comes near to it in more prosaic moments, as in his assertion "What the Imagination seizes as Beauty must be Truth."[17] It is not just truth that is hard to tie down here but beauty itself. Perhaps the underlying idea is not that different from the truth Iris Murdoch sees in an artist's "just and compassionate vision." What is beautifully expressed under the clarity of such a vision cannot but be true.

Departing from the scientific paradigm: propositional truth

What is notable about all these conceptions is that they depart from a simple paradigm of truth familiar to science, history, and philosophy, nicely encapsulated in Aristotle's dictum: "to say of what is that it is, and of what is not that it is not, is true." This paradigm is propositional truth. Defenders of poetic truth rarely seem satisfied with it. If literature is to be valued for its truth, the thought seems to be, then it cannot be ordinary empirical or conceptual truth. But this puts pro-truth theorists in an uncomfortable position. They might well make a case for truth as a literary value if they define a *sui generis* notion of truth that suits the literary application. The trouble is if this is not the standard kind of truth with a time-honored connection to knowledge then literature can seem a poor relation in the battle for ideas. If literary truth is too remote from philosophical (or scientific) truth then literature cannot seem to compete for the high-ground of truth to which human cognition aspires.

There is no doubt that many of the "poetic" conceptions of truth just outlined do indeed connect with literary value. A good case could be made that a kind of sincerity, authenticity, or clarity in literary writing is a mark of value in the literary sphere. Also if attention is given to plot structure, characterization, or general subject-matter then plausibility, verisimilitude, and "acceptability" are (exceptional cases aside) likely to be valued over their opposites. With a little help from examples, and a bit more precision and filling out, it does seem that under some at least of these conceptions a substantial Yes can be given to our initial question, whether truth is a criterion of literary value. If truth means acceptability or sincerity, then truth, arguably, is a value of literature. But this can seem a hollow victory for the pro-truth camp. After all no one supposes for a moment that sincerity (or beauty or "ringing true") is a mark of truth in the discourses of philosophy, history, or science. Can poems or novels or dramas really not hold their own in that company?

Propositional Truth and Literature

When Aristotle, Dr Johnson, and Wordsworth spoke of "universal" or "general" truth it is not hard to see how their suggestion might be recast in terms of propositional truth. Some propositional truths are universal in nature and arguably it is just such that are at the heart of philosophy and science. Perhaps, after all, literature can make a claim to truth at roughly the level (that of "universal truth") sought in these other discourses.

Where there is language, propositions cannot be far away and it is not hard to find propositions, of a kind eligible for truth-valuation, in poetry or works of fiction. First, then, we must identify such propositions, then inquire into their status and the relevance of their truth-assessment.

Distinctions concerning content

Some preliminary distinctions are helpful. One is between *explicit* propositional content, in the form of indicative sentences within works, and *derived* propositional content, the result of a reader's reconstruction of explicit content through inference and "filling in." Another distinction is between subject-level content and thematic-level content. The distinctions cut across each other. Subject-level content can be both explicit and derived, as can thematic-level content. By subject-level content is meant the characters, events, episodes, experiences presented in a work, from an emotional predicament in a short lyric to a complex narrative in a novel. Such content is often, but not necessarily, fictional, in the sense of being made up. Derived subject content is that supplementary content filled in, imaginatively or inferentially, by a reader. Thematic-level content, in contrast, is rarely fictional and involves generalizations, sometimes explicitly given, sometimes derived by readers, on the work's subject.

Explicit thematic reflections

Writers often offer their own thematic reflections. Here is Wordsworth reflecting on human mortality in his "Valedictory Sonnet to the River Duddon":

> While we, the brave, the mighty, and the wise,
> We Men, who in our morn of youth defied
> The elements, must vanish; – be it so!

And what more impassioned and chilling statement of the fear of death could there be than Claudio's speech in *Measure for Measure*:

> Ay, but to die, and go we know not where;
> To lie in cold obstruction and to rot;
> This sensible warm motion to become
> A kneaded clod; and the delighted spirit
> To bathe in fiery floods, or to reside
> In thrilling region of thick-ribbed ice;
> To be imprison'd in the viewless winds,
> And blown with restless violence round about
> The pendent world. . . .
>   – 'tis too horrible.
> The weariest and most loathed worldly life
> That age, ache, penury, and imprisonment,
> Can lay on nature, is a paradise
> To what we fear of death.[18]

Sometimes fictional characters almost incidentally set out a universal proposition, as when Macbeth describes sleep, the very sleep that he fears he has "murdered":

>   the innocent sleep,
> Sleep that knits up the ravell'd sleave of care,
> The death of each day's life, sore labour's bath,
> Balm of hurt minds, great nature's second course,
> Chief nourisher in life's feast.[19]

Explicit generalizations in literature, of this kind, are the stuff of the quotation industry.

Derived thematic reflections

Not all thematic reflections, though, are explicit. Some are constructed, or derived, by readers. Here is a critic summarizing a theme in Dostoyevsky's *Crime and Punishment*:

> the criminal must, and wants to, accept retribution for the act that expresses the metaphysical self-determination of his free will. It is unjust to deny to the criminal that responsibility that raises him above the beasts, and also to deny him the punishment that purifies him and gives him new being.[20]

Here is an even more pithy statement about Tolstoy's *War and Peace*:

> simplicity [is] the supreme beauty of man; goodness and truth, the supreme aims for which man should live and work.[21]

Such generalizations are common at thematic level. Here we have plausible candidates for propositional truth of a kind recognizable in philosophy and the social sciences. The question is what bearing their truth (if they are true) has on the literary value of the works from which they arise. This will be pursued shortly.

Propositional truth at subject level

But propositional truth at subject level should not be left out of the equation. Most novels have some grounding in the real world against which fictional events take place. Sometimes explicit factual description characterizes this background, as when the narrator in Malcolm Bradbury's novel *To the Hermitage* offers travelogue-like descriptions of Stockholm and St Petersburg:

> To one end of the square outside lies the busy Nevsky Prospekt, filled with its rushing traffic and its whirring trolley buses; to the other is a grand classical façade, the front of the Pushkin Drama Theatre; everything in this city is named after one writer or another.[22]

Factual mistakes in works of fiction

But what happens when mistakes creep into this factual background? This is surprisingly common. In the proofs of *Barnaby Rudge* Dickens had to change a passage where a man was hanged "for passing bad one pound notes" after it was pointed out that there were no one pound notes at the historical period when the novel was set.[23] George Eliot, in *Middlemarch*, described Lydgate "with bright dilated eyes" from taking opium; when she learned that pupils *contract* from opium she changed the passage, in a later edition, to "with a strange light in his eyes." Not all mistakes get corrected. In William Golding's *Lord of the Flies*, Piggy's glasses are used to light a fire. The scene is pivotal in the book. But Piggy is shortsighted and the concave lenses in his glasses could never focus the sun's rays as required. Making him longsighted would have changed the dynamics of the plot for that would not so obviously have been a disadvantage to him.[24]

Are these clear cases of truth affecting literary value? The issue of falsehood – at the subject level – in literature is complicated. Authors will sometimes deliberately distort fact for literary ends. Even scrupulously researched historical novels involve fabrication when invented dialogue is attributed to historical characters. No one would suppose this is an artistic flaw, although the *kind* and *manner* of things said might be deemed inappropriate or anachronistic. A crucial consideration is genre. In some genres – historical fiction, science fiction of certain kinds, even political satire – departures from fact based on mistakes can seriously affect the overall achievement. Perhaps the best way to treat these cases is as breaches in genre conventions, rather than as general failures of literary truth. Factual accuracy is a convention of the genres mentioned. Just as it is a breach of convention in classical tragedy to depict the tragic hero as wicked or dishonorable, so it is a breach of convention to get the background facts wrong in certain kinds of fiction. Unintentional falsehood with no literary purpose then becomes a recognizable kind of literary failure.

Truth and vacuity at the thematic level

Returning to our thematic generalizations, how important is truth in this context? When critics, such as Dr Johnson, praise literature for its truth it is "universal" rather than straightforward factual truth that they have in mind. But universal propositions like those illustrated present problems of their own. It is not so much the risk of falsehood but the risk of vacuity that besets them. That man must "vanish" (i.e. die), that death is "horrible," that sleep is a "balm of hurt minds," that criminals should accept punishment, that "goodness and truth" are "supreme aims," seem true but curiously empty. Defenders of literary truth can find it difficult to articulate substantial truths from the works they admire and it is perhaps for this reason that non-propositional conceptions of truth are preferred. Jerome Stolnitz pokes fun at the search for an artistic truth derivable from Jane Austen's *Pride and Prejudice*. Could it be, he asks, the "distressingly impoverished" thought that "Stubborn pride and ignorant prejudice keep attractive people apart"?[25]

But the triviality argument only goes so far. There is nothing trivial about the reflections on crime and punishment in Dostoyevsky's novel and some of the complexity is manifest in the discussions of critics. The critical observation, for example, that "Man must suffer . . . because man, his intellect a delusion and its power demonic, trapped by his instinctive brutality and the conspiracy of his victims, does not will his destiny" is complex and, taken as a universal truth, far from uncontroversial.[26]

Cognitive triviality and expressive triviality

In the normal run of cases, though, it might be helpful to distinguish cognitive triviality from expressive triviality. Shakespeare's description of sleep (as above) might not tell us anything we did not know about sleep. Boiled down to its cognitive, truth-bearing, core it says only that sleep "nourishes" and eases our cares. But Shakespeare embodies this truth in quite remarkable metaphors, far from trivial. Alexander Pope famously captures the poetic achievement: "What oft was thought, but ne'er so well expressed."[27] It is surely right that the literary contribution in this and similar cases rests in the *way* something is said. Saying something aptly and tellingly is an important literary skill. There is nothing trivial or banal in Shakespeare's extraordinarily powerful expression of what "innocent sleep" is like. Strictly speaking, though, if we contrast the *mode* of expression with *what* is expressed then it might seem that truth – bare propositional truth – again takes a step back.

Truth and argument in literary works

Other concerns are sometimes raised about the explicit or derived "universal" truths in propositional form. For example, they are seldom *defended* or *argued* either in the literary works themselves or in the critical works that uncover them.[28] This makes the literary context seem very different from the philosophic or scientific one where reasoning and evidence are paramount. This concern is the basis for the rationalist suspicion felt by Plato against the seductive charms of poetry. If an existentialist novel, by Camus, say, or Sartre, or indeed Dostoyevsky, "shows" a world where choice is inescapable this can hardly count as an *argument* for free will, even if the novels strike readers as powerfully persuasive. Likewise a Kafka novel, or perhaps a Greek tragedy, that rejects free will in place of metaphysical determinism or implacable "fate" could not be said to "contradict" existentialism, far less "refute" free will. These works are not pitted against each other as rival theories but justifiably embraced as powerful alternative visions of human life. But care should be taken in the weight given to the lack of argument in fictional literature. It would beg the question against the special contribution of imaginative literature to insist that it employ the very methods of truth advancement found in science and philosophy. Literary works, the defender of truth might reasonably insist, simply have different rhetorical strategies and different means of support from other truth-promoting modes of discourse; that's what's special about them.

Thematic reflection and authorial assertion

A more serious concern is with the status of the thematic propositions. Their propositional form and their truth-assessability can be deceptive. It would be wrong to suppose that every such proposition is being *asserted* as a *worldly truth*. In fact these notions can be taken separately. It is a conventional assumption in reading poetry that sentiments expressed are not directly asserted by the poet but, at most, issued by a "dramatic speaker." When Keats in his poem *Lamia* writes "Philosophy will clip an Angel's wings, / Conquer all mysteries by rule and line" we should not take this as an *assertion* by Keats, expressing his considered view on philosophy, any more than we suppose he is expecting an answer to his (rhetorical) question a few lines earlier: "Do not all charms fly / At the mere touch of cold philosophy?" Literature has been defined as "discourse whose sentences lack the illocutionary forces that would normally attach to them,"[29] and that idea captures the distance between a poet *in propria persona* and a dramatic speaker. Again, though, care must be taken in how the point is generalized. There is no reason in principle why a work of fiction should not be used to make assertions and indeed didactic uses of fiction are common enough. Telling a story can be a good way of drumming home a point, as everyone from Plato with his myths, to Christ with his parables, knows well.

Derived themes and assertion

If caution is needed in attributing a belief to an author equal care must be taken in how to assess thematic hypotheses advanced by critics. When the critic, discussing *Crime and Punishment*, states "the criminal must . . . accept retribution for the act that expresses the metaphysical self-determination of his free will" this is not an assertion about the *world*, an assertion in moral philosophy; it is rather a claim about the novel, an interpretation and reconstruction of one of the novel's central themes. To state a theme in a work, as part of an interpretation of the work, and to make a statement about the world at large are utterly different enterprises. There is no reason to suppose that the critic supports the ethical stance in the theme. Significantly there is no further attempt in the critical discussion to debate that stance independently of its role in the novel. The critic is not a moral philosopher. A derived thematic proposition might be true of the work but not true, or not uncontroversially so, of the world at large. The job of the critic is to make sense of a work, to identify its major themes and characterize them in an illuminating way. Although some of the claims of the critic can look like general propositions in philosophy and psychology, their primary focus, and thus the primary context of their assessment, should be their applicability to the work.

Thematic propositions taken out of context

The distinction between being *about the world* and being *about the work* applies also to universal "truths" found explicitly in works themselves. The trouble with the examples offered earlier – the trouble with the whole quotation industry – is that propositions are wrenched out of context. If we are looking to make a speech or reflect more deeply on some subject or merely impress with our literary knowledge we might well appropriate "sayings" from great works. That is what dictionaries of quotations can offer. Taken out of context we can propound these sayings as worldly truths. But none of this has much relevance to literary value as such. If literary works are to be valued for their truth then the truths had better be integrally connected to the works.

Our examples show how easy it is for quotations to become cut off from the context. The lines (above) from Wordsworth's "Valedictory Sonnet to the River Duddon" suggest (blandly) man's mortality and an attitude to it of calm acceptance. But consider the complete context:

> I THOUGHT of Thee, my partner and my guide,
> As being past away. – Vain sympathies!
> For, backward, Duddon! as I cast my eyes,
> I see what was, and is, and will abide;
> Still glides the Stream, and shall for ever glide;
> The Form remains, the Function never dies;
> While we, the brave, the mighty, and the wise,
> We Men, who in our morn of youth defied
> The elements, must vanish; – be it so!
> Enough, if something from our hands have power
> To live, and act, and serve the future hour;
> And if, as toward the silent tomb we go,
> Through love, through hope, and faith's transcendent dower,
> We feel that we are greater than we know.

The poem itself offers far more than the abstracted lines suggest and perhaps even contradicts them, hinting at a kind of immortality "Through love, through hope, and faith's transcendent dower." It offers a complex reflection on "Form" and "Function" in nature and a suggestion of the eternal: "I see what was, and is, and will abide." Any supposed triviality vanishes in the wider context. But so perhaps does a concern for *truth*. Is it *true* that "the Stream . . . shall for ever glide" (the capital letter implies something greater, more god-like, than the river itself). Is it *true* that "the Function never dies," that there is something eternal in nature and in man? There is no way of knowing, for this is not verifiable truth, it is not science. Propositional truth on the scientific paradigm seems hopelessly irrelevant. Our thoughts are not bound up with verification but with poetic reflection, with the imagination, with the vision that the poem proposes.

Contextualization weakens, but also makes more interesting, the truth status of the other quotations. Claudio in the lines from *Measure for Measure* is pleading with his sister Isabella to spare his own life by giving up her chastity to the odious Angelo. Are his remarks about the horrors of death not tinged with self-pity? Does their eloquence not conceal self-serving exaggeration? Is Claudio, as Isabella wails, not a "faithless coward"? Is there not irony in the fact that his characterization of "The weariest and most loathed worldly life" that he prefers to death fails to mention defilement and loss of purity (Isabella's fate)? When Macbeth describes "innocent sleep," only moments after murdering Duncan, his lines are resonant with the wider assault on innocence. What he says about sleep is, in the context of the play, as telling about his own guilt and state of mind as it is effective as a general reflection on sleep itself. More often than not when explicit universal propositions crop up within works it can be more rewarding to reflect on them not just as abstractable quasi-philosophical observations about the world but more as inwardly directed characterizations of events and persons helping to structure an artistic vision.

Worldly content and the function of propositional description

The defender of literary truth is perhaps over-impressed by a feature of all literary works, fiction and non-fiction alike, that their content is inevitably and deeply implicated in "real world" concerns, both at subject and thematic levels. At the subject level, particularities of plot and character will be presented in world-familiar ways, and at the more universal thematic level, concepts involved (free will, innocence, desire, despair, etc.) will be those that figure in world-focused discourses like philosophy or psychology. But although worldly truth is often available it is not always sought or even relevant in this context. Propositions can be found or formulated but there is a fundamental distinction between a proposition used to *characterize an organizing principle in a literary work* and a proposition (which might be expressed by the very same words) used to *state a truth about the world at large*. These quite different aims should not be conflated. In fact the propositional form itself can be misleading in this regard. What a work is *about*, in the sense of its literary thematic content, need not be propositional. Works can be about pride and prejudice, unrequited love and social responsibility, the conflict of duty and desire, without expressing or implying propositions on these. Monroe Beardsley's distinction between theme and thesis[30] is not really a distinction between a theme and something else but between two ways in which themes can be characterized. The propositional way is not obligatory.

Thematic truth-valuation and value

What about falsehood at the level of thematic propositions? In contrast to factual background it is hard to see how authors might *make mistakes* when proposing a general vision of the world. The vision might be uninteresting, incoherent, undeveloped, uninspired, clichéd, far-fetched, or in general unappealing. It might also be insincere but it is hard to see how it could be *mistaken*. One reason, as we saw with the Wordsworth example, is that the universal "truths" characteristic of literary works are often unverifiable: they are too general, they have an essential value component, they are grounded in a highly personal outlook, and so forth. Of course that is not to say that readers might not disagree with the point of view propounded or implied in a work. Existentialists might disagree with the implied determinism in Kafka, social realists might reject the nihilistic individualism in Beckett, atheists might be unsympathetic to Donne's religious sonnets. But it would be odd for any of these critics to describe the authors as *mistaken*. The critics are making a value judgment, but not one comparable to objections against writers who get their facts wrong. Usually serious readers of literature are remarkably tolerant towards outlooks different from their own, and often value works in spite of these differences. For example, even someone of a naturally optimistic disposition could admire the despairing vision in Matthew Arnold's "Dover Beach":

> the world, which seems
> To lie before us like a land of dreams,
> So various, so beautiful, so new,
> Hath really neither joy, nor love, nor light,
> Nor certitude, nor peace, nor help for pain;
>
> And we are here as on a darkling plain
> Swept with confused alarms of struggle and flight,
> Where ignorant armies clash by night.

A reader does not have to believe it is *true* that the world has "neither joy, nor love, nor light, / Nor certitude, nor peace, nor help for pain" to appreciate and value Arnold's poem. Such simple cases, easily multiplied, illustrate how thematic truth or falsity can be irrelevant to literary value. Hilary Putnam remarks of Celine's *Journey to the End of the Night*:

> I do not learn that love does not exist, that all human beings are hateful and hating. . . . What I learn is to see the world as it looks to someone who is sure that hypothesis is correct.[31]

Empathetic Knowledge and Clarification

There are close relatives of literary truth that shift away from truth *per se*, or propositional truth, towards other "cognitive" benefits: what it is like to see the world from a certain perspective (as with Putnam above), what it is like to be in a certain predicament, changing our outlook on life, educating our emotions. Jenefer Robinson, for example, associates a kind of emotional learning, a "sentimental education," with certain novels. This involves more than just acquiring beliefs: "the idea that learning emotionally through fiction consists primarily in the acquisition of beliefs does not do justice to the experience of reading a novel."[32] She elaborates:

> The emotional education of . . . readers . . . takes place via a series of emotional episodes in which *beliefs* are less important than such things as unexpected physiological responses, non-cognitive affective appraisals, shifts in focus of attention, the perception of new aspects of situations, and the revelation of previously hidden wants and interests.[33]

Often, Robinson believes, a reader's emotional education will be paralleled by that of certain characters. As the characters confront their predicaments and seek ways to understand and overcome them (through the controlling hands, of course, of the author), so a reader empathetically follows their path. David Novitz in this context has spoken of "empathetic knowledge" arising from fiction:

> If the problems which confront fictional characters are seen to arise in the actual world, any reader who has acquired empathetic beliefs pertinent to such problems may well be more aware of, and hence more sensitive to, the difficulties involved in solving them. . . . [If so,] we are justified in saying that the fiction has imparted empathetic *knowledge* of the situation, that it has given readers a "pretty good idea of," or enabled them to know something about, what it feels like to be ensnared in such a situation.[34]

Thus, "knowing what it is like" becomes a cognitive payoff, related to, but not identical with, the acquiring of true beliefs.

Cognitive strengthening

A similar view, which has gained currency in recent years, might be called *cognitive strengthening*. Again the emphasis is away from the acquisition of newly found worldly truths towards "clarification" (Noël Carroll) or an "enriched understanding" (Gordon Graham) or an "acknowledgement" (John Gibson) of beliefs readers are likely to hold already.[35] As Noël Carroll puts it,

> in mobilising what we already know and what we can already feel, the narrative artwork can become an occasion for us to deepen our understanding of what we know and what we feel.[36]

It can do this by "reorganis[ing] the hierarchical orderings of our moral categories and premises" or "reinterpret[ing] those categories and premises in the light of new paradigm instances and hard cases" or "reclassify[ing] barely acknowledged phenomena afresh."[37] The idea is that literary works – notably narratives – do not educate readers merely by imparting truths that the readers had not thought before, but by "clarifying" or "enriching" or giving fresh impetus to beliefs that readers already possess but rarely attend to. Perhaps on a small scale something similar occurs in reflecting on Macbeth's observations about sleep. Shakespeare's powerfully expressive metaphors might not *inform* us about sleep but they provide a unique perspective for re-conceiving only vaguely considered aspects of sleep.

The idea of cognitive strengthening identifies an important and familiar phenomenon in the reading of novels and other literary works. It is a further question, though, how far it boosts the pro-truth case about literary value. By moving away from beliefs and propositional truth it becomes distanced from paradigmatic cases of truth. Also, it might seem to weaken certain kinds of pro-truth accounts by in effect conceding the triviality objection. Why would literary works need to "clarify" or "enhance" truths if these were already substantial in themselves (as they might be in a philosophical treatise)? And is it characteristically the case that the "clarification" or "enrichment" offered by literature merely builds on beliefs that readers already possess? Is it so rare for new beliefs to be in the offing?

An Enduring Contrast: Philosophy and Literature

The debate about truth in literature – the debate over whether truth is a fundamental value in literary works – is not, as noted from the start, one that affords any final or easy resolution. Novels, poems, and plays offer numerous instances of truths and can be the occasion for learning and acquiring beliefs. They afford other cognitive payoffs as well, as shown. But is a didactic function a central achievement or aspiration of such works? Do those works that fail to teach fail as literature? Must the reading of novels always strive for self-improvement or education? The specter of Plato still haunts the debate.

Those skeptical that truth is a fundamental value of literature like to emphasize a contrast between paradigmatic literary works (fiction and poetry) and what can be called *constitutively cognitive* discourses, such as philosophy. Philosophy, they will insist, *essentially* aims at advancing understanding and is valued accordingly. The core focus of interest in a philosophical work is on the claims it makes and the arguments in support of them. Ill-supported, poorly argued, or unoriginal works are devalued for that reason. To read philosophy is to read for truth. In contrast, to read and value a work *from a literary point of view* seems quite different. For one thing, literary works that are too overtly didactic are seldom valued highly. For another, one of the pleasures of a literary reading is to notice different ways that the content can be imaginatively construed, not necessarily focused on a single "message" or "thesis" to be conveyed. Also the expectations readers have in coming to a novel or poem for the first time are seldom cognitive expectations: readers are not commonly motivated to read by the thought that they will learn something. They might learn something and might value that learning, what they learn might even change their lives (for the better), but all that seems like a bonus gained not a demand made. More characteristically, readers seek a distinctive kind of pleasure from their reading. The very process of reading a novel or poem is quite unlike that conventionally associated with philosophical or historical works. Readers like to be imaginatively involved with the narrative or subject content, they like to find coherence and interest at a broader thematic level, they enjoy and look out for formal qualities of structure and design. Do they seek truth as well? Some do, some don't.

Notes

1 Samuel Johnson, *Preface to Shakespeare's Plays* (London: Scholar Press, 1969), lines 280–2.
2 Samuel Johnson, *Milton* (*Lives of the Poets*).
3 William Shakespeare, *As You Like It*, 3.3.16.
4 Friedrich Nietzsche, "On Truth and Falsity in Their Extramoral Sense."
5 Roland Barthes, "The Death of the Author," in *Image-Music-Text*, trans. Stephen Heath (London: Fontana, 1977), 145–6.
6 Paul de Man, *The Resistance to Theory* (Manchester: Manchester University Press, 1986), 11.
7 Plato, *Republic*, 607d–e, trans. Robin Waterfield (Oxford: Oxford University Press, 1998), 362.
8 Aristotle, *Poetics*, 1460b10–11, trans. Ingram Bywater, in Jonathan Barnes, ed., *The Complete Works of Aristotle: The Revised Oxford Translation*, vol. 2 (Princeton, NJ: Princeton University Press, 1984).
9 Aristotle, *Poetics*, 1451b2–10, trans. Bywater.
10 I. A. Richards, *Principles of Literary Criticism* (London: Routledge, 1967), 212.
11 Iris Murdoch, *Metaphysics as a Guide to Morals* (Harmondsworth: Penguin), 86, 321.
12 Iris Murdoch, *The Sovereignty of Good* (London: Routledge, 1970), 65.
13 Cecil Day Lewis, *The Poetic Image* (New York: Oxford University Press, 1947), chapter 1.
14 W. K. Wimsatt, *The Verbal Icon* (Lexington, KY: University of Kentucky Press, 1954).
15 Morris Weitz, "Truth in Literature," *Revue Internationale de Philosophie* 9 (1955): 1–14.
16 Colin Falck, *Myth, Truth and Literature* (Cambridge: Cambridge University Press, 1989), 74.
17 John Keats, Letter to Benjamin Bailey, November 22, 1817.
18 William Shakespeare, *Measure for Measure*, 3.1.119–33.
19 William Shakespeare, *Macbeth*, 2.2.
20 Vyacheslav Ivanov, "The Revolt Against Mother Earth," in Feodor Dostoyevsky, *Crime and Punishment*, ed. George Gibian (New York: W. W. Norton & Co, 1975), 584.
21 Rosemary Edmonds, "Introduction," in Leo Tolstoy, *War and Peace* (Harmondsworth: Penguin, 1969), vol. 1, xii.
22 Malcolm Bradbury, *To the Hermitage* (London: Picador, 2000), 386.
23 This and the following examples come from Christopher Ricks, "Literature and the Matter of Fact," in *Essays in Appreciation* (Oxford: Clarendon Press, 1996).
24 The case is discussed in M. W. Rowe, "Lamarque and Olsen on Literature and Truth," *Philosophical Quarterly* 47:188 (1997): 322–41, 334.
25 Jerome Stolnitz, "On the Cognitive Triviality of Art," in Peter Lamarque and Stein Haugom Olsen, eds., *Aesthetics and the Philosophy of Art: The Analytic Tradition: An Anthology* (Oxford: Blackwell, 2003), 338–9.
26 Maurice Beebe, "The Three Motives of Rasknolnikov: A Reinterpretation of *Crime and Punishment*," in Feodor Dostoyevsky, *Crime and Punishment*, ed. George Gibian (New York: W. W. Norton & Co, 1975), 596.

27 Alexander Pope, *An Essay On Criticism* (1711), part 2, line 298.
28 The point is emphasized by Stein Haugom Olsen in *The Structure of Literary Understanding* (Cambridge: Cambridge University Press, 1978), 69f. It is also discussed in Noël Carroll, "The Wheel of Virtue: Art, Literature, and Moral Knowledge," *Journal of Aesthetics and Art Criticism* 60 (2002), 6ff.
29 Richard Ohmann, "Speech Acts and the Definition of Literature," *Philosophy and Rhetoric* 4 (1971): 14. A similar view is advanced by Monroe C. Beardsley: e.g. "Fiction as Representation," *Synthese* 46 (1981); "Aesthetic Intentions and Fictive Illocutions," in Paul Hernadi, ed., *What is Literature?* (Bloomington, IN: Indiana University Press, 1978); and *Aesthetics: Problems in the Philosophy of Criticism*, 2nd edn. (Indianapolis, IN: Hackett, 1981), xliv.
30 Beardsley, *Aesthetics: Problems in the Philosophy of Criticism*, 404.
31 Hilary Putnam, "Literature, Science, and Reflection," in Hilary Putnam, *Meaning and the Moral Sciences* (London: Routledge, 1978), 89.
32 Jenefer Robinson, *Deeper than Reason* (Oxford: Oxford University Press, 2005), 155. See also her chapter in this volume: 5, EMOTION AND THE UNDERSTANDING OF NARRATIVE.
33 Robinson, *Deeper than Reason*, 157.
34 David Novitz, *Knowledge, Fiction and Imagination* (Philadelphia: Temple University Press, 1987), 135–6.
35 Noël Carroll, "Art, Narrative, and Moral Understanding," in *Beyond Aesthetics* (Cambridge: Cambridge University Press, 2001), 270–93; Gordon Graham, *Philosophy of the Arts: An Introduction to Aesthetics* (London: Routledge, 1997); John Gibson, "Between Truth and Triviality," *British Journal of Aesthetics* 43 (2003): 224–37.
36 Carroll, "Art, Narrative, and Moral Understanding," 283.
37 Ibid.

20

Truth in Poetry: Particulars and Universals

RICHARD ELDRIDGE

Any account of truth in poetry must begin by facing the fact that poems are artifacts made neither for any immediate practical-material purpose, such as the satisfaction of bodily needs, nor with reference to measurements of material realities. Aristotle marks this difference between poems and other things by calling them imitations (*mimemata*) that are products of *poiesis*, as opposed either to actions that are products of *praxis* or accounts (*logoi*) that are products of *theoria*. Since for us, as for Aristotle, *logoi* or accounts or theories that are generated by reliable procedures (experimentation, measurement, calculation, and their cousins) are significant paradigms of the presentation of truth, a natural question arises as to how poems specifically, and literary works generally, could be true at all. What, if anything, do Petrarch's longings for Laura, or the verbalized plights of consciousness of Hamlet or Prufrock, or the effusions of Wordsworth over daffodils, or Whitman's songs of himself and America, or Plath's musings upon cutting her thumb, have to do with the recording of the real? It is, moreover, equally natural to think that the particular way in which a poem thematizes its subject matter – its use of just these words – matters to its nature and value in a way that presentation does not matter in other, more scientific paradigms of recording truth. Although it has been said to be a kind of heresy, a paraphrase of a poem is often a useful way of coming to grips with it, especially when exploring important verbal densities and specificities. In contrast, there is, in mathematics and the natural sciences, no significance to verbal density and specificity "for their own sake" apart from reliable investigative procedures.

Taking these differences between truth-representation in theoretical inquiries and the nature of the poetic work into account, we may be tempted to suppose that poetry presents no truths at all. Monroe Beardsley, for example, claims that the work of fiction "does not make an assertion, at least on the Report level" – that is, nothing about the world that is assessable as true or false is claimed in the literary work. A poem "is not an assertion and therefore claims to convey no information."[1] Similarly, Peter Lamarque and Stein Haugom Olsen note that "we can imagine, ponder, entertain thoughts, or speculate about something without any commitment to the truth of our

---

A Companion to the Philosophy of Literature, First Edition. Edited by Garry L. Hagberg and Walter Jost.
© 2010 John Wiley & Sons Ltd. Published 2015 by John Wiley & Sons, Ltd.

ruminations," and they argue that literary works invite us to undertake imagining "without advancing propositions, statements, or hypotheses."[2] In each case, the argument turns on a comparison between science, with its objective procedures of experimentation, and "mere" imagining, and in each case we are urged to turn our attention to the literary work as a vehicle not for the presentation of truth, but rather for the delivery of an absorbing pleasure.

Here we may already begin to suspect that the argument has moved too quickly, particularly when we remember that imagination may plausibly be supposed to play some role within the practices of science, including its pursuit of confirmations of claims. Not only does imagining help us to frame hypotheses, it also helps us to "see" the phenomena at hand in the laboratory as falling into certain classes. For example, as Thomas Kuhn has notoriously emphasized, it takes a background of ongoing commitments, themselves not established through measurement, in order to see the motion of a stone swinging on a chain as a case of motion subject to independent horizontal and vertical force vectors rather than as constrained fall towards a "natural" place. The practice of science, including the discovery of confirmations, is not simple measurement "all the way down."[3] It is plausible to regard comparatively well-confirmed natural scientific theories as *better* representations of phenomena (e.g. gravitational attraction, electrical charge, solubility) that "really exist" apart from human beings and their doings; but the natural sciences themselves do not make "direct contact" with "fundamental reality" via measurement or observation alone, without drawing on imagination.

Nonetheless, important differences are evident between *theoria* (and *praxis*), on the one hand, and *poiesis*, on the other. A successful poetic imitation must in some way produce an experience that is "like" the experience of its subject matter, whereas the equation that correctly represents projectile motion on the earth does not in any sense look like what it represents. Given the important roles of history, traditions, and conventions (including linguistic traditions) within artistic practice, it is notoriously difficult to specify the sort of resemblance that is relevant to poetic imitation. Visual depiction, for example, plays no role in successful poetic imitation in words. Yet, like viewers of paintings, readers of successful poems (and other literary works) often report a feeling of "knowing what it is like" to have been struck by a certain scene, to have had or overheard a train of thought and feeling, or to have been "involved in" a course of action. Successful poetic imitations have some sort of significant phenomenal presence.

Second, and perhaps more important, unlike theoretical representations that present phenomena that exist "on their own," such as the melting point of lead or the composition of the atmosphere of Jupiter, poetic imitations present scenes, incidents, actions, and thoughts and feelings about them all, in relation to how they matter to and for human life. In poetry, scene (as object of attention and reflection), incident, action, thought and feeling all exist *for* a responding intelligence. Poetic imitations, it is plausible to suppose, exist not primarily in order to record material realities that are independent of human life, but rather to model aptness of feeling and response: to model how things matter for us.

Aristotle captures this point effectively in explaining how it is that "plot is the origin and as it were the soul of tragedy" – tragedy in particular, and by implication of imitative verbal art in general. Plot presents a complete course of action as having "a beginning, a middle, and a conclusion," where "a beginning is that after which there naturally is, or comes into being, something else. A conclusion, conversely, is that which itself naturally follows something else, either of necessity or for the most part, but has nothing else after it. A middle is that which itself naturally follows something else, and has something else after it."[4] The notion of "naturally following after" is crucial here. This relation is not that of material causation according to a law of mathematical physics, but rather that of an intelligible unfolding of action in a way that makes sense to a rational audience, given the natures of things:

> It is the function of the poet to relate not things that have happened [which may all have their own material causes or be referable to physical laws, or may not], but things that may happen, i.e. that are possible in accordance with probability or necessity.[5]

The probability or necessity that is displayed by a successful poetic plot is neither a statistical likelihood nor a physical determination, but rather *how things* (including people, with their rational natures and specific characters) *reveal their essential natures over time and in interaction with other things, fitfully perhaps but discernibly, to and for an attentive audience.*

More specifically, that human beings as rational animals, capable of understanding their situation and best possibilities of life, are naturally directed toward *eudaimonia* or rational activity in accordance with virtue, but under imperfect conditions, shows itself, according to Aristotle, in the successful plot of a tragic drama. Directedness by reason toward *eudaimonia* is the universal that informs or structures human life. Human beings have rational souls, where the soul just *is* the form or organization of the body, and being rational just *is* being so organized as to be capable of *logos* and reflection, and so of theoretical and practical reasoning. Rationality in human beings is, however, combined with other, more animal propensities, such as fearfulness, anger, or patience. The mixtures of animal qualities with reason vary from person to person, giving each person a distinctive character or *hexis*, in which reason plays a part but is not the whole. In addition, the circumstances of action – geographic, economic, and cultural, among others – differ among people, so that conflict results as mixtures of rational and animal propensities are played out in specific circumstances. No actual human life is one perpetual rational progress, smooth and bright.

Poetry in general and tragic drama in particular discern and track the expression of character or *hexis* (including rationality) in particular circumstances, where that expression is not always immediately evident to the senses alone. What happens "with probability or necessity" is that the pursuit of *eudaimonia* is undertaken by a rational agent with a type of character, who then further meets with good or ill fortune, in the form of material circumstances, social relations, cultural affordances, and so on. Poetry makes manifest how this happens.

> For this reason poetry is a more philosophical and more serious business than [chronicle] history; poetry tends to speak of universals, history of particulars. A universal is the sort of thing that a certain kind of person may well say or do in accordance with probability or necessity – this is what poetry aims at, although it assigns [particular] names to the people.[6]

A successful poem will, therefore, discern and clarify how, with probability or necessity, a specific character possessed by a rational animal is lived out in specific, imperfect circumstances.

In the Homeric poems and other early sagas, the hero typically excels in strength and military virtue, and his exploits either on behalf of or in spite of his culture are celebrated in songs that remember them. Thus Homer's *Iliad* begins:

> Rage, Goddess, sing the rage of Peleus' son Achilles,
> murderous, doomed, that cost the Achaeans countless losses,
> hurling down to the House of Death so many sturdy souls,
> great fighters' souls, but made their bodies carrion,
> feasts for the dogs and birds,
> and the will of Zeus was moving toward its end.
> Begin, Muse, when the two first broke and clashed,
> Agamemnon lord of men and brilliant Achilles.[7]

Pindar's odes celebrate the victors in Greek athletic festivals. Many of Sappho's lyrics celebrate more or less natural human beauty and erotic attractiveness. As cultures become more urbanized, more knowledge-based, and more complex, however, concentration on martial, athletic, and "natural" virtues wanes. In the *Republic*, Plato simultaneously criticizes warrior society, the preeminence of military virtue, and the presentational form of the heroic epic. Instead of seeing the universal – a shared rational-animal character informing all distinctively human life – exemplified predominantly in violent struggle and "outdoing" (*pleonexia*), Plato argues that reason (or at least a measure of reason) is itself a human universal, one that, properly exercised, leads to stability in life and command of the self that is properly devoted to the contemplative grasp of "higher" intellectual realities. Aristotle significantly follows Plato in this emphasis on reason, conceding that the life of intellectual contemplation is highest, but he argues also that practical reason motivates the pursuit of *eudaimonia* through civic friendship. The tragedies of Sophocles and Euripides and the comedies of Aristophanes focus on yet further formations of individual character that are varieties of general human character, and they track the careers that flow from them. Antigone's devotion to family life, ritual, and the unwritten, eternal law of the gods, is admirable, but also one-sided, as is Creon's devotion to political life and civic order; in their circumstances, their respective casts of character bring them both to heroic grief.

The result of increasing urbanization, of more complex and more knowledge-based life, and of the accompanying pluralism of poetic forms (traditional epics, odes, comedies, tragedies, philosophical pleas for an intellectualized restoration of unified self-command), is that confidence in the availability of any single, authoritatively correct account of human directedness toward an end in nature falters. Both Aristophanes' *The Clouds* and the self-interested prudentialism of the Sophists, with their insistences on the inevitable varieties of human commitments in different contexts, express a sense of this faltering and oppose the hubris of the philosopher who would still seek a final account of value in human life. Perhaps, then, there is no such thing as a human universal – an underlying, given, non-optional directedness toward an end, together with a set of virtues or skills for achieving it – to be discerned poetically. Plato and Aristotle protect themselves against this thought by arguing that nature itself, and so human life along with it, is comprehensively organized for the sake of the good. As Socrates puts it in the *Republic*,

> one must conclude that [the form of the good] is the cause of all that is correct and beautiful in anything, that it produces both light and its source in the visible realm, and that in the intelligible realm it controls and provides truth and understanding, so that anyone who is to act sensibly in public or private must see it.[8]

Any account – any poetic imitation of human life – that denies this presiding role of the form of the good in nature and in human life must be false, and it must be possible poetically to discern in a favored, ordered way what human life is all about. Aristotle argues that God or Divine Intelligence (*Noûs*) exists eternally as a first cause that through its self-moving activity of thinking contributes form, identity, and value to finite material things. "If [this account] were not true, the world would have proceeded out of night and 'all things together' and out of non-being."[9] Since that cannot happen, this account must be true. The best life for us is, then, the life that most resembles the life of this divine activity. Tragic poetry can track how the pursuit of the best life can go wrong, while comedy can track good fortune, and epic can track the exercise of heroic virtues. Underlying each case, however, there remains something (albeit subject to contingency and imperfection) that human life is inherently all about: directedness toward a well-ordered household and public life of *eudaimonia* and further toward intellectual contemplation as the fullest exercise of central and centrally valuable inherent human powers.

It is easy to suspect, however, that these metaphysical accounts of nature in general and of human nature in particular suffer from reactionary defensiveness and lack of grounding. Exactly why "must one conclude" that the form of the good presides over all finite being? Why must there be a self-moving, divine first cause, rather than the world proceeding "out of night and 'all things together' "? If these claims are unfounded, is there then any genuine human universal that can be discerned poetically? Perhaps both the metaphysical claims and the moral and artistic stances of Plato and Aristotle are functions more of their psychological-cultural needs than of insight into the ultimate natures of things. Hegel makes exactly this charge against Plato:

> Plato, aware that the [dominant, Hellenic, warrior] ethics of his time were being penetrated by a deeper principle [subjective freedom or freedom of choice of commitments] which,

within this context, could appear immediately only as an as yet unsatisfied longing and hence only as a destructive force, was obliged, in order to counteract it, to seek the help of that very longing itself. But the help he required had to come from above, and he could seek it at first only in a particular *external* form of Greek ethics. By this means, he imagined he could overcome the destructive force, and he thereby inflicted the gravest damage on the deeper drive behind it, namely free infinite personality.[10]

Nietzsche similarly claims to have "recognized Socrates and Plato as symptoms of decay, as tools of the Greek dissolution, as [*having*] to have the same negative attitude towards life."[11] In both cases the charge is that Plato posited an overarching metaphysical system that undergirds a moral stance not out of metaphysical insight but simply out of a need to find some source of stability, even stasis, against the onward movement of life in increasingly chaotic cultural conditions. The ideas that there is no presiding form of the good to be discerned, no *Nôus* as first cause, and so no inherent human directedness toward a specific end or any accompanying objective virtues or powers for achieving that end – all become only more plausible with the rise of modern physical science, with its conception of a meaningless or disenchanted ("merely physical") nature, where motion, growth, and development take place (so it is thought) only in accordance with value-independent, mathematically formulable laws.

It can seem, then, that poetry even at its best can only record particular experiences, thoughts, or emotions, where the occurrence of any of these has nothing necessarily to do with their place in any general, mandatory human project or purpose. At best then, poetry might be a window into the particulars of individual souls and their experiences, for anyone who might happen contingently to take an interest in what is going on with another person.

Yet this suggestion that poetry is only about the presentation of experiences of particulars also faces problems. Politically and morally, it unhappily encourages Thrasymachanism or competitive individualism, curbed only by the practical necessities of cooperating with others when one must. Free-riding and covert exploitativeness become reasonable life strategies when one can get away with them, and human intimacy is thereby made problematic. More important, the idea that poetry presents only particular experiences is false to the experience of poetry itself, where we continue to find something of general significance in a successful poetic work, even if it remains very difficult to unpack that significance into a philosophical doctrine of essential directedness toward an end. The poetic work remains both interesting in its own right, in its verbal density and specificity, and interesting as something we feel we know somehow to be an exemplification to some degree of human life as such.

In the modern period, poets have consciously struggled to balance a sense of the particularities of their lives, experiences, and verbal art with the working out of a claim to general significance. Among early modern writers, this struggle is especially clear in Petrarch (1304–1374), and its presence in his work is a mark of his bearing a distinctively modern sense of individual self. In a "Letter to Posterity," Petrarch describes explicitly his sense of his individuality and his failure to be bound in his commitments by any detailed, comprehensive, moral doctrine.

TRUTH IN POETRY: PARTICULARS AND UNIVERSALS

> To begin with myself, then, the utterances of men concerning me will differ widely, since in passing judgment almost every one is influenced not so much by truth as by preference, and good and evil report alike know no bounds.[12]

To say that good and evil report know no bounds, but are rather rooted in preferences, is to say that full truth about moral matters is unavailable. There are only multiple perspectives on what is worth doing, and these are never fully reconcilable with one another. Despite his perspectival individualism, however, Petrarch continues nonetheless to claim and court general significance in and for his verse.

Building on a tradition of medieval court poetry in praise of an idealized object of love, but going beyond that tradition in self-consciousness, Petrarch describes, in the first sonnet of his *Canzoniere* or *Songbook*, the nature of his love for Laura:

> O you, who list in scatter'd verse the sound
> Of all those sighs with which my heart I fed,
> When I, by youthful error first misled,
> Unlike my present self in heart was found;
>
> Who list the plaints, the reasonings that abound
> Throughout my song, by hopes and vain griefs bred;
> If e'er true love its influence o'er ye shed,
> Oh! let your pity be with pardon crown'd.
>
> But now full well I see how to the crowd
> For length of time I proved a public jest:
> E'en by myself my folly is allow'd:
>
> And of my vanity the fruit is shame,
> Repentance, and a knowledge strong imprest,
> That worldly pleasure is a passing dream.[13]

Petrarch's focus here is first of all on himself as a particular, suffering individual. He knows he has changed since his first errant youthful days; he asks for pity and forgiveness for his failings (rather than wholehearted approval of his deportment); he knows other people gossip about his folly (rather than endorsing his commitments); and he hopes for repentance and change, not merely approval for having done well. "The reasonings that abound" throughout the sonnets that follow are the products of passion and error, not sound understanding. And yet he also continues to regard his love for a particular individual as at least conjecturally a central point of essential likeness with his readers. If any have suffered as he has suffered, then they should be or may be ready to pity and to pardon. The poem is also distinctively formally unified, both rhythmically and metrically. This achieved unity is a self-conscious display of verbal art and of self-control that have either survived or been in part the product of the suffering of passion, and Petrarch surely hopes that his readers will respond to this verbal art and self-control as exemplary. The sonnet as a whole is a complex performance and recording of a human subjectivity lodged within historical time, capable of acknowledging its finitude and of accepting the impossibility of an essential understanding of humanity that is specifically action guiding. Folly and vanity (and contingency and reversal) cannot be avoided altogether. Declaration of the plights of the self, in the hope of uncovering likenesses and soliciting forgiveness, supplants any triumphal, rational discovery of the specific essential end of humanity as such.

Petrarch's stance is here exemplary for modern poetry and perhaps for poetry and literature in general. (Homer, Hesiod, and Pindar stage their own works self-consciously and variously as witness, therapy, inspiration, and verbal art, but not as products of abstract and general reasoning.[14]) Everywhere there is perplexity and uncertainty. Poetic work is strongly pluralized in both form and subject matter. There no single style, theme, or message that is consistently dominant. Hamlet, for example, exists as a freethinking individual decathected from a culture of honor, yet not knowing where to turn or how to act. Romeo's love for Juliet as a thinking, feeling, individualized person who speaks and refuses to be mere sexual booty lifts him out of a cycle of masculine conquest and dynastic loyalty and into something uncertain. Don Quixote pursues older values in a world that cannot recognize them. Wordsworth is brought to reverie by the light of a setting sun or to awe by a rushing torrent. As Friedrich Schlegel remarks in his "Critical Fragments,"

> All the classical poetical genres have now become ridiculous in their rigid purity. Poetry is republican speech: a speech which is its own law and end unto itself, and in which all the parts are free citizens and have the right to vote.[15]

Modern poetry continues, nonetheless, to do work in relation to its initiating perplexities. It does not simply record particulars of thought and feeling. Rather, it "works them through," until the initiating perplexity and shock of strong feeling are somehow clarified and calmed, without reversion to moral dogma. Regarding poetry, the best philosophical model for "working through" perplexity and feeling is provided by Spinoza in his account of the transformation by reflection of an inadequate idea of an affection into an adequate idea. One begins by caring about some things, but inchoately and confusedly. Perhaps there is an experience of attraction to or repulsion from some scene, incident, or person, or perhaps one is caught up in conflicting attractions and aversions, loyalties and animosities, ideals and senses of the shameful. One has an idea, perhaps too many ideas, of what is worth doing and what is worth shunning, but one's ideas are unclear, ill-formed, and incomplete. Confusion, drift, or simple reactivity without coherent purpose threaten to dominate one's doings. Through reflection, one comes to see what here and now is more worth caring about in which specific ways.

According to Spinoza, the result of correct reflection is commitment to a substantive, Stoic intellectualism.

> We would do well to become aware how effective against the emotions is clear and distinct knowledge, and especially the kind of knowledge whose basis is the knowledge of [an impersonal and immutable] God [whose being is the whole of nature].[16]

Knowledge of God as the one, whole, substance of nature

> begets love towards something immutable and eternal which we can truly possess, and which therefore cannot be defiled by any of the faults that are to be found in the common sort of love, but can continue to grow more and more and engage the greatest part of the mind and pervade it.[17]

Here Spinoza echoes Plato and the philosophers in holding that there is a single correct method of reflection (realized in his proofs) with a single correct outcome, the stance of intellectual reflection itself. This position has its charms, and the consolations of detached thought may be especially compelling in times of personal or social chaos. But Spinoza's stance does not quite answer to the kinds of perplexities involving sudden emotion due to receptivity or to conflicting senses of self to which poets particularly attend.

The solution of the poets, therefore, is to take up the Spinozistic labor of reflection in order to work through perplexities so as to achieve a greater calm and composure, but without any assurance of arriving in the end at a single, coherent, and formulable stance. Among modern poet-theorists, Friedrich Hölderlin and William Wordsworth give the best accounts of this neo-Spinozistic work of poetry in reorienting and calming the soul without final assurances. Both Hölderlin and Wordsworth begin from a sharp sense of the unavailability to human beings of any ultimate metaphysical knowledge that might guide us toward a specific course of exemplary and successful life, and both think of the achievement of a *comparative*, good-enough, momentary composure as the central task of poetic thinking and writing.[18]

Hölderlin begins his reflections on poetic thinking with the thought that we have, as finite discursive beings capable of reflection, fallen out of simple, unreflective immersion in the whole of being. "I am as such necessarily restricted, even if it were only within time, hence not absolute."[19] Therefore my thinking and reflecting – my having any object or content of my consciousness at all – take place always from a particularized location or point of view. From a particular point of view, I am unable to bring the whole of reality into view "before" me, as something I can survey. Thinking always instead begins from an *Ahnung* – a presentiment or surmise that is evident in feeling and that remains to be unpacked or worked out, where, in light of human finitude, the working out remains marked by what Thomas Pfau has aptly called "the absence of any totalizing figure."[20] The task of the poet in carrying out the unpacking of initiating felt presentiment is "to bear the momentarily incomplete"[21] – the incompleteness of thinking at every moment – in such a way that relative composure is nonetheless achieved. Modulation from one feeling to another and the achievement of relative composure supplant triumphant moral discovery as the available and appropriate end of the work of poetic thinking. This modulation and achievement of composure can remain exemplary for readers by holding their emotional engagement and modeling its development, but not by commanding any doctrinal conclusion.

Like Hölderlin, Wordsworth sees discursive thought as emerging out of an irrecuperable fall from immersion in the whole of nature. For Wordsworth, as for Hölderlin, it is not possible to trace the process of this emergence from within the register of discursivity: the having of particular thoughts as a particular individual entails that one is *not* grasping the whole.

> Hard task, vain hope, to analyze the mind,
> If each most obvious and particular thought,
> Not in a mystical or idle sense,
> But in the words of Reason deeply weighed,
> Hath no beginning.[22]

As a result, it is impossible also to ground foundationally in a proof from indubitable first principles any claim about how discursive thought and human life ought to develop and about the proper cares of human beings. Poems show a protagonist moving through a sequence of interested feelings and of reflections on them, and the poet hopes to achieve exemplarity in this sequence. But the claim to exemplarity cannot be supported by general metaphysical reasoning: it must stand, if at all, on its own. It is a "selfish and foolish hope" to undertake "*reasoning* [the Reader] into approbation of these particular Poems."[23] Any such reasoning would require a full deduction of the origins of human mindedness in general, its course of development in sociocultural life, and its proper end, and no such deduction is available.

The task of poetry, then, is not to announce general truths about a merely material world, but instead to exemplify and so to cultivate in attentive readers an apt, sensitive responsiveness to the significances of things. The poet

> shall describe objects, and utter sentiments, of such a nature, *and in such connection with each other*, that the understanding of the Reader must necessarily be in some degree enlightened, and his affections strengthened and purified.[24]

Without this poetic work of the exemplification and communication of felt interest in objects, scenes, incidents, and persons, human life is in danger of becoming pale. "Savage torpor" and "a degrading thirst after outrageous stimulations"[25] can result. The only way out of this situation is through the improvisatory poetic work (either in composition or in attentive reading that follows it) of experiencing and rendering feeling in relation to things, so as "to *make* incidents and situations interesting"[26] in relation to apt emotional and reflective attention. This poetic work of the disclosure of the significances of things in relation to feeling can never be made otiose by advances in science. The aim of this work is

> truth not standing upon external testimony, but carried alive into the heart by passion; truth which is its own testimony, which gives competence and confidence to the tribunal to which it appeals, and receives them from the same tribunal.[27]

Here confidence in feeling and its aptness is received only from like responsive feeling in others, so that poet (or any precursor figure) and audience (or any responsive figure) are continually bootstrapping one another's emotional investments. Within this bootstrapping circuit, the poet is distinguished only by greater promptness of feeling and "a greater readiness and power in expressing what he thinks and feels."[28] Poetic thinking takes place from within a framework of ongoing human emotional life, not from a point apart, and its work is to make the materials of this framework – the emotions that undergird action and response to life – healthy from within.

These basic ideas of Hölderlin and Wordsworth, regarding how poetry helps to achieve (without reifying) apt, truthful emotional orientations and actions, have been endorsed and developed by subsequent theorists. R. G. Collingwood extends this picture of the work of poetic thinking to elucidate the work of philosophy as well, which he sees not as general discovery that can properly be modeled on the procedures of either scientific experimentation or mathematical proof, but rather as the clearing up of disturbing incoherencies in our concepts. This work of clarification is not referred to anything external to it, such as Platonic forms or Aristotelian essences or scientific discoveries, but is rather governed, like poetry, by the effort to achieve greater fluency in (conceptual) performance and in coherence of emotional engagement in life.

> Good philosophy and good poetry are not two different kinds of writing, but one; each is simply good writing; and in the limiting case where each was as good as it ought to be, the distinction would disappear.[29]

Ludwig Wittgenstein holds a similar position in remarking that "philosophy ought really to be written only as a *poetic composition* [Philosophie dürfte man eigentlich nur *dichten*]"[30] so that "your mental cramp is relieved."[31]

In *The Sense of an Ending*, Frank Kermode emphasizes the role of plot as falling somehow between discovery and contrivance in tracing human orientation and directedness toward an end. We can no longer believe in archaic, mythical, presiding purposes: the cognitive achievements of the modern sciences, our modern sense of our free inwardness as subjects, and the attractions of value pluralism are too strong for that. Yet we cannot live either without some sense of an objectively appropriate shape for a life. Poetically formed plots then enable us to cope with "the tension or dissonance between paradigmatic form and contingent reality."[32] In generating them and in following them, we work through both our senses of what it is appropriate for us to do when and our attitudes toward actual and possible commitments. They offer us models of orientation toward commanding values in the absence of any comprehensive, completed metaphysics.

Barbara Herrnstein Smith concentrates on how poems achieve closure or a sense of arriving at their appropriate endings through a combination of formal arrangement and the achievement of thematic and emotional coherence amidst complexity. The task of poetry is to enable "us to know what we know, including our illusions and desires, by giving us the language in which to acknowledge it."[33] Crucially, what a successful poem enables us to acknowledge is our own emotions and attitudes toward incidents, attractions, aversions, scenes, or persons that were initially confusing and troubling. Through the work of the poem, these initiating phenomena are set in a larger context – that is, thematized as having significance in relation to human life in general – and a more stable emotion in relation to them is achieved. As with Kermode, however, this poetic work of acknowledgment and the achievement of more stable, composed emotion remains importantly open-ended and improvisatory, ungoverned by either any single master metaphysics or any single formal device of poetic tradition alone. We find in the successful poem the sense that the poet is achieving closure anew and in a complex way, in relation to troublesome phenomena that demand a newer emotional and attitudinal stance.

Charles Altieri focuses somewhat more on the delights that poets self-consciously take in their formal and thematic improvisations. Poets are alert to and pursue "the kinds of satisfactions that are available for agents simply because of the qualities of consciousness they bring to what they are feeling."[34] They render these qualities of consciousness formally and thematically so as to achieve these satisfactions. These achievements model for us kinds of satisfactions that we may also find – emotionally, attitudinally, and cognitively as acknowledgment – whenever we find ourselves in straits that are similar enough to those of the poet. Since new conditions of perplexity and confusion will continue to arise, new forms of poetic rendering will always be in order.

T. W. Adorno integrates each of these various emphases – on innovative plots of orientation, on formal-thematic working through, and on satisfaction in poetic forming – in his account of lyric, as he concentrates on the voice that *takes shape* in the poem.

> The substance of a poem is not merely an expression of individual impulses and experiences. [The lyric poems works] by making manifest something not distorted, not grasped, not yet subsumed. It thereby anticipates, spiritually, a situation in which no false universality, that is, nothing profoundly particular, continues to fetter what is other than itself, the human. The lyric work hopes to attain universality through unrestrained individuation.[35]

> The "I" whose voice is heard in the lyric is an "I" that defines and expresses itself as something opposed to the collective, to objectivity; it is not immediately at one with the nature to which its expression refers. It has lost it, as it were, and attempts to restore it through animation, through immersion in the "I" itself.[36]

The picture here is of an "I" – all at once the author, the implied speaker of a poem, and the readers who identify with the speaking voice – that has, as a discursive subject, fallen out of immediate unity with nature. Under the pressures of socialization, that "I" takes up various repertoires of action and of self-presentation, as it becomes husband or wife or single person, manual worker or bureaucrat, engineer or politician, athlete or artist, and so on. In this way the "I" is subsumed under the requirements of one or many social roles, where these social roles exist as historically achieved and posited (as merely particularly willed and informed by "false universality," at least in part), rather than being transparently reasonable, mutually self-supporting, satisfying, and continuously freedom-enabling for all. Something in experience – it may be a scene, a person, an incident, a memory, or a complex of any of these – then attracts, in perplexity, the attentions and emotions (which may be those of absorption or recoil, in any of many shades) of the "I," and the "I" is moved to speak, as if not from its social role, but from nothing other than its own natural and human stores of attention, energy, and emotion. If its speech is well-plotted enough, if the emotion is contextually thematized enough, if originality in the crafting of form yields enough stability and composure without the shirking of attention, then the resulting poetic speech or writing can appear as an expression of "unrestrained individuation" – that is, the expression of a subject who is fully and naturally at home in this moment of the voicing of experience. In this way the achievement of poetic voice serves as a model of what we continue to aspire to, inchoately, without guiding plan, and always constrained also by what remain the complex and changing requirements of social life. The lyric voice is in the end transcended by the forces from which it seeks to withdraw (it "anticipates" and "hopes to attain" rather than fully attaining its end), yet nonetheless retains its exemplary power. The truth of poetry is to voice ever anew, in ever-changing circumstances, this aspiration that continues to haunt the lives of subjects. Poetry courts effectiveness in thinking about values, ends, stances, and commitments, without denying human finitude.

Notes

1 Monroe C. Beardsley, *Aesthetics: Problems in the Philosophy of Criticism*, 2nd edn., (Indianapolis, IN: Hackett Publishing Company, 1981), 29.
2 Peter Lamarque and Stein Haugom Olsen, *Truth, Fiction, and Literature* (Oxford: Clarendon Press, 1996), 11, 22.
3 Thomas S. Kuhn, *The Structure of Scientific Revolutions*, 2nd edn. (Chicago: University of Chicago Press, 1970), 118–25.
4 Aristotle, *Poetics*, 50a, trans. Richard Janko (Indianapolis, IN: Hackett Publishing Company, 1987), 9.
5 Ibid., 51a–b, 12.
6 Ibid., 50b, 10.
7 Homer, *The Iliad*, trans. Robert Fagles (New York: Penguin, 1990), 77, lines 1–8.
8 Plato, *Republic*, 517b–c, trans. G. M. A. Grube, revised C. D. C. Reeve (Indianapolis, IN: Hackett Publishing Company, 1992), 189.
9 Aristotle, *Metaphysics*, 1072a, trans. W. D. Ross, in Richard McKeon, ed., *The Basic Works of Aristotle* (New York: Random House, 1941), 879.
10 G. W. F. Hegel, *Elements of the Philosophy of Right*, trans. H. B. Nisbet (Cambridge: Cambridge University Press, 1991), 20; interpolations mine.
11 Friedrich Nietzsche, *The Twilight of the Idols*, trans. Duncan Large (Oxford: Oxford University Press, 1998), 11.
12 Petrarch, "Letter to Posterity," in James Harvey Robinson, ed. and trans., *Petrarch: The First Modern Scholar and Man of Letters* (New York: G. P. Putnam, 1898), 60.
13 Petrarch, "sonnet I: To Laura in Life" in *The Sonnets, Triumphs, and Other Poems of Petrarch*, trans. Revd Dr Nott (London: George Bell & Sons, 1893), 1–2. Stanza breaks introduced to match original Italian. I have preferred this translation for its preservation of the sonnet rhyme scheme. For an unrhymed modern translation as well as the original Italian, see Petrarch, *Canzoniere*, trans. Mark Musa (Bloomington, IN: Indiana University Press, 1996), 2–3.

14. See Grace M. Ledbetter, *Poetics Before Plato: Interpretation and Authority in Early Greek Theories of Poetry* (Princeton, NJ: Princeton University Press, 2002).
15. Friedrich Schlegel, "Critical Fragments," in Schlegel, *Philosophical Fragments*, trans. Peter Firchow (Minneapolis: University of Minnesota Press, 1991), nos. 60, 65, p. 8.
16. See Spinoza, Baruch, *Ethics* in Spinoza, *Ethics, Treatise on the Emendation of the Intellect, and Selected Letters*, trans. Samuel Shirley (Indianapolis, IN: Hackett Publishing Company, 1992), part 5, propositions 3–9, 204–9.
17. Ibid., part 5, scholium to proposition 20, 212–13.
18. For a longer account of Wordsworth's theory of poetry, see Richard Eldridge, "Wordsworth and the Life of a Subject," in Ross Wilson, ed., *The Meaning of "Life" in Romantic Poetry and Poetics* (London: Routledge 2008). For a longer account of Hölderlin's theory of poetry, see Eldridge, "Rotating the Axis of our Investigation: Wittgenstein's Investigations and Hölderlin's Poetology," in John Gibson and Wolfgang Huemer, eds., *The Literary Wittgenstein* (London: Routledge, 2004), 211–27.
19. Hölderlin, "Letter No. 94, to Hegel, January 26, 1795," in Hölderlin, *Essays and Letters on Theory*, ed. and trans. Thomas Pfau (Albany, NY: State University of New York Press, 1988), 125.
20. Thomas Pfau, "Critical Introduction," in Hölderlin, *Essays and Letters on Theory*, 28.
21. Hölderlin, "Reflection," in *Essays and Letters on Theory*, 46.
22. William Wordsworth, *The Prelude*, in Wordsworth, *Selected Poems and Prefaces*, ed. Jack Stillinger (Boston: Houghton Mifflin Company, 1965), book 2, lines 228–32, p. 212.
23. *Selected Poems and Prefaces*, 448.
24. Ibid., 449; emphasis added.
25. Ibid., 447; emphasis added.
26. See ibid., 456.
27. Ibid., 454.
28. Ibid., 453.
29. R. G. Collingwood, *The Principles of Art* (Oxford: Oxford University Press, 1938), 298.
30. Ludwig Wittgenstein, *Culture and Value*, ed. G. H. Von Wright with Heikki Nyman, trans. Peter Winch (Chicago, IL: University of Chicago Press, 1980), 11e, 11.
31. Wittgenstein, quoted in Malcolm, Norman, *Ludwig Wittgenstein: A Memoir* (Oxford: Oxford University Press, 1958), 50. See also Wittgenstein, *The Blue Book*, in Wittgenstein, *The Blue and Brown Books* (Oxford: Basil Blackwell, 1958), 1.
32. Frank Kermode, *The Sense of an Ending: Studies in the Theory of Fiction, with a New Epilogue* (Oxford: Oxford University Press, 2000), 133.
33. Barbara Herrnstein Smith, *Poetic Closure: A Study of How Poems End* (Chicago, IL: University of Chicago Press, 1968), 154.
34. Charles Altieri, *The Particulars of Rapture: An Aesthetics of the Affects* (Ithaca, NY: Cornell University Press, 2003), 107.
35. Theodor W. Adorno, "On Lyric Poetry and Society," in Adorno, *Notes to Literature*, vol. 1, ed. Rolf Tiedemann, trans. Shierry Weber Nicholsen (New York: Columbia University Press, 1991), 38.
36. Ibid., 41.

Part VI

Intention and Biography in Criticism

21

Authorial Intention and the Varieties of Intentionalism

PAISLEY LIVINGSTON

Although a comprehensive survey of these complex topics is out of reach in this essay, nevertheless I hope to provide a schematic overview of some of the main positions and arguments in this area. Recent monographs and collections on the topic include Krausz (2002), Livingston (2005), Margolis and Rockmore (2000), Stecker (2003), and Thom (2000).

Intention

Rather diverse theoretical positions have been taken on the question of the nature of intentions (Anscombe 1957; Audi 1997; Bratman 1990). A first dimension of variation concerns assumptions about the link between intentions and consciousness. It is sometimes held that intentions must be at least "accessible" to conscious introspection, if they are not actually the object of some form of occurrent or "focal" awareness. A stronger claim is that all intentions must actually be conscious to some degree. Many theorists have acknowledged the existence of wholly unconscious intentions as well as conscious ones.

Another set of options pertains to the relation between intentions and the other mental items that figure within the preferred psychological model. Reductionist accounts include proposals in which intention is equated with volition or trying (Ginet 1990), as well as proposals in which intention is reduced to belief and desire (Audi 1973; Beardsley 1978; Davidson 1963; Davis 1984) or some more complex constellation of states or attitudes. Some theorists eschew such reductions and identify intention as a type of mental state characterized by its function(s). In Alfred R. Mele's influential proposal (1988, 1992), intention plays a special motivational and cognitive role because it is an executive attitude towards some plan or means–end scheme. Someone with an intention has a goal as well as a schematic means to the realization of that goal; the intending person's attitude towards this plan is a firm yet defeasible commitment to acting on it. The agent's actual motivation at the time of intending is a separate issue, since motivation can diminish or strengthen before the intended time for action arrives. One can strongly want to do something, for example, without having any intention of doing this thing; conversely, one can intend to do one's duty without really wanting to do so when one settles on that intention. And the fact that someone does not actually act on a scheme does not mean that the person never genuinely intended to do so. These sorts of cases drive a conceptual wedge between intentions, reasons composed of beliefs and desires, and the actions to which intentions sometimes give rise.

There is room for disagreement about what sorts of items can and cannot fill in the blank in "S intends _____." Many philosophers have claimed that only actions that some intending agent, S, could perform should figure in such clauses (Fleming 1964; Meiland 1970). Some philosophers require that at the time of intending, the action be one that S does not deem it impossible for S to perform. Other philosophers (Davis 1984; Harman 1986; Vermazen 1993, 1998) take a more liberal view and allow that intentions can range over any number of propositions or states of affairs. Can someone intend "that a friend get a raise" without having any intention of doing something to bring about this desired result? If so, how is intending different from wishing? This topic is related to the difficult question of how authorial intentions should be explicated. Can an author intend "that the audience grasp a given idea or theme?" The question concerning the possible contents of intentions also has implications for our thinking about collective intentions and actions, such as artistic collaboration. Some philosophers (Kutz 2000; Searle 1990; Velleman 1997) ask whether such activities involve a form of intending that is not reducible to a collection of individual intentions – as in "I intend that we lift the table."

There is disagreement as well about the temporal dimensions of intentions. One formulation of the basic situation of intending runs: "Some agent, S, intends now (at t_1) to perform some action, A, during t_2." When $t_1 < t_2$, the intention is future-directed or distal; when t_1 converges on t_2, the intention is a proximal one.

A concept of intentions as future-directed mental states that may or may not lead or even contribute to some intended, successful action stands in contrast to a notion that John R. Searle (1983) has labeled "intention in action." This is a term of art for a type of mental item that is necessarily acted upon and embodied in active trying. It is doubtful, however, whether all of our discourse about intentions and intendings can be captured by the notion of "intention in action." Even an abandoned intention, that is, one that never triggers and guides an action and so cannot be an "intention in action," may influence behavior by temporarily ruling out incompatible schemes (Bratman 1987). For example, S's planning on writing a comedy (which was never successfully completed) could prevent S from intentionally creating a tragedy.

The intention someone has now to do something later is logically distinct from that person's actually acting on that intention, and both intending and acting on an intention are distinct from actually bringing about the target result. An intention is "realized" or "successful" when the results of acting on that intention match the contents of the intention, and where this match or fit is brought about in the right sort of way, as specified, at least schematically, by the content of the intention (Mele and Moser 1994).

Intentions play a variety of roles in the lives of deliberating agents who must negotiate the passage of time, deal with cognitive limitations, and anticipate the activities of other deliberating, strategic agents (Brand 1984; Bratman 1987; Mele 1992, 1995). Publicly avowed intentions help us coordinate our activities; commitment to intentions or personal policies helps us budget our resources and achieve long-term goals. In some cases, commitment to longstanding intentions allows us to avoid wasting time on deliberation and helps us resist temptation. Intentions help us organize our ongoing activities. A writer who has committed herself to a long-term artistic scheme can develop a range of intentions subordinate to that scheme. Some of these intentions will arise spontaneously within the framework of ongoing activity, while others may be the product of more or less systematic deliberation over options.

Authorial Intention

Any attempt to survey opinion on the nature of authorial intention is complicated by ongoing controversy surrounding rival conceptions of authorship (Irwin 2002). There may, however, be some significant measure of agreement that authorship requires the performance of actions informed by certain semantic intentions. Someone who produces reams of texts as part of a typing exercise is not thereby an author; on the other hand, someone who copies someone else's words verbatim, but presents them as his or her own essay, is the author of a plagiarism. A first question, then, concerns the nature of the semantic intentions (and corresponding actions) *necessary* to authorship. The question of what conditions are *sufficient* to authorship cannot be surveyed here.

H. Paul Grice's (1989) proposals have dominated philosophical discussions of the question of the nature of an utterer's intentions. Grice's basic aim in this regard was to reduce the semantic intention of a speaker or writer to a complex communicative intention. In one of its most influential versions, the Gricean analysis runs as follows. Someone authors an utterance just in case that person, S, utters (writes, speaks, etc.) something with an intention comprised of the following three sub-intentions:

1 S's utterance, U, is to produce a certain response, R, should there be an audience, A, having some characteristic, C;
2 The audience, A, is to recognize S's intention (1);
3 The audience's recognition of S's intention (1) is to function as at least part of A's reason for having response R.

If, for example, the target response, or R, is the acquisition of a particular belief by some audience, A, what the speaker intends is that the audience's recognition of the speaker's intention to give rise to that belief in the audience will be a reason for the formation of the belief. So the author of the utterance targets not only an idea to be conveyed, but an intended way of conveying it, namely, a mode whereby success is at least partly a matter of the recognition of the intention.

A first complaint about this proposal is that its inclusion of a complicated reflexive or "looped" intention places speaker's meaning beyond the cognitive capacities of small children, who nonetheless do manage sometimes to speak their minds. Is there no less complex form that the speaker's semantic intentions might take?

A second objection moves in the opposite direction, and has led Grice and his followers to propose even more complicated accounts of communicative intentions. Sir Peter Strawson (1964) and others (e.g. Schiffer 1972) introduced counterexamples suggesting that the reflexive, looped intentions, described above as (1)–(3), are not sufficient to rule out cases of tricky, less than fully communicative speaker's meaning. Suppose someone knows she is being watched but also knows that the observer is not aware of this fact; the person being watched can do something with the intention of giving rise to a given response in the observer, and may also act on the intention of having this first intention be recognized by the observer. But this latter intention is not itself meant to be recognized. Adding in an additional "loop" of intentions can cover this case, but in principle the objection could be reiterated. The full array of potential counterexamples can be dealt with by building an infinite hierarchy of reflexive intentions into the analysis, but such a move is made at the cost of sacrificing psychological plausibility, since it is unlikely that the minds of actual speakers have any such furnishings. In response to this problem, Grice opted for a strikingly unrealistic notion of speaker's meaning as a regulative ideal of rationality, in relation to which actual utterer's intentions stand as "pre-rational counterparts." Others (e.g. Recanati 1987) have followed up on a different option that Grice mentioned, in which a single negative clause rules out sneaky, unrecognized intentions. Whether such negative intentions are themselves necessary components of ordinary speaker's meaning is not so obvious.

Wayne A. Davis (2003, 2005) has explored a different way of thinking about semantic intentions. Sometimes we communicate something unintentionally, and when we do communicate intentionally, our intentions need not satisfy Gricean strictures. In particular, the intended recognition of the speaker's intention to communicate is not a necessary means to the communication of a thought. Davis also argues that not all speaker's meaning is communicative in the sense of primarily targeting uptake by some audience. Some speaker's meaning is expressive without being communicative in Grice's sense. Expressive speaker's meaning can be analyzed as the intentional performance of an observable action as an *indication* of some attitude, where some x indicates some y whenever x provides some possibly unreliable evidence that y is the case. Evidence of an attitude is effectively provided whenever a "well-positioned observer" would be likely to draw an inference to the attitude. Questions may be raised about what this condition entails with regard to that observer's inferential capacities and background information. Such an observer is not, in any case, an ideal knower or omniscient mind-reader.

Semantic intentions do not exhaust the intentions constitutive of authorship. Another relevant type of intention is what Jerrold Levinson (1992) has called "categorial" intentions, which pertain to the category or genre of work the author means to create. Authors intend to write a work of fiction or non-fiction; they may settle on trying to create a work belonging to some well-established genre or literary form, or they may have a more or less innovative hybrid in view. Categorial and semantic intentions are often interrelated; for example, the standard features of an artistic category may require that certain types of semantic elements belong to any particular work in the category; and some meanings are inimical to an utterance's belonging to some categories.

So much for a brief survey of views on intention and authorial intention. Many options have been left out, but those mentioned suffice to indicate some of the many variables that may be carried over into the theory of interpretation.

Varieties of Intentionalism

Intentionalism in the philosophy of art interpretation is, in general, a thesis about intention's determination of the meaning *or* the value of works of art. Intentionalism can also be characterized as a family of principles that are supposed to describe apt interpretation or appreciation, namely, those in which authorial intention is the target of some if not all attributions.

It is coherent to be an intentionalist about the meaning of works without also being an intentionalist about their value, and vice versa. Yet there are hybrid, axiological and semantic intentionalist theses, such as the idea that appreciation and interpretation should be attuned to a type of artistic excellence partly realized through the artist's skilful accomplishment of semantic intentions.

In a selective survey of some of the most salient proposals, we may start with *fictionalist intentionalism* (Nehamas 1981, 1986, 1987), which instructs interpreters to attribute the meanings of a text to an imagined or make-believe author. *Textualist intentionalism* would have the interpreter write as if *the text* were the locus of the relevant semantic intentions (Eco 1992). A *conditionalist intentionalism* invites the interpreter to describe the meanings that the author of the text *could have* intended, as opposed to only those that this person actually intended. Such an invitation to imagine "possible" meanings may be guided by some more or less precise indication of the constraints within which such imaginings are to be developed. For example, the intentions in question must square with the text and be psychologically or intellectually possible given what is known about the actual author. *Actualist intentionalism* (Carroll 1986, 1992, 1993, 2000, 2002; Dutton 1987; Hirsch 1967, 1976a; Iseminger 1992, 1996; Juhl 1980) codifies the idea that it is the actual author's actual intentions that are ideally to be identified in the interpretation of the meaning of a work, at least in cases where those intentions have been successfully acted upon. In cases of collaborative authorship, the relevant intentions would be the joint intentions, and related individual intentions, of the actual persons involved in the making of the work (Livingston 2005).

A variety of theses have been proposed with regard to the question of the nature and extent of the specific contribution made by intentions to the meanings of a work of art. An extreme thesis holds that for all works of art, a work's meanings are all and only those intended by the author(s). This extreme or *absolute intentionalist* thesis is challenged by adverting to counterexamples where the linguistic expression someone has uttered or written turns out to have meanings not intended by that person (Gaut 1993).

There are also cases where an author fails to create a work that genuinely expresses the meanings intended. Proponents of absolute intentionalism (e.g. Irwin 1999) may deny that there are any such counterexamples. At least some, if not all, failed intentions may be reclassified as not falling into some privileged category of intentions, designated as the "final" or "effective" ones (Hancher 1972). As for unintended meanings of a work, some if not all of these may be assigned to the category of a work's *significance*, as opposed to its meaning (Hirsch 1967).

A central contention advanced by advocates of absolute intentionalism is that texts are semantically indeterminate in the absence of the anchoring provided by an actual utterer's referential and semantic aims or decisions. Although this thesis clearly holds with regard to pronouns and indexicals, it has been extended to embrace the linguistic meaning of strings of characters as such, the thought being that all such meaning depends on specific instances of use in a particular context. Either a text has no determinate meanings, or it has one as a result of authorial intentions of the final or decisive variety. Cases where the interpreter appears to be describing unintended meanings in the text are parasitic on a prior interpretative anchoring corresponding to intentionalist strictures.

Against this line of thought it has been retorted that, while it should be conceded that linguistic meaning in general may be correctly viewed as a matter of conventions related in complex ways to patterns of usage in a given community, once a linguistic convention is in place, at least some of the determinate meanings of the words in a particular utterance are not decided by the intentions of the speaker (Nathan 1973, 1982, 1992). And sometimes speakers produce expressions having conventionally determined meanings that were not part of the content of the intentions with which the expression was produced. It is a dubious "Humpty Dumpty" semantics that allows that an individual speaker freely determines the meaning of a sequence of words. Humpty tells Alice that "glory" means "a nice knock-down argument," and she rightly protests that this simply is not the case. Humpty seems to enjoy semantic mastery over his nonce words like "mimsy," but when he wants to get his meaning across, he has to employ standard usage in the definitions he communicates to Alice.

A weaker intentionalist thesis is the moderate or partial intentionalist contention (Carroll 2000; Livingston 2005) that intentions determine some, but not all, of the semantic properties of at least some works of art. This weaker thesis is nonetheless contested by those who argue that a work's actual meanings are determined not by fallible, future-directed intentions, but by the nature of the finished text as it stands in relation to relevant linguistic and contextual facts. Another claim raised against even a moderate variety of intentionalism is that it is the reader's interpretative efforts that determine meaning; in one variant, it is an "interpretive community" that determines the meanings of texts (Fish 1980, 1991). Although the writer's intentions may be recognized as having played a crucial role "upstream" in the causal process whereby this text has been generated, once the text is finished, what it means is not determined by those prior intentions and actions, but by its actual, completed features. Another proposal (Barthes 1971) has it that readerly constructions determine the text's meanings, an idea that appeals to those who believe that authors or authorial intentions are more or less contingent constructions or fictions. Some advocates (e.g. Pappas 1989) of the interpretative freedom of the reader have described such authorial constructions as an unnecessary constraint on the interpreter's options: the reader's semantic freedom may not require the death of the author, but it does call for a wholesale neglect of his or her intentions.

The Utterance Model

Intentionalists of various kinds tend to think about the meaning of literary works along the same lines as one thinks about the meaning of an utterance, and one anti-intentionalist objection is that this "utterance model" is simply inappropriate (Lamarque 2000; Olsen 1982). A first reason is that while it usually makes perfect sense to ask what the meaning of an utterance is, it may sound ill-conceived or even foolhardy to ask for *the* overall or total meaning of a sprawling text like Proust's *Recherche*. This could be because literary and other artistic works are not utterances in any case and so just aren't the sort of thing to have such a meaning. In response, it may be agreed that it is hard to spell out the meaning of imposing and complex artistic achievements, especially Proust's fragmentary concatenation of drafts and versions, but this does not suffice to establish the more general thesis that most or even all artworks are not utterances. As long as we accept a classificatory and non-honorific concept of literary works, we can identify short and simple literary works, the utterance meaning of which is not so hard to identify. Also, there are some very long non-literary utterances the meaning of which it would be difficult if not impossible to elucidate completely, but that does not entail that these discourses are not utterances, as long as we understand the term as referring to expressive or communicative actions indicative of attitudes. So the distinction between utterances having meanings, and the sorts of things that do not have meanings of this kind, does not map neatly onto the distinction between things having a meaning that can and cannot be readily paraphrased or elucidated. The meaning can be too complex to allow of an exhaustive restatement, which does not imply that more partial elucidations, in keeping with our cognitive limitations, cannot be provided.

Another reason given in support of the thesis that works are not utterances is that the utterance model of meaning equates the meaning of an utterance with the speaker's meaning. Assuming that the meanings of a literary work are not reducible to the author's semantic intentions, it follows that the utterance model is inappropriate (Olsen 1982). In response, one may reply that one reason why a concept of utterance meaning is attractive as a way of understanding works of art is that it offers an alternative to absolute intentionalism. Utterance meaning is not equivalent to speaker meaning, but emerges in a relation between utterer's meaning, conventional or linguistic meaning, and contextual factors. Utterances have plenty of unintended meanings, such as symptomatic meanings discovered by statistical analysis of lexical frequencies. So one does not have to reject the utterance model in a swerve away from absolute intentionalism.

A third main reason given in support of the thesis that works are not utterances is that works, unlike utterances, should be understood as having an interest and relevance independent of the situation in which they were initially produced (Ellis 1974). To read a text as literature, then, is to detach it from its context of origin. In response to this line of thought, intentionalists may advert to the many reasons why features of the context of creation are crucial to adequate appreciation of a work's aesthetic, artistic, and artistically relevant semantic properties (Wollheim 1980).

Hypothetical Intentionalism

Another variety of intentionalism is William Tolhurst's (1979) *hypothetical intentionalism*, the central thesis of which is that utterance meaning is determined by an intention that a member of the intended audience would be justified in attributing to the author on the basis of evidence that defines membership in the intended audience. In other words, authors not only have an intention with regard to what meanings they wish to include in a work; they also have intentions with regard to their preferred or target audience, and this audience is identified in terms of the kind of evidence its members are to use in reasoning about the work's content.

An objection to this approach is that it is unclear why authors' intentions concerning types of relevant and irrelevant evidence should be deemed infallible or decisive. One author wants statements in a diary, personal correspondence, or an interview to be taken as decisive indications about the meaning of her poem; yet another author has contrasting intentions and sets herself the task of getting implicit meanings across without the help of such "external" means. According to the principle under consideration, evidence from a diary would be decisive in the case of the first author but not in the case of the second. Yet one may wonder why utterance meaning should be determined in this manner. If we are persuaded in the first case that the diary reveals some implicit content *of the poem*, why would we not be similarly persuaded in the second case? One response could be that we think that it ought to be up to the author to determine what does and does not count as part of a work, and we allow that this inclination ought to be extended to the means by which intentions are revealed and thereby realized. Yet reasonable doubts could be raised with regard to this extension. What the audience ought to be interested in is the author's relevant semantic intentions, and not intentions about evidence pertaining to the latter. The interpreter's goal in this respect is to assess the relation between the intentions and the text, and restrictions with regard to evidence can only hinder the pursuit of this goal.

Another type of hypothetical intentionalism, proposed by Jerrold Levinson (1992, 2002), is not based on the notion that it is the writer's intentions that infallibly select the audience whose interpretation will constitute the work's meaning; instead, the distinction between appropriate and inappropriate evidence is independently drawn, and is said to be part of the rules constitutive of artistic communication. More specifically, Levinson includes as appropriate evidence various sorts of contextual information, including information about the author and the categorial intentions on which the author has acted. What Levinson rules out is "any fact about the author's actual mental state or attitude during composition, in particular what I have called his semantic intentions for a text" (1992, 206). The hypothetical intentionalist is supposed to take the text and interpret it in keeping with the contextual information just evoked; yet, when it comes to semantic intentions, the interpreter should construct a reading that maximizes the artistic or aesthetic value of the work.

Levinson illustrates an important feature of the interpretative principles of hypothetical intentionalism by constructing an imaginary example. Suppose a diary or letter reveals that Franz Kafka had very pedestrian intentions when he wrote a short story translated as "A Country Doctor." Instead of the allegorical ideas critics have associated with this text, Kafka just wanted to criticize rural medical practices. We should ignore this evidence, and using everything else we know about Kafka, devise an interpretation that grants the text the greatest range of meanings. These will be the meanings intended by a "hypothetical" Kafka, as in some cases, there could be a discrepancy between what the actual Kafka intended and the attribution yielded by an interpretation guided by Levinson's principles.

Hypothetical Intentionalism and Actualist Intentionalism Compared

What reasons do proponents of actualist intentionalism and hypothetical intentionalism offer that could justify preferring one of them over the other?

One objection to hypothetical intentionalism is that it is odd to ask an interpreter to defend a "hypothesis" about the intention of Franz Kafka or any other author in a context where evidence indicates that the author in question in fact had some semantic intention that is incompatible with the hypothesized attribution. The hypothetical intentionalist responds that what the hypothesis refers to, finally, is the meaning of the utterance, not the empirical author's state of mind. And the meaning of the utterance corresponds to the intentions of the hypothetical author. The critic of this account of interpretation may then complain that such principles do not allow for unintended meanings, or at least for meanings not intended by the *hypothetical* author. This is only a shortcoming if it is desirable to say that some of the *utterance's* meanings are unintended.

One line of thought set forth in favor of hypothetical intentionalism is the idea that literature is a public phenomenon and that the author's literary communications ought not to be understood or assessed in terms of private information, such as the contents of personal correspondence or diaries. In response, the proponents of actual intentionalism contend that this use of a public/private dichotomy is problematic. A document may have originally been intended for personal use or for some small, "private" audience, but what is its status once it has been published or cited by critics and scholars? For example, Thomas Hardy provided some information about the characters in *Jude the Obscure* in a personal letter to Sir Edmund Gosse, where he could be far more frank than the censors would allow. Even though the letter is not part of the novel, it provides evidence about the imaginings constitutive of the work's fictional content. Hardy got his imaginings across to those of us who have the letter, which is now included in at least one scholarly edition of the novel, and we can and should understand the work along those very lines.

In response, a proponent of hypothetical intentionalism may say that the key point about private letters and diaries is not that they were initially meant to be kept out of the public eye. *Rather*, the important point is that we should reject the notion that such sources reveal a decisive semantic intention. It is the ban on this latter idea that hypothetical intentionalism's principles express, and in so doing, they reflect a valuable and well-entrenched rule in the "game" of literary appreciation. The author of a novel or poem should try to get his or her meanings across in the novel or poem, and not by other means. Similarly, critics should respect this rule by not building their interpretations on the contents of diaries, interviews, and such. What matters in the context of the interpretation of a work of art *as a work of art* is the artistic structure or text as understood in the relevant artistic context. In response to this, proponents of actualist intentionalism dispute the claim that there is any such agreed upon, well-entrenched rule. Many critics have proposed interpretations based partly on the proscribed sources, and thus hypothetical intentionalism must be assessed as a revisionary proposal. What is it, the critic of hypothetical intentionalism asks, which makes this a better principle of interpretation, one in light of which critical practice must be revised?

To this the proponent of hypothetical intentionalism may respond that the strictures of this doctrine are to be preferred because they enhance literary value, since an actual author's mediocre intentions can be replaced by the superior intentions a critic can attribute to the hypothetical author of the work. Critics of hypothetical intentionalism respond that in some cases actual authorial intentions as revealed by diaries and interviews reveal meanings that indicate previously unknown qualities contributing positively to a work's artistic value. Such qualities could be superior to those attributed by a critic who has followed hypothetical intentionalism in categorizing this evidence as inadmissible. Yet the proponent of hypothetical intentionalism may respond that there are far more cases where the "external" sources reveal that actual authorial intention was disappointing, and that in all such cases hypothetical intentionalism opens the way for an interpretation according to which the work is a better one than it would have been had actualist intentionalism been correct. A response to this contention is that this is a recipe for an unwelcome ersatz artistic value as opposed to actual artistic accomplishments. Many if not all inferior works would be better if we replaced actual artistic intentions with parodic or ironic ones, and it is not clear whether the strictures of hypothetical intentionalism suffice to prohibit enough of the artificial interpretative operations that could be undertaken along these lines. Proponents of hypothetical intentionalism need to argue convincingly that the interpretative inflation of semantic and related artistic successes has, on balance, a positive impact on the world of art.

A similar challenge may be raised for the advocates of actualist intentionalism, however, since their interpretative principles are also regularly ignored by many literary scholars. How would criticism, and literary culture more generally, stand to benefit from a widespread observance of the strictures of actualist intentionalism? One response is that actualist intentionalism correctly codifies the orientation of a type of interpretation and criticism that seeks to assess the actual author's intentional accomplishment, and that such an assessment corresponds to our interest in an important type of artistic value, which derives from the quality of the author's imaginative and expressive achievements, not those of the critic. Yet one consequence of actualist intentionalism is that it is hard and sometimes impossible to produce well-justified interpretations that target work-meaning; we need to acquire sufficient evidence about the artist and the making of the work, and there are many cases where the evidence is simply not to be had. Another consequence of actualist intentionalism is that sensible criticism in which the evidence is sifted in a reasonable way makes it harder and harder to come up with new, yet evidentially responsible, readings. This can seem to make life difficult for academic critics who need to publish innovative readings. Yet it may be responded that a raising of interpretative and/or evaluative standards is on the whole a desirable move.

Proponents of hypothetical intentionalism contend that their view has the advantage of not needing to give a non-circular answer to the difficult question whether the actual author's semantic intentions are successfully realized in the utterance. The success of a categorial intention is another matter, since it is determined by finding out whether the work in fact has the standard features required by categorial membership, as well as no contra-standard features that would preclude such a classification. Yet the advocate of actualist intentionalism assails this reliance upon the distinction between categorial and semantic intentions. The problem is not that this distinction is unsound or can never be applied. The problem, rather, is that in the creation and appreciation of literary works, categorical and semantic intentions are frequently entangled, since many of the literary categories of art have standard features involving constraints on the contents of the fiction. It is not clear that hypothetical intentionalism offers a principled manner of dealing with such hybrid cases. Another problem is that the differential treatment of categorical and semantic intentions is insufficiently motivated. Why not replace mediocre categorial intentions with superior ones hypothesized by the interpreter? It is not promising to respond to this question by saying that categorial intentions, unlike semantic ones, are most often successfully realized by the artist. What is more, successful realization of the one type of intention is linked to that of the other. For example, if Henry James's categorial intention in *The Turn of the Screw* was to write a gothic-style ghost story, then either he failed to realize this intention, or we must recognize the success of his intention to include implied ghosts in the story and not merely ghosts imagined by a deranged narrator. It follows that in a range of significant cases, hypothetical intentionalism does not in fact relieve the interpreter of the problem of ascertaining whether semantic intentions have been successfully realized in the work. Both actualist and hypothetical intentionalism must find a viable way of dealing with the problem of success conditions.

Success Conditions and the Dilemma Argument

One of the strongest arguments against actualist intentionalism takes the form of a dilemma: either intentions are successfully realized in the artistic structure or text, or they are not so realized; if they are realized, reference to intentions is not necessary to a correct understanding of the work's meaning; if they are not realized, reference to the fact that the author intended to make a work with a particular meaning is not sufficient to establish that the work actually has that meaning (Wimsatt and Beardsley 1946).

One intentionalist response to this argument finds its point of departure in the observation that not all meaning need be explicit or "realized in the text" in the manner required by the dilemma. A work of art may have *implicit* content, some of which depends on relations between the features of the text and the intentions with which the text was made. A paradigm is provided by ironic utterances. Although irony is often marked explicitly by intonation or other features of what is said or written, instances of "deadpan" irony show that such properties are not strictly necessary to establish the ironic status of an utterance. What the speaker says is one thing, but what the speaker *and ironic utterance* mean is the reverse. Ironic content, which is often crucial to both the understanding and evaluation of a work, remains implicit, and so cannot be expected to be realized uniquely "in" the text.

Although it may be plausible to contend in this manner that intentions are necessary to some *implicit* content of literary utterances, it may still be asked under what conditions the intended meanings are actually those that belong to the utterance. While it is a truism to say that intention, or at least intended meaning, is crucial to what the *speaker* means, it is not at all obvious that the identification of the speaker's or writer's meaning is essential to the determination of the meaning of the *utterance or work*. If actualist intentionalism rests on the claim that some utterance meaning depends on what the speaker intends, it is crucial for the intentionalist to establish which cases these are, as only an extreme and hard-to-defend variety of intentionalism allows that intentions infallibly determine the meaning of the work.

The problem just raised has at times been illustrated by means of striking, outlandish examples. We are invited, for example, to imagine a Conan Doyle who secretly intends his stories to be implicitly but not explicitly inhabited by purple gnomes who consistently present themselves as human beings. Nothing that is explicitly said in the texts, at least as these might be interpreted standardly in terms of the relevant linguistic conventions, is logically incompatible with such intentions. Does it follow that intentionalist strictures require us to include some propositions about purple gnomes as part of the implicit content of these fictional works? As it is generally agreed that this is an unacceptable option, any viable variety of actualist intentionalism must include some sort of constraint taking the form of a success condition on the determination of implicit work meaning by intention. A large part of the contemporary story about the varieties of intentionalism can be aptly recounted as a series of attempts to formulate an adequate solution to this problem. The key question here can be framed as follows:

assuming that some speaker or writer says or writes something that means *p* in order to imply some *q*, under what condition does the utterance actually mean *q*? Presumably, "if and only if S intends *q*" is not the correct response that question.

One influential approach to this problem is the Gricean attempt to anchor the justification of implicature in a norm arising from cooperative rationality. Grice's central conjecture in this vein was that the following imperative guides conversational exchanges: "Make your contribution such as required, at the stage at which it occurs, by the accepted purpose or direction of the talk exchange in which you are engaged" (Grice 1975, 45). Grice further claimed that it is a "well-recognized empirical fact" that this *ceteris paribus* principle, and some related maxims said to be derivable from it, applies to all talk exchanges that do not consist of wholly disconnected remarks. In an effort to argue that the principle is grounded in rationality, Grice contends that persons participating in conversational exchanges share such purposes as exchanging information. Only if conversation is conducted in accordance with the cooperative principle can such shared purposes be realized. Given knowledge of this fact, it is rational to behave in accordance with the cooperative principle and to expect others to do so as well. Given assumptions about shared conversational ends, effective means to those ends, and rationality, the cooperative principle and presumption are rational. And indeed, on one salient reading of Grice's imperative, the cooperative principle includes a norm of rationality within it, since it is *rational* to make one's contribution fit the purpose of the conversation.

With regard to the question of the success conditions on the expression of implicit meaning in an utterance, the upshot of the Gricean approach is that intended meanings are those of the utterance just in case they are ones that would be attributed to the writer or speaker by interpreters rationally working with the cooperative principle. In other words, the speaker who says *p* in order to imply *q* successfully produces an utterance with that implicature just in case the audience can derive *q* from the cooperative principle and the other relevant information, which includes contextual factors and linguistic conventions.

One worry about this approach targets the assumption that authors and their audiences are always engaged in a (primarily) cooperative endeavor, as well as the subsidiary idea that their shared goal in such an endeavor is the transparent communication of thoughts or propositional content (Kasher 1976; Davis 1998). What determines a work's meaning is not necessarily a collaborative activity, but the author's pursuit of his or her aims. It follows that what is decisive in the determination of meaning is not what the audience "presumes" about the writer's cooperative rationality, but the writer's actual literary performance or accomplishment, which may or may not be cooperative.

A different strategy is to frame the question as an empirical problem: the intention to imply some thought, *p*, with utterance U is successfully realized just in case the audience understands U as meaning *p*. Such a formulation is, however, far too simple, for it offers no indication concerning which audience's judgments are supposed to be decisive. One might prefer a probabilistic formulation involving the likelihood of a target response amongst the members of some target audience. The upshot would be that if the audience in question fails to make a given inference (with sufficient frequency), then the author has failed to realize the intention in question. If, on the other hand, the target audience does make the inference (with sufficient frequency), then the intended meanings are part of the utterance's meaning. It may be objected to this approach, however, that some actual audience might perform incompetently and fail to register the implicit meaning of a work. Another objection points to the possibility of cases where the audience's "uptake" in fact corresponds to authorial intention but only does so in a wayward or haphazard manner. If the audience's uptake is to be decisive, it must be warranted or reliable.

A proposal for the needed success condition that takes this problem into account has been set forth by Robert Stecker, who writes that

> An utterance does mean what a speaker intends if the intention is apt to be recognized in part because of the conventional meaning of the words used, or of a context that extends those meanings. I will say an intention is successful if it is apt to be recognized on the basis just mentioned, and otherwise unsuccessful or failed. (2003,14)

This success condition is partly couched in terms of an audience's tendency to recognize the intention, but what is decisive is not the vagaries of actual reception but the grounds upon which the recognition of intention is to be based. These grounds involve the sorts of factors that anti-intentionalists have tended to identify as determinative of the meaning of a work or text, namely, the conventional meanings of its sentences and the ways in which these meanings are inflected by non-intentional contextual factors. Stecker's success condition thus provides an intention-independent standard of success, that is, one that does not itself rely on an intention-determined textual meaning. One respect in which this proposal remains sketchy is the nature of the conditions under which a context can and cannot "extend" the conventional linguistic meanings of a text. Stecker admits that the interplay between the various factors contributing to the meaning of an utterance is complex, and he does not try to provide a detailed mapping of the conditions under which the recognition of intentions is warranted.

A kindred proposal (Livingston 2005) links actualist intentionalism to a minimal success condition based on a model of implicative relations that diverges from Grice's theory of conversational implicature. On this account, the intention to mean q by saying p is successful whenever the intention to imply q *meshes* sufficiently with what is written or spoken. Such an intention may be signaled or indicated by a diary, letter, or some other source that is not the literary work itself, but it is not successfully realized by the literary work unless the text or verbal performance of that work meshes sufficiently with the intention. That some well-informed audience is apt to infer the intention from the text is a *symptom* of meshing, but not a necessary condition. Another symptom of meshing is the interpreter's ability, given independent knowledge of the intention, to develop a detailed and systematic interpretation of the text consonant with the ideas intended.

The meshing condition applies to the relation between the content of the intention and the text's conventional meanings, including those explicit and implied ideational relations that give the text its coherence, such as rhetorical connections between its clauses and sentences (Asher and Lascarides 2003). The meshing of text and intention requires a high degree of coherence between the content of the intention and the text's rhetorical patterns. This requirement is satisfied when the intended ideas are articulated with such internal semantic relations as contrast, parallelism, exemplification, generalization, explication, and elaboration. Suppose, for example, that an author's intention in writing a novella was to express the thought that wealth corrupts, and this intention is matched by a text that explicitly describes story events that contrast a protagonist's condition before and after his sudden acquisition of a large fortune. The virtues of a simple, honest fisherman's life are exemplified in a host of narrative details and are further articulated by means of parallels to the similar lives of other characters in the village; these descriptions stand in stark contrast to the narrative of the vices and misfortunes that follow from the initially joyous windfall. The rhetorical relations between the text's individual sentences and larger segments serve to elaborate this more general contrast, which in turn instantiates the intended explanation of the events of the story. It is implied, but nowhere overtly stated in the text, that the disastrous changes in the lives of the fisherman and his companions are the result of wealth's inevitably baleful influence.

The ideational connections constitutive of meshing can take many forms, but as some discourse theorists have hypothesized, many of them involve such basic categories of thought as part–whole relations, cause and effect, similarity and difference, and spatio-temporal links or contiguity. It is important to note that as such ideational connections and rhetorical structures can be found in texts independently of reference to corresponding authorial intentions, they thereby provide an independent source of evidence of the successful realization of intended meaning in the utterance.

The meshing condition does not require that the intention regarding implicit content correspond to or bear a strong conceptual association with each and every feature of the text. Yet cases where intentions mesh with a text contrast with those where intentions about content fall woefully short of cohering sufficiently with the meaningful elements of the text. Although there is no explicit method or procedure for the application of the meshing condition, many particular cases can be readily classified as either satisfying or failing to satisfy this condition. In cases where the meshing condition is satisfied, competent readers find that the intentions readily integrate with the linguistic meanings of the text and with the rhetorical structures and other patterns of coherence established by the text's conventional meanings. In contrasting cases, the interpreter finds that coherence breaks down. Sometimes an author intends to introduce an implicit, explanatory rationale for a large sequence of imagined story events, but the intentions in question were too impoverished, or too imperfectly thought through and acted upon, to provide anything like a consistent and reasonably detailed fleshing out of the story elements and rhetorical structures conveyed by the text, so it would be a mistake for anyone to identify the work's meaning along those intended lines. An example is provided by the crude materialist designs that pop up here and there in Theodore Dreiser's narratives. There is good reason to believe that this is an important and serious authorial intention, as there is ample, external evidence that Dreiser had such leanings, including philosophical ruminations in manuscripts. Yet the related novelistic intentions do not engage adequately with the text, and thereby fail to warrant a generalized replacement of attitude psychology with a pseudo-neuroscience that is only barely gestured at by the narrator.

One last consideration in favor of actualist intentionalism will be mentioned in this selective survey of ongoing debates on this topic. In a range of central cases, the object of interpretation or appreciation is the completed or final text of a literary work. Ideally, the text has been determined largely if not entirely by authorial decisions, including the decision that a given text forms a completed whole that is ready to be appreciated as a literary work. One may be tempted to think that the literary appreciator is only interested in the result of the author's efforts, which is a text that can be detached from the process in which it was made. Yet in fact interpreters do have an interest in the *manner* in which a text has been created. They are interested, for example, in knowing whether the text has been produced freely or under coercion. They may also be interested in other aspects of the process of composition. Although such things may be uncommon, a text that has the appearance of having been produced in a haphazard or frenzied manner could in fact be produced by someone acting calmly on a carefully deliberated scheme; and contrariwise, episodes of chance and unthinking spontaneity could yield an orderly and neatly composed text. Similar considerations may be set forth with regard to the various semantic intentions and related creative processes and results. Given that such matters can be relevant to our assessment of the writer's skill, the appreciator may want to eschew any interpretative strictures that make it impossible to recognize and assess the relation between the result and the process through which this result has been achieved. For example, a theory of interpretation that instructs the reader to make up or imagine the text's meanings or the fictional or postulated author's intentions without reference to the actual history of the text's production has a constitutive blind spot in this regard. Actualist intentionalism, on the other hand, has the advantage of recognizing that the way in which something is created can make an artistic difference, and of allowing that evidence pertaining to such differences is germane to criticism.

Note

The work described in this paper was partially supported by a grant from the Research Grants Council of the Hong Kong Special Administrative Region, China (Project No. LU3401/06H). I am very grateful for this support.

Bibliography

Anscombe, G. E. M. (1957). *Intention* (Oxford: Blackwell).
Asher, Nicholas, and Lascarides, Alex (2003). *Logics of Conversation* (Cambridge: Cambridge University Press).
Audi, Robert (1973). "Intending," *Journal of Philosophy* 70: 387–403.

Audi, Robert (1997). "Intending and its Place in the Theory of Action," in Ghita Holmström-Hintikka and Raimo Tuomela, eds., *Contemporary Action Theory*, vol. 1, *Individual Action* (Dordrecht: Kluwer), 177–96.
Barthes, Roland (1971). "De l'œuvre au texte," *La Revue d'esthétique* 3 : 225–32. Translated as "From Work to Text," in Josué. V. Harari, ed., *Textual Strategies: Perspectives in Post-Structuralist Criticism* (Ithaca, NY: Cornell University Press, 1979), 73–81.
Beardsley, Monroe C. (1978). "Intending," in Alvin Goldman and Jaegwon Kim, eds., *Values and Morals* (Dordrecht, Reidel), 163–84.
Brand, Myles (1984). *Intending and Acting: Toward a Naturalized Action Theory* (Cambridge, MA: MIT Press).
Bratman, Michael E. (1987). *Intention, Plans, and Practical Reason* (Cambridge, MA: Harvard University Press).
Bratman, Michael E. (1990). "What is Intention?" in Philip R. Cohen, Jerry Morgan, and Martha E. Pollack, eds., *Intentions in Communication* (Cambridge, MA: MIT Press), 15–31.
Carroll, Noël (1986). "Art and Interaction," *Journal of Aesthetics and Art Criticism* 45: 57–68.
Carroll, Noël (1992). "Art, Intention, and Conversation," in Gary Iseminger, ed., *Intention and Interpretation* (Philadelphia: Temple University Press), 97–131.
Carroll, Noël (1993). "Anglo-American Aesthetics and Contemporary Criticism: Intention and the Hermeneutics of Suspicion," *Journal of Aesthetics and Art Criticism* 51: 245–52.
Carroll, Noël (2000). "Interpretation and Intention: The Debate between Hypothetical and Actual Intentionalism," *Metaphilosophy* 31: 75–95.
Carroll, Noël (2002). "Andy Kaufman and the Philosophy of Interpretation," in Michael Krausz, ed., *Is There a Single Right Interpretation?* (University Park, PA: Pennsylvania State University Press), 319–44.
Davidson, Donald (1963). "Actions, Reasons, and Causes," *Journal of Philosophy* 60: 685–700.
Davis, Wayne A. (1984). "A Causal Theory of Intending," *American Philosophical Quarterly* 21: 43–54.
Davis, Wayne A. (1998). *Implicature: Intention, Convention, and Principle in the Failure of Gricean Theory* (Cambridge: Cambridge University Press).
Davis, Wayne A. (2003). *Meaning, Expression, and Thought* (Cambridge: Cambridge University Press).
Davis, Wayne A. (2005). *Nondescriptive Meaning and Reference* (New York: Oxford University Press).
Dutton, Dennis (1987). "Why Intentionalism Won't Go Away," in Anthony J. Cascardi, ed., *Literature and the Question of Philosophy* (Baltimore, MD: Johns Hopkins University Press), 194–209.
Eco, Umberto (1992). "Overinterpreting Texts," in Stefan Collini, ed., *Interpretation and Overinterpretation* (Cambridge: Cambridge University Press), 45–66.
Ellis, John M. (1974). *Theory of Literary Criticism: A Logical Analysis* (Berkeley, CA: University of California Press).
Fish, Stanley (1980). *Is there a Text in this Class?* (Cambridge, MA: Harvard University Press).
Fish, Stanley (1991). "Biography and Intention," in W. H. Epstein, ed., *Contesting the Subject: Essays in the Postmodern Theory and Practice of Biography and Biographical Criticism* (West Lafayette, IN: Purdue University Press), 9–16.
Fleming, Bruce Noel (1964). "On Intention," *Philosophical Review* 73, 301–20.
Gaut, Berys (1993). "Interpreting the Arts: The Patchwork Theory," *Journal of Aesthetics and Art Criticism* 51: 597–610.
Ginet, Carl (1990). *On Action* (Cambridge: Cambridge University Press).

Grice, H. Paul (1975). "Logic and Conversation," in P. Cole and J. Morgan, eds., *Syntax and Semantics*, vol. 3, *Speech Acts* (New York: Academic Press), 41–58.
Grice, H. Paul (1989). *Studies in the Way of Words* (Cambridge, MA: Harvard University Press).
Hancher, Michael (1972). "Three Kinds of Intention," *MLN* 87, 827–51.
Harman, Gilbert (1986). *Change of View: Principles of Reasoning* (Cambridge, MA: MIT Press).
Hirsch, E. D., Jr. (1967). *Validity in Interpretation* (New Haven, CN: Yale University Press).
Hirsch, E. D., Jr. (1976a). *The Aims of Interpretation* (Chicago, IL: University of Chicago Press).
Hirsch, E. D., Jr. (1976b). "In Defense of the Author," in David Newton-de Molina, ed., *On Literary Intention* (Edinburgh: Edinburgh University Press), 87–103.
Irwin, William (1999). *Intentionalist Interpretation: A Philosophical Explanation and Defense* (Westport, CT: Greenwood Press).
Irwin, William (ed.) (2002). *The Death and Resurrection of the Author?* (Westerport, CT: Greenwood Press).
Iseminger, Gary (1992). "An Intentional Demonstration?" in Gary Iseminger, ed., *Intention and Interpretation* (Philadelphia: Temple University Press), 76–96.
Iseminger, Gary (1996). "Actual vs. Hypothetical Intentionalism," *Journal of Aesthetics and Art Criticism* 54: 319–26.
Juhl, P. D. (1980). *Interpretation: An Essay in the Philosophy of Literary Criticism* (Princeton, NJ: Princeton University Press).
Kasher, Asa (1976). "Conversational Maxims and Rationality," in A. Kasher, *Language in Focus: Foundations, Methods, and Systems* (Dordrecht: Reidel), 197–211.
Krausz, Michael (ed.) (2002). *Is There a Single Right Interpretation?* (University Park, PA: Pennsylvania State University Press).
Kutz, Christopher (2000). "Acting Together," *Philosophy and Phenomenological Research* 61: 1–31.
Lamarque, Peter (2000). "Objects of Interpretation," *Metaphilosophy* 31: 96–124.
Levinson, Jerrold (1992). "Intention and Interpretation: A Last Look," in Gary Iseminger, ed., *Intention and Interpretation* (Philadelphia: Temple University Press), 221–56.
Levinson, Jerrold (2002). "Hypothetical Intentionalism: Statement, Objections, Replies," in Michael Krausz, ed., *Is There a Single Right Interpretation?* (University Park, PA: Pennsylvania State University Press), 309–18.
Livingston, Paisley (2005). *Art and Intention: A Philosophical Study* (Oxford: Clarendon Press).
Margolis, Joseph, and Rockmore, Tom (eds.) (2000). *The Philosophy of Interpretation* (Oxford: Blackwell).
Meiland, Jack W. (1970). *The Nature of Intention* (London: Methuen).
Mele, Alfred R. (1988). "Against a Belief/Desire Analysis of Intention," *Philosophia* 18: 239–42.
Mele, Alfred R. (1992). *Springs of Action* (New York: Oxford University Press).
Mele, Alfred R. (1995). *Autonomous Agents: From Self-Control to Autonomy* (New York: Oxford University Press).
Mele, Alfred R., and Moser, Paul K. (1994). "Intentional Action," *Noûs* 28: 39–68.
Nathan, Daniel. O. (1973). "Categories and Intentions," *Journal of Aesthetics and Art Criticism* 31: 539–41.
Nathan, Daniel. O. (1982). "Irony and the Author's Intentions," *British Journal of Aesthetics* 22: 246–56.
Nathan, Daniel. O. (1992). "Irony, Metaphor, and the Problem of Intention," in Gary Iseminger, ed., *Intention and Interpretation* (Philadelphia, PA: Temple University Press), 183–202.

Nehamas, Alexander (1981). "The Postulated Author: Critical Monism as a Regulative Ideal," *Critical Inquiry* 8: 131–49.

Nehamas, Alexander (1986). "What an Author Is," *Journal of Philosophy* 83: 685–91.

Nehamas, Alexander (1987). "Writer, Text, Work, Author," in Anthony J. Cascardi, ed., *Literature and the Question of Philosophy* (Baltimore, MD: Johns Hopkins University Press), 265–91.

Olsen, Stein Haugom (1982). "The 'Meaning' of a Literary Work," *New Literary History* 14:1: 13–32.

Pappas, Nickolas (1989). "Authorship and Authority," *Journal of Aesthetics and Art Criticism* 47: 325–32.

Recanati, François (1987). *Meaning and Force: The Pragmatics of Performative Utterances* (Cambridge: Cambridge University Press).

Schiffer, Stephen (1972). *Meaning* (Oxford: Clarendon Press).

Searle, John R. (1983). *Intentionality: An Essay in the Philosophy of Mind* (Cambridge: Cambridge University Press).

Searle, John R. (1990). "Collective Intentions and Actions," in Philip R. Cohen, Jerry Morgan, and Martha E. Pollack, eds., *Intentions in Communication* (Cambridge, MA: MIT Press), 401–15.

Stecker, Robert (2003). *Interpretation and Construction: Art, Speech, and the Law* (Oxford: Blackwell).

Strawson, Peter F. (1964). "Intention and Convention in Speech Acts," *Philosophical Review* 73: 439–60.

Tolhurst, William (1979). "On What a Text is and How it Means," *British Journal of Aesthetics* 19: 3–14.

Thom, Paul (2000). *Making Sense: A Theory of Interpretation* (Lanham, MD: Rowman & Littlefield).

Velleman, J. David (1997). "How to Share an Intention," *Philosophy and Phenomenological Research* 57: 29–50.

Vermazen, Bruce (1993). "Objects of Intention," *Philosophical Studies* 71: 223–65.

Vermazen, Bruce (1998). "Questionable Intentions," *Philosophical Studies* 90: 264–79.

Wimsatt, William K., and Beardsley, Monroe C. (1946). "The Intentional Fallacy," *Sewanee Review* 54: 468–88. Reprinted in David Newton-de Molina, ed., *On Literary Intention* (Edinburgh: Edinburgh University Press, 1976), 1–13.

Wollheim, Richard (1980). *Art and its Objects*, revised 2nd edn. (Oxford: Oxford University Press).

22

Art as Techne, or, The Intentional Fallacy and the Unfinished Project of Formalism

HENRY STATEN

> "... the meaning of art is inseparable from all the details of its material body."
> Bakhtin and Medvedev, *Theory of the Formal Method*

W. K. Wimsatt and Monroe Beardsley declared in 1946 that it is a mistake to consult authorial intention in order to judge the value, or determine the meaning, of a literary text. They named the notion that sponsors this mistake "the intentional fallacy," in an essay with the same name. "Critical inquiry," they argued, must look to "the text itself," rather than authorial intention.[1] "The Intentional Fallacy" became the authoritative statement of the principles of the already-established movement called the New Criticism, and touched off a debate that continues to the present day.

As the Russian Formalists had already shown decades earlier, the logic of anti-intentionalism rigorously followed out leads to strict formalism; but Wimsatt and Beardsley, along with the other New Critics, failed to carry through the logic of their own argument to this conclusion. This failure has led to persistent confusions in the ensuing debate over the purported fallacy, confusions that I try to clear up as much as possible in the first four sections of this essay.[2] The fifth and final section is a reading of Blake's short poem "London" in which I attempt to bring the New Critical practice of "close reading" nearer to the formalist standard set by the Russian group.

Since the intentional fallacy debate belongs to general aesthetics, I will move freely among the terms "art," "literature," and "poetry" or "the poem," as appropriate to the generality or specificity of the argument at that moment. All of these terms are deployed in their classic, non-Duchampian senses.[3]

The Intentions of Art

Wimsatt and Beardsley's argument in "The Intentional Fallacy" has been widely misunderstood to exclude intentionality as such, in any sense of the term, from the work of art. No less a figure than Paul de Man expounded this misconception, and

---

A Companion to the Philosophy of Literature, First Edition. Edited by Garry L. Hagberg and Walter Jost.
© 2010 John Wiley & Sons Ltd. Published 2015 by John Wiley & Sons, Ltd.

philosophers of aesthetics have routinely interpreted Wimsatt and Beardsley's doctrine as what Gregory Currie calls "aesthetic empiricism" – the notion that artworks can be understood apart from any kind of context at all.[4] In fact, however, the only kind of intention Wimsatt and Beardsley ruled out of bounds to the critic is the author's *private* intention, something "mental," "inside the head" of the author that, if the author does not directly reveal it, must be guessed by the critic on the basis of historical and biographical clues.[5] In challenging this kind of mentalistic intentionalism, Wimsatt and Beardsley were bringing into literary criticism the rejection of "psychologism" that had been basic to both analytic philosophy and phenomenology since the nineteenth century, and which culminated in the later philosophy of Wittgenstein.

But intention can be conceived otherwise than in this mentalistic way. It can be conceived as something that is intrinsic or structural to the poem or artwork in general. Wimsatt and Beardsley point toward artistic intentionality of this intrinsic or structural type – surprisingly, in view of the strict line that the New Critics drew between poetry and science – by a *machine* analogy. "A poem is like . . . a machine. . . . It is only because an artifact works that we infer the intention of its artificer."[6] Artificer's intention defined in this way is essentially social, external, open to view – and it is precisely on behalf of the social character of a poem's meaning that the attack on the "intentional fallacy" was devised. What is "internal" to the text "is also public," and the "public" includes "all that makes a language and culture" – a very expansive affirmation of the relevance of "context."[7] For those who have misread them, Wimsatt and Beardsley's distinction between what is "internal" and what is "external" to the text has overshadowed the criterion on which the distinction is based: anything that is *internal* to the poem is essentially social or cultural in nature, and therefore *external* to private, psychological interiority.

In fact, the phrase "all that makes a language and culture" is too vague in its inclusiveness to be useful as a theoretical rule (I will touch on this again in my final section); but it indicates unequivocally the tendency of Wimsatt and Beardsley's anti-intentionalism, and of formalism in general. The intentionality of the work of art is not locked away in the privacy of an individual artist's or poet's mind; it can be read off from the structure of the work "itself," *given appropriate knowledge of the appropriate context.*

What precisely constitutes "appropriateness" in this definition is an enormous question, but both the Russian and the American groups clearly believed that one kind of context, at least, is indispensable for construing the structural intentionality of literary texts. Thus, for example, Wimsatt's celebrated essay "The Structure of Romantic Nature Imagery" analyzed a phase in the historical evolution of the techniques of lyric poetry, showing what is "in" a poem by Coleridge by placing it in a compendious sketch of its literary precedents and intellectual context;[8] and the most influential "practical" critic among the New Critics, Cleanth Brooks, acknowledged the dependence of each poet's art on the historical state of the art itself.[9] Similarly, according to Boris Eichenbaum, he and the other Russian Formalists found that "we could not see the literary work in isolation, that we had to see its form against a background of other works rather than by itself," a relation the Formalists came to see as a "dialectic" between old and new forms.[10]

The machine analogy used by Wimsatt and Beardsley invites us to consider formalist criticism as a sort of critical "reverse engineering," related to that by which the design of industrial artifacts is deciphered.[11] As Peter Steiner has shown, the Russian Formalists, in particular Victor Shklovsky, had already by the 1920s developed this line of thought. "[W]e approached art as a production," wrote Shklovsky; "Spoke of it alone."[12] For the "mechanistic Formalists," says Steiner, "The perception of the work is ... nothing but the re-presentation of the intentional creative process which gave birth to the perceived work," a process that is a matter not of authorial psychology but of the "general technology of literary production and the laws that govern it."[13] Reverse engineering obviously cannot discover the "technology of literary production" on strict empiricist grounds; it requires an understanding of what a device is supposed to do, as well as the history of its predecessor machines and the techniques involved in their creation.

In fact, the notion of *technique* – historically evolved productive knowledge/power that is inherited and actualized by an individual artist, but which transcends the psychological intentionality of the individual – is the key to the logic of formalist criticism, on the basis of which critical reverse engineering of the sort intuited by Wimsatt and Beardsley can be effectively carried out. In the end, as Eichenbaum noted, his group found this notion "much more significant ... than ... the notion of form."[14] Form is the *product* of technique; hence, to be properly understood, it has to be tracked back to the technique that shaped it.

With their concept of technique the Russians came close to the ancient Greek concept of *techne* that is central to the thought of Aristotle. Techne is the socially accumulated, impersonal, productive knowledge of how to produce a specific kind of object, and the Russians, like Aristotle, considered the analysis of this power/knowledge to be the deepest level at which critical intelligence can probe the mystery of artistic agency. Aristotle stated the primacy of techne in his own philosophical language in a way that is unacceptable today but which gives us an intriguing starting point: "Techne is the origin [*arkhe*] and the form [*eidos*] of the object that is made" (*Generation of Animals* 735a).

This is not the place for an extended exposition of the relation between formalism and Aristotle's thought; but the term "techne" and the concept to which it refers are indispensable here because they draw together into a single, sharply focused notion the threads of formalist thought that I have been tracing.[15] I can now say simply that formalism considers art as a form of techne, and I can refer to the type of form-making intention that is to be distinguished from the psychologistic or mentalistic intention decried by Wimsatt and Beardsley as a *techne-intention*.

The word *technique* is inadequate because it means to us something more mechanical and superficial than techne, and suggests the distinction between "mere technique" and "inspiration" or "genius." This simplistic dichotomy is a distraction from the task of understanding art as techne – the task that every artist in order to become an artist necessarily has to undertake, and which the formalist critic is obliged to tackle in the artist's wake.

Can Private Intentions Go Public?

It is possible, in a given case, that our efforts at inferring an artwork's form by a strictly formalist contextualization will fail; from a formalist standpoint, however, this means, not that the design is inscrutable in itself, but that we are not yet adequately informed about the techne in question. Once the method of formalism is accurately conceived, the standard arguments for the irreducible importance of artist's (private) intention show up as cases of *giving up too soon* – often, startlingly soon – in the attempt to understand the relevant techne. Thus Kendall Walton in an influential essay jumped to the conclusion that only our knowledge of Schönberg's intention that his works be heard as twelve-tone compositions could "account for the correctness of our hearing them this way."[16] He completely ignored the alternate possibility subsequently pointed out by Stephen Davies: that Schönberg's music developed by stages out of the tradition of tonal music, and, consequently, close study of its development by someone who knows this tradition should, in principle, be able to arrive at the correct understanding of the twelve-tone works, without guidance by the composer.[17]

Walton's argument appeared to posit an irreducible residue of privacy in some aspects of artistic intention that are essential to the construal of a work; yet, as is often the case with intentionalist arguments, he left vague the precise nature of the type of intention in question. Is it strictly private in the mentalistic sense that Wittgenstein and "The Intentional Fallacy" attacked? Having taken to heart Wittgenstein's critique of mentalism, few philosophers today explicitly defend private intentions of this type; yet they are reluctant to give them up altogether.[18] Even someone like Paisley Livingston who, unlike Walton, actually articulates a strictly mentalistic notion of intention, in the end stops ambiguously short of it.[19] Livingston explicitly posits "meanings . . . in [the author's] mind" that "constitute the links" binding the work together but which remain undiscoverable without such aids as the author's diaries[20] – just the sorts of notions Wimsatt and Beardsley attacked. Yet he concludes his book with a much more modest claim: that raku tea bowls from seventeenth-century Japan cannot be appreciated if we do not know "the ideal of *wabi* and the artist's attendant designs, that is, if we do not know that they were intentionally made to have irregularities."[21] Since Livingston himself describes the artist's designs as "attendant" on an aesthetic ideal that persisted for centuries, he implicitly concedes the fundamental point he apparently meant to contest: that artistic intentions may *in principle* be read off from the work, given knowledge of the techne-context, with no essentially private mental residue.

But if Walton and Livingston are unable to defend a strictly mentalistic conception of artist's intention, their intentionalism becomes nothing but a confused restatement of the standard anti-intentionalist doctrine of formalism: that a work must be seen against the background of the history of the art by which it was made. Only the mischaracterization of formalism as "aesthetic empiricism" makes it seem as though intentionalism is needed as a corrective to it.

Livingston, however, seems to suggest a "third way," an accommodation between formalism and intentionalism that would do justice to the claims of both. He argues that the intention of the author can be taken to determine objective features of the text, but if and only if *these assumptions "mesh sufficiently" with the "features" of the text.*[22] Livingston thus apparently projects the existence of objective but *extremely subtle* features of an artwork – features so subtle that no one but the author can give us the clue to their presence. Walton's Schönberg argument appears also to presuppose qualities of this sort. Such qualities would, it seems, form an intermediate case between the strictly public and the strictly private – a subtle yet still objective medium in which a statement or guess about intention could apply the feather-touch by which private mental activity would "mesh" with the public techne conventions that are the realm of formalist analysis.

Livingston's proposal suggests the following thought experiment. Imagine that a puzzle picture is drawn by its maker in a way that she intends to have the figure of a fish hidden in it. She puts in this line *here* and this color *there* with the purpose of suggesting a fish; but, because this is a puzzle picture, she makes the relation of elements difficult to discern, so difficult in fact that all attempts by viewers to find the hidden picture fail. Now imagine, further, that when the creator reveals what she intended, or this intention is guessed by someone from study of the creator's letters and journals, viewers apprised of this intention quickly begin to see *this* line and *this* one as related to each other in such a way as to suggest a fish.

The preceding thought experiment seems to support the idea that objective, yet super-subtle, art qualities exist. Now let's consider it more closely. We have imagined that all efforts by all viewers, no matter how expert they are, fail to discern the fish; and yet the fish is "there." In what sense, then, can the fish be said to be *there*? One might conclude, alternately, that this is a bad puzzle picture – that the maker has not made it properly. The crucial question is how much authority we are going to concede to the maker's statement of intention. We can "imagine" that this intention provides the key to the perception of formal, public features of the work only if we antecedently assume that the viewer is obligated to bow to this authority; in which case the entire question is begged.

Small children make marks on paper and then explain that this is a horse or an airplane or Mommy, and we willingly concede this; but ought we to do the same with artists' intentions? In 2005 I saw in the Pompidou Center a Cy Twombly painting titled *Achilles Mourning the Death of Patroclus*, the main features of which were a red and a black swirl of paint, the first labeled "Achilles" and the second "Patroclus"; on the wall next to the painting were quotations from Twombly to the effect that this painting expressed how much he had been moved by the *Iliad*. The way they presented Twombly's remarks suggested that the curators of the exhibition were as willing to find, and as willing for the public to find, all the pathos of Achilles' grief in these swirls of paint as a parent is to see Mommy in the child's squiggle. And of course once one's imagination is set in motion one can "discover" all sorts of "mesh" between the work and its presumed meaning – for example, between the color red and Achilles' anger, the color black and death.

But suppose it had been the red swirl that was labeled Patroclus and the black one Achilles. This would form no impediment to the imaginative critic, who could then, if he desires, fabricate an even more interesting "mesh" between the canvas and Twombly's expressed intention. Anyone familiar with the machinery of criticism can easily imagine such a reinterpretation as the following: "In a movement of supreme and touching irony, the artist assigns the color of death to the living and paints the dead with a vividness of color denied to the living. As T. S. Eliot wrote in a similar vein: 'The communication of the dead is tongued with fire beyond the language of the living.'" (The connoisseur's reference to another great work of art is a crucial rhetorical touch here; it gives an apparent solidity to the arbitrary dance of fantasy. Nothing is more characteristic of non-formalist art-critical discourse than this dance.[23])

From the formalist standpoint, by contrast, the creative contribution of the viewer's imagination is severely circumscribed – and so is that of the critic. The *public* conventions by which the class of qualified viewers, or some significant subset of this class, judges that x is indeed being depicted or expressed must license these lines as a depiction or expression of x, without guidance from behind the arras, for it to count as an actual depiction or expression of x. Guidance of this kind makes Livingston's promising notion of "sufficient mesh" too flexible to serve as a standard for what can validly, by the public standards "outside" the work, be found "in" the work. If the most highly qualified puzzle-picture decipherers must *in principle* be defeated in their attempts to find the fish, absent knowledge or assumptions about maker's intention, this means simply that the maker's intention to depict has failed of its mark. An intermediate class of super-subtle art-features that are at once public and private does not exist.

The Intention to Make a Poem

Art as a concrete social phenomenon includes many types of intentions and responses on the part of both audiences and artists, and it is senseless to attempt to legislate away the vast majority of them by a formalist definition. The formula "art as techne," unlike "art as art," does not imply that all other interests in art are alien to the nature of art as such; it only brings to center stage the question of art's intentional structure at one specific level, that of the objective, socially accumulated power/knowledge that the artist brought into play in its making. And, since techne in the Greek sense is any historically evolved, systematized method by which some end is attained, whether in the "fine arts" or in any other activity of making or doing, to speak of art as techne is to focus on perhaps its least sublime aspect – the one it shares with the crafts and social practices in general.

This power/knowledge is, nevertheless, in an irreducible sense and in every case, what produces the *difference* between art and non-art of any kind or genre. The techne of poetry, for instance, produces the difference between poem and non-poem; for, even if the artist's most profound and passionate purpose in making art is to save mankind or communicate his innermost self, if what he makes is to be recognized as art (in a non-Duchampian sense), the work must have been made in accord with the constructive principles relevant to the making of the kind of artwork that it is.[24] Poems, artworks in general, can embody intentions of different and sometimes much more important kinds than the bare techne-intention; but *every* poem necessarily embodies the intention to *make a poem*, and this intention structurally implies the techne of poem-making (just as the intention to play a game of chess structurally implies the techne of chess-playing).

Techne-intentionality has of course an essential relation to the psychological reality of living, breathing human beings; yet it has a fundamentally different nature than psychological reality. The intentionality of techne is not something about the living subjectivity of an individual human being; it is "deposited" or "sedimented" in a given techne as the anonymous accumulation of intentional activity by many generations of agents who structure their intentions in terms of the techne as it exists when they come on the scene and who then contribute in large or small measure to its further evolution or devolution. And the earliest beginnings of techne are in the anonymity of the history of the human race. There is no better example of the productive power of the techne itself than the poems of Homer, which grew out of devices, forms, and techniques developed communally in Greece over hundreds of years, and which were themselves developments of still older techniques that date back to Indo-European times.[25]

When I choose to write a poem, what I choose is the intentionality of the art of poetry in whatever specific form it has come down to me, whether in its stricter established varieties or in some direction of innovation which nevertheless, to the degree that it is still *poetry* that I intend to make, must give form to my own subjective intentionality "from outside."

Poems Are Made out of Words

Cleanth Brooks's famous rejection of paraphrase as an equivalent for the poem has obscured the fact that for him and for the other New Critics something essential continued to hover *behind* "the poem itself" conceived as an arrangement of words. Brooks described the "structure" of poetry as "a structure of meanings, evaluations, and interpretations,"[26] a heterogeneous and not very clear grouping, but one that clearly privileges the level of meaning. When he said that "the poet is a maker, not a communicator,"[27] thus, he was not thinking of what the poet made as *these words in this arrangement* but rather – in common with the other New Critics – as the structure of meanings that the interpreter must reconstruct from the arrangement of words, always somewhat inadequately (hence – and not, as is commonly said, from some sort of fetishization of the text – the vanity of paraphrase).

The difference between the New Critics' conception of "the text itself" and the corresponding techne-conception can be clarified through Jerrold Levinson's notion that a writer *directly intends* "a text that means M" and only *indirectly intends* the meaning M itself.[28] M, on this account, is whatever the author might have had in mind in composing a text, the "message" that he hoped his work would convey. But even though the author intends the text to mean M, the text will do so, to the degree that it does do so, not by virtue of the fact that it is so intended but by virtue of how well the text has actually been constructed with this end in view.[29] Thus, for Levinson as for the New Critics, the proper object of interpretation is not M itself; rather, it is *the text that means M*.

The reason the formula *the text that means M* is worth introducing here is that, understood in terms of the distinction between direct and indirect authorial intention, it makes visible an ambiguity obscured by Wimsatt and Beardsley's phrase "the text itself." *The text that means M* implies two incompatible things. On the one hand, it means that *meaning is inseparable from the text*, thus that the text "itself" is a matter of primary concern, because it is only in the arrangement of words that meaning dwells. According to this sense of Levinson's formula, it points toward formalism. But, on the other hand, *the text that means M* implies that *the text is inseparable from the meaning*, thus that the task of the interpreter is to go *through* the text *to* its meaning. This second sense points away from formalism, and accounts for the fact that neither Levinson nor the New Critics have quite gotten at the techne-conception that characterizes the most rigorous formalism.

For techne-oriented formalism, poetry, as Mallarmé famously said, "is not made of meanings, it is made of words." Words, of course, have meanings; but the Russian Formalists' crucial discovery as they went decisively beyond the form–content distinction was that meaning can be treated as itself one of the materials of which poetry is made.[30] Meaning may be the most important material of poetry; but from a formalist standpoint it is, like the other materials on which the poetic art works, subordinate to its form-giving techniques.

If we reconsider the question of artist's intention from this techne standpoint, it becomes truly an intention not to *mean* but to *make*, and once the text is treated in this way, the notions of the unity and wholeness of a poem are demystified. Poems are wholes because, at the most general level, the intention "I will write a poem," unless modified by a supplementary or revisionary techne-intention (such as the German Romantics' notion of the *fragment*) that aims to disrupt the ideal of wholeness, is intrinsically structured by the practice-guiding aim at wholeness – even as when one intends to play a game of chess one's intention, just because one knows how to play chess, structurally involves *beginning* and *ending* the game. Most social practices involve rules concerned with beginning and ending, norms of well-formedness (think of a wedding), and, further, standards of correct, inferior, and superior execution. This is in particular true of linguistic practices; as Mary Louise Pratt has shown, the formal norms of literature are not essentially different from those that govern a vast diversity of ordinary language games, such as telling jokes and anecdotes, and even ordinary conversation.[31] The wholeness of the form of a joke is neither the unity nor the disunity of the structure of meanings; it is a function of how well the language of the joke has been "joined," as this join is judged by the norms of the joke-telling techne in the relevant group. Similarly, the quality of the form of a poem is normed by the historical practice of poets within a given tradition, and to speak of the unity of this form is nothing more than a judgment, ideally based on adequate knowledge of poetic techne, on the level of skill with which the poem has been executed, compared with the skill of normative exemplars. All poems can be shown at this level or that to be full of fissures and disunities, but at some other level they had better manifest skillful joining, or they lose the title of poems; and if all poems lack wholeness and "unity" *even at the techne level* then by definition the art of poetry does not exist.

Literature is the most difficult of the arts to conceive in terms of techne because the sheer meaningfulness of its material, language, tends to overwhelm the reader's sense of its "materiality." But there is no escaping the dominance of the quest for M unless the "join" of the poem's elements is conceived in the most material way possible – by analogy, for example, with the join of two angles in a wooden cabinet made by a skilled cabinetmaker. As has often been pointed out, the application of notions of materiality to poetry is misguided when it ignores the intentional structure of the artwork. But techne formalism does not ignore it.[32]

A craftsman's material is not bare materiality; it is defined as just the kind of material that it is by its relation to the intentionality of the craftsman's techne. The qualities of marble for the sculptor are not the qualities it has for the geologist; further, when marble is chosen, quarried, and prepared for the sculptor it is already, as material, being worked over with the intentionality of the subordinate technai by which these procedures are carried out. Moreover, the more thoroughly the materials of an art are culturally processed by subordinate technai with the aim of the superordinate techne in view, the more deeply their materiality will already embody the intentionality of the latter. For example, the ingredients of paint are chosen, combined, and processed for the specific purpose of making them into a suitable medium, not for painting in general, but for very specific types of painting involving specific techniques. These preliminary elaborations of the materials of art are themselves applications of types of techne, historically evolved forms of know-how that structure the intentionality of the craftsman or laborer who brings them to bear; the new intentionality of the artwork is then laid over these underlying layers of intentionality.[33]

In the case of language, the situation is of course considerably different. The language material with which poetic techne works is pre-formed into words, locutions, tones, networks of relation on the levels of meaning and feeling, trajectories of ideological force, and so forth, by socio-historical forces that do not have poetry in view. But this indifference to the poet's aim is precisely what gives pre-existent language-forms properties to which the poetic art must adapt itself, as other makers must adapt themselves to the partial autonomy of their own materials.

Blake's "London"

I will now illustrate the distinctiveness of techne-oriented formalist reading, using the example of Blake's "London." Here is Blake's poem:

> I wander thro' each charter'd street
> Near where the charter'd Thames does flow,
> And mark in every face I meet,
> Marks of weakness, marks of woe.

> In every cry of every Man,
> In every Infant's cry of fear,
> In every voice, in every ban,
> The mind-forg'd manacles I hear:
>
> How the chimney-sweeper's cry
> Every black'ning Church appalls;
> And the hapless Soldier's sigh
> Runs in blood down palace walls.
>
> But most, thro' midnight streets I hear
> How the youthful Harlot's curse
> Blasts the new-born Infant's tear,
> And blights with plagues the Marriage-hearse.

In an important late essay in which he reaffirmed the doctrine of the intentional fallacy Wimsatt attacked E. D. Hirsch's purportedly intentionalist reading of the final stanza of this poem; yet he did so in a way that is remarkably inattentive to its linguistic architecture.[34] In his preliminary summary account of the poem Wimsatt says that it "is about human 'weakness' and 'woe' as they may be observed in certain (uncertain) visual and auditory betrayals ('marks' and 'cries') and . . . imputed human causes. . . ."[35] This summary succinctly identifies the basic meaning-structure of the poem, yet makes little contact with the formal arrangement of the poem's language. Most strikingly, Wimsatt elides the "I" who figures as the perceiver of the "visual and auditory betrayals," even though the grammatical presence of this "I" creates the dominant, framing, visible structure of the poem as an arrangement of words, what could be called its "manifest architecture." The poem opens with "I wander," and moves to "I meet"; then, following the structural shift between the first and second stanzas (from the seeing of faces to the hearing of voices and cries), the final three stanzas are syntactically ruled by the phrase "I hear" which occurs at the end of the second stanza and again in the first line of the fourth. The syntactic force of the initial "I hear," intensified by the syntactic inversion that postpones its appearance to the end of the second stanza, is one of the most salient formal effects of the poem. More generally, the series of first-person present-tense perceptual acts (including "I mark" and "I hear") is the basis of the aural structure of the poem, which in the last three stanzas forms a crescendo, the crest of which is marked by the first two words of the final stanza, "But most": I wander, I meet, I hear, *But most . . . I hear.*

This structural skeleton, at once syntactic, discursive, and aural, on which the linguistic architecture of the poem is based, is the manifest techne-intention of the poet – the *public* linguistic "machine," object of critical reverse engineering, that Blake, whatever his private thoughts and feelings might have been, left to function on its own.

Wimsatt, however, jumps from his quick summary to a criticism of Hirsch's interpretation of the phrase "Marriage-hearse" in the last line. In Hirsch's interpretation, this phrase should be understood in light of the belief, imputed to Blake by Hirsch, that "If there were no marriage, there would be no ungratified desires, and therefore no prostitution." According to Wimsatt, however, Hirsch is illegitimately reading into this particular poem "certain soreheaded antinomian attitudes" that Blake indeed held at one time, but which from Wimsatt's own severe Christian standpoint are merely silly.[36] In Wimsatt's view, we should read the poem as saying that marriage, birth, and love are all blighted by a deathly plague that both Blake and his audience would have had in mind. "For an initiate reading of the last stanza, consult the career of an eighteenth-century Londoner like James Boswell or Charles Hanbury Williams."[37] Wimsatt rather delicately implies by these references that "harlot's curse" should be understood, on the basis of public evidence, as venereal disease.[38]

Neither Wimsatt nor Hirsch feels compelled to present, as the prerequisite for significant debate, an account of the intentionality of the poem as *immediately bound* to its linguistic architecture, considered *in detail* and *as a whole*. Hirsch's remarks are actually based on "closer" reading than Wimsatt's, yet the results of this reading are unsystematically culled and thrown into an unprincipled mix of historical evidence and interpretive remark. It is as though for both critics the mere "poem itself" considered as expression of poetic techne is *not enough;* it must have a "meaning" that only critical divination based on the accidents of individual erudition can reveal.

What if, by contrast, we give ourselves over to the poem in its *literal* presence, what I have called its "manifest architecture"? A series of perceptual acts placed in a specific setting is narrated, and that is all. The sense of literal seeing and hearing is (as so often in poetry) the *primary conceit* of the poem, and this conceit motivates the specification of details of time and place: in the first stanza the streets are placed in central London ("near . . . the Thames") and it is implied that the speaker walks them intensively ("*each* chartered street"); in the final stanza the setting is reiterated, and in addition placed in time ("through *midnight* streets"). The principles of "reverse engineering" demand that we ask why these details are there. Perhaps they are mere space-fillers, put in for purposes of meter or rhyme; but formalist method requires us to test the hypothesis that they are an expression of architectonic techne.

In the middle of the night, then, on the streets of central London, the speaker hears, and registers with supreme intensity, the harlot's curse, as he had heard the sweep's cry and the soldier's sigh.[39] The description of these scenes of hearing contains a profusion of metaphorical language that grammatically complicates the organizing structure. The sounds mentioned in the poem are not the direct objects of the hearing verbs; grammatically, what is heard is what the sounds *do*: "In every cry . . . I hear *how*". This metonymy evokes in an immensely compressed way the full social meaning, for the hearer, of the suffering of the persons involved, implying both the structure of oppression and its baleful repercussions for the ruling institutions themselves. It remains the case that, according to the organizing conceit, what is *literally heard* is not this meaning but the sounds themselves; yet the act of literal hearing is folded into an act of figurative hearing. Strikingly, the only direct object of "I hear" is figurative: the notorious "mind-forg'd manacles." Although strictly figurative, the word "manacles" evokes the clanking of the heavy metal restraints that prisoners wore in Blake's time, and as a direct object is grammatically integrated into the narrative of literal perception.[40] This clanking is in fact what the speaker hears "in every cry": the formal intertwining of the poem's figures shows up as the "literal" sound of imagined manacles nested within the "figured" meaning of actual cries (their *how*), itself nested within the "literal" sound of the cries.[41] This is a layering of figures worthy of Baudelaire; yet they are all contained within the tightly organized literal narrative.

A decisive objection to reading the harlot's curse as venereal disease now becomes apparent. Since venereal disease is not in any sense "hearable," Wimsatt's reading implies a sudden, unsignaled switch in register between the preceding series of literally hearable sounds to a "curse" that belongs to the same "literal" level of the poem as these sounds and is said in fact to be what is *most* heard, and yet (if taken in Wimsatt's sense) would be impossible to hear – *even in the figurative way that imagined manacles could be heard.* The reader would have to mentally inscribe the required meaning in a way that makes a certain historical sense, but throws the manifest structure of the poem into confusion.

The argument here is not that the genius Blake could not make what I am identifying as a clumsy switch in register. It is, rather, that the techne of poetry, like any other craft, is a craft of detail, and that the details in question in this poem can be shown, without recourse to interpretive epicycles, to be motivated by well-known and evident structural devices. The reader who isn't interested in the text as a well-joined "material" structure of words (that is, in the difference between poem and non-poem) need not concede that this switch *is* clumsy. But even such a critic might be interested in the fact that if, instead of imposing a meaning on the poem that requires either "external" evidence or interpretive ingenuity, one merely takes the poem at its word, everything works in a straightforward way.

In fact, the significance of the harlot's curse is much more fully realized in the literal scene of utterance than are the other sounds. For once the curse is restored to its primary status as something *heard,* it becomes evident that its effectuality, its "how," unlike that of the sigh and the cry, is not distinct from the utterance itself; the harlot's curse is an *effectual speech-act.* What the speaker hears is the set forms of curses transposed into a description of the destructive action accomplished by a genuine curse; the harlot is represented not as *saying* "Blast you" but as *blasting;* not as saying "a plague on you," but as *blighting with plagues.* This is the grand, final effect of the grammatical figure "I hear . . . how." And once we restore her curse to its primary status as speech-act, another, crucial difference from the previously heard expressions of suffering, the sigh and the cry, becomes visible. Unlike these, a curse is an articulate utterance, and one of a highly formalized, ritual type – one that marks, along with blessing, one of the two limit points of expressiveness of archaic human speech. A curse justly uttered, by the appropriate person against the appropriate object, implies the fitness for damnation of what is cursed, and therefore the intrinsic effectuality of the curse; and everything in this poem implies that the harlot's curse is justly uttered.

As for "Marriage-hearse": once we take the scene of cursing literally, the phrase readily suggests a passing carriage in which a bourgeois couple makes its stately, and deathly, progress down a London street, and which, like the crying neonate (who could easily be in the same carriage), draws down the resentful wrath of a young whore. "Marriage-hearse" indeed suggests that its own internal corruption has already overwhelmed the object of her curse.

Yet in the poem's most surprising turn, a turn that takes it beyond the measured reasonableness of the modern protest against injustice, it is the *most* helpless, the *most* innocent of human beings, a newborn babe, that the harlot curses first, and literally not even the infant itself but rather the infant's expression of suffering ("the new-born Infant's tear"). The poem might have, less surprisingly, culminated with "Most I hear the new-born Infant's cry" – a cry that has been evoked in the second stanza ("In every Infant's cry of fear") as one of those to which the speaker so passionately responds; and then the poem would have been digestible without residue by the liberal moralist. Instead, there is a kind of moral savagery in the poem's passionately empathic reception of a curse that takes as its first object an infant's tear – a savagery that restores all its archaic dignity and force to the speech-act of cursing, and wrings notes from the poem's utterance that have rarely been attained in English poetry. Occurring as it does at the lyrical climax of the poem, the young harlot's curse, simply as speech-act, is as impressive as any uttered by an Old Testament patriarch, with which – as blasting the inmost intestines of an unjust society, and carrying the innocent along with the guilty – it has a great deal in common. It is not, of course, "Blake" who utters this curse, but the represented persona of the harlot; yet the poet has put all his techne in the service of her voice.

None of what I have said implies that the prevalence of venereal disease in Blake's London, or Blake's antinomian attitudes toward marriage (soreheaded or not) are *ultimately* irrelevant to the poem, so that we should never at any point bring them into the discussion. My suggestion is that there is a salutary discipline, recently neglected, in learning to track those meanings that are explicitly located in close relation to the linguistic architecture of the poem, and to distinguish them from those that are farther away. The meaning-effects of a poem that are tied as closely as possible to its linguistic architecture shade off into an illimitable series of further, and potentially (but not necessarily) more profound and resonant effects, and there is no rigid boundary between the two. But that doesn't mean there's no difference. Formalism is the critical techne by which this difference is discerned.

Notes

1 W. K. Wimsatt and Monroe C. Beardsley, "The Intentional Fallacy," published originally in the *Sewanee Review* 54 (1946): 468–88; reprinted in W. K. Wimsatt, *The Verbal Icon: Studies in the Meaning of Poetry* (University of Kentucky Press, 1954), 3–18. (Page citations here refer to the reprint edition.)

2 The standard account of the Russian movement is still Victor Erlich, *Russian Formalism: History and Doctrine* (New Haven, CT: Yale University Press, 1965). See also the penetrating analysis of the conceptual evolution of the movement by Peter Steiner in *Russian Formalism: A Metapoetics* (Ithaca, NY: Cornell University Press, 1984).

3 On the question of art as "anything whatever," see Thierry du Duve, *Kant after Duchamp* (Cambridge, MA: MIT Press, 1996). I agree with Stephen Davies' account of art after Duchamp as "parasitic" on the practices and definitions of art in the traditional sense. See Stephen Davies, *Definitions of Art* (Ithaca, NY: Cornell University Press, 1991).

4 Paul de Man, *Blindness and Insight*, 2nd edn. (Minneapolis, MN: University of Minnesota Press, 1983), 23–7; Gregory Currie, *An Ontology of Art* (London: Macmillan, 1989), 17. According to Currie, Wimsatt and Beardsley are aligned with "aesthetic empiricism" because they believed that "the text has a meaning that is independent of facts about the text's history" (18).

5 The most acute and comprehensive critical account of what Wimsatt and Beardsley really said, and meant, is J. Timothy Bagwell, *American Formalism and the Problem of Interpretation* (Houston, TX: Rice University Press, 1986).

6 Wimsatt and Beardsley, "The Intentional Fallacy," 4.

7 Wimsatt and Beardsley, "The Intentional Fallacy," 10.

8 In Wimsatt, *The Verbal Icon*, 103–16.

9 Cleanth Brooks, *The Well-Wrought Urn: Studies in the Structure of Poetry* (New York: Harcourt, Brace, Jovanovich, 1947), 215.

10 Boris Eichenbaum, "The Theory of the Formal Method," in Lee T. Lemon and Marion J. Reis, eds. and trans., *Russian Formalist Criticism: Four Essays* (Lincoln, NE: University of Nebraska Press, 1965), 99–139, 119.

11 On the notion of "reverse engineering" see Daniel Dennett, *Darwin's Dangerous Idea: Evolution and the Meanings of Life* (New York: Simon and Shuster, 1995), 212ff. There is a close analogy between intentionalism in aesthetics and the "argument from design" in evolutionary biology; both jump from the evident fact of complex "design" (in the mammalian eye or in a Shakespeare sonnet) to the conclusion that an inexplicable power of intelligence must have created it. These arguments have been soundly rejected in biology, but still linger in aesthetics.

12 Quoted in Steiner, *Russian Formalism*, 65.

13 Ibid.

14 Boris Eichenbaum, "The Theory of the Formal Method," 115.

15 Steiner casually says that "mechanistic Formalism" was "concerned with the literary *techné*" (47), but does not develop this insight; on the contrary, he argues that Shklovsky's approach was merely "mechanistic."

16 Kendall Walton, "Categories of Art," *The Philosophical Review* 79:3 (July, 1970): 334–67.

17 Davies, *Definitions of Art*, 199–200. Davies does not write explicitly in support of formalism, but his position on this point and many others is fully compatible with it.

18 It must be noted that Wimsatt and Beardsley themselves never gave a full and philosophically rigorous account of intention, and actually contributed to the confusion with their statement that intention "in the head," although irrelevant to how we judge the poem, is its *cause* or *origin*. In contemporary aesthetics, confusion over intention reaches its maximum in the arguments of certain intentionalists who adapt Wittgenstein's critique of mentalism as a basis for their own mentalistic views. Thus in their contributions to the important collection *Intention and Interpretation*, ed. Gary Iseminger (Philadelphia: Temple University Press, 1992), Colin Lyas and Noël Carroll in standard Wittgensteinian fashion assert that intention is made possible by the appropriate public context and is not a private mental occurrence, concluding from this that the intention can be read off from the artwork plus its context; yet they then treat the intention that can be read off as something proper to the author's psychological reality. Lyas looks to the work in order to discover "the state of mind of the agent" (142), whose intentions are "displayed" in the work (148), and Carroll unabashedly looks behind the "implied author" for the "actual" author, with whom he proposes to pursue "an I-Thou relationship" (108–9, 118).

19 Paisley Livingston, *Art and Intention: A Philosophical Study* (Oxford: Clarendon Press, 1995). See also Livingston's chapter in this volume, 21 AUTHORIAL INTENTION AND THE VARIETIES OF INTENTIONALISM.
20 Ibid., 160, 164.
21 Ibid., 210.
22 Ibid., 207.
23 See, by contrast, the impressive formalistically oriented works of Yves-Alain Bois, *Painting as Model* (Cambridge, MA: MIT Press, 1990), and Rosalind Krauss, *The Originality of the Avant-Garde and Other Modernist Myths* (Cambridge, MA: MIT Press, 1986).
24 Of course there is no such thing as a pure artistic kind. This observation is not an objection to techne-theory; it is an integral part of it.
25 On the Indo-European roots of Homer's poetics, see Gregory Nagy, *Comparative Studies in Greek and Indic Meter* (Cambridge, MA: Harvard University Press, 1974).
26 Cleanth Brooks, *The Well-Wrought Urn*, 195.
27 Ibid., 74–5.
28 Jerrold Levinson, *The Pleasures of Aesthetics* (Ithaca: Cornell University Press, 1996), 211–12.
29 Levinson adds that the text must be evaluated in relation to its appropriate audience. His analysis of the concept of appropriate audience, and its relation to the text, is an important contribution to the debate over artistic intention; but it does not affect my point here.
30 Boris Eichenbaum, "The Theory of the Formal Method," 129–30.
31 Mary Louise Pratt, *Toward a Speech-Act Theory of Literary Discourse* (Bloomington, IN: Indiana University Press, 1977).
32 Notably, Bakhtin and Medvedev in their critique of the Formalists did not quarrel with their notion that language was the material of literature.
33 At this point the theory of art as techne abuts on the general theory of labor, on which see Georg Lukacs, *The Ontology of Social Being*, vol. 2, chapter 3, "Labor." This chapter has appeared as a separate volume in English: *Labour* (London: Merlin, 1978), trans. David Fernbach.
34 W. K. Wimsatt, *Day of the Leopards: Essays in Defense of Poems* (New Haven, CT: Yale University Press, 1976), 30–35. Hirsch's comments on Blake are in his *Innocence and Experience: An Introduction to Blake* (New Haven, CT: Yale University Press, 1964).
35 Wimsatt, *Day of the Leopards*, 31–2.
36 Ibid., 34–5.
37 Ibid., 34.
38 This shows the vagueness of the criterion of publicness as conceived by Wimsatt; at the limit, as here, it sanctions the loose historicism of traditional literary scholarship.
39 The soldier's sigh seems a far less typical city sound, and less literally hearable, than the sweep's cry and the harlot's curse, and therefore appears less fully motivated by the conceit of literality. This sort of apparent flaw in verbal architecture legitimately opens the door to historical research; and it turns out that there was indeed a historical sense of "soldier's sigh" that makes good perceptual sense here, something like "murmur of revolt." See David V. Erdman, *Blake: Prophet Against Empire*, revised edn. (Princeton, NJ: Princeton University Press, 1969), 278–9. This sort of concern should not, however, obscure the formal structure within which the sigh functions. The formal structure of poems can be near-perfect at the level of "manifest architecture," but the deeper we dig the more the manifest symmetries inevitably give way to an underlying, much less tidy, profusion of effects. Critics tend to be mainly interested in this underlying profusion; but the poem as product

of poem-techne is precisely the *appearing form* of what I have been calling the "linguistic architecture."

40 Hirsch makes casual reference to this clanking, but does not address its structural significance.

41 The figure of manacles, embedded in the meaning of all the other sounds, implies a fourth institution set beside those of the church, the palace, and marriage: that of the prison; it thus evokes what today we might call the "carceral essence" of them all. This last observation, however, begins to cross the line between formal analysis and broader considerations, and I include it here precisely to show the necessity of drawing such a line.

23

Biography in Literary Criticism

STEIN HAUGOM OLSEN

In spite of the fact that dominant theoretical "schools" over the last forty years have pronounced against the use of biography in criticism and have even pronounced the author dead, biographical information and biographical accounts are regularly used in literary criticism to establish interpretative conclusions, to enhance readers' understanding of literary works and literary oeuvres, and/or to provide insight into the writing practices of authors. What is more, while biography has survived as a critical instrument, the theories that banished references to the author have faded away. This being the case, it may be time to raise again the question about the role of biographical accounts and biographical information in criticism.

The answer to this question will be determined partly by the way in which the question is formulated. Those arguing against the employment of biographical information have made use of the concept of "legitimacy" rather than concepts like "relevance" or "usefulness." The notion that some kinds of criticism are "illegitimate" because they employ biographical information is a difficult one since this criticism often, though not always, seems useful or relevant. Usefulness and relevance are practice-based notions and their normative force is based in shared perceptions which are a result of mastering the practice. Once the notion of "legitimacy" is cut off from these practice-based notions, it has to be based in a theory. This makes the notion vulnerable as theories about literature and criticism tend to change rather quickly.[1] When the question about the role of biographical information in criticism is addressed in the last part of this article, it will be formulated in terms of "usefulness" and "relevance" rather than "legitimacy." This may not make possible the sort of theoretically neat answer that questions of legitimacy permit, but in the longer perspective one may hope that the answer to these questions may be more useful for and relevant to criticism than answers to questions about legitimacy have been.

Critical Theory's Attack on Biography

There have been two different attacks on the use of biographical information in literary criticism. Critical theory (structuralism/post-structuralism) developed a conceptual

A Companion to the Philosophy of Literature, First Edition. Edited by Garry L. Hagberg and Walter Jost.
© 2010 John Wiley & Sons Ltd. Published 2015 by John Wiley & Sons, Ltd.

scheme for the description of literature that left no room at all for the concept of a real, flesh and blood author. Structuralist theories conceived of the literary work as an autonomous structural unit, the meaning of which was a function of a syntagmatic combination of minimal units. There was no provision in that conceptual scheme for the notion of an utterer or an author as an *origin* of the literary work. In post-structuralist criticism a notion of "author" is reintroduced, but as the "figure in the carpet," a function of the text, and not as a person-in-the-world:

> If the author is a novelist, he inscribes himself in his text as one of his characters, as another figure sewn into the rug; his signature is no longer privileged and paternal, the locus of genuine truth, but rather, ludic. He becomes a "paper author": his life is no longer the origin of his fables, but a fable that runs concurrently with his work. There is a reversal, and it is the work which affects the life, not the life which affects the work: the work of Proust and Genet allows us to read their lives as text. The word "biography" reassumes its strong meaning, in accordance with its etymology. At the same time, the enunciation's sincerity, which has been a veritable "cross" of literary morality, becomes a false problem: the *I* that writes the text, is never, itself, anything more than a paper I.[2]

In this type of theory the notion of an independent, individual self is held to be a bourgeois fiction. Consequently, all one can mean when one talks about the author is the author-inscribed-in-the-text. Only reference to other texts and codes will figure in *genuine* criticism: the text is an intertext constituting the author-in-the-text. Facts about the-person-in-the-world would not be relevant in genuine, "non-naïve" understanding of texts: since there are no persons-in-the-world, there are no such facts, but only fictions masquerading as facts.

It is, strictly speaking, wrong to say that structuralist and post-structuralist theories attack the use of biographical accounts in criticism. These types of theory develop conceptual schemes where biographical accounts simply have no place. What is more, they also throw out the traditional notion of literary criticism. They take their point of departure in theoretical frameworks developed in linguistics, and any connection or analogy between the sort of "textual practice" which is given recognition in their conceptual schemes, and traditional literary practice is incidental. Since they exclude from their conceptual schemes the concept of literary criticism as well as the concept of an author, biographical accounts in criticism present no theoretical problem for these types of theory. Consequently, they have no contribution to make to the discussion about the role and usefulness of biography in literary criticism, nor do they have any implications for critical practice that need to be heeded by the critic who makes use of biographical accounts and biographical information in his criticism, except perhaps the consequence that these and other *literary* critics are engaged in a futile activity and should start doing something else, i.e. criticism of texts. Structuralism and post-structuralism are revolutionary in the sense that they do not aim at throwing light on an already existing practice but rather recommend exchanging that practice for another. These theories may have prevented some critics from availing themselves of the biographical instrument and left others wondering if the use of biography was illicit,

437

but in general they have had little success in reducing the use of references to the author's biography in literary criticism.

The Attack from within Literary Criticism

While the attack from Critical Theory came from outside critical practice, the other type of attack came from within criticism itself. It came a as reaction against what its opponents variously called "the factualist system," "the biographical fashion in criticism," or the "personal heresy," and was directed against what was seen as an accumulation of facts about authors that had little or no bearing on the understanding or appreciation of the works produced by those authors:

> The principal and characteristic manifestation of the factualistic perversion of poetic-artistic meaning is the insistence on exclusively external documentation of literary meaning. Any sort of authenticated record by the author and his contemporaries concerning the occasions, the intentions, the values, of his works, and the actual and supposed experiences, opinions of persons and events, moral and intellectual attitudes; letters written and received by the author, contemporary criticism, attitudes toward him; records of conversations; any documents bearing upon his modes of life and work, are treated as primary evidence of literary meaning.[3]

A parodic example was given by Harold Cherniss:

> Several years ago a professor of English literature was widely acclaimed for having made an important discovery in his field of research; he had found in certain English archives the record of sale of a house belonging to John Milton. This may seem like a parody of what I call the biographical fashion in literary interpretation rather than like a fair example of that fashion; but I suspect that few professors of Greek literature see anything comic in their scholarly debates concerning the number of Euripides' wives, the question of Sophocles' indictment of his son, Iophon, and the reasons for Aeschylus' removal from Athens. None of these questions, however, affects the works of these poets or our understanding of them. Neither has the discovery in the English archives elucidated a single word or line in the writings of John Milton; and yet that discovery, far from being taken lightly by any of the journals that announced it, was treated by all of them as an addition to our knowledge of the history of English literature.[4]

The debate between those representing the "biographical fashion" and the attackers was epitomized by an exchange between E. M. W. Tillyard and C. S. Lewis that started in *Essays and Studies of the English Association*, volume 19 (1934) and ended with a book of altogether six essays being published by Oxford University Press in 1939 under the title *The Personal Heresy: A Controversy*. This controversy started with C. S. Lewis attacking the "widely held belief" that poetry is an "expression of personality," and the concomitant assumptions that "the end which we are supposed to pursue in reading it is a certain contact with the poet's soul," and that " 'Life' and 'Works' are simply two diverse expressions of this single quiddity."[5] One of the examples adduced by C. S. Lewis was the approach to Milton adopted by E. M. W. Tillyard in his book on that author and the assumption that *Paradise Lost* is "really about" "the true state of Milton's mind when he wrote it."[6] C. S. Lewis presents what is essentially an autonomy view of literature:

> I shall maintain that when we read poetry as poetry should be read, we have before us no representation which claims to be the poet, and frequently no representation of a *man*, a *character*, or a *personality* at all.[7]

And as time passes the literary work "is continually taking on . . . new colours which the artist neither foresaw nor intended." "There can be poetry without a poet."[8]

The attack on the biographical fashion in criticism culminated in W. K. Wimsatt's and Monroe Beardsley's "The Intentional Fallacy" (1946).[9] This article put forward in magisterial tone but without much argument a number of theses which had been developed and repeated in articles in journals of literary criticism since the early 1930s. It established as orthodoxy within the discipline of criticism for the next twenty years the autonomy view of the literary work:

> "A poem should not mean but be." A poem can *be* only through its meaning – since its medium is words – yet it *is*, simply *is*, in the sense that we have no excuse for inquiring what part is intended or meant. Poetry is a feat of style by which a complex of meaning is handled all at once.[10]

This autonomy view gave a theoretical grounding to the intuition on which the attack on the biographical was based: that a good deal of biographical information has no bearing on the understanding and appreciation of literature. It seemed to explain why the record of sale of a house belonging to John Milton, or Shakespeare willing his second-best bed to his wife Ann Hathaway, seem irrelevant to any of the works written by these authors.

It is interesting that all the critics mentioned above as attacking the biographical fashion see themselves as a vanguard opposing a critical orthodoxy.[11] However, the fact that the autonomy view itself became dominant in the few years after the publication of "The Intentional Fallacy," does indicate that there was a widespread and growing frustration among academic critics in the Anglophone world with the accumulation of biographical facts that apparently bore no relations to the understanding or appreciation of works of the authors under discussion.

Distinguishing a Category of Relevant Biographical Information

The autonomy view faced an immediate and obvious problem: it went too far. It not only provided theoretical justification for excluding from "proper criticism" biographical information that had no obvious relevance to works of literature under discussion. It provided theoretical justification for excluding from "proper criticism" *all* information "extrinsic" to the work of literature. Those who opposed the autonomy view pointed out that though a great deal of private/external information is certainly irrelevant, "There are many instances on the other side of the account":

> Doubtless there would be a touching pathos in "All, all are gone, the old familiar faces," if the poem were anonymous, but there is much more when I know that it was written by Charles Lamb – a fact which is no part of the poem – and know something of the tragic circumstances in his life. Or consider Coleridge's "Dejection, an Ode": our present knowledge (which we owe to his biographers and the collectors of his letters) of the experiences out of which it arose, and of the fact that it marked the end of his great creative period as a poet, makes the poem far more moving than it can have been to the generality of the readers of the *Morning Post* in 1802.[12]

Instances "on the other side of the account" comprise not only single works of literature, but also the understanding and appreciation of an author's oeuvre. Writing about his experience of doing a critical study of the oeuvre of Ford Madox Ford, John Meixner makes a point which seems obvious but which, at least in the 1960s, had to be insisted on:

> If my book was to have unity, inner logic, significance, and scale, and to offer a balanced evaluation, I had to refer the novels to a single center. They were not nominally the novels of Ford Madox Ford, a convenient fiction, but Ford Madox Ford's novels actually. ... Successively, one had to come to terms with Ford's view of history, of England, of Roman Catholicism, of America, of Toryism, of the Jews, of Henry VIII and Katharine Howard, of votes for women, of various Protestant heresies, of love, of the official intelligentsia, of France, of the first world war, of the moral changes of the twenties, of the impact of the depression – and, more and more, in his later years, of the ideal conditions for a society that would be fit for "a proper man." Now all of these are, clearly, not matters of autonomous art, but of biography, of period, and of life.[13]

Wimsatt and Beardsley tried to deal with the role of biographical information in criticism by introducing a double distinction between "internal"/"external" and "public"/"private" information:

> There is a difference between internal and external evidence for the meaning of a poem. And the paradox is only verbal and superficial that what is (1) internal is also public: it is discovered through the semantics and syntax of a poem, through our habitual knowledge of the language, through grammars, dictionaries, and all the literature which is the source of dictionaries, in general through all that makes a language and culture; while what is (2) external is private or idiosyncratic; not a part of the work as a linguistic fact: it consists of revelations (in journals, for example, or letters or reported conversations) about how or why the poet wrote the poem – to what lady, while sitting on what lawn, or at the death of what friend or brother.[14]

However, the distinction between internal-public and the external-private is unhelpful because it does not clarify the intuition that some collateral information is critically useful and relevant to the understanding and appreciation of a literary work of art while other collateral information is not. There is indeed a wide range of *public information* related to the content and meaning of a literary work that appears to be irrelevant to the reader's grasp of those qualities of a work that is characteristic of it as a literary work. "It is not difficult," says a critic, writing about Shylock in 1933,

> in our present state of knowledge to reconstruct Shylock's actual background and to depict, without leaving much margin for error, those details which Shakespeare relegated to the imagination.[15]

And in the rest of his article this critic, taking as his point of departure what is said about Shylock in the play, builds up a detailed picture of Shylock: what Jewish "nation" he belonged to; where in Venice he would have lived; what his social status would have been; what "treasures" and "pledges" he would have been likely to have had in his possession; what was his ancestry; etc. However, none of this information seems to contribute to the reader's understanding of the role of Shylock in the play.

There are two options open to theories which reject "external" information in the sense defined by Wimsatt and Beardsley.[16] They can legislate against all use of biographical information or they can explain away cases which use biographical information in what is an apparently illuminating way. Since a wide range of various types of examples in which illuminating biographical information is used to support critical conclusions can be marshaled, there must be strong initial doubt whether it is possible to explain away the use of biographical information in all these cases. Nor is legislating against such use an attractive option since this will in the end weaken or destroy this kind of theory.

"The Intentional Fallacy" was the culmination of an attack on the abuse of biographical information and as such it pointed backwards rather than forwards to a constructive development of principles for clarifying what biographical information could be critically useful. One major reason for this failure was the reconceptualization of the problem of the relevance of historical and biographical information in criticism as a problem about authorial intention. The problem of how far reference to the author's intentions should enter into the identification and interpretation of a literary work is related only marginally, if at all, to the question concerning the use and usefulness of biographical information as a critical instrument. The problem of the artist's intentions may be an interesting question in its own right, but the long debate about authorial intention that followed on the Wimsatt and Beardsley article and is still going on prevented the different question about the usefulness of biographical information as a critical instrument from being pursued.[17]

Reconceptualization of the problem of the usefulness of historical and biographical information in criticism as a problem about authorial intention also narrowed the discussion to the role of biographical information as "evidence" in the interpretation and appreciation of literary works. Granted that this question is crucial, biographical information is also used in a variety of other ways in criticism. Even should one conclude that there is no role for biographical evidence as an integral part of literary interpretation, it does not follow from this that there are no further uses of biographical information that are illuminating and critically useful.

STEIN HAUGOM OLSEN

Biographical Information as an Aid to Understanding

As a preliminary to a discussion of the role of biographical information in criticism, one must make an initial a distinction between biography as a historical discipline and biography as an instrument for literary criticism. As a *historical discipline* biography will make use of any work an author may have written, as a source for saying something about the poet's life. The aim of biography, in this sense, will be to give a historically correct presentation of the author and his environment, and the works of art he may have produced will be source material, among other types of source material, for drawing conclusions about the author's personality, opinions, emotional life, etc. It is the greatness of the works of art that makes the author an interesting subject for biography, but these works do not have any special status as sources for drawing these conclusions. As a historical discipline biography does not belong to criticism and does not present any special philosophical problems that have to be addressed by literary aesthetics. In this discussion it is without further interest. As a *critical instrument* biographical information is used to understand the works produced by the author. The focus is not on the life of the author, but on his works, and biographical information is used to illuminate the works. The point seems obvious, but is worth making since much that passes for criticism is actually "critical biography." "We are all familiar," says John Meixner,

> with that hybrid monstrosity, the critical biography, the ideal form beloved of publishers. Pure critical studies, alas, do not sell. And straight biographies of literary men would appear a shirking of duties, a confession by the biographer of critical incompetence. But how rarely are the interpretations in such works more than passes at criticism. Most often, they are simply smuggled, not infrequently pernicious, procedures for presenting the life. When the biographical and the critical principles of organization come into conflict, both are likely to be diverted from clear method.[18]

A second distinction that will be useful in such a discussion is that between the *appreciation* of a literary work and an *understanding* of it. Both appreciation and understanding are *modes of apprehension*. Appreciation differs from understanding in that it is a form of apprehension that involves the recognition of a type of value, aesthetic value. Understanding involves merely a recognition of features of the literary work and its relationships, not a recognition of these features as constituting a value. The concept of appreciation is thus meant to focus the mode of apprehension which constitutes a production of some sort as a work of art for the reader or audience. Appreciation of a literary work is, in its turn, constituted through literary interpretation. This is a logical or formal point: literary interpretation can be distinguished from other types of interpretation of literary works which constitute modes of understanding rather than appreciation.

Consider now the following example. In *The Rise of the Novel* Ian Watt has a discussion of the incoherence and discontinuities of Defoe's *Moll Flanders*. The most striking example that he mentions, is the meeting-house scene where Moll attempts, but fails, to steal a gold watch from "a gentlewoman." When she is transported to Virginia she gives a watch to her son that she maintains to have stolen from "a gentlewoman's side, at a meeting house in London." Says Watt,

> Since there is no other episode in *Moll Flanders* dealing with watches, gentlewomen and meeting-houses, we must surely infer that Defoe had a faint recollection of what he had written a hundred pages earlier about the attempt on the gentlewoman's gold watch, but forgot that it had failed.
>
> These discontinuities strongly suggest that Defoe did not plan his novel as a coherent whole, but worked piecemeal, very rapidly, and without any subsequent revision. This is indeed very likely on other grounds. His main aim as a writer was to achieve a large and effective output – over fifteen hundred pages of print in the year that saw *Moll Flanders*; and this output was not primarily intended for a careful and critical audience.[19]

And Watt goes on to give further facts from Defoe's personal history to make the point that Defoe's attitude to his writing was "casual." He identifies apparent incoherence and inconsistencies in Defoe's work, and he explains them as a consequence of Defoe's way of working, of his aims, and of his attitudes, all of which are documented biographical facts. His explanation contributes to an understanding of *Moll Flanders*, in the sense that the reader comes to see how these inconsistencies have arisen, what attitudes Defoe had to his novel, and how the attitudes which Defoe probably had as a man manifest themselves in this novel. Watt's discussion contributes to an understanding in general of Defoe as an artist, of his artistic methods, and his attitudes to his art. The argument explains by linking certain features of the work to Defoe's habits, aims, and attitudes. It does not draw attention away from the works of Defoe but promotes a better understanding of their shortcomings as works of art.

In this example the biographical information does not figure as "evidence" in a literary interpretation constituting an appreciation of the novel. Nevertheless, it contrasts with information that relates to experiences of Defoe's that have nothing to do with his practices as an artist, i.e. the information that Defoe was imprisoned in Newgate for five months after having published *The Shortest Way with the Dissenters*. This may give us the assurance that Defoe knew Newgate and did not "make up" the horrors of the Newgate scenes in *Moll Flanders* but it does not relate to his art. This second piece of information does not contribute to our understanding of *Moll Flanders* or of Defoe as an artist. In cases where understanding rather than appreciation is involved it seems relatively unproblematic to state a principle for distinguishing between use and abuse of biographical information: only such biographical information is critically useful as relates to the role of the author as artist, i.e. to the author's conception of himself as an artist, to his artistic methods, to his artistic aims etc.

Biographical Information as an Aid to Appreciation

The use of biographical information to gain a deeper insight into the artistry of an author also contrasts with information that more directly influences interpretation and appreciation. Consider one of the most celebrated discussions in modern critical history: the discussion of Defoe's artistic control in *Moll Flanders*. In her book *The English Novel: Form and Function* Dorothy Van Ghent makes the following statement:

> Either *Moll Flanders* is a collection of scandal sheet anecdotes naively patched together with the platitudes that form the morality of an impoverished soul (Defoe's), a "sincere" soul but a confused and degraded one; or *Moll Flanders* is a great novel, coherent in structure, unified and given its shape and significance by a complex system of ironies.

She concludes that it must be a great novel because we reread it with pleasure:

> That it may be the latter is justified by the analysis it yields itself to, as an ironic structure, and most of all justified by our pleasure in it. Shall we, then, waive the question of Defoe's "intention" and "sincerity"? Speculations as to these apparently can add nothing to the book nor can they take anything from it; the book remains what it is.[20]

This view is attacked by Ian Watt in *The Rise of the Novel* by pointing out that apparently central examples of such use of irony are much more plausibly understood as non-ironic expressions of Defoe's values. Watt identifies groups of apparent ironies in *Moll Flanders* that can be explained in this way. In particular he focuses on the episodes where Moll takes a moralizing stance and episodes where Moll is concerned with the value of worldly goods. One such example is the episode where Moll gives an account of how the reception of the rich gifts given her by her son in Virginia, made a sincere penitent of her Lancashire husband. "No writer," says Watt,

> who had allowed himself to contemplate either his heroine's conscience, or the actual moral implications of her career, in a spirit of irony, could have written seriously . . . the account of James' moral reformation, in which Moll Flanders tells us how she brought him the riches given her by her son, not forgetting "the horses, hogs, and cows and other stores for our plantation" and concludes "from this time forward I believe he was as sincere a penitent and as thoroughly a reformed man as ever God's goodness brought back from a profligate, a highwayman and a robber." We, not Defoe, laugh at the concept of reformation through hogs and cows.[21]

It is impossible to see Defoe as displaying ironical awareness here, Watt argues, because Defoe

> was not ashamed to make economic self-interest his major premise about life; he did not think such a premise conflicted either with social or religious values and nor did his age. It is likely therefore that one group of apparent ironies in *Moll Flanders* can be explained as products of an unresolved and largely unconscious conflict in Defoe's own outlook, a conflict which is typical of the late puritan disengagement of economic matters and moral sanctions.[22]

In this argument Watt uses biographical information to *block* a certain kind of appreciation. "Watt warns that what we have taken to be ironic masterstrokes are very often perceptions we bring to rather than get from Defoe."[23] The biographical information does not enter into and form an integral part of literary interpretation, but is provided as a background against which appreciation has to take place.

Legislating against such use of biographical information, as does Dorothy Van Ghent, has proved useless.[24] The debate about the coherence of and possible ironies in *Moll Flanders* has continued to the present day, but the arguments against Watt have not been theoretical arguments to show that his evidence cannot be admitted because it is illegitimate. They have been arguments paying more and detailed attention to the work itself, supported by literary precedents and facts about Defoe's artistic practice,[25] as well as arguments aimed at showing that the biographical evidence that Watt marshals is unconvincing or simply wrong and that from what we know about Defoe there is every reason to believe that he did appreciate irony and employed it across his oeuvre. "What I want to do in this article," says Maximillian E. Novak in an early response to Watt,

> is to outline some of the general areas of irony which the reader may pick out of *Moll Flanders*, to indicate those themes and elements of human behaviour which Defoe regarded as inherently paradoxical and hence subject to ironic treatment, and to assure those readers who have found irony in *Moll Flanders* that Defoe was being consciously ironic.
>
> Of course in order to do this, the critic must have read a good part of the five hundred and forty-seven items which appear in Professor John Robert Moore's *Checklist of the Writings of Daniel Defoe* (Professor Moore has subsequently added several more), but this is precisely what none of the critics appear to have done. Many of these works are long, some are dull, but all of them give us some insight into Defoe's mind.[26]

The critical usefulness of this kind of background information is summed up by Jacques Barzun:

> a work as a whole or in detail is easy to misconceive, . . . its substance and value are at the mercy of preconceptions which create *pre-perceptions*, and . . . the main task of criticism is to clear this foreground of obstacles – nothing more.[27]

This is exactly what Watt is doing in his comments on *Moll Flanders*, performing the critical task of clearing the ground, preventing preconceptions from creating pre-perceptions. The criticism leveled at Watt by other critics is that he really fails to clear the ground properly.

Biographical Information as an Integral Part of Appreciation

There is a point to distinguishing between, on the one hand, biographical information that contributes to the understanding of the artistry of an author and biographical information that provides a background for appreciation and, on the other hand, biographical information that constitutes an integral part of literary interpretation.

The motivation for the attack on the biographical fashion in criticism was that biographical information led the reader and the critic away from the work of literature where the focus *should* be. Underlying the autonomy theory there is an ontological anxiety based in an evaluative concern. The anxiety and the concern were summed up in one sentence in C. S. Lewis's 1934 article: "Very few care for beauty; but any one can be interested in gossip."[28] The concept of a literature current in our culture is the concept of a canon of works embodying some of the most fundamental values of our civilization, what Lewis in this quote calls "beauty." The values these works embody are what justifies our interest in them. The values are constituted by the literary work and collateral information has no role in *constituting* that value. Therefore the focus of critical interest must be the work itself and references to collateral information must be irrelevant in the appreciation of the literary work of art. If collateral information is assumed to be *necessary* to appreciation then the concept of literature as a canon of works embodying fundamental humanistic values is threatened. These values then reside in not in the work itself but in the work *plus* the collateral information. But if this is so, the very integrity of the concept of literary work would be threatened as no line could be drawn between the literary work itself and the text that provides the collateral information.

Biographical information that contributes to the understanding of the artistry of an author as well as biographical information that provides a background for appreciation poses no real challenge to the integrity of the literary work. Background information both constrains interpretation and suggests possible ways that interpretation may take. Such background information is *always* presupposed by an author. It consists in a set of assumptions about the real physical and social world into which the work is introduced. The author then makes use of these assumptions to constitute the world of the work. For it is a part of the conventions governing literary practice that the readers should assume, unless they are informed otherwise, directly or by implication, that the world of the work is similar to the real world. The assumptions constituting the background information will concern social and ethical as well as physical aspects of this world. That is, it includes assumptions about social structures, relations, and values as well as assumptions about the physical appearance and laws of this world. In the Defoe example from *The Rise of the Novel* Watt bases his argument on the possibilities for evaluating the character of Moll Flanders offered by the society and community in which Defoe lived and whose ideas and attitudes he was likely to share. The biographical information that Defoe was a dissenter and a tradesman is important since he must be assumed to share the values of economic individualism which were important to these classes. If he had been a high-church Tory, the world he would have assumed his readers to know would have been different. Providing this background information is only to "clear the foreground" to prevent such preconceptions as the reader has from creating pre-perceptions. The literary work remains ontologically speaking separate from the background.

On the other hand, when biographical information enters into the very process of appreciation, the ontological separateness of the work may appear to be compromised. Yet the kind of argument that makes biographical information part and parcel

BIOGRAPHY IN LITERARY CRITICISM

of appreciation is relatively widespread in criticism. Consider the following comment on Yeats' *Meditations in Time of Civil War*:

> Yeats wrote *Meditations in Time of Civil War* during the summer of 1922 – the war broke out in June – and, significant enough in his country's history, the event had a particular meaning for the poet. He had already (certainly by 1922, but the following passage was probably drafted in 1916–17) come to accept that fact that
>
>> the dream of my early manhood, that a modern nation can return to Unity of Culture, is false; though it may be we can achieve it for some small circle of men and women, and there leave it till the moon brings round its century.
>
> He had, that is, given up the hope that Ireland would produce, and that he would contribute to, an art both major and popular. What remained was the limited achievement of writing for a sympathetic coterie, and the verse-play of *Four Plays for Dancers* (1921) are precisely that. "In writing these little plays I knew that I was creating something which could only fully succeed in a civilization *very unlike ours*" – Yeats is adjusting his ambition to the restricted community of "some fifty people in a drawing room," and the achieved content is correspondingly thin. But in *Meditations*, the old dream reasserts itself in a painful yet fruitful way. The fact that Ireland is no exception to the historical rule has come true in the most tragic terms: the fact of the war resurrects in Yeats' mind the whole structure of youthful hopes, and involves him in a more thorough abandonment of those hopes than he had expected.[29]

This critic goes on to develop the point that *Meditations* are Yeats' response to his disillusionment with the Irish people as a nation that could realize his dream of a sound national culture that would inspire love and not hate. With the coming of the Civil War, the critic argues, Yeats had to live through the consequences of the failure of the dream of sound nationalism. What is more, Yeats himself felt guilty about the "troubles" because he saw the dream of a sound national culture, that he had helped to foster, as a partial cause of the violence to which the Civil War led. This, according to this critic, is what the following stanza (from "The Stare's Nest by My Window," part 6 of *Meditations*) is about:

> We had fed the heart on fantasies,
> The heart's grown brutal from the fare;
> More substance in our enmities
> Than in our love; O honey-bees,
> Come build in the empty house of the stare.

The critic sketches an intellectual biography for Yeats and places *Meditations* in that intellectual biography. This also permits him to see a thematic development from "Easter 1916" (1916), where "Yeats could describe the bloody Easter Rising which destroyed a good part of O'Connell Street, as having given birth to 'a terrible beauty,'" to the *Meditations* where the bloody violence has become a metaphor for the modern condition of destructive social change that isolates the poet and dissolves culture."[30] Yeats' intellectual biography is used as a point of departure for a thematic analysis of the poems:

> There are seven sections to the poem. In the first, "Ancestral Houses," Yeats evokes only to discard a familiar image for Unity of Culture, the house-and-garden of the eighteenth-century Anglo-Ireland.
>
> ... now it seems
> As if some marvellous empty sea-shell flung
> Out of the obscure dark of the rich streams,
>
> And not a fountain, were the symbol which
> Shadows the inherited glory of the rich.
>
> The very excellence of past creations has exhausted the creative energies, and the present impulses have yet to crystallize. In poems II to IV, he erects symbols appropriate for a poet isolated by destructive social change. In poems V and VI he shows his response – part-envy, part-revulsion – to the actual business of war. Finally, in poem VII he prophesies the threatening future which "the indifferent multitude" is likely to command.[31]

Without the knowledge of Yeats' dream of a sound national culture and the loss of that dream, stanza 4 of "The Stare's Nest by My Window" becomes, it may be argued, even in the context of the whole poem, vague, if not unintelligible. Knowledge of Yeats' dream and what he suffered makes the content clear and gives the poem a poignancy which it would not otherwise have had.

If one does accept that this kind of criticism does indeed compromise the integrity of the literary work of art, then the temptation to legislate against it may become irresistible. However, the ontological anxiety seems overstated. Logically speaking, the kind of criticism that ties a literary work to the concerns, values, and intellectual development of the author does function in the same way as background information: it defines parameters and suggests directions for interpretation. Such information is always subject to evaluation in light of the various features of structure, diction, character, etc., that the reader is able to recognize *without* reference to this information – though not without reference to further collateral information: how a work relates to other works in an author's oeuvre (how the *Meditations in Time of Civil War* relates to "Nineteen Hundred and Nineteen"); how it exemplifies the author's artistic practice (e.g. Yeats' use of sculpture and monuments which figure prominently in the *Meditations*[32]); the author's knowledge of culture and history that will explain his use of symbols (e.g. What did Yeats know that would explain the following line from part VII of *Meditations*: " 'Vengeance upon the murderers,' the cry goes up, / 'Vengeance for Jacques Molay' "?); etc.

Though the ontological anxiety is unjustified, this kind of criticism does evoke an evaluative concern of the same type as that expressed by Dorothy Van Ghent in her treatment of *Moll Flanders*: that this kind of criticism will come into conflict with the basic critical principle of identifying and explaining such features of a work of literature as make it good or great literature. The concern is related to, though it is not identical with, the concern that underpinned the attack on the biographical fashion in criticism: that criticism should focus on the work and not lead the reader away from the work. When biographical information becomes an integral part of the interpretative argument there is always the danger that it will lead to a view of the literary work as a purely personal statement that has an interest for the author alone but fails to have a public interest. In the above example, the critic is justified in his use of biographical information by the results of the critical argument. Yeats' intellectual biography is used as a point of departure for a thematic analysis of the poems, an analysis which demonstrates to the reader how the poem develops deeply interesting themes concerning the breakdown of culture and civilization in orgies of violence that has as its partial roots complaisant romantic visions of freedom and brotherhood. It is always possible to read a work of literature as a personal utterance, but insofar as a reader attempts to *appreciate* the utterance as a literary work of art, he is trying to apprehend the value which, as a literary work, such an utterance is conventionally expected to yield. The information that Yeats in the years from 1916 to 1921 finally gave up the dream of a sound national culture and came to see the Irish for what they were, is critically useful to the reader of the *Meditations* because it provides the perspective that the poem can be seen as Yeats' *Waste Land* poem, where a situation is presented in which culture is shattered in war and violence. A reader who approaches *Meditations* as a poem is trying to grasp not what Yeats may have meant by a personal utterance to which he incidentally gave the form of a poem, but how Yeats meant the poem he wrote to be appreciated. Biographical information is critically useful when it promotes this aim.

Conclusion

Biographical information is useful in criticism when it increases our understanding of such aspects of an author's personal life and behavior that relate to and define his artistic practice, his artistic methods, his attitudes to his art, etc. Such criticism illuminates the work of an author by linking certain features of his work to his habits, techniques, aims, and attitudes. Biographical information is also useful when it provides a background which constrains and provides direction for literary interpretation and appreciation, and when it enters into interpretative arguments as an integral part of the effort to appreciate a work. These are the principles that have emerged from the above discussion for distinguishing between the informative use and uninformative abuse of collateral information of the biographical kind. Or, to revert to the idiom of legitimacy, they provide a set of norms, though vaguely formulated, for distinguishing between legitimate and illegitimate use of biographical information in criticism. The principles also meet the main concerns voiced by those who attacked the biographical fashion in criticism, i.e. they secure that the focus of criticism is the work and not the author, as well as the evaluative concern that criticism should be concerned with, in Lewis's terms, "beauty" rather than "gossip."

These principles may seem trivial, but if they do it is because they are grounded in a familiar practice.

One may, however, raise the question why, if the principles formulated are obvious, there is a need to make them explicit. The answer may be found in C. S. Lewis's remark that "Very few care for beauty; but anyone can be interested in gossip." There is no longer a biographical fashion in criticism, but there is a universal curiosity about great men, authors among them, that is similar to that catered to by the "human interest story" in journalism. The principles of relevant use may be obvious, but they may not always be observed or even easy to keep in mind when biographical information introduces the human interest angle. As to the power of the human interest angle "I shall merely cite," says a critic

> the extraordinary sensation which has been caused by the recent announcement of A. L. Rowse's biographical study of Shakespeare – with its revelations of Shakespeare's relationship to the Earl of Southampton and the identification of Marlowe as Shakespeare's rival poet. The most distinguished newspapers of London, New York, and Washington devoted news columns and editorials to Professor Rowse's book even before its publication. If Shakespeare's sonnets represent, as has been claimed, "the greatest puzzle in the history of English literature," they represent the classic example of biography in the interpretation of poetry. No purely esthetic criticism has ever stimulated the same public interest – not even the most astounding discoveries of verbal tensions, zeugmas, or many-splendored ambiguities in Shakespeare or any other poet.[33]

That is why it is useful to have explicitly formulated principles even if they are obvious.

Notes

1. Practices do, of course, change over time as indeed has critical practice. This change has not, however, been driven by theory. For an interesting comment on the relative independence of literary theory and critical practice, see Wallace Martin, "Criticism and the Academy," in A. Walton Litz, Louis Menand, and Lawrence Rainey, eds., *The Cambridge History of Literary Criticism*, vol. 7, *Modernism and the New Criticism* (Cambridge: Cambridge University Press, 2000), 301–2.
2. Roland Barthes, "From Work to Text," in Josué V. Harari, ed., *Textual Strategies. Perspectives in Post-Structuralist Criticism* (London: Methuen, 1979), 78–9 (originally published in *Revue d'Esthetique* 3 (1971) as "De l'oeuvre au texte"). See also Roland Barthes, "The Death of the Author," in Roland Barthes, *Image-Music-Text* (sel. and trans. Stephen Heath, London: Fontana Books, 1977), 142–8 (originally published as "La mort de l'auteur," *Mantéla* 5 (1968)); and Michel Foucault, "What Is an Author?" in Harari, ed., *Textual Strategies*, 141–60 (revised version of Michel Foucault, "Qu'est-ce qu'un auteur?" *Bulletin de la Société française de Philosophie* 63 (1969), trans. Josué V. Harari). For an excellent evaluation of these arguments see Peter Lamarque, "The Death of the Author: An Analytical Autopsy," *British Journal of Aesthetics* 30 (1990): 319–31.
3. Martin Schütze, *Academic Illusions in the Field of Letters and the Arts* (Hamden: Archon Books, 1962), 238–9. Originally published by the University of Chicago Press in 1933. The 1962

reprint has a preface by René Wellek where Wellek says that "This book was originally published in 1933 and thus anticipates the New Criticism on the central issue: the focus on the text and the rejection of irrelevant origins or intentions" (viii). For someone writing from within the framework of the New Criticism it may possibly look like that. However, the attack on the "biographical fashion in criticism" was widely supported among critics in the 1930s.

4   Harold Fredrik Cherniss, "The Biographical Fashion in Literary Criticism," *University of California Publications in Classical Philology* 12:15 (1943): 279.

5   E. M. W. Tillyard and C. S. Lewis, *The Personal Heresy: A Controversy* (London: Oxford University Press, 1939), 1–2.

6   E. M. W. Tillyard, *Milton* (London: Chatto and Windus, 1930), 237.

7   Tillyard and Lewis, *The Personal Heresy*, 4.

8   Ibid., 16.

9   William K. Wimsatt and Monroe C. Beardsley, "The Intentional Fallacy," *Sewanee Review* 54 (1946), 468–88; revised and republished in William K. Wimsatt, *The Verbal Icon: Studies in the Meaning of Poetry and Two Preliminary Essays Written in Collaboration with Monroe C. Beardsley* (Kentucky: University of Kentucky Press, 1954), 3–18.

10 Wimsatt and Beardsley, "The Intentional Fallacy," *The Verbal Icon*, 4. The line "A poem should not mean / But be" is the final couplet in Archibald Macleish "*ArsPoetica*" (1936) which became a summary of modernist literary aesthetics.

11 "The factualist system," says Schütze, "is at present the ruling system in America" ("Introduction," xi). "Few will deny," says C. S. Lewis, "that the role of biography in our literary studies is steadily increasing. . . ." (*The Personal Heresy*, 1). And Cherniss in the quoted paragraph emphasizes the absence of any reaction among critics to the biographical facts that he finds absurd.

12 Arthur O. Lovejoy, "Reflections on the History of Ideas," *Journal of the History of Ideas* 1:1 (1940): 12. Lovejoy's main concern is to argue the case for the role of history and in particular intellectual history in literary interpretation, but he also makes the point that "even knowledge from external sources about the *artist*, his 'personality' or his life, is one of the sorts of collateral information" which will enhance the aesthetic experience of a literary work of art (12–14). The necessity of historical information for the full understanding and appreciation of literary works was also discussed in terms of scholarship versus criticism. See Louis Teeter, "Scholarship and the Art of Criticism," *ELH* 5:3 (1938): 173–94.

Instances of this type can be multiplied. Alfred Owen Aldridge, "Biography in the Interpretation of Poetry," *College English* 25:6 (1964): 412–20 marshals a number of examples of different kinds.

13 John A. Meixner, "The Uses of Biography in Criticism," *College English* 28:2 (1966): 110–11.

14 Wimsatt and Beardsley, "The Intentional Fallacy," *The Verbal Icon*, 10.

15 Cecil Roth, "The Background of Shylock," *Review of English Studies* 9:34 (1933): 149–50.

16 As is clear from the above quote from "The Intentional Fallacy," the distinction between "external" ("extrinsic") and "internal" ("intrinsic") is problematic. To avoid the obvious problems I shall in the following use the term employed by Lovejoy: "collateral," i.e. the information "placed side by side" with the work of literature.

17 After "The Intentional Fallacy" one can find only a very few articles on this topic, and after the end of the 1960s the topic disappears altogether from the theoretical/critical discussion. The discussion about authorial intention has, however, mushroomed. See

e.g. the number of items on artistic intention in the bibliography in Paisley Livingston's recent book *Art and Intention: A Philosophical Study* (Oxford: Oxford University Press, 2005). In a review of *Intention and Interpretation* (Philadelphia: Temple University Press, 1992) edited by Gary Iseminger, I remarked that the title of Jerry Levinson's final article in the volume, "Intention and Interpretation: A Last Look," "must undoubtedly be construed as intentionally ironic." In the light of the number of items produced about this question in the last 15 years, it is today difficult not to read that title as at least hypothetically intended as ironic. For an amusing comment, see Gary Iseminger, "Actual Intentionalism vs. Hypothetical Intentionalism," *Journal of Aesthetics and Art Criticism* 54 (1996): 326, n.20.

18 Meixner, "The Uses of Biography in Criticism," 108.
19 Ian Watt, *The Rise of the Novel. Studies in Defoe, Richardson, and Fielding* (London: Chatto and Windus, 1957), 99.
20 Van Ghent, Dorothy, *The English Novel: Form and Function* (New York: Holt, Rinehart and Winston, 1953), 42.
21 Watt, *The Rise of the Novel*, 125–6.
22 Ibid., 127.
23 Howard L. Koonce, "Moll's Muddle: Defoe's Use of Irony in Moll Flanders," *ELH* 30:4 (1963): 377.
24 It is interesting that the last printing of Van Ghent's *The English Novel* was in 1967, while Watt's *The Rise of the Novel* has been reprinted again and again by various paperback presses such as Penguin and Pimlico, the latest reprint being a new edition brought out by the University of California Press in 2001. It is perhaps also worth noting that the attack on the biographical fashion in criticism did not prevent E. M. W. Tillyard's book *Milton* from being frequently reprinted over a period of almost 40 years, the last reprint being a Peregrine edition in 1968.
25 As does Koonce in "Moll's Muddle: Defoe's Use of Irony in Moll Flanders."
26 Maximillian E. Novak, "Conscious Irony in Moll Flanders: Facts and Problems," *College English* 26:3 (1964): 199.
27 Jacques Barzun, "Biography and Criticism: A Misalliance Disputed," *Critical Inquiry* 1:3 (1975): 482–3.
28 Tillyard and Lewis, *The Personal Heresy*, 28.
29 Graham Martin, "The Later Poetry of W. B. Yeats," in Boris Ford ed., *The New Pelican Guide to English Literature*, vol. 7, *From James to Eliot* (Harmondsworth: Penguin Books, 1983), 233–4.
30 Martin, "The Later Poetry of W. B. Yeats," 236–40.
31 Ibid., 236.
32 For a general account of Yeats' use of sculpture, see Michael North, "The Ambiguity of Repose: Sculpture and the Public Art of W. B. Yeats," *ELH* 50:2 (1983): 379–400.
33 Aldridge, "Biography in the Interpretation of Poetry," 415.

24

Getting Inside Heisenberg's Head

RAY MONK

In the fascinating "Postscript" that he has added to the printed version of his play, *Copenhagen*, Michael Frayn writes that: "The great challenge facing the storyteller and the historian alike is to get inside people's heads" (Frayn 1998, 97). Philosophers are accustomed to looking askance at phrases such as this, but, perhaps speaking first and foremost as a biographer, it seems to me that there is a perfectly unobjectionable way of understanding the notion of "getting inside people's heads," and that Frayn himself articulates this well when he glosses the great challenge he has identified as the attempt "to stand where they [the people whose heads we are attempting to get inside] stood and to see the world as they saw it, to make some informed estimate of their motives and intentions" (97).

Put like this, the task facing the story-teller, the historian, and (I would insist on adding) the biographer is indeed challenging, but not impossible. After all, why shouldn't we be able to see the world as another sees it, and thereby grasp the other's motives and intentions? However, Frayn adds to this way of putting it a skepticism about the identification and ascription of mental processes which, if accepted, would appear to make history and biography, if not story-telling, impossible. According to him: "There is not one single thought or intention of any sort that can ever be precisely established" (99). Thus, the "great challenge" of getting inside another person's head is one that we are doomed never to be able to meet. In the attempt to grasp the thoughts, motives and intentions of others, we are dogged by uncertainty at every step, an uncertainty that, like that of Werner Heisenberg's celebrated *Ungenauigkeit* or *Unbestimmtheit* with regard to the position and velocity of sub-atomic particles, is, in Frayn's words, "not just a practical [difficulty], but a systematic limitation which cannot even in theory be circumnavigated" (99). So, the inside of people's heads, which is where Frayn says the historian endeavors to place himself, is, as he puts it, "precisely where recorded and recordable history cannot reach" (97). "Even when all the external evidence has been mastered," he adds, "the only way into the protagonists' heads is through the imagination" (97). In that sense, it seems to be implied (though Frayn himself rather delicately refrains from spelling this out), the playwright is at an advantage over the historian in meeting the great challenge that both of them face.

A Companion to the Philosophy of Literature, First Edition. Edited by Garry L. Hagberg and Walter Jost.
© 2010 John Wiley & Sons Ltd. Published 2015 by John Wiley & Sons, Ltd.

Frayn's argument here mirrors in a rather interesting way an argument put forward by Virginia Woolf in the essays she published on biography in the 1920s. Like Frayn, Virginia Woolf distinguishes sharply between the external and the internal, and is skeptical that the "external" documented record that is the raw material of history and biography can provide what one is really looking for, namely an insight into the "inner" mental lives of one's subjects. To accomplish this latter task, she insists, again like Frayn, we need, not the discovery of facts, but the exercise of our imaginative powers. Unlike Frayn, however, Woolf explicitly draws from this the conclusion that the faithful representation of our inner lives is a task to which fiction is better suited than history or biography.

In one such essay, called "The Art of Biography" (Woolf 1967a), she appraises the work of her friend Lytton Strachey and concludes that what is revealed by Strachey's work is that biography is a craft rather than an art. Her argument takes the form of contrasting the success of Strachey's *Queen Victoria* with the failure of his *Elizabeth and Essex*. In the former, she claims, Strachey treated biography as a craft and submitted to its limitations; in the latter he treated it as an art and flouted its limitations. Thus, she says: "it was not Lytton Strachey who failed; it was the art of biography" (223).

At the heart of her argument is the dependence of the biographer on what Frayn refers to as "the recorded and recordable history." The crucial difference between Strachey's two subjects, according to Virginia Woolf, is one of documentation. "About Queen Victoria," she says, "everything was known":

> No one has ever been more closely verified and exactly authenticated than Queen Victoria. The biographer could not invent her, because at every moment some document was at hand to check his invention. And, in writing of Victoria, Lytton Strachey submitted to the conditions. He used to the full the biographer's power of selection and relation, but he kept strictly within the world of fact. Every statement was verified; every fact was authenticated. And the result is a life which, very possibly, will do for the old Queen what Boswell did for the old dictionary-maker. (224)

When writing about Elizabeth I, however, Strachey was forced, through lack of documented evidence, to use his powers of invention to recreate the "tragic history" that he claimed to see lying dormant, half-revealed and half-concealed, in the available facts about the Virgin Queen and Lord Essex. And so, Woolf claims, Strachey formed the ambition of writing a book that was "not only a biography but also a work of art" (224). Nevertheless, she argues,

> the combination proved unworkable; fact and fiction refused to mix. Elizabeth never became real in the sense that Queen Victoria had been real, yet she never became fictitious in the sense that Cleopatra or Falstaff are fictitious. The reason would seem to be that very little was known – he was urged to invent; yet something was known – his invention was checked. The Queen thus moves in an ambiguous world, between fact and fiction, neither embodied nor disembodied. (224–5)

It is in this way that "the trouble lies with biography itself":

It imposes conditions, and those conditions are that it must be based on fact. And by fact in biography we mean facts that can be verified by other people besides the artist. If he invents facts as an artist invents them – facts that no one else can verify – and tries to combine them with facts of the other sort, they destroy each other. (225)

In order for Strachey's ambitions for *Elizabeth and Essex* to be realized, in order to create a real work of art, Strachey needed the freedom from fact, the freedom to invent, enjoyed by the novelist. The invented character, Woolf writes,

> lives in a free world where the facts are verified by one person only – the artist himself. Their authenticity lies in the truth of his own vision. The world created by that vision is rarer, intenser, and more wholly of a piece than the world that is largely made of authentic information supplied by other people. (225)

In another essay on the subject, "The New Biography" (Woolf 1967b), Virginia Woolf begins by quoting the dictum of Sir Sidney Lee that: "The aim of biography is the truthful transmission of personality."[1] "No such single sentence," Woolf declares,

> could more neatly split up into two parts the whole problem of biography as it presents itself to us today. On the one hand there is truth; on the other there is personality. And if we think of truth as something of granite-like solidity and of personality as something of rainbow-like intangibility and reflect that the aim of biography is to weld these two into one seamless whole, we shall admit that the problem is a stiff one and that we need not wonder if biographers have for the most part failed to solve it. (229)

From this perspective, biography looks less like an honest craft that fails only when it aspires to the status of an art, and more like an endeavor doomed to present itself with a challenge that is intrinsically impossible to meet. Striving to create a rainbow, the biographer has at his or her disposal only a block of granite. Or, to put it another way, striving for a truthful transmission of personality, of thought and intention – things, that, as Michael Frayn puts it, remain intractably "shifting and elusive" – the biographer has merely a body of "external" evidence. And so, Virginia Woolf writes, some biographers take the easy way out and insist that the true life of their subjects reveals itself in action, "rather than in that inner life of thought and emotion which meanders darkly and obscurely through the hidden channels of the soul" (229–30). The only way of being faithful to this meandering, dark, obscure, hidden inner life, Woolf insists, is through the imagination, a route that, for the biographer, but not for the novelist, is fraught with danger. In seeking to be truthful to the fragile, insubstantial nature of the rainbow – of thoughts, intentions, desires, and personality – the biographer is forced to write like a novelist, and thus flirts with the danger of producing a work of fiction, a work that by its very nature cannot hope to be true to the granite-like world of documented fact, and becomes therefore a betrayal of the craft of biography. "Truth of fact and truth of fiction are incompatible," states Woolf, and yet the biographer somehow has to combine them:

> For it would seem that the life which is increasingly real to us is the fictitious life; it dwells in the personality rather than in the act. Each of us is more Hamlet, Prince of Denmark, than he is John Smith of the Corn Exchange. Thus, the biographer's imagination is always being stimulated to use the novelist's art of arrangement, suggestion, dramatic effect to expound the private life. Yet if he carries the use of fiction too far, so that he disregards the truth, or can only introduce it with incongruity, he loses both worlds. (234)

The dangers of mixing the worlds of fact and fiction to which Virginia Woolf draws attention in her critique, both of Strachey's *Elizabeth and Essex* and of the entire genre of biography, are vividly illustrated by Heisenberg's autobiography, *Physics and Beyond*, in which he provides dialogues between himself and his friends and colleagues which, he freely admits, are not reproductions of conversations that actually took place, but imaginative creations designed to illustrate the protagonists' points of view. In defense of this technique, Heisenberg cites Thucydides, who in the preface to his *History of the Peloponnesian War*, explains that the speeches contained in his book were, to put it bluntly, made up by Thucydides himself, who, however, claims to have endeavored to keep as close as he could to "the train of thought that guided [the] actual speech" (Heisenberg 1971, v) of his characters.

This is a rather puzzling claim. We are accustomed to regarding the words that a person says as evidence for what he or she thinks, and yet here we are expected to turn this around and accept the veracity of direct quotation on the basis that it follows pretty closely what the person thought. Of course, in the cases where Thucydides is reporting speeches that he himself heard, he is doing little more than following the practice we all follow on those occasions when we are asked to recall what somebody said and we reply: "Well, I don't remember his actual words, but the gist of it was...." However, that "little more" – the shift from reported speech to direct quotation – is, we may feel, the line that separates fact from fiction. And, where Thucydides is attempting to reconstruct speeches that he himself did not hear and the text of which he does not have access to, he is, I would suggest, in a fairly straightforward sense, writing fiction.

Frayn's "Postscript" begins with the question: how much of his play is fiction and how much of it is history? He answers this in two ways; first, by itemizing those parts of the play that are based on the historical record and those which are his own invention, and second, by some general reflections on the difficulties involved in getting inside other people's heads, reflections that seem to lead to the conclusion that, in the ascription of thoughts and intentions to others (and perhaps even to ourselves), *some* element of fiction is ineradicable. He is led to this series of reflections by a consideration of what he calls the "Thucydidean principle," the principle, that is, that invented quotations are legitimate in a work of non-fiction in so far as they keep close to the trains of thought of the historical characters to which they are attributed. "The actual words spoken by my characters," Frayn says, "are of course entirely their own" (Frayn 1998, 96), but, he adds, they "follow in so far as possible the original protagonists' train of thought" (97). But how far *is* it possible? It is at this point that Frayn invokes the analogy between Heisenbergian uncertainty in quantum theory and the difficulties of determining thoughts and intentions, an analogy that allows him to claim that, in reproducing the train of thought of his characters, he has departed, not only from the established historical record, but from *any possible* historical record.

So, to return to the original question, how much of the play is fiction? The answer would seem to be: nearly all of it. Every time a character expresses a thought (that is to say, in every utterance contained in the play) the historical record has been left behind. And this, as Wittgenstein would say, is a grammatical remark, since the historical record, no matter how detailed, is doomed to remain silent on the question of the thoughts and intentions that people had. In this sense, Frayn's position is more radical than that of Virginia Woolf. Where she had claimed that fiction is *better* at representing the inner life of thought, intention, and emotion (largely because of the *incompleteness* of the historical record), Frayn insists that fiction – or at least a departure from the historical record – is *necessary* when conveying that inner life, not because of the incompleteness of the historical record, but because of its very nature as a body of "external" evidence.

On Frayn's view, historical documents *cannot possibly* tell us what we really want to know, namely what was in the heads of the people whose thoughts and intentions we seek to understand. It would seem to follow that in inventing a solution to the vexed question of what Heisenberg hoped to achieve from his visit to Niels Bohr in 1941, Frayn was doing no more than submitting to the inevitable. In the attempt to understand the thoughts and intentions of people, the historical record will *always* be insufficient, because, by their very nature, thoughts and intentions are "shifting and elusive" and subject to an indeterminacy that leaves their precise identification forever uncertain. Thus, the problem in understanding what Heisenberg had in mind when he travelled to Copenhagen in 1941 is not that the historical record *in this particular case* is inconclusive and contradictory. The problem is deeper and more general than that: at bottom it is but one example of the universal uncertainty that arises in attributing to anyone *any* mental process. "The uncertainty would have existed," Frayn claims, "even if he [Heisenberg] had been as open, honest, and helpful as it is humanly possible to be." For:

> What people say about their own motives and intentions, even when they are not caught in the traps that entangled Heisenberg, is always subject to question – as subject to question as what anybody else says about them. Thoughts and intentions, even one's own – perhaps one's own most of all – remain shifting and elusive. There is not one thought or intention of any sort that can ever be precisely established. (99)

I would not dispute the suggestion that what people say about their motives and intentions is always subject to question, and I readily accept, on the basis of personal experience as a biographer, that thoughts and intentions are very often shifting and elusive. However, at the risk of stating the obvious, I do want to insist that in many, many cases the ascription of thought and intention is no more problematic, no more "uncertain," than the judgment of any other kind of fact. Of course, it is open for Frayn to say that this is part of his point: *everything* is uncertain; our judgments about the physical world are bedeviled by Heisenbergian uncertainty and our judgments about the mental world are similarly compromised by the uncertainty that forms the subject of his play. But this entirely generalized form of the claim – the idea that we cannot know *anything* with certainty – strips Frayn's claims about the nature of historical documents of any bite they might have. Consider these two statements:

1   Heisenberg traveled to Copenhagen on September 14, 1941.
2   Heisenberg went to see Bohr in order to learn what he could about the allied plans to build an atomic bomb.

I take it that Frayn considers the first of these to be a matter of historical record and to be knowable with a greater degree of certainty than the second, which, because it attributes an intention to Heisenberg, lies beyond any possible historical record, its truth or falsity forever enshrouded in uncertainty. But now, if we say that *all* judgments are uncertain, the force of this distinction is entirely lost. For this reason, I think we can dispense with the generalized form of the "Uncertainty Principle" and concentrate on the more specific claim that attributions of thought and intention are subject, intrinsically, to a degree of systematic uncertainty that other kinds of judgment are not.

In order to show that this claim is false I do not think we need to do any more than invent a possible historical record that would suffice to establish the truth of statement (2) beyond any reasonable doubt, and this, I think, can be easily done. Suppose, for example, that Bohr and Heisenberg in their later recollections of this meeting were agreed in remembering that its purpose was for Heisenberg to learn something about the allied bomb project, and that these recollections were supported by notes that each of them made shortly after the meeting, notes which tallied with each other and which recorded Heisenberg asking Bohr a stream of questions about the allied effort. Suppose also that these recollections were supported by surviving letters of Bohr and Heisenberg and by reports from friends and family members of conversations they had with the protagonists about the meeting, and that, because of the wealth of documentation revealing Heisenberg's purpose in visiting Copenhagen, no controversy about it had ever arisen. If these conditions were fulfilled, I do not think it would have occurred to anyone to doubt the truth of statement (2), and it would generally be regarded as a historical fact, established with as much certainty as it is possible to establish *any* historical fact. We would be in no more doubt about its truth than we would about the truth of statement (1).

Thus, it is clearly *not* true that no possible historical record could settle the question of Heisenberg's intention in visiting Copenhagen. What *is* true is that, as it happens, the historical record in this particular case, as no doubt in scores of others, does not, in fact, settle the issue as clearly and as unambiguously as we would like. On the basis of the surviving evidence – which includes Heisenberg's published accounts of the meeting, the scattered remarks about it found in Bohr's correspondence, and the conflicting recollections by wives, children, and friends of comments made by Bohr and Heisenberg – it is possible to believe any number of different things about Heisenberg's intentions. Among them are: (a) that he was seeking Bohr's blessing, or possibly absolution, for working on the Nazi bomb project; (b) that he was seeking to alert Bohr, and, through him, the allies, about the progress made by the Nazis; (c) that he was looking for Bohr's support for an international agreement among scientists not to work on the construction of atomic bombs; (d) that he was on an intelligence mission to find out what progress the allies had made; and (e) that he was trying to enlist Bohr to work on the Nazi project. With varying degrees of plausibility, cases could be made for each of these possibilities, and, no doubt, for many others besides.

The question of which, if any, of these possibilities is the truth may well be, on the basis of the available evidence, unresolvable, but this is not, I would claim, because of the nature of historical records, or because of the nature of intention. And, in particular, it is not because historical evidence is, by its very nature, silent on the subject of intention. Frayn himself implicitly concedes this when, in his "Postscript," he argues against Gitta Sereny's suggestion that Heisenberg was trying to enlist Bohr to work on the German bomb, a suggestion he dismisses as "the least plausible out of all the possible interpretations that have been offered" (109). His reasons for dismissing the suggestion are that: "It is completely at odds with what Weisskopf recalls Bohr as saying in 1948, and with what Bohr is on record as telling Chadwick at the time" (109). In other words: the suggestion is incompatible with the historical record.

In the play itself, Frayn offers a clever and intriguing answer to the question of Heisenberg's intention in visiting Bohr. Heisenberg, it is suggested, was not conscious himself of his real purpose. As he enters Bohr's house, he comments that "at once the clear purposes inside my head lose all definite shape" (86). His thoughts about the physics of atomic weapons are muddled, and, unconsciously, he has visited Bohr in order to clarify them. Clarification comes when Bohr asks him why he is so confident that it is going to be so reassuringly difficult to build an atom bomb using uranium-235. "Is it", he asks, "because you have done the calculation?" (89). He then forces Heisenberg to admit that, in fact, he had not done the calculation required to accurately estimate the critical mass of uranium-235, and, indeed, had not consciously realized there was a calculation to be made. Upon which Heisenberg's thoughts on the question become suddenly clear and, as Otto Frisch and Rudolf Peierls had done in 1939, he realizes that the quantity of uranium required to build a bomb is in fact very much smaller than he, in the absence of a precise calculation of the question, had supposed. At that moment, when the leader of the Nazi bomb project suddenly understands that an atomic bomb is, after all, a practical possibility, "a very different and very terrible new world begins to take shape" (89), a world in which Nazi Germany stands a realistic chance of matching the achievement of the Manhattan Project.

But, of course, all this is, even in the context of the play, hypothetical. In real life Bohr performed no such service of clarification to the muddled Heisenberg. One thing on which the conflicting accounts agree is that Bohr cut the conversation abruptly short when he realized that Heisenberg was working on the Nazi project. So, on Frayn's version, both Bohr and Heisenberg remained unaware of Heisenberg's real purpose, and, as a result, Heisenberg was relieved of the awful burden of providing Hitler with the bomb and the world was saved from a Nazi Germany armed with atomic weapons. As Bohr's wife, Margrethe, sums it up in the play: the last and greatest demand that Heisenberg made on his friendship with Bohr was "to be understood when he couldn't understand himself," and the last and greatest act of friendship that Bohr performed for Heisenberg was: "To leave him misunderstood" (89).

As a speculative, fictitious solution to the riddle presented by the historical evidence, Frayn's version of why Heisenberg visited Bohr is brilliantly neat. It has, however, the merits of a brilliant work of fiction, rather than those of a persuasive work of history. To recall Virginia Woolf's words, it "lives in a free world where the facts are verified by one person only – the artist himself," a world that is "rarer, intenser, and more wholly of a piece than the world that is largely made of authentic information supplied by other people." What it lacks is any reason to suppose that it is true.

This does not matter, or ought not to matter, in a work of fiction, and it is, I think, as Virginia Woolf insisted, important to separate fictional from non-fictional genres. Non-fiction, as Woolf says, "imposes conditions, and those conditions are that it must be based on fact. And by fact . . . we mean facts that can be verified by other people besides the artist." We must not be misled here by Frayn's argument in the "Postscript" that any attempt to identify Heisenberg's intention in visiting Copenhagen, any attempt, that is, to "get inside his head," must necessarily depart from any possible historical record. As I hope to have shown this is, in general, simply not true.

Of course, the attribution of *unconscious* intentions does raise acute questions of verification, and it may be tempting to think that what Frayn says about the need to depart from any possible historical record when trying to get inside someone's head, though in general false, may be true when it comes to identifying unconscious thoughts, motives, and intentions. Certainly it is true that, for the reasons Virginia Woolf has identified, the novelist and the playwright have a much easier time of it when dealing with unconscious mental processes than does the historian or the biographer. But I think this should be resisted as well. For I think it is indeed frequently the case that our own thinking is muddled with regard to why we say or do things, and that other people can sometimes clarify our thoughts on these questions in such a way as to make it natural to say that, though we were not conscious of it at the time, our intention in doing such-and-such has been successfully identified by someone else.

And, given that this sort of thing can happen, I do not see any reason in principle why there should not be some historical record of it happening. Take, for example, the case studies of psychoanalysts: would it not sometimes be reasonable to regard these as providing evidence for the attribution to someone of an unconscious intention?[2] So, though it is true that no historical record, in fact, supports Frayn's suggestion as to what Heisenberg's intention was in visiting Bohr, it is not true that no *possible* historical record could provide evidence for it. Let us suppose, for example, that Heisenberg later underwent psychoanalysis and was thereby brought to the self-understanding that, unconsciously, he was looking to Bohr to force him to realize that he was avoiding the question of calculating the critical mass of uranium-235, and that both Heisenberg and the psychoanalyst kept notes of these sessions that tallied with each other. Would we not then have documentary evidence that supported Frayn's speculative solution to this question?

Despite his skepticism about the determinacy of the historical record with regard to psychological states, Frayn in his "Postscript" makes some attempt to show that the solution to the question of Heisenberg's intention in visiting Copenhagen in 1941 is at least a serious contender for historical truth. After picking his way carefully and tentatively through the divergent opinions of historians and scientists about Heisenberg's work during the war, he concludes: "In the end, it seems to me, your judgment of Heisenberg comes down to what you make of his failure to attempt that fundamental calculation" (123). Does it, he asks, suggest incompetence:

> Or does the failure suggest something rather different? An unconscious reluctance to challenge the comforting and convenient assumption that the thing was not a practical possibility? Comforting and convenient, that is, if what he was trying to do was *not* to build a bomb. (123)

Both the play and the "Postscript" show which of these alternatives Frayn favors.

Whether he is right or not can only be decided, if at all (and it is, I think, perfectly possible that it cannot be decided, given the conflicting nature of the evidence) by a careful consideration of the historical record. For what it is worth, after examining the record in as much detail as I was able to, it seems to me that Frayn's way of posing the problem rests on an overly simple presentation of Heisenberg's failure to correctly calculate the critical mass of uranium-235. Frayn seems to assume that there was a more or less simple mathematical calculation that Heisenberg neglected to carry out, a sum that was waiting for him to perform and which he avoided performing. But the evidence suggests that this is not how it was. It may or may not be true that Heisenberg did not attempt to calculate the precise critical mass of 235 during the war (the evidence is radically inconclusive on this point), but what is revealed by the Farm Hall transcripts (Bernstein 2001) is that, even if Heisenberg had made the calculation during the war, he would have got it very wrong, not because his mathematics was faulty, but because he was in thrall to a fundamentally misconceived model of how an atom bomb might work. In other words, the problem lies not with Heisenberg's neglect or refusal to carry out a piece of arithmetic, but rather with his understanding of *which* piece of arithmetic needed to be carried out. The problem was not with Heisenberg's mathematics, or his (conscious or unconscious) refusal to do a bit of mathematics; it was, rather, with his physics.

Frayn argues that, with regard to calculating the critical mass of 235, Heisenberg was trapped in a circle: "he didn't try the calculation because he didn't think it was worth doing – he didn't think it was worth doing because he didn't try it" (123). For him, "the phenomenon that requires explaining is not this non-occurrence but its opposite – the escape of Frisch and Peierls from that same circle." This latter, he says, "seems almost like a random quantum event" (123). But this, it seems to me, is to misrepresent the advance made by Frisch and Peierls, and the advantage their work gave the allies over the Nazis in the race to build an atom bomb.

As I understand it, the breakthrough achieved by Frisch and Peierls was to realize that the crucial factor in estimating how much, or, more crucially still in this case, how little, uranium-235 was required to achieve an atomic explosion was not, as Heisenberg thought, the mean free path of the neutrons which initiated the chain reaction, but the speed with which the chain reaction occurred. So, the question they asked was significantly different to the question Heisenberg would have asked if he had chosen to "do the calculation." What they asked was: How much uranium-235 do you need to guarantee that 80 generations of fission could occur before the chain reaction fizzled because the neutrons were escaping to the surface before they could set up further reactions? What they realized was that, using fast neutrons, the speed of the reaction compensated for the loss of neutrons from the surface in such a way that the radius of the sphere of uranium could actually be a good deal shorter than the mean free path of the neutrons. Until he was forced by the Hiroshima bomb to radically rethink his views, Heisenberg never realized this. The formula that guided his thinking about critical mass was one taken from the random walk model of diffusion that gave central place, not to the speed of the reaction, but to the length of the mean free path, i.e., Diffusion = Mean free path multiplied by the square root of n, the average number of collisions. In the Farm Hall transcripts, using this formula and taking the mean free path to be 6 cm, he calculates the critical mass of 235 to be that of a sphere with a radius of 54 cm, which he estimates wrongly to be "about a ton" (Bernstein 2001, 129).[3] His calculation is compromised by false values, both for the mean free path (which is actually 13 cm) and for the density of uranium-235. If the correct values are inserted into his formula, the result is an even greater exaggeration of the amount of 235 needed to make a bomb.

Some attempt to understand the model of critical mass that Heisenberg had adopted during the war is, it seems to me, an indispensable part of the historian's duty to try to "get inside Heisenberg's head." And this is where Thomas Powers in his book, *Heisenberg's War*, conspicuously fails. During the war, Heisenberg produced many reports outlining his thinking about the prospects for the utilization of fission for industrial and military purposes, reports that have now been published in Heisenberg's *Gesammelte Werke*. Rather scandalously, to my mind, Powers gives no indication in his book that he is even aware that this edition of Heisenberg's collected works even exists. Certainly, he never cites it. Neither does he cite any of the reports that Heisenberg wrote during the war, with the isolated exception of an English translation of his 1942 report. In this respect, Paul Lawrence Rose's book, *Heisenberg and the Nazi Atomic Bomb Project: A Study in German Culture*, is immeasurably superior, containing as it does detailed analysis of every significant paper on bomb physics which Heisenberg ever wrote. Though I share Frayn's distaste of the high moral tone adopted by Rose throughout his book, it seems to me to represent a far more serious attempt to "get inside Heisenberg's head" than Powers's book. Interestingly, when Rose attempts to explain the muddled thinking about the physics of atomic bombs that bedeviled Heisenberg's work on the Nazi bomb project, he begins by saying: "Let us try to get inside Heisenberg's mind in 1939 and to summarise the peculiar assumptions and perspectives that shaped and constrained his understanding of the problems of a uranium bomb" (Rose 1998, 113).

Whether or not Rose is successful in his stated aim of getting inside Heisenberg's mind, I would want to insist on two things: (a) that it is an appropriate aim for a historian (or a biographer) to adopt (it is, as Frayn himself has said, the "great challenge" facing the historian); and (b) that there is no reason, in principle, why this aim should not be realized. Neither the historian nor the biographer should succumb to the thought that a person's inner life, his or her thoughts, intentions, motives, and desires, are intrinsically hidden from others. This is a tempting thought, because all too often a person's inner life *is* hidden from us. It is fruitless to deny, as some philosophers have sought to deny, that there are thoughts that we do not express and intentions that we do not reveal. But, when we sit opposite someone on a train and torture ourselves with the question of what they are thinking about, or when we find ourselves stumped, as historians and biographers *have* found themselves stumped in the case of Heisenberg's visit to Copenhagen in 1941, with the question of what a person had in mind when he or she undertook some action, we should not fall into the trap of thinking that *everything* that is inner is hidden.

It is a trap into which many, perhaps most, modern discussions of biography have fallen. Bernard Crick, the biographer of George Orwell, has written that: "We can only know actual persons by observing their behaviour in a variety of different situations and through different perspectives" (quoted in Ellis 2000, 12). In his book about biography, *Literary Lives*, David Ellis, the biographer of D. H. Lawrence, appears to endorse Crick's view that the claim of biographers to "enter into another person's mind" is no more than an "affable pretence" (12).

At the root of these confusions, it seems to me, is a faulty understanding of the distinction between "inner" and "outer," and, therefore, of the notion of getting inside another person's mind or head. There is indeed a sensible distinction to be made between a person's inner and outer lives, and it frequently happens that a person's inner life – his or her thoughts, intentions, motives, etc. – is hidden from us. But, if we find ourselves tempted to think that a person's inner life is hidden from us *because* it is inner, we should reflect on the many, many occasions on which the ascription of thoughts, intentions, and motives is as uncomplicated and as free from uncertainty as any other judgments. When I see my youngest child distressed because his older brother has stopped playing with him, am I making an "affable pretence" to understand his state of mind? When my dog sits upright next to his bowl and fixes me with a long, imploring stare, am I being over-hasty in attributing to him the intention of persuading me to feed him? Consider too that in many everyday cases the best, the most natural description of a person's appearance is via an attribution of a psychological state. How did my daughter look when she left for school this morning? She looked tired and apprehensive. How did my son look when he finally completed the computer game that he has been playing all summer? He looked pleased and triumphant. These are the ways we customarily describe the people around us. There is no gulf to be bridged between the "external appearance" and the "inner state"; rather, the easiest way of describing the former is via the latter. If I tried to describe my daughter's appearance *without* reference to her tiredness and anxiety, or my son's without reference to his pleasure and triumph, I would most likely be stumped.

"An 'inner process' stands in need of outward criteria" (Wittgenstein 1953, paragraph 580). But the extent to which we can interpret the outward criteria varies with respect to our knowledge, our experience, and our sensitivity. To "get inside

Heisenberg's head" we have to attend very closely to all the outward criteria available, and, even then, we are not guaranteed success. We can, of course, take a shortcut by inventing for ourselves a fictional character whose thoughts and intentions are within our control. But then it will not be *Heisenberg's* head we have got inside, but that of a fictional character who happens to share the same name.

Notes

1. Woolf does not provide any references, but the sentence she (mis)quotes here comes from "The Principles of Biography," Sidney Lee's Leslie Stephen Lecture, given at Cambridge in 1911. What Lee actually said was: "The aim of biography is not the moral edification which may flow from the survey of either vice or virtue; it is the truthful transmission of personality" (Lee, 1929, 43).
2. This claim is not, in any way, dependent on an acceptance of psychoanalysis as a science or even as an effective form of therapy. It is dependent only on the suggestion that, in undergoing psychoanalysis, a person might leave evidence for attributing to them this or that unconscious intention.
3. It would actually be about 13 tons (see Bernstein 2001, 130).

Bibliography

Bernstein, Jeremy (2001). *Hitler's Uranium Club: The Secret Recordings at Farm Hall* (New York: Copernicus).

Ellis, David (2000). *Literary Lives: Biography and the Search for Understanding* (Edinburgh: Edinburgh University Press).

Frayn, Michael (1998). *Copenhagen* (London: Methuen).

Lee, Sir Sidney (1929). *Elizabethan and Other Essays* (London).

Rose, Paul Lawrence (1998). *Heisenberg and the Nazi Atomic Bomb Project: A Study in German Culture* (London: University of California Press).

Wittgenstein, Ludwig (1953). *Philosophical Investigations* (Oxford: Basil Blackwell).

Woolf, Virginia (1967a). "The Art of Biography," in Leonard Woolf, ed., *Collected Essays*, vol. 4 (London: Hogarth), 221–8.

Woolf, Virginia (1967b). "The New Biography" in Leonard Woolf, ed., *Collected Essays*, vol. 4 (London: Hogarth), 229–35.

Part VII

On Literary Language

25

Wittgenstein and Literary Language

JON COOK AND RUPERT READ

Is there a way in which literature distinctively shows us something about the world or about language? For more than a generation a number of philosophers and critics have argued that this question is best answered by thinking about literature's distinctive contribution to our ethical understanding. In her account[1] of Dickens's novel, *Hard Times*, for example, Martha Nussbaum has argued that the imaginative achievement of the book is to show us the limits of either Kantian or utilitarian ethical systems. There is something about living ethically that eludes a systematic philosophy of ethics, however well-intentioned, and it is the distinctive property of literature to show a sensitivity to this aspect of ethical life in a way that is nonetheless wholly rational. And this distinctive, rational property is closely connected to literature's concern with detail, with a kind of showing of how it is that people live together and treat each other, an understanding that we need if we are to be sensitive both to the importance of ethics in our lives and to its limitations.

J. Hillis Miller, in his book *The Ethics of Reading*,[2] has argued with great subtlety for a properly ethical moment in the act of reading literature, one that can and must be distinguished from the cognitive, political, and social aspects of reading. We do not in this sense apply ethics to the reading of literature or justify it by appeal to the ethical outcomes it might have. To think this way is to misunderstand the intimate connection between a major element in literary experience and a crucial dimension of ethics, its reliance on story-telling – stories of the kind that Kant tells about promising, for example. For Hillis Miller, our response to a literary work is necessarily a responsibility to it, an action that respects what is read. This responsibility is imbued with a familiar dilemma in ethical thought: Is my respect for a text or a person a respect for them in their specific individuality or a respect for the law they represent?

For Nussbaum one important philosophical precedent is Aristotle and for Hillis Miller it is Kant. But in the works of Richard Rorty and Cora Diamond, Wittgenstein's influence is perhaps most strongly at work in their thinking about literature as a special, non-categorical, kind of ethical reasoning. What each of these writers tries to do is develop an idea of literature's educational power, and, in Nussbaum's case at least, this is connected to a defense of literature as a public good, a justification of its place in

---

A Companion to the Philosophy of Literature, First Edition. Edited by Garry L. Hagberg and Walter Jost.
© 2010 John Wiley & Sons Ltd. Published 2015 by John Wiley & Sons, Ltd.

the curricula of schools and universities. Each, in seeking to identify what it is that literature distinctively does or is, also discovers a justification for literature in its ethically educative effects. An attempt to understand literature's autonomy becomes an argument that justifies its existence. There are two distinct but entangled inflections of value at work here: one that arises from identifying what something distinctively is or does; the other from identifying its effects or outcomes.

In this paper we want to pursue another way of thinking about literature's distinctiveness, and one that owes a great deal to Wittgenstein. While acknowledging the importance of "the ethical turn," we would like to remark that *there is a danger that it ignores the "intransitivity" of literature*; that is, there is a value in literature that does not have to do with its being the instrument or the midwife of an ethical understanding. James Guetti in his book *Wittgenstein and the Grammar of Literary Experience*[3] provides a valuable starting point and example for this kind of thinking. At the centre of his argument is what he takes to be Wittgenstein's preoccupation with "the philosophical necessity of marking one difference above all: the difference between verbal expressions that are meaningful and those that are not, the difference between the active and applied use of words and the 'mere' saying of them" (3).

Before we can understand the relevance of this difference to an experience of reading (and writing?) literature, we need to briefly outline its importance in Wittgenstein's thought. As Guetti acknowledges, the difference between meaningful verbal expressions and the "mere" saying of words did not mostly interest Wittgenstein because he wanted to say something specifically about literature. On the one hand, and famously, Wittgenstein argued that language is meaningful in its use and, as Guetti points out, "a use of language for him is not a mere saying of words; it is an application of words to do something, an application that is both purposive and consequential" (3). "Pass the salt," "Yes, I am here!", "I pronounce you husband and wife": all might serve as paradigms here. This account of meaning is not far from Austin's idea of a speech act.

But Wittgenstein's concern to describe and delimit meaningful uses of language is also and endlessly engaged in thinking about how language happens in another way. He finds a source of confusion here in our tendency to believe that we are using language meaningfully when we are not, and a lot of philosophy in his view is prone to just this misunderstanding. Consider here this passage from his *On Certainty*[4] (§467), a tiny tale of a certain philosopher:

> I am sitting with a philosopher in the garden; he says again and again "I know that that's a tree," pointing to a tree that is near us. Someone else arrives and hears this and I tell him: "This fellow isn't insane. We are only doing philosophy."

One might even imagine the following poem:

> I know that that's a tree
> I *know* that that's a tree
> I <u>know</u> that that's a tree
> I ***know*** that that's a tree . . .

What then is happening in this other and ubiquitous condition of language? Guetti argues that it is best understood as a form of "grammatical display."[5] Language in this condition is *on show*; it is in some sense language about language, or language that draws attention to itself. In meaningful uses of language the words themselves are in the background. It is what we are doing with them in order to get something done that is to the fore. In "grammatical displays" we experience language in a way that we do not when it is in use.

In order to better understand the schematic difference between meaningful use and grammatical display Guetti proposes another – and we suggest, equally therapeutic – distinction:

> Some expressions, we might say, are "about" the world, and describe our experience of it, and these are "empirical." But others, in one way or another, are statements about our language, and draw our attention to its rules, and these are "grammatical." (5)

The use of inverted commas around the words "about," "empirical," and "grammatical" indicates the tentativeness and the difficulty of these provisional, "transitional"[6] distinctions. One source of the difficulty is that we confuse one kind of expression with another, believe that we are making statements about the world when we are making statements about language. (If this is a valid reading of Wittgenstein it suggests that his philosophy is part of a tradition that is concerned with the central role that illusion or error plays in our lives, a tradition that would include the work of Freud, Hegel, and Plato.)

Another is that this is only Guetti's first attempt to describe or elicit a distinction that is crucial to his whole argument about literature's distinctiveness. He goes on to invoke another important theme in Wittgenstein's philosophy – the question of what is "shown" in language – to develop his analysis of "grammatical displays." One source of this thinking comes from the *Tractatus*[7] and Wittgenstein's thinking about the logical form of propositions. It is there that he makes the famously gnomic remark that "What expresses *itself* in language we cannot express by means of language" (4.121). This fascination with something that manifests itself in language that paradoxically cannot be said by language is evident in Wittgenstein's later writings as well, for instance in some of his reflections on the "dawning of an aspect."

According to Guetti something momentous in our understanding of language is at issue here:

> every proposition, even as it says what is says – as it describes a case, provides new information, generates meaning, and so on – also displays its *form* of doing so, comprising both the "elements" and the "mode" of representation, and this grammar is the most fundamental property of our world. . . . (8)

One further therapeutic or "grammatical" distinction is important to this sketch of what Guetti wants us to understand by "grammatical displays." Language has a "sense" that is not exhausted by its capacity for meaningful application (for the first occurrence of this idea, see p. 7 of Wittgenstein's *Notebooks 1914–16*, 2nd edition). Sense is the capacity of language for meaningful application, the capacity of a proposition to be judged true or false, rather than any actual application of language in a context. To grasp these distinctions and potentials is to understand, in post-Kantian vocabulary, a fundamental property of human experience. (To grasp the point here, try the following would-be thought experiment: imagine a human experience without language. This would not be an experience of language's absence or its limitation, both of which would presuppose language's prior existence.)

Grammatical displays are not unique to literature. They are, as Guetti makes clear, a part of ordinary verbal behavior. We often, and not necessarily deliberately, put language on display by echoing an utterance, parodying it, inventing puns, or taking it out of its context of intended use. In literature, however, grammatical displays are especially evident and powerful. For Guetti our receptivity to a literary text is akin to the experience of learning a language. We are not quite sure what it means or are fascinated by the possibility that words and utterances familiar to us are being displayed in ways that suspend or challenge our understanding of their customary applications. They are compelling precisely because we become aware of a power or capacity in language that had hitherto been unknown to us. In this condition we do not understand literary utterances in the way that we do everyday meaningful applications of language. And it may be a mistake of a certain (widespread) kind (or kinds) of literary criticism that it tries to make literary language applicable in just this way, to deny its peculiar – suspended? – "sense," its grammatical display, in order to find uses for it (this is an issue we return to in the conclusion of this paper). We need, according to Guetti, to move away from the idea that the most important thing we can do with a work of literature is to interpret it, as though it was simply waiting to be translated into some master code that would show its real or hidden meaning. Literature just does not have meaning in that way; it is not context dependent in a way that many current theories of literature assume it must be. Instead:

> When we perceive language "as such," therefore, language isolated and more forceful than any use of it, we should also recognize that it cannot be turned to any immediate use. This is to say that because it is not "interpretable" in any single direction, because it seems irreplaceable and untranslatable, it cannot be used. Thus to be aware of language's presence and potential in the ways I am considering is not, at the moment, to "understand" anything in the ordinary, workable sense of that term. In Wittgenstein's conception, once again, language is "idling," though one would want to add here that when the revolutions per minute get as high as they can in some literary expressions, "idling" is no longer the right word for verbal forms whose inertia – their resistance to singular employments – is enormous but whose activity within themselves – in the integral and complex play of their exposed possibilities – is very quick indeed. (12–13)

One may want to argue by this point that all Guetti is doing is invoking the authority of Wittgenstein to restate a very familiar understanding of what happens when we read literature. One common assumption about literary language is that it works more personally and associatively than language in everyday use. We can discover emotional resonances, images, or special associations when we read them in a literary text. We dream with the language rather than put it to practical use. These lead us to think that literary language has a special "atmosphere," one that may be created, for example, by the sounds and rhythms of language or its capacity to invoke pictures in our mind:

> In Xanadu did Kubla Khan
> A stately pleasure dome decree.

These first two lines of Coleridge's famous poem, "Kubla Khan," seem to work in just this way, evoking images of something at once strange and powerful, a building created by decree, dedicated to pleasure, in a language that displays all sorts of sound effects: through internal rhyme, alliteration, modulations in vowel sounds, the pulsing four-beat rhythm in each line, and the way that all these things, in their turn, create a sense of an enraptured and compelled voice.

Guetti might well agree that there is a connection between his argument and this common assumption about the associative power of language in literature; that, indeed, it might be timely to restate the fact that the common assumption has quite a lot going for it. But his agreement only goes so far:

> It is true that in "grammatical exhibitions" the normal *accompaniments* of meaning – certain feelings for certain words, for example – are foregrounded with the words they are attached to. And it is equally true that our perceptions in these cases involve imaginative "experiences" that seem deeply personal, but these are not necessarily secret or hidden, nor are they restricted or determined by one's individual history. For it is not so much what particular associations we have for the words of a text that matters – since one could never insist on the exclusive relevance of his associations as opposed to someone else's – but that the imaginative act of *having* associations is built in, or evidently called for, by "grammatical displays." (13)

So, to return to the two lines of Kubla Khan, there is nothing especially private or hidden about their effect. Rather something that is in the background of language when it is in ordinary use – namely the capacity of language to provoke associations – comes to the fore in literature. These associations may be "personal," evoking particular memories or scenes, but it does not follow that literature works in ways that are irredeemably private and hidden, just to do with what it "means" to me without the possibility of further discussion. If that was true, the experience of finding that another reader's experience of a text enhances my own would be impossible. Nor is it simply the case, as Guetti makes clear in his discussion of metaphor, that the associative power of language is dependent on its evocation of memories. One effect of metaphor, an effect not to be mistaken for its meaning (as if there was some hidden kernel of meaning lurking within it), is to mark what Shelley called the "before unapprehended relations of things." Metaphor brings words not ordinarily used together into grammatical and syntactical connection. Metaphor has a predicative quality. It does not simply remind us of resemblances that already exist but may have been forgotten. It creates new resemblances, but it creates them in a distinctive grammatical and logical space where the rules governing the connections between disparate terms do not ordinarily apply.

We are not going to understand an extravagant metaphor if we insist on making it work in the way that language in ordinary use works.

Guetti invites us to reconsider our "pre-critical" experiences of literature – that there is something personal and associative about it and so on – not as something to do with what is going on in the supposedly private space of a mind, but as an impersonal matter of language, its capacity for grammatical display. But his attempt to describe literary experience in terms of grammatical display may be familiar to some readers not because it builds on a pre-critical experience of literature but for the ways it echoes arguments put forward by some twentieth-century theorists who were not followers of Wittgenstein. Two figures, Mukarowski and Jakobson, both associated with the Prague School of Linguistics, are relevant here. Both were concerned to identify the features of poetic language. They raise the important question of whether Guetti, in following Wittgenstein, is telling us something more about the nature of poetic or literary language, and its distinctive mode of action, than they do. Telling us something valuable, specific, new.

In his influential essay, "Standard Language and Poetic Language,"[8] first published in 1932, Mukarowski proposes that the crucial criterion of poetic language is its deviation from some more or less pronounced version or versions of a standard language. He extends this notion of the standard to include what is canonically understood to be appropriately poetic language. The proportions and kinds of deviation in poetic language are many and various. They may be grammatical, syntactic, semantic, typographic, or all of these together. Poetic language is not simply made up of this "deviation" but emerges as a "foreground" of deviation against some background of standard use. Mukarowski goes on to argue that when this foregrounding is particularly pronounced something happens to language's communicative capacity:

> In poetic language, foregrounding achieves maximum intensity to the extent of pushing communication into the background as the objective of expression and of being used for its own sake; it is not used in the service of communication, but in order to place in the foreground the act of expression, the act of speech itself.

Mukarowski seems to be addressing the same phenomena as Guetti: replace Guetti's "grammatical displays" with the "act of speech itself" and his "language in use" with Mukarowski's "communication" and it appears that both are proposing very similar understandings of the poetic.

Similarly, Jakobson, in his 1960 paper "Linguistics and Poetics: Concluding Statement"[9] attempts to answer the question of what it is that makes a verbal message into a work of art by identifying a poetic dimension in all kinds of communication. This dimension is one amongst a number – according to Jakobson the most common form of communication is when the context or frame of reference is dominant, when that is, people are attending to what the message is saying about the world – and, in every case, linguistic form is affected by whichever of the dimensions is dominant. In the case of the poetic, the "set" or "orientation" is towards the "form of the message for its own sake" and this takes priority over what it might be telling us about the world, or the state of the speaker, although those and other elements will be in play. There is not a categorical distinction to be drawn between poetic and non-poetic language. Rather there is a series of planes of emergence in which different properties and capacities of language will become evident.

Like Mukarowski and Guetti, Jakobson argues that when the poetic is dominant ordinary meaning is put into abeyance. The dominance of the poetic function promotes the "palpability of the sign" – its grammatical, syntactic, and material form – and in doing this it "deepens the fundamental dichotomy of signs and objects" (335). When the referential function of language is dominant, the dichotomy between signs and objects tends to fall into abeyance. We are not so intensely aware that words might have a life other than the one they have when they refer to a world.

Jakobson, like Guetti, sees a continuum between literary and everyday uses of language, a continuum discriminated by what in any particular utterance is the dominant function. He is like Guetti too in his sense that the poetic suspends the ordinary, taken-for-granted rules for meaning. And he sees all the elements of language as taking on a new kind of life when the poetic predominates. The poetic function builds equivalences between words that are unlike in their ordinary meanings; it cuts across the sequential flow of language by linking together phrases and other syntactic, and in some cases typographic, units of language that are ordinarily held apart. In doing this a new kind of "sense" is created by the poetic. It makes "meanings" that cannot be found by looking up the dictionary definitions of words or by relying on their customary usages.

The ideas exemplified by Mukarowski and Jakobson are not apparently part of Guetti's intellectual world. At least he makes no explicit reference to them in *Wittgenstein and the Grammar of Literary Experience*. Yet there are clearly some elements in common. All agree that a particular aspect of "language in general" comes into especial prominence in works of literature. All agree that this happens when the ordinary or standard conditions of language give way to something else, a heightened awareness of linguistic form or potential. And all agree that in the process something happens to our standard expectations of meaning.

The value of the comparison for our purposes is this: Are there important differences amongst the similarities that might illuminate the special value of thinking about literature in a Wittgensteinian way as distinct from the Saussurian and sociolinguistic perspectives that inform the arguments of Mukarowski and Jakobson? An answer to that question can only be sketched here. Guetti offers a fuller account of the experience of the act of reading poetry or fiction than either Mukarowski or Jakobson. He includes the associative, affective, and subjective aspects of reading literature without sacrificing the conceptual complications of understanding language in the continuum of its everyday uses and its literary manifestations. In short we might argue that he takes us some way towards something that is singularly lacking in contemporary critical theory, *a phenomenology of the experience of reading literature*. Jakobson's and Mukarowski's rigorous analyses of the conditions of poetic language nonetheless constantly risk an impoverished account of what it is like to read or encounter it.

We now want to further explore this idea by developing an example. That is, following Guetti's lead, we want to (try to) produce a suitably aesthetic and sensitive reading of a poem by Wallace Stevens, a contemporary of Wittgenstein – and one whose work we think is thrown into sharp relief against a background of Wittgenstein's philosophy. Not: Stevens as expressing the content of Wittgenstein's philosophy. But rather: Stevens's poetry more easily and more fully appreciated, when one understands Wittgenstein's philosophical method or when one understands the implications of Wittgenstein's "account" of meaning for our experience of reading literature. For: What we have urged is a Wittgensteinian take on literary language is sharply supported by some of the finest of Stevens's writing.

Stevens published "Thirteen Ways of Looking at a Blackbird" in his 1923 collection *Harmonium*. In its entirety the poem appears to be what its title indicates. It records or reports or proposes 13 ways of looking at a blackbird. Each section of the poem contains one of these 13 ways, often in haiku-like three- or four- or five-line stanzas. In each section there is a perhaps deceptive simplicity of utterance, as though nothing in the poem required further elaboration or commentary by the poet. Each stanza contains the word "blackbird" or "blackbirds," and there are other less insistent repetitions: the signs of winter for example in stanzas 1, 6, and 13; and these, in turn, interweave with direct or indirect allusions to other seasons, autumn in stanza 3, and spring or summer in stanza 10.

In ways that playfully allude to a Romantic tradition of nature poetry (a tradition that would include poems like Keats's "Ode to a Nightingale" or Hardy's "The Darkling Thrush") Stevens's poem seems to ask us to see the blackbird as a creature both of nature and of art. In the first stanza, for example, the bird is "seen" in a winter landscape:

> Among twenty snowy mountains,
> The only moving thing
> Was the eye of a blackbird.

The fifth stanza starts to "place" it in the context of a speculation about art:

> I do not know which to prefer,
> The beauty of inflections
> Or the beauty of innuendos,
> The blackbird whistling
> Or just after.

The eighth and tenth stanzas continue this line of speculation or assertion in a way that seems to put the blackbird in some assertively resistant relation to conventional ideas about poetry. The blackbird is, so to speak, not just a bird in Stevens's poem. It is (also) a challenge, or, more precisely, the echo of a polemical mood that would set the bird in the poem, its word, as a qualification of "noble accents / And lucid, inescapable rhythms" or in opposition to the "bawds of euphony." In its simplicity or bare presence the blackbird disrupts the attractions of a certain kind of melodious or "euphonic" poetry that Stevens knew only too well how to write.

Yet these thoughts may still be awry. Writing of the poem's first stanza

> Among twenty snowy mountains,
> The only moving thing,
> Was the eye of the blackbird

Guetti remarks:

> [T]here may be no difficulty in visualizing the parts of this sentence, the "snowy mountains," even if not exactly twenty of them, and a small, bright eye. But there would seem to be a problem in organizing them into an entire image. . . .
>
> The simplest problem here is one of visual scale and perspective. What single "picture" could be of a blackbird's eye? One might think of a "surreal" superimposition of pictures – some extravagant sort of double exposure – but that would appear to generate more possibilities and so more problems. Is that eye in a head, and by virtue of what contrast of light and colour would it then be visible? . . . But after all, it is difficult to estimate how far this shuffling of representational techniques would go, given the problem created by the pivotal line, by the fact that the blackbird's eye is "moving."

Guetti finds the playful challenge of the poem in the way that it invites us to "visualize" through words and then discover the impossibility of doing so. As such his commentary on Stevens's poem is part of a larger argument in his work about the need to challenge the dominance of the visual in our ways of thinking about imagination, and to recover or discover the resources and pleasures of an "auditory imagination." Its motto about reading literature might almost be "for those who have ears to hear let them hear," and Guetti's worry about the teaching of literature is that so much of it inhibits our capacity to listen imaginatively to the subtle "voicings" that arise in powerful literary works.

A central question raised by this stanza, then, and we believe it to be raised in one way or another by every single stanza in the remainder of the poem too, is simply this: In what sense exactly (if any, indeed) can we justly regard this as a description of a way of *looking* at a blackbird?

For sure, there are other "ways of looking" than the ways involved in and with visual perception. And so, for sure, part of what is in process in Stevens's poem is the relatively straightforward task of "reminding" readers of the many meanings, which we can crudely refer to as variously "literal" and "non-literal," of "looking." *But* what fascinates, what grips about this first stanza of the poem – and several at least of the other stanzas have the same feature – is that it *looks* so like it involves a visual looking. One so naturally *experiences* this little haiku-like piece of literature as generating an image. But, just as Guetti says, when one presses on this experience, when one "looks" closer, the "image" starts to collapse on one; or rather: either quite to disintegrate, or to become an image of such a strange sort that it is not clear one can easily succeed in imagining it, let alone draw or paint it (even if one were a very good artist).

Borrowing from Cora Diamond,[10] we should like to say that some of the ways of looking that appear to be natural to the implied reader of "Thirteen Ways," one only imagines that one can succeed in realizing: for instance, one merely imagines that one can successfully *image* or *visualize* this first stanza. And *what* one imagines that one can thus image is itself nonsensical: "it" cannot be put into prose without falsifying it, and its poetical presentation remains forever strange to one. One just doesn't know what it would be – it doesn't as yet *mean* anything – to know that and to see (that) only a blackbird's eye (is) moving, among twenty snowy mountains. It is, we are arguing, Stevens's genius to allow one to learn from gradually figuring this out for oneself, when at first the stanza seems so overwhelmingly to yield one something that can be seen, a way literally of looking at a blackbird.[11]

One imagines that one can visualize *this*, what the poem "describes." What is it to imagine this, at least as a way of looking at *a* blackbird, without imaging it? The poem lets one learn gradually that there may be a limit to one's imagination and it is at that limit that it can most vividly come into play. Reading the poem with understanding is giving up the illusion that it is, in the ordinary sense, to be understood *at all*. This first stanza, as more obviously others, such as the second,

> I was of three minds
> Like a tree
> In which there are three blackbirds

and the fourth,

> A man and a woman
> Are one.
> A man and a woman and a blackbird
> Are one

undermine one's sense, as one "works" through them, that there is, first impressions notwithstanding, anything to be understood here.

Because, for instance: In what sense "Like"?! One is supposed to be able to make any simile work. But one hasn't the foggiest how to put stanza 2 to work. The ease and the confidence of the utterance lead us to expect something obvious. Instead we discover a strange bafflement. Similarly in the fourth stanza: "A man and a woman are one" has a sanctioned, proverbial quality to it but not so "A man and a woman and a blackbird are one." And now one perhaps looks back at "A man and a woman are one," and wonders whether one understood any one thing by it, clearly, after all.[12]

Part of the effect of this poem, then, is that when what one most appears to have on one's hands is something visual, visualizable, something like an image, something that can be – or is a product of being – looked at in the most straightforward of ways, then in just those cases one should beware, or *look out* (to coin a phrase). *In this most natural way of reading the expression "looking," it is not clear that there are any such lookings at blackbirds at all, present(-ed) in Stevens's poem.*[13]

And this is so, we would submit, even in the wonderfully still and apparently least strange of the poem's stanzas, the last:

> It was evening all afternoon.
> It was snowing
> And it was going to snow.
> The blackbird sat
> In the cedar-limbs.

There is much to discuss here, much to say for instance about the peculiar apparent duration of the image apparently created here.[14] We will restrict ourselves in the present context only to the following points: Firstly, the first two lines appear to set a scene, straightforwardly. They appear to tell you simply and vividly what was happening (viz., it was snowing a lot). But the repetition of that deeply simple phrase, "It was," is deceptive. The first "It was" characterizes how things were over a long period of time ("all afternoon"), whereas the second is actually apposite only to moments: "It was snowing" is past continuous, and applies to what was happening at some given moment in the past. One can tell this by "And it was going to snow": that is only so when it carries on snowing. So, unless it snows forever, this can only be so at certain specified times. Thus the first line establishes a time – *the whole* afternoon. The second (re-)establishes a/the time – *some particular point in* the afternoon. And now one seems bound to ask: *Did the blackbird sit in the cedar limbs for the whole afternoon? Or just at some point in it?*

But perhaps to say this is to push too hard on the language of the thirteenth "way." Perhaps we are overanalyzing the poem. There's no great harm in doing that, so long as one is aware that one is or may be doing it. But let us try going more gently, to be surer of staying in touch with Stevens's method. We can then say at least the following.

The stanza works by incrementally creating a winter scene. Once we grasp this, the paradoxical first line can be understood as a description of the kind of twilight that comes when snow falls from grey skies. Reading the first two lines together we can discern how the second not only adds to the first but also explains its semantic strangeness. By implication we read the lines as "It was evening all afternoon and it was snowing all afternoon, and because of the second of these happenings the afternoon took on some of the characteristics of evening." But again it is important to stress here that description is not just of what can be visualized. The sense of time passing, of afternoon moving to evening, of what has happened in the past and of what will happen in the future are gently and teasingly disturbed. "It was snowing," as we have noted is in the past continuous tense. What happened in the past happened not just once but continually, and this is what happens when snow falls, when, so to speak, it really falls, and bits of snow just keep on falling. There is a lulled sense of something that has happened and will continue to happen – hence the line "And it was going to snow." Then the blackbird makes its entrance on the scene – on this occasion as on so many others as a static, not a moving, element. If there is something white falling in the midst of twilight, now we have something black in the midst of or on the periphery of something white. The stanza is poised on the edge of the figural and the abstract, of something that one might actually experience on an afternoon in winter and something that could only take place in a work of art, where the imagination freely plays with color relations, imaginary objects, and times, no longer subject to the constraints of what really could have happened or been seen. There is a drawing together of nature and art and, simultaneously, a tension between them. And it is just in its occupation of this space between something deeply familiar and something deeply strange that the power of the stanza resides.

Consider too the delicately conceptual eighth stanza, again so seemingly ordinary and so subtly strange at the very same time:

> When the blackbird flew out of sight
> It marked the edge
> Of one of many circles.

The nearest one can get to imagining this is to imagine something like a (series of) diagram(s), with the blackbird included on it (them) at its (their) limit. But so near and yet so very far: for the blackbird, at the moment at which the poem focuses, is *ex hypothesi* not visible/representable. There is no such thing as seeing the horizon of what one can see, neither at the "far" edge of that horizon, "beyond" which is the unseen or invisible, nor at the "near" edge of that horizon, "beyond" (or "before") which is the seer. The horizon of vision is not like the limit of, say, a football field. It makes *no sense* to look across the former, while the latter is *defined* by its visibility and measurability.

The crucial guiding words for how to read Wittgenstein, and how to understand his talk of "limits" come from the preface to the *Tractatus*:

> [T]he aim of the book is to draw a limit to thought, or rather – not to thought, but to the expression of thoughts: for in order to draw a limit to thought, we should have to be able to think both sides of this limit (we should therefore have to be able to think what cannot be thought).

As Diamond remarks, of this, "He then draws the conclusion from those remarks that it will therefore only be in language that the limit can be drawn, and what lies on the other side of the limit will simply be nonsense."[15] The circle that Stevens's blackbird marks is precisely a circle that cannot be drawn; or, better, as the blackbird draws it, it does so in a way that is not visible. What is "blackbirdy" outside the circle is for the observer nothing. It *makes no sense* for one to hope to see this invisible. Stevens "teaches" here a "lesson" that Wittgenstein too teaches. One seems to see the blackbird flying out of sight, in one's mind's eye. But in this stanza, as in the others, it would be a complete mistake to try to force what one seems to see into being a real seeing; it would be a deep conceptual mistake indefinitely to try to will oneself to suspend the disbelief that one will still probably feel in the middle of this. For belief here, acquiescence in the image – the would-be stable imagination – seemingly generated, in this poem, leads one in just the wrong direction. The *point* of the thing is to *learn* from the *collapse* of many of one's efforts to obey the poet's implied instruction, "Try out these 13 'ways of looking' at a 'blackbird' for yourself."[16] In the case of the eighth stanza, the absurdity of the effort to capture in vision *or, by analogy, in thought of any kind* the limit, the "far" horizon, is (we would submit) entirely of a piece with the method of Wittgenstein's work. For this "blackbird" at the end – at the edge, at the limit – of the mind, is the same delicate deliberate nonsense as the limit drawn by Wittgenstein in the *Tractatus*.

It might be countered, against our argument/interpretation thus far, that we are overplaying the limits of image-ability, and neglecting the power of imagination. Isn't there more to the imagination than what can be visually imag(in)ed? And of course there is: for instance, a million-sided figure can be imagined, but not imaged in one's mind's eye (at any rate, not in a way that efficaciously distinguishes it from a million-and-one-sided figure). But the important point is that much of what we are "asked" to imagine by Stevens is *not* something sensical that simply cannot be imaged in one's mind's eye. As we have intimated and illustrated: the limits of image-ability are a clue to the more fundamental point: the limits of imaginability, full-stop. The crucial degree to which we have not in truth been asked to imagine anything which there can be any such thing as imagining, when we are asked to imagine more than one thing at once, and the things in question are non-cotenable. The crucial degree to which there is *more* that can be "said"/written than can be imagined: though *not* more that can actually be intelligibly meant. Thus: Stevens opens up what "looking" can mean, and undermines the prejudice that looking need be visual – but *not* in service of a merely reactive counter-prejudice (the kind of prejudice that some post-modernists or deconstructionists[17] might assume or enjoy, for instance), that (say) visual looking is bad or oppressive, or that "looking" can mean just anything one pleases. Rather, one has to be reminded of and to figure out, simultaneously, what "looking" actually does mean and can mean for one. One can see that roughly *this* might usefully be said to be the "teaching" – or the "upshot" – of the poem, by considering the following question, a question we suggest is more or less implicit in the cumulative action of the poem as one reads to its end and then re-reads: Is *any and every* sentence with the word "blackbird" featuring in it a vehicle for "looking" at a blackbird, in some suitably loose sense of the word "looking"? Surely not: for instance, a mere mention of the word "blackbird," as in the sentence, "Pronounce the word 'blackbird' " hardly seems well described as involving or implicating a way of looking at a blackbird. *Likewise*, nonsense-sentences or ungrammatical sentences involving the word "blackbird." And it is in *approximately* these ways – though of course more subtly; that is how the poetry gets to work its magic – that we claim the word "blackbird" – and *thus* the word "looking" and its cognates – typically appears, in this poem. That is, the word is "used" very roughly in the way words are "used" in nonsense-poetry, but with a more enduring *appearance* of sense. You can of course (if you wish) insist that all the same such occurrences or mentions *are* <u>uses</u> of the word "blackbird" (and "looking"); fine... only notice the qualitative difference between such uses and other things we call "uses."

We would suggest that an important aspect of the poem is obscured if one fails to see that the word "blackbird" in Stevens's poem tends to veer for instance toward mention more than toward use, and that the language of the poem as a whole is *"idling"*

479

as a car engine idles: it is not working language, it is not going anywhere (except perhaps on holiday). It shows language and the life that goes with it mainly *by contrast*, via absurdities. It does not show nor even necessarily point toward any blackbird, real *or imaginary*.

If Stevens's poem tests the limits of what it means to imagine something, why do we want to describe this testing as "playful," and how might this playfulness connect to what the poem can be heard as teaching us? Here we need to pay renewed attention to the auditory qualities of the poem, and the way in which it appears as, or sounds like, a set of "sayings," "sayings" that have an aphoristic quality, as though they might be passing on a wisdom about blackbirds, about the world and its weather, about poetry and its sounds. It is an effect of the poem as a grammatical display that each of these sayings has a formal completeness. Each stanza is a shapely sentence, "grammatically correct" in a conventional sense. Each sounds as though its imagined and imaginary speaker knows what he is saying, that he has something to impart.

This aspect of the poem can be illuminated by Guetti's discussion of metaphor, alluded to earlier. One response to the poem is to say that it consists of a series of metaphors, that its title might as well be "Thirteen Metaphors about a Blackbird," or "Blackbird in Thirteen Metaphors," as "Thirteen Ways of Looking at a Blackbird." One characteristic of metaphor, the juxtaposition and implied connection of apparently unrelated things, pervades the poem: between "three minds" and three blackbirds in a tree, for example, or, in stanza 12, between a seemingly banal statement of fact "The river is moving" and the implication that because of this "The blackbird must be flying." In the first of these two examples, one effect of "I was in three minds" is at once to echo and transform a familiar phrase about uncertainty, "I was in two minds," thus creating the impression that the language of the poem is somehow very close to – and yet of course, humorously distant from – ordinary speech. In the second example we see how Stevens has invoked and subtly displaced the haiku-like form of the poem. Where a haiku typically juxtaposes two perceptions and allows them to resonate, Stevens adds a language of cognition: not "The river is moving / The blackbird is flying," but "The river is moving / The blackbird *must* be flying," as though a language of perceptual description is (endlessly?) mutating into a language of certain knowledge. These echoes of familiar language combined with the confident certainty with which each of its stanzas is "said" repeatedly creates the effect of being in the presence of someone who knows what he is talking about even if we are not at all certain of what it is he is saying! We begin to believe what he is saying because he so clearly believes – is able to believe it – himself.

This is at once to acknowledge the force of voice in this poem (not Stevens's voice, but the rhetorical voice created by the poem's language) and to see how it provokes a kind of subdued comedy out of our capacity to believe the unbelievable. But this, in turn, is part of the poem's capacity for metaphor. And, as Ricoeur and Guetti following him have shown, this capacity for metaphor consists in what Ricoeur has called "predicative assimilation." What Ricoeur means by this phrase is clarified by his description of what a metaphor does:

> It is as though a change of distance between meanings occurred within a logical space. The *new* pertinence or congruence proper to a meaningful metaphoric utterance proceeds from the kind of semantic proximity which suddenly obtains between terms in spite of their distance. Things or ideas which were remote now appear as close. (Ricoeur, 1978, 147)

Ricoeur's claim is that what a metaphor brings together in the logical and grammatical form of a predication is also brought together at a semantic level, at the level of meaning. There is a danger in this description that we might think that metaphors contain hidden meanings. Rather, as Guetti himself proposes, the "logical space" is also the space of what he calls grammatical displays, and in this space we breathe a heady air, created out of the freewheeling "associativeness of words," released from their obligations to meaningful use.

Our attempt here is to say something helpful, using Guetti and his reading of Wittgenstein, about what Stevens's poem does, not to interpret what it means. Of course what it does has endlessly to do with the capacity of words to be meaningful; but it also has to do with their capacity to be meaningless or nonsensical, and in ways that are moving, effective, and funny, as though we are being invited by Stevens, in this and many other of his poems, to acknowledge that language's capacity for meaningful use is not its only value. "Thirteen Ways of Looking at a Blackbird" displays what strange and enticing inventions language can make – "He rode over Connecticut / In a glass coach," for example – and how these inventions can live in a world of imagination, or of language "out of use." Yet at the same time the poem tests the limits of these inventions. The poem acts out two of Stevens's preoccupations. One is with our ability to participate in imaginative invention, a difficult task given the pressures of skepticism or the requirement that what is imagined must be readily translated into what is conventionally meaningful. In his essay, "The Noble Rider and the Sound of Words," he described the poet's work in this way:

> What is his function? Certainly it is not to lead people out of the confusion in which they find themselves. Nor is it, I think to comfort them while they follow their readers to and fro. I think that his function is to make his imagination theirs and that he fulfils himself only as he sees his imagination become the light in the minds of others. (Stevens, 2004, 264)

For Stevens this imaginative making was something more than just getting readers to accept whatever the poet, or the language working through him, happened to invent. It was also a matter of an endless and subtle adjustment:

> It is not only that the imagination adheres to reality, but, also, that reality adheres to the imagination and that the interdependence is essential. (266)

These adherences cannot be predicted in advance. As Stevens knew, reality and imagination are repeatedly falling apart, to the impoverishment of both. A poem such as "Thirteen Ways of Looking at a Blackbird" is a series of verbal experiments in the ways in which the imaginative and the real separate and coalesce.

By this point in our essay, a gradual shift has occurred. The cusp of a new way of looking at – or using – Stevens is perhaps at hand. There have been a number of moments, in the above discussion of "Thirteen Ways," wherein it appeared less that we, (Wittgensteinian) philosophers/critics of literature, were seeking to render Stevens clearly by means of using Wittgenstein as a tool with which to place or illumine his words; and more: that we were actually finding the kind of therapeutic maneuvers that are Wittgenstein's teaching *in* Stevens's poetry. And that *is* a key point of the present paper: to see what one can learn by trying to read Stevens *as* "a Wittgensteinian"; as *making*, through his "strong-grammared" poetry, a set of moves that invite the reader to learn almost exactly the kinds of thing about themselves and about their tendencies to mire themselves in misunderstanding and delusion that Wittgenstein invites his reader to learn, through his therapeutic writing, his philosophy of delusion *and its overcomings*.[18] But now something *else* interesting starts to happen, or is or has been happening, beyond (even) seeing Stevens as a roughly "Wittgensteinian philosopher" doing his own literary philosophizing. We start to see how Stevens's poetry *might be able to help us get further with (understanding) Wittgenstein* (and with practicing philosophy, after Wittgenstein) than we normally manage.

Take Wittgenstein's rather famous (or infamous) "woodsellers," who have been ably dissected in recent years by "New Wittgensteinians" such as Cavell, Conant, Crary, and Cerbone.[19] These characters, the "woodsellers," seem to have a different logic, for they pay more for wood that is spread out, and less when the wood is piled up. Indeed, they say there IS more wood, when it is spread out, even when they witness the spreading. But what Cavell et al. have submitted is that Wittgenstein wants us all to see for ourselves that we will, if we keep on failing to establish a context of significant use for the woodsellers' talk, if we ongoingly fail to understand what game is being played here, eventually cease to regard a scenario as having successfully been sketched here at all. We may, for instance, withdraw the claim that the woodsellers are really doing the same thing as what we would call "counting" (or "pricing"). We will not be content to say that they have an arithmetic, only a different arithmetic, if that leaves us unhappily hovering between the claim that they have something which recognizably is an arithmetic, with a comprehensible logic to it, only one slightly different from our own, and the claim that they do not have what we would call an arithmetic or a logic at all.

In other words, "New Wittgensteinians," truly therapeutic readers of the philosopher, urge that Wittgenstein has deceived one into the truth here. He has made one confront an unclarity in the ways one wants to use words such as "arithmetic" or "logic," through deceiving one into thinking that a coherent scenario has definitely been sketched, in sketching the woodsellers.

The use of the term "the woodsellers" is arguably crucial to the deceit one tends to impose on oneself here: this term instantly makes it seem as though a group or "tribe" *has* been indexed. So "they" *must* be describable, one thinks. But perhaps this "they" *in the form that we want to describe them* (e.g. as *buying* and *selling*) are nothing but a fiction. Or rather: a complete fantasy, an illusion of sense, *a fiction of a fiction*. (And isn't that a nice description of what poems like "Thirteen Ways" ultimately mostly give us? A – supreme – *fiction* of a fiction. Once one has figured out the kind of thing that "Thirteen

Ways" really is, one is, we submit, better placed to see clearly the true nature of Wittgenstein's famous so-called "imaginary" scenarios.)

Our *desires* with regard to our words must and do give out: the mistake is to imagine that one can succeed in imagining successfully the "scenarios" depicted here. Or again: one *merely* imagines that one can imagine them. Or again: one may well withdraw the use of the word "scenario" or even of "description," on reflection.

So we have now outlined a suggestion: that Stevens encourages one to form a kind of belief about what one can succeed in imagining, and then facilitates one's learning from the collapse of that belief under its own weight. We believe that Stevens exposes more clearly to view actual life, everyday language and life, through exposing to us, marvelously, language as it goes on holiday. Stevens *discloses* the sensical *through* "*violating*" *the limits of language*.[20] But one needn't think he thereby succeeds in saying the unsayable, nor need one think any other such *non sequiturs*. Rather, what lies on the other side of the limit is simply nonsense. Stevens makes that nonsense fun, and a thing of beauty, as thus he acts as midwife to one's coming to find and feel where the "limit" is. He allows one to bump one's head up against it with pleasure, and with a growing self-awareness.

The fun[21] and the glorious absurdity or almost schizoid bizarreness in Wittgenstein's discussion is less often appreciated. This again inclines us to think that Stevens cannot only do Wittgensteinian philosophy, but also can help to render perspicuous – "visible" – what Wittgensteinian philosophy *is*. Compare the opening section of the *Investigations*:

> [T]hink of the following use of language: I send someone shopping. I give him a slip marked "five red apples." He takes the slip to the shopkeeper, who opens the drawer marked "apples"; then he looks up the word "red" in a table and finds a colour sample opposite it; then he says the series of cardinal numbers – I assume he knows them by heart – up to the word "five" and for each number he takes an apple of the same colour as the sample out of the drawer. – It is in this and similar ways that one operates with words.

Oh yeah? Wittgenstein's blunt apparent insistence at the end here has silenced most Wittgensteinians (though not Cavell, and his "school," including Stephen Mulhall and David Stern, on whose work we loosely draw here). Most "Wittgensteinians" tend to meekly swallow that this is how language is: that this is a shop in which a practical – paradigmatic – use of language is shown one. But surely a more *reasonable* response, on re-reading, is to be struck by the unreasonable character of Wittgenstein's "It is in this and similar ways . . ." and in particular by the frankly utterly bizarre character of this "grocer's shop." A moment's reflection probably suffices to show that none of us in our adult lives has seen or heard of a shop where anything remotely like this happens (A color chart in a grocers?!). This is a *parody* of a shop. One should instantly suspect that it yields a parody of how language works. And this is what we find. Language as it is embodied in this "example" is *not* a paradigm of how Wittgenstein thinks language actually works; it is a parody of how language works according to the very picture of language that Wittgenstein is wishing to undermine in us. When one overcomes that picture *and* the parody (not: *embraces* the latter, as for instance some behaviorism does), then one can start to see language aright. Riffing on T. S. Eliot a little: one can return to the beginning of all one's philosophical journeyings, and know the place – know one's way about – for the first time.

There is then a "hidden" strangeness in the founding example/scenario of Wittgenstein's masterpiece. The same is true of his other most famous such scenarios: crucially, of course, in his "builders" (in §2ff. of the *Investigations*: these builders have a "language" that consists of just four words) and in the "woodsellers" (mentioned above, who pay more for wood when it is spread out on the ground than when it is piled up), among others. One learns about the human "form of life," one gets reminded of features of our lives with language so obvious that usually we cannot *see* them, cannot bring them into focus, not just, and indeed not best, through the plain focus on ordinary, everyday, practical examples that is the staple of "Ordinary Language Philosophy," but through the collapse of "imaginary" fantasy "examples," *which at first we were much attracted/tempted by*. Wittgenstein "exposes" or discloses ordinary language and life most tellingly when he exposes language ("language") as it is when he sends it covertly on holiday, as it passes beyond this horizon that is not visible, speakable, or thinkable, the ultimate limit that limits us from nothing that we actually want, and beyond which there are *only* what Stevens calls "The Creations of Sound"; creations which try their best to resist our misfiring attempts to domesticate them; creations which delight in their self-deconstruction.

(One could then imagine a series of short stories:[22] "Thirteen Ways of Looking at Language," the first "way" of which would be Wittgenstein's "grocer's shop"; and then second his "builders" yard"; and so forth . . . and the point of the series would be: to get one to worry about whether one was actually being presented here with anything that was recognizably and truly: *language*. But actually, one doesn't have to imagine that series: Wittgenstein did actually write it. It's called *Philosophical Investigations* (and *Remarks on the Foundations of Mathematics*).)

Stevens invites one to *look* "at a blackbird" in the ways he proposes; and it seems so much as if visual looking is possible here! And then one gradually comes to see that it is mostly not, and that in fact one may even want to give up the claim that *any* kind of looking is. Wittgenstein invites one to look at the scenarios, the activities he proposes (the "grocer's shop," the "builders," the "naming of one's *private* sensations," the "woodsellers," etc.) as if they were real, as if they were languages that we could speak, or at least understand, and then we gradually come to see that they are not – to be precise, that they are not *what one wanted them to be*. And that is philosophy, after Wittgenstein: returning to your concepts, in and with which you live, and knowing them for the first time. But the best route to where you are right now lies for Wittgenstein, as for Stevens, *via* the nothing that is the delusions of sense one entertains when one appears to be saying or "showing" what allegedly lies beyond the limits of thought or language.

Many have perhaps missed many of the willing – willed – absurdities of Stevens's texts. But how many more, including the very philosophers and scholars who have claimed to be Wittgenstein's truest commentators or heirs, have missed almost entirely the absurdist atmosphere that permeates so much of Wittgenstein's best work! So much of Wittgenstein's writing, especially in the last 15 years or so of his life, crucially involves scenarios that are subtly (or in some cases even fairly obviously) quite "mad." This is an absolutely vital aspect of his method. Dusty Wittgenstein scholarship has occluded or domesticated this "madness" – to its and (all of our) great cost. Wittgenstein has come to seem more assimilable with the philosophical tradition than he actually is: his "arguments" have been brought to bear against those of more traditional philosophic voices – and have (rightly) been found wanting. One can only understand Wittgenstein's real point – he can only *win* – if his texts are allowed to "self-deconstruct" on one, and if this is understood to be *the point* of them, *not* an argument against them!

If one approaches the *Investigations* not from the likes of Russell but from the likes of (poets such as) Stevens, one may be in a better frame of mind to *hear* what Wittgenstein is actually up to. Rather than shoehorning Wittgenstein into the constraints of analytic philosophy, one should perhaps learn to see his kinship with Stevens's educative poetry of the absurd. Less of a tired emphasis on logic, more of a journey via "illogic" – via blackbirds seen at the point of flying out of sight – will help one to understand (to practice) the true, therapeutic nature of Wittgenstein's philosophy of logic – *throughout* his career. Wittgenstein believes that one has to go by the way of delusion, if one wants to arrive at truth. Stevens agrees, unlike Russell, and (on balance) unlike Frege.[23]

Simon Critchley, in his intriguing book, *Things Merely Are: Philosophy in the Poetry of Wallace Stevens*,[24] rightly paints Stevens as transcending/overcoming Kantianism. Wittgenstein's philosophy can helpfully be seen as above all doing precisely the same.[25] Kant sought to show the limits of knowledge and reason, via his effort to set out the transcendental conditions of possibility for these things. To sum up what we have argued in this paper: Stevens, as Wittgenstein(-ian), takes one to "the other side" of language, "beyond the limit." And finds the "place" then reached to contain not ineffable truths, nor thoughts that can't be uttered, nor an indescribable formless realm, nor even successful acts of imagination, but simply: the words, the sounds, the fabulous, sensuous, delicious, sometimes hysterical, sometimes weird or mad or unpleasant delusions of sense that they produce, that they *are the creations of*. "Thirteen Ways" – and many other poems such as for instance "Anecdote of a Jar" and "Fabliau of Florida' – are, in the end, neither about imagining nor about looking – they are ("about") language. The language, language "out of use," language which iconically "represents" only itself, and which seemingly "gestures at" a nothing that presents itself as a something about which nothing can be said. Language's possible aspect of non-transparency is wonderfully displayed by Stevens, much as it is "displayed" and in play in the literary presentations – the "imaginary scenarios" etc. – in Wittgenstein, and furthermore is explicitly discussed by him at scattered points, as a kind of necessary complement to what seems to be his "philosophy of the ordinary," *throughout* his later writing; for instance at quite a number of points in part 2 of the *Investigations*.

That is what is presented to one, by Stevens as we read him. Language, and its fantasized other, "the signified" (as opposed to its real other and *confrere*: reality). Language playing, and noth-ing.

We have focused here on one of Stevens's *early* poems. But later Stevens also has real genius, and has we suspect just as deep a philosophical interest for his readers. Early Stevens, to generalize very crudely, tends to focus one's attention most helpfully and concentratedly on the nature of our human (and, in particular, English) *language*, of our mindedness, and on the world as involving our mindedness. Later Stevens tends to focus one's attention most helpfully on the nature of the *world*, including the world thought of as independent of thought.[26] These are two slightly differing emphases, two sides of the same coin. Things merely are, as Critchley points out (later) Stevens "says." But among the things that ("merely') are, as (early) Stevens "says," are poems and imaginations, words and their speakers, and much more. Literary and philosophic works – including those works that rail against mere being, against things as they are, those works that do not leave everything as it is – are real, and part of what Stevens calls "absolute fact." Thus Stevens's corpus *overcomes* the apparent tension between "where there is no imagination, there no thing may be," and "things merely are [whether we imagine them or no]," and Stevens need not be seen, as Critchley sees him,[27] as torn between these two aspects.

We have pointed up how Stevens shows us all our language – just as Critchley points up how Stevens shows one the world. There is a therapeutic aspect to both (interrelated) tasks, as Critchley rightly points out.[28] But what is most therapeutic of all is seeing how the two tasks are *entirely complementary.*[29]

We human animals could never not be nature, even though – no; in fact, *because* – nature is not there *for us.* (This is part of what one sees when one "sees" "Blackbird" or a blackbird clearly.) So Stevens's poetry does not ultimately fail, as Critchley claims it does.[30] It succeeds, as Wittgenstein succeeds, *in the only way one can*: intermittently (even: rarely). For non-intermittent – final – success in attaining clarity, beautifully, would mean and be: no more poetry. Such a "success" would be in some ways regrettable: it would mean that we no longer had a recognizably human life. The psychological, cultural, linguistic roots of the need to philosophize and poetize are so deep and widespread that we know not what it would be, in fact, to be entirely beyond them. (Except that it would not be anything like the human.)

We have not attempted here anything remotely resembling a complete reading of even one poem by Stevens – indeed such completeness is, from our perspective, "not possible," not a coherently described endeavor – still less to extend such a reading or such a treatment to any substantial degree at all further into his oeuvre. We have rather attempted to display some aspects of a poem we think important, and even revelatory of a number of ways in which philosophy and literature can interact and mutually inflect.

For the conclusion to this paper is a perhaps triply surprising one. On the one hand, we can be helped to read Stevens through understanding and following a Wittgensteinian "philosophy of language." (This much, James Guetti we think already proved, over a decade ago.) On the other hand, when we thus read Stevens, at deep and crucial moments *we find him following a (very roughly) Wittgensteinian line of approach in the substance or "content" of his poetry.* But it is crucial not to read this wrongly: we violate Guetti's methodological injunctions and critical discoveries / aspect-revelations, if we take Stevens to be *expressing* a Wittgensteinian philosophy.

Rather, his poems remain strange.[31] They do not get successfully *translated* or paraphrased. They do philosophical work *of their own*; this is poetry as philosophy, but poetry that *remains* poetry, all the same.[32] And so then, on the third hand: *this sheds some helpful light on Wittgenstein's* own *writing*. The "action" of Stevens's poetry, as its invitations to the reader dissolve upon that reader, makes more strikingly perspicuous what has eluded many readers of Wittgenstein: much the same method, of inviting the reader to adopt a perspective or an idea, and then seeing whether it really does or yields what s/he wants from it, or whether rather it collapses on one. And then of seeing what one can learn from that.

Our title is "Wittgenstein and Literary Language." Our paper is ultimately as much about thinking of the philosophically active – the philosophically crucial – literariness of Wittgenstein's own style, as it is about the helpfulness of Wittgenstein to the task of appreciating and perspicuously presenting the language of those more standardly recognized as poets.

Moreover: *our* paradoxical or poetical flourishes (whether or not they work) are no accident. One cannot do philosophy properly without engaging with – without *inhabiting* – one's own and others' inclinations to mire oneself in nonsense. One cannot do justice to literary language without inhabiting its literariness, its paradoxicality. The meaning of a poem is always another poem (though usually of course not as good a poem as the one started with). The language of philosophy of literature, and of good literary criticism, is of necessity the language of paradox.

In other words: *our* paper needs must have consisted in considerable measure of "grammatical display," and not just of "grammatical remarks." Or, to put the point perhaps just slightly too strongly in order to make quite clear what that point *is*: It may be good or bad, but the genre of our paper too at times necessarily aspires to be something akin to "literature," and not just "philosophy."

Notes

Parts of this essay draw upon bits of material present in earlier forms in our "Recent work: The Philosophy of Literature," in *Philosophical Books* 43:2 (April 2001): 118–31, and in Read's "Wittgensteinian Poetry," in his *Applying Wittgenstein*. And our thanks in particular to Alun Davies, Cathy Osborne, Kate Campbell, Laura Cook, Garrett Caples, and our students in LitPhil over the past decade, for some helpful thoughts on this material.

1 *Poetic Justice: The Literary Imagination and Public Life* (Boston, MA: Beacon Press, 1995).
2 *The Ethics of Reading: Kant, De Man, Eliot, Trollope, James, and Benjamin* (New York: Columbia University Press, 1986).
3 *Wittgenstein and the Grammar of Literary Experience* (Athens and London: University of Georgia Press, 1993). Page references for this work are given in parenthesis in the text of this chapter.
4 *On Certainty*, ed. G. E. M. Anscombe and G. H. von Wright, trans. Denis Paul and G. E. M. Anscombe (Oxford: Basil Blackwell, 1969).
5 We say that this condition of language too is "ubiquitous." This gives a clue to something which we hope to write about in detail on a future occasion: the *limits* of the concept of

"mastery of a natural language." This concept, which plays a critically important role in Wittgenstein's and Guetti's understanding of "meaningful use," is *an object of comparison*, not a universalizing theoretical claim. It reaches and breaches a limit, when it encounters – as it does, continually – "grammatical display." We are not masters of such displays; we are not in full *control* of them – even if we are the greatest of poets. No more than we are – anyone is – masters of all philosophical temptations and confusions. (And indeed, one place in which this can be seen is in the uncontrollable, even when deliberately created, self-deconstruction of Wittgenstein's own "poetic" language, discussed toward the end of this paper. One might perhaps venture to say: the collective unconscious is structured like a language, just *insofar* as language is unmasterable. Insofar, very roughly, as language has, sometimes, the form of poetic literature.) If Guetti or Wittgenstein ever suggest otherwise, then so much the worse for them.

6   For more on what we mean by "transitional," see Cora Diamond's writing on Wittgenstein.
7   *Tractatus Logico-Philosophicus*, trans. D. F. Pears and B. F. McGuinness (London: Routledge and Kegan Paul, 1961).
8   http://ecmd.nju.edu.cn/UploadFile/17/8076/standard.doc.
9   In T. Sebeok, ed., *Style in Language* (New York: Wiley, 1960), reprinted 2004. Subsequent page citations of Jakobson in this chapter are of the 2004 reprint.
10 In her "Ethics, Imagination and the Method of the *Tractatus*," in Rupert Read and Alice Crary, eds., *The New Wittgenstein* (London: Routledge, 2000), wherein (*passim*) Diamond argues that much of what interests Wittgenstein philosophically is what in fact we (can) only imagine that we can imagine.
11 Again, let our use of the word "literally" not cause offence here: it is simply a quick index of the important – "grammatical" – distinction between looking with the eyes and other things that we call "looking."
12 A very similar process is at work in the process and progress of another of Stevens's early poems, "Metaphors of a Magnifico."
13 And such teaching of the poem naturally extends into the following kind of point: *that the reader has to come to decide for themselves what is well described as one or another way of looking, and what isn't*, among what is presented here. We shall return to this point below, in discussion of Wittgenstein's method in his greatest writing, such as in the opening of *Philosophical Investigations*.
14 See for instance the – different – points discussed by Guetti on p. 169 of his *Wittgenstein and the Grammar of Literary Experience*.
15 Read and Crary, *The New Wittgenstein*, 149.
16 Stevens's poems are marvelously replete with such *faux* instructions. Check out for instance the nonsensical commands explicitly encoded into "Fabliau of Florida."
17 We have in mind for instance Derrida's infamous – and signally misleading – claim in "Signature, Event, Context" that using a bit of language as an example of agrammaticality or of error is at all the same kind of thing as using a bit of language, such as the same bit of language to undertake a speech act.
18 We refer here to Wittgenstein throughout his career.
19 See especially Stanley Cavell, *The Claim of Reason* (Oxford: Oxford University Press, 1979), 115–25; and Alice Crary's and David Cerbone's essays in Read and Crary, *The New Wittgenstein*.
20 Other great artists who we believe do the same include W. S. Graham, William Faulkner (on this, see Read's essay in John Gibson, Wolfgang Huemer, eds. *The Literary Wittgenstein*,

21 Routledge, 2004), and Peter Greenaway (in his early films, especially the shorts and *The Draughtsman's Contract* and *Drowning by Numbers*; perhaps also in *Prospero's Books*).
21 One fails to understand Wittgenstein, we submit, if one never or only very rarely giggles or laughs out loud at his text.
22 One might think of Wittgenstein therefore as offering us literature: the thematic collection of short stories, a little like Hemingway's *The First Forty-Nine*, that constitutes *Philosophical Investigations*; the more epic-poetic approach that constituted the *Tractatus*. . . . Though it would in fact be misleading to characterize the later work as prose and the earlier as poetry – there are counterexamples, in *each* case (Consider for instance the quasi-poem we earlier constructed easily from a line of *On Certainty*: "I know that that's a tree.")
23 The proviso here references the moments when Frege appears to recognize, albeit reluctantly, that such trafficking in delusion might be necessary. Compare Frege's invocation at some crucial moments in his work of "hints," or of "a pinch of salt," and his audacious reply to Kerry on concepts and objects.
24 Simon Critchley, *Things Merely Are: Philosophy in the Poetry of Wallace Stevens* (London: Routledge, 2005).
25 Read argues this in his "The New Hume's New Antagonists," in Rupert Read and Kenneth Richman, eds., *The New Hume Debate* (London: Routledge, 2000; rev. edn. 2007).
26 Critchley is broadly right, then, about our being able to encounter "the things themselves" most especially in Stevens's later work. Though they are also present in his early work: not only in poems like "The Snowman" and "The Comedian as the letter C," but also in many more. We might put the point this way: jars, blackbirds, mountains, poems, etc. *are things in themselves*.
27 See Critchley, *Things Merely Are*, 85, 61.
28 See ibid., 83, 59. There is indeed a kind of wish to bring poetry to an end in Stevens, as there is in Wittgenstein a kind of wish to bring philosophy to an end. These are wishes that one can act on or attempt to act on; they are not, however (*contra* "end of philosophy" philosophers, etc.) wishes that one can often *realize*.
29 Critchley writes,

> On the one hand, literature is an act of idealization governed by the desire to assimilate all reality to the ego and to view the latter as the former's projection . . . On the other hand . . . literature does not aim to reduce reality to the imagination, but rather to let things be in their separateness from us. (86)

Our suggestion is that these two tendencies are happily married in Stevens's corpus.
30 See, e.g., Critchley, *Things Merely Are*, 6, 87.
31 And this is one of the points at which we part company with Critchley. Critchley is willing to understand great poetry as involving the submergence of philosophical "preoccupations into the particular grain of the poems" (32). Whereas we think that we have to let poetry *be*, to let it *stand*. Poetry is *a way we speak*; great poetry is never merely philosophy in another form. If we thought that Stevens merely "submerged" a philosophy "into the particular grain" of certain poems, we would not think him a great poet. We agree with Frank Kermode that later Stevens sometimes does do this, and when he does, his poems fall away from the true greatness of his oeuvre, which is most undoubted, it seems to us, in the early poems of his such as those on which we have focused in this essay. Those are poems which remain strange to us, remain poetical, even "after" we have worked through them to find their provision for philosophical insight.

32 In this respect, it is akin to J. M. Coetzee's oeuvre; and to "film as philosophy" as discussed in Rupert Read and Jerry Goodenough, eds., *Film as Philosophy: Essays in Cinema After Wittgenstein and Cavell* (Palgrave Macmillan, 2005). Films such as *Memento* and *Last Year at Marienbad* remain films, even after one has described the philosophical work they accomplish. Or, better: one can only fully understand that philosophical work by seeing how it is inextricably tied to its filmic presentation. Or, better: accounts of the philosophical work accomplished are only ever allegories of the work – the film – itself.

26

Exemplification and Expression

CHARLES ALTIERI

The "Grammaticalization of Experience"

Last year I wrote an essay using Wittgenstein's *On Certainty* to develop a Wittgenstein who might provide an alternative to the therapeutic values Stanley Cavell finds in the *Philosophical Investigations*.[1] I had no idea at the time that many philosophers had been elaborating a "third" Wittgenstein (after the first of the *Tractatus* and the second, "therapeutic," of *Philosophical Investigations*, part 1). It was this third Wittgenstein (especially in *On Certainty* and *Last Writings*) who, from 1946 to the end of his life, was at work developing what Daniéle Moyal-Sharrock calls "the grammaticalization of experience."[2] Having now discovered these claims, I want to engage them here, because the ideas developed by this third Wittgenstein can, I think, be very helpful for literary criticism. For one thing, I find the turn away from the second, more therapeutically inclined Wittgenstein a significant therapeutic possibility for my own profession. But I am much more excited by the positive values informing this turn, because this "grammaticalization of experience" proves immensely useful for thinking about exemplification and expression, two motifs rarely addressed by critics with the scope and intricacy Wittgenstein offers.

To make my case I will have to assert something that most commentators on the third Wittgenstein reject – that this third Wittgenstein breaks from the author of part 1 of *Philosophical Investigations* because he sees a new way to apply the model for logical analysis that had been fundamental to his *Tractatus*.[3] Wittgenstein was clearly no longer interested in repeating his account of how language can establish truthful propositions. But he does seem quite eager to extend what Matthew Ostrow calls "the logical transcendentalism" of the *Tractatus*[4] so that he might establish a comprehensive sense of how philosophical grammar also provides a "ground" for the achieving of meaningful statements.

This transcendental position – both early and late – depends in large part on wielding the distinction between display and depiction.[5] In the *Tractatus* Wittgenstein had seen logic as a conceptual space defining the boundaries of the world; within logic lies what can be said, outside logic (or on its boundaries) lie the subject and all

---

A Companion to the Philosophy of Literature, First Edition. Edited by Garry L. Hagberg and Walter Jost.
© 2010 John Wiley & Sons Ltd. Published 2015 by John Wiley & Sons, Ltd.

determinations of value. Because logic displays the truth conditions for what can be said, logic itself cannot be described. It too lies outside the world. That is, the propositions of logic cannot themselves satisfy truth conditions because they are the preconditions or frameworks for the very idea of truth. Moreover, because logic must be objective and mechanical, it cannot account for or even characterize values, so that the domain of value must also lie beyond its ken, and hence beyond the world characterized by propositions.

In *On Certainty* it is the foundational role of grammar, not logic, that is displayed rather than asserted (cf. *OC* 501). The situation is now different, because grammar is not one definable system but rather an interlocking field of systems. Therefore, one can only illustrate the foundational role of grammar by analyzing representative instances of how it works. There is no characterizing the network as a whole. On the other hand, the multiplicity of frameworks provides something that was not available to the *Tractatus*. When the emphasis is on objective truth conditions, there is simply no place for the subject. Subjects must be silent – not by any means absent, but present only in their coloring of the facts with values that cannot be described in truth-functional terms. However, when one is talking about grammar as a foundation for meanings, value is not something separate from the world but is embedded in the very practices it enables. There remains an existential dimension, for individuals can transfigure values; but those transfigurations occur against a backdrop of practices and not simply of the facts of the world.

This "grammaticalization of experience" necessarily challenges the emphasis of modern philosophy on epistemic questions asking how one knows what one claims.[6] Grammaticalization becomes a matter of how agents can be oriented toward particular actions, only some of which emphasize the subject–object relations characteristic of knowledge claims. Because "Language did not emerge from some kind of ratiocination" (*OC* 475), Wittgenstein insists there is no reason to believe that a language game should "rest on some form of knowledge" (*OC* 477). "Display" matters, then, because there emerges a great deal that cannot be said on a Tractarian model of saying, and yet must be recognized in concrete terms if we are to appreciate how grammar governs our practices. And display matters because it is a practice in its own right. That is, giving examples is the basic way we test our understanding of what is appropriate within a practice. To learn a grammar is in most cases to learn by example rather than by rule.

We can display how grammar provides various means of representation only by establishing perspicuous representations of the frameworks making possible certain kinds of actions. Examples orient us to the powers inherent in our ways of making sense. Hence, as early as the first part of *Philosophical Investigations*, Wittgenstein insisted on a sharp contrast between a language game that concentrates on descriptions of color and a language game that focuses not on something represented but on "a means of representation" (*PI* 50). Color can be invoked in a description. But many of our assertions about color refer, not to the color itself, but to aspects of color charts, hence to the means by which specific colors are denoted. And the more Wittgenstein attended to grammatical features that "ground" cultural competence, the more fully he recognized that an emphasis on doing rather than on knowing requires also an emphasis on what the conditions are that guide those doings. Displaying grammatical relations entails showing that many sentences occupy "a shifting border between logic and the empirical, so that their meaning changes back and forth and they count now as expressions of norms, now as expressions of experience" (*Remarks on Colour*, 1.32).

Conversely, philosophical error occurs primarily when we confuse example with depiction. A theory of language as use is strongest when it also contains perspicuous examples of our continual temptations to misuse. And in that respect G. E. Moore provides Wittgenstein with his version of Flaubert's Saint Anthony. Moore claims that "empiricist" statements like Moore's "Here is one hand" provide a paradigmatic depiction that can be taken as secure knowledge. Against Moore, Wittgenstein sees that sentence functioning typically as a *display* of a capacity for performing certain actions. Only if there is doubt that this is a hand would the sentence provide a knowledge claim.

Obviously, the "grammaticalization of experience" makes enormous differences in how we approach philosophical problems. It is probably less obvious, but almost equally important, that the roles of exemplification emphasized in this enterprise also modify substantially how we might approach a variety of literary issues. Grammaticalization affords a means of talking about how perspicuous particulars can have representative value for our understanding of experience even though they do not represent or imitate any particular event. Because grammaticalization finesses epistemic disciplines, there need be no invidious contrast with what is "merely" imagined. Positively speaking, we can envision works of art as displaying at least three forms of perspicuous exemplification. First, exemplification in art can make concrete and intense realizations of the cultural forces at work in establishing criteria for meaning and for significance; second, it can provide models for expressive activity that honor how subjects display their individual concerns and investments without requiring that one speculate on chains of "inner experiences"; and third, it can offer exemplary attitudes inviting provisional identifications so that an audience can imagine exploring possible selves (and possible others that these selves encounter).

I presume that I needn't illustrate my first claim – that Wittgenstein's critique of epistemic values makes especially important the ways that the arts come to exemplify various possibilities for developing meanings within cultural practices (both practices devoted to the arts and practices that elicit commentary in the mode of works of art). The arts elaborate examples articulating norms of what is entailed in social practices, even as they simultaneously display how it might be possible to change those entailments. The arts offer exemplary attitudes and orientations of attention that display models for making sense of experience that parallel the work done when we show how grammar structures possibilities for meaningfulness. One must admit that in the arts the focus is on psychological means of gaining access to the world rather than on pragmatic means of coming to appreciate what our practices might afford. Yet even characteristic typologies like "Oedipus complex" or "Hamlet-like delay" indicate the close parallel between what a color chart provides and what literary experience might do to sort and relate types of experience.

Unfortunately, attempting to demonstrate such claims on any general level would either be a fruitless exercise in preaching to the converted or a hopeless attempt to secure, by abstract means, the language of appreciation that has to be developed in practices of reading and discussing particular works. Yet I hope that I can do something useful by shifting to two more subtle features of display that Wittgenstein explores for their grammatical intricacies. First, I will examine how Wittgenstein links the psychological realm of expressive behavior to the grammatical possibilities of exemplification. These linkings go a long way toward showing how subjects can manifest intensely personal states without needing any rhetoric of inner lives. And that, in turn, goes a long way toward helping to read the personality in impersonal modernist art.

Next, I take up the question of what kind of example Wittgenstein offers by his overall use of Moore's somewhat blind empiricism. Wittgenstein's choice seems a case where a philosophical text not only uses examples but wants to be read as an example of investments and attitudes that themselves cannot be represented in epistemic terms. Therefore, we need a distinction between the function involved in being an "example of" some general properties and the function of being an "example as," which serves as the bearer of desirable imaginative properties. And we need to be able to characterize the kind of speech act that can not only use examples but serves as an example by offering to others its mode of organizing energies and attitudes.

What is Exemplification?

I begin with some fundamental distinctions offered by Nelson Goodman which, while they lack Wittgenstein's subtlety, nevertheless establish a more systematic sense of why examples do not picture the world but refer us "forward" to our frameworks for making sense of that world rather than "back" to an existent object or situation.[7] Goodman treats exemplification as one of three, tightly connected basic modes of symbolic functioning, each of which selects from and organizes its universe, therefore becoming "itself in turn informed and transformed":

> Representation and description relate a symbol to things it applies to. Exemplification relates a symbol to a label that denotes it, and hence indirectly to the things (including the symbol itself) in the range of that label. Expression relates the symbol to the label that metaphorically denotes it, and hence indirectly not only to the given metaphorical but also to the literal range of that label.[8]

This is difficult material to process, but it helps that Goodman's primary examples are works of art, since it is crucial in that domain to keep distinct what a picture describes or represents and what kind of a picture or act of picturing the work demonstrates. The history of art provides clear examples of how taste shifts among the three modes of symbolization. Denotation is stressed when art is prized for what it represents or describes; exemplification when what matters is the display of formal or decorative properties for which the work provides a label; and expression when art is valued for evoking psychological states (93) by the metaphoric extension of those formal properties. A shade of red in a painting might *describe* what the artist sees, or it might *exemplify* a possible color tone capable of achieving certain contrasts with other colors, or it might *express* anger or vengeance as the artist tilts the metaphoric aspects of what the label is denoted by. (Notice here that "denoted by" is a tricky concept, inasmuch as the properties possessed by the label get very difficult to fix when metaphorical possession of properties comes in to play.) And we can also arrange these functions synchronically. A painting like Munch's *The Scream* can *describe* an anguished vision, *exemplify* distorted shapes and intense color for their direct power to *express* a mode of anguish.

Wittgenstein offers a much more intricate connection between exemplification and expressivity by bringing into play issues of intentionality that are anathema to Goodman. He shares Goodman's suspicion of any effort to characterize intentional states by describing interior events. Such description at best turns the subject into an object; worst it displaces agency into abstract and fantasized categories. But there are other options for preserving what Richard Moran calls "an asymmetry between first and third person positions." Rather than characterize the intending agent by attempting to describe inner states, one can see the example as directly making visible something that we have to process as a first-person state. For we can mine Goodman's distinction between what references to self might denote and how they might call attention to what they are denoted by. And in so doing we can also emphasize a shift from treating the self as if it were observable matter and treating the self as something made visible by the manner of its expressive activity.

Consider two exemplary Wittgensteinian interpretations of expressive exemplification. The first statement occurs in a discussion of description. The passage defines description in a language reminiscent of the *Tractatus* as "a representation of a distribution in space." Then Wittgenstein invents this way of dramatizing what cannot be included within such distributions but *can* be displayed: "If I let my gaze wander round a room and suddenly it lights on an object of striking red colour, and I say 'Red!' – that is not a description" (*PI* 187). The exclamation "Red!" does not *describe* anything because attention is not focused on the object. Rather, the statement *exemplifies* what Wittgenstein calls "the dawning of an aspect," and so calls attention to a state the subject experiences in relation to how the object appears. "Red!" still functions as a label for that appearance. Yet it is denoted not only by the color it evokes but by the exclamation which that appearance elicits. The force of the label now leads us to two aspects of the scene which we have to attribute to the capacity to establish denotations: the background by which we determine colors, and the backgrounds by which we determine attitudes. More precisely, we have to characterize the exclamation in terms of *this* person who might utter this exclamation to account for how *this* situation dawns on the activity of observing.

I am not sure whether Goodman would say that the exclamation brings into play a metaphoric register for interpreting the properties the label possesses. Yet this attribution seems appropriate to me, for the exclamatory force cannot derive just from the properties the label literally possesses. Rather, as Geoffrey Hellman puts it,

495

the exemplified red "has been transferred from a domain of literal application to a different domain."[9]

In this case, "Red!" toggles between literal exemplification as an invoked label and something resembling metaphoric exemplification. The expression characterizes the person because, here, the property red is subsumed under properties involving surprise and wonder. That the scene evokes a label red need not entail any specific affective response. But that the scene invokes an exclamation projects this red as affording a site where the agent gets to express something about himself or herself. Moreover, as an exclamation, "Red!" suggests that there are shades of the color that have hitherto not been noticed or not used in this conjunction with other color tones.

Exemplification now bears the force of an expression. But then, shouldn't we be able to say what the exclamation serves as expression of or expression for? Minimally, Wittgenstein wants to make the point that what is being expressed *cannot* be described. What is being expressed can only be exhibited – largely because it establishes in public something that is not observable except through the speaker's utterance. Expression does not invite description of the person but exemplifies an aspect of the person. In this case, the exclamation becomes a means of making the speaker's state a distinctive feature of the scene that cannot be explained simply by the scene. This label possesses the property of testifying to the speaker's willingness to make an affective investment in what he or she sees. The subject still occupies the boundary marking the limit of the world of fact, as in the *Tractatus*; but now it need not be silent, because the grammar of our language includes these expressive possibilities.

More important, the agent need not fear that his calling attention to himself will displace the phenomenon eliciting the self-reference. In the case with "Red!" the agent's exclamation does not depend on any narrative that would risk turning the subject into an object of the forces that the narrative recounts. In fact, the exclamation "Red!" simply renders the subject as the recipient of the dawning of an aspect. The subject of perception is primarily acted upon. But it is quite a different case for the subject of the exclamation, who makes possible a second-order bringing of the will to bear on what is perceived. Once the exclamation point contextualizes how the label is being used, this way of using the label invites further accounts that may clarify why this particular agent is so moved by this particular red. Now, the assertion of the color provides a label for a specific state of the subject; and this state is not merely observed, it is asserted, as if the subject were affirming this capacity for recognition as fundamental to its sense of agency. As Wittgenstein put it in a quite different context,

> The criteria for the truth of the *confession* that I thought such-and-such are not the criteria for a true *description* of a process. And the importance of the true confession does not reside in its being a correct and certain report of a process. It resides rather in the special consequences which can be drawn from a confession whose truth is guaranteed by the special criteria of truthfulness. (*PI* 222)[10]

Perhaps the role of confession here is simply to thicken the context enabling us to develop more fully how this particular exclamation can be denoted.

Exemplifying Feeling

I am painfully aware that I am imposing a heavy conceptual burden on Wittgenstein's example of an exclamation. My only defense is that taking up this burden will clarify and deepen another enigmatic passage that I think is even more suggestive about the strange grammar of first-person expression as a mode of exemplification directed toward what the subject offers as its own investments. The following passage is so supple in its abstract concreteness that it could be the work of a modern poet, and in fact it elaborates themes that bring these poets quite close to Wittgensteinian concerns: "'*This* looks *so*; *this* tastes *so*, *this* feels *so*.' 'This' and 'so' must be differently explained'" (*PI* 186).

In the first instance, "*This*" refers to an object and thus calls for some version of testing the adequacy of the description offered. But adding "feels so" contrasts a domain of description with another grammatical domain, since "feels so" does not refer to the object but calls attention to the subject's reactions. In Goodman's terms, "feels so" shifts from denoting the object to states that can be denoted by predications about the subject. "Feels so" invites our taking the experience as a concrete example that makes manifest how the subject processes the object. Only the subject can flesh out this "so," because that task calls not for description but for specifying how some aspect of the situation engages the agent or dawns on the agent (like a new sense of "red"). If one were still to insist on treating the object eliciting "feels so" in strictly epistemic terms that must be made explicit, the expression would call attention only to the object, losing the equivalences or identifications between subject and object that "so" grammatically puts on stage.

How do we honor these equivalences, and what powers can the subject exhibit in elaborating these equivalences? The first step is to realize that "feels so" insists on a specific moment of subjective experience. Indeed, that is why we have to talk about exemplification rather than description. The crucial issue is what is displayed in the agent's expression of the feelings involved so that they can be claimed as aspects of its involvement in the scene. Second, we have to honor the fact that this specificity involves equivalences between two domains – what is involved in the dawning of the object, and what is involved in the states projected by the subject in order to render the apprehension of that dawning. The best way to honor such equivalence is to apply Wittgenstein's account of "seeing as," since "as-ness" is the richest counterpart to "so." We can see "so" as the moment of self-consciousness where the speaker recognizes that its apprehension modifies the object. Then "as" provides the grammatical resources for characterizing the equivalences that shape and sustain the feelings aroused.

We need a contrast between "seeing that" and "seeing as" in order to show how the speaker's responsiveness does not consist in a mental picture that can then be checked for its truth value. "Seeing as" preserves the capacity to treat the properties informing the experience as a combination of the material and the metaphoric. Therefore, we can honor the fact that the speaker cannot describe his or her responsiveness because the

497

responsiveness is an aspect of the situation and not a separable object within it. And yet, even though the speaker cannot describe that responsiveness, he or she can display it. Then the speaker can engage this display – not by describing it but by contextualizing it. The speaker brings to bear a kind of confession filling out the expression of interest. But the confession will not be very helpful if it seeks a picture of the inner life activated by the event eliciting the feelings. Rather, confession proves useful if it can offer information about the priorities and interests and desired applications that further denote the sensibility informing the construction of that particular example.

In other words, the confession brings to bear the capacity of the speaker to see the particular in terms of qualities that matter for the individual. The speaker does not have to have an idea of these qualities. Rather, the specific force of the qualities emerges in the process of expressing the feeling. While "so" does not offer specific metaphoric properties, it elicits them because the reference of "so" has to be denoted by what the subject might bring to it. "So" establishes the opening to a world that can only be completed by the subject as he or she fleshes out what provokes the exclamation. In turn, "as" provides the perfect grammatical complement to the way in which "so" deviates from the world of description. For "as" specifies by concrete examples the equivalences that flesh out "so," while avoiding the kinds of generalization that would transform the subject's experience into an object in its own right. Grammatically the "as" relations bring into play temporal and modal equivalences between what is happening and what the agent invests in that happening. And psychologically these equivalences make possible rich subjective states that we need not turn into pictures or stories – that is, into the kinds of narratives that provide an imaginary substance for the self by in fact depriving it of its powers to abide in these concrete expressions.

Poetry and the Resources of Grammar

Now I need poetry to display the intricate resources of this grammar. I have to show how authors can establish identifications that do not depend on concepts of the self, and I have to expand my scenario by illustrating what is at stake for readers in attuning to the expressive activity. Early in his career Wallace Stevens wrote "Nomad Exquisite," a playful rendering of the relation between "so" and "as" that exhibits how a sensibility might revel in equivalences, bringing the personal to bear in experience without needing an idea of personal identity:

> As the immense dew of Florida
> Brings forth
> The big-finned palm
> And green vine angering for life,

> As the immense dew of Florida
> Brings forth hymn and hymn
> From the beholder,
> Beholding all these green sides,
>
> And blessed mornings,
> Meet for the eye of the young alligator,
> And lightning colors
> So, in me, come flinging
> Forms, flames, and the flakes of flame.[11]

The basic force here is the grammatical power of "as" and "so" to set in motion a chain of equivalents that draw worlds together without relying on the abstracting power of ideas. The first means of drawing worlds together is temporal: the poem wants to catch the precise feel of aligning with the Florida sunrise. Then we realize that this temporal equivalence is reinforced by an intricate set of modal equivalences. The emerging scene elicits the grammar of "so" because that sunrise brings the psyche alive to a series of qualitative parallels – identifying with the motion of the palm, seeing the breeze as producing hymns, awakening to a sense of sight that allows comparisons of the self with the young alligator, and finally feeling general powers of self in giving the form of flakes of flame to the sun's light.

I especially like how "the eyes of the young alligator" deploy the grammar of "as" to merge concrete observation with possibilities of identifying with what and how that creature sees. Then the closing lines boldly state the transition from what the eye sees to metaphors emphasizing the intensity of what is seen. Finally, there is another level of metaphor established by the formal qualities of what is displayed. For the single sentence absorbs the literal exemplified properties into a self-organizing attitude, as if the "so" had the power to gather all these potential identifications in one completed feeling. The period that closes the sentence opens the domain of identification, enabling the imagined speaker to provide future narratives characterizing the investments displayed.

It is not a great leap then to the effort in Stevens's late poems to understand what might be involved in the possibility that "is and as are one" (*CPP* 406). But now he is sufficiently confident to blend abstraction and sensuous properties into more comprehensive celebrations of the chain of examples that elicit provisional identifications:

> The poem is the cry of its occasion,
> Part of the res itself and not about it.
> The poet speaks the poem as it is
>
> Not as it was: part of the reverberation
> Of a windy night as it is, when the marble statues
> Are like newspapers blown by the wind. He speaks
>
> By sight and insight as they are. (*CPP* 404)

Here, becoming and being now seem inseparable. Analogously, the poem offers the simile of the newspapers blown by the wind to make clear that being "a part" is also fusing literal and metaphoric properties into an act expressing "sight and insight as they are." Aspects of mental life are no less dependent on temporal and modal adjustments than perceptions are.

A final brief segment from Stevens makes visible the basic reward for making the adjustment to treating expression as a condition always in process and always adapting to shifting circumstances:

> We are two that use these roses as we are
> In seeing them. This is what makes them seem
> So far beyond the rhetorician's touch. (*CPP* 371)

In the heyday of deconstruction it seemed important to stress the ironic potential of this "seem." But in the light of the argument I am making, "seem" becomes a very confident assertion. Because "as" brings becoming and being together, it also has the power to elaborate equivalences between seeming and being. And when examples can do that, there is no place in the process of reverberation for rhetoric to wield its heavy and dangerous hand. Examples are not assertions, and that is why they can suffice as means of sustaining identifications.

Example "Of" and Example "As"

Reference to poems adds another kind of example to my narrative. We have dealt with how examples make visible our capacities for representation. Labels clarify what we can depict, so they indicate the powers of grammar to develop the significance of those observations. Then we spent considerable time on specific expressive and evaluative uses of example that specify a kind of agency that is lost when we make it the stuff of narrative. Now I want to address another aspect of exemplification that occurs when texts project a stance defined by the power to integrate specific examples into comprehensive synthetic structures. These structures do not provide arguments but offer stances or attitudes or modes of attention that establish the stakes for future arguments and that model their possible consequences.

Take Stevens's "Nomad Exquisite" as our example. As a synthetic act, the poem cannot be denoted only by what denotes the sum of its labels. If the poem exemplifies as an act, we must ask how that act also makes itself manifest. To capture this distinctive act we have to distinguish between serving as an example *of* something and being an example *as* this particular conjunction of properties.

My reasoning here depends on and interprets an application for another aspect of Goodman's argument. He makes an important distinction between two-place and one-place predicates. Two-place predicates are the more common since terms like "picture" or "represents" invoke a model of name and referent, each with their separate role to play. In contrast, expressions like " 'picture of Pickwick' and 'represents a unicorn' are better considered one-piece predicates or class terms, like 'desk' and 'table,' rather than a divisible series of assertions." Dickens does not offer a picture of Pickwick; Dickens offers a Pickwick-representing picture: "we cannot reach inside the picture and quantify over parts of it" (21–2). Or we could say that rather than being asked to see what the picture of Pickwick refers to, the readers of Dickens's novel are asked to treat the picture as referring to all the traits that the picture exemplifies.

Standard examples seem to be built on the logic of two-place predicates, since they denote some feature that they are denoted by. They are examples of these properties. But elaborate examples that can be projected as works of art require a more synthetic model. Insofar as they perform something or hold together complex features they function as one place predicates – we cannot reach inside the example and quantify over parts of it without doing serious harm to what holds it together. To capture this distinction I want to separate these acts of exemplifying as examples *as* rather than examples *of*.

I labor to make this distinction because it strikes me as a good, quasi-technical way of clarifying how some philosophical texts invite comparison with literary works in their ways of offering alternatives to propositional arguments. One might say, for example, that the more one appreciates what Wittgenstein does in his staging of Moore, the more those aspects of *On Certainty* approach the status of a "one-place predicate." Moreover, this attribution of status suggests that becoming a one-place predicate does not banish the work to a formal aesthetic domain but only establishes a different way of working within the public world. In *On Certainty* Wittgenstein is not content to describe Moore's arguments and then respond to them. He wants his audience to interpret the desires that shape these arguments and that probably blind Moore to what is limited in his whole approach to argument. In other words, Moore is given the status of something like a literary character because he becomes a figure defining a stance that not only fails to establish a refutation of the skeptic but elicits the very skepticism he is committed to refuting.

Consider this passage: "When one hears Moore say 'I know that's a tree' one suddenly understands those who think that that has by no means been settled" (*OC* 481). Here Wittgenstein points out that what is at issue is more than a matter of particular arguments. We have to ask why the "I know" is so important a frame for the statement that "that is a tree". Moore seems to seek two modes of certainty – that the tree exists, and that the "I" has a stable existence because it can anchor itself in the certainty that the tree exists. But if the "I" is actually invoking knowledge where there is no knowledge, the stability of the "I" also seems called into question. What does the "I" have to gain by asserting its own certainty in situations where the assertion is problematic? (And what does Wittgenstein have to gain by insisting on this issue?) Each claim becomes the more vulnerable because its counterpart so visibly wobbles. Eventually, the "I's" assertions of knowledge seem to be excessive, to attempt to provide reinforcement for its own lack of certainty about what could possibly anchor it in resistance to the skeptic's unsettling gaze. Therefore, the entire effort to refute the skeptic serves as an invitation for the skeptic to examine closely the psychodynamics of our uses of "I know." In deconstructive terms, the "I" needs a supplement that can postulate for the world a stability it sees itself as lacking. So the skeptic seems warranted in suspicions that the anxious "I" will become so eager to defend the possibility of certainty that it might take labels for certainty as evidence of what they assert.

Wittgenstein's citations of Moore and of Moore's characteristic ways of arguing stand as *examples of* Moore's philosophy and they are denoted by what Moore has come to stand for in philosophic culture. The connection between these examples and the world presuppose an already public understanding of Moore's positions. But the ironic case of Moore's helping to produce the skepticism he resists presents a different Moore. This Moore has his identity primarily because of how Wittgenstein reconstructs him. It still matters that Wittgenstein be accurate in summarizing Moore's positions. The philosopher is not free in the ways Stevens is to invent how agent and world can mutually construct one another. It matters that thinking like Moore's takes place, and it matters that this thinking has the self-defeating effect of encouraging skepticism. Ultimately, it may not matter much that it is Moore who thinks this way. The text becomes an expressive act displaying Wittgenstein's own investments in assessing what Moore exemplifies. And we see how the writing of philosophy is continually threatened by, and continually exalted by, the possibility that it can be read for what it is denoted by rather than for what it denotes.[12] That possibility requires only that we take the text as itself providing the denotation for the picture of Moore that it establishes.

We have arrived, then, at one measure that can distinguish texts devoted to exposition and description and texts devoted to expressing and establishing attitudes. The former texts can make use of examples (*examples of*); the latter texts offer *examples as* that concentrate an author's interests in rendering the subject matter in a particular way. But this is not just a matter of distinguishing kinds of texts. I think the differences are important enough to suggest a different kind of speech act devoted to foregrounding the text's status as exemplification through and through. If texts are to resist being subsumed under epistemic practices, there ought be a way to define the authorial intentions underlying this resistance. So I want, in closing, to propose that there is a distinctive speech act, which I call "the demonstrative," devoted to the conjunctions between exemplification and expression that we have been exploring.

The "demonstrative" must be considered in the context of Austin's case for performative expressions. Both speech acts involve doing something within the language uttered so that it has effects beyond illocutionary assertions. But Austin saw the performative as covering only those speech acts which accomplish something through language by invoking social ritual. He rightly banished from his account all fictional expressions and all discourse that expresses individual intentions and states. Austin does not countenance any metaphoric exemplification. Therefore, many philosophers and literary critics have claimed that Austin's analysis is severely limited because he banishes precisely the domain of individual performance from his performative. *By doing so, however,* he also managed to secure the case for how social action can take place in language. And in doing that, he made clear the signifying capacity of many features of language that are not suited for the making and testing of descriptions. Postulating a "demonstrative" speech act allows us to address other features of performance and expression while stabilizing Austin's account by accepting its self-imposed limitations.

I choose "demonstrative" because of a felicitous conjunction of semantic properties. Expressive people tend to be demonstrative, so the term picks up an affective element or orientation toward the expression of affects. And "demonstrative" leads us to indexical pronouns that often play deictic roles. This dimension of self-reference in turn seems crucial to the power of exemplification – hence Goodman's concern for expressive properties.

Elemental demonstrative speech acts are of two kinds, each with parallels to actions that do not involve language; and the two kinds obviously extend into each other. The first is actual demonstration of something, ranging from the display of how to use a word, to showing someone how to ride a bike, where the example is much more effective than a description of the principles involved. Here the paradigm sentence is "Do it like this." The second brings in the expressive component. Demonstrative speech acts consist in specifying an attitude by offering a linguistic embodiment of it. I think shouting or exclaiming or speaking through tears are decent examples. But the best example came from my Dean, Janet Broughton, who suggested the case of asking a teenager how he or she feels and getting the response "Blurghh" or some similar construction. With demonstratives the underlying concern might be: "Please care for how I am doing this."

Works of art and rhetorical performances use these elemental demonstratives. But in order to characterize the overall speech act involved in such work, one has to shift to the notion of "metaphoric demonstratives." (The proliferation of "metaphoric" as modifier should be acceptable here, for the entire notion of a single speech act for an extended work is itself a metaphoric construct.) Metaphoric demonstratives emphasize two aspects of exemplification. First, they display an attitude that the work can try to contextualize, qualify, justify, and test by elaborating how it possesses (or fails to possess) various capacities for interpreting the situation presented. Here the metaphoric register consists in the work's interest in overwriting the details presented so that they will carry an intended interpretation. Second, metaphoric demonstratives call attention to how the performing presence is at every moment taking responsibility for constructing an imaginary world (usually as a possible real world) that has its primary appeal directly because of this constructive activity. Here performance is necessarily self-reflexive. But that does not necessarily entail irony or endless self-referentiality. Rather, the self-reflexiveness can be focused simply on the effort to share with the audience an explicitness about the possible values in the constructive activity shaping how the work unfolds. This self-referentiality is no different in kind from the self-referentiality that allows the exclamation "Red!" to serve also as a taking of responsibility for one's enthusiasms.

I have written two essays elaborating how we might apply the notion of demonstrative speech act to literary works.[13] So I need say here only that this concept matters because, in most accounts of literary art, there is insufficient attention to the ways authors insist on their presence in the form of a constant purposiveness at work in making the choices that shape what kind of world the fiction establishes. This lack of attention is not surprising when philosophers talk about writing, since philosophy almost always chooses as its exemplars representational fiction or drama, that is, works where one can easily concentrate on the world presented rather than the author presenting. But literary critics, too, are often reluctant to stake anything on authorial agency. Critics now are typically content with attributing meaning to the effect of social text or to the critic's own hypothetical construct. They can then draw quite interesting connections among texts. However, they surrender much of the imaginative potential inherent in responding to the drama of how the work creates and thickens what it displays. These literal and figurative elements present a unique configuration of forces continually being shaped by an authorial will.

Finally, criticism attentive to this demonstrative dimension can ultimately test the powers of example to make alternative worlds available and so to effect large-scale change, even though the examples bypass the route of description and argument. As the second and "third" Wittgenstein often reminded us, the concreteness of example affords the best means of bringing people to "look at the world in a different way" (*OC* 92). Examples address not just our attitudes but also our understanding of how the attitudes fit into larger practices and frameworks. And demonstratives can be especially effective in modifying how people look at the world because they directly offer examples emphasizing how needs and desires lead us to develop stances toward the world. In that way they articulate how change might be both possible and necessary. In fact, in offering a direct claim on our capacities for appreciation and respect, the demonstrative is fundamental to keeping human achievement central in any world we might work to compose. Examples help us sort the methods of representation that make any world possible. Demonstratives help us appreciate the worlds in which we might live.

Notes

1. More specifically, Cavell makes four basic claims about how *Philosophical Investigations* calls upon that very subjectivity that the *Tractatus* banishes to the boundaries of sense. First, *Philosophical Investigations* introduces the need to internalize the skeptic without submitting to the skeptic's epistemic commitments; second, it calls for the agent's accepting finitude (cf. *Cities of Words: Pedagogical Letters on a Register of the Moral Life*, Cambridge, MA: Harvard University Press, 2004, 4) rather than adapting the skeptic's disappointment over the failures of certainty; third, it dramatizes the pragmatic and ethical significance of "acknowledgement" and "attunement" as means of pursuing trust in developing criteria for meaning; and last, it promises the perfectionist possibility of philosophy's leading "the soul, imprisoned and distorted by confusion and darkness, into the freedom of day (4).

2. Daniéle Moyal-Sharrock , "Introduction: The Idea of a Third Wittgenstein," in Daniéle Moyal-Sharrock, ed., *The Third Wittgenstein: The Post-Investigations Works* (Hampshire: Ashgate Publishing, 2004), 5. Moyal-Sharrock's essay in *The Third Wittgenstein*, "On Certainty and the Grammaticalization of Experience" (43–62) makes a strong case for Wittgenstein's shift from a concern for the grammar expressed by rules to the expressions of grammar "in our ways of acting." And she also makes a strong case for having "the therapeutic nature of Wittgenstein's thinking moved off centre-stage in Wittgenstein studies" (5). To reinforce

her point I would like to emphasize Wittgenstein's concern in *On Certainty* to distinguish logical from psychological remarks (*OC* 447). Psychological remarks address states of mind; logical remarks address the structures within cultural frameworks providing possibilities for a society's actions being intelligible to its various agents.

3   Avrum Stroll, "Wittgenstein's Foundational Metaphors," in Moyal-Sharrock, ed., *The Third Wittgenstein*, 13–24, offers an intelligent version of the argument that, in *On Certainty*, Wittgenstein rejects the contrast between what can be seen and what can shown. But I think one can best accommodate Stroll's observations about Wittgenstein's renewed concern for foundations by showing that Wittgenstein applies the saying–showing distinction in a new way. I find support for my position in Daniel D. Hutto's helpful essay "Two Wittgenstein's Too Many: Wittgenstein's Foundationalism," in Moyal-Sharrock, *The Third Wittgenstein*, 25–41.

4   Matthew Ostrow, *Wittgenstein's Tractatus: A Dialectical Interpretation* (Cambridge: Cambridge University Press, 2002).

5   I am using the following texts of Wittgenstein: *Tractatus Logico Philosophicus*, trans. D. F. Pears and B. F. McGuiness (London: Routledge and Kegan Paul, 1961); *Philosophical Investigations* (cited as *PI* in my text), trans. G. E. M. Anscombe (London: Basil Blackwell, 1958); *On Certainty* (cited as *OC* in my text), trans. Denis Paul and G. E. M. Anscombe (New York: Harper Torchbooks, 1969); *Remarks on Colour*, trans. Linda L. McAlister and Margaret Schattle (Berkeley: University of California Press, 1977).

6   "Epistemic practices" are those that depend first on establishing how one can be said to know something, and then on developing methods of inquiry that show how a particular discipline can emerge to secure the knowledge claims. Exemplification promises another practice, one that examines manner rather than matter, modes of signification rather than the stability of what is signified. John Koethe (in "Wittgenstein and Epistemology," in Moyal-Sharrock, *The Third Wittgenstein*, 93–105), makes a radical but interesting case that from the start Wittgenstein was concerned with semantics and not with "epistemological significance."

7   Here I share Richard Wollheim's concern that Goodman's nominalism unnecessarily limits what Goodman's example of example can offer. See his essay, "Nelson Goodman's *Languages of Art*, reprinted in Catherine Z. Elgin, ed., *The Philosophy of Nelson Goodman: Nelson Goodman's Philosophy of Art* (New York: Garland Publishing, 1997), 18–42. In a second essay in that volume, "Are the Criteria of Identity That Hold for a Work of Art in the Different Arts Aesthetically Relevant?" (73–92), Wollheim supports this with the powerful argument that "disagreement between us begins only when notational requirements are taken as providing not just necessary but also sufficient conditions for identity." From Wollheim's perspective, "sufficient conditions for identification occur only when some reference to the history of production is added" (91). Without that supplement, Goodman's account seems too generous in offering possibilities for exemplification, because possession of properties is the only criterion (88–92). Therefore, there must be this additional feature that will actually signify that the property is relevant for the situation – hence the need to add conditions of production as contexts for works of art (30–31). However, I will argue that this need for context is best met when we can project an authorial purposiveness.

I might also point out that there is a similar difference between Goodman and Wittgenstein in their thinking about example. Because Wittgenstein embeds the working of symbols within a grammar of practices, he can offer a directionality to exemplification that is not possible in Goodman. By showing how the symbol can vary between expressions of experience and expressions of norms, Wittgenstein suggests that the analysis is incomplete until one can determine how the practice involved best defines what are the exemplary qualities. I conclude from this that we need speculation about intentions to process examples in use – whether the intentions come from authors or audiences or even from the expectations built into practices. But we do not need to equate intentionality with the constant presence of decision that makes deconstructive theory argue that ultimately examples can neither denote nor be denoted by some category. Examples closely read become singular events with their own irreducible dynamic. However anything read closely enough for its possibilities becomes singular – that is a tautological feature of the explanatory framework and not anything specific to the roles examples actually play in the grammars of European languages. See for a representative version of this deconstructive approach to examples, the introduction and part 1 in Thomas Keenan, *Fables of Responsibility: Aberrations and Predicaments in Ethics and Politics* (Palo Alto: Stanford University Press, 1997).

8 *Languages of Art* (Indianapolis, IN: Bobbs Merrill, 1968), 92. Subsequent references to this work are made by page numbers in the text.

9 Geoffrey Hellman, "Symbol System and Artistic Styles" in Elgin, *The Philosophy of Nelson Goodman*, 297.

10 Wittgenstein is terrific at showing what objective accounts of experience cannot handle because of how first-person states so pervade phenomena that we cannot isolate subject from object. That means that accounts that meet standards of objectivity are not discerning enough to be trusted. But also accounts that stress a purported inner life turn out to be mirror images of accounts that reduce the world to objects. For example Cavell's talk about owning the self depends on a possibility of the subject treating its own force as an object. Cavell tends to ignore concepts of expressivity that might locate the self within activities rather than as their source and possessor. This tendency does not stem from ignorance of Wittgenstein's effort to separate confession as process from confession as a narrative of what the person thought about his or her experiences. Cavell distinguishes between enacting the self and describing the self. But as long as one's ambition is to "own" the self, even as just a condition of the activity the self performs, there will be serious temptations to treat the self as expressible in narrative. Talk of ownership risks giving the self an interest in turning its experiences into something that can be described, and hence in treating subjectivity as somehow available in the narratives one tells about oneself. It comes as no surprise then that in Cavell's perfectionist stage he turns to a language of self-knowledge. In contrast, I rely on Wittgenstein's turn from therapeutic psychology to grammar as a logic. For him one simply displays various relations of the self to its experiences, various ways of manifesting "as" and "so" by a series of equivalences. One does not own the self; one makes present its abilities to complement what elicits desires and interests by showing how the experience elicits investments by the agent. "True confession" contextualizes why wonder might matter on this occasion. It does not substitute some aspect of ownership for what can be exhibited of the state of wonder the agent undergoes.

11 Wallace Stevens, *Collected Poetry and Prose* (New York: Library of America, 1997), 77. (This work is cited in the text as *CPP*.)

12 The ending of Ian McEwan's *Atonement* offers a striking account of the pleasures and pains of dealing with historical matters under conditions that establish one-place predicates.

13 Altieri, "Tractatus Logico-Poeticus," *Critical Inquiry* 33 (2007): 527–42, and "Why Style Still Matters," forthcoming in Richard Eldridge, ed., *Oxford Companion to the Study of Philosophy and Literature*.

27

At Play in the Fields of Metaphor

TED COHEN

Introduction

In current discussions of metaphor two matters remain debated or at least awaiting clarification. This essay neither settles a debate nor offers much clarification. It only introduces considerations that may have some bearing on these matters.

One current controversy concerns how to describe what happens when a metaphor succeeds, with a central question being whether to suppose that a metaphor presents a new meaning, a metaphorical meaning in addition to the meaning the expression has when taken literally.

The other matter, no doubt related to the controversy, is the question of what it is to deny a metaphor, seemingly to advance its negation.

The Logic of Freedom

A metaphor is an irregular use of language. Regular uses of language, we may suppose, conform to what we may think of as the rules of that language. As Donald Davidson puts it,

> understanding a metaphor is as much a creative endeavor as making a metaphor, and as little guided by rules.[1]

Literal uses of language *are* guided by rules. What are these rules? I cannot say, nor can anyone else with finality, although contemporary linguists and philosophers of language do wonderful work in attempting to formulate rules of syntax and semantics.

Think of the whole of the rules of English, the "grammar" of English, if you like, as R. Now consider Shakespeare's "Macbeth doth murder sleep." Something is irregular in this sentence. However R is spelled out, and whatever semantics it advances, it will incorporate a requirement to the effect that the use of the word "murder" as a transitive verb requires a direct object that is (or was) a living thing, perhaps also requiring

---

A Companion to the Philosophy of Literature, First Edition. Edited by Garry L. Hagberg and Walter Jost.
© 2010 John Wiley & Sons Ltd. Published 2015 by John Wiley & Sons, Ltd.

that the living thing be a person. The noun "sleep" which occupies the syntactic position of the direct object of "murder" does not refer to such a thing.

It is critical to note that this use of "murder" is not merely *novel*. Words used in metaphors do exhibit novelty, but this cannot be their only feature. This point may have been underappreciated by Nelson Goodman in his powerful theory.

Goodman, mobilizing his remarkably parsimonious metaphysics and philosophy of language says that in a metaphor the word in question, which Goodman calls a "label" (strictly: a set of inscriptions), has been applied to something outside its normal extension.[2]

When, a few years ago, the term "bacteria-caused" was first applied to some ulcers, this was a new use of the term, but "This ulcer is caused by bacteria" isn't and wasn't a metaphor, and those who countenance new meanings in metaphors are not even tempted to think that "bacteria-caused" has a new meaning when applied to ulcers. Indeed it is exactly because the term has its old, standard meaning that it is medically significant to note that some ulcers are caused by bacteria. Saying bacteria cause some ulcers was new, but it did not depart from R, the rules of standard English.

Suppose that the literal sense of a sentence is somehow generated by and grasped in terms of R, the language's rules. This is why dictionaries and grammar books can be used to find the literal meanings of enigmatic sentences. But then how is the metaphorical import of a sentence generated and grasped, given that this cannot be done in terms of R precisely because R has been transgressed? Is it that an amended set of rules has been invoked, an R^*? This is implausible for a number of reasons. Here are two: (a) How could the hearer or reader be expected to know R^*, rules he has never before encountered? (b) This would make metaphor a matter of simple polysemy, more or less like ambiguity. Metaphors would be exactly like ambiguity except that a metaphor presents its extra, second, meaning for the first time.

The ambiguous sentence "Last night I slept on a cape" might mean I spent the night at Peter Kivy's in Falmouth on Cape Cod, or that, wherever I was, instead of sheets I lay upon a garment of the kind favored by Sherlock Holmes. Both these readings can be found in R, although it may be uncertain which to choose.

What of the metaphorical import of "Macbeth doth murder sleep" or of "Hitler was an animal"? R assigns no meaning to "Macbeth doth murder sleep." It does assign a literal meaning to "Hitler was an animal," but the metaphorical readings of both sentences are beyond R's purview.

It is the depreciating conception of metaphor, thinking of it as just another way of introducing a novel meaning, that Davidson rejected, after which he concluded that there simply is no extra meaning, no metaphorical meaning, and that metaphors work their effects non-semantically. Perhaps Davidson was too quick to embrace this strong conclusion. We do speak of *understanding* metaphors, even though meanings are not the only things available to be understood, and there may be something systematic in such understanding. For instance, if sleep can be murdered – say by Macbeth – then can't someone or something heal sleep? Give birth to sleep? Injure sleep? Resurrect sleep? Poets far less gifted than Shakespeare could answer yes to all these and give examples. I think you and I could.

If, when a metaphor comes forth, *R* has been abandoned, at least in some critical parts, and no *R** has taken its place, then the metaphor is effectively cut loose. I think this is true. If the metaphor does present a second meaning, there is no canonical way to determine what it is. If it advances a proposition, there is no way to formulate it uniquely. If, as Davidson has it, there is no second meaning and thus no extra proposition, then the grasping of a metaphor is an unconstricted act of imagination. There are constraints, no doubt, but there is bound to be ample room for innovation and improvisation. And this will be so however we understand what metaphorical import is. Perhaps it is a meaning with an attendant proposition, perhaps it is a presentation of a way of seeing or thinking of things, perhaps it is an inducement to speculation. None of these will be rigidly controlled.

This means that grasping a metaphor is pretty much like interpreting, understanding, and appreciating a work of art. Good. A metaphor is an invitation and inducement to a kind of freedom. Examples abound in one of the most striking books of the Bible.

The Song of Songs is a short work, running to only eight chapters, less than four pages in the King James Version. It is chock full of figures of speech. By my quick, unsystematic count there are more than three dozen figures, and it is not uncommon to regard the entire text as a single extended allegory or parable.[3]

Here are about a dozen samples. I quote them from the splendid translation by Chana Bloch and Ariel Bloch.[4] In presenting these quotations I preserve a useful convention introduced by the Blochs. They identify four distinct speakers in the poem, and use a different typeface for each: the young woman (italics), the young man (roman), the daughters of Jerusalem (boldface italics), the woman's brothers (boldface roman). These identifications do not matter much for the purposes of this essay, but it is a great help in finding the figurative sense of some lines to know who speaks them. (There are no lines quoted here that are spoken by the daughters of Jerusalem.)

I divide the samples into three groups, metaphors, similes, and "other." The others may seem to you to be metaphors or it might be better to call them allegories. It does not matter for present purposes: they are all figurative.

Metaphors

I am the rose of Sharon,
the wild lily of the valleys. (2:1)

My love is a gazelle, a wild stag. (2:9)

Your neck is a tower of David
raised in splendor,
a thousand bucklers hang upon it,
all the shields of the warriors.

Your breasts are two fawns,
twins of a gazelle,
grazing in a field of lilies. (4:4–5)

Your lips are honey, honey and milk
are under your tongue,
your clothes hold the scent of Lebanon. (4:11)

An enclosed garden is my sister, my bride,
a hidden well, a sealed spring.

Your branches are an orchard
of pomegranate trees heavy with fruit,
flowering henna and spikenard,
spikenard and saffron, cane and cinnamon,
with every tree of frankincense,
myrrh and aloes,
all the rare spices.

You are a fountain in the garden,
a well of living waters
that stream from Lebanon. (4:12–15)

If she is a wall, we will build
a silver turret upon her.
If she is a door, we will bolt her
with beams of cedarwood.

I am a wall
and my breasts are towers.
But for my lover I am
a city of peace. (8:9–10)

Similes

Like a lily in a field
of thistles,
such is my love
among the young women. (2:2)

his thighs like marble pillars
on pedestals of gold. (5:15)

That day you seemed to me a tall palm tree
and your breasts
the clusters of its fruit. (7:8)

And oh, may your breasts be like clusters
of grapes on a vine, the scent
of your breath like apricots,
your mouth good wine – (7:9–10)

Other

> **Catch us the foxes,**
> **the quick little foxes**
> **that raid our vineyards**
> **now, when the vines are in blossom.** (2:15)
>
> You have ravished my heart,
> my sister, my bride,
> ravished me with one glance of your eyes,
> one link of your necklace. (4:9)
>
> My vineyard is all my own.
> Keep your thousand, Solomon! And pay
> two hundred to those
> who must guard the fruit. (8:12)

In their excellent introduction to their wonderful translation of the Song of Songs the Blochs take a curious and charming false step.[5] Writing about various ways in which the Song has been taken, they say,

> Early audiences would have no trouble understanding the Song in its literal sense. . . . (30)

What they mean is an understanding of the Song as having to do with physical lovemaking. As they claim at the beginning of their introduction,

> The Song of Songs is a poem about the sexual awakening of a young woman and her lover. (3)

And the Blochs are saying that early audiences took the Song in just that way. I have absolutely no standing from which I might dispute the Blochs on either of these points – what the Song is "about," or how early audiences understood the Song. In fact I think they are right about both matters. But they are wrong to speak of a "literal sense." Here are two consecutive sections, from chapters 4 and 5 of the Song:

> Awake, north wind! O south wind, come,
> breathe upon my garden,
> let its spices stream out.
> Let my lover come into his garden
> and taste its delicious fruit.
>
> I have come into my garden,
> my sister, my bride,
> I have gathered my myrrh and my spices,
> I have eaten from the honeycomb,
> I have drunk the milk and the wine.

What is the literal sense of these lines? The woman asks the winds to blow so that her garden, wherein are herbs, spices, and fruits, will be fragrant; and she asks that her lover enter that garden which she says is now his garden and taste his fruit. The man then says that he has indeed entered the garden and enjoyed its contents. And that is all the man and woman literally say.

If the lines are "about" a young woman offering her body to her lover and his appreciative possession of it, then this is a figurative upshot of the lines and is not their literal sense.

Perhaps when the Blochs speak of taking the Song of Songs "literally," they do not mean taking it non-metaphorically (a primary meaning of "literal"), but they mean taking it in its real or obvious or correct sense (a subsidiary meaning of "literal"). It seems likely that this is what the Blochs have in mind, that the erotic reading is the "correct" reading and they put this by calling that reading literal.[6] If so, then they are not denying that the Song is figurative, but they are begging the question against those who opt for a different figurative meaning.[7]

Various commentators, including rabbis and Church fathers have attempted to domesticate the Song of Songs, to avoid reading it as a poem about physical lovemaking.[8] What they have done is not to impose figurative understandings in place of a literal one. They have advanced one figurative reading over another. It is surely possible to resist these domestications and insist on a human erotic reading, as the Blochs do and I agree, but not on the grounds that these other readings are only figurative. The physically erotic reading is already figurative.

As the Bloch's note, citing Robert Alter, the Song of Songs virtually flaunts its use of simile and metaphor, and perhaps allegory and parable as well. But when one moves to figuration, the rules that constrained literal meaning are gone, and no one – not even the maker of the metaphors – can control how these figures are taken. One may well argue against the rabbis and Church fathers, but not on the grounds that they have introduced figures of speech when none were present.

Robert Alter argues (successfully, I think) that the King James translators have rendered the Hebrew expression *bi-msibbo* as meaning reclining or sitting at a table when they should have understood it to mean reclining or lying on a bed.[9] They got a wrong literal meaning. When the domesticators argue that the Song is about Godly love, not human physical love, they are not arguing about literal meaning, nor are we when we argue against them.

There are lines in the Song of Songs that are literally about a man entering and taking possession of a garden. The lines are read metaphorically as being about a man making love to a woman. Then they are read again metaphorically, but now as being about love between God and Israel. Call these the garden reading, the erotic reading, and the spiritual reading. It is possible that the spiritual reading arose directly from the garden reading, that is, as a metaphorical understanding of literal lines; but it seems likely that it arose from the erotic reading. Indeed the erotic reading can seem so inescapably in place that readers like the Blochs think of it as a literal reading. If the spiritual reading does arise from the erotic reading, then we have an example of one metaphor giving rise to another, a new metaphor that displaces the earlier one.

The garden reading is the grandparent of the spiritual reading, and the intermediate generation is the erotic reading.[10]

The Song of Songs contains many cues that its figurative passages can and perhaps should be understood in terms of physical love. William Blake's "The Sick Rose" contains few such cues, if any – in fact it is possible to understand it only as an address to a pest-ridden flower – but it is customarily understood, like the Song, to be about sex.

> O Rose, thou art sick!
> The invisible worm
> That flies in the night,
> In the howling storm,
>
> Has found out thy bed
> Of crimson joy:
> And his dark secret love
> Does thy life destroy.

At certain times in certain places it may be difficult to write or speak about sex literally, leaving authors in need of figures of speech, lines not literally about sex but understood that way when taken figuratively. But when an author relies upon figurative understandings, there is no longer any guarantee that the figures will be read in the intended sense.

There is some temptation to suppose that metaphors are not, so to speak, invertible. That is to say that if *A* (understood literally) can be understood metaphorically as *B*, it is unlikely that *B* (understood literally) can be understood metaphorically as *A*. Thus Richard Moran notes,

> But, on the other hand, the floral and culinary stock in trade of erotic metaphor is rarely reversible. If we are enjoined to imagine a garden in her face or lips like cherries, we may be sure we are not to read against the grain in the direction of a face in the garden or cherries like lips.[11]

But it can happen, and does. Here is an example in which a literal description of physical lovemaking, a kind of pre-positional foreplay, leads to a piece of geography.

> License my roving hands, and let them go
> Before, behind, between, above, below.
> O, my America, my Newfoundland,
> My kingdom, safest when with one man mann'd,
> My mine of precious stones, my empery.[12]

I hope this section has shown, or at least strongly suggested, that metaphorical import is not rigidly fixed. If metaphorical import is not exactly and entirely up for grabs, then it is still *free* in a way that rule-bound literal meaning is not. And if that is so, the question naturally arises of *what* is being denied when a metaphor is negated.

513

The Logic of Denial

There is something powerful and penetrating about some metaphors, even insinuating, one might say, and they can be hard to resist. Richard Moran has noted this, and he says,

> And the full appreciative comprehension of a metaphor can make any subsequent denial of the point it makes seem feeble or disingenuous, in much the same way that appreciative understanding of a joke can overpower any subsequent refusal of the point *it* makes.[13]

And yet it is possible to deny a metaphor, to refuse it, and some metaphors themselves are denials of metaphors.

Whatever metaphorical import is, and however it gets across, when it is delivered by way of a declarative sentence, that sentence will have a (logical) negation, and someone embracing that negation is denying the metaphor.

If we disregard the specifics of grammatical and logical form, we may think generically of a metaphor as "*A* is *B*." The denial of a metaphor, then, is "*A* is not *B*" or something that implies that "*A* is *B*" is false. This denial can be, as I will call it, either *internal* or *external*. When the denial is internal, it is within a (written or spoken) text. When the denial is external, the text presents only "*A* is *B*" and it is left to us (readers or hearers) to produce a denial.

A metaphor can be denied neither externally nor internally but in a kind of *ignoratio*, by someone simply unwilling or unable to take it as a metaphor. Here is a contrived example.

> Romeo's doctor is concerned that Romeo shows signs of suffering a vitamin deficiency, and recommends that Romeo spend more time outdoors during daylight hours. Romeo protests that he wishes to spend as much time as possible with Juliet, and that he can do this only indoors, in places where they are hidden from their families.
>
> Expressing his great need to be with Juliet, to be in her presence, Romeo declares "Juliet is the sun." The doctor objects: "Juliet is not the sun," indicating, of course, that Juliet is not a source of the vitamin D Romeo needs.

Has the doctor contradicted Romeo? Well, yes and no. The doctor has uttered a sentence which plainly is a negation of Romeo's sentence, but still, we might say, what Romeo has "said" or "suggested" is not what the doctor has denied. Here we have what might be called simply a *refusal* of a metaphor, a refusal to respond as if the sentence were a metaphor at all.

The external denial of a metaphor does take the sentence as a metaphor, acknowledges the content of the metaphor, but refuses to accept that content. Here is an example.

> I respond to T. S. Eliot's "We are the hollow men" in this way.
>
> Who is this "we," Mr Eliot? Include me out. Perhaps you are a hollow man, and you may speak for yourself, although it seems to me that you, becoming ever more

desiccated as you moved east, finally moving out of America itself, and having found yourself unable to accept and appreciate America, having failed at everything Walt Whitman achieved, took yourself to Europe where you could not find what you hoped was there and continue to believe was once there, and so you have projected your own sense of loss upon a great collection of humanity. We will not let you speak for us. If you like, say "I and some of my acquaintances, especially Ezra Pound, are hollow men, or seem to one another to be hollow men," but leave the rest of us out of it.

Furthermore, April is not the cruelest month. Far from it.

That is an external denial of a metaphor. Here are some examples of internally denied figures, figures that appear negated in their texts.

> No man is an island entire of itself. . . .[14]

> The first long shadows in the fields
> Are like mortal difficulty.
> The first birdsong is not like that at all.[15]

We have no further interest in the example of Romeo's doctor. He may well not be denying Romeo's metaphor. He might accept Romeo's metaphorical description of Juliet and be insisting only that however much the sunny Juliet does for Romeo, she does not supply him with vitamin D.

When a metaphor "A is B" is successful, presumably there is something – call it "X" – that A and B can be thought to have in common, even if A has X only metaphorically. Or, if you prefer not to think of metaphors in terms of meanings and propositions, perhaps you would like to say that A can be thought of as B, or seen as B. If so, then A will be thought of or seen as being X. (Thus Romeo thinks of or sees Juliet as being warm, like the sun.)

Then what is being denied when it is asserted that A is not B? It cannot be sensibly asserted that there is *no* X common to A and B, for as anyone even slightly infected by metaphysics will tell you, any two things are similar in some respect or another. This guarantees that "A is like B" is invariably a literal truth, and if so, this promises that "A is like B" is even more strongly guaranteed to be a successful figurative simile.

It must be with reference to some specific X, and not to X's in general, that it is being denied that A is B. When Robert Hass says that the first birdsong is not like mortal difficulty, perhaps he is not saying that there is no way in which they are alike, but only that the first birdsong is not like mortal difficulty in the way in which the first long shadows in the fields are like mortal difficulty. And, as shall be noted presently, Donne's denial that any man is an island is to be understood in terms of a specified feature. An internal denial of a metaphor, as with these lines of Robert Hass and John Donne, customarily supplies, in one way or another, the X which is being denied to A.[16]

There are two ways in which one might contest a metaphor without exactly contradicting it. One is to concede that the metaphor may be apt for its maker but refuse its applicability to oneself.

The other way of disarming or parrying a metaphor is to concede its probity with regard to a certain point of similarity but to note another point at which there is no similarity.

It is possible and not uncommon to admit the salience of a metaphor but not to accept it for oneself. Then the metaphor-maker speaks only for himself, and to understand him you do not have to see things as he does. When Romeo says "Juliet is the sun," you are not required to see Juliet as Romeo does. What is required of you is that you grasp how Romeo sees Juliet.[17]

In Kafka's writing, the figurative devices of allegory, parable, metaphor, and simile are used to present the world, or part of it, and its people seen and felt in a bleak light. I do not see things in that light. When I wonder at this difference between Kafka and me, I imagine Kafka as a frail, young, Jewish man coming of age as a German speaker, with a domineering father, in Czechoslovakia more than a century ago, while I came of age in rural Illinois after World War II, with loving and supportive parents, living in a town displaying no trace of anti-Semitism.

Such a comparison irresistibly recalls Wittgenstein's well-known remark, "The world of the happy man is not the same as the world of the sad man." Indeed. Sometimes different views of the world seem to be only that – different *views* – and to be independent of what may or may not be the facts.

There is a group of academics and quasi-academics vocationally engaged in telling us how dismal things are. This group includes various lower-level devotees of Nietzsche, Marx, Freud, Heidegger, and Wittgenstein.[18]

When resisting this *kvetching*, one is often annoyed yet again when one is told that it is because of one's failure of vision and insight that one doesn't see the gloomy prospect. Thus it is stupid or ignorant of me to be happy. This is an especially annoying indictment when it comes from highly paid, underworked professors. These seem to be people telling us how wretched things are while they enjoy their fat, happy lives. They are forensic pathologists, perhaps sorry about the mayhem, but glad to have the business.

Annoyance aside, however, if these complainers are not entitled to write off my happy satisfaction to my opacity, then neither am I secure in assigning their gloominess to their dyspepsia or their unearned smugness.

Here we have conflicting metaphors. Neither is an obvious *denial* of the other, and yet they feel incompatible. One describes the world in terms implying that the world is happy, pleasant, beautiful. The other's terms suggest that the world is painful, ugly, endlessly disappointing. Is it possible to accept both metaphors, at least to understand them? Perhaps it is like looking at a Necker cube, struggling to see it in one way and then in the other, unable to see it in both ways at once but certain that it is the same one thing being seen. Are philosophers telling us about the world bound to be either Laughing Philosophers or Weeping Philosophers?

Suppose someone (perhaps the very same gloomy Mr Eliot) opines that Western civilization is a wasteland. You disagree, but instead of simply denying that assessment, you offer a different metaphor. Then there will be two metaphors:

Western civilization is a wasteland.
Western civilization is a spiritual and material cornucopia.

Not only is it impossible to see the West in both ways at once, but each view seems to exclude the other permanently – that is, it may be impossible to pass from one view to the other even if both metaphor-makers are understandable.

It is possible for two metaphors of the same subject to be, if not exactly complementary, certainly not contradictory. John Donne is such a double-metaphor-maker. His "no man is an island" is part of an extended metaphor. Here is a part of that:

> No man is an island entire of itself; every man is a piece of the continent, a part of the main; if a clod be washed away by the sea, Europe is the less, as well as if a promontory were, as well as any manner of thy friends or of thine own were; any man's death diminishes me, because I am involved in mankind. And therefore never send to know for whom the bell tolls; it tolls for thee.[19]

And within the same text there is this:

> all mankind is of one author and is one volume; when one man dies, one chapter is not torn out of the book, but is translated into a better language; and every chapter must be so translated. God employs several translators; some pieces are translated by age, some by sickness, some by war, some by justice; but God's hand is in every translation, and his hand shall bind up all our scattered leaves again for that library where every book shall lie open to one another.

Two ways of looking at a human life. It is not possible to see both views at once, but neither otherwise excludes the other.

These ways of denying metaphors are markedly different. My imagined response to Eliot's remark about hollow men offers no competing metaphor. All I have said is that I do not – perhaps cannot – see myself as a hollow man.

The response to Eliot's appraisal of the West – a "wasteland," on the other hand, is in the form of a metaphor, a metaphor that implies that Eliot's is wrong, or presents a view of the West that precludes Eliot's view.

Donne's "no man is an island" is different yet again. No doubt it is a negative metaphor, understandable as the negation of a metaphor, but it is contained, as it were, within an affirmative metaphor. Its reasoned background is this:

Every man is part of mankind.
Mankind is a continent.
No part of a continent is an island.
Therefore, no man is an island.

This is an illustration of how it is with some metaphors. First, in their creation, they flout the rules of logic and language, but then, in working their effects, they exploit those very rules, including those having to do with negation.

Conclusion

We do not know exactly how metaphors work, and perhaps we never shall, although we know more than before thanks especially to recent work by Josef Stern and Roger White.[20]

We do know that a metaphor-maker is exploiting the freedom he gains when he ventures beyond the standard rules of his language. It follows that in grasping his metaphor we will have to follow him in his exodus with no firm guarantee that we will join him in the promised land. Furthermore, should we decide that we do not want the fruit of his excursion we may still have to venture outside the bounds, into the field, just in order to find a way to deny his figure. It can be exhilarating. And dangerous.

Notes

1. Donald Davidson, "What Metaphors Mean," *Critical Inquiry* 5:1 (Autumn 1978): 31.
2. Nelson Goodman, *Languages of Art* (Indianapolis, IN: Bobbs-Merrill, 1968), especially chapter 2. Goodman either failed to note or neglected to explain cases in which the metaphorically denoted object does lie within a word's normal extension, as in "Hitler was an animal" and "the sun is a gas." An ingenious Goodmanian explanation has been proposed by Israel Scheffler in his *Beyond the Letter* (London: Routledge and Kegan Paul, 1979).
3. In their study *Idolatry* (Cambridge, MA: Harvard University Press, 1992), a fascinating discussion of the use of the terms of illicit sex through which Israel is denounced sometimes as a whore, sometimes as a faithless husband who patronizes whores, Moshe Halbertal and Avishai Margalit say the Song of Songs is interpreted as a parable (29), and as an allegory (50). I am not concerned with what are otherwise perfectly legitimate distinctions between parable, allegory, simile, metaphor, metonymy, litotes, oxymoron, meiosis, and the rest.
4. *The Song of Songs*, trans., with an introduction and commentary, Chana Bloch and Ariel Bloch, with a foreword by Stephen Mitchell and an afterword by Robert Alter (New York: Modern Library, 2006). (The book was published originally by Random House in 1995, and then as a University of California Press paper edition in 1998.) When referring to the translation of the Biblical text I will use traditional chapter and verse numbers. Other references, to the Bloch commentary and the Alter afterword, are by page number.
5. Although the introduction is credited to Chana Bloch, the Blochs report that they consulted one another extensively, and so I assume they took this step together.
6. As likely as this is, as a guess about what the Blochs intend, it had not occurred to me until Amos Cohen pointed it out.
7. It is diverting to consider uses of the word "literally" in which it functions as a kind of intensifier, and has nothing to do with figuration, as in "I was literally horrified." Things become especially interesting when what is asserted to be "literal" is itself not literal, as in "I was literally beside myself with rage (or laughter)." It may not be so, but what if the use of "literal" to mean correct or exact were once a figurative use of the word, with its literal sense meaning non-metaphorical? Then Romeo might say "Juliet is literally the sun" meaning Juliet is not literally the sun. Oh my! No one is more sensitive to or adept at such

twists of language than James Joyce, and if you have a taste for such things you might consider the first line of Joyce's "The Dead." It reads, "Lily, the caretaker's daughter, was literally run off her feet." In conversations with the late Frank Kinahan, a profound Joyce scholar, I became persuaded that a full appreciation of this sentence is, approximately, a full appreciation of the entire story.

8   The Blocks canvass a number of these sanitized readings on pp. 14–15. An excellent discussion of what happens when a text is canonized is in Moshe Halbertal, *People of the Book: Canon, Meaning, and Authority* (Cambridge, MA: Harvard University Press, 1997).

9   In Bloch and Bloch, *The Song of Songs*, 120.

10 If the erotic reading was already securely in place when the Song of Songs was canonized, the question arises of why the canonizers took on the burden of the book, given that they could not leave it with its erotic reading. Devorah Shubowitz has made the excellent suggestion (in conversation) that the book may already have been canonized in the sense of having become so widely popular that it seemed bound to be a permanent part of the people's literature, and therefore had to be acknowledged. That may well be true, and when the powerfully attractive and engaging character of the book is acknowledged, the canonizers might have felt a need to adopt the book and make use of it. For a discussion of canon-making see Halbertal, *People of the Book*.

11 Richard Moran, "Seeing and Believing: Metaphor, Image, and Force," *Critical Inquiry* 16:1 (Autumn, 1989): 87–112. In his very careful and exceptionally useful essay Moran is careful not to say there is never such a reversal. His essay, valuable in many respects, is also one of the few texts on metaphor to take a significant interest in negated metaphors, the next topic in the present essay.

12 John Donne, from his elegy "To His Mistress Going to Bed."

13 Moran, "Seeing and Believing," 91.

14 John Donne, from his devotional Meditation 17.

15 Robert Hass. This is the first of his "Three Dawn Songs in Summer," printed in Hass's collection *Time and Materials* (New York: Harper-Collins, 2007). Hass says that it was proposed to him that he should write a sequence of poems that were in succession simile, metaphor, and allegory. The lines just quoted, then, are the simile. The following metaphor and allegory are

> The light in summer is very young and wholly unsupervised.
> No one has made it sit down to breakfast.
> It's the first one up, the first one out,

and

> Because he has opened his eyes, he must be light
> And she, sleeping beside him, must be the visible.
> One ringlet of hair curled about her ear.
> Into which he whispers, "Wake up!"
> "Wake up!" he whispers.

16 The relevant point of similarity is determined by the "context" in which a metaphor appears. The character of this context has been investigated in two excellent studies, Josef Stern, *Metaphor in Context* (Cambridge, MA: MIT Press, 2000), and Roger White, *The Structure of Metaphor* (Oxford: Blackwell, 1996). Both these texts are acutely and sensitively concerned with the contexts in which metaphors occur. Stern's work is a meticulous

and imaginative effort to understand the semantics of metaphor in terms of very sophisticated and up-to-date linguistics and philosophy of language. White's work is less technical but more concerned with the subtleties to be found in a great many extended literary examples.

17 The use of metaphor in this quintessential achievement of art, communicating to others how the artist sees and feels, is a topic of my *Thinking of Others: On the Talent for Metaphor* (Princeton, NJ: Princeton University Press, 2008).

18 A curious quintet, I think, composed entirely of Jews and possible anti-Semites, sometimes in the same person.

19 This and the following passage are from his devotional Meditation 17.

20 Stern, *Metaphor in Context*, and White, *The Structure of Metaphor*.

28

Macbeth Appalled

STANLEY CAVELL

When a given text is claimed to work in the light, or in the shadow, of another – taking obvious extremes, as one of a given work's sources or as one of its commentaries – a measure of the responsibility of such a linking is the degree to which each is found responsive to the other, to tap the other, as for its closer attention. *Macbeth* is a likely work to turn to in these terms on a number of counts. Being Shakespearean melodrama, it takes up the question of responsiveness, the question, we might say, of the truth of response, of whether an action or reaction is – or can be – sensually or emotionally adequate to its cause, neither withholding nor excessive (Macbeth's to news of his wife's death, or Macduff's to his wife's and his childrens', or Macbeth's to Banquo's reappearance, or Lady Macbeth's to Macbeth's return from the wars). More than any other Shakespearean tragedy, *Macbeth* thematically shows melodramatic responsiveness as a contest over interpretations, hence over whether an understanding is – or can be – intellectually adequate to its question, neither denying what is there, nor affirming what is not there (a deed, a dagger). As if what is at stake is the intelligibility of the human to itself.

The question of human intelligibility takes the form, in what I want to begin to work through in *Macbeth*, of a question of the intelligibility of human history, a question whether we can see what we make happen and tell its difference from what happens to us, as in the difference between human action and human suffering. I conceive of *Macbeth* as belonging as much with Shakespearean histories as with the tragedies, but not as a history that takes for granted the importance of the political and of what constitutes a pertinent representation of its present condition. It raises, rather, the question of what history is a history of, hence the question of how its present is to be thought of. This continues the direction I was taking the last time I was caught up in a text of Shakespeare's, in thinking about *Antony and Cleopatra*. There, accepting as uncontroversial the ideas that a Shakespeare history play forms some precedent or parable for its own political present, and that the playing of Antony and Cleopatra and their company is a setting for world catastrophe, I proposed thinking through the play as a representation of the catastrophe of the modern advent of skepticism (hence also of the advent of the new science, a new form of knowing), taken as an individual

---

A Companion to the Philosophy of Literature, First Edition. Edited by Garry L. Hagberg and Walter Jost.
© 2010 John Wiley & Sons Ltd. Published 2015 by John Wiley & Sons, Ltd.

and a historical process. (This is recorded in the introduction to my *Disowning Knowledge*.) But while certain contemporary historical events are accepted as sources for *Macbeth* – accounts of the Gowrie Conspiracy and of the Gunpowder Plot – there is not, to my knowledge, an uncontroversial sense of the play as unfolding, in its claustrophobic setting, its own sense of its present politics and of human history. On the reading of the play proposed here this lack of clarity itself becomes a certain confirmation of the play's invocation of its sense of its own matrix, specifically a sense of the political as itself changing, as itself a scene of obscurity, even, one might say, of the occult.

I might describe the drift of this reading as following out my sense that the texts of *Macbeth* and of *Antony and Cleopatra* – I am glad to accept them as dating within a year or so of one another – are opposite faces of a study of the interpenetration of the erotic and the political. Here is a way I described the changeover of worlds envisioned in *Antony and Cleopatra*: "Hegel says that with the birth of Christianity a new subjectivity enters the world. I want to say that with the birth of skepticism, hence of modern philosophy, a new intimacy, or wish for it, enters the world; call it privacy shared (not shared with the public, but from it)." *Macbeth*, I conjecture, secretes its own environment of a new intimacy, of privacy shared, a setting not exactly of world catastrophe but of a catastrophe of privacy, hence of a certain politics. This privacy is expressed in philosophy as a catastrophe of knowledge. It may be thought of as the skeptical isolation of the mind from the body, simultaneously a sense that everything is closed to, occluded in, human knowledge (in philosophy?) and at the same time that everything is open to human knowledge (in science? in magic?). The aspiration and eroticization of the new science invoked at the opening of *Antony and Cleopatra* ("Then must you needs find out new heaven, new earth") marks its relation to and distance from the closing of the world of *Macbeth* within magic, science's origin and shadow.

It matters to me, in ways some of which will become explicit, to mention in passing another sort of unfinished or continuing business of mine determining my interest in history in *Macbeth* – my attention in recent years to the work of Emerson, in which narrative history, let us say, is under incessant attack. It is clear enough that Emerson's mission as a writer of the philosophical constitution of a new nation is in part to free its potential members from an enslaving worship of the past and its institutions, in religion, in politics, in literature, in philosophy. But the anticipation is quite uncanny, in his "History," the first essay of his First Series of Essays, of the spirit of the Annales historians' disdain for great events, their pursuit of the uneventful, a pursuit requiring an altered sense of time and of change, an interpretation of what I call the ordinary or the everyday. I had thought that Emerson's formulations concerning history would play a more extensive role in this text – or in some unwritten one of which the present text is perhaps a fragment – than has so far proven the case. At present I will be content with four citations from "History":

> I have no expectation that any man will read history aright, who thinks that what was done in a remote age, by men whose names have resounded far, has any deeper sense than what he is doing to-day.

> But along with the civil and metaphysical history of man, another history goes daily forward – that of the external world, – in which he is not less strictly implicated.

> I am ashamed to see what a shallow village tale our so-called History is. . . . What does Rome know of rat and lizard? What are Olympiads and Consulates to these neighboring systems of being? Nay, what food or experience or succor have they for the Esquimaux seal-hunter, for the Kanaka in his canoe, for the fisherman, the stevedore, the porter?

> When a thought of Plato becomes a thought to me, – when a truth that fired the soul of Pindar fires mine, time is no more.

The immediate background for what follows formed itself in an unpredicted interaction of two seminars I was teaching two springs ago. The more elaborate of these was a large seminar on recent trends in Shakespearean criticism that my colleague Marjorie Garber and I were offering on an experimental basis to a group of students divided between the study of literature and of philosophy. The division itself is one that various trends in contemporary literary theory have promised to move beyond, but which, in my part of the academic forest, is kept in place by all but immovable institutional forces. The trends in criticism we proposed to consider fell, not surprisingly, into the more or less recognizable categories of feminist, psychoanalytic, and new historicist work; but while as an outsider to the institutions of Shakespeare study I was happy for the instruction in recontextualizing this material, and while the feminist and the psychoanalytic continued to seem to me about what I expected criticism to be, the new historicist, for all its evident attractions, kept presenting itself to me as combating something that I kept failing to grasp steadily or clearly. Put otherwise, in reading the feminist and/or the psychoanalytic critics I did not feel that I had in *advance* to answer the questions, What does Shakespeare think women are, or think psychology is?, but that I could read these pieces as part of thinking about these questions; whereas I found myself, in reading the new historicist critics, somehow required to have an independent answer to the question, What does Shakespeare think history is?

The form the question took for me more particularly was, How does Shakespeare think things happen? – is it in the way science thinks, in the way magic thinks, or religion, or politics, or perhaps in the way works of art, for example, works of poetic drama think? It is not clear that these questions make good sense. You may even feel in them a certain unstable frame of mind, as if there is already palpable in them a response to *Macbeth*.

This form of the question of history was shaped for me by the other seminar I was offering that spring, on Romanticism and skepticism, in which the romantic fantasy of a union between philosophy and poetry was a recurrent topic, particularized in the question to what extent Emerson is to be thought of as a philosopher and the question of the extent to which, or sense in which, Wittgenstein's thinking is a function of his writing. An important theoretical statement of the questions of philosophy and writing for the seminar was Heidegger's "On the Origin of the Work of Art," taking up its formulation according to which the *work* of the work of art is that of letting truth happen; and taking up Heidegger's relating, as the German does, of the idea of happening to the idea of history; so that the implied notion is that truth becomes historical in art. This can be seen as a contesting of Hegel's finding that the belief in art as the highest expression of truth is a thing of the past. Behind both Heidegger and Emerson we read Friedrich Schlegel, the great translator and follower of Shakespeare, who had called for the union of philosophy and poetry, who had said that what happens in poetry happens in a given work always or never, whose concept of *poesis*, or poetic making or work, evidently inspires Heidegger's idea of the particular, irreplaceable work art does, and who in his extraordinary essay "On Incomprehensibility" cites Shakespeare's "infinitely many depths, subterfuges, and intentions" as an example of the conscious artist enabled to carry on "ironically, hundreds of years after their deaths, with their most faithful followers and admirers," and who also in that essay on incomprehensibility had said, "I absolutely detest incomprehension, not only the incomprehension of the uncomprehending but even more the incomprehension of the comprehending" – the moral of which I take to concern the present human intellectual task as one of undoing our present understanding of understanding, a task I find continued with startling faithfulness to Schlegel's terms in Emerson's "Self-Reliance," understanding this essay to be, as it quite explicitly declares itself to be, an essay on human understanding.

In the reading we assigned ourselves for our Shakespeare seminar, I found *Macbeth* to be the text of Shakespeare's about which the most interesting concentration of current critical intelligence had been brought to bear. Both Marjorie Garber and Janet Adelman have recently published major discussions of the play, as has Steven Mullaney, whose work cites its affiliation with, and is cited in the work of, Stephen Greenblatt. While *Macbeth* is not given special attention in Greenblatt's *Shakespearean Negotiations*, certain sentences from that book's introduction – entitled "The Circulation of Social Energy" – rather haunt the preoccupations that will guide my remarks here. Greenblatt's introduction concludes with the sentence, "The speech of the dead, like my own speech, is not private property," about which I feel both that I agree with the intuition or impulse being expressed, and at the same time, that this expression invites me to deny something – something about the privacy of language – that I have never affirmed, that no one can simply have affirmed. I must try, even briefly, to articulate this double feeling. I am not alone in finding the most significant work of this century on the idea of the privacy of language to be Wittgenstein's *Philosophical Investigations*. Wittgenstein rather cultivates the impression – which the prevailing view of him takes *as* his thesis – that he denies language is private; whereas his teaching is that the assertion or the denial either of the publicness or of the privateness of my language is empty. Philosophers, typically modern philosophers, do chronically seem to be denying something, typically that we can know there is a world and others and we in it, and then denying that they are denying it. Wittgenstein is distinguished by asking (as it were non-rhetorically), "What gives the impression that I want to deny anything?" His answer has to do with his efforts to destroy philosophical illusions (ones he takes apparently as endemic in Western philosophical thought): denial is in the effect of a presiding, locked philosophical struggle between, let us say, skepticism and metaphysics. To understand this effect or impression is part of Wittgenstein's philosophical mission. For him simply to *deny* that he is *denying* privacy, say by asserting publicness, would accordingly amount to no intellectual advance. It would merely constitute a private assertion of publicness, as though publicness itself had become private property. Something of the sort is a way of putting my intuition of what *Macbeth* is about; one might call it the privatization of politics or think of it as a discovery of the state of nature.

Because at the moment I see my contribution to the study of *Macbeth* to lie perhaps in addressing certain features of its language that I find peculiar to it, I shall mostly forgo discussion of recent important work, and its conflicts, on the question of gender in *Macbeth*, as for instance Janet Adelman's proposal (in "Born of Woman"[1]) that the play embodies at once fantasies of absolute maternal domination and of absolute escape from that domination (a discussion, besides, whose generosity in the notation of the critical literature goes beyond my scholarship); and as Marjorie Garber's rather conflicting proposal (in "Macbeth: The Male Medusa"[2]) that the play studies gender indeterminacy. I mark this elision here and at the same time give a little warm-up, out-of-context exercise in the way I read Shakespeare's lines, by taking a certain exception to Garber's interpretation in that piece of a familiar exchange in *Macbeth*, one that can be taken as involving a discourse of gender.

When Macbeth says, "I dare do all that may become a man. / Who dares do more is none," Lady Macbeth replies, "What beast was't then / That made you break this enterprise to me? / When you durst do it, then you were a man" (1.7.46–9). Garber reads this as an all-too-familiar sexual taunt, a questioning of her partner's masculinity. Without denying the taunt in Lady Macbeth's question, I find myself struck by her taunting interpretation of Macbeth's idea of excessive daring as meaning that to strike beyond certain human limits is to be a beast. If we take it – something that will come back – that Lady Macbeth shares with Macbeth, as they share every other idea, something like the idea of men as beasts, then this tells another way to hear her puzzling continuation: "To be more than what you were, you would / Be so much more the man" (1.7.50–51). That is: To be more beast *is* to be more man. On this way of thinking, her sexual taunt is something more than, or is prejudicially confined in being called, an "attack upon his masculinity, his male identity." It is as much an attack on human sexuality as such, as it has revealed itself; surely including an attack on its presence in her.

My fastening on to the species reading of the sexual taunt – its expression of an anxiety about *human* identity – has been prepared by the way I have over the years addressed the issue of philosophical skepticism as an expression of the human wish to escape the bounds or bonds of the human, if not from above then from below. I call it the human craving for, and horror of, the inhuman, of limitlessness, of monstrousness. (Besides being a beast, another species-like contrast with being human is being a monster. It may be that Macbeth and Lady Macbeth have reason to suppress this possibility while they can, to cover it with a somewhat different horror.) There is in me, accordingly, a standing possibility that I use the more general, or less historical (is it? and is it more metaphysical?) species anxiety to cover a wish to avoid thinking

525

through the anxiety of gender. If there is a good reason to run this risk it is that the reverse covering is also a risk, since knowing what is to be thought about the human is part of knowing what is to be thought about gender.

The risks of confining interpretation – to move now further into the play – are exemplified in the much-considered announcement of Macduff's that he was untimely ripped from the womb. Macbeth's response is to denounce, or pray for, or command disbelief in, the "fiends / That palter with us in a double sense; / That keep the word of promise to our ear, / And break it to our hope" (3.8.19–22). The picture here is that to wish to rule out equivocation, the work of witches, is the prayer of tyranny. The picture is itself equivocal, however, since it must be asked why Macbeth believes Macduff. That means both: Why does he believe this man? and Why does he believe what this man says? Here I can merely assert something. In turning against Macduff (to "try the last against him"), Macbeth is contesting not simply a man (whatever that is) but an interpretation; or really a double interpretation. The first interpretation, I believe uncontested, is that being of no woman born just means being untimely ripped from the womb. Some critics have expressed puzzlement and dissatisfaction over this interpretation, feeling that a fateful moment is made to depend on a quibble, as if Shakespeare is being superficial or sloppy; yet they feel forced to accept it, presumably because Macbeth accepts it. But I do not know that any have expressed a sense that Macbeth may himself (though he has suggested other possibilities – that Macduff derives from a girl, or from witches) have felt forced.

This is the burden of what I suggest as the second interpretation Macbeth contests in his fatal encounter with Macduff, one that associates with the name of Caesar the procedure of delivering a child by an incision through the abdominal wall and uterus. Macbeth had identified Banquo as the one "under [whom] / My genius is rebuk'd; as, it is said, / Mark Antony's was by Caesar" (3.1.53–5). It is congenial to my sense of things that this fact of Caesar's rebuke cited by Macbeth about Mark Antony is notable in *Antony and Cleopatra*; beyond this, my suggestion that Macbeth silently associates Macduff's origin as partaking of Caesar's and so transfers to the antagonist before him the power to rebuke or subdue his spirit (for example the power to force his acceptance of that other's interpretation of what is between them), is a reading which reveals Macbeth to be afraid of domination by a masculine as much as by a feminine figure. I say he is contesting an interpretation (or fantasy), and it is one to which, this being tragedy, he succumbs, having (always) already accepted an interpretation (that of witchery) – as if the other face of tyranny (or a redescription of its fear of equivocation) is fixation, say superstition. (Of course my second interpretation depends on granting that Shakespeare knew the surgical procedure in question under the Caesarean interpretation.)

Since (what proves to be) the equivocation of "no woman born" is a construction of the witches, and since fixating its meaning as being ripped untimely is Macbeth's response to Macduff's fixing of himself as rebuker and subduer, I am taking the play to characterize interpretation as a kind of inner or private contest between witchcraft and tyranny, which it almost identifies as a war between the feminine and the masculine. This formulation contests, while to an unassessed extent it agrees with, the perception of the play in Steven Mullaney's "Lying Like Truth."[3] I agree particularly with

Mullaney's sense that the play virtually announces its topic as, whatever else, equivocation, and that standing interpretations of equivocation, or ambiguity, do not account for the extraordinary language of this play. But, putting aside here Mullaney's elegant presentation of the play as a presentation of treasonous language (which nevertheless seems to me a confined interpretation), he cites too few of the actual words of the play to clarify his claim of their specialness. For example, he claims that the "language [Macbeth] would use [to lie] instead masters him." How shall we assess whether Mullaney's idea of being mastered comes to more than an assertion of one of the common facts of words, that they have associations beyond their use on a particular occasion? Certainly we must not deny it: A word's reach exceeds a speaker's grasp, or what's a language for?

This is to say: words recur, in unforetellable contexts; there would be no words otherwise; and no intentions otherwise, none beyond the, let me say, natural expression of instinct; nothing would be the expression of desire, or ambition, or the making of a promise, or the acceptance of a prophecy. Unpredictable recurrence is not a sign of language's ambiguity but is a fact of language as such, that there are words.

I strew my reservation concerning Mullaney's description of *Macbeth's* language with references to various of the play's famous topics – ambition, prophecy, promise – to register my awareness that in claiming, despite my reservation, to share a sense of the play's specialness of language, the weight of this reservation depends on proposing an alternative account. I shall sketch two elements of such a proposal, isolating two common features or conditions of the medium of the play – its language to begin with – that the text of *Macbeth* particularly acknowledges, or interprets. One can think of the idea of a text's uniqueness, or difference, as the theory of language the text holds of itself, as Friedrich Schlegel more or less puts it. I will call these features of language language as prophecy and as magic or mind-reading.

These features interpret conditions of what can be called the possibility of language as such. Prophecy, or foretelling, takes up the condition of words as recurrent; mind-reading takes up words as shared. Philosophy has wished to explain the recurrence of words (which may present itself as their evanescence) by a theory of what it calls universals; and similarly (taking universals *as* concepts or as rules) to explain their sharing or mutuality, so far as this is seen to be a separate question. Wittgenstein's *Investigations* questions precisely the necessity and possibility of these places of philosophical explanation. In this light, *Macbeth* represents the world whose existence philosophy is horrified by, and created by – the possibility that there is no end to our irrationalities, to our will to intellectual emptiness.

My idea of the first of the conditions of language acknowledged by this play – language as prophecy – is that a kind of foretelling is effected by the way the play, at what prove to be charged moments, will bond a small group of generally small words so that they may then at any time fall upon one another and discharge or expel meaning. The play dramatizes the fact that a word does not exist until it is understood as repeated. Examples I specify a bit here are the foretelling of the words *face*, *hand*, *do* and *done*, *success* and *succession*, *time*, *sleep*, and *walk*. That the acknowledgement of words as foretelling is a specific strain within the Shakespearean virtuosity is indicated in contrasting it with words as telling or counting in *The Winter's Tale* (as recounted in *Disowning Knowledge*). Foretelling emphasizes the unpredictable *time* of telling, unguarded as it were from the time of understanding. Take the case of *do* and *done*. The word leaps from a witch's "I'll do, I'll do, and I'll do," to Lady Macbeth's "What's done cannot be undone," and Macbeth's "[I] wish the estate o' th' world were now undone." I take up the word from what is perhaps its most intricate instance: "If it were done, when 'tis done, then 'twere well / It were done quickly" (1.7.1–2).

As a statement is grammatically what can prove to be true or false, and be verified or modified, so a human action is what can prove to succeed or fail, and be justified or excused – words and deeds carry within themselves the terms, or intentions, of their satisfaction. With recurrence on my mind, and having said that without the recurrence of words there are no words (hence no expression beyond that of organic need, no expression, we might say, that *contains* desire), I hear Macbeth's speculation of deeds done in the doing, without consequence, when surcease is success, to be a wish for there to be no human action, no separation of consequence from intention, no gratification of desire, no showing of one's hand in what happens. It is a wish to escape a condition of the human which, while developing terms of Emerson's essay "Fate," I have described as the human fatedness to significance, ourselves as victims of intelligibility. And I have claimed that it is this perception that Wittgenstein captures in identifying the human form of life as that of language. Something of the sort is, I believe, meant in recent years when it is said that language speaks us, or that the self is created by language. The implication in these formulations seems often to be that we are not exactly or fully responsible for what we say, or that we do not have selves. And yet the only point of such assertions – cast in a skeptical tone – is to deny a prior stance or tone of metaphysics, a metaphysical "picture" of what it is to "be" responsible or to "have" a self (a picture no doubt at the service of politics, but what is not?). Such skeptical assertions would deny that the self is everything by asserting that it is nothing, or deny that we are in control of a present plenum of meaning by denying that we have so much as a single human hand in what we say. These assertions and denials of metaphysics are the victories of tyranny over witchcraft, Macbeth's occupation. Whose story is it that the self is self-presence, that meaning is the fullness of a word? It is not truer than it is false.

A famous registration of what I am calling the fatedness to significance is Freud's idea of the overdetermination of meaning in human action and passion. If we follow Jean Laplanche (in *Life and Death in Psychoanalysis*) in watching the origins of human significance in the emergence of human sexuality, tracing the transfiguration of psychic drives out of biological instincts, then may we not further recognize in this origin of desire the origin of time, say of the delay or interval or containment in human satisfaction; hence the origin of the end of time, say of the repetitiveness of desire's wants and satisfactions; hence the origin of reality, say of something "beyond" me in which my satisfaction is provided, or not? Then we have a way of thinking about why Macbeth, in wishing for the success of his act to be a surcease of the need of action, for a deed that undoes doing, must (logically) wish for an end to time. For to destroy time is what he would, with paralyzing paradox, risk the future for: "that but this blow / Might be the be-all and the end-all – here, / But here, upon this bank and shoal of time" (1.7.4–6). This is what "We'd jump the life to come" in favor of (whether the life to come is taken to mean the rest of his time, or the rest of time). Why? (And suppose the life to come suggests the life to come *from* him. He says that the worth of his kingship is bound up for him with the question of his succession. But we have just heard him say in effect that success would consist for him in surcease, in remaining, with respect to the act which is the type of the consequential – producing progeny – "unlineal," "unfruitful." Well, does he want babies or not? Is this undecidable? If we say so, then Macbeth is the picture of undecidability.)

Both he and Lady Macbeth associate doing, in addition to time, with thinking: "I am afraid to think what I have done," he says (2.2.50); and a few lines earlier she had said, "These deeds must not be thought / After these ways; so, it will make us mad" (2.2.32–3). If there were nothing done or to do there would be nothing to think about. Before we come to ponder what it is they have to think about, I note that the opposite of thinking in Macbeth's mind is sleep ("sore labour's bath, / Balm of hurt minds" (2.2.37–8), and that in acting to kill action and end time Macbeth "does murther Sleep" (2.2.35); so that in acting metaphysically to end thought he consigns himself absolutely to thinking, to unending watchfulness. Lady Macbeth at last finds a solution to the problem of thinking how not to think, when there is no obvious way not to think, in sleepwalking, which her witness describes as a version of watchfulness.

Before moving from language as foretelling to the second of the conditions of language which I hypothesize the play particularly to acknowledge – language as magic or mind-reading – I simply note two foretellings or occurrences of the idea of walking (or walking as sleeping) that bond with the ambiguity or reciprocity, real or imagined, of action without consequence, say of the active and the passive becoming one another. First, the witnessing Doctor's description of Lady Macbeth's sleepwalking – "to receive at once the benefit of sleep, and do the effects of watching" – seems most literally a description of the conditions of a play's audience, and play-watching becomes, along with (or as an interpretation of) sleepwalking, exemplary of human action as such, as conceived in this play – yet another of Shakespeare's apparently unending figurations, or explorations, of theater; here, theater as the scene, and as the perception or witnessing of the scene, that is, of human existence, as sleepwalking. Macbeth's all but literal equivalent of sleepwalking is his walking, striding, pacing (all words of his), to his appointment to murder, led by "a dagger of the mind, a false creation" (2.1.38), moving like a ghost (2.1.56).

Another bonding of the idea of walking with that of acting without acting is Macbeth's description of life as "but a walking shadow; a poor player" (5.5.24). While in this inaudibly familiar speech about all our tomorrows I remark that Macbeth has a use for something like the idea that life, construed as a tale, signifies nothing – he has, as said, been trying to achieve the condition of insignificance ever since his speech about ending time, and before that. That life's but a walking shadow, a poor player, like both mad Lady Macbeth and sad Macbeth and like the perhaps sane players playing them, is a tremendous thought, but not something Macbeth learned just now, upon hearing of his wife's death. Perhaps it is something he can *say* now, say for himself, now that she is dead – that human life does not, any more than a human player, signify its course for and beyond itself; it is instead the scene or medium in which significance is found, or not. She is apt to have found this idea unmanly, anyway as diverging from her point of view. To speak of a player who "struts and frets" is simply, minus the melodramatic mode, to speak of someone who walks and cares, hence signifies acting and suffering and talking about both in view of others, which pretty well covers the human territory. And what is wrong with strutting and fretting for an "hour on the stage" that is not wrong with time altogether? Is "signifying nothing" the decay of their having been "promised greatness" (favorite words of both Macbeth and Lady Macbeth in their opening speeches)? And is this announcement of greatness taken as a hint of pregnancy and issue, or is it perhaps the promise of exemption from time (if that is different); or is it, given the hints of religious contestation in the play, a charge against the promise of eternity, against something Macbeth calls, thinking of the witches, the "metaphysical"? It is imaginable that Macbeth is taking revenge against any and all of these promises of consequence, perhaps against the idea of history as fulfilling promises.

Of course this speech about insignificance, or say inexpressiveness, is an expression of limitlessly painful melancholy; but again, that pain is not new to Macbeth, not caused by the news of his wife's death. His response to that news I find in full – before the metaphysics of time and meaning, so to speak, take over – to be: "She should have died hereafter; / There would have been a time for such a word." That is all. Is it so little? He says that like everything else that happens her death is untimely, as if not hers: nothing is on or in time when nothing is desired, when desire is nothing, is not yours. And he says that he is incapable of mourning now; and if not capable now, then when not? The wrong time for death is an ultimately missed appointment; no time for mourning death sets an ultimate stake in disappointment. Here is a view of human history, history as unmournable disappointment. Macbeth's speech goes on to explore it. Perhaps it is a perception Lady Macbeth perished in trying to protect her husband from. This is something he can say now, no longer protecting her from her failure to protect him. If so, then the play's study of history is a study of their relationship, this marriage. What is this marriage?

In arriving at the question I have opened what is for myself the encompassing question of why, in thinking about Shakespearean tragedy, I have previously avoided turning to this play. Two questions have, it seems forever, dogged me about *Macbeth*. What is the source of the attractiveness of this terrible pair? And why have I always felt intimate yet unengaged with their famous moments? As if I have and have not wanted to consider that this pair, representing the most extensive description the Shakespearean corpus devotes to an undoubted marriage (that of Cleopatra's with Antony is not undoubted), represents, to some as yet unmeasured extent, an always standing possibility of marriage itself.

Masculine disappointment together with feminine deflection of that disappointment indicates a more or less familiarly cursed marriage; and I was suggesting that the mood of "Tomorrow and tomorrow and tomorrow" is informed by knowledge Macbeth brings onto the stage from the beginning. If that is so, then the events of the play, the ambition for and against greatness and exemption, are in defense against this knowledge. In asking what this marriage is we have crossed to the second of the conditions of language that I have been claiming this play particularly to acknowledge: the first was language as prophesy, as foretelling; the second is language as mind-reading, a particular sharing of words, as if by magic.

As foretelling in *Macbeth* may be contrasted with telling or counting in *The Winters Tale*, so sharing words in *Macbeth* may be compared with sharing words in *Coriolanus*, namely with words figured as food; in *Macbeth* words may rather, it seems, be something like potions: "Hie thee hither, / That I may pour my spirits in thine ear" (1.5.25–6). There recurrently seems to me a phantasm glancing in these words of Lady Macbeth, beyond the idea of her wishing to inspire her husband, or give him courage, through her words; some more literal or imagined posture in which she invades him with her essence. Anyone might note that the play associates the production of words with the production and reception of blood: "We but teach / Bloody instructions, which, being taught, return / To plague th' inventor. This even-handed justice / Commends th' ingredience of our poison'd chalice / To our own lips" (1.7.8–12); "My gashes cry for help" / "So well thy words become thee, as thy wounds" (1.2.43–4), as if in a tragedy of blood – and in this one, as the Arden editor reports, blood is mentioned over one hundred times – words are wounds, and the causes of wounds. I am drawn to test for the phantasm I allude to because of my sense of the pairs of certain cursed marriages, as in a relation of a sort I have elsewhere called spiritual vampirism.

The idea of words as mind-reading is a conception of reading as such – or playwatching – reading the text of another as being read by the other. Uttering words as mind-reading is represented in the language of this marriage, in which each of the pair says what the other already knows or has already said; or does not say something the other does not say, either assuming the other knows, or keeping a pledge of silence. They exemplify exchanges of words that are not exchanges, that represent a kind of negation of conversation. For example: Macbeth prays to "let that be, / Which the eye fears, when it is done, to see" (1.4.52–3), and Lady Macbeth is soon incanting "That my keen knife see not the wound it makes" (1.5.52); again, she fears that he is "without / The illness that should attend" ambition (1.5.19–20), and later he says to her, "Things bad begun make strong themselves by ill" (3.3.55); and earlier, Macbeth's letter tells Lady Macbeth that greatness is promised her, and she repeats this in her ensuing soliloquy as something promised him. And let us add that before she reads, while sleepwalking, the letter she has in that condition written herself, as a kind of script of the play (a suggestion of Marjorie Garber's), Macbeth at the opposite end of the play had already written a letter which forms a script for her words; the first words we hear her say are his. But my hypothesis is that the play's sense of mind-reading, of being trapped in one another's mind, in false, draining intimacies (the idea of vampirism), is expressed preeminently in what the pair of the marriage do not, or not in good time, say to, or say for, one another. I note three topics about which they are silent: the plan to kill Duncan, their childlessness, and the relation of Lady Macbeth to the witches. I imagine there are different causes for silence in the three cases.

The pair's initial implicitness to one another over the plan to kill Duncan means to me not that each had the idea independently but that each thinks it is the other's idea, that each does the deed somehow for the other. It is an omen that neither knows why it is done. This will come back.

The compulsively repeated critical sneer expressed in the question "how many children had Lady Macbeth?" expresses anxiety over the question of the marriage's sexuality and childlessness, as if critics are spooked by the marriage. But I speak for myself. Is there any good reason, otherwise, to deny or to slight the one break in Lady Macbeth's silence on the subject of her childlessness, her assertion that she has suckled a (male) child? There may be good reason for her husband to deny or doubt it, in his considering whose it might be. If we do not deny her assertion, then the question how many children she had is of no interest that I can see; the interesting question is what happened, in fact or in fantasy, to the child she remembers. (David Willbern, as I recall, in a fine essay suggests in passing that her suckling is a fantasy. If so, then what is the fantasy of remembering a (fantasied) child?) And if we do not deny or slight her assertion then the fate of the child is their question, a fact or issue for them of a magnitude to cause the magnitude and intimacy of guilt and melancholy Macbeth begins with and Lady Macbeth ends with. Its massive unspokenness is registered by the reverse of the procedure of the recurrence of words, namely by the dispersal or dissemination of words for birth throughout the play – deliver, issue, breed, labour, hatch'd, birthdom, bring forth. I would like to include the punning use of borne, repeated by Lenox in his nervously ironic "Men must not walk too late" speech (a nice instance of the prophetic or foretelling use of "walk," especially of Lady Macbeth's last appearance). This listing of terms for child-bearing perhaps tells us nothing about early references in the play to becoming great or to "the swelling act / Of the imperial theme" (1.3.128–9). But when one is caught by the power – it will not happen predictably – of the vanished child, one may wonder even over Lady Macbeth's response upon the initial entrance to her of Macbeth, "I feel now / The future in the present," which in turn is, and is not, Macbeth's perception of history. (A sense of pregnancy, but without assurance of reproduction, may suggest the monstrous as much as it does the sterile.)

Anticipating for some reason an especially negative reaction to the last instance of deflected birth and death I am about to adduce, I emphasize that I am not undertaking to persuade anyone of unspoken presence. I am testifying to something guiding me that I cannot distinguish from a valid intuition. If I do not eventually discover a satisfying tuition for it, I will have to give it up as a guide. Perhaps it is not an intuition of free interpretation but a dagger of the mind, precisely not to be followed. But if one could know this in advance, or settle it, there would be no spiritual danger of the kind criticism runs, no such acts and thoughts to be responsible for or to; one would be either a witch or a tyrant. I would like to say: The great responsibility of philosophy is responsiveness – to be awake after all the others have fallen asleep.

The instance I am thinking of is the opening human question of the play, I mean the first words spoken after the witches have delivered themselves of their opening questions and answers about their meeting again. Duncan enters and encounters something that brings forth his response, "What bloody man is that?" If we take it to heart that in this tragedy, or say medium, of blood, blood is associated both with death and with birth, and that bloody figures and figures of children originate or appear from, as it were, the witches' cauldron, then this appearance of the questionable bloody man – as from the cauldron – may be seen to begin the play. It figures beginnings – of plays, of human actions – as consequences, as conclusions manifested, synthesized, conjured. The witches' cauldron accordingly appears as the origin of theater, as the scene of apparitions or appearances, and as the source or representation of the human as that which identifies and denies itself – or, as Hamlet virtually says, as that which imitates itself so "abominably," in the form of abominations, objects of horror to themselves.

That a first-night, or a first-day, audience may not at first recognize a connection between the bloody man and the cauldron is true enough, but not obviously more surprising than anything else not recognized, on the first, or on the hundred-and-first, encounter. I assume that any complexity the average mortal finds in a play of Shakespeare's is something Shakespeare is capable of having placed there. The critical question is: How? By what means? The question whether an author intends any or all of what happens is a convenient defense against this critical question. Recent attacks on intentionality share the (metaphysical) picture of intention that they would criticize, one that makes its importance absolute, as if, if intention counts for anything in meaning, it counts for everything. (We have seen the pattern before.) Metaphysics, so described, here concerning intention, might be called magic thinking. So let us say: Intention is merely of the last importance. Everything (else) has first to be in place for it to do what it does – as in putting a flame to a fuse. And of course accidents can happen. Would one like to imagine that the man of blood follows the witches' incantations by accident? Magicless, impotent witches are no easier to imagine than the other kind.

But I cannot stop the intuition here, the intuition of the magic of theater and its voices and its other apparitions, of the declaration of theater as the power of making things appear, along of course with the powers of equivocation and of casting spells. (Are only witches and warlocks so empowered? Or are they only convenient paranoid projections of what we accept as humdrum human power? Glendower's metaphysical claim to call up monsters, together with Hotspur's skeptical question as to whether they will come when he calls them, forms another instance of fixated philosophical sides that Shakespeare may be taken as bringing to confusion. Is this the accomplishment of philosophy, or its cue?) What has happened to Macbeth? What is the element of difference to his consciousness that brings forth his guilt and private violence and melancholy, as if settling something? This question draws me to imagine the bloody man – a poor player whom we never see again, who in Shakespeare's source was killed – against the question I impute to Macbeth (granted as it were that Lady Macbeth knows the answer) about what happened at the death and birth of his child. (Macbeth is not the only Shakespearean male to find birth mysterious and unnatural, who might believe anything about it and about those to whom and from whom it happens. This is cardinal in the essay of Janet Adelman's that I cited above.) I do not look for a stable answer to be found by Macbeth: he protests his acceptance and his doubt of the witches throughout. But that there are witches and that they bring forth children may provide him with a glance of explanation, perhaps of hope, perhaps of despair; an explanation at once of the presence of the absence of his child and of the absence in the presence of his wife.

I ask here only that we allow Macbeth to have posed for himself the issue that so many critics now so readily take as answered – that there is some inner connection between Lady Macbeth and witchery. Some approve the idea that in her opening scene she is casting a spell on herself ("unsex me here . . . fill me, from the crown to the toe, top-full / Of direst cruelty" (1.5.41–3) – though here I seem to have heard every interpretation of these frightening words except the one that seems unforced to me; that it expresses rage, human as can be, at the violence and obligation of sexual intercourse, at what Laplanche calls, in *Life and Death in Psychoanalysis*, the traumatic nature of human sexuality: her husband is returning any moment from the wars. And none fail to remark that she is presenting herself as a mother, in her fashion ("Take my milk for gall, you murth'ring ministers" [1.5.48]). If she is a witch it follows both that witches are mothers and presumably that she is capable of destroying their child with her own hands. (Is there a difference supposed in the pronunciation of "murth'ring" and "mothering"? Or is this identity a critical commonplace?)

We are, of course, in the middle of the third of the three topics I said the pair are silent about; the first two were their plan of Duncan's murder and their vanished child; the third is the topic and the logic of monstrousness. What is there for them to discuss about this? Others may speculate with detachment over the belief in witches, but it is the likes of Macbeth who, finding themselves confronted with witches, have to ask how you tell who is a witch (the commonest question there could be about witches); and have to carry through the logic that if anyone is a witch then his wife may be one; that hence he may be the master and the minister of a witch, figures named in the play (and he has perhaps tasted his wife's milk or gall and had her pour her spirits in his ear and felt chastised by the valor of her tongue, but I will not speculate here); hence that he has had a child with a witch, produced something monstrous that has to die, as if he were a devil, not a man (he is called "Hell-hound" by Macduff [5.8.3]). There is nothing to discuss: No individual human knows more than any other what the difference is between the human and the monstrous, as no human is exempt from the wish for exemption from the human. I mean no one is in a position to tell another that there are or are not witches, any more than to tell another that there are or are not humans.

Here is a way of considering this play's contribution to the continuing European discussion of witches contemporary with it – its sense of metaphysical denial (say denial of our fundamental metaphysical ignorance of difference between the human and the monstrous) projected through human society by legalizing the identification of witches. It seems to me just like Shakespeare to have already infiltrated this discussion (as noted in *Disowning Knowledge*) by coloring Othello's psychological torture of Desdemona (who, on the pattern of Lady Macbeth, is anything but a witch) as a witch trial – a sense of the erotic denial introduced into one's human identity by the projection of one's sense of bewitchment. (Another of Shakespeare's indirections with his sources is his hedging of Mark Antony, who, on the pattern of Coriolanus, is anything but a Christ, with signs of Christ.)

By the time of Macbeth's last encounter with the witches, at the opening of act 4, he seems to have accepted his participation in their realm, undertaking, successfully, to "conjure" them (4.1.50). In the ensuing appearances or apparitions from the cauldron to Macbeth (and to us) of the armed head and of the bloody child and of the child crowned, we have the pattest declaration by the play of its theory of the work of theater as the conjuring of apparitions; and I am taking it, if you like in deferred action, to figure for us (and for Macbeth, whoever, in identification with us, he is), what we see (saw) when at the beginning we encounter(ed) the bloody man, the origin and destiny of his child, hence of himself. Now one may feel that all this takes Macbeth's sense of bewitchment or exemption to be a function of an incredible capacity for literalization on his part. But is it really more than is shown by his sense that he is to be dominated by a man who exists from no woman? Moreover, literalization is perhaps not so uncommon, but is an ordinary part of magic thinking, like imagining that to claim that an author means what he or she says is to claim that his or her intention has created all the conditions in conjunction with which intention does what it does, as if the striking match creates the fuse it lights, together with the anger and the enemy and the opportunity in and for and from which it is struck. (In a sense, no doubt, it does. What sense?)

To work toward a close of these remarks, one that takes them back to my opening intuitions of *Macbeth* as a history play that questions whether anything can be known – or known to be made – to happen, I come back to the murder of Duncan. What I have said or implied about this so far is that Macbeth walks to it in a sleep and that each of the pair acts it out as for the other, assuming its origination in the other, so that the desire for the deed and the time of the deed can never be appropriate, never quite intelligible. To raise the question of what it is that is thus done on borrowed time, with stolen words, let us take it that it is performed with that dagger of the mind Macbeth speculates might be the instrument of murder and ask what wound in the mind it makes, one that each of the pair asks not to see – which we now understand as impossibly asking the other not to see.

I pause to remark that it is probably the sense of their silence to one another about unsilenceable topics that has above all prompted critics to suggest that scenes are missing from the play. I am in effect claiming that what is missing is not absent but is present in the play's specific ways of saying nothing, say of showing the unspeakable. A methodological point of interest thus arises concerning the subject of what you might call critical responsibility. My claim is that readers/watchers of the play are meant to read its silences; that, in effect, the speculation about a missing scene is a cover for the speculator's missing response to scenes that are present. This implies that should, as it were, a missing scene show up for this play, it could prove neither the truth nor the falsity of what I claim the silence is about. To accept such a scene is to be willing to rethink the play; perhaps it would contain further silences. There is, by my definition, no scene missing from the play I mean to be considering here, the one constituted in the Arden edition I cite from. (How many plays have the Macbeths?)

535

My account of the pair's silence about the plan to kill Duncan depends here mostly on three elements that indicate that they each imagine Macbeth's deathblow to direct itself to Lady Macbeth.

The first element is Macbeth's speech as he reenters from having gone, after the discovery of Duncan's body, to see his handiwork: "From this instant, / There's nothing serious in mortality; / All is but toys" (2.3.90–92). Good readers have characteristically felt that something is horrifyingly disproportionate in these words of Macbeth's, disagreeing about Macbeth's sincerity or degree of consciousness in saying them. My sense is that these words cannot take their direction from the figure of Duncan, however they may recognize his disfigurement; but that the only object whose loss for Macbeth could amount to the radical devaluation of the human world is Lady Macbeth, together with some phantasm in the idea of "toys," as of some existence left behind. (A measure of the disproportion in Macbeth's speech on Duncan's death – "nothing serious in mortality" – is to set it with Cleopatra's on Antony's death – "nothing left remarkable / Beneath the visiting moon" (4.15) – where I assume no sense of disproportion. How far this connection verifies my general sense of these plays as history plays about a break in history, as turns in the history of privacy, or say skepticism, hence in the history of marriage, hence in the history of legitimacy and succession, I do not guess now.)

That Lady Macbeth shares this knowledge of herself as the object of the killing is how I take the second element I cite in this connection, that of her fainting upon Macbeth's words that recount in vivid and livid detail his killing of Duncan's grooms: "Who could refrain / That had a heart to love, and in that heart / Courage, to make 's love known?" (2.3.114–16.) It is she alone who knows what Macbeth loves, to whom whatever he does makes his love known. (But the sincerity or reality of her fainting is a matter of controversy. Am I simply assuming it? I might say I have provided an argument in favor of its reality. But I would rather say that it is still perfectly possible to insist that the fainting is insincere, put on by her to divert the attention of the company, only this will now have to include her knowledge of what Macbeth's deed was in killing his love; and then the idea of her insincerity will perhaps seem less attractive.) After Lady Macbeth is helped to exit from this scene, she is never an active presence in the play's events. This is why the fact of her death comes to Macbeth as no shock.

The third element in defining the object of Macbeth's killing is Lady Macbeth's entrance to him upon his words, "I have no spur / To prick the sides of my intent, but only / Vaulting ambition, which o'erleaps itself / And falls on th' other" (1.7.25–6). By now I will take no one by surprise in expressing my sense that the line should be left alone (I mean, to begin with, that it should not be taken to be incomplete) to nominate Lady Macbeth as the other. (This at the same time leaves the line to mark this entrance as a cardinal declaration in this play that its study or acknowledgment of theatrical entrances is of their quality as appearances or apparitions, called forth, conjured.) Critics have wished to see in Macbeth's image of "overleaping" here an image of himself as the rider of a horse, mounting it or jumping it, overeagerly. I do not say this is wrong; but since Macbeth's words are that it is *his* intent whose sides are, or are not, to be pricked, there is a suggestion that he is identifying himself also as the horse (as earlier he associates himself with a wolf and later identifies himself as a baited bear); a horse by whom or by what ridden is unclear, ambiguous: perhaps it is by his ambition, perhaps by the ambition of another, so that "falling on the other" means falling to the other, to be responsible for it, but perhaps it means falling upon the other, as its casualty. Then the falling is not overeager, but an inevitable self-projection of human promise. (If one insists that not he but strictly his intent is the horse, he remaining strictly the rider, then again his intent outruns his control not because of overeagerness but because of the separate lives of intention and of the world, we riding, as best we can, between.)

If we take it as ambiguous whether Macbeth is imagining himself as the rider or as the horse, the ambiguity is then an expression of the pair's mutual mind-reading, their being as it were over-literally of one mind: whatever occurs to one occurs to the other; whatever one does the other does; in striking at her he strikes at himself; his action is something he suffers. Sleepwalking seems a fair instance of a condition ambiguous as between doing something and having something happen to you. Other actions pertinent to this play, exemplary of the ambiguity or reciprocity of acting and suffering, or in Emerson's words, between getting and having, are giving birth and the play of sexual gratification. The reciprocity presents itself to Macbeth as requiring an assassination that trammels up consequence, all consequence, an act of metaphysics whose consequence is of being assassinated; as if acts of realizing your world, acts of self-empowerment, are acts of self-assassination, the openest case in which doing a deed and suffering the deed are inseparable. The logic is that of narcissism, and the sense is that there is a narcissism under a negative sign, with love replaced by hatred. You need not think that masculinity and femininity are determined by a prior determination of activity and passivity in order to think that prior to the individuation that begins individuating others – to the formation of the human self that is subject to others and subjects others, that knows passion and that knows action, that is bewitchable and tyrannical – there is nothing either decidable or undecidable about the self's gender. And if "being" a gender (one rather than another) is a mode like, or is part of, "having" a self (this one rather than another), is individuation ever over? There are always others to tell you so and others to tell you otherwise. Are they others?

A psychological account of the state in which punishment of an object (or former object) of love is a state of self-punishment is given by Freud in his statement of the etiology of melancholia. I shall quote some sentences from Freud's "Mourning and Melancholia" and then close with a few sentences about why I find their association with Macbeth, through Nietzsche, significant, I mean why I want to follow them on.

> An object-choice, an attachment of the libido to a particular person, had at one time existed; then, owing to a real slight or disappointment coming from this loved person, the object-relationship was shattered. The result was not the normal one of a withdrawal of the libido from this object and a displacement of it onto a new one, but something different. . . . It was withdrawn into the ego . . . [where] it served to establish an identification of the ego with the abandoned object. Thus the shadow of the object fell upon the ego, so that the

> [ego] could henceforth be criticized by a special mental faculty, the forsaken object.... The melancholic displays ... an impoverishment of his ego on a grand scale. In mourning it is the world which has become poor and empty; in the melancholic, it is the ego itself.

"Impoverishment of his ego on a grand scale" – it seems a move in an auction of nothingness, self-punishment as for the murder, finally, of the world. Guilt as melancholia seems a reasonable formulation of Macbeth's frame of mind. It is a suggestion from which to reenter the texts from which I reported that I have begun asking tuition for my intuitions about this play.

The passages from "Mourning and Melancholia" just quoted were adduced a few years ago in Timothy Gould's study of Nietzsche's Pale Criminal (a figure in an early section of *Thus Spoke Zarathustra*), which appeared in the Summer 1986 issue of *Soundings*.[4] In readducing the passages here I am in effect claiming that Nietzsche's Pale Criminal, whatever else, is a study of Macbeth. That section of *Zarathustra* speaks of guilt that expresses itself in madness after the deed and madness before the deed, and it proposes a problematic of blood and of human action in which performing a deed is taken over by an image of the performance of the deed, an image which functions to fixate or exhaust the doer's identity so that he becomes nothing but the doer of this deed, suffering subjective extinction as it were in the doing of what he does. It speaks, accordingly, to why Macbeth thinks of himself (thinking shared, as it must be, by Lady Macbeth) as in a sea of blood of his own giving, so as pale. (Macbeth once asks "seeling Night," with its "bloody and invisible hand" to release him from that "which keeps me pale" [3.2.46–50] and in her sleepwalking Lady Macbeth will say, or say again, "Look not so pale ... give me your hand" [5.1.59, 63].) In a world of blood, to be pale, exceptional, exempt, without kin, without kind, is to want there to be no world, none outside of you, nothing to be or not to be yours, neither from nor not from your hand; but to be pale is to be drained and to demand blood, to absorb what is absorbing you.

And the bearing of Macbeth as Nietzsche's Pale Criminal is significant for me, to be followed on, because of Nietzsche's response (so I claim) to Emerson's "Experience," a centerpiece of the seminar on romanticism and skepticism I mentioned at the outset of this essay. (Emerson's essay opens with the question, "Where do we find ourselves?" The introduction to Nietzsche's *Genealogy of Morals* opens with the two sentences: "We are unknown to ourselves, we knowers. How should we have found ourselves when we have never looked for ourselves?") Emerson's "Experience" is about the inability, and the ability, to mourn the death of his five-year-old son; the essay works toward the discovery of the social, call it America, toward the discovery of succession, imaged by Emerson as coming to walk, to take steps, beginning in what is quite explicitly described as walking in your sleep. Emerson here responds to, takes responsibility for, Shakespeare's and Kant's and America's ideas of success and succession: in effect, he is claiming to enter history by becoming their successor. It is an essay, as I have put it in the first chapter of *This New Yet Unapproachable America*, where the image of the human hand emblematizes the question of how deeds enter and work in the world, the question of how, as Emerson phrases it, you "realize your world," something Emerson's critics, as he reports in his essay, keep complaining that he has himself failed to do. But realizing his world is of course precisely what Emerson takes himself to be doing, in his writing, in the way only humans can; non-magically, as it were; by letting something happen, the reversal of denial. This is more or less, not for unrelated reasons, how Heidegger and Wittgenstein also think, so that what is most active is what is most passive, or receptive. This suggests that we do not know whether knowing – for example, knowing whether one is human or inhuman – is a masculine or a feminine affair.

I am citing bits of what might, in another world, be called the history of the reception of *Macbeth*, or part of its historical circulation or exchange or energy, say of its money or blood of the mind, as a way of saying that if Shakespeare's play is a distinctive event in the history it remembers and enacts – if it is to continue to happen to its culture, to the extent that it, or anything, has ever happened to its culture as art happens, as truth happens in art, not alone as conclusion but as premise, not alone as document but as event – that is because events happen as this work shows them to happen, contains them, no more nor less clearly. In emphasizing, rather than Shakespeare's sources, Shakespeare's writing as a source variously open to appropriation, I may find my own provocation in it, without claiming to speak for it – as for example fixing its own mode of appropriating sources. Then I am in effect claiming that the Shakespearean play here claims a power to challenge authority that is based on birth and inheritance; that the political as realm of royal blood never recovers from this portrait which locates its causes in unsayable privacy (as in this marriage), in royal authority's sleek imitability (as in Malcolm's apparent libeling of himself, and in Macbeth's bloody hand as the imitation and inheritor of the king's healing touch); nor recovers from its support by treasonableness in expansive masculinity (as in Macduff); nor from its vanity (as in Banquo's narcissistic mirror).

So I am in effect verifying the familiar idea that a Shakespeare history play develops from the morality tradition, but taking its moral direction to put a kink in the old history – taking it not as directed to teach the proper conduct of king and subject, but instead to constitute a moral about what history is, or has become – that what happens is not what is news, not a tale of a world, real or fictional; that such things are accounts merely of trivial horrors, consequences of old deeds, revenge returning, as Macbeth learns, as kings typically learn, too late; that learning what has happened is exemplified by the learning of what is happening now, or as Emerson more or less puts the matter, that history is not of the past, but for example is in our sleep-watching of this play; so that you need not become a horror-dealing, horror-dealt tyrant in order to recognize what is worth doing and worth having. And might you learn how not to become the victim of a tyrant? But what if, after the passing of tyrants, you yourself play the confiner?

Notes

1 Janet Adelman, "'Born of Woman': Fantasies of Maternal Power in *Macbeth*," in Marjorie Garber, ed., *Cannibals, Witches, and Divorce: Estranging the Renaissance* (Baltimore, MD: Johns Hopkins University Press, 1987), 90–121.

2 Marjorie Garber, "Macbeth: The Male Medusa," in Susanne L. Wofford, ed., *Shakespeare's Late Tragedies: A Collection of Critical Essays* (Upper Saddle River, NJ: Prentice Hall, 1996), 74–103.
3 Steven Mullaney, "Lying Like Truth: Riddle, Representation and Treason in Renaissance England," *ELH* 47:1 (Spring 1980): 32–47.
4 Timothy Gould, "What Makes the Pale Criminal Pale: Nietzsche and the Image of the Deed," *Soundings: An Interdisciplinary Journal* 58 (1985): 510–36.

Index

absolute intentionalism, 405–6
absurdity, Wittgenstein, 483–5
acceptability, 371, 372–3
Achilles Mourning the Death of Patroclus (Twombly), 424–5
actualist intentionalism, 405, 409–11, 412–16
Adelman, Janet, 524, 525, 533
Adorno, T. W., 15, 396
adventure, moral, 296–7
Aeneid (Virgil), 140–5
aesthetic orientation, characters', 307–11, 316–17
aestheticism, as term of criticism, 275–6
aesthetics, intentional fallacy, 420–32
"Against Dryness" (Murdoch), 300
Alcibiades (Plato), 9–10, 12–13
allographic arts, 107
Alter, Robert, 512
Altieri, Charles, 396
The Ambassadors (James)
  literary–ethical theory balance, 241, 244, 247–61, 262, 263–4
  moralism, 273, 275–6, 282n22
  point of view narration, 334, 336, 340–1, 346n23
  understanding through emotion, 77, 78–82, 87
American modernist poetry
  language, 474–87, 498–500
  rhetorical reading, 38–49
anamnesis (theory of recollection), 189
anti-rhetoric, 46–9

Antigone (Sophocles), 169–70, 225
Antony and Cleopatra (Shakespeare), 521–2, 526
appreciation, biography for, 442, 443–9
Arendt, Hannah, 16–17
Aristophanes, 389
Aristotle
  feeling fictions, 97
  formalism, 422
  influence on Shakespeare, 178, 180, 186
  literary–ethical theory balance, 244, 245, 246, 253–4
  need to philosophize, 227
  poet–historian distinction, 61, 62–3, 202–3
  styles of selfishness, 300
  tragedy, 163, 166–9, 387
  tragic catharsis, 193–211, 222–3
  truth, 369–70, 372, 385, 387–8, 389
Arnold, Matthew, 380
art, reading as, 113–16
"The Art of Biography" (Woolf), 454–5
"as", exemplification, 497, 498–500, 501, 502
Asian philosophical traditions, 18–19
ataraxia, feeling nothing, 226–9
atom bomb project, 456–64
Attridge, Derek, 304, 310, 321
Augustine, 14
Austen, Jane, 236n39, 376
Austin, J. L., 502–3
authenticity, 371, 372–3
author biography, 436–50

INDEX

authorial intention, 401–16
  intentional fallacy, 420–32, 439, 441
authorial manipulation, 86–7
autism, 90–1n29
autographic arts, 107

Baier, Annette, 272, 273, 274
Barnaby Rudge (Dickens), 375
Barnes, Julian, 152n2
Barthes, Roland, 369
Barzun, Jacques, 445
Beach, John Warren, 334
Beardsley, Monroe, 379, 385, 420–2, 439, 440–1
beauty, 372
Beauvoir, Simone de, 16, 17
Beckett, Samuel, 226–8
Being, 27–9
beliefs
  orientation compared, 317–18
  self-defining reading, 122–52
Bellow, Saul, 301, 311–22
Bernays, Jacob, 211–12n3
Bernstein, Charles, 38–9
Bible, 53, 58, 60, 509–13
biography
  intention, 439, 441, 453–64
  in literary criticism, 436–50
  philosophy as literature, 8–9
Blake, William, 428–32, 513
Bloch, Ariel, 509–12
Bloch, Chana, 509–12
blogs, debt, 17–18
Bohr, Niels, 457, 458–60
"The Book of Sand" (Borges), 135–6
Booth, Stephen, 166, 167
Borges, Jorge Luis, 135–6, 292–3
The Bostonians (James), 272, 273
Bradbury, Malcolm, 375
Brave New World (Huxley), 360
Brewer, W. F., 83
Brighton Rock (Greene), 289
Brontë, Emily, 102, 103
Brooks, Cleanth, 421, 426
Brothers Karamazov (Dostoevsky), 236n39
Bruns, Gerald L., 39

Calvino, Italo, 82
Camus, Albert, 28

Canzoniere (*Songbook*; Petrarch), 391–2
Carroll, Noel, 298n5, 381, 433n18
categorial intentions, 404–5, 411
catharsis, 193–211, 222–3, 228–9
Cato, Marcus, 45
Cavell, Stanley, 22, 29–31, 33, 40, 323–4n20, 482, 491
Cervantes, Miguel de, 64–5
character change, 321–2
Charmides (Plato), 185
Chekhov, Anton, 288
Cherniss, Harold, 438
Cicero, 42–3, 45
clarification of truths, 382
clarity, 371, 372–3
The Clouds (Aristophanes), 389
Coetzee, J. M., 301, 304–11, 316–22
cognitive modeling, 339–40
cognitive monitoring, 72, 73–5, 79, 80–2, 86, 87, 88
cognitive pleasure, 199–202
cognitive strengthening, 381–2
cognitive triviality, 376
cognitivism, literary, 352–4
Cohn, Dorrit, 342
Coleridge, Samuel Taylor, 471
Collingwood, R. G., 395
commonplaces, 40–9
Conant, James, 282n22
conditionalist intentionalism, 405
Confessions (Augustine), 14
Confucius, 19
Conrad, Joseph, 306–7, 318
conservatism, literary, 357
contingency of selfhood, 127–9, 133–4, 135, 151
cooperative principle, intention, 413
Coover, Robert, 82
Copenhagen (Frayn), 453, 456–61
counterfactual reasoning, 357, 360–1
Crary, Alice, 301, 324n22
Crick, Bernard, 463
Crime and Punishment (Dostoevsky), 374, 376, 377
Critchley, Simon, 485, 486
criticism
  biography in, 436–50
  intention, 401–16, 420–32

542

The Curious Incident of the Dog in the Night-Time (Haddon), 363
Currie, Gregory, 95, 104, 105n5, 421

Damasio, Antonio, 73, 81–2
Danto, Arthur C., 145–9, 302
Davidson, Donald, 122–3, 124, 125, 131, 507, 508
Davies, Paul, 423
Davis, Lydia, 152n2
Davis, Wayne A., 404
De Man, Paul, 369, 420–1
de se suppositions, 362–4
De Sousa, Ronald, 318
"The Dead" (Joyce), 519n7
death
   practicing philosophy in, 18
   tragedy and philosophy, 171–2
debt, blogs devoted to, 17–18
definition problem, tragedy, 165–8
Defoe, Daniel, 442–3, 444–5, 446
Déjeuner sur l'herbe (Manet), 59
demonstratives, 502–4
Dennett, Daniel, 111, 116
Derrida, Jacques, 243
dialectic, Plato, 164–6
Diamond, Cora, 301, 478
diarēsis, 165–6
Dickens, Charles, 375
Dickinson, Emily, 41–6
Dijksterhuis, Ap, 339, 340
dilemma argument, intention, 412–16
direct reporting of speech (DRS), 338–9, 342–3
Disgrace (Coetzee), 301, 304–11, 316–22
disgust
   literature on, 91n41
   tragic catharsis, 206
divided self, 38, 39, 47–8
Don Quixote (Cervantes), 64–5
Donne, John, 515, 517
Dostoevsky, Fyodor, 236n39, 374, 376, 377
double takes, morally evaluative, 287–90, 297–8
double-focused reader–protagonist identification, 132–52
"Dover Beach" (Arnold), 380
Drabble, Margaret, 28

Dreiser, Theodore, 415–16
Duchamp, Marcel, 62

earth, the, 26–31, 33–4
Edel, Leon, 274
Eichenbaum, Boris, 421–2
Either/Or (Kierkegaard), 300, 306
Ekman, Paul, 81, 84
elenctic method, *Othello*, 174, 181–9
Eliot, George, 61, 74–5, 77–82, 84–5, 87, 375
Eliot, T. S., 12, 15, 32, 121–2, 151–2, 516–17
Elizabeth and Essex (Strachey), 454–5, 456
Ellis, David, 463
Emerson, Ralph Waldo, 522–3, 524, 538–9
emotion
   empathetic knowledge, 380–2
   exemplifying, 497–8
   feeling fictions, 93–104
   feeling nothing, 218–29
   literary–ethical theory balance, 252–6, 257, 258–61
   orientation compared, 318–19
   tragic catharsis, 193–211, 222–3, 228–9
   truth in poetry, 394–7
   understanding of narrative, 71–88
emotional intelligence, 81
emotional knowledge, 98–9
empathetic knowledge, 380–2
empathy
   imitative narrating, 341–2
   tragic catharsis, 222–6, 228–9
enhancement of truths, 382
enthymemes, 43–4, 46, 48
epistolary self-examination, 14–15, 16–17
Esrock, Ellen, 23, 24
ethical theory, moral philosophy distinguished, 265n2
   see also morality in literature
The Europeans (James), 272, 273
Euthyphro (Plato), 178–80, 181
exemplification, 491, 494–504
expressive triviality, 376
expressivity, 491, 495–504

factual mistakes, 375, 380
Falck, Colin, 372
falsehoods, 375, 380

Feagin, Susan, 86
fear, 193, 194, 195–8, 200–1, 203, 204–9, 211, 222–3
feeling fictions, 71–88, 93–104
feeling nothing, 218–29
fictionalist intentionalism, 405
Fielding, Henry, 269–70, 271
fixity, self-defining reading, 121–32, 151–2
Flaubert, Gustave, 60, 218–22, 225–6, 228–9
Fletcher, Angus, 39
Fletcher, C. R., 76
fluidity, self-defining reading, 121–32, 151–2
focalization, 336
Ford, Ford Madox, 440
foretelling, language as prophecy, 527–31
formalism, 420–32
Forster, E. M., 288
Foucault, Michel, 13, 16
Four Quartets (T. S. Eliot), 121–2, 152
"403" (Dickinson), 42–4
Franklin, Benjamin, 11–12
Frayn, Michael, 453, 456–61
free indirect discourse (FID), 337–9, 342, 343–4
free speech, 164–5
Frege, Gottlob, 104
Freud, Sigmund, 528, 537–8
frivolousness, 275–6
Frye, Northrop, 58
fun, Wittgenstein, 483–5

Gaita, Rai, 270
game, morality not a, 287, 290–3, 295–7
Garber, Marjorie, 523, 524, 525
Gaut, Berys, 350, 358
gender, *Macbeth*, 525–6, 537
Genette, Gerard, 334, 336
genres, fiction, 356–8, 361, 375
Gerrig, Richard J., 77
Ghosts (Ibsen), 282n18
God, 389–90, 392–3
Goethe, J. W. von, 10–11, 14–15, 16, 132–5
Goldie, Peter, 318
Golding, William, 375
"A Good Man is Hard to Find" (O'Connor), 289

Goodman, Nelson, 57, 107, 494–5, 500–1, 508
Gorgias (Plato), 181–2, 184
Gosse, Sir Edmund, 410
Gould, Timothy, 538
grammar, metaphor, 507–8
grammatical displays, 469–72
grammatical resources, 498–500
grammaticalization of experience, 491–4
Greek epic poems, 108–9, 110–11, 117–18, 388
Greenblatt, Stephen, 524
Greene, Graham, 289
Grice, H. Paul, 403–4, 413
grocer's shop, Wittgenstein, 483–4
Groundwork of the Metaphysics of Morals (Kant), 274–5
Guetti, James, 468, 469–72, 473, 475, 480, 481

Haddon, Mark, 363
Halbertal, Moshe, 518n3
Hamilton, Jane, 351, 359
Hamlet (Shakespeare), 176–7, 179, 181, 185
Hardin, Russell, 324n28
Hardy, Thomas, 102–3, 104, 409–10
Harries, Karsten, 27, 29, 34
Harris, Paul, 83, 86
Hass, Robert, 515, 519n15
hearing voices, 111–12, 116
Hedda Gabler (Ibsen), 274–5, 277
Hegel, G. F. W., 38, 52, 63, 145, 169–71, 389–90
Heidegger, Martin, 26–8, 29, 30, 33–4, 164, 523–4
Heisenberg, Werner, 453, 456–64
Hellman, Geoffrey, 495–6
Hemingway, Ernest, 291–2
Henry V (Shakespeare), 175–6, 181
Herzog (Bellow), 301, 311–22
high modernism, 46–9
Hillis Miller, J., 467–8
"Hills Like White Elephants" (Hemingway), 291–2
Hindu philosophy, 19
Hirsch, E. D., 429–30
Hirshfield, Jane, 39
historical records, intention, 453–64

history, *Macbeth*, 521–39
History of the Peloponnesian War (Thucydides), 456
Hölderlin, Friedrich, 393–5
Homeric epics, 108–9, 110–11, 117–18, 388
Hopkins, Gerard Manley, 25–6
Horace, 11, 368
The House of Mirth (Wharton), 288–9, 291
Housman, A. E., 103–4
Howards End (Forster), 288
Hume, David, 272, 274, 275, 368
Hunt, Lynn, 234n30
Huxley, Aldous, 360
hypothetical intentionalism, 408–11

"I"
    self-defining reading, 120–52
    truth in poetry, 396–7
Ibsen, Henrik, 274–5, 277, 282n18, 294–5, 296
identification, with characters, 302–3
Iliad (Homer), 388
imagination
    feeling fictions, 95–6, 100–2, 104
    learning from fiction, 354–8, 362–4
    literary language, 479–80, 481–4, 486
    literary truth–value relation, 368–9
imitation
    emotion through, 97–9, 100–1, 104
    point of view narration, 331–2, 336–44
    tragedy, 162, 168
    tragic catharsis, 193, 196, 198–200, 205, 210–11
    truth in poetry, 369–70, 385, 386
    see also mimesis
imperfection, 287, 294–5
individualism, 390–1
inescapability of morality, 295–6
inheritance metaphor, 30–2, 33–4
intellect, abdication of, 226–8
intellectualism, Stoic, 392–3
intelligence, imitation, 339–40
intention, 401–16
    biography, 453–64
    Macbeth, 533
    Wittgenstein, 423, 495
    see also intentional fallacy
intentional fallacy, 420–32, 439, 441

intentionalism, 405–16
    see also intentional fallacy
internet, debt blogs, 17–18
interpretation
    reading as, 112–13
    role of emotion in, 71–88
introspection, 9–15, 16, 17
Ion (Plato), 110–11, 117–18, 177, 181
ironic utterances, 412
Iser, Wolfgang, 75–6

Jakobson, Roman, 472–3
James, Henry
    literary–ethical theory balance, 241–64
    moralism, 268–79
    point of view narration, 334, 336, 340–1, 346n23
    understanding through emotion, 77, 78–82, 87
James, M. R., 342–4
James, William, 12, 268, 279
Johnson, Samuel, 368, 370
jokes, 22, 273–4, 427
Jonson, Ben, 179
Jose, P. E., 83
Journey to the End of the Night (Putnam), 380
Joyce, James, 157n60, 519n7
Jude the Obscure, 410
judging, moral, 271–2, 277–8
    double takes, 287–90, 297–8
judgment theory of emotion, 84–5
Julius Caesar (Shakespeare), 176, 177, 179, 181

Kafka, Franz, 516
Kant, Immanuel
    character change, 321–2
    literary–ethical theory balance, 244, 250, 251, 256–7
    moralism, 272, 273, 274–5, 277–8
    self-knowledge, 10
Kazin, Alfred, 314
Keats, John, 302–3, 372, 377
Kermode, Frank, 314, 395
Kierkegaard, Søren, 300, 306
King Lear (Shakespeare), 167, 171–2
Kivy, Peter, 358
"know thyself", 9, 16, 18
    see also self-knowledge; self-transformation

545

INDEX

knowledge
  empathetic, 380–2
  learning from fiction, 350–64, 381–2
  see also narrative understanding
Krook, Dorothea, 275
Krumhansl, Carol, 84
"Kubla Khan" (Coleridge), 471
Kuhn, Thomas, 386

Lamarque, Peter, 385–6
Lamia (Keats), 377
Lanchester, John, 310–11
language
  Macbeth, 521–39
  metaphor, 471–2, 480–1, 507–18
  ontological function of literature and philosophy, 25–31, 33–4, 35
  point of view narration, 337–9, 342–4
  self-defining reading, 121–52
  shaping thought, 12
  techne-intention, 427–8, 429–32
  Wittgenstein, 467–87, 491–504, 524–5, 527–8
Laplanche, Jean, 528
Larkin, Philip, 127
Last Writings (Wittgenstein), 491
Le Guin, Ursula, 355
Lear, Jonathan, 168
learning
  from fiction, 350–64, 381–2
  through imitation see imitation
  see also narrative understanding
Leavis, F. R., 102–3, 262
LeDoux, Joseph, 73
The Left Hand of Darkness (Le Guin), 355
"Letter to Posterity" (Petrarch), 390–1
Levinson, Jerrold, 404–5, 408–9, 426–7
Lewis, C. S., 438–9, 446, 450
Lewis, Cecil Day, 372
Lewis, David, 354
life
  philosophy as way of, 8, 14, 18–19
  visions of, 301
  see also orientations, characters'
"Linguistics and Poetics" (Jakobson), 472–3
literary cognitivism, 352–4
literary criticism
  biography in, 436–50
  intention, 401–16, 420–32

literary language see language
literary text–self relation, 145–52
literary theory, balance with ethical, 241–64
literary truth
  learning from fiction, 350–64, 381–2
  literary value, 367–83
  in poetry, 368, 369–74, 376–7, 378–9, 380, 385–97
literary value
  moral relevance, 303–4
  truth and, 367–83
literature, philosophy and see philosophy and literature
Livingston, Paisley, 423–4, 425
logic, Wittgenstein, 491–2
Lolita (Nabokov), 224–5
"London" (Blake), 428–32
Lord of the Flies (Golding), 375
Lord Jim (Conrad), 306–7, 318
love
  literary–ethical theory balance, 258–61, 264
  moralism, 270–1
Lovejoy, Arthur O., 451n12
The Lovely Bones (Sebold), 351, 362–3
Lubbock, Percy, 334
Lyas, Colin, 433n18

Macbeth (Shakespeare), 167, 168, 180, 374, 379, 507–8, 521–39
Machiavellian intelligence, 224
Madame Bovary (Flaubert), 218–22, 225–6, 228–9
Madonna della sedia (Raphael), 58–9
magic, language as, 529, 531–7
Manet, Edouard, 59
A Map of the World (Hamilton), 351, 359
Margalit, Avishai, 518n3
Marlowe, Christopher, 191n18
Márquez, Gabriel García, 351
McEwan, Ian, 82
McKoon, M., 76
McTaggart, J. M. E., 23, 29
meaning
  intentionalism, 405–7, 412–16
  techne-intention, 426–32
Measure for Measure (Shakespeare), 180, 374, 379

546

Meditations in Time of Civil War (Yeats), 447–9
Meixner, John, 440, 442
melancholia, 537–8
Mele, Alfred R., 401
Meno (Plato), 189
mentalistic intention, 420–2, 423
meshing condition, intention, 414–16, 424–5
metaphoric demonstratives, 503
metaphorical identification, 145–52
metaphors
    literary language, 471–2, 480–1, 507–18
    philosophy as literature, 64, 65–6, 67
    ontological function, 29–32, 33–4
Metaphysics (Aristotle), 167, 201
Middlemarch (George Eliot), 61, 74–5, 77–82, 84–5, 87, 375
Milosz, Czeslaw, 38
Milton, John, 439
mimesis
    literary truth–value relation, 369–70
    self-defining reading, 124, 146
    tragic catharsis, 193, 196, 198–200, 205, 210–11
    see also imitation
mind-reading, language as, 529, 531–7
mistakes, factual, 375, 380
modernist poetry
    language, 474–87, 498–500
    rhetorical reading, 38–49
Moll Flanders (Defoe), 442–3, 444–5, 446
Molloy (Beckett), 226, 227
Montaigne, Michel de, 8, 10, 18
Moore, G. E., 493, 501–2
morality in literature
    Aeneid, 144–5
    empathy and, 223–5
    ethical order in tragedy, 169–71
    ethical turn, 467–8
    ethical–literary theory balance, 241–64
    literary role, 285–98
    metaphorical self-individuation, 148
    moralism, 268–79
    tragedy for ethical education, 196–9, 204
Moran, Richard, 150–1, 495, 513, 514
"Mourning and Melancholia" (Freud), 537–8

Moyal-Sharrock, Daniéle, 491
Mukarowski, Jan, 472, 473
Mullaney, Steven, 524, 526–7
Murdoch, Iris, 138–9, 300–1, 371
music
    catharsis, 194, 196–7
    experience of reading and, 110, 111, 113, 114
    intention, 423

Nabokov, Vladimir, 224–5
narration, point of view, 331–44
narrative understanding
    biography in criticism, 442–3
    emotion, 71–88
networks of reciprocal effects, 60–1, 62
"The New Biography" (Woolf), 455–6
New Criticism, 420–32
Nicomachean Ethics (Aristotle), 97, 178, 180, 186, 300
Nietzsche, Friedrich
    literary truth–value relation, 369
    literary–ethical theory balance, 243
    Macbeth, 538
    moralism, 282n22
    self-knowledge, 10, 16
    selfhood, 127–9
    truth in poetry, 390
"The Noble Rider and the Sound of Words" (Stevens), 481
"Nomad Exquisite" (Stevens), 498–9
Novak, Maximillian E., 445
novels
    learning from, 350–64, 381–2
        see also role of emotion in interpreting *below*
    literary–ethical theory balance, 241–64
    moralism, 268–79
    role of emotion in interpreting, 71–88
    silent reading of as performance, 106–18
    styles of selfishness, 300–22
Novitz, David, 381
Nussbaum, Martha
    empathy, 234–5n30, 235n31
    literature's distinctiveness, 467–8
    moral adventure, 296
    moral life, 301
    moralism, 273, 282n22
    tragedy and philosophy, 162, 163

INDEX

O'Connor, Flannery, 289
Oedipus Tyrannus (Sophocles), 163, 164, 166–8, 211
Olsen, Stein Haugom, 385–6
On Certainty (Wittgenstein), 468, 491, 492, 501–2
One Hundred Years of Solitude (Márquez), 351
one-place predicates, 500–1
O'Neill, Onora, 282n22
Ong, Walter, 39
ontology
   biography in criticism, 446–9
   experience of reading, 107, 118
   philosophy as literature, 22–36, 56–7
orientations, characters', 301, 306–22
"The Origin of the Work of Art" (Heidegger), 26–7, 523–4
Ostrow, Matthew, 491
Othello (Shakespeare), 171, 174, 180, 181–9
The Outsider (Camus), 28

Paradise Lost (Milton), 439
paradox
   of fiction, 84–6, 93, 96–100
   function of literature and philosophy, 32
parody, Wittgenstein, 483–5
particulars/particularity
   literary–ethical theory balance, 247, 248–56, 257
   ontological function of literature and philosophy, 25
   self-defining reading, 127–31
   truth in poetry, 385–97
Parts of Animals (Aristotle), 199–200
Paterson (Williams), 47
peace of mind, 226–9
perception, 251–61, 264, 332
performing art, the novel as, 107–18
Petrarch, 390–2
Phaedo (Plato), 175, 181, 189
Phaedrus (Plato), 9
phenomenology
   of ethical thought, 278–9
   of the experience of reading, 473–87
   fictional narratives, 302–3
Philosophical Investigations (Wittgenstein), 483, 484, 485, 491, 495, 496, 497, 524–5

philosophy and literature
   biography
      intention, 439, 441, 453–64
      in literary criticism, 436–50
      philosophy as literature, 8–9
   emotion
      empathetic knowledge, 380–2
      exemplifying, 497–8
      feeling fictions, 93–104
      feeling nothing, 218–29
      literary–ethical theory balance, 252–6, 257, 258–61
      orientation compared, 318–19
      tragic catharsis, 193–211, 222–3, 228–9
      truth in poetry, 394–7
      understanding of narrative, 71–88
   intention, 401–16
      biography, 439, 441, 453–64
      intentional fallacy, 420–32, 439, 441
   literary language
      Macbeth, 521–39
      metaphor, 471–2, 480–1, 507–18
      Wittgenstein, 467–87, 491–504, 524–5, 527–8
   morality in literature
      ethical–literary theory balance, 241–64
      literary role, 285–98
      moralism, 268–79
      styles of selfishness, 300–22
   philosophy as literature, 7–18, 52–67
      or as more than literature, 18–19
      ontological function, 22–36, 56–7
      rhetorical reading, 38–49
   point of view narration, 331–44
   reading
      self-defining, 120–52
      silent, as performance, 106–18
   tragedy and, 161–72
      catharsis, 193–211, 222–3, 228–9
      feeling fictions, 99–100, 101, 102–3
      feeling nothing, 218–29
      Platonic influences on Shakespeare, 174–89
   truth
      learning from fiction, 350–64, 381–2
      literary value, 367–83
      in poetry, 368, 369–74, 376–7, 378–9, 380, 385–97

Physics and Beyond (Heisenberg), 456
pictorial semantics, 57, 58–9
Pippin, Robert, 298n6
pity, 193, 194, 195–8, 200–1, 203, 204–9, 222–3
place, rhetorical reading of poetry, 38–49
Plato
   influence on Shakespeare, 174–89
   literary truth–value relation, 369–70
   moralism, 274
   philosophy as literature, 9–10, 12–13, 22
   philosophy as more than literature, 18
   silent reading as performance, 110–11, 117–18
   tragedy and philosophy, 161–6, 198
   truth in poetry, 388, 389–90
plots
   tragedy, 200–1, 205–7, 211, 387
   truth in poetry, 395
Poetics (Aristotle), 166, 168, 199–200, 201–3, 205–8
poetry
   biography in criticism, 438–40, 447–9
   Confucius, 19
   experience of reading, 107–9, 110–11
   feeling fictions, 102–4
   language, 471, 472–87, 498–500, 509–13
   ontological function of philosophy and literature, 25–6, 28, 29–30, 32, 33, 34–5
   reference, 58, 59–60, 61, 62–3
   rhetorical reading, 38–49
   techne-intention, 425–6, 427–32
   truth in, 368, 369–74, 376–7, 378–9, 380, 385–97
point of view narration, 331–44
political correctness, 273–4
Politics (Aristotle), 193, 194–5, 196–7
Polytopia, 38–49
Pope, Alexander, 376
possible selves, 120, 121–32
post-modern novels, emotion and, 82–3
post-structuralism
   biography, 436–8
   literary truth–value relation, 369
Powers, Thomas, 462
Pratt, Mary Louise, 427
predicative assimilation, 480–1

Pride and Prejudice (Austen), 376
privacy of language, 524–5
prophecy, language as, 527–31
propositional truth, 372–80
Pulp Fiction (Tarantino), 86
purgation of the emotions, 193, 194–6, 204, 222–3
purity, ideal of, 296
Putnam, Hilary, 380

Queen Victoria (Strachey), 454

Raimondi, Marcantonio, 59
Raphael, 58–9
Ratcliff, R., 76
Rawls, John, 246–7, 254
readers' emotions
   feeling fictions, 93–104
   understanding narrative, 71–88
The Reader (Schlink), 355
reading
   emotional engagement, 324n22
   mind-reading, 531
   a phenomenology of the experience, 473–87
   philosophy as literature, 66–7
   self-defining, 120–52
   silent, as performance, 106–18
"Reality and Sincerity" (Leavis), 102–3
Recanati, François, 347n29
recollection, theory of (anamnesis), 189
reductio ad absurdum arguments, 359, 360
reference, 25–9, 56–67
reflection, 392–5
reflective equilibrium, 246–7, 254, 258
rehearsing emotions, 97–9, 100–2
Remarks on Colour (Wittgenstein), 493
Republic (Plato)
   influence on Shakespeare, 176, 177–8, 181, 187–8
   tragedy and philosophy, 161–3, 164–5
   truth, 388, 389
responsibility, moralism, 269, 270, 275–6
responsiveness
   Macbeth, 521
   to moralism, 269, 270, 273–9
reverse engineering, 422
Reznikoff, Charles, 38–9
rhetoric, illuminating poetry, 38–49

INDEX

Rhetoric (Aristotle), 201, 211
Richards, D. A. J., 270–1
Richards, I. A., 371
Richardson, Henry, 254
Ricks, Christopher, 103–4
Ricoeur, Paul, 27, 480–1
"ringing true", 371
The Rise of the Novel (Watt), 442–3, 444–5, 446
Robinson, Jenefer, 96–7, 381
Romeo and Juliet (Shakespeare), 171
Rortification of philosophy, 24
Rorty, Richard, 23, 127–31, 136, 234n30, 235n35
Rose, Paul Lawrence, 462
Rowse, A. L., 450
Russian Formalism, 420, 421–2, 427

Saenger, Paul, 108
Said, Edward, 136–7
Salovey, Peter, 81
Santayana, George, 55–6
Sartre, Jean-Paul, 137, 153n5, 342
Scheffler, Samuel, 310
Schlegel, Friedrich, 392, 524
Schlink, Bernhard, 355
Schönberg, Arnold, 423
science fiction, 28–9, 361
The Sea, The Sea (Murdoch), 138–9
The Seagull (Chekhov), 288
Searle, John R., 402
Sebold, Alice, 351, 362–3
secondary extensions theory, 57
The Second Sex (Beauvoir), 17
self, divided, 38, 39, 47–8
self-defining reading, 120–52
self-knowledge
　de se suppositions, 362
　literary–ethical theory balance, 263
　philosophy as literature, 9–16, 18–19, 22
　see also self-defining reading
self-transformation, 15–19
selfishness, styles of, 300–22
selves, possible, 120, 121–32
semantic intentions, 403–5, 408–10, 411
semantics
　feeling fictions, 105n5
　intentionalism, 405, 406–7
　philosophy as literature, 56–63

Seneca, 8, 13
Seventh Letter (Plato), 183–4
"76" (Dickinson), 44–6
Shakespeare, William
　biography in criticism, 450
　language of *Macbeth*, 507–8, 521–39
　literary truth–value relation, 369, 374, 376, 379
　metaphor, 507–8
　Platonic influences on, 174–89
　tragedy and philosophy, 167, 168, 171–2
Shih Ching (*Book of Songs*), 19
Shklovsky, Victor, 422
"The Sick Rose" (Blake), 513
silent reading, as performance, 106–18
similes, *Song of Songs*, 510
sincerity, 371, 372–3
skepticism
　Antony and Cleopatra, 521–2
　feeling nothing, 226–8, 229
　literary truth–value relation, 369
Slow Man (Coetzee), 310–11
Smith, Adam, 99–100, 224
Smith, Barbara Hernstein, 395
"so", exemplification, 497, 498–9
Socrates, 8, 9, 10, 12–13, 18, 174–89, 389
Solomon, Robert, 326–7n63
Solotaroff, Theodore, 314
Song of Songs, 509–13
Songbook (*Canzoniere*; Petrarch), 391–2
Sophist (Plato), 165
Sophocles, 163, 164, 166–8, 169–70, 225, 388
Sparshott, Francis, 34
speech
　in biographies, 456–7
　demonstratives, 502–4
　freedom of, 164–5
　point of view narration, 337–9, 340–1, 342–4
　thought–speech relations, 12, 121–52
Spinoza, Baruch, 392–3
"Standard Language and Poetic Language" (Mukarowski), 472
state, the, tragedy, 161–3, 164–5, 170–1, 172, 198
Stecker, Robert, 414
Stein, Gertrude, 47
Steiner, Peter, 422

550

Stevens, Wallace, 46–9, 474–87, 498–500
Stoic intellectualism, 392–3
Stolnitz, Jerome, 376
Stoppard, Tom, 32
Strachey, Lytton, 454–5, 456
Strawson, Peter, 404
structuralism, 436–8
"The Structure of Romantic Nature Imagery" (Wimsatt), 421
styles of selfishness, 300–22
subject-level content, propositional truth, 373, 375, 376–7
success conditions, intention, 411, 412–16, 424–5
supposition, learning from fiction, 358–64
symbolization, 494–5
sympathy, 99–104
Symposium (Plato), 184, 185

The Taming of the Shrew (Shakespeare), 174–5, 180, 181, 191n18
Tarantino, Quentin, 86
techne-intention, 420–32
temperament, orientation compared, 317
Tender Buttons (Stein), 47
textual authority *see* literary value
textualist intentionalism, 405
Thackeray, William Makepeace, 101
theatricality, *Herzog*, 312–13, 315, 316–17
thematic-level content, propositional truth, 373–5, 376, 377–80
"Theory" (Stevens), 46–8
A Theory of Justice (Rawls), 246–7
thinking
    poetic, 392–7
    reading and, 117–18
    see also thought
"Thirteen Ways of Looking at a Blackbird" (Stevens), 474–86
Thoreau, Henry David, 8
thought, phenomenology of ethical, 278–9
thought experiments, 354–6
thought–speech relations, 12, 121–52
Thrasymachanism, 390
"Three Dawn Songs in Summer" (Hass), 515, 519n15
Thucydides, 456
Thus Spoke Zarathustra (Nietzsche), 538
Tillyard, E. M. W., 438–9

"Tlön, Uqbar, Orbis Tertius" (Borges), 292–3
To the Hermitage (Bradbury), 375
Tolhurst, William, 408
Tolstoy, Leo, 282n18, 374
Tom Jones (Fielding), 269–70
Trabasso, Tom, 76
Tractatus (Wittgenstein), 478, 491–2
tradition, 24
tragedy
    catharsis, 193–211, 222–3, 228–9
    feeling fictions, 99–100, 101, 102–3
    feeling nothing, 218–29
    language in *Macbeth*, 521–39
    philosophy's response to, 161–72
    Platonic influences on Shakespeare, 174–89
    truth in poetry, 387, 388, 389
The Tragic Muse (James), 268–9, 275, 276
Treatise on Human Nature (Hume), 368
Trilling, Lionel, 262
triviality, 376
Troilus and Cressida (Shakespeare), 177–80, 181, 186
"true to", 372
Trumbull, John, 59
truth
    learning from fiction, 350–64, 381–2
    literary value, 367–83
    philosophy as literature, 53–6, 63, 64–7
    in poetry, 368, 369–74, 376–7, 378–9, 380, 385–97
Turgenev, Ivan, 271, 273
two-place predicates, 500–1
Twombly, Cy, 424–5

universals/universality
    literary truth–value relation, 370, 376–7, 378
    philosophy as literature, 25–7, 63–4, 66–7
    self-defining reading, 127–31, 145–6
    tragic catharsis, 202–3
    truth in poetry, 385–97
The Unnamable (Beckett), 226
utterance model, intention, 407–8, 412–14

"Valedictory Sonnet to the River Duddon" (Wordsworth), 373, 378–9
Van Ghent, Dorothy, 444, 452n24

INDEX

van Knippenberg, Ad, 340
Vanity Fair (Thackeray), 101
Varnhagen, Rahel, 16–17
verisimilitude, 372–3
Virgil, 140–5
virtues, orientation and, 319–20
visions of life, 301
   see also orientations, characters'
Vrana, S. R., 83

Walton, Kendall, 93–5, 101, 423
War and Peace (Tolstoy), 374
Washington, George, 59
Watt, Ian, 341, 346n23, 442–3, 444–5, 446
way of life, philosophy as, 8, 14, 18–19
webs of belief, 122–32, 135–42, 147, 151
Weitz, Morris, 372
Wharton, Edith, 288–9, 291
What Maisie Knew (James), 276–7, 345n12
The Wild Duck (Ibsen), 294–5, 296
Willbern, David, 532
Williams, Bernard, 162, 270–1, 295–6
Williams, William Carlos, 47
Wimsatt, William, 372, 420–2, 429–31, 439, 440–1

Wisdom, John, 31–2
Wittgenstein, Ludwig
   intention, 423, 495
   language, 467–87, 491–504, 524–5, 527–8
   literature and philosophy's function, 30, 31, 33, 35
   peace of mind, 236–7n43
   self-examining thoughts, 12
   truth in poetry, 395
   universalizing, 129
Wollheim, Richard, 295
women, self-realization, 16–17
woodsellers, the, 482
Woolf, Virginia, 454–6, 460
Wordsworth, William, 58, 59–60, 373, 378–9, 393–5
worldly truth, 379
writing
   novel as performance, 108–9
   philosophy as literature, 8, 9–10, 11–14, 16–18, 23

Yeats, W. B., 447–9

Zwicky, Jan, 35

Printed and bound by CPI Group (UK) Ltd, Croydon, CR0 4YY